CORNWALL AND ITS PEOPLE

CORNWALL
and its People

*being a new impression of the
composite work including:*

CORNISH SEAFARERS, 1932
CORNWALL AND THE CORNISH, 1933
CORNISH HOMES AND CUSTOMS, 1934

by

A. K. HAMILTON JENKIN
M.A., B.Litt. (Oxon.)

With an Introduction by
SIR ARTHUR QUILLER-COUCH

This impression introduced by
David St John Thomas

DAVID & CHARLES REPRINTS

7153 4702 0

This work was first published in composite form by
J M Dent & Sons Ltd in 1945

This impression published 1970

© 1970 A. K. HAMILTON JENKIN

Printed in Great Britain by
Redwood Press Limited Trowbridge and London
for David & Charles (Publishers) Limited
South Devon House Newton Abbot
Devon

PUBLISHER'S NOTE TO THE 1970 REPRINT

THIS is one of the classics of Cornish history, and it is a privilege to be able to reprint it for the benefit of a new generation of readers.

I well remember buying my copy of the first combined edition at the end of the war. To a boy still at school, in Devon, Hamilton Jenkin's book was a dramatic introduction to the different world that then still lay beyond Brunel's Royal Albert Bridge over the Tamar. I had many many a foray by train, to Looe and St Ives, then still essentially fishing ports, to Padstow, scarcely on the tourist map, and on by bus from Penzance to St Just where in those days there were hardly more visitors than you would see in North country mining towns. Already, of course, Cornwall was remorselessly being brought into the national scheme of affairs, but it was not until the early 1950s that motorised tourists, television and other forces finally broke down age-old patterns and some of the local customs became consciously-preserved publicity attractions.

Cornwall is still very Cornish, and its unique natural and man-scarred landscape will ensure that it remains so. But today's young readers must rely ever more on the printed word for accounts of how life used to be lived, livelihoods earned, and leisure filled in a land with almost more comings and goings by sea with the great outside world than across the Tamar with England. This book will have a unique role to play in revealing the past, and it should be in every school library in the county. For it brings old Cornwall to life. It is of course written by a Cornishman who deeply understands his Cornwall and the relationship between its past and more recent history. It was written to be read with enjoyment, but is accurate and non-sentimental. It will take its place alongside classics such as Crossing's *Guide to Dartmoor* and Nicholls' *Forest of Dean*.

DAVID ST JOHN THOMAS

INTRODUCTION

BOOKS about Cornwall have multiplied in my lifetime at an astonishing rate and with gathering volume. In my infancy the railway had scarcely begun to awaken curiosity in this remote, but recently accessible, land and its people : many of whom—and some of them well known to me—lived and died contentedly without ever having set eyes on a locomotive. The arrival of the motor, moderately priced, has swelled the number of guide-books, illustrated books, chatty books for the tourist, little books of legendary stuff (some of it surprisingly well invented), handy folding maps, obliging descriptions of the Cornish, their manners, customs, foibles, eccentricities ; almost to a ' harmonical progression '. While of late a most careful Survey prepared by Mr W. Harding Thompson for the Council for the Preservation of Rural England, sumptuously printed and illustrated, has not only shown what the many characteristic beauties of Cornwall are, but attempted winningly to teach how they should be preserved from the tooth of Time, rescued from spoiling by commercial greed, and even improved by intelligent planting and planning for the future.

But before all this book-making actively began, lovers of our land—here and there, in sequestered spots and with no prospect of earning a penny by it—were laboriously collecting, shaping, indexing all records they could lay hold on, by document or tradition, of their chosen corner, its history, its topography, the fauna and flora of the country-side, their neighbours' family traditions, events that now and then excite a village and startle it even into public importance for a while. I pay a small pious debt to the memory of my own grandfather, who happened to be such a man—a naturalist in the line of Gilbert White of Selborne, accurate to observe, faithful to record, setting the result down in the severe English of a man who had trained himself to quiet, scholarly prose. His modest contribution in its kind—' Polperro, its History, etc.'—I mention here because, with its documents and records of ' natural phenomena', it includes descriptions of his lifelong neighbours, the fishermen, their ways and modes of industry ; as also because the book contained a chapter on Privateers and Smugglers from which the late Captain H. N. Shore (afterwards Lord Teignmouth), so often quoted in the following pages, derived much of the material he reproduced in more popular language.

But, for our good fortune, concurrently with this spate of ' topical ' books about Cornwall there has established itself a quiet group of genuine seekers into her past. The old race of devoted inquirers—the sort of men who founded the Royal Institution of Cornwall—were scattered, worked sporadically. Many of them, like so many local antiquarians, even to-day, were cranks, holding theories about Druids, or intent to prove the Cornish (God forbid !) one of the Lost Tribes. Given an obsession, and a heated brain working in solitude, there is no telling to what lengths of speculation we may not be carried. But Cornwall to-day has somehow found a group of workers, of whom Mr A. K. Hamilton Jenkin is among the foremost, who seriously devote themselves to keeping alive an interesting, if almost defunct, language ; in reviving the embers of ancient festivities, almost extinct in Cornwall, as, for example, the happy social art of chamber-music lies almost extinct to-day, crushed by the same heat of a mistaken Puritanism : in re-capturing (more scientifically to-day than did Bottrell, Hunt, and some others for whose pains we yet give thanks) the racial legends and household tales before they quite fade out—as a last loiterer beside the inn-fire will rise and remove himself into the night.

> The race of yore
> Who danced our infancy upon their knee
> And told our marvelling boyhood legends store
> Of their strange ventures happ'd by land or sea,
> How are they blotted from the things that be !

But there are other records, less ' romantic ' perhaps to the superficial mind, perhaps even more evanescent in memory—recollections of the ways, habits, and daily occupations of the Cornish in quite recent generations—which also, to the discerning reader, have the deep import of actual life, with its struggles, anxieties, frequent and astonishing heroism. Beneath a pile of dusty newspaper entries, share-lists, sailings of emigrant ships, etc., or hidden in treasured private letters, must lie the heroic tale of the Cornish ' forty-niners ', of the shutting-down of work at home, dwindling wage, semi-starvation, sudden hope, decision (at what cost !), the break-up of homes in home-devoted families, the great adventure to Nevada or California. The event of those days in the small port of Fowey, where my home is, would be the arrival or departure of one of its two sailing-brigs : bringing home, in lessening quantity, timber for mine-props, carrying away, in gathering numbers, the Duchy's adventurous youth.

To this tale of the Cornish miner Mr Hamilton Jenkin gave his time and toil in a previous book. He here turns an equal care to serve the story of our seafarers and fishermen. I thank him particularly for having, without prejudice or *parti pris*, reduced the old legend of ' wrecking ' to history and proportion.

ARTHUR QUILLER-COUCH.

1932.

AUTHOR'S PREFACE

It is not without reason that the Cornish people have always been regarded as a race apart. Even to-day, despite the loss of their native language, they retain, to a surprising degree, the characteristics which mark them still as Celts. It is not only the distance of Cornwall from the great centres of population which has helped to preserve this distinctive character in its inhabitants. The land itself is different from any other English county—a long bony ridge reaching far out by west and south into the immensity of the Atlantic Ocean. Though in latter years becoming known as ' England's Riviera', the essential attributes of Cornwall are in truth the reverse of tropical luxuriance. It was not indeed in the cultivation of its, frequently, barren surface that the people of Cornwall formerly looked for a return on their labour. The wealth of the Duchy, as they knew it, lay buried deep in the hills of granite, and in the waters which surrounded their cliff-girt home. Hence it was that, in times past, but two forms of occupation lay open to the majority of Cornishmen, and it was by instinct rather than conscious choice that one generation followed another to the mine, or to the boat. The narrative of the former has been told by the writer in his book, *The Cornish Miner*. This present volume, incorporating three other books originally published separately in the years 1932–34, opens with the story of those who followed the sea for their livelihood. In it lies the epic of the little Cornish ports and fishing coves which throughout their long history produced alike the privateer, the smuggler, the wrecker and the poor toiling fisherman. As the background to this life of enterprise and struggle can be viewed the social changes which I have attempted to describe in *Cornwall and the Cornish*. Into that old Cornwall wherein wheeled traffic was unknown and the lives of rich and poor alike lay untouched by any outside influence, there came the figure of John Wesley whose influence in the conversion of the people to Methodism marks one of the chief milestones in Cornish history. Alongside this can be seen how many of the old beliefs still lingered, lending currency to many a wild tale of 'pisky' and 'knackers' and the practice of ancient rites which are scarcely forgotten at this day. Lastly, in *Cornish Homes and Customs*, I have pictured for the reader the home-life of the people in the cottages and farms, the conditions under which they lived, the food they ate and, not least, the pastimes and recreations which served to lighten the burden of their lives, and which have survived, as ancient customs like the Furry-dance, into our own time. In this series, intended, as it is, to present a general view of the richly coloured life of this once remote and still 'delectable' corner of Celtic Britain, I have profited directly or indirectly by the help of many friends. To them I offer my grateful thanks. Of myself I will only say that 'though I have milked from many people's cows, the butter', I believe, 'is my own'.

A. K. HAMILTON JENKIN.

Mullion, near Helston
April, 1945

CONTENTS

CUSTOMS AND OBSERVANCES

LIST OF ILLUSTRATIONS

CORNISH SEAFARERS

CORNWALL AND THE CORNISH

CORNISH HOMES AND CUSTOMS

CORNISH SEAFARERS

THE SMUGGLERS

I

THE story of the 'long-shore' life of Cornwall, rich as it is in colour, incident, and high romance, has never yet been told in full by any writer, for the very reason perhaps that its many-sidedness and complexity forbid its telling within the limits of any book of ordinary length. Throughout that varied length of coastline, from Hartland Point to the Land's End and onward thence to Plymouth Sound where the dividing waters of the Tamar reach the sea, secluded coves and rocky inlets, frowning cliffs, sandy towans and deep sea-creeks— the latter often biting far inwards upon the bosom of the land —are all rich in the unwritten stories of a population who as smugglers, wreckers, pirates, and fishermen have looked to the sea for their livelihood and support. For it is thus that the Cornishman has ever regarded the waters that surround the far-outstretching promontory which constitutes his home. Living as he does within sight and sound of the sea, he has little in common with the townsman who glorifies it for its beauty or sentimentalizes over its treachery and untamable power. To the Cornishman rather it is a harvest-field from which it is possible to wrest a hard-earned living, sometimes a battle-field upon which he may be called to fight for his very life. In consequence of this he neither dreads nor romantically loves the sea, for he knows it for what it is. Part and parcel of his life, he has seen it in its every mood, conscious all the while that each must be watched and studied if he is to gain the mastery in that never-ending contest wherein man is pitting his intelligence against the forces of nature.

It is, perhaps, only natural that with the passing of time, the realities of a life which is now receding into the background of the past should become overlaid by the imaginative conceptions of a later day. Particularly does this apply to that branch of the old seafaring life of the west which falls under the heading of smuggling. It is true that anyone who is sufficiently steeped in the stories of the smugglers and who has visited the coves wherein some of their most daring deeds were enacted, will probably have found it easy to conjure up some not unsatisfactory vision of the past. As the dusk of an autumn evening descends, it is not hard to fancy that one sees again the rough bearded men and their hardy little ponies, waiting by the sea's edge for the kegs of brandy, packets of lace and tobacco, or barrels of rum, which are shortly to be raced away up the rocky paths to the villages where the arrival of the ' goods ' is eagerly expected. This is well as far as it goes ; but smuggling among the Cornishmen of old was not, as has been truly said, the outcome of a mere love of adventure or desire to cheat the revenue authorities. Rather, it was something which was vital to the very existence of the people. The extreme poverty of the working-classes, especially of those engaged in the precarious occupations of fishing and mining, created a condition which was peculiarly favourable to the development of this form of Free Trade. Without going so far as to say, as one writer has done, that the frequently recurring periods of economic stress *enforced* smuggling on the Cornish people, one can at least find in the state of the times some clue to the character of such a man as Captain Harry Carter, brother of the still more famous ' King of Prussia', who, when already at the age of eighteen in command of a smuggling craft of his own, forbade all swearing and unseemly conversation on board his ship ' under pain of punishment ', and in later life when residing at Roscoff with a price upon his head, was in the habit of conducting religious services on Sunday afternoons for the benefit of the twenty or thirty other English smugglers staying in the town. ' The men took off their hats,' he notes in his diary after one of these occasions, ' all very serious, no laffing, no trifling conversations.' [1]

It is clear that such men regarded themselves not so much as smugglers as ' fair traders ', a term which they often applied to the enterprise in which they were engaged. They knew the law and, had it been in their power to do so, they would no doubt have changed the law and legalized their position, but this being impossible, they set themselves above such a man-made institution. In doing so they clearly had the sympathy of more than one celebrated spokesman.

' It is impossible,' declared Lord Holland in a speech before the House of Lords, 9 July 1805, ' totally to prevent smuggling, all that the legislature can do is to compromise with a crime which, whatever laws may be made to constitute it a high offence, the mind of man can never conceive as at all

[1] *Autobiography of a Cornish Smuggler*, 1749–1809, Edited by J. B. Cornish (1894).

equalling in turpitude those acts which are breaches of clear moral virtues.'

Adam Smith in his famous definition of a smuggler as ' a person who, though no doubt highly blamable for violating the laws of his country, is frequently incapable of violating those of natural justice and who would have been in every respect an excellent citizen had not the laws of his country made that a crime which Nature never meant to be so ', states the defence for smuggling with an even greater directness.[1]

On the other hand it must be admitted that there was a dark side to the smuggling trade, whose practitioners could not truthfully be described in all cases either as excellent citizens or as incapable, when provoked, of violating the laws of natural justice. Even so it must be remembered that if the smugglers were armed men, so in like manner were those whose business it was to prevent smuggling. If, under such circumstances, the conflicts which were bound to take place resulted in bloodshed and, occasionally, even loss of life, neither side could be held solely responsible. In most cases, however, it was the smugglers' reputation which suffered. Thus, when, in the year 1735, a quantity of rum which had been discovered in a barn near Fowey was being taken to the custom-house, we read that the excisemen were attacked by an armed body of smugglers who had acquired such a reputation for violence in that district that in the words of the official report : ' If the officers attempt to make any seizure they go in danger of their lives, the smugglers having entered into a combination to rescue any person who shall be arrested '.[2] How far the words ' go in danger of their lives ' should bear a literal interpretation it is difficult to say, seeing that the report, being an official one, must necessarily have been somewhat biased.

Nevertheless, there is plenty of evidence to show that serious clashes between the Government officers and the local population were at one time not infrequent. In 1768, William Odgers, one of the officers of the excise stationed at Porthleven, was murdered by a party of smugglers in a most barbarous manner. The case was made the subject of a searching inquiry and £100 reward was offered by the commissioners

---

[1] Cf., however, Dr Johnson's definition of a smuggler as ' A wretch who, in defiance of justice and the laws, imports or exports goods either contraband or without payment of the customs '.

[2] M. Oppenheim, *Victoria History of Cornwall*, 505.

to anyone who would lay the necessary information. At the inquest, a verdict of wilful murder was returned against Melchisideck Kinsman, of Gwennap, and others unknown. The controller stated at the time that he feared four of the men implicated had escaped to Guernsey and Morlaix. Later, he advised the commissioners that he believed the men had not gone abroad but were skulking underground in the tin mines. The next year, he reported that £500 had been offered to Hampton, the principal witness for the Crown against the murderers, to go out of the country and stay away for two years. This Hampton refused, and the commissioners granted him seven shillings a week, as he was afraid to go about on his ordinary work. In 1780, this man was receiving ten shillings a week. Eventually three of the supposed murderers gave themselves up and promised to effect the capture of Kinsman, which they succeeded in doing after an affray in which one of them was seriously wounded. All four were tried at the assizes, but, contrary to the opinion of the judge, and to the amazement of the whole court, were found not guilty. The collector stated in his report that there was no doubt that the jury had been bribed by Kinsman's relatives and that three of the jury had disappeared after the case.[1]

Another story, based though it is on tradition rather than on written evidence, will serve to illustrate further the violence to which the smuggling trade gave rise.

On a rough piece of moorland forming the western slope of Trencrom Hill, in the parish of Lelant, may still be seen two old granite-built cottages which locally go by the name of ' Newcastle '.[2] One of these, a century or more years ago, was occupied as a ' kiddleywink ' or beershop, a noted haunt of the smugglers who had excavated a cave (which may still be seen in the hedge outside) where supplies of contraband goods were regularly stored. At this particular time, the kiddleywink happened to be owned by two brothers, one of whom had joined the army. Finding, however, that the disciplined life of the service was less exhilarating than smuggling, the latter at length deserted and returned to his home where he lay for some time in hiding. It so happened that

[1] Quoted by Mr J. A. D. Bridger, *West Briton*, 22 October 1931.
[2] ' Castle ' is commonly used in a derisive sense in Cornwall, houses built in a pretentious style or in inconvenient situations being often nicknamed ' Booby's Castle,' a term corresponding to ' —— Folly ' in other shires.

about this time the press-gang came into the district and getting wind of the deserter's whereabouts a party of soldiery suddenly descended one day upon the cottage. The door was opened by the other brother who, on learning the cause of the party's arrival, immediately put up a fight. The press-gang, however, proved too strong for him and in the course of the struggle he was killed. Meantime, the deserter brother, unaware of the desperate nature of the fight proceeding below, had made a hole in the roof and succeeded in escaping to some hiding-place outside. On entering the house and finding the bird flown, the press-gang took their departure, and the deserter, though he long continued to live in the neighbourhood, was never troubled with their attentions again. The reason popularly given for this was that having killed one brother they were debarred from laying hands on the other, since the law did not allow of the taking of two men for one.[1]

It is certainly a fact that the excisemen were sometimes guilty of grave errors of judgment, as more than one innocent traveller learnt at the cost of his life. In the year 1799, a couple of preventive men, travelling between Bodmin and Truro, fell in with two persons whom, for some reason or other, they suspected of carrying smuggled goods. 'This, however,' as a correspondent states in the *Gentleman's Magazine*, 27 June 1799, 'not being the case, the suspects put up an obdurate resistance, until at length being overpowered by their desperate antagonists they were left dead on the spot. The excisemen then absconded.' Whether the Government took any action in the matter does not appear. Perhaps, as in the case of the American judge of the pioneer days who, on finding that he had hanged an innocent man by mistake, is said to have ' apologized ' to the widow with the words : ' Gee, marm, I guess you 've got the laugh over us this time ', the Government considered that they had already paid sufficiently in loss of prestige. Though this must have provided small consolation for the relatives of the unfortunate victims, there can be no doubt that keen satisfaction was felt by the country-side at large at such a discomfiture of the hated ' sarchers '. This, however, was not the only occasion on which the justice of the law miscarried with tragic results, as is revealed by the inscription on a tombstone, dated 1814, standing in the little churchyard of Mylor, near Falmouth :

[1] Per Mr R. J. Noall, of St Ives.

We have not a moment we can call our own.
Officious zeal in luckless hour laid wait
And wilful sent the murderous ball of Fate !
James to his home, which late in health he left,
Wounded returns—of life is soon bereft.

Notwithstanding the unconscious humour of the opening line, the memorial leaves little doubt of the strength of popular feeling which was aroused on this occasion. For in this case the victim of the excisemen's aggression was no mere stranger but a young man of the village who, returning in his boat one evening after having been out fishing, was fired upon by the officers and thus fatally wounded.

The smugglers themselves, however, sometimes made mistakes, and since attacks upon the detested minions of the law were generally made under cover of darkness, a hard fate occasionally awaited the individual who happened to look, ride, or walk like an exciseman ! One night in the early part of the last century, a Truro gentleman was riding home from Redruth at a late hour, when he suddenly found himself surrounded by a band of miners, who shouted : ' Knack 'un down ! Knack 'un down ! and scat his head abroad 'pon the floor'. The gentleman realizing the mistake which had been made quickly undeceived them, when the miners, in tones of deepest repentance, exclaimed : ' Arreah ! why 'tes Maister S—— from ovver to Trura, why we wud'n hurt a heer of hes head '. Saying which they remounted Mr S—— on his horse and escorted him far on his way home, finally taking leave with renewed apologies for the inconvenience which had been caused by his mistaken identity.

Though they hated the ' sarchers ' for their interference in what was locally regarded as an honest trade, the Cornish people could be generous even to their enemies when in distress. During one bitterly cold and pitch-black night in the month of December 1805, two excise officers, travelling from Luxillian to Lostwithiel, lost their way, and after proceeding for several miles across country, at length found themselves in the desolate region of the Goss Moors. There they wandered for several hours, and at last became so exhausted that they sank down on the ground unable to proceed any farther. Fortunately for them, soon afterwards two tinners on their way to their night's labour chanced to hear their groans, and on discovering from whence they proceeded, immediately went to their relief, thereby in all probability saving them from death by exposure.[1]

In smuggling, indeed, as in other of the more adventurous games of life, the strands of humour and tragedy, generosity and meanness, were closely interwoven. Nowhere is this better illustrated than in the following story which was pieced together from traditional sources by that indefatigable researcher into ' Old Cornwall '—Mr R. J. Noall, of St Ives.

During the earlier half of the last century, there flourished in west Cornwall a certain smuggler called Trevaskis, who had acquired more than a local reputation for his success in running ' goods ' upon the coast, and in finding safe hiding-places for them afterwards till the danger of discovery was past. It so happened that on one occasion a cargo was expected in a little cove to the west of St Ives, a secluded spot admirably suited for the smuggler's needs. Among the few inhabitants of the valley was the owner of a grist mill, a simple old fellow who had never had any dealings with the smugglers himself, but who, on being approached by Trevaskis, good-naturedly gave permission for the storage of some of the goods on his property. This was done and all seemed well until a few weeks later when a party of excisemen arrived one day at the cove. The latter immediately began poking about the place, and in so doing discovered a nest of brandy-kegs cunningly concealed in one of the old man's furze ricks. The miller, needless to say, was terribly upset, dreading the loss of his reputation as an honest man even more than the legal consequences of his complicity. At length, however, he succeeded, in return for a bribe of £200, which comprised his life's savings, in getting the king's officer to hush the matter up. It would appear, however, that in the course of the inquiry the miller must have revealed the part which Trevaskis had had in the business, for shortly afterwards the ' sarcher ', hoping no doubt for another fat reward if he succeeded in catching so notorious a smuggler, called on the former and charged him with what he knew. The smuggler, being of a very different type from his confederate, told the exciseman bluntly that he ' warn't going to pay no bribe ', and that ' they could put him up to Bodmin (the assize town) if they 'd a mind to '. To Bodmin, accordingly, he had to go, accompanied by the exciseman, who no doubt felt in high spirits. At Hayle, the couple boarded the train at the little station

[1] *Cornwall Gazette*, 21 December 1805.

which may still be seen in Foundry Square, beneath the arches of the more modern railway line. Passing along under Clifton Terrace and through the grounds of the present Penmare House, the train at length reached the foot of 'Steamer's Hill', near Angarrack, where a stationary engine at that time pulled the trucks up a steep incline to a point near the present Gwinear Road station. On this occasion, however, the train had not got more than half-way up the incline when the wire rope attached to the front carriage parted. Back rushed the trucks gathering terrible speed, till finally, reaching the bottom, they crashed into a bank and overturned. Strange to relate, few of the passengers were seriously hurt and only one was killed, that one being the exciseman ! With no one who could now act as a witness against him, Trevaskis took his own release and returned home, amidst universal triumph, to his own village.

The story, however, ends on a tragic note. The miller's wife hearing of Trevaskis's escape never ceased to reproach her husband for his folly in having bribed the exciseman, and at length the worry of this so much preyed on the old man's mind that one morning he was found hanging dead from a beam in his own mill.

II

A complete history of Cornish smuggling has, for various reasons, never yet been attempted, and it is impossible, therefore, to assign any definite date to the beginning of the contraband trade. It is certain, however, that smuggling everywhere reached the zenith of its prosperity during the eighteenth century. In 1783, a committee which had been appointed by the Government to inquire into the matter, found that in some cases vessels of three hundred tons, manned by as many as a hundred men, were engaged in bringing ' goods ' across the Channel. ' The most considerable of these vessels,' states the Report, ' are able to make seven or eight voyages a year. The largest of them can bring, in one freight, the enormous quantity of three thousand half-ankers of spirits, and ten or twelve tons of tea, whilst their strength is such as to enable them to bid defiance to the revenue cruisers. It is also a practice for the large armed vessels to take under convoy the small defenceless craft employed in the same trade.

The landing of the cargo is regulated by signals, and the proceedings are guarded by scouts who give warning of any approach of strangers. The cargo is placed in wagons or on horses, being packed for that purpose in casks and oil-skin bags. Batteries have been established on the coast to assist and protect these illicit landings. The commodities thus imported are distributed on the coast at little more than half the usual price, or brought to the metropolis under insurance, and delivered to retail traders or private housekeepers at about two-thirds of their proper price.' [1]

Of this flourishing and important branch of the country's commerce Cornwall took its full share, and the records of the Cornish custom-houses of this date provide a complete corroboration of the truth of the above report. The hardihood and daring of the smugglers during this period knew no bounds. In 1748, the collector of customs at Penzance complained that a St Keverne boat had anchored off the pier with contraband, and that the crew had sworn bitterly at the officers when they had approached, and endeavoured to knock out their brains with a boat-hook, besides throwing large stones at them, presumably from the ballast. On a subsequent occasion, a store of contraband wine was discovered at Gunwalloe. Finding no one who would lend them a ' plough ' (i.e. wheeled cart) for its removal, the officers sealed up the goods in a room. On calling two days later, however, with the required ' plough ' they discovered that the wine was gone. That evening, the collector and surveyor being in bed, four of the excisemen went off on their own, and found a quantity of goods in the charge of nine smugglers who threatened their lives with corn pikes. The excisemen came to an agreement that if they had the goods, the horses should go free. For this, however, they were severely reprimanded by their superior officers. Later on, the collector found at Ludgvan, on two different dates, thirty-three casks of brandy, forming part of this cargo. In June of the same year, he complained of the vast number and assurance of the smugglers. ' They do smuggle so much,' he writes, ' that the seized brandy will not sell at the reserve price of 5s. 6d. a gallon, the smugglers supplying any quantity at 3s. 3d. a gallon.'

In November, the collector reported that the custom warehouse had been broken open, the new locks shattered, and eighty-five gallons of brandy taken away. He added that

[1] Report of Committee on Smuggling, Parl. Pap. (1783).

but for an alarm which was raised by some, presumably, jealous neighbours, the whole store would have been cleared. A reward of ten pounds was offered but without result, whereupon the surveyor suggested that a free pardon and a more handsome reward should be offered to anyone who would turn informer.

Later on in the same year, a warrant was obtained to arrest certain other smugglers. The constables, however, excused themselves from doing their duty on the grounds that the offenders had already fled, though it appears that the collector himself knew well enough that they might have been found had the men chosen to exert themselves.

In 1750, the collector seized a cargo of wool in a vessel lying off Penzance, but the justices (John Borlase, Christopher Hawkins, and Walter Borlase) dismissed the case, and the collectors were forced to ask for protection in case they should be served with writs by the smugglers, ' who are got to that height they take all opportunity to insult the officers '. On a subsequent occasion, a custom officer, whilst taking charge of a quantity of contraband found in a house at Marazion, had a silver spoon slipped into his pocket. This, he was charged by the smugglers with stealing. Happily for him the grand jury at the assizes threw out the bill. Some years later, two excisemen were severely injured by a certain James Rogers, of Breage, who attacked them with a hanger and a poleaxe whilst they were engaged in removing a cask of smuggled brandy from his house. For this, the officers were summoned by Rogers at Helston, on the charge of having entered upon his property without a warrant.

In 1774, the custom officers and a party of marines from the *Wolf* intercepted some smugglers, one of whom was shot dead by a marine. The coroner's jury found the latter guilty of murder. When the trial came on at Launceston, however, it was adjourned because no counsel would come to the town, the gaol fever being very bad there at the time.

In October 1751, a good haul of smugglers was made, including one Green, a notorious character. The Penzance magistrates committed them to Launceston gaol, from which, however, they escaped in November ' through the wall '. On another occasion, the controller obtained evidence against a certain John Maddern, who struck a servant of the custom with a silver tankard and ' cut his head in a vile manner, so that he was presently in a gore of blood '. His informer,

John Bodilley, afterwards came forward and said that when he swore the affidavit he was excessively overcome with liquor. Indeed, he went so far as to add that he had not been sober for several days.

In 1757, William Allen Cutler, of Penzance, broke open the custom warehouse and stole fifteen bags of tea, for which he was sentenced to seven years' transportation. The unfortunate officer, however, who was sent to retrieve the goods was promptly seized by two other smugglers, William Keigwin, of Mousehole, and John Yeoman (alias 'Lean Jack'), and locked up in a room, from which he was not released until everything had been removed.

Smuggling in Mousehole, indeed, had arrived at such a pitch that the goods were commonly carried at noonday, the local exciseman excusing himself on one of these occasions by stating that he was confined to his bed through having been pelted with stones a few days before.

In 1759, the local controller entered a plea against seized goods being sold on the Scilly Islands, adding that there were ' nought but smugglers there to sell the goods to '. In 1761, he and his men seized a French cutter, having as its cargo one hundred and thirty-four half-ankers and twenty ankers (tubs) of brandy, four casks and two small bags of tea, and two bags of tobacco. This, the captain affirmed, was the entire lading of the vessel. Further search, however, revealed two other large casks of tea, cunningly hidden behind a false bulkhead. In this year, the collector again made representation that he should be allowed a boat in order to go out to vessels moored in the bay. ' The inhabitants,' he complained, ' that have boats will never assist us, being in link with the smugglers.'

Two years later, the new controller of Scilly asked that, as smuggling had got so bad, his men might be armed, and suggested that he might have sent him, six blunderbusses, six fusils, twenty pair of pistols of different sizes, twenty hangers, two dozen tucks, two dozen long tucks, and two dozen lanterns. Whether he was provided with these, does not appear.[1]

In any case, the arming of the excisemen in no way served to check the daring of the smugglers. In 1762, two hundred and eighteen ankers of brandy were landed by the men of ' Proustock ' (Porthoustock) in one night. Five years later,

[1] Penzance custom-house books, quoted by Mr J. A. D. Bridger, *West Briton*, 22 October 1931.

a smuggling fleet of nine sail of large boats and armed sloops passed out from Penzance, in full daylight, and under the very eyes of a man-of-war.

In 1771, a very fast-sailing sloop was boarded by the excise officers in Mounts Bay. She had a crew of twelve men, and was armed with eight carriage guns. The captain declared her cargo to be salt, but, on a search being made, a false bulkhead was discovered, behind which were artfully concealed some hundreds of dozens of silk handkerchiefs. In the ceiling of the cabin, which was hung with paper, were likewise found a large store of silk cambrics, muslin, lace, snuff-boxes, and trinkets.[1]

In 1772, a Penzance custom boat was plundered and sunk by a smuggler, and on 29th November of the same year, another sailed into Penzance harbour and carried off the revenue cutter *Brilliant*, which was lying there with captured cargo in her hold.[2] In 1775, two vessels lay off Penzance for three days discharging cargo, the custom collector looking on helplessly meanwhile, since everyone ashore was either actively interested in the success of the 'run', or a passive sympathizer. About the same time an excise ship off Padstow, instead of chasing, was chased into the port by a large Irish vessel which ' by way of bravado fired seven guns at the mouth of the harbour and hung out a flag in triumph', afterwards sailing away to discharge her cargo at Newquay, in which place the smugglers and excise officers were stated to be on excellent terms. It was not uncommon, indeed, for a hundred horses to be awaiting the arrival of such cargoes here nearly every day of the week.[3]

Much of the reckless daring of the smugglers at this time was undoubtedly due to the fact that they enjoyed the protection of, and not infrequently an actual alliance with, persons of local standing and position. In 1770, the Mayor of Penzance was himself bound over in a considerable sum ' not to be again guilty of smuggling '. In 1779, four persons belonging to Poughill and Madron were prosecuted for having evaded the customs on smuggled goods to the extent of £18,600. They offered £160 in composition. One was a small farmer, whose property was worth but £15 a year ; another a labourer,

[1] Penzance custom-house books, quoted by Mr J. A. D. Bridger, *West Briton*, 22 October 1931.
[2] J. B. Cornish, *Cornish Magazine*, I, 118.
[3] M. Oppenheim, *Victoria History of Cornwall*.

working for him.   The two others were small yeomen.   These men were, of course, financed by well-to-do people.

In 1780, the custom officials seized no less than 636 lb. of tea *in one day* in the parishes of Sithney and Breage.   This valuable haul was derived almost entirely from the cottages, where the goods were concealed under beds or in haystacks. About the same time, a charge was brought against all the custom officials at Mousehole for themselves assisting the smugglers and receiving bribes.[1]

' The riches of the land and sea is in full gallop to France, and the countenance given to the smugglers by those whose business it is to restrain these pernicious practices hath brot 'm so bold and daring that nobody can venture to come near them with safety whilst they are at their work,' wrote Mr George Borlase in 1753.   ' The coasts here swarm with smugglers from the Land's End to the Lizard, so that I wonder the soldiers (which were late quartered here) should have been ordered off without being replaced by others.'[2]   One would have thought that Mr Borlase, being a Cornishman, and knowing something of the propensities of the local squires (who were also the magistrates), might have found a possible answer to his own question.   Be that as it may, it is quite clear from the scale on which much of the smuggling of these days was conducted that a large amount of capital was invested in the trade.   The vessels used in the Cornish ports ranged, as we know, from fifty to two hundred and fifty tons burthen, and were often heavily armed.   Mevagissey-built craft in particular were so noted for their fast-sailing qualities as to be in demand from Dover to the Land's End.   Some of these luggers carried a thousand yards of canvas in their mainsail, and with a fair wind would cross the Channel in eight hours. ' In those days,' wrote Mr Matthias Dunn, ' the purchase price of a cargo of brandy for one of these ships in France or the Channel Islands was £1,500, and the same would be sold for £3,000 in this country.   As a consequence, when smuggling was in its full swing, money became so plentiful that neighbours lent guineas to each other by the handful, not stopping to count, or being so particular as to reckon by ones or twos.'[3]

[1] Penzance .custom-house books, quoted by Mr J. A. D. Bridger, *West Briton*, 22 October 1931.

[2] Lanisley Letters, printed in *Journal of Royal Institution of Cornwall* (1881), XXIII, 374–9.

[3] *Western Morning News*, 8 March 1930.

As the result of the encouragement and protection which they received on land, and the absence of interference at sea, owing to the forces of the navy being otherwise requisitioned during the European wars, the latter half of the eighteenth century was indeed the Golden Age of smuggling. ' In the western part of this county,' wrote Mr Edward Giddy, of Tredrea, to the chief custom officer in 1778, ' smuggling, since the soldiers have been drawn off, has been carried on almost without control. Irish wherries, carrying fourteen, sixteen, or more guns, and well manned, frequently land large quantities of goods in defiance of the officers of the customs and excise, and their crews, armed with swords and pistols, escort the smugglers a considerable distance from the sea. In this way, goods are carried from one part of the country to another almost every night. About a fortnight since, a large wherry landed, according to the best information I can obtain, from fifteen hundred to two thousand ankers of spirits (containing $9\frac{1}{2}$ gallons on an average), about twenty tons of tea, and other kinds of smuggled goods, on a sandy beach in Mounts Bay, between the towns of Penzance and Marazion. This beach lies near a public road which, whilst the goods were discharging, was filled with armed men, in order to stop every traveller in whom they could not confide, till the goods were safely lodged in the country.

' A few days after, two officers got information that a very considerable quantity of goods was concealed in the house and premises of a well-known smuggler. They obtained from me a search warrant, but were forcibly hindered from executing it by four men, one armed with a pistol and a large whip, the others with sticks and bludgeons. They were told that if they persisted they would have their brains blown out. As the law now stands, I fear a criminal prosecution would have been useless for the reason, which it shocks me to mention, that a Cornish jury would certainly acquit the smugglers.

' These, my lord, are facts. It would be mere pedantry to attempt to describe to your lordship the shocking effects, the moral and political consequences of smuggling carried to such a daring height, but I cannot help saying that perjury, drunkenness, idleness, poverty, and contempt of the law, and a universal corruption of manners are, in this neighbourhood, too plainly seen to accompany it.

' It is a very unlucky circumstance that Patrick Plunkett, who was lately discharged from our county gaol by an order from your lordship, should have escaped without a prosecution, for he is a very daring fellow, and I fear his advice, example, and impunity will increase the audacity and inhumanity of the smugglers which the civil power, such at least as we can obtain from it, seems too weak to oppose with effect.—Yours, etc., Edward Giddy.' [1]

The state of affairs which the writer describes was by no means confined to west Cornwall, but appears to have been more or less general to the county at this period. ' I well remember, some time before the conclusion of the peace,' stated a writer from St Columb in 1765, ' that having occasion to land some goods out of one of my vessels at the port of Padstow, my servants set out some time before day, but by fine moonlight, when, crossing the common about three miles from us, they met sixty horses having each three bags of tea on them of fifty-six or fifty-eight pounds weight. All this was landed on a beach about two miles to the west of Padstow, and carried from thence through this county and into Devon.' [2]

Though the contemporary records are soberly worded, they suffice to show the influence which the astonishing exploits of the smuggler kings of this date must have had upon the public imagination. Nor is it strange that in course of time and through oft recounting, the lives and actions of such men should at length have passed beyond history and become enshrined in popular romance.

Of all the figures associated by tradition with the smuggling trade of the north coast of Cornwall during the eighteenth century, none has acquired a more lasting notoriety than that of ' Cruel Coppinger', the Dane, concerning whom the Rev. R. S. Hawker has catalogued a series of dreadful tales in his book, entitled *Footprints of Former Men in Far Cornwall*. Very little is actually known of this wild and, perhaps, half-mythical personage. Local tradition, however, relates that one day in the midst of a fearful storm a foreign-rigged vessel was seen in the offing, drifting in towards the shore. Whether or not she was actually wrecked was never known, for the ship was soon afterwards lost sight of in the driving clouds and rain. One man, however, came ashore from her, swimming powerfully through the boiling surf. Wrapped in a

---

[1] Penzance custom-house books, quoted in *West Briton*, 22 October 1931.

[2] Letters from William Rawlings to Earl of Dartmouth.—Hist. MSS. Comm., XV, 176.

cloak that he is said to have torn from the shoulders of an old woman who was on the beach, the stranger leaped up behind a farmer's daughter who had ridden down to see the wreck, and was taken by her to her father's house, where he was fed, clothed, and most hospitably received. He was a fine, handsome, well-built man, and gave himself out as being highly connected in his own country. He soon won the young woman's affections, and at her father's death, which occurred not long after, he easily induced her to marry him. The union was not a happy one, and, fortunately perhaps, there was only one child—a deaf and dumb idiot who inherited his father's cruel disposition and delighted in torturing all living things. It is even said that he cunningly killed one of his young playmates. After his marriage, Coppinger made himself captain of an organized band of smugglers, and through his black deeds quickly earned the title by which he is remembered. Hawker in his book refers to Coppinger's ship as the *Black Prince*, and says that he had it built for himself in Denmark, and that men who had made themselves in any way obnoxious to him on land were carried on board this vessel, and compelled, by fearful oaths, to enrol themselves as members of her crew. Although Hawker was a novelist, rather than an historian, there is no reason for doubting this particular assertion. In the year 1835, an old man of the age of ninety-seven, told Miss M. A. Courtney, of Penzance, that when a youth he had been abducted in a precisely similar manner, and had only been ransomed by his friends after two years' service on board a smuggling craft. ' And all,' said the old man, very simply, ' because I happened to see one man kill another, and they thought I should mention it.'

Hawker, who delighted in flights of the imagination, whether his own or those of the simple countryfolk among whom he lived, credits Coppinger with a wondrous and fearful end. His account, however, tallies so closely with that given by Bottrell of the passing of a wicked and notorious wrecker near St Just that we prefer quoting from the latter on account of its admirable word-painting. ' At length,' states this writer, ' the time came for the fiend to claim his own. Several parsons and other pious folks were sent for and readily came, for the dying sinner was rich. Although it was harvest-time and high-by-day, the old wrecker's chamber became, at times, as dark as night. The parsons saw the devil in the room when others could not ; and by their reading they drove him to take many shapes, but for all that he would not be put out, and at last, when he took the form of a fly and buzzed about the dying wretch, they saw that it was vain for them to try any longer. During all the time the exorcists were thus engaged the chamber seemed—by the sound—to be filled with the sea splashing around the bed, and waves were heard as if surging and breaking against the house, though it was a good bit inland. Whilst this was taking place at the dying man's bedside, two men, who were about harvest work in one of his fields near the cliff, heard a hollow voice, as if coming from the sea, which said, " The hour is come but the man is not come ". Looking in the direction from whence the words proceeded, they saw no person, but far out to sea they beheld a black, heavy, square-rigged ship, with all sail set, coming in fast, against wind and tide and not a hand to be seen aboard her. She came so close under the cliff that only her topmast could be seen ; when black clouds—that seemed to rise out of the deep—gathered around her, and extended thence straight to the dying man's chamber. The harvesters, terrified at the sight of this ship-of-doom so near them, ran up to the town-place, just at the moment as the old sinner died, when his dwelling shook as if about to fall. Everybody, in great fright, rushed out and saw the black clouds roll off towards the death-ship, which at once sailed away—amidst a blaze of lightning—over the sea, and disappeared. The weather immediately cleared, and nothing unusual occurred until a. few men assembled to put the wrecker's ghastly remains quickly off the face of the earth. Then, as the coffin was borne towards the churchyard, the sky again became suddenly overcast, and a tempest sprang up with such violence that they could scarcely keep on their legs to reach the churchyard stile, where such sheets of blinding lightning flashed around them that they dropped the coffin and rushed into the church. The storm having at length abated, they ventured out to find nothing of the coffin but its handles and a few nails, all else having been set on fire and consumed by the lightning.' [1]

So in like manner was Cruel Coppinger overtaken by his fate, as the story was related by the old droll-tellers from whom Hawker derived his account. Despite the mythical nature of this and many of the other stories which are associated with

[1] William Bottrell, *Traditions and Hearthside Stories of West Cornwall*, second series, 247–9.

him, there is reason for supposing that an actual smuggler of this name did at one time flourish on the north coast of Cornwall. It would appear also that he amassed enough money by his ill-doings to purchase a small freehold estate near the sea, the title-deeds of which, bearing his signature, were in existence not long since.[1]

III

It has often been claimed that the teaching of Wesley and the spread of the Methodist movement was responsible for putting an almost complete check upon smuggling. In point of fact, however, this was far from being the case, since, as already shown, smuggling and Methodism long went hand in hand, and impossible as the association may seem to-day it is none the less true, that in the past some of the most notorious of Cornish smugglers were also staunch supporters of the dissenting cause. Even their natural enemies, the officers of the excise, were fain to admit the sterling qualities of many of these men, the collector of custom at Penzance in 1771 describing Richard Pentreath of Mousehole, otherwise 'Doga', as 'an honest man in all his dealings though a notorious smuggler', whilst Thomas Mann, of the same place, is likewise spoken of in the official records as a 'reputed smuggler', but 'an honest man'.[2]

In all the annals of Cornish smuggling, no better illustration is provided of this strange, but not entirely incomprehensible, mixture of honest bravery with an inclination to break a certain man-made law, than in the case of the Carter family of Prussia Cove. The most famous member of this gang, John Carter, the 'King of Prussia', is still remembered on account of the high standard of integrity which he adopted in all his commercial dealings. Characteristic of this is the time-honoured story which relates how, on a certain occasion, he broke open the custom-house store at Penzance in order to recover some goods which had been confiscated during his absence from home, explaining to his comrades who demurred at the risk, that he had agreed to deliver the same to his customers by a

---

[1] M. A. Gourtney, *Cornish Feasts and Folklore*, 91.
[2] J. B. Cornish, *Cornish Magazine*, I, 118.

specified date, and that to fail in this obligation would be to forfeit his reputation as an honest trader. Nor is it yet forgotten how, when the excisemen arrived the next morning and found that the place had been broken open, they said amongst themselves, ' John Carter has been here, and we know it because he is an upright man, and has taken away nothing which was not his own '.[1]

Such, indeed, were the ethics of Cornish smuggling in its palmiest days and among its most celebrated practitioners. It is not so surprising, therefore, in the light of this, to find that the diary of Harry Carter,[2] brother of ' the king', reads more like a circuit minister's commonplace book than the annals of a daring smuggler, and whilst page after page is filled with religious ' experiences', only such occasional entries as ' bought a cutter of 160 tons and 19 guns ', or ' surprised by two man-of-war boats while landing at Costan', show that the worthy captain was still engaged in a worldly vocation of a strangely different nature.

The story of Prussia Cove, and of the daring adventurers whose deeds have made it famous for all time, has been well told by the late Mr J. B. Cornish, of Penzance, in an interesting article contributed to the *Cornish Magazine*. The very name of the cove (which lies immediately to the eastward of Cuddan Point in Mounts Bay) is John Carter's own, it being said that the latter, when a boy and playing at soldiers with other children, so regularly claimed to be the ' King of Prussia ', that for his sake the cove where he dwelt at length lost its older name of Porthleah and became known as ' The King of Prussia's Cove '. The degree of fame which attended the doings of the local ' king ' during the hey-day of his prosperity is amusingly illustrated by the story told of a sailor who on his return between voyages during the Napoleonic wars used regularly to visit an old farmer residing in the neighbourhood of Gwithian.

' Well, what 's the news this time, my son ? ' was the question which greeted the traveller on one of these occasions.

' Why, the latest thing I 've heard, Uncle Caleb, is that the King of Prussia has suffered a big loss.'

' My dear life, that so, es 'a ? ' exclaimed the farmer. ' I tell 'ee, Maister Joe, I 'm downright sorry for that man. 'Twas

---

[1] J. B. Cornish, *Cornish Magazine*, I, 118.

[2] *The Autobiography of a Cornish Smuggler*, edited by J. B. Cornish (1894).

only last month he lost nigh upon forty ankers of brandy—
by information, so I 'm told ! ' [1]

There is little doubt that for the majority of poor people
living in west Cornwall at this time, there was only *one* King
of Prussia, a fact which is the less marvellous when one
recollects that newspapers were still a rarity in all but the
houses of the well-to-do, whilst the deeds of the smuggling
king at their doors had reached a pitch of notoriety almost
eclipsing the fame of Bonaparte himself.

The site chosen by the Carter family for the headquarters
of their operations had every natural advantage to recommend
it. ' A spot,' as Mr J. B. Cornish has said, ' so sheltered and
secluded that it is impossible to see what boats are in the
little harbour until one literally leans over the edge of the cliff
above ; a harbour cut out of the solid rock and a roadway
with wheel-tracks, partly cut and partly worn, climbing up the
face of the cliff on either side of the cove, caves and remains of
caves everywhere, some of them with their mouths built up
which are reputed to be connected with the house above by
secret passages—these are still existing trademarks left by one
of the most enterprising smuggling gangs that Cornwall has
ever known.' In this favoured spot lived and reigned John
Carter, the King of Prussia, during the years 1770 to 1807.
Many a stirring and exciting tale has been recorded by Mr
Cornish of the exploits of that adventurous reign, probably
the best known being that of the smugglers firing upon a
revenue cutter from their little battery which lay stationed
on the point between Bessie's and the ' King's ' Cove.[2] This
act, though it marks an epoch in the history of Cornish
smuggling, was in reality purely one of bravado, little damage
being done, either by the guns of the smugglers or by the
return fire which was opened upon the latter from the decks
of the ship-of-war.

Indeed, the annals of Mounts Bay smuggling as a whole
are remarkably free from tales of bloodshed. How far this
was due to restraint on the part of the smugglers, or to the
tact of the revenue men in keeping out of harm's way, it is, of
course, not easy to say. For it is clear that very often when the
excise officers were not actually terrorized, ' they wore fog
spectacles with bank-note shades', as a writer has said.
Smuggling, indeed, was carried on even in the official Falmouth

[1] Per Miss B. Vivian.
[2] ' Annals of the Smugglers,' *Cornish Magazine*, I, 122.

packet boats, running to and from Lisbon and the West Indies, and wine from the former was sold in Cornwall at this time at little more than half the ordinary price. 'The captains themselves,' states a contemporary, ' smuggle large quantities, and connive at the men doing the same, not allowing them sufficient wages whereon to live without it. When the *Vansittart*, East Indiaman, recently arrived in Falmouth, people came together on horse and foot from twenty miles around and flocked on board every day, including Sundays, as to a fair. Muslins, silks, and other valuable and dutiable goods were sold to the value of at least £5,000.' [1]

It was a notorious fact that scarcely any seizures were ever made at this port by the excise.

With a whole country-side in league against them, it is small wonder that the excisemen occasionally showed themselves not over-zealous in the cause of duty, preferring to take the line of least resistance rather than risk their lives in the attempt of an impossible task. Chief among the aiders and abettors of the smugglers on land were the miners and alluvial tin streamers, and liquor brought ashore anywhere in the neighbourhood of Penzance was always certain of a safe hiding-place among the stream-banks and moors in the secluded valleys of the West Penwith mining area. Many of the streamers themselves, moreover, indulged in smuggling, and during the summer-time, when water was scarce, found a profitable outlet for their activities in the taking of three or four trips to Roscoff, in Brittany, for the purchase of brandy, silk handkerchiefs, lace, and other articles of contraband. ' Our Free Traders ran but little risk then,' writes Mr Bottrell, ' as there was no Preventive Service of any note. If the revenue cutters came near our western land their crews dreaded more to fall in with the Cornish traders than our smugglers ever feared the king's men. As for the riding officers and excisemen, they would rather ride anywhere than on the cliffs in the dark nights when the beacon fires blazed from the rocky cairns to guide the smugglers' boats into the coves. Still less would the officers care to venture among the stream-leats and bogs where scores of ankers (barrels) of brandy used formerly to be left, till the innkeepers, gentry, and other regular customers wanted them. Now and then, of course, there was a bit of a shindy between the streamers and excisemen for mere sham, and in return the smugglers would leave an anker or two to be taken, in places

[1] M. Oppenheim, *Victoria History of Cornwall*, 506.

where they never kept their stock. This served for a decoy and the Government crew knew well enow that that was their share, and they had better not look for any more.' [1]

During those good old roystering days, many of the young 'West Country' blades, sons of the yeoman squires who farmed the ancestral tenements of West Penwith, were in the habit of fitting out fast-sailing, well-armed little craft which they kept in Porth-gwarra, Porth-Curnow, and other of the secluded coves which lie deep-hidden in that romantic strip of coastline between Penzance and the Land's End. The work of seedtime or harvest being over, the boats would be got ready for a trip to France, and they and their crews would then disappear for weeks or months on end, often returning at the end of that time with goods of such richness and rarity as an over-curious person would scarcely have credited as being *bought* from our neighbours across the Channel. Little inquiry was made, however, of the exact doings of these wild young rovers when away on their mysterious voyages, and if rumours occasionally hinted at some rich foreign merchantman having been relieved of portions of its cargo, they were soon quieted ; for at that time little distinction was made between smuggler, privateer, and pirate. Indeed, with money to spend on one and all, with their gifts of jewels and lace for the women, and their brandy, rum, and tobacco for the squire, such reckless young adventurers were the heroes of the hour, and for long after their return the halls of the old decaying mansions which were their homes resounded far into the night with the shouts and songs of the feasters, who kept open house for all who cared to join them in their wild and care-free revels. [2]

IV

Whilst the wars with France continued, cutters and luggers armed with eighteen or twenty guns apiece, and manned by reckless adventurers of this sort, had more or less their own way in the Channel between Ushant and the Smalls. With the declaration of the Peace of Amiens, however, in 1802, the armed smuggler began to prove a definite source of embarrass-

[1] *Traditions and Hearthside Stories of West Cornwall* (1870), 70.
[2] *Traditions and Hearthside Stories of West Cornwall* (1870), 192 *et seq.*

ment to the Government, and measures were put in hand to stay their practices, which were rightly considered a menace to our international relationships. This decision, however, was regarded in Cornwall with a lack of enthusiasm which would appear to signify that considerable interests were at stake. ' A squadron of frigates being ordered to cruise on the Cornish coasts against the smugglers,' comments the *Cornwall Gazette*, a Tory newspaper, on 13th February 1802, ' has raised a formidable idea in the public mind of the extent of the illicit trade carried on here. We shall be much surprised, however, if these frigates shall, at the end of twelve months, have seized as much spirits as will be equal to the regular consumption of their crews. The fact is that while the war establishment is kept up, some employment must be found for it—" When children are doing nothing they are doing mischief ".'

Despite such protestations, however, the surveillance of the Government forces at this time, on sea and land, was not without its effect. Whether through the over-recklessness of their crews or because their malpractices had marked them out for special attention, Polperro boats seem to have suffered most during these years. Among the losses sustained by this port may be mentioned the *Unity*, which after having made, as it is said, no less than five hundred successful trips across the Channel, was at length captured with one hundred and seventy casks of spirits on board, besides large quantities of tobacco. As a measure of the smugglers' daring, it is interesting to note that when seized this vessel was lying in Plymouth Sound, with the king's ships ranked about her on every side ! The *Expedition* of Polperro met with a like fate during the same month, when she was brought into Plymouth with nine hundred ankers of brandy in her hold, ' besides bale goods and tobacco'. About six weeks later, another of the Polperro fleet, the *Three Friends*, fell to the king, being surprised by H.M.S. *Spitfire* whilst discharging her illicit cargo into boats outside her home port. On this occasion, as in that of the *Lottery*, another Polperro capture, we find the crew making armed resistance, and one smuggler was killed on the spot. A few months later, yet another Polperro craft, the lugger *Providence*, was seized by a revenue cutter when on her voyage home from Guernsey with eight hundred ankers on board.[1]

Polperro, however, was not the only sufferer. In February 1802, the *Nymphe* frigate captured, and sent into Plymouth,

[1] C. K. C. Andrew, *Western Morning News*, 13 March 1930.

a smuggling cutter of Fowey with nine hundred and forty-four ankers of spirits and some dry goods on board,[1] whilst in the following month we read of one hundred and thirty kegs of spirits being seized in the parish of St Hilary by the officers of the excise.[2]

Such incidents, though they read coldly enough upon paper, were often of an exciting nature, and took place under romantic circumstances. On one occasion in the summer of 1801, a smuggler, with two ankers of brandy on the horse under him, was discovered by an exciseman on the steep and precipitous road leading down to King Harry Passage on the River Fal. Without waiting to be challenged, the smuggler immediately rode off at full speed, closely pursued by the officer who was also on horseback. Despite the breakneck speed with which he descended the hill, the smuggler, on reaching the passage, found his pursuer pressing so hard upon him that he immediately plunged his horse into the water, in an attempt to gain the opposite shore. The horse, however, had not swum half-way over, before, exhausted with fatigue and the load on his back, he was on the point of sinking. Realizing this, the intrepid rider slid from the animal's back, and with his knife cut the slings which bound the ankers. Swimming then alongside his horse, the smuggler exerted himself in the attempt to keep the animal's head above water, but all to no purpose, for the horse was drowned, and the man only with the utmost difficulty reached the opposite shore. Meantime, the less mettlesome exciseman had halted on the nearer bank, from whence he surveyed the ineffectual struggle ; afterwards, with the help of the ferryman, getting possession of the kegs.[3]

Still, as events proved, the anxiety of Cornwall at the possibility of any serious check to smuggling at this time was premature. With renewal of hostilities in 1803, the forces of the Crown were once again diverted to more pressing matters, and smuggling took on a new lease of life. One might even say that the Government was in some measure responsible for stimulating it. For in the early months of the war, owing to the need of men for the services and home defence, Royal Proclamation was made that any smuggler who had fled the country should, provided he was not charged with murder, be permitted to return without fear of arrest, on his entering

---

[1] *Cornwall Gazette*, 6 February 1802.
[2] *Cornwall Gazette*, 13 March 1802.
[3] *Cornwall Gazette*, 29 August 1801.

into bond to refrain from smuggling practices for the future. Copies of this proclamation were posted in all Cornish villages, and it was not long before the news filtered through to those who were lying in exile overseas. Among the first to take advantage of the amnesty was a certain Christopher Pollard, of Madron. The latter had been charged some years before with obstructing and assaulting the revenue officers, and had fled to Guernsey in order to escape the consequences of his crimes. He now returned to Cornwall and signed the requisite bond, his brother, Joseph Pollard, standing surety for the sum of £200. But for him, as for many another, the allurements of the old adventurous life were too strong, and little more than six months had elapsed before Pollard, as appears from a brief to counsel, dated 1805, was again concerned in a charge of smuggling. The prosecution states that on this occasion the accused had assaulted the officers of H.M. excise when occupied in their duty at Sennen, and had incited a crowd of three or four hundred persons to attack the excisemen with a view to carrying off the smuggled goods which they had captured and were defending on the beach. This landing was indeed a valuable one, consisting as it did of one thousand gallons of brandy, one thousand gallons of rum, one thousand gallons of Geneva, and five hundred pounds of tobacco. In addition to the general charge of inciting the mob, Pollard was accused of having offered £100 for the rescue of a hundred ankers of the spirits and ' of using other violent and improper language '. The counsel for the defence admitted that Pollard was part-owner of these goods, but stated that what had actually happened was that on going to Sennen he had found the cargo in the possession of the revenue authorities, and that so far from inciting the mob to a rescue he had gone straight home, only calling in on the excise officer at Newlyn in order to advise him to go to Sennen at once ' lest any unforeseen circumstances might ensue '. It further appears that in the evening of the same day on which the cargo had been landed, Pollard was in a public-house at Penzance trying to sell a yoke of oxen to a farmer of Nancothnan, named Pool. The latter afterwards accompanied Pollard to Sennen and agreed to provide him with horses wherewith to remove the cargo in return for the promise of a cask of brandy for his own use— ' he having a number of workmen and tradesmen about him at the time '. On arriving at the beach, however, about eleven o'clock at night and finding a huge crowd firing muskets and throwing stones at the excisemen, ' they decided that that was no place for them to stay for that they would be killed '. So both returned home.

The principal witness for the prosecution was a certain Anne George. This woman, it appears, was a person of notorious character. At the time of the trial she is described as being the wife of Joseph George who, up to a short time before, had been the keeper of the Sennen inn—a place which had the reputation of being ' the resort of all the idle blackguards in the county '. During the time in which he had kept the inn, Joseph George had acted as a smuggling agent for his landlord, a well-to-do farmer of the parish, named Dionysius Williams. Presuming on the secret hold which they possessed over their landlord, through the knowledge of his illicit transactions, the Georges had for some time refused to pay any rent for the inn, and at length the owner, very unwisely, had decided to eject them. Infuriated by this, the innkeeper's wife had thereupon turned king's evidence against Williams, and reaped her revenge in seeing the latter served with a long term of imprisonment.

The villainy of the woman's character, however, is best revealed by the account, given in the same brief, of a quarrel which she had had some years previously with her brother-in-law, John George, over a few pounds of tobacco. In this case also she had turned king's evidence, accused the victim of her malice of firing on a revenue officer, and so incriminated him that the poor wretch was actually convicted and hanged on 5th June 1802. In a district in which almost every inhabitant had probably had some hand in smuggling at one time or another, the presence of such a malicious and wholly unscrupulous informer caused widespread fear, and no doubt accounted for the difficulty which was experienced in obtaining witnesses for the defence. ' The terror and dismay, indeed, which this woman has been the means of spreading throughout the county are not to be described,' stated the counsel's brief. ' Independent of the present prosecution no less than five persons have been capitally indicted by her means, one of whom had already been executed, and so callous is her conscience, and deadly her revenge, that persons who may have given her slight cause for offence are now trembling for fear of the consequences, expecting to be made the next victim of the detestable passion with which she is actuated.' [1]

[1] Brief to Counsel, seen by kind permission of Mr J. A. D. Bridger, Penzance.

It was probably due to the discreditable character of the chief witness against him, rather than to any proof of his own innocence, that Pollard in this case owed his acquittal. His narrow escape from justice, however, appears to have taught him no lesson, and ten years later he was serving a term of imprisonment in Devon gaol as the result of his having been arrested off Plymouth when in the possession of a large quantity of smuggled goods.

It was not until the actual signing of peace after Waterloo that the changes which mark a definite epoch in the history of smuggling came about. The termination of the war, whilst it greatly augmented the ranks of the smugglers through the release of men from the services, also had the effect of enabling the Government at long last to deal seriously with the contraband trade. In 1816–17 a new and much more efficient preventive force was established along the south coast of England, and a regular watch began to be kept upon the activities of the smaller fishing coves and ports. The consequences seem to have borne particularly hardly upon the inhabitants of the Scilly Islands, who had hitherto looked upon smuggling as their chief source of revenue. In 1818, seven magistrates from Penzance and the district went over to the Scillies to make a report on the condition of the people. They concluded their findings with the following interesting statement : ' And above all, by the entire suppression of smuggling on these islands (a measure which has been accomplished by the preventive boat system established there) the islanders, who had too long and too successfully depended on their contraband trade, are now deprived of their chief means of support '.[1]

Actually, the claim that smuggling had been entirely suppressed on the Scillies at this date was somewhat too sweeping, for records show that the trade continued to linger in the islands for many years after this. Here, as elsewhere, however, the increasing watchfulness of the preventive service was giving the smugglers serious cause for concern. About this time, therefore, the latter began to change their methods and, abandoning the large, heavily-armed craft which they had hitherto employed, took to a smaller class of vessel. For this, the half-decked fishing boats of Cawsand Bay and other ports along the south coast proved particularly suited. During the ten years 1832–42 no less than fifty-two boats and eighty-one

[1] *West Briton*, 22 October 1931.

men belonging to Cawsand were engaged in the smuggling trade with the ports across the Channel—a fairly good record for one village.[1]

Roscoff was now the chief entrepôt of the smugglers, as Guernsey had been in earlier times. In one month, November 1824, the following Cornish smuggling craft left Roscoff: *Marie I*, of Cawsand, with cargo for the west of Dodman; *Marie II*, of Cawsand, for Hemwick Cove; *Cruzier*, of Polperro, for St Austell Bay; *Ant*, of Mevagissey, for the Black Head; *Arethusa*, of Cawsand, for St Austell Bay; and *Exchange*, of Polperro, for near the Black Head.[2]

In March 1832, a ' well-informed ' correspondent reported from Roscoff that ' smuggling had not been carried on so extensively at any time during the last twenty years as it is now '. In the following year, the same writer gave information concerning nineteen West Country boats which had arrived or departed from this port within a fortnight.[3] These were, for the most part, small craft, varying from nine to a hundred tons. Crossing the hundred miles of water between Roscoff and the Cornish coast in the bitter gales of a hard winter can have been no child's play even in decked vessels of this size, and, as Commander Shore has written, one can scarcely imagine what it must have been in the open boats, to which the more adventurous souls entrusted their persons and their cargoes.[4] Nevertheless, there were always men to be found who were eager to play the risky game, and willing to stake their all in the attempt to bring in the articles of contraband for which there was still such a ready sale.

A story told of Prussia Cove somewhat after the days of the ' king ', serves to illustrate the humours of smuggling as also the hardiness and endurance of the men who were engaged at this period in the trade. On a certain occasion, two Prussia Cove men were returning home from Roscoff in a small sailing boat well laden with contraband. The wind having dropped, they had been forced for the latter part of their crossing to labour at the oars and, thinking to save themselves the last few miles, decided to put in to Mullion. On arriving here, however, they found two excisemen waiting on the beach. Exhausted after their long and arduous passage, the smugglers

[1] H. N. Shore, *Smuggling Days and Smuggling Ways*, 109 (edn. 1929).
[2] H. N. Shore, *Smuggling Days*, 99.
[3] H. N. Shore, *Smuggling Days*, 102, 105.
[4] H. N. Shore, *Smuggling Days*, 110 (edn. 1929).

offered five pounds in order to be allowed to land. Bribery in this case, however, proved of no avail, and so with heavy hearts they bent themselves once more to the task of rowing on to the Cove. Meantime, the officers mounted their horses and kept pace with them along the cliffs. Just short of the Cove, the smugglers passed out of sight of the excisemen behind a headland, and here, much to their delight, they found a Cover out in his boat, hauling crab-pots. Making good use of their opportunity, they quickly exchanged the contents of their boat with that of their neighbour, and rowed on their way. They had hardly drawn into the Cove before the officers arrived, and immediately set about a search—but in vain ! It was not until some hours later, when the coast was once more clear, that an innocent-looking fisherman came into shore bringing with him a catch which is not often taken in crab-pots.[1]

In 1818, there arose a curious case which illustrates not only the ingenuity of the smugglers, but the shady practices to which the legal fraternity were willing to lend themselves in the cause of such clients. About this time, two St Just smugglers, named Oats and Permewan, had been very success-ful in running goods upon the north coast of Cornwall. Their activities extended over a considerable area, and in the course of a few months they are stated to have landed no less than six cargoes. In order to ensure greater secrecy, the smugglers had adopted the method of employing an agent—by name Pridham—to whom they made payment for the goods and whose duty it was to settle their accounts with the French merchants. For some time the arrangement appears to have worked fairly well. At length, however, a report reached the smugglers that the remittances, which were always promptly made on their part, were not being forwarded by their agent. Realizing that the latter was no longer to be trusted, the smugglers decided to sever the connection. On this, Pridham announced that he would turn king's evidence against them. A meeting between Permewan and the agent was accordingly arranged, with a view, if possible, to buying off the evidence, although the lawyer in charge of the smugglers' defence must have realized as clearly as his clients that there was but slight hope of achieving this. It appears, however, that a short time before the meeting was to take place, Permewan suggested that he had doubts as to Pridham's

[1] J. B. Cornish, *Cornish Magazine*, I, 123.

ability to recognize him, seeing that they had only met on two occasions, for a few minutes at a time. They therefore decided to take the risk of dressing up a brother of Permewan's in the latter's clothes, and sending him to Devonshire to the appointed interview. In the meantime, the smuggler brother was at pains on the day on which the meeting took place to be seen walking about the streets of Penzance, where he was spoken to by all and sundry. By this means an indisputable alibi was established, which so entirely discredited Pridham's evidence as to render it wholly worthless in a court of law.[1]

By the forties of the last century, the palmiest days of Cornish smuggling were over. Nevertheless, the trade continued on a fairly extensive scale ; whilst the smugglers themselves had lost none of their former daring. On 18th September 1840, we learn that H.M. custom-house at Helford, within the port of Gweek, was attacked by a body of men, ' consisting, as it is supposed, of upwards of thirty persons, who broke open the heavy doors and strong locks, and robbed the cellars of one hundred and twenty-six kegs of contraband brandy (each keg containing four and a half gallons of spirit) which had been seized some days before at Coverack '. The burglars commenced their work about 1 a.m., and in the course of half an hour had succeeded in removing all the kegs except three, which they left for the benefit of the officers at Helford ! The man and his wife who lived at the custom-house had heard the sound of the cellar doors being broken open, but had been afraid to give the alarm, which, indeed, they could not well have done in any case, as the house was a remote building nearly three-quarters of a mile from any other dwelling. From the tracks of the wheels which were seen next day, it was supposed that at least three wagons had been employed in removing the spirit, a fact which accounted for the rapidity with which the whole business had been effected.[2]

The smugglers, however, were no longer in the position of being able to ' get away with it ' every time, and the task of bringing the goods to land now involved even more difficulty and danger than that of their subsequent distribution, once they were ashore. On 27th September 1840, the Government cruiser *Harpy*, whilst patrolling in the Channel, made capture of the *Five Brothers*, a smuggling craft belonging to Cawsand,

[1] Brief to Counsel, seen by permission of Mr J. A. D. Bridger.
[2] *West Briton*, 25 September 1840.

together with seventy-two half-ankers of foreign spirits which had been thrown overboard by the latter in the course of an exciting chase. The remainder of the cargo was sunk with large stones ' so that the people of the *Harpy* could not recover them '—though it is more than probable that the inhabitants of Cawsand could, and did, since the fishing up of sunken tubs by means of crooks or ' creepers ' was an art which was well known to the smugglers of this date. In the following week the *Harpy* was successful in capturing, about fifteen miles off the Lizard, another Cawsand vessel, called the *Fox*, having on board one hundred and twenty-six half-ankers of contraband spirit, and four men, including ' the notorious smuggler, Peter Benallack, tailor, of Veryan. This', states the correspondent of the *West Briton*, ' makes eleven smuggling boats that Lieutenant Drew has taken since he has held command of the *Harpy*, whilst eleven more have been compelled to throw overboard their cargo in order to effect escape when being chased '.[1]

The penalty now imposed on the ' fair trader ' who was caught in the act was certainly severe enough to damp the ardour of all but the most reckless ; consisting, as it did, in having his vessel sawn up into three parts. As Commander H. N. Shore has remarked, ' the consequent feelings—and language—of the owner, as he watched the slow disintegration of the smart little craft which was the centre of all his hopes, and the source of so much profit, can only be left to the imagination of the reader '. Such, however, was the fate which overtook not a few of the Cornish-owned smuggling vessels of this period.

' Last Wednesday week,' states the *West Briton*, 24 May 1839, ' the schooner, *Marie Victoire*, laden with coals, entered Falmouth harbour, when she was boarded by one of the preventive men, who, as she had long been a suspected vessel, remained with her whilst she was unloading her cargo off Malpas. The exciseman suspected there was something wrong, but the sailors conducted themselves in such a careless and unaffected manner, as very much to shake these suspicions. On Saturday, however, when a great part of her coal was cleared, the exciseman commenced boring in different parts of the vessel and at length sent his gimlet into a cask of brandy. He immediately sent after the seamen who had gone ashore, but they had effected their escape. The vessel was

[1] *West Briton*, 6 November 1840.

then brought up to Truro Quay, where it was found she had a false bottom, and that she was well stored with spirits. On Sunday, the officers began to remove their booty, which amounted to two hundred and seventy-six tubs of brandy and Geneva, and the vessel, which was registered in the name of Mr Jago, of Redruth, is now being cut up. She has been in active operation for nearly three years, and has several times been examined in different ports without any discovery being made.'

The sequel to the story is to be found in the brief notice which appeared in the press some two months later, announcing the ' sale of the broken-up hull and boat of the schooner *Marie Victoire*, with her sails and ropes reduced to paper-stuff, and her masts and yards reduced to firewood '.[1]

The consequence of such a severe penalty was that the smugglers once again began to change their methods, and instead of risking their own boats, chartered French vessels with which the revenue cruisers had no power to interfere as long as they remained outside of territorial waters. Cruising up and down the Channel during the day, these ships were distinguishable to the smugglers by the cut of their sails, and the farmers also working in the fields kept a close look out for them. In these vessels the goods were brought across, and either sunk near the shore, from whence they could be conveniently ' worked ' ; or else were taken off direct by the local boats which went out to meet them. Dark, moonless nights were, of course, particularly favoured for these operations, and at such times the French ships would draw in close under the cliffs, and a pre-arranged signal having been flashed across the intervening water, the smugglers' boats immediately put off.[2] The number of landing-places along an extensive coastline, endowed by Nature with innumerable coves, inlets, backwaters, and creeks, made detection by the Crown officers very difficult, but it none the less happened on more than one occasion that the occupants of the local boats were surprised and, being unable to land without being captured and identified, embarked on the French ship, and spent an unexpected holiday in France before returning to their homes. Occasionally the Frenchmen themselves, by approaching too near the shore, paid the price of their complicity. In December 1838, the schooner *La Vigilante* of Roscoff, with

[1] *West Briton*, 20 September 1839.
[2] Stanley Old, *Western Morning News*, 17 January 1930.

ninety-two tubs of contraband spirit on board, and a crew of six Frenchmen (i.e. Bretons) and two Englishmen, was seized by the coastguards off Carter's Island, near Newquay.[1]

Two years later the French sloop *La Commerce* met with the same fate about a mile off the ' Gurnet's Head ', to the west of St Ives, where she was discovered to have one hundred and fifty-eight tubs of brandy in her hold, and a crew consisting of five Frenchmen and one Cornishman, the latter being Philip Light, of Cawsand.[2]

V

Although, by the middle of the last century, the difficulty of landing goods upon the coast was ever increasing, the facilities for their subsequent distribution through the country-side had reached the highest pitch of efficiency.   Once a cargo was safely ashore it could almost always be stowed away within a few hours among the innumerable caves, peaths (wells), barns, furze, ricks, or other safe hiding-places belonging to the many landowners who were friendly to the trade.   From thence it was dispatched into the interior as time and opportunity allowed.   In the eastern part of the county, Millbrook was one of the chief depots for the sale of contraband spirit, which was frequently conveyed into Plymouth in skins, concealed by innocent-looking old market woman under their long cloaks.[3]   The ancient fishing ports of Cawsand, Polperro, Looe, and Mevagissey were likewise riddled with secret hiding-places, some of which may still be seen in the older houses of these towns to-day.

The smugglers' successes, however, in most cases, involved arduous and exacting toil, and were accompanied by hair-breadth escapes.   The goods had to be carried by night, and frequently across country over the fields in order to minimize the risk of detection.

' On one occasion,' writes Mr Stanley Old, ' a quantity of wines and spirits which had been landed on the coast near Padstow, was " warehoused " at a farm some three or four

---

[1] *West Briton*, 21 December 1838.
[2] *West Briton*, 6 November 1840.
[3] H. N. Shore, *Cornish Magazine*, I, 117.

miles inland. By some means or other the excise officers had got wind of this and in consequence a raid was expected. It happened, however, that just at this time the farmer's wife was anticipating " a happy event ", and accordingly the smugglers were seized with the idea of stowing the goods in one of the bedrooms of the house. Immediately after this had been done, the woman retired to bed and the doctor was sent for. Arriving before the search party, the latter at once took charge of the bedroom, into which he forbade the excisemen to enter, on account of the critical condition of his patient. The remainder of the house, however, and the farm outbuildings, were thoroughly searched, but no dutiable goods being found, the party went away satisfied. Exactly how much of the contraband the doctor received for the part he had played is unknown ! ' [1]

That the smugglers were in the habit of paying in a free-hearted and generous way for the favours which they received, there is no doubt, and this fact in all probability accounts for the affection with which their memory is still regarded. An illustration of this was given to the writer by an old resident of St Just not long since.

' The night my youngest sister was born, I can remember we were all sitting up late in the kitchen, and about one o'clock in the morning a knock came to the door. Father got up to open it and found several men standing outside.

' " What 's up here, this time of night ? " they asked, pointing to the lights in the windows.

' Father explained that a baby was expected.

' " Well," said the smugglers—for such they were, " will 'ee 'ave a drop of spirits to cheer yourselves up ? If so bring out a bottle and we 'll fill 'un for 'ee."

' Father came in and started looking for a bottle, but not one could be found. The only thing he could lay hands on was one of those great glass carboids, like they use for bringing acid to the mines.

' " Will this do ? " asked father, taking it to the door.

' " Aais, all right, my dear," replied the men—though they must have been a bit surprised at its size. However, they filled it all the same, and then father gave them leave to put a few kegs in his mowy, which was what they wanted. I was a small boy then, but I remember the night clearly enough, and I 've

[1] *Western Morning News*, 17 January 1930.

got the carboid in the house still, though it 's never been filled since ! ' [1]

Though the profits made by smuggling were generally hard won, the demand for the goods themselves had never been keener than it was some seventy or eighty years ago. At that period, the consumption of a certain amount of alcohol was still looked upon as a necessity even by persons of strictly temperate habits, whilst heavy drinking characterized many households in all classes of society. There are persons still living, indeed, who can remember the time when the small town of St Ives boasted no less than twenty public-houses, *in addition* to beershops and spirit shops. In all such houses of entertainment ' Cousin Jack ', as the cognac of the smugglers was familiarly known, found a ready sale, and though the parson and squire sipping their strong waters before the fire in the raging nights of winter might have frowned at the mention of smuggling, they were willing enough, in their secret hearts, to bless the daring men who brought them such liquor at the risk of their lives, and for such absurdly moderate prices. Indeed, the fact that the excisemen's grip was tightening, and that greater daring and cunning were required for the trade now than ever before, only seemed to add spice and flavour to the game. Old ladies sitting at ease in their little parlours over a fragrant dish of tea, knew the joys of smuggling without its risks and hardships, as they handled the rare old egg-shell china cups and whispered to each other : ' All smuggled, my dear, like the tay that 's in them ! ' ; whilst, in the kiddleywink close by, the miner or fisherman calling for a pint of beer, and seeing a drop of something added to ' take the chill off ', rejoiced in the knowledge that once again the Cornish boys had outwitted the ' sarcher's gang '.

The success of the smuggling trade entirely depended, of course, on the loyalty of all parties concerned, and, true to the Cornish motto of ' One and All ', it was rarely that this loyalty was ever betrayed. Such cases, however, naturally did occur from time to time. In the village of Shuffley, near Redruth—formerly one of the greatest resorts of the smugglers in the mining districts—one particular family continued to bear until recent times the contemptuous nickname ' Informer ', in commemoration of the never-to-be-forgotten crime of an ancestor who had betrayed the sacred trust by

[1] Per Mr Henry Thomas, St Just.

which almost every member of the hamlet had once been bound.[1]

The quickness of wit and nimble action required by the latter-day smugglers is well illustrated by a story told of a certain quaint old journeyman tailor—Lewis Grenfell—of St Just. One cold mid-winter day, Grenfell and a companion were engaged in removing a cask of brandy from one of the mine adits which formed a favourite hiding-place for smuggled goods in this district. They had just brought out the cask from the tunnel in question when, as luck would have it, an exciseman was seen approaching. The tailor's companion, thinking discretion the better part of valour, promptly took to flight and hid himself in a thick furze brake near at hand, leaving the other man to face the situation as best he could. In answer to the officer's stern inquiries, Grenfell, who appeared to be shaking with the cold, admitted his offence— indeed, with the incriminating cask beside him he could do no other—but pleaded in extenuation his extreme poverty and the needs of a large family and a sick wife. Finding, however, that pathos produced no effect upon the exciseman, the old man begged only that he might be allowed to taste a drop of the precious liquor to warm his shivering bones. To this the officer agreed, and handed him a gimlet with which to make a hole in the cask. The tailor's hands were numb, however, and his movements so slow that at length the ' sarcher', who was also quite ready for a drink, leapt down from his horse and, handing the reins to Grenfell, began ' spiling ' the cask himself. Hardly had he begun to do so, when the tailor, perceiving his chance, jumped on to the horse's back and made off at a gallop. The officer thereupon gave chase, and scarcely were both men out of sight round the shoulder of the hill, when the tailor's companion crept out from his hiding-place and quickly secured the cask, which, needless to say, the exciseman never saw again ! [2]

Stories similar to this are, of course, told in many parts of Cornwall. Adjoining a certain farm in the Padstow district there is a narrow lane which takes its winding course down to the shores of the neighbouring bay. On one occasion, a number of years since, the farmer was carrying a keg of brandy through his lane when he was observed from some distance off by an exciseman. The latter, who was on horseback,

[1] Per Mr William Michell, Redruth.
[2] Per Mr Henry Thomas, St Just.

galloped towards the farmer and fired his pistol as he went, in order to attract attention. Hurrying along the lane, the farmer dropped his load at a certain spot, removed a gate post from its socket, deposited the keg therein and replaced the post, in time to greet the officer as he rode up with a cheery ' Good day'. In answer to the exciseman's question, the farmer denied all knowledge of the keg, and although the officer was sure that he had seen him carrying it, a search revealed nothing ! [1]

The smugglers themselves sometimes showed their high spirits by acts of extreme bravado. On one occasion which is remembered by the grandparents of persons still living in the town of Redruth, a band of smugglers rode into the streets by night and stopping under the exciseman's window, called forth in mocking tones : ' Would 'ee like to see our " kags " (kegs), maister ? ' [2] At this particular period, a certain farm in Gwithian parish was a noted haunt of the smugglers. Passing here on a dark night, the traveller would sometimes find the whole place lit up and numbers of horses and ponies tethered outside. Within the house, meat and drink was going in plenty for all who had a mind to it. Not a word would be said at these strangely convivial parties of the work in hand, and a ' sarcher ' himself might have mingled with the assembly without being one whit the wiser. Only when the feasting was over, and news had come that the coast was clear, a significant nod from the farmer warned the guests that the time had come for action. Mounting his horse, each man betook himself to a certain spot on the cliffs, where the kegs would be found ready laid. Two of these were slung across the back of each horse and everyone rode his way. On one occasion, however, a Redruth man (whose family is still resident in the neighbourhood) was pursued by an exciseman. Reaching as far as St Erth bridge, he found that his horse was unequal to the burden of himself and the kegs and, accordingly, leaping to the ground, he lashed the animal into a gallop and then ran down and hid himself beneath one of the arches. Not long afterwards, just as he was beginning to feel the water decidedly cold to his feet, he was relieved to hear the thundering hoofs of his pursuer's horse passing overhead. Freed from all further anxiety, he at once came out from his hiding-place and started for his home on foot, to find, on reaching Redruth,

[1] Stanley Old, *Western Morning News*, 17 January 1930.
[2] Per Mr William Michell.

that his horse had safely arrived some hours before, together with the precious burden of kegs.[1]

Many are the stories of this sort which are still told of the last days of smuggling, and many more could, no doubt, be brought to light by persons still living were they only considered sufficiently ' respectable ' for the ears of the modern generation. ' My father, at the age of fourteen,' wrote an old gentleman on a recent occasion, ' was bound apprentice for the term of seven years to a certain well-known shoemaker in the village in which he lived. The fee required for such an apprenticeship was ten pounds, a great sum of money for poor people in those days, but in return, the shoemaker was required to teach the apprentice his trade, to feed, clothe, lodge him, and pay him sixpence a week, rising to two shillings by the end of his time. My father had good food whilst he was thus apprenticed, but the hours were long—from 7 a.m. to 8 p.m., ordinarily, but on some occasions much longer. The only recognized holidays were Christmas Day, Boxing Day; Feast Monday, and Good Friday, with sometimes a half-day at Truro Whitsun Fair and Summercourt Fair. To vary the monotony of work, however, they often turned out for a night's poaching, also going to Gorran or Portloe, ten miles away, to fetch home smuggled goods—chiefly brandy. This latter was carried in small kegs, slung by a rope over the shoulders. On one occasion, when returning, they espied at some distance a party of excisemen, and were forced to take to hiding in a field of standing corn, where they remained all day beneath a hot sun, with nothing to eat or drink. On arriving home, the liquor was poured into a wash tray and coloured the right shade with burnt sugar, after which it was returned to the kegs and sold to trusty customers.' [2]

Tactful and sympathetic inquiry among the older generation of persons still living in west Cornwall confirms the fact that fifty or sixty years ago, smuggled goods had by no means ceased to find a sale in the county. On a recent occasion, a lady residing in the village of Troon, near Camborne, told the writer that she clearly recollected as a child, how an old woman used to call at regular intervals at her home, offering her parents the chance of purchasing ' a little cheap brandy '. Where the spirit came from, the old woman

[1] Per Mr William Michell.
[2] Reminiscences of Mr J. C. Hoare, Madron.

refrained from saying, but it is certain that she never lacked customers.[1]

Spirits, of course, were not the only form of contraband dealt in by the smugglers. One day, a man named George Michell drove up at the door of the Angel Hotel at Helston, in a spring cart, the back portion of which was closely covered with a sheet of tarpaulin. ' What 'ave 'ee got in there ? ' inquired the landlady, coming to the door to meet him. ' Silk, my dear,' replied the man, ' do 'ee want to buy some ? ' ' Hush,' replied the landlady, ' I thoft as much, and what 's more there 's others know of it. There 's a party of sarchers in the bar waiting for you now. They 'll be out any minute. What are 'ee going to do ? '   Without a word the man jumped down from his cart, and throwing the reins to his son, bade him drive into the inn yard. Proceeding himself towards the bar, he greeted the excisemen with a friendly nod.

' A cold day, gentlemen,' he remarked. ' What about a drink all round ? '

The excisemen, having their man in sight, willingly agreed.

' I expect you found the wind pretty cold crossing Goonhilly Downs this morning,' said the officer with a knowing glance ; ' you come from St Keverne, I believe. Do you know if there 's been much smuggling out that way lately ? '

' Aw, ais, pretty fair, I believe,' replied the other, ' and there would be plenty more if you chaps wasn't always so darned smart. No good for the poor smugglers to try and deceive you. You can see through their tricks every time. It beats me how you do knaw so much.'

Between drinking and chatting, the man contrived to spin out a considerable time. Suddenly, however, there was a rumble of cart-wheels and the sound of horse-hoofs outside. One of the men rushed to the window, in time to see an old-fashioned box-hearse being driven out of the inn yard.

' Only a pauper's funeral,' he remarked, as he rejoined the others by the fire.

They finished their glasses and then the officer rose and, putting on an official air, turned to the other and said, ' George Michell, for that, I believe, is your name, I have a warrant here to search you and the cart in which you drove up just now. I must ask you to accompany me into the yard '.

Nothing loth, the other led the way. The tarpaulin was removed, only to disclose to the ' sarcher's ' gaze the usual

[1] Mrs J. Davies, Troon.

market produce—several baskets of eggs, a few fowls, and some butter.

' Is that all, friends ? ' inquired the owner, ' because, if so, I must be going about my business—and you, I expect, have yours ! ' [1]

It must be admitted, of course, that such tales as these represent the smugglers' version of the story, and it is necessary, as Mr Cornish has pointed out, to make some allowances for this when considering them in the light of history. The official records of the custom-houses, however, are not open to the same criticism, and these bear overwhelming testimony to the daring and success which attended the smugglers' activities over a long period of time.

VI

The end of the smuggling trade, as already shown, did not come suddenly, but its decline, though gradual, was inevitable. As late as the eighteen-seventies, the trade still lingered in some of the western ports. ' About this time,' writes Mr William Paynter, ' a great deal of rum found its way to St Ives, being brought there from Holland in a vessel locally known as the *Old Dutchy*. The fishermen used to get the spirit when they were out in their boats at night, disposing of it in the town afterwards with great profit to themselves. This went on for some time, for though the preventive men were suspicious, they had no definite knowledge to work on. At length, they managed to obtain indisputable proof of what was happening by sending spies among the fishermen. The new-comers were very friendly and talkative, liberal with their tobacco, and always ready to stand drinks. As a result, the spies were soon in possession of all the facts they wanted to know. Several houses were raided, and such heavy fines were imposed on the delinquents that they sorrowfully realized that smuggling was no longer a safe or a profitable calling.' [2]

With the exception of one trifling incident over a few bottles of scent, little has been heard since of smuggling in St Ives, or, for that matter, in any other Cornish port. It was but a few months ago that a worthy tradesman, occupying an

[1] Per Mr Michell, Penzance.
[2] *Old St Ives* (1927), 36.

honourable position in the affairs of his town, told the writer that he believed that his father was the last person to be summoned in Cornwall for smuggling, and added with more than a trace of regret in his voice, ' and the last person that is ever likely to be now'. A subsequent conversation with an old coastguard commander, whose experience certainly entitled him to speak with authority on the subject, served only to confirm this unromantic point of view. Despite all the very sound arguments which could be put forward in favour of reviving an industry which might help to replace fishing (now, alas ! in such poor plight), modern conditions are over-whelmingly against smuggling. Not only has the elaborate organization for the disposal of the goods throughout the country-side been swept away, but the demand for the goods themselves is infinitely less than it was. Whether the coming of the aeroplane will cause a partial revival of smuggling in a different form can hardly be said as yet, but it is certain that the contraband trade itself can never partake again of the romance associated with it in those great days of the past when scores of well-found vessels, and hundreds of honest, daring, reckless men put out from the western ports, and served a sea apprenticeship which made them sailors the like of whom the world will never know again.

WRECKS AND WRECKERS

I

FEW aspects of Cornish life have excited more popular interest than the tales of the wreckers, whose misdoings figure so largely in the pages of sensational fiction. At some time or other, every Cornishman, one may suppose, has been asked what his opinion is on this subject, and to such a question an honest man may well be hard put for a definite answer. So much depends on what is really meant by ' wrecking'. If the latter simply implies a propensity to regard as his own the flotsam and jetsam which the sea casts up upon the coastline, or to be willing at any moment to risk a wet suit of clothes in order to recover such spoil from the waves, then it is probably true to say that the average Cornishman is a wrecker still at heart. To take in thankfulness, however, the harvest which the gods have provided is surely not reprehensible but praiseworthy, whilst the instinctive desire to get something for nothing is one which is scarcely confined to Cornish people.

The writer has in mind an illustration of this which occurred during the war, when the pilot of an aeroplane who had been stunting over a certain Cornish seaside town, at length paid the penalty of his daring by crashing precipitately into the waves. Much to the relief of everyone it was soon learnt that the pilot was unhurt, and the genuine concern which had been felt on this head was quickly turned to joy when it was perceived that the machine itself was about to become a ' total wreck'. By one o'clock in the morning, practically the whole population of the town was assembled on the beach, anxiously awaiting the going down of the tide. Foremost among the crowd were a number of visitors who, corrupted, no doubt, by the Cornish element amongst which they found themselves, nevertheless showed surprising acumen in seizing many of the most valuable portions of the wreck when once the looting began ! One remembers in particular a clock which was one of the most coveted of the spoils and which went to an up-country visitor, despite the efforts of a local fisherman who was heard to remark afterwards : ' Ais, I had my eye on that, too, but, darn 'ee, the London fellow was too quick. Anyone would think he 'd been a wrecker all his days ! '

Most people, indeed, have only to experience for themselves the white heat of excitement which the circumstances of a wreck breeds, in order to understand how the Cornishman's reputation in this respect was gained. On such occasions, the most prosaic and respectable people will often reveal a predatory instinct of which they themselves were previously quite unconscious, and in the darkness of the night, with the sound of the breaking surf, and the singing of the gale in one's ears, old instincts and desires will awake to life again in a most surprising way.

Nor are the spoils of wrecking always spurned by those who benefit from them second-hand, as was amusingly revealed by a story told to the writer not long since. During the visit of a lady to the Lizard some forty years ago, a wreck occurred, in the neighbourhood, of a ship which was laden with a cargo of potted goods and other tinned delicacies. Many of the cases in which these were contained came in on to the beach undamaged, and even in those which had been broken by the waves, the majority of the tins were found to be intact. The latter were, of course, soon dispersed throughout the neighbourhood, several of them finding their way on to the table of the friends with whom the lady was staying. This fact caused much distress to her parents who, on learning that the goods were unpaid for, wrote at once to say how surprised they were that such a thing could ever have been countenanced by her hosts. Judging that in such circumstances attack might perhaps be the best method of defence, a parcel containing several more of the offending tins was immediately dispatched by the lady to her parents, with a request that they should first sample the good things for themselves before delivering any final judgment on her conduct. So successful did this procedure prove, that within a few days she received a most cordial letter from her mother, who concluded with a postscript : ' Your father and I have much enjoyed the delicious tinned meats which you sent us, and we wonder if it would be possible to obtain any more, if, as you say, everyone is doing it, and your friends think that it is *really quite all right* '. The story has a no less amusing sequel. For some weeks after the wreck had occurred, the salvage officials were busily employed in removing the undamaged cases to the top of the cliff, an arduous undertaking in which they received considerable help from many of the natives of the district. At length, on a certain day, a sale was called, and dealers came from far and wide, attracted by the likelihood of good bargains. Taking his stand in the midst of the assembled crowd of onlookers and buyers, the auctioneer with a flourish of his hammer announced the terms of the sale, and bade his assistant open the first case, in order to display the excellent condition of its contents. Scarcely had the cover been removed, however, when a gasp of consternation showed that something was wrong, and, drawing nearer, the crowd perceived with mingled amusement and chagrin, that in place of the much advertised goods the contents consisted of nothing but stones ! Once again old instincts had proved too strong, and the people who had been so kind in assisting the officials to bring up the cases by day, had been assisting themselves to the contents of the same by night.

For the latter-day Cornishman, wrecking has come to mean little more than a pastime, representing at the most an occasional opportunity of gaining a few perquisites of a more or less illegitimate kind. Very different from this was the businesslike spirit in which wrecking was conducted in the more distant past. From the earliest records which throw light on the subject, it would appear that the right to wreckage in Cornwall was originally vested in the Crown. As may be gathered, however, from various incidents, private landowners began at an early period to make their claims felt in a forceful manner. Thus, in the year 1305, William Le Poer, coroner of the Scilly Islands, arriving in Tresco to inquire into a wreck and to take charge of the salved cargo, found himself seized and imprisoned by a mob, led by the prior of St Nicholas, from whose clutches he only escaped by buying his freedom at a high price.[1] Shortly after this, on the occasion of a Spanish ship being wrecked on the mainland, the cargo was plundered, and the owner kept in confinement for the space of a year.[2]

As time went on the right of wreck appears to have fallen more and more into the hands of the lords of the coast-lying manors, some of whom possessed very extensive 'royalties'. Thus, the lord of Connerton, in Gwithian, claimed all the wreck from Cudden Point in Mounts Bay right around the Land's End to Gwithian beach.[3] It is clear, however, that the Crown did not forgo this valuable right without some show of protest. In '36, Henry VIII, two Norman ships laden with fish from Newfoundland were driven into St Ives Bay by stress of weather, in a time of war. The townspeople, we are told, seized the vessels, and Sir William Godolphin and many of the gentlemen thereabout came and put the fish into the cellars. The Lord Admiral claimed the ship and cargo as droits of Admiralty ; Sir John Arundel also claimed them in right of his Hundred of Penwith. The Lord Admiral issued a citation against the seizure, but afterwards did not prosecute his claim, and the jury determined that Sir John Arundel had most right to the ship and goods, ' and so he had them quietly '.[4]

Adjoining the claim which was thus successfully defended by the manor of Connerton, came the royalties claimed respectively by the lords of Tehidy, Nancekuke, Tywarnhayle, and Ellenglaze, these together covering the whole of the wreckage along that cruel stretch of coast from Godrevy to

[1] M. Oppenheim, *Victoria History of Cornwall*, 478.
[2] M. Oppenheim, *Victoria History of Cornwall*, 478.
[3] C. G. Henderson, *Western Morning News*, 21 January 1929.
[4] Quoted by C. Bowles, *Short Account of the Hundred of Penwith* (1805).

Newquay. Going back to Mounts Bay, the lord of Methleigh claimed all the rights of wreck from Cudden Point to Looe Bar, whilst from Looe Bar to Polurrian the manor of Winnianton held sway. Beyond that again came the lord of the manor of Predannack. 'The court-rolls of these manors are full of references to wrecks all through the centuries,' states Mr Henderson, ' and in some cases the value of the commodities which came ashore have never been surpassed except perhaps in the case of the wreck of Prince Charles's wardrobe at Godrevy, during the Civil War.' [1]

On 19th January 1526, a great ship of the King of Portugal, called the *St Andrew*, freighted with bullion, silver plate, and other treasure, was driven ashore at Gunwalloe by ' the outrageous tempest of the sea '. Here the vessel became a complete wreck, but, as Francis Person, the King of Portugal's factor, states, ' by the grace and mercy of Almighty God, the greater part of the crew got safely to land '. Not only were the country people, who had assembled in great numbers on the beach, largely responsible for this, but he adds that by their exertions, which continued throughout that day and the following night, a great part of the cargo was also saved. The latter was extremely valuable, comprising as it did eight thousand cakes of copper, worth £3,224 ; eighteen blocks of silver bullion, worth £2,250 ; silver vessels, plates, ewers, and pots, pearls, precious stones, chains, brooches, and jewels of gold ; together with a chest of ready money containing £6,240. From further details in the careful inventory drawn up by the Portuguese factor, we learn that the ship was also laden with cloth of arras, tapestry, rich hangings, satins, velvets, silks, chamlets, sayes, and Flemish and English cloth. This was by no means all, however, for other curious entries show that there were on board twenty-one hundred barbers' basins, thirty-two hundred latten candlesticks, a great chest of shalmers, and other instruments of music, besides four sets of armour for the King of Portugal, and harness for his horses, etc., the whole amounting in value to about £160,000 in present money. The work of the natives and the crew, however, in saving much of this cargo proved to little purpose. Person, in his declaration, goes on to state that shortly after it was landed, three local magistrates, representatives of the leading families of the district, viz. Thomas St Aubyn, of Clowance ; William Godolphin, of Godolphin ; and John

[1] *Western Morning News*, 21 January 1929.

Milaton, of Pengersick Castle and the Mount, arrived on the scene with about sixty retainers, armed in manner of war with bows and swords, and made an assault on the shipwrecked sailors, putting them in great fear and jeopardy, and eventually taking from them all they had saved from the wreck. ' This,' he adds plaintively, ' they will not return, although they have been called on to do so.' It is true that a very different complexion was given to the affair by the account written by Thomas St Aubyn himself. In this he states that being in the neighbourhood of Gunwalloe, he heard of the wreck, rode to it and assisted in saving the men ; Godolphin and Milaton afterwards joining him with the same object. They found, he states, very little that could be rescued and, seeing that the men were destitute, without money to buy meat or drink, they bought the goods of the ship in lawful bargain with the captain. He further denied any assault, or that they had taken goods to the value of £10,000 from the sailors, adding that, in fact, they had only saved £20 altogether, the bulk lying in the ship still, and that although they had tried to recover more, they had failed even to pay the cost of the labour employed.[1] So the two stories run, but those who have studied the propensities of the Cornish gentry in those far-off days will probably not find it hard to make up their minds which one approximates more nearly to the truth.

At a later date than this, the Arundells of Lanherne (afterwards of Wardour Castle, in Wiltshire) were among those who continued to derive a handsome income every year from the wrecks which occurred all along the Cornish coast. Not only did this great family possess the manor of Winnianton, but also the valuable Liberty of Connerton which, as already described, gave them the right to all wrecks from Marazion to St Ives. ' In addition,' states Mr Henderson, ' they had the wrecks near Mawgan Porth and in several other places. At Wardour Castle, built by Lord Arundell in the eighteenth century, the splendid stateroom doors of Spanish oak are said to have come ashore as wreckage on one of the Cornish manors.'[2]

The ' Royalty of Wreck ', as may thus be seen, often provided the coast-lying landlords with most valuable perquisites, and it is not surprising, therefore, to find that in some

[1] Cf. H. M. Whitley, ' The Treasure Ship of Gunwalloe ', *Journal of the Royal Institution of Cornwall* (1890), X, Pt I.
[2] *Western Morning News*, 21 January 1929.

instances the claim to such a privilege was hotly contested. Proof of this may be found in the bitter dispute, which broke out during the earlier part of the eighteenth century, between the Penrose family and the lord of the manor of Methleigh, both of whom claimed the right of wreck between Porthleven and the Looe Bar.

' In July 1743,' writes Mr Henderson, ' matters came to a head when some wreckage, including a cask of salted pork, was washed ashore at Porthleven. Edward Coode, whose father, Samuel, was lord of Methleigh, wearing only his great coat, gloves, and walking-stick, went down to the shore to see that his father's rights were preserved. Squire Edward Penrose, however, appeared on the scene with some men armed with fixed bayonets, who declared that they would shoot the first man who touched the cask. One of them struck Mr Coode on the breast, and they all appeared to be much in liquor. Squire Penrose seized a musket, and cried, " Damn him, shoot him, or by God, I 'll shoot him ". A great uproar thereupon ensued, but young Mr Coode managed to escape, and legal proceedings were the inevitable sequel.' [1]

II

Wrecking, therefore, as may thus be seen, was by no means confined to the lower orders of Cornish society, its greatest and most successful practitioners being those to whom rank and privilege had granted the power to pillage and plunder on a scale undreamt of by the poor. Nevertheless, all classes benefited therein to a greater or lesser degree. When Sir John Killigrew erected the first lighthouse at the Lizard in 1619, he stated that most of the houses in the district were built of ruined ships, and that the inhabitants were enraged by his action, complaining that ' I take away God's grace from them, meaning that they shall receive no more benefit from shipwrecks. They have so long been used to reap profit by the calamity of the ruin of shipping that they claim it as hereditary [2].'

As has been pointed out, however, a Killigrew was ever

---

[1] *West Briton*, 24 January 1929.
[2] Quoted by C. G. Henderson, *West Briton*, 1 August 1929.

A CORNISH SEAFARER

(*See page 10*)

THE SMUGGLERS
(after Rowlandson)

willing to pose as a Christian philanthropist living among savages, when it suited his purpose ; as in this case it obviously did. Such sentiments, however, coming from such a quarter, must have caused no little astonishment to a generation whose fathers, at any rate, had known these same Killigrews as some of the most out-and-out pirates that ever sailed the seas. No doubt there were people still living at this time who could recall how, in 1557, three members of the Killigrew family had attacked a ship off the Land's End and subsequently divided amongst themselves the cargo, which was said to have been worth £10,000. Even clearer in the public memory must have been the exploits of the notorious Lady Killigrew, who, in 1582, had seized a Spanish vessel which was sheltering in Falmouth harbour, removed its cargo to Arwenacke and drowned most of the crew.[1] Perhaps these facts were not overlooked by the Trinity House Brethren ; at any rate, the latter refused to assist Sir John Killigrew in his scheme for getting a patent to levy toll on all shipping passing the Lizard, excusing themselves on the plea that the light was useful only as a guide to pirates ! In 1680, however, the ' brethren ' themselves erected the first light tower on the Scillies. Unfortunately, the keepers appointed appear to have been Scillonians who, as Mr Henderson writes, following Oppenheim and Heath, ' used their light to assist, rather than hinder, their relations engaged in the family occupation of wrecking. For over a century the St Agnes light was a public scandal. Sometimes it shone brightly ; sometimes so dimly that it could not be seen from St Mary's ; sometimes it was put out altogether '.[2]

This is, in point of fact, the only authenticated statement, known to the writer, which in any way supports the oft-quoted charge, that the men of the west were in the habit of deliberately causing wrecks, and even here, it may be noted, it applies, not to the Cornish people, but to the inhabitants of Scilly ! No doubt, however, Parson Troutbeck, who dwelt among the latter, expressed even more correctly the attitude of his

[1] *Victoria History of Cornwall*, 490.
[2] *West Briton*, 1 August 1929. See also Robert Heath, *Account of the Islands of Scilly* (1750), 88. Elsewhere, however, Heath writes : ' As to the Scillonians, whom a late author has reflected upon for their conduct towards persons shipwrecked on their coast, they are certainly much more known for their services to strangers, in such times of distress, than the Cornish, or any other inhabitants on the coast of England .'—*Account of the Islands of Scilly*, 138.

parishioners towards wrecking when, as it is said, he added to the litany his famous petition : ' We pray Thee, O Lord, not that wrecks should happen, but that if wrecks do happen, Thou wilt guide them into the Scilly Isles, for the benefit of the poor inhabitants '.[1] This, no doubt, would quite as truly have expressed the feelings of those who dwelt on the mainland also. Before judging either of them too harshly, however, it would be well to understand something of what that phrase ' the poor inhabitants ' implied.

Of all the parishes in Cornwall which were addicted to wrecking—and very few of those which abutted on the coast-line were not—Breage and Germoe certainly attained to the greatest notoriety in this respect. The district embraced by these two parishes, even to-day, is sparsely cultivated, rocky, bleak, and windswept, and its general characteristics are sufficient to give some clue to the degree of poverty which must have prevailed among its inhabitants two hundred years ago. Mining at that time provided the parishioners with their sole means of subsistence, but the account books of ' Great Work ', which during the eighteenth century was the foremost mine in the area, show clearly enough the standard of wages on which a miner and his family had to attempt the task of keeping body and soul together. Between the years 1759–64, the average pay for miners working underground in this district seems to have varied between sixteen shillings and twenty-one shillings a month, from which sum considerable ' spales ' or fines were often deducted for misdemeanours arising out of the conditions of their employment. Further-more, when any ' lett ' or misfortune occurred in the mine in which he was normally employed, the tinner became at once deprived of even this wretched pittance. ' We have had the greatest floods of rain here that has ever been seen in any man's remembrance now living,' wrote Lieutenant-General Onslow's agent from Gulval on 30th January 1749, ' the tyn-works are all drowned almost and many thousand tynners by that means deprived of employ, and starving, ours amongst the rest.' [2] What wonder, then, that to men of this sort, a wreck, with its promise of food for the belly, wine to cheer the heart, and perquisites wherewith to furnish their miserable hovels, came as a veritable godsend, and that, at the merest possibility of a vessel being driven upon their shore, the

---

[1] *Cornish Notes and Queries* (1906), 282.
[2] See Hamilton Jenkin, *The Cornish Miner*, 169.

tinners would leave their work, and in bands 'two thousand strong' follow the same for miles along the coast, trusting only that that Providence which watcheth over all might deem it righteous to deliver the spoil into their outstretched hands.

That under such circumstances, when a wreck actually occurred, small pity was shown by the half-starved tinners towards those who were struggling to escape the fury of the sea, seems more than likely. ' The late storms have brought several vessels ashore and some dead wrecks,' wrote Mr George Borlase, from Gulval, 1st February 1753, ' and in the former case great barbaritys have been committed. My situation in life hath obliged me sometimes to be a spectator of things which shock humanity. The people who make it their business to attend these wrecks are generally tynners and, as soon as they observe a ship on the coast, they first arm themselves with sharp axes and hatchetts, and leave their tynn works to follow those ships. Sometimes the ship is not wrecked, but whether 'tis or not the mines suffer greatly, not only by the loss of their labour which may be about £100 per diem if they are two thousand in quest of the ship, but where the water is quick the mine is entirely drowned, and they seldom go in a less number than two thousand. Now 'tis hardly to be imagined,' continues Mr Borlase, ' how farr the taking of this infamous practice in its budd, and laying the loss of all wages due and some further penalty on every labouring tynner who should leave his tyn work in order to go to a wreck, would contribute to keep them home and break the neck of it. Next, I apprehend no person should be allowed to attend a wreck armed with an axse or the like, unless lawfully required. They'll cut a large trading vessell to pieces in one tide, and cut down everybody that offers to oppose them. Two or three years ago, a Dutchman was stranded near Helston, every man saved, and the ship whole, burthen 250 tons, laden with claret. In twenty-four hours' time the tinners cleared all. A few months before this, they murdered a poor man just by Helston who came in aid of a custom-house officer to seize some brandy. Next, I humbly apprehend the Bill (then before Parliament to prevent wrecking) does not sufficiently provide against the monstrous barbarity practised by these savages upon the poor sufferers. I have seen many a poor man, half dead, cast ashore and crawling out of the reach of the waves, fallen upon and in a manner stripped naked by those villains, and if afterwards he has saved his chest or any more cloaths they have been taken from him.' [1]

It might perhaps be thought that such remarks, coming as they did from the agent of a coast-lying manor with important privileges of its own in regard to wrecking, were to some extent biased against the humbler participants in the spoils. Evidence, however, derived from other sources shows that the writer's accusations of occasional brutality on the part of the wreckers were not without foundation. In 1764, when a French ship was wrecked at Perranzabuloe, not only was the whole of the cargo carried away, but the crew themselves were stripped to their very shirts. Unable to obtain a hearing in Cornwall, the captain petitioned the Crown through the French ambassador, and was eventually awarded compensation. [2]

It must be admitted that the local population were veritable artists in the task of ' clearing ' a wreck. In 1738, a large ship, the *Vigilante*, from Hamburg, was cast ashore at Perran Uthnoe, in Mounts Bay. Captain Vyvyan who was in command of the soldiers quartered at Penzance, immediately repaired to the spot, but not the least part of the cargo could be preserved, even the sails and rigging being carried away by the country people. Two anchors and nine small guns were all that was saved.

A short while after this, the *Lady Lucy* was wrecked at Gunwalloe, and again the country people did well. A few days after the wreck, five casks of wine were found in the possession of the Vicar of Cury !

By 1748, the soldiers had been removed, and with them all possibility of restraint. In December of that year, the *Alcida*, of Bordeaux, was wrecked at Porthleven, with a cargo of one hundred and sixty-seven tuns of wine. The collector, surveyor, and other officers of the excise arrived soon afterwards, but to no purpose. The violence and brutality of the country people, states the report, were such that they could not save a single cask, and were indeed in danger of their lives. The collector wrote afterwards pointing out how hopeless was their position unless they had troops. [3]

Though the tinners of west Cornwall suffered most in their

[1] *Journal of Royal Institution of Cornwall* (1881), XXIII, 374–9.
[2] H. O. Papers, 24 September, 21 November 1764.
[3] Penzance custom-house books, quoted *West Briton*, 22 October 1931.

reputation, they were far from being the only delinquents as regards wrecking. 'A ship has just been thrown on the rocks near Looe,' states a writer from Liskeard on 20th January 1750, ' seven men and a boy, being all the hands on board, perished. 'Tis said that all the horses in the neighbourhood are taken up about the plunder. Even our town, at eight miles distance, is much depopulated both of men and women —a most melancholy scene.'[1] In the following year the custom surveyor at Looe stated that on a ship being wrecked, he endeavoured to form a guard of the townspeople, but that, instead of helping him, they only got out their carts and filled them with the cargo.[2]

Though in the face of all the evidence which exists, it would be impossible to exculpate the inhabitants of the duchy during this century from the charge of practising wrecking to a notorious degree, it is worth while noting that Mr Borlase, the severest of all contemporary critics, makes no mention whatever of the time-honoured fable of ships being *lured* in on to the rocks. As the writer has said elsewhere, the foul deeds which were done, and they were doubtless not a few, were performed in that white heat of excitement which a wreck breeds, and not as the result of any cold-blooded scheming to deprive others of their lives and property.

Nor is it justifiable in every case to judge the actions of one generation by the ethical code of another. At a time, for instance, when brutality and violence passed for discipline in Britain's proudest service, her Royal Navy, little surprise can be felt if such qualities sometimes informed the actions of those who constituted the lower ranks and orders of the contemporary civil life.

Of all the wrecks which have met their fate on the western peninsula, none is more famous than that of the disaster which overtook Sir Cloudesley Shovel in the year 1707. The event itself is, of course, a matter of history, but so many traditions have gathered around the story, which are illustrative of the temper of those times, that, as Miss Courtney has said, no account of the old sea-life of the west would be complete without it. It was on the afternoon of 22nd October 1707, that the admiral, returning home with the whole fleet, after the capture of Gibraltar, reached the Scilly Isles. The weather being thick and dirty at the time, orders were at first

[1] MS. *penes*, Duchy of Cornwall office.
[2] *Gentleman's Magazine*, quoted in *Victoria History of Cornwall*, 508.

given ' to lie-to ', but later, about dusk, the fleet again made sail. An hour or two afterwards the *Association*, which carried the commander on board, showed signals of distress, these being answered from several of the others. Two minutes later the *Association* struck on the Gilston rock in Porth Hellick Bay, St Mary's, and sank immediately, all on board perishing. The *Eagle* and the *Romney* with their crews shared the same fate ; the *Firebrand* also was lost, but most of her crew were saved. ' The other men-of-war,' we read, ' with difficulty escaped, by having timely warning.' As the result of this disaster, between fifteen hundred and two thousand men and boys were drowned in one night.

So much for the bare facts of history. Tradition, however, affirms that, a day or two before the event took place, a sailor aboard the *Association*, who was a native of Scilly, had persistently warned the officer of the watch that, unless their ship's course was altered, she, with all the fleet, would soon be on the Scilly rocks, amidst the breakers. These repeated warnings, it is supposed, so exasperated the officer that he reported them to the admiral. The latter, vexed that a common sailor should presume to know better than his superiors how to navigate a vessel, gave orders, in accordance with the savage disciplinary methods of those days, that the man should be forthwith hanged at the yard-arm for inciting the others to insubordination. Before his execution, the sailor begged, as a great favour, that the chaplain should be allowed to read him one of the psalms. His request was granted, and he chose the 109th, repeating after the reader in a loud voice the curses it contains, and finally prophesying that the admiral, with all those who saw him hanged, would find a watery grave. Up to that time the weather had been fair, but hardly had the sailor's body been committed to the sea before conditions changed, the wind began to blow, and his shipmates were horrified to see the corpse, released of its winding sheet, following in their wake. Long before the vessel struck, most of the men, it is said, had already given themselves up for lost. According to some of the traditions, Sir Cloudesley's body came ashore on a hatch, on which he had endeavoured to save himself, with his favourite little dog dead by his side. Others relate that, after the wreck, the admiral's body was cast up naked on Porth Hellick beach, where it was discovered by a soldier, who took off a ring which was still on his finger, afterwards burying the corpse in the sands. Yet another account, given on the authority of Robert, second Lord Romney, Sir Cloudesley Shovel's grandson, runs thus : ' There is one circumstance relating to Sir Cloudesley Shovel's death that is known to very few persons, namely that he was *not* drowned, having got to shore, where, by the confession of an ancient woman, he was put to death. This she revealed many years after, when on her death-bed, to the minister of the parish, declaring she could not die in peace until she had made this confession, as she was led to commit this horrid deed for the sake of plunder. She acknowledged having, amongst other things, an emerald ring in her possession, which she had been afraid to sell lest it should lead to a discovery. The ring, which she delivered to the minister, was by him given to James, Earl of Berkeley, at his particular request, Sir Cloudesley Shovel and himself having lived on the strictest footing of friendship '. ' As to the place and manner of his burial,' writes Miss Courtney, ' all traditions agree. Where he lay (the body was subsequently removed to Westminster Abbey) is still pointed out—a bare spot surrounded by green grass—and the Scillonians will tell you that, because he so obstinately refused to hear a warning and wantonly threw away so many lives, God, to keep alive the memory of this great wickedness, permits nothing to grow on his grave.' [1]

III

Whatever truth there may or may not be in the tradition that Sir Cloudesley Shovel met his death at the hand of a Scillonian, and that this alleged act was inspired by revenge, it must be remembered that English law, as it stood at this time, was a direct incitement to the callous treatment of shipwrecked men. Corpses washed ashore were not allowed Christian burial until about 1808, when a Cornishman, Davies Gilbert, President of the Royal Society, and Member of Parliament for Bodmin, succeeded in getting an Act of Parliament passed for their burial in churchyards at the expense of the parish. [2] Up to this time, the bodies which the sea brought in were buried anywhere and anyhow, in the cliffs,

[1] M. A. Courtney, *Cornish Feasts and Folklore*, 115–17.
[2] S. Baring-Gould, *Cornish Characters and Strange Events*, 62.

or upon the margin of the beaches, the expense being, in some cases, grudgingly allowed by the lords of the coastal manors. A vivid light is cast on this bad old system by the following letter (quoted by Mr C. G. Henderson) from the vicar of Breage to the lord of Methleigh, in September 1796 :

' Dear sir,—By the inclosed paper you will find that the number of dead bodies, and such parts of bodies as with respect to interment should, we think, be considered and paid for as whole bodies, taken up within the precincts of your manor and buried there after the late unhappy wreck, amounts to sixty-two. The extraordinary charge of two men attending constantly, one of them twelve days, the other thirteen days at 1s. 6d., was thought to be necessary in order to secure the bodies, as soon as they should be cast ashore, from being torn by dogs and other carnivorous animals, and to prepare graves for their immediate reception, being at that time very offensive. This circumstance accounts for the great consumption of liquor, without which the people would hardly have been prevailed with to touch the broken bodies, and also for the pack and rope by which they were drawn up over the cliffs and to the graves. Some of the bodies having been buried where the sand was very loose and shallow, Mr Tregear was induced to employ four men to hedge the graves about with stones and to lay on large heaps of earth, in order to prevent their being torn up by pigs and dogs. Young Carter's and Laity's journey to Newlyn was not without my advice and approbation. You have the result of their inquiries in the paper respecting the goods that were salved or carried off by the boats belonging to Newlyn and the Mount. . . . It was very unfortunate that your own ill-health and your son's business would not permit either of you to come to the parish at the time. I am well assured that, by proper exertions, goods to a considerable amount might have been secured for you, and even now I cannot but think that enough may be recovered for reimbursing the expenses.

' I remain, dear sir, your most obedient servant,

E. MARSHALL.' [1]

Further, English law defined ' a wreck of the sea ' as anything from which no creature, man or beast, escaped to shore alive. Thus, as has been pointed out, the inhabitants of the district, by their endeavours to save life, were virtually

[1] *West Briton*, 24 January 1929.

depriving themselves of what might be a valuable prize. Notwithstanding this, evidence shows that the Cornish coast-dwellers often exerted themselves to the utmost in rescuing shipwrecked mariners who were cast upon their shores, even when at the same time maintaining their ' rights ' with regard to the wreck itself. This is very clearly illustrated by an extract from the journal of that famous eighteenth-century privateer, Commodore George Walker, whose ship the *Boscawen*, as a result of encountering a terrific storm, became a total wreck at St Ives, on 19th April 1745. ' The people of the sea coast of Cornwall,' states the writer of the journal, ' have for some years undergone the censure of being savage devourers of all wrecks that strike against their coast. How weak a creature is general belief, the dupe of idle fame ! Humanity never exercised its virtues more conspicuously than in this instance in the inhabitants and people of St Ives. They flocked down in numbers to our assistance and, at the risk of their own lives, saved ours. Mr Walker would not be prevailed upon to quit the ship till he had seen the sick lifted through the cabin windows into the boats, bidding all, without distinction, provide for themselves, as he was capable of swimming, but he was himself, at last, lifted out by two of the townsmen, strangers to him, who went upon the deck to bring him off. When we came into the town, everybody's house was open to us in all the offices of assistance ; but above all other instances which could be given of the generosity of the place, gratitude must here pay her greatest debt in remembering John Stevens, Esq. (of Tregenna) whose unwearied activity, liberality, and prudence in aiding, befriending, and directing our affairs are without parallel, except in other like actions of his own. When we mention this gentleman as most distinguishable amongst others, we do not forget to acknow-ledge the debt of obligation we owe to the mayor, the magis-trates, and other gentlemen of the town, whose invitations, readiness to serve, and other acts of civility rendered them ever worthy the best report of their deserving.' The wretched miners, it is true, did not share in the same general commendation, but then, as the writer goes on to explain— ' these are a people the civil power is scarcely answerable for, at least for their good manners, as they live almost out of the districts of human society, and may be said to be no visible inhabitants of the earth, though they act in the world. Conscious of this fact, the first night Mr Walker made all his officers sleep under arms, in order to be in readiness for any attack against the wreck ; and accordingly so it happened, for in the night the miners came down and were setting about sharing the wreck amongst themselves. At the very first alarm, the mayor himself was up, and a party of the town who went in arms with Mr Walker dispersed the crowd, and took some of the men prisoners. The remainder of the time during our stay, which was upwards of three weeks, was solely employed in taking care of the wreck and, through the assist-ance of the aforesaid gentlemen and others, everything was taken care of with as much exactness as if the wreck had lain at the doors of the proprietors, and a great part was saved to a considerable amount '. (*Voyages and Cruises of Commo-dore Walker*. Edited by H. S. Vaughan, 1928.)

Living as they did under conditions of extraordinary severity and hardship, and deprived of even such civilizing influences as the society of the slightly more educated town-dwellers might have afforded them, it is little wonder that the tinners long continued to bear the worst possible name as wreckers. Courage, at any rate, they certainly did not lack, and not infrequently they paid the penalty for the risks they took, by the loss of their own lives. ' The stiffness of the shore adds much to the power of the returning backwater,' stated a writer in 1817, describing the wrecking scenes which he had witnessed near the Looe Bar and Gunwalloe, ' and it is astonishing with what rapidity the sand is carried away under a person's feet. Once this happens, and he is thrown off his legs, he becomes in jeopardy immediately, and has a very poor chance of escaping unless prompt assistance is afforded. Hence it is that so many persons in the neighbour-hood get drowned or have the most hairbreadth escapes when in the course of " going a-wrecking ". An instance of this occurred but a few years ago when several persons attending a wreck, and not being sufficiently on their guard, were surrounded by the run of a large wave, and four of their number were thrown off their legs and carried away. They were all, however, cast in again by the following wave and three of them, having immediate assistance, were saved. The fourth was floated out once more by an " out-haul ", which carried him in a sitting posture as regularly and smoothly as though he had been sliding on an inclined plane of ice. In this manner he was hurried into the " truck " of the waves, from whence, alas ! there was no return. At the wreck of the *Resolution* brig at Porthleven, only last January,' he adds, ' a young man was drowned in an exactly similar way, entirely owing to the dangerous nature of the sand.' [1]

Although with the passage of time wrecking began to assume a somewhat less savage aspect than in the past, the practice itself continued far into the nineteenth century. Early in the morning of Saturday, 4th January 1817, with the wind blowing at gale force, a brig was observed approaching the then unfinished harbour of Porthleven, in Mounts Bay. When within about two miles of the shore, the vessel came to anchor, and succeeded in riding out the storm until about six o'clock the same evening. At that time, finding that no boat could approach her, and having parted one anchor, the master gave orders to cut the other and ran the ship ashore, this appearing to be the only chance of preserving the lives of the crew. As it turned out, the vessel grounded on a fine, sandy beach to the eastward of the new pier, and the tide having begun to ebb, the crew were enabled to reach the land in safety. No sooner, however, had the tide gone down than the ship itself was boarded by a great concourse of the local population who straightway set about plundering. The whole of the private property of the captain and crew was carried off ; the heads of the pipes and hogsheads of wine, which formed a large part of the vessel's lading, were staved in, and kegs and other receptacles filled with the liquor. The arrival of some fourteen dismounted dragoons from Helston, though it must have added a touch of colour to the scene, appears to have served no other purpose, their number being wholly insufficient to restrain the lawless multitude who rushed in from all sides. Out of a cargo of three hundred and seventy-five pipes and twenty-five hogsheads of wine, between fifty and sixty pipes only were saved by the agents. As often happened on these occasions, severe contests took place among the plunderers themselves, each being anxious to secure the largest possible share of the booty. The only casualties, however, appeared to have been a young man of Wendron, who was drowned by the violence of the sea ; and two local men who got so much intoxicated with the wine that they were unable to reach home, and perished during the night by the roadside, the weather being very severe at the time. Although the vessel in the first instance had sustained but little damage, by the following Monday she had

[1] Henry Trengrouse, *Shipwreck Investigated* (1817).

become a complete wreck, and the country people had ripped up the hull and carried off a large part of the timber.[1]

Some three months later, another brig, the *Mary*, of Ilfracombe, was driven ashore at Fassel Geaver Cove, near Godrevy, in a violent snowstorm and a gale of wind. By a miracle of Providence, the crew were all saved and the captain, assisted by some of the local farmers and the custom officers of the port of St Ives, succeeded in getting out the necessary cables to hold the ship in a position of safety. During that night and the succeeding day, parties of men were employed about the ship in securing her stores, and keeping watch over what had been saved, with the result that everything was conducted with the greatest regularity, and not the smallest pillage took place. On the second evening, however, a party of Camborne miners arrived on the scene, ' determined for a wreck '. Within a short time they had cut the ship's cable, carried off two of her small anchors, stolen all the beef and biscuit on board, and even had the hardihood, before it became dark, to steal some of the seamen's clothes, which had been washed for the poor fellows by the people of the adjacent village, and had been hung out to dry. In pillaging the ship they set the watch at defiance, threatening to cut them down with their ' dags ' or hatchets if they showed the least sign of resistance. The captain who owned the ship and most of the cargo, which was uninsured, was practically ruined as a result of this more than usually infamous conduct on the part of the wreckers, and it is not without a feeling of satisfaction that one learns that the ringleaders were subsequently apprehended and committed to the assizes to take their trial.[2]

Seeing that, during the years 1823–46, no less than one hundred and thirty-one vessels were lost between the Land's End and Trevose Head,[3] a distance of little more than forty miles, the Cornish people certainly could not complain of being bereft of what they had once naïvely termed ' God's grace '. ' I have the honour to acquaint you,' wrote Mr Alexander Shairp to the comptroller-general of coastguards, 4th October 1838, ' that on the 1st instant I received intelligence that a French brig, *Les Landois*, was wrecked between Sennen and Priest Coves. On arriving at the spot, I found the beach

[1] *West Briton*, 10 January 1817.
[2] *West Briton*, 28 March 1817.
[3] Parl. Pap. (1859), X.

covered, for the space of a mile, with the ship's cargo, which the coastguards of the adjoining stations were doing their utmost to protect. The cargo consisted of pipes of wine, casks of brandy, tobacco, cotton, liqueurs, etc. There were four or five thousand people of all classes present, who were engaged in staving in the casks, drinking the liquor and wine, and plundering the property of every description—hundreds of women with pails, pots, jars, and other vessels carrying it off into the country in all directions. We destroyed and upset many hundreds of these vessels in our passage down to the wreck, where we proceeded to protect the full casks which were surrounded by many hundreds of armed men, who threatened to destroy the coastguard, and were armed with staves and pieces of iron from the wreck. It was impossible, in such a case, with our force of twenty-five men, and upon such an extent of coast, to preserve the whole of the property, but, after every exertion had been made, forty-one casks of wine, with a quantity of cotton, cork, staves, etc., were secured and placed in safety for removal to Penzance. . . . The names of some of the parties who committed assault upon the coast-guard or in whose possession plundered property was found, have been given to the local authorities but, as some special constables, who arrived late at night, were unable or un-willing to identify the parties who were taken, the number of obstructors, in the execution of this our duty, who have been recognized, amounts only to two, and those with property in their possession to fifteen, which cases are now before the magistrate for further proceedings.' [1]

It would be a very great mistake to suppose that wrecking, at this or any other date, was confined to the inhabitants of Cornwall. The report of the Constabulary Force Commis-sioners of 1839 asserts that on the Cheshire coast hundreds of people were known to assemble on such occasions, carrying off the wine and spirits in kettles or other receptacles. It also describes how, on an Italian vessel being wrecked on the coast of North Wales, the inhabitants robbed the sailors who had escaped from the wreck, and ' took the clothes out of their chests before their very faces '. Furthermore, we learn from the same source that at Deal, and at other places on the coast of Kent, the country people were in the habit of assembling in such numbers for plundering purposes that the coastguards were sometimes obliged to discharge their

[1] First Report of the Constabulary Force Commissioners, 1839.

fire-arms over their heads before they could be sufficiently intimidated to disperse. Reports of like happenings were also given to the Commissioners from many other districts, including Durham, Yorkshire, Norfolk, Suffolk, the Isle of Wight, Dorset, and Devon. It is true that in most of these places the wrecking consisted chiefly in pilfering small articles of property under cover of darkness, or when the coastguards' backs were turned, and the open conflicts which took place in Cornwall between the representatives of the law and the local population seem to have been rare elsewhere. Furthermore, as the report itself concludes : ' whilst in other parts of the English coast, persons may assemble by hundreds for plunder on the occasion of a wreck, on the Cornish coast they assemble in thousands '.

IV

By the latter half of the last century, the ever-increasing vigilance of the coastguards was beginning to make wrecking, even in Cornwall, a more hazardous and far less profitable occupation than it had been in earlier times. Like their close confederates, the smugglers, those who continued to indulge in wrecking found that nimble wits and a ready hand were increasingly necessary in order to evade the officers of the law. A story recently told by Mr Stanley Old, of St Merryn, is illustrative of this. ' During the month of January 1860, a ship named the *James Alexander* was driven ashore by a heavy gale at Porthmeor, near Porthcothan Bay. On board the vessel was found a live pig, for which a general scramble took place amongst the spoilers who had collected from the surrounding countryside. The pig was eventually secured and brought ashore by a man from Penrose. Half-way across the fields, as he was driving the animal towards his home, he was suddenly met by a preventive officer. Now, anyone coming from a wreck was always suspected by the officers of being in possession of something to which he had no right, and accordingly the Penrose man was challenged with the words : " Hallo ! what are you up to ? " Quick as a flash came the answer : " There's a wreck out there on the cliffs, and the blackguards have gone and left all the gates open and I have had to round up my stock and drive 'em home." With a " Get out, you ! " to the pig, the man continued his course, and eventually got the animal safely to his house.' [1]

Not infrequently in those days of wooden ships, valuable timber would be washed ashore after the prolonged gales of winter. On one occasion it so happened that large baulks of mahogany had been coming in under St Merryn cliffs, and several of these valuable prizes had been secured by the farmers of the district and safely hidden in their rickyards. This fact, by some means or other, becoming known to the custom officer at Padstow, the latter journeyed out one evening in order to make inquiries. On his arrival, one of the farmers in question confessed that he knew where the timber was, and offered to take him to the spot where he could see it. Before doing so, however, he suggested their taking a jug of cider, which the officer, after his four-mile walk, was nothing loth to accept. One jug led to another, and it was growing dusk before a start was made. Calling to his labourer to bring a rope and a lantern, the trio set out across the fields to Mackerel Cove, near Trevose Head. On arrival there, the farmer proposed that he and the labourer should tie the rope round the officer's body and lower him down the face of the cliff to the spot where he told him that the baulks could be seen. As already stated, it was by this time practically dark, and as he peered over the two-hundred-feet drop, at the bottom of which could be heard the roar and thunder of a heavy breaking sea, the officer's courage completely failed him. Rather than venture his life in such an awful situation, he told the farmer that he would be willing to say no more about it, and with this agreement, which must have proved equally satisfactory to both parties, the inquiry was brought to a close. [2]

Beach-combing, though an unadventurous form of wrecking, sometimes yielded rich rewards to the dwellers by the coast. Gold coinage used often to be carried on ships trading with foreign countries, and when one of these came to disaster, the coins themselves were frequently found upon the beaches for months or years afterwards. In many places, stories are still told of the existence of hoards of gold and silver coins, though unfortunately for the descendants of the people who put them there, the description of the hiding-places seems always too vague to allow of their recovery ! It is a fact,

[1] *Western Morning News*, 13 August 1930.
[2] *Western Morning News*, 17 January 1930.

however, as Mr Old has said, that in the past, farms were sometimes bought and paid for in gold currency on such a scale that, if the money had been saved by ordinary methods, the purchasers must indeed have been thrifty. Some sixty or more years ago, masons were called in to make some structural alterations in a large house in the Padstow district. In removing the old plaster from the ceiling of a bedroom, a shower of gold coins suddenly descended upon the workmen, and it is said that more than one of the ladies' apron-strings snapped under the weight of gold which was recovered. On the death of the owner of another house in the same district, a relation of the deceased and the housekeeper excused themselves from attending the funeral, on the grounds that it was necessary for them to stay and prepare a meal for the mourners on their return. As soon as the coffin had left the house, the relative told her companion that she was going to make a search, and that the two should go fifty-fifty with the spoils. What they actually discovered is not known, but shortly afterwards the relative, who was married to a ne'er-do-well, who was unlikely to have saved a penny-piece of his own, departed to south Cornwall, where she bought a two-hundred-acre farm and soon retired, as did also her sons at an early age.[1]

Near the church of Gunwalloe, on the shores of Mounts Bay, specimens of the large old-fashioned dollar coins have been frequently recovered by residents in the neighbourhood. These are believed to come from a foreign vessel which was wrecked here in the latter part of the eighteenth century. About the year 1820, the number of these coins which had been found led to the formation of a company, which set about a systematic search in a miner-like way. An iron shaft was made and let down through the sand. The work, however, was hindered by the constant gales and rough seas, and soon afterwards the project was abandoned. About the year 1863 another attempt was made to secure the treasure by the employment of divers.[2] This, however, proved equally unsuccessful, but the fact that silver coins are still occasionally picked up on these beaches, shows that the stories told in the neighbourhood are not wholly legendary.

The ill-fame of this district, both as regards wrecks and the lawless character of its inhabitants, lasted far into the nineteenth century. 'The dangers of the coast from St

[1] *Western Morning News*, 17 January 1930.
Thomas Spargo, *Mines of Cornwall and Devon* (1868).

(See page 21)

"THE KING OF PRUSSIA'S" COVE

(See page 52)

CLEARING A WRECK IN CORNWALL
(after Rowlandson)

Michael's Mount to the Lizard are too well known to need description,' wrote the Rev. G. C. Smith—better known to his contemporaries as 'Bo'sun'. Smith—in a letter composed shortly before his death in 1860. ' Many vessels, especially foreigners from the East and West Indies, South America, and other parts, frequently, in the winter, at night, make the light-house at St Agnes in Scilly, and that on the Longships, off the Land's End, as their first landfall: and if a strong gale from the south-west sets in, they find it impossible to weather the Lizard. They then fall deeper into the bay and are frequently driven, with a violence that nothing can surpass, on to the coast between the Mount and the Lizard. Here they are often dashed to atoms in a moment : or at other times, through the concurrence of some favourable circumstances, are thrown up into places where the greater part of the cargo might be saved. Natural depravity and the custom of centuries have inspired the inhabitants of the coast with a rapacity for plundering those wrecks, and the name " wreckers " applies, therefore, to vast numbers who look for the season of booty. When the news of a wreck flies along the coast, thousands of these people collect near the fatal spot, armed with pickaxes, hatchets, crowbars, and ropes, not for helping the sufferers, but for breaking up and carrying off all they can. The moment the vessel touches the shores, she is considered as fair plunder ; and men, women, and children are working on her, night and day, to break her up. The hardships they, especially the women, endure, are incredible. Should a vessel be laden with wine or spirit, she brings them certain death. The rage and fighting to stave in the casks, and bring away the spoil in kettles and all kinds of vessels, are brutal and shocking ; to drunkenness and fighting succeed fatigue, cold, sleep, wet, suffocation, and death ! Once last winter, a wreck happened on Sunday ; they had everything ready and sallied forth, not, however, until the clock had struck twelve at midnight, when all checks of conscience were thought to be removed. Five hundred little children in a parish are brought up in this way, and encouraged by precept and example to pursue this horrid system. The practices of these wreckers have, by one severe instance, awakened the attention of the Bishop of St David's, who lately exhorted his clergy to preach everywhere against it. To this method may be added, with as great effect, the persuasion of those who will visit their cottages. It appears for the credit of the county, however, that these practices are confined to a few western parishes, *and that even there, no deeds of personal inhumanity towards the unhappy sufferers have been permitted in modern times, even by the plunderers themselves.* Inheriting from their ancestors, however, an opinion that they have a right to such spoils as the ocean may place within their reach, many even among the more enlightened inhabitants secure whatever they can seize, and conclude without any hesitation that nothing but injustice, supported by power, and sanctioned by law, can wrench it from their hands.' [1]

The fame of Bo'sun Smith, it may be well to recall, rested upon his power as a popular preacher and, like many another of his kind, he was gifted, in no small degree, with the histrionic art. The scenes, therefore, which he depicts, though doubtless not without foundation, cannot be assumed in all respects to constitute a literal presentation of the facts. Less sensational, but probably far truer to type, is the picture given by Mrs Bonham in her book, *A Corner of Old Cornwall,* which recalls more intimately than any other of its kind, the state of life which obtained in the isolated Lizard promontory in the earlier part of the last century. That the people were ' wreckers ', the authoress makes no attempt to disguise, but her account entirely dispels the illusion that the majority of the wrecks were attended by such scenes of drunkenness as the former writer has conjured up. Indeed, the reverse seems to have been true since, in certain cases, wrecks were the means of introducing to the people teetotal drinks of a kind which they had formerly scarcely known. ' Many useful things are stowed away in the cottages after a good wreck,' writes Mrs Bonham. ' The " tea-wreck ", in particular, was a wonderful piece of good fortune for folks, very few of whom could ever indulge in such an expensive luxury. There was also the " coffee-wreck ", when many tasted that delicious stimulant for the first time.'

Of all the ' useful ' wrecks of this sort which have occurred on the coast of Cornwall, none has better reason for being remembered than that of the *Good Samaritan,* which came ashore at Bedruthan Steps on 22nd October 1846—a year before the Trevose Lighthouse was completed :

> *The* Good Samaritan *came ashore*
> *To feed the hungry and clothe the poor,*
> *Barrels of beef and bales of linen,*
> *No poor man shall want a shillin'.*

[1] Quoted by C. G. Cooke.   *Topographical Description of Cornwall.*

The vessel, whose untimely end gave rise to this well-known panegyric, was bound from Liverpool to Constantinople with a valuable cargo of silk and cotton goods. The night on which the disaster occurred was an unusually wild one, and the vessel was dashed to pieces and completely destroyed within a few hours after she had struck. Out of her crew of ten, two only survived the horrors of the night. The gale, as not infrequently happens, was succeeded by glorious weather, and next morning crowds of people from all the surrounding country-side were gathered on the beach. Nothing remained of the wreck itself but the pieces of smashed-up timber and her bottom, which lay embedded in the sand close to what is now known as the Samaritan Rock. The cargo, contained in iron-bound bales, many of which had burst, lay scattered around on the sands, whilst strips of the finest silks and cotton hung waving in the breeze from the topmost points of the rocks, on to which they had been tossed by the sport of the waves. ' Looting,' writes a local resident, ' was carried on incessantly. Never before, or perhaps since, have the ladies of the neighbourhood been clothed in such rich silks and other fineries. After the wreck, excise officers searched practically every house in the district, where much of the spoil was discovered and its possessors arrested. It is said that at the time Bodmin gaol was half full of St Eval men. In many more cases, however, the officers were outwitted. News quickly spread when a search was in progress, and in one house where a cupboard was crammed chock-full of material, the kitchen dresser was placed in front of it, and although the premises were searched, the finds were nil ! ' Amongst those who did well out of the wreck was a certain George Lee, of St Merryn, a noted character of his day, concerning whom many stories of wrecking are told. In his younger days Lee had been in the navy and, as an illustration of his vigorous constitution, it is said that when his ship was in Plymouth, he would think little of walking the fifty-odd miles during the night in order to reach his home. On the occasion of the wreck of the *Samaritan*, it is recorded that George Lee, whilst working in partnership with a boon companion, discovered a quantity of gold coins. The cliffs at Bedruthan Steps are nearly four hundred feet high, and then, as now, there was only one track leading up from the beach, and this was guarded by a preventive officer. How to get past the latter was the question that had to be solved. Eventually, it was decided that the gold coins should be transferred to Lee's pocket, after which the pair separated, his companion, Northcott, going straight to his home, there to await Lee's arrival and the sharing of the spoil. This was done ; but actually, it was many hours that Northcott had to wait before his partner arrived. When he did so, Lee presented a sorry spectacle. With clothes covered in mud, he informed Northcott that he had been attacked and robbed, his pockets and their contents having been cut clean out of his clothes. ' This tale,' states Mr Old, ' was evidently believed by Northcott and others ; but,' he adds, ' it is a significant fact that soon after this affair George Lee was in a position to buy a cottage and the adjoining meadow.' [1]

V

Though many of the tales and incidents related above might seem to reflect small credit on the character of the Cornish people, it would be a very unjust statement of the case which made no attempt to show the reverse side of the picture. For if the dwellers by the Cornish sea have harvested for long centuries where they have not sown, they have time and again given of their best with an unstinting hand. Nor is this only true of latter days, when the lifeboats of Cornwall, manned by their gallant crews of local fishermen, have done such signal service to mariners passing these storm-vexed shores. As long ago as 1802, when according to popular conception the average Cornish coast-dweller was still the brutal wrecker, dear to the heart of the novelist, local records show that the bulk of the population were none the less ready to risk their own lives in the attempt to save those of the chance strangers whom Fate had made dependent on them for aid. ' On Thursday last,' states the St Ives correspondent of the *Cornwall Gazette*, 6 March 1802, 'there was driven on shore in this bay, by a violent gale of wind at north-east, the ship *Suffolk*, of London, laden with bale goods and rice from Bengal. She came on shore in a shocking and distressed condition, having split all her sails to pieces the night before, the ship leaking badly, and of the twenty-one hands on board, six only able to do duty, the rest being sick. The crew remained on board in a

[1] Stanley Old, *Western Morning News*, 17 January 1930.

perilous situation for some hours ; but by the vigilant exertions of the people from the shore (*who always in such cases distinguish themselves by manly alacrity*), boats were got from the creek at Hayle, and another large eight-oar boat was *carried* from St Ives (three miles) by land, which being well manned, attempted at all hazards to get to the ship. In the meantime the captain and crew on board fastened a line to a keg, and let it drift to the shore, and the boat's crew, having got hold of it, by that means hauled all the people, one by one, to land, except two who were so ill as not to be able to struggle, and who accordingly died in their hammocks. The weather the next day proving favourable, the bale goods, consisting of raw silk and muslins with some hundreds of bags of rice, were brought to St Ives by boats ; and yesterday the ship itself, with part of the cargo, was brought into St Ives pier much damaged.'

In the year 1817, a similar wreck occurred at Gunwalloe Cove, near Helston. Here again conspicuous bravery was shown by the local population in rescuing the sailors who had jumped overboard amidst the heavy breakers. Among the rescuers was a certain William Triggs, of Mullion, who, perceiving one of the less fortunate sailors surrounded by the waves, and being carried out in an exhausted state by the violent ' undertow ', rushed into the surf, and succeeded in getting hold of the man by the sleeve of his coat. ' They were now,' states an eye-witness, ' both off their feet, and beaten and tossed about by the surf. Perceiving this, the people who had the end of the rope which was about Triggs's waist, being eager to get them both to land, hauled on it somewhat violently. As a result, the sailor's coat rent, and the piece coming off in Triggs's hand, the latter was hauled in to the beach without the other man. Another young man, however, a farmer named John Curtis, observing the mishap, immediately dashed into the water, and by his gallant action succeeded in bringing the sailor to shore in safety, though at the peril of his own life.' [1]

Some ten years before this, there had gone ashore on the Looe Bar, a short distance southward of Gunwalloe Cove, H.M. frigate *Anson*, among the most famous of all the wrecks which have occurred on the Cornish coast, and worthy, as results proved, to be regarded as one of the outstanding events of British maritime history. The *Anson*, forty-four guns, had

[1] Henry Trengrouse, *Shipwreck Investigated* (1817), 84.

left Falmouth on Christmas Eve, 1807, for her station off Brest, as a look-out ship for the Channel Fleet. A gale from the west-south-west having sprung up shortly after her leaving port, she continued to be buffeted about for some days in the seas off Mounts Bay, and at length, on the 28th, the wind still increasing, the captain determined to put back to Falmouth. Owing, however, to mistaking the Land's End for the Lizard, the ship became embayed, and at the cry of ' Breakers ahead ! ' from the man on the lookout, both cables were let go. The *Anson* rode to these till the morning of the 29th, when they parted, and the captain, in order to save as many lives as possible, decided to beach her on the sands off the Looe Pool. ' By this time,' as the Rev. Baring-Gould has written, ' a tremendous sea was running, and as she took the beach, only sixty yards from the bar, she was dashed broadside on, but happily for those on board, heeled landwards. Seas mountains high rolled over her, sweeping everything before them.' The captain, realizing that no chance of rescue was possible for those who remained on board, gave orders to the men to save themselves as best they could. Whilst a small proportion succeeded in fighting their way to safety through the boiling surf, the majority of those who leaped over the side were instantly swept off their feet by the terrific ' under tow ', and carried out into the trough of the waves, never to return. In consequence of this, though the wreck lay under the very eyes of the crowd which was gathered on the beach, upwards of a hundred men are believed to have been drowned, including the captain, who stood by the frigate to the last.

In the meantime, those who had got to shore reported that two women, and a like number of children, were yet remaining on board. On learning this, to the lasting honour of Cornwall, several local men, including Mr Tobias Roberts, of Helston, and Mr Foxwell, of Mullion, determined to give their own lives, if necessary, in making the hazardous attempt to reach the ship.[1] In this act of almost unparalleled bravery they succeeded ; but at what risk and peril to themselves may be judged from Mr Foxwell's own statement. ' I went into the surf as far as I could,' he writes, ' and got so near the ship as to have a child handed to me, and Mr R—— at the same time had one handed to him. I carried the child under one arm, and held by the rope with the other. Mr R——, though I begged him, refused the assistance of the rope. After a

[1] S. Baring-Gould, *Cornish Characters and Strange Events*, 60–1.

few moments, however, a tremendous wave broke in upon the beach, so we were both enclosed by the waters. As I was holding by the rope, I sustained myself, but Mr R—— was washed off his legs. I saw his danger, but feared if I quitted the rope, I should get into the like difficulty. My apprehension, however, for his safety, and that of the child, prevailed and I ran the risk (being a tall man), and seized him by the collar, and succeeded in getting him upon his legs again, otherwise I do not doubt that both he and the child would have been drowned.' [1]

Whilst these agonizing scenes were taking place, there was standing amongst the crowd of spectators on the beach a certain Henry Trengrouse, of Helston, whose subsequent devotion to the cause of life-saving, were it but one-half as famous as it deserves to be, would surely atone for all the sins which have been attributed to his countrymen in the pages of popular fiction. By one of those curious chances of fortune, however, which ever seem to deprive the true inventor of his recognition and reward, Trengrouse's service to humanity in the evolution of the rocket apparatus is still almost unknown to the world at large. And yet, in actual fact, it is to him, above all others, that the world is indebted for the invention which has since saved many thousands of lives and which is now a commonplace to all who dwell by English shores. From the day of the wreck of the *Anson*, it is said that Trengrouse's mind never ceased to be exercised by the thought of how some means of communication might be established between vessels and the shore, and throughout the remainder of his life he freely sacrificed his money, business, and health, in the effort to achieve, and to get others to adopt, the substance of his grand invention. Something of the same idea, it is true, had occurred to Lieutenant John Bell in 1791 ; and in 1807 Captain G. W. Manby had carried the proposal a stage farther by experimenting with a mortar for throwing a shot, with a line attached, to stranded ships. Manby's mortar, however, notwithstanding that its inventor was rewarded by the Government with a sum of £2,000, was cumbrous and dangerous, and after several men had been killed during tests, it was definitely abandoned by the authorities. The superior advantages of Trengrouse's apparatus are too manifold to be discussed in detail, but it will suffice to point out that the rocket apparatus, being much lighter than

[1] H. Trengrouse, *Shipwreck Investigated* (1817), 21.

the mortar, could be readily carried to situations on the cliffs whither it would have been well nigh impossible to have conveyed the latter. Moreover the velocity of a rocket, increasing gradually, was much less likely to cause the breaking of the life-line than a mortar, whose action was so sudden and violent as frequently to snap the rope by the force of its discharge. In addition to all this, Trengrouse's rocket could either be fired from the shore to the ship or vice versa, and had the added advantage over a shot, of showing its track by a trail of fire, thus rendering it visible to the crew and their rescuers at night time when the wrecks most commonly occur. It was Trengrouse's earnest desire to see every ship supplied with a rocket apparatus, since vessels being almost invariably wrecked *before* the wind, the line might the more easily be fired from a ship than from the shore. For years, however, Parliament continued to haggle over the matter and little was done. Nevertheless, the ardour of the inventor survived every discouragement, and his last words to his son as he lay on his death-bed on 19th February 1854 were : ' If you live to be as old as I am, you will find my rocket apparatus all along our shores'. The prophecy has, indeed, been fulfilled, and the world of to-day is still benefiting from the achievement for which Trengrouse had sacrificed his all. In return for the outlay on his experiments, however, of over £3,000, the inventor received only two money grants to the value of £50 and thirty guineas, together with a silver medal and a diamond ring. Even the latter, which had been presented to him by the Czar of Russia in recognition of the services which his apparatus had rendered in saving shipwrecked lives in the Baltic and the Black Sea, Trengrouse had been constrained to pawn, in order to carry out the further investigations for which his own country was not sufficiently grateful to pay ! [1]

VI

Meantime, however, the gallant work of rescuing ship-wrecked lives went on. Numbered among the many disastrous wrecks which have occurred on the Scilly Islands was that of the steamer *Thames*, which went ashore in a violent gale in the

[1] See S. Baring-Gould, *Cornish Characters and Strange Events*, 63–7.

year 1841. Immediately the discovery of the wreck had been made, we learn that boats began putting off from the islands, despite the imminent danger from the tremendous seas which were running. ' Indeed,' wrote an eye-witness, ' the distress on land appeared to be almost as great as that on the vessel, for crowds of women were out on the hills bewailing the anticipated fate of their nearest relatives. It should further be recorded,' he adds, ' to the lasting honour of the islanders, that although in the course of their task they frequently fell in with various parts of the cargo (such as casks of porter, whisky, etc.), they gave not a moment's thought to securing these as objects of salvage. Their sole meritorious object was to render prompt and efficient aid for the preservation of life.' [1] Those who escaped from the sea, moreover, found that the islanders were as generous as they were brave, the latter, despite their own poverty, putting everything which they possessed at the service of the shipwrecked passengers and crew.

In the pages of an old diary kept by a resident of St Ives, during the years 1806–48, many other instances are recorded of the bravery of the local population. Under the date 24th December 1838 the writer notes : ' A very heavy gale from north-west to north-east with thick rain. At 1 p.m. a vessel was seen running in for Porthmeor beach, but, by hoisting a flag on the island, she hauled to more, and came round the head and let go her anchor at the back of the quay. The anchor, however, not holding and it being low water, she struck, and the sea made one complete breach over her. Two light seine boats were manned in attempt to rescue the crew, but being struck with a heavy sea were thrown so far to leeward, that they were obliged to run them on shore on Porth-minster beach. A tow-boat was next manned, but filled with water by being struck with a heavy sea. A gig got near, but was struck with a sea and filled. The tow-boat was again manned with a fresh crew, a sea again filled her and washed two men out of her. She was a third time manned, when they succeeded in rescuing the crew. Afterwards the vessel beat in near the rocks on Porthminster beach, but was got off by the pilots the following day (Christmas) on the flowing tide '. [2]

On 7th April 1840 the sloop *Mary Anne*, of Poole, in the

[1] Rev. G. Woodly, *Narrative of the Loss of the Steamer ' Thames ' at Scilly* (1841).
[2] Diary in the possession of Col T. J. Chellew, St Ives.

course of a heavy gale from the north-east, split her sails, and in running for the pier at St Ives was struck by a sea on the Ridge. As a result of this, she became unmanageable and shortly afterwards went on shore under the ' Mills '. The lifeboat was manned, but owing to bad seamanship was likewise thrown on shore. By a most daring attempt, however, on the part of two local fisherman—Sam Uren, jr., and R. Welch, jr—who swam out to the vessel through the sea, a line was eventually got on board, and by this means the crew, consisting of the master, one man, and a boy, were hauled to shore in safety. On 24th August 1842, the writer of the above-quoted diary notes: ' Heavy gale north-north-east. At 1 a.m. a large barque discovered in the bay. The quay light was put in, and a tar barrel burnt at Cairn Crowse. The vessel wore and made for the light. The *William* gig succeeded in boarding her after great risk of their lives in getting over the Ridge (it being low water), and brought the vessel to an anchor to the eastward of the Carrack. Proved to be the *Bosphorus* for Jamaica, with a general cargo. Pilotage claimed £400, settled for £150 '. [1]

The last sentence of this entry throws an interesting light on Cornish character. Willing to risk all at the moment of danger and prepared, as he is, to gamble his own life on the chance of saving those of others, the typical Cornishman sees no reason why he should not drive the best possible bargain once the crisis is over. The profits of pilotage were in some cases very considerable. On 28th February 1838 two St Ives boats, who managed to bring in a French brig which had been abandoned off the Land's End, were awarded £1,000 for their services by the Admiralty Court. A year later, some Newlyn and St Ives boats received £450 for salving the derelict *John*, of Sunderland. On another occasion, the St Ives pilots demanded £120 for bringing in the French brig *Normand*, of Cherbourg. After a good deal of haggling they were at length granted £100, as a result of the captain's own statement that it was fully due, although as the writer of the diary naïvely adds, ' had they been offered £50 or £60 at first it is very likely it would have been accepted ! ' In some instances, however, the pilots overreached themselves in their demands. On 8th November 1838 the French barque *Joséphine*, which had been brought up by the Scilly pilot, was handed over to the charge of the St Ives men. The latter anchored in the bay that night,

[1] Diary in the possession of Col T. J. Chellew, St Ives.

and the next morning slipped the cables, warped her in, and demanded £170 for their services ! This was, not unnaturally, refused by the owners ; and the court before whom the case was brought, considering the charge to be a shameful one for so trifling a matter, gave the pilots nothing, and ordered them to pay their own costs.[1]

Although it might perhaps be claimed that the profits of salvage and pilotage were, in some cases, sufficient to inspire the coast-dwelling population with motives for service which were not wholly disinterested, there is no such charge which can ever detract from the heroism of the crews who have manned the lifeboats. As Mr Claude Berry has finely written in his foreword to the story of Cornwall's oldest lifeboat station which passed its centenary a few years ago : ' No hundred years has been more crowded with daring deeds, acts of supreme courage and self-sacrifice than the century of lifeboat service which has elapsed since the founding of the first Cornish station at Padstow in 1827. No distressed vessel within sight of the cliffs ever sought help from the lifeboat and was denied it. Sometimes, within the space of twenty-four hours, Padstow lifeboatmen have been out on three distinct services. Twice their lifeboats have been wrecked—on one occasion five men being drowned, and on the other every man of the crew perishing in the sweeping waters. But the great work of life-saving has continued, and to-day our lifeboatmen are as ready as their splendid predecessors to man the boats when precious lives are in danger'. [2]

What is true of this particular station, is true of all. ' Never shall I forget,' wrote an old inhabitant of Penzance on a recent occasion, ' the wreck of the *North Britain*, a barque of seven hundred tons which, when homeward bound from America, got lost in a fog and went ashore on the Eastern Green. It was on a Sunday afternoon, early in December 1868, and a terrible day it was, with the wind blowing a hurricane. As soon as the signal went, hundreds of people were swarming down on the beach, and very soon by their aid the lifeboat was got out ; Higgins as usual in the bow, and Tom Carbis steering. There were no engines, of course, in those days, and the boats had to be pulled through the water by oars. However, they managed at length to struggle through the terrific seas until they got quite close to the wreck when, all of a

[1] Diary in the possession of Col T. J. Chellew, St Ives.
[2] *The Story of Padstow's Lifeboats.*

sudden, a great wave struck the lifeboat, and over she went with the crew underneath. Somehow, they managed to struggle out, and by a superhuman effort righted her. No sooner had they done so, than another sea struck her and over she went again. Once more they got her on to her keel, and all except one man struggled aboard. He was called Hodge, and a wave carried him away from the boat. He tried to swim ashore in his cork jacket, and how we were thrilled when a man named Desraux rode out amongst the breakers on horseback and hauled Hodge in by the collar ! The lifeboat then gave up the attempt to reach the wreck, for the crew were so exhausted by their experiences as to have scarcely strength to pull ashore. As soon as she was beached, however, a volunteer crew was called for, and, despite the fact that what had happened to her before had been clearly visible to those on the beach, she was quickly manned and launched again. In the meantime, the crew of the barque, thinking that their chance of rescue had gone when the lifeboat capsized, had lowered their whaler. This was smashed to pieces almost immediately. They then got out their jolly-boat, filled her with men and began to row ashore. They had got about three-quarters of the way in, when she was up-ended by a sea and the men were flung out. Spectators waded into the water as far as they dared and pulled some ashore, but four of the sailors were drowned. Those who remained on the barque, however, were saved, for the volunteer lifeboat crew managed to get to them.' [1]

A plain record of facts, told in a plain unvarnished manner, this story is characteristic of countless others which illustrate the heroism of the crews who man the lifeboats of the Cornish coast. Although the introduction of wireless and the passing of the sailing ship have happily rendered wrecks a much less frequent occurrence than formerly, still, when the worst comes to the worst, and vessels are driven landwards to their fate, the lifeboats are out on their work of humanity, and the gallantry which distinguished their crews in the past is being perpetuated by their descendants of to-day. These matters are well known to all those who dwell within sight and sound of the Cornish seas ; but it is none the less an ironical fact that for the world at large, the deeds attributed by fiction to the wreckers of long ago still excite more attention than all the life-saving by which their sins have surely been atoned.

[1] John Richards, *Western Morning News*, 13 January 1930.

THE FISHERMAN'S TRADE

I

THE smuggling days of Cornwall are over and past, and the wrecker of history and romance has become the mere gatherer of driftwood upon her beaches, but still the fisherman plies his ancient trade, the first of all the long-shore types to take to the sea for a livelihood, the last to leave it.

To visit a port like St Ives in the fall of a winter's afternoon, and to watch the herring fleet as it goes streaking out across the darkening waters of the bay, is to recapture something of the spirit of the old sea-life of the past. True, the days of mast and sail are over, and the throb of petrol-engines has replaced the creaking of ropes in the pulley-blocks and the strain of canvas tautening in the wind, but the appearance of the men on deck in their heavy oilskins and great sea-boots, or the proud and anxious women who, with shawls gathered about their heads, stand watching them off from the end of the granite quays, has little changed in all the centuries of similarly enacted scenes which such ancient ports have witnessed.

It has been truly said that of all those who have followed the sea for a livelihood, the fisherman has had least glory and most toil. In the cold bluster-nights of winter, with the salt spray freezing his hands and limbs to the very marrow, the fisherman still spends in labour the hours when others sleep. Out in their tiny boats, or in undecked 'gigs', the latter exposing their crews to all the rigours and hardships of wind and rain, they know, as few landsmen ever can, what the struggle for existence means on the open sea. Some have paid the penalty of their calling, even within the most recent years, by being swept overboard when their hands have become too numbed with cold to grasp the means of safety. Others, again, have gone to their fate when returning to port, full-laden with the harvest. Often enough at such times no sound or cry has been heard above the roaring of the wind, only the sudden disappearance of one of the gleaming lights has warned those who were following that a boat had foundered. Though friends might be not far off, slender indeed are the chances of rescuing those whom the sea engulfs in the blackness of the night, when never a shout may be heard, and a sinking man may see his last hope of deliverance pass by but a few yards distant from his eyes. Or, again, in the thick and dirty weather, when the mist and rain come down and hide the very lighthouse beams, how many a fisherman must have seen, in his mind's eye, the blackness of the ' Stones ', and the jagged reefs where the deep-sea weed floats upward on the swell of a rising wave, or sinks again to hang in horrible festoons before the gulfs where conger lie, and where the waters suck and moan, like vampires awaiting the dead. For though the fisherman, like his comrade the miner, may be a man of few words in regard to danger, he is gifted with all the imagination of the Celt, and when in conversation he speaks of some spot or other as being an ' ugly plaace in a ground say ' (sea), his words suffice, for those who know him, to conjure up visions of danger more fearful than those described in any work of fiction.

Despite all the changes of a mechanized world, therefore, the fisherman's life is a hard one still, dependent, as he is, not only on the unforeseen chances of Nature in the prosecution of his work, but on the verdict of others for the ultimate reward of his toil. For, in the simple, hard-working share-fisherman of the west, striving to maintain himself in the possession of his own boat and tackle, may be seen one of the last outposts of an older order of individualism engaged in an heroic struggle with the massed forces of the highly organized economic world of to-day. Out in his boat at night, perhaps, whilst riding beneath the stars, the fisherman may almost forget the thraldom in which he lies ; but, with the return to port in the morning, any dreams which he may have had of being still his own master are quickly shattered. For between him and the consumer of his catches, the middlemen now stand, masters of his fate, no less than of the countless town-dwellers who might, but so infrequently are permitted to, benefit from the cheap food which the fisherman's labour should provide. When fish is scarce in the ports, the price is good, and herrings may fetch as much as sixteen shillings a hundred (120 in reality) for those who have them to sell. At this price the buyers are clearly able to make a profit or they would not give it. The next night, maybe, the fishing is more general, and, with fairly large landings, the price sinks, perhaps to eight shillings. Shortly after this, the whole fleet of sixty or more boats may return to port one day heavily laden with an abundant harvest, which has to be ' given ' to the buyers for two shillings and sixpence per hundred or even less. In the meantime a box of one hundred and twenty herrings may be sent to London for approximately two shillings, so that, assuming the price of the fish in the shops throughout the country to average twopence each (a very modest estimate), it would appear that of every £1 worth of herrings consumed by the public after a large catch the chain of middlemen will receive fifteen shillings and sixpence, in comparison with the fisherman's two shillings and sixpence.

Were the problem to be presented to them thus, the middle-men would, of course, point to their overhead charges, such as cellar rents, and the like, which have to be met, be the quantity of fish landed great or small. This, however, is a mere begging of the question, seeing that the same conditions apply equally to the men who have to pay not only for the purchase of their boats, nets, and gear, and the instalments on their engines (which are rented), but to provide the running expenses of petrol and oil, to say nothing of their labour which is performed under conditions of such hardship and peril. Indeed, of the two, the fisherman's overhead costs are the more constant, for the latter has still to meet the upkeep of his boat and its running expenses whether he catches any fish or not, whereas in the case of the buyers, the railway freights which, as they never tire of pointing out, constitute their heaviest charges, are variable, being less in proportion when they are dispatching large quantities of fish, and obviously not being incurred at all when they have none to send.

As things stand at present, therefore, owing to the inadequacy of the price which he receives when his catches are good, and the heavy losses which are frequently incurred when the fishing is poor, the share-fisherman, whose luck has once been against him, sinks deeper and deeper into the slough of insolvency, finding himself in the unhappy position of neither receiving the living wages of a hireling nor a proper participation in the profits of independent ownership. That the system whereby the fish, for which he has risked his capital, and in some cases even his life, and has in return been paid a farthing, should be sold in a shop round the corner for twopence or twopence-halfpenny, is all wrong, the share-fisherman has no doubt ; but failing to see any solution to this problem, he has developed an attitude of fatalism which renders the organization of any co-operative method of selling extremely difficult. His children, however, are growing up with the fixed determination that they, at any rate, will no longer endure the hardships which their fathers face for such an inadequate return, and so, year by year, the inshore fishery is dwindling, and a valuable part of the nation's food supply is being strangled at its source.

Formerly the actual work of selling the fish occupied more time than it does to-day, with the result that many of the fishermen, after being out all night, were detained at the auctions until almost midday. By the time, therefore, they had returned home and had dinner, it was necessary for them to be getting ready to go to sea again, so that in the busy part of the season many of the fishermen never took off their clothes or got a regular period of sleep from Monday to Saturday. Small wonder, then, that, apart from any religious consideration, the fishermen of Cornwall have so earnestly striven for the preservation of Sunday as a day of rest, realizing from their own experience, the human wisdom which underlay the Old Testament command.

The St Ives fishermen in particular can claim to have shown for at least three centuries that they have been willing to observe the Sabbath even to their own hindrance. In 1622, we find a minute recorded in the borough accounts to the effect that ' no owner of boats or nets shall dryve or sett their nets or owners of seines row to stem the Sunday night or any time befor day of that night', under penalty of a fine of ten shillings for each owner and three shillings and threepence for each fisherman. That this regulation was strictly enforced, is proved by the entries for money received for Sabbath-breaking which appear in subsequent pages of the same accounts. Moreover, such lapses when they occurred were always severely criticized by the leaders of local society. In a scarce little volume recording the life of Thomas Tregosse, of St Ives, a seventeenth-century Puritan divine, we read that in the summer of 1658, ' the fishermen taking a great number of pilchards on a Saturday, all the night was spent in saving of them, and the seamen were very intent in drying their nets on the Lord's day. This, Mr Tregosse rebuked them for, withal giving them to understand that they provoked the Lord de-servedly to withdraw His blessings from them, which happened accordingly. For from that time to the end of the fishing season they had not another opportunity of employing their nets '.[1]

In 1827 the Sabbath was still being observed with all its former strictness, and we learn from an old diary that on 12 August of that year ' two shoals, by colour, passed out, but no " Hevva " (cry, proclaiming appearance of a shoal) it being Sunday'. In 1831, the seine owners renewed their agreement not to catch fish on the Sabbath day, and, in consequence, although on 28th August of that year immense quantities of pilchards passed through all the stems, close to the rocks, one small shoal actually coming inside the quay-head under the seine-boats, ' no one attempted to catch them (it being Sunday)—until the evening, when Mr. Tremearne caught five hundred hogsheads at Porthminster '. The temptation, indeed, must have been strong, and it is small wonder that the fishermen sometimes partially yielded to it, as in this case. On Sunday, 16 October 1836, five seine boats at St Ives again shot their nets, ' but only one reaped any benefit '. During the next year, the diary records : ' *Tantivy* shot on an immense body of fish, but the men did not obey the huer and the fish were lost. The *Francis* then shot on the same shoal, which when taken was supposed to be from four to five thousand hogsheads '. Apparently this occurred on a Saturday, for we read that ' the seine being so full, they were obliged to shoot another outside it on Sunday '. The results, however, do not seem to have justified the Sabbath-breakers, for the diary adds, ' it is supposed two to three thousand hogsheads must have escaped and died, immense piles of dead fish washed ashore every day, and carted away as manure by the country people '. In 1838, a large body of fish was again discovered on a Sunday morning, close to the point at Carrack Gladden. ' The finders immediately made hevva, but *no notice was taken*. Charles Tremearne then ran home to St Ives, when all the boats were immediately manned ; but . . . the fish had gone ! ' [2]

A year later, another incident occurred which was no doubt regarded by many of the fishermen as a Divine intervention. ' On Sunday se'nnight,' states the *West Briton*, 15 November 1839, ' a man employed as a huer (watcher) to one of the seines at Newquay, ran to the neighbouring church to inform the

---

[1] Quoted by Mr C. G. Henderson, *Western Morning News*, 19 September 1929.

[2] From an old diary in the possession of Col T. J. Chellew, St Ives.

gentleman who superintended the seine in question that the bay was full of fish and to rally the crew that might be assembled there. Not being a very frequent attendant at the church himself, the huer had much trouble in finding the agent, but at length, after searching the different pews, he espied him to his great satisfaction, and delivered the glad tidings. They both left the place immediately, followed at full speed by a long train of persons whose curiosity had been excited. But lo and behold ! to their great surprise and disappointment, when they arrived at the cliff there was no fish in the bay, whilst the huer had forgotten to keep the boats afloat ! '

II

The mention of fishing regulations at St Ives in the early seventeenth century proves that the industry is of no recent growth. Its beginnings, however, though certainly dating from a period many centuries before this, are impossible to define. Prior to the Norman Conquest, as Mr Howard Dunn has pointed out, the difficulties of obtaining salt for curing must have kept the trade in fish within very narrow limits. Though there is evidence of small quantities of salt having been obtained by the evaporation of sea water (' salt works ' are mentioned in Domesday Book), the common method of preserving fish was by sun-drying. Only those fish which carry their fat in their livers were thus ' curable', and the method was not applicable to pilchards or herrings whose fat is contained in their bodily tissue.[1]

Early in the thirteenth century, however, King John granted licences to merchants of Bayonne to fish ' for whales, conger, and hake, from St Michael's Mount to Dartmouth ', and this association with France brought French salt into the country, as well as better material for nets than that provided locally.[2] From this time onwards, the fishing industry of Cornwall and Devon began to prosper, until, under Tudor administration, it had assumed a position of national importance.

During the reign of Elizabeth, the Council of State itself set about formulating a mass of petty regulations with the

[1] Cornwall ' Education Week ' Handbook (1927), 108.
[2] Cornwall ' Education Week ' Handbook (1927), 108.

twofold object of encouraging the development of the industry, and 'the conserving of the profytable foode (fish) for the liege people of the realme'. In respect of the latter, the orders were primarily concerned with the best means of distributing the fish. Thus, in 1588, it was ordained that of the pilchards taken at Cawsand Bay, ' two parts should be distributed among the towns of Plymouth, Milbrooke, etc., and one-third at Cawsand'. Needless to say, the complications which arose out of such orders were endless ; and, from the first, they were generally evaded by the inhabitants of Cawsand who, besides knowing something about fish, and the length of time which it would keep, were determined, for pecuniary reasons, to salt in their catches on the spot, and make better prices by exporting them overseas. Such an idea, however, was abhorrent to Elizabethan government. In 1590, came another order requiring that ' all shadds, cellars and pentises, called " Linns", which had been erected since 1588 should forthwith be plucked down'. It was stipulated, however, that if after the requisite two-thirds of the fish had been brought to Plymouth, ' it have not a ready sale within fowre tydes, it shall then be lawful for the seynars to carrie the same away by water or land to anie other place within the same counties, but in no sort to carry or sell the same beyond the seas'. [1] As the fish had generally gone bad by this time, this concession seems to have awakened little enthusiasm among the merchants. Oblivious of this fact, the council proceeded in a fatherly manner to explain that the principal intention of the order was not, as might well have been supposed, to put difficulties in the way of trade, but ' to preserve the use of this kind of fish called pilchards, to serve for the food of the people of the said counties, and not to be for private gaine carried out of the realme to strangers and to defraude the naturall inhabitants of their profytable foode. Moreover', the council continued, ' it is not meant but when it shall please God to grant encrease of the same kind of fish, more than sufficient to serve the necessities of the people of the realme, upon signification thereof to the Lords of the Council by the Justices of the Peace of the same county, etc.—leave may be granted to export the same'. [2]

With this somewhat indefinite assurance, the more law-abiding merchants and fish-curers had presumably to be

[1] Acts of Privy Council, 1590–1, 137–42.
[2] Acts of Privy Council, 1590–1, 137–42.

content, but there were obviously many others who continued to evade the regulations, esteeming their own profit above their country's weal.

The Government, however, did not merely confine its attention to restricting the exports of fish, but showed that it was willing to extend its paternal care to the industry by stimulating the consumption of the former in the home markets. Amongst the various steps which were taken to this end, the most important, perhaps, was the continuing of the national fast-days, long after the religious significance which had attached to them in pre-Reformation times had passed away. It has been calculated that during the Elizabethan period there were no less than one hundred and fifty-three days in the year on which it was officially forbidden to eat meat.

Nevertheless, despite all the efforts of the Council of State, the development of the fishing industry of Great Britain, apart from that of Devon and Cornwall, still left much to be desired. The chief reason for this seems to have lain in the curious prejudice or apathy which caused the herring fishery to be almost completely neglected by English fishermen, who were content to allow the Dutch to come over to their very shores in the pursuit of this fish, and afterwards to sell it to English buyers for handsome prices. ' All these herrings the Dutch do catch in the Yarmouth seas,' wrote a pamphleteer in 1614, ' they sell for ready money or gold to the Yarmouth men that be no fishermen, but only merchants and ingrossers.' [1] The result was that when Carew published his *Survey of Cornwall* in 1602, the ancient fisheries of Cornwall and Devon were still of much greater importance than those of the eastern counties. From a muster of ships and mariners made in the year 1582, it appears that Cornwall had a sea-going population of nearly two thousand, which was slightly exceeded only by that of Devon. The next two counties, Norfolk and Suffolk, claimed but sixteen hundred and twelve hundred respectively, so that altogether the mariners and fishermen of Cornwall and Devon exceeded those of the two eastern counties by more than a thousand. [2]

This preponderance is partly accounted for by the fact that the herring was much less neglected in the west, where the

---

[1] ' England's Way to Win Wealth.'   See Arber, *English Garner*, IV, 333.

[2] Sir William Monson, *Naval Tracts*, ed. Oppenheim, 188.

fishermen were not only accustomed to take large catches of these fish upon the coast but, by the beginning of the seventeenth century, at any rate, had begun to follow them as far afield as the shores of Ireland.[1] The chief cause, however, of the flourishing state of the West Country industry lay, as already shown, in the valuable monopoly which it enjoyed of the pilchard, a fish whose taking and curing continued until recent times to be the mainstay and support of the inhabitants of the Cornish coast.

These fish, which Carew describes as being 'the least in bigness, greatest for gaine, and most in number', were formerly wont to reach the Cornish shores 'betweene harvest and Alhallon-tyde', when their coming was eagerly awaited by all classes of the population. They were taken by two different methods, known to the fishermen as 'driving' (or drifting), and 'seining'. 'The drovers,' writes Carew, 'hang certain square nets athwart the tyde, thorow which the schoell of pilchards passing, leave many behind intangled in the meashes. When the nets are so filled, the drovers take them up, cleanse them and let them fall again.'[2] Straightforward and innocuous as such a method sounds, it nevertheless caused infinite contention, the seiners complaining 'with open mouth' at the drivers' short-sighted greed in thus breaking up and scattering the shoals of fish before they reached the shore, where they might be taken in far greater quantities by the use of the seine-net. This dispute, long, loud, and violent, as subsequent history proves it to have been, continued to vex the minds of the local population until, at length, the time came when both seiner and drifter alike were overwhelmed by their common enemy—the trawler.

A 'sayne', in Carew's time, commonly consisted of three or four boats carrying about six men apiece, 'with which, when the season of the year and weather serveth, they lie hovering upon the coast, and are directed in their works by a balker (Dutch *balken*, to shout) or huer who standeth on the cliffe side and from thence best discerneth the quantitie and course of the pilchard, according whereunto he cundeth (as they call it) the master of each boate by crying with a lowd voice, whistling through his fingers, and wheazing certain diversified and significant signs with a bush which he holdeth in his hand. At his appointment, the sayners in the boats cast out their net,

---

[1] Hobson Matthews, *History of St Ives*, 339.
[2] *Survey of Cornwall.*

drawing it round to either hand as the schoell lyeth, beating
with their oars to keep in the fish (as the ends of the net were
being drawn together) and at last either close and tuck it up
in the sea, or draw the same on land with more certain profit,
if the ground be not rough of rockes. After one companie
have thus shot their net, another beginneth behind them, and
so a third, as opportunitie serveth. Being taken, some, the
countrie people, who attend with horses and ponies at the
cliffes side, in great numbers, doe buy and carrie home ;
the large remainder is, by the merchant, greedily and speedily
seized upon '. [1]

To those who have themselves watched the ' shooting ' of a
seine, this brief, but strikingly vivid account of a scene which
must often have been witnessed by the writer near his home at
East Antony three hundred years and more ago, shows clearly
enough how little the methods of this particular branch of
the fishing industry were destined to change. On many a
high look-out along the Cornish coast may still be seen the
' huer's hut ', or ' balking-house ', wherein, until recent years,
patient watch was kept for the great shoals of pilchards which
once so regularly enriched these shores. Hanging within such
huts, might be seen the ' bushes ', consisting of wooden hoops
covered with white bags, and the long tin speaking-horns or
trumpets, by means of which the modern huer ' cunded ' or
signalled to the boats which still lay ' hovering upon the
coast '. It was not until the year 1924, in fact, that seining was
at length brought to a close at St Ives. In 1928, the last of
the seine-boats was sent to the Scilly Islands, the whole of the
remainder of the great fleet once possessed by this port having
been ruthlessly broken up for firewood. The bushes, trumpets, and other paraphernalia from the balking-house were
fortunately preserved, and are now in the possession of the
St Ives Old Cornwall Society.

Before entering upon a description of the all-important
seining industry, however, and showing how much the latter
formerly meant to Cornwall, it is desirable to glance back once
more on another early development of West Country fishing,
which proves that as long as four hundred years ago the
inhabitants of these areas were willing to risk even the hazards
of an Atlantic crossing in the pursuance of their calling. For
it is indeed an astonishing fact, and one which has scarcely
received the notice which it deserves, that within less than

[1] *Survey of Cornwall.*

thirty years after the voyages of Columbus and Cabot to the American continent, the hardy fishermen of Devon and Cornwall had already embarked on that most exacting of all sea enterprises—the great Newfoundland trade. As early as the year 1527, we read of the little Devonshire ships being unable to carry home more than a portion of their huge catches derived from this source.[1] On 20 July 1594 Sir Walter Raleigh wrote to Sir Robert Cecil pointing out that certain ' great Spanish men-of-war ' had recently given chase to several British vessels as far as Dartmouth. ' It is likely,' he adds, ' that all our Newfoundland men will be taken up by them if they be not speedily driven from the coast for, in the beginning of August, our " Newland " fleet are expected, which are above a hundred sail. If those should be lost, it would be the greatest blow ever given to England.' [2] Two years later, another correspondent, writing to Cecil from Plymouth, states : ' There is arrived in these ports within these fourteen days past, to the number of fifty sail, this country shipping, all laden with Newfoundland fish which, as it is thought, will be laden away by Flemmings and Frenchmen that have their ships here ready for the same '. [3]

By the early decades of the seventeenth century, as many as two hundred West Country vessels were engaged in the Newfoundland trade.[4] In 1626, the number dispatched from Devonshire alone was estimated at one hundred and fifty, whilst, in Cornwall, the ports of Saltash, Looe, Fowey, Mevagissey, Falmouth, St Mawes, St Keverne, Penzance, St Ives and Padstow were all taking their share in the great adventure.[5] Every year, hundreds of West Country fishermen signed on, and shipped away for a period which involved two summers and a winter of separation from home, and a life of indescribable hardship. Down to about a century ago, many ships, locally manned and built, still annually sailed from Devonshire to the Newfoundland shores. The principal ports concerned during this period were Dartmouth, Teignmouth, and Exmouth, the central recruiting station for these being at Newton Abbot. Here, according to a recent correspondence

---

[1] Newfoundland Fishery.—*Encycl. Brit.*
[2] Hist. MSS. Comm. (Salisbury). Report IV, 566.
[3] Hist. MSS. Comm. (Salisbury). Report V, 387.
[4] Newfoundland Fishery.—*Encycl. Brit.*
[5] *Victoria History of Cornwall*, 491.

in the *Western Morning News*, many agreements were formally signed at the local hostelries, being afterwards clinched with cider, beer, or rum—and not infrequently all three.[1]

Quite apart from the special rigours of the Newfoundland trade, the toil of the fishermen generally during the sixteenth and seventeenth centuries was subject to a variety of hardships and perils which now seem scarcely conceivable. ' Poor, painful fishermen,' Monson calls them, ' who get their living with more pains, with more cold and watching than any other trade or people whatsoever ; but,' he adds, ' indeed their greatest danger is interruption by pirates.' [2]

During the period of the wars with Spain, the kidnapping by the enemy of West Country fishermen was a favourite method of attempting to gain information concerning the doings of the English fleet. Actually, the value of such a policy to the Spaniards would appear to have been extremely doubtful since, judging by the depositions of those who were allowed to return, they generally contrived to bring back as much information as they could ever have given. Nevertheless, the practice long continued. Thus we read that in June 1595, one Sampson Porth, of St Keverne, whilst fishing with three others in Falmouth Bay, ' was taken by a shallop of Bluett ', and brought before Don Diego, ' who, by an Englishman that was in one of the galleys, examined them on oath as to what preparation of shipping was being made in England '.[3] A year later, another Cornishman, Richard Perne or Peren, of Penryn, was likewise seized by a Spanish galleon as he was out fishing by night, and carried away to Spain, where he was held captive for the space of six months.[4] Nor were such incidents confined to the western parts of Cornwall. In 1599, Richard Carew informed the Privy Council ' that yesterday four ships and a pinnace came before Plymouth harbour and took five fishing boats and most of their men '.[5]

So far from ceasing at the conclusion of the war with Spain, these terrors increased tenfold. When Englishmen would probably fain have had peace, others had learnt their piratical ways of war, and the ' Dunkirkers ' had begun to harass

---

[1] *Western Morning News*, 21 March 1929.
[2] Monson, *Churchill's Collections*, Vol. III, bk. vi, p. 497.
[3] Cal. S.P. Dom., 1595–7, 59.
[4] Cal. S.P. Dom., 1595–7, 172.
[5] Cal. S.P. Dom., 1598–1601, 188.

British shipping. On 31 December 1600 William Stallenge wrote to Sir Robert Cecil, from Plymouth : ' The Dunkerk's men-of-war remain about the Lizard, where they have taken divers ships and barks, taking out their principal men and suffering the rest to depart '.[1] By 1608, it was estimated that there were five hundred sail of pirates in English waters.[2] Shortly after this, the Algerian and Sallee rovers began to make their appearance in the Channel. In 1625, Penzance was petitioning for a fort ' because of late terribly terrified by the Turks '.[3] In the following year it was stated that the Turkish men-of-war were sighted daily off the shore, ' so that no fishermen dare go forth '.[4] In 1631, the inhabitants of Fowey stated that their town was ' so decayed in shipping, mariners, fishermen, and all sorts of people living by trade, being spoiled by Turks and pirates, and daily sustaining infinite other losses at sea, that through poverty many people have abandoned the town and gone to other places to seek their living '.[5] Five years later, it was reported that fifteen fishing-boats belonging to Looe and Helford had been taken within a month.[6] In the same year, 1636, Edmond Percivall wrote to Sir Phillip Percivall : ' I advise you to send no more cattle over (to Ireland) whilst the Turks are so busy, lest both your cattle and your gentlemen should suffer, there having been a multitude of passengers taken this summer. Sir Francis Godolphin and his lady and his servants, with his brother Captain Godolphin and his wife, going to the Isles of Scilly, some three or four leagues off the shore, were taken by the Turks, and one of the Turks attempting to abuse the captain's wife, he presently ran him through, whereupon they cut him in a hundred pieces, and they carried Sir Francis and the rest away captives. God of His mercy send us some relief '.[7]

Such were the perils under which the local seagoing population laboured, until the time came when the Sallee men and Dunkirkers were at length driven out of the Channel by the very efficient Commonwealth navy.

[1] Hist. MSS. Comm. (Hatfield House), X, 431–2.
[2] Cal. S.P. Venetian, 1607–10, 192.
[3] *Victoria History of Cornwall*, 495.
[4] Cal. S.P. Dom., 1625–6, 370.
[5] Duchy of Cornwall Records, per Mr R. L. Clowes.
[6] *Victoria History of Cornwall*, 495.
[7] Hist. MSS. Comm. (Egmont Papers). Quoted by ' Lanje ', *Western Morning News*, 27 January 1931.

III

From this time onwards, the fishing industry continued to make great strides. That there were fluctuations, of course, goes without saying. Tonkin, at the beginning of the eighteenth century, noted that at times when fish was scarce upon the coast, the fishermen might often be seen lying about basking in the sun for weeks together ' rather than earn a penny at husbandry, though their wives and children were starving at home '. [1] In another period of great scarcity towards the end of the same century, Maton describes how the fishermen of Fowey and their families were reduced to such straits as to be dependent on limpets and other small shellfish gathered from the rocks as their sole means of support. [2]

On the whole, however, the fishing trade, and, in particular, the inshore seining for pilchards, developed on a tremendous scale during the course of the eighteenth century. ' This fish ' (i.e. the pilchard), wrote Doctor Borlase in 1758, ' comes from the north seas in immense shoals, and about the middle of July reaches the islands of Scilly and the Land's End of Cornwall. The pilchard continues off and on in the south channel, principally from Fowey harbour westward, and is taken sometimes in great numbers at Mevagissy, in the creeks of Falmouth and Helford harbours, at St Keverne and in the Mount's Bay, as also in St Ives Bay and the northern channel. [3] With the taking this fish by seine-nets and drift-nets, the

[1] R. Carew, *Survey of Cornwall* (edit. 1811), 35 n.
[2] *Tour of the Western Counties*, I, 143.
[3] The pilchards were taken throughout three stretches of the coast. The first extended east of the Lizard Point to Bolt Head in Devonshire, a second area was included between the Lizard and Land's End, whilst the third area was centred around St Ives. It was common for one of these districts to be full of fish, whilst in neither of the others was a ' school ' to be seen, but towards the end of the season the fish often changed from one area to another.—J. Couch, Royal Cornwall Polytechnic Society, Report 1835, p. 70. After about 1840, the pilchard fishery of the south-eastern extremity of Cornwall greatly declined, whilst in the St Ives area, where in Dr Borlase's day it had been of less importance than in the other two, the seining showed a rapid increase in development.—J. S. Courtenay, Royal Cornwall Polytechnic Society, Report 1838, 121. In 1877, St Ives was by far the greatest seining centre of the county, possessing no less than 288 seines. It is doubtful, however, if half this number were in actual use.—Royal Cornwall Polytechnic Society, Report 1878, p. 98.

curing of them with salt and exporting them to foreign markets, the world is so well acquainted that I need only suggest in a summary manner the advantages of this fish to the county of Cornwall—it employs a great number of men on the sea, training them thereby to naval affairs ; it employs men, women, and children at land, in salting, pressing, washing, and cleaning the fish. In making boats, nets, ropes, casks, many other trades are dependent on the same ; the poor is fed with the offal of the captures, the land with the refuse of the fish and salt, the merchants find the gain of commission and honest commerce, the fisherman, the gains of the fish. Ships, likewise, are often freighted hither with salt and into foreign countries with the fish, carrying off at the same time part of our tin.' [1]

During the ten years 1747–56, the total quantity of pilchards dispatched from the four principal Cornish ports—Fowey, Falmouth, Penzance, and St Ives—averaged thirty thousand hogsheads, or ninety millions of fish, annually, and the value of these, including the extracted oil and the Government bounty of eight shillings and sixpence on each hogshead, was estimated at approximately £50,000 a year,[2] a very great sum, considering the value of money in those days. In 1790, after several years in which the seining had been practically a failure, the fisheries produced fifty-two thousand hogs heads; whilst in 1796, the quantity of pilchards taken exceeded sixty-five thousand hogsheads. The huge catches of this year surpassed all the expectations of the merchants, and Gilbert notes that ' such was the scarcity of salt, the fish-owners were obliged to send several vessels to France for a sufficient quantity to cure the fish that were taken '. [3] It is quite clear, however, that the catches of 1790 and 1796 were exceptional, and between the latter year and 1802, the normal exports varied between thirty to forty-four thousand hogsheads per annum. [4]

The Reverend J. Skinner, who made an extensive tour through Cornwall about the year 1798, estimated the initial cost of a seine, with its full complement of boats and nets, at approximately £1,000, and he states that each seine employed

[1] *Natural History of Cornwall*, 273.
[2] *Natural History of Cornwall*, 272–3.
[3] See J. S. Courtenay, Royal Cornwall Polytechnic Society, Report 1838, 118–19.
[4] *Cornwall Gazette*, 31 July 1802.

an average of nineteen hands. In addition to these, at least
five thousand persons, of whom four-fifths were women, were
engaged in salting, packing, pressing, and preparing the fish ;
whilst ropemakers, blacksmiths, shipwrights, and sailmakers,
to the number of over four hundred, and not less than one
hundred and fifty female ' twine-spinners ', found subsidiary
employment in catering for the needs of the industry. In all,
some six hundred nets were commonly made during each
winter season. As regards wages, the same writer states,
' the men at Newquay have seven shillings a week, and one
quarter of the net proceeds of the fish and oil. The general
sum obtained by the men, exclusive of their wages, is from £15
to £25 each for the season. The expense of curing a hogshead
of fish is from a guinea to twenty-three shillings, of which
charge the cost of salt alone is six shillings. The fish have
lately sold from thirty-five to forty-two shillings per hogshead '.[1] Whilst this price was in advance of the average
obtaining forty years earlier—estimated by Borlase at thirty-
three shillings—it probably did not represent any great
difference in real money, as the cost of living had risen rapidly
during the latter decades of the eighteenth century.

The fishing industry, moreover, then as now, was subject
to those wild fluctuations, both in regard to prices and in the
quantity of fish taken, which have ever tended to make the
fishermen's livelihood a most precarious and uncertain one.
The home market for pilchards has always been extremely
limited, and from early times the greater part of this fish has
been exported to Italy, where, as a writer once humorously
remarked, ' they enable the Holy Father and his Catholic
children to keep their Lent, by filling their bellies and fasting
at the same time '.[2] Herein lies the explanation of the once
popular Cornish toast :

> *Here's a Health to the Pope! may he live to repent*
> *And add just six months to the term of his Lent,*
> *And tell all his vassals from Rome to the Poles*
> *There's nothing like pilchards for saving their Souls!*

' Long life to the Pope, death to our best friends, and may
our streets run in blood ' was another favourite toast which
illustrates the same point.

The principal ports of delivery for pilchards were Genoa,

[1] Brit. Mus., Add. MSS. 28793.
[2] *Cornwall Gazette*, 31 July 1892.

Leghorn, Civita Vecchia, Naples, Venice, and Trieste, and great numbers of small Cornish-owned vessels were employed in carrying the fish thither and in bringing home fruit, olive oil, and other miscellaneous cargo. As may well be imagined, correspondence between the local fish merchants of the past and their Italian customers often presented considerable difficulties, a fact which is clearly shown by the following letter from Mr Antony, of St Ives, to Bernadina Polomba, of Civita Vecchia :

'11 October 1779.

'SIR,—I received your favour of 13th ult., and am surprised you should write me in such bad language as I cannot make sense of, particularly that letter of 26 July, and that of 9 August are so writ as not to be well understood. I mentioned to you in my letter of 4 September desiring you would get some friend to write your English letters ; as I cannot comprehend the true meaning of those I have received, how is it possible to understand so unintelligible writing. Yours of 21 December 1778, was a well wrote letter, from which you gave me encouragement to correspond with you, this your favour of 13 September, I cannot rightly understand. This is the third I have received writ by a novice who do not understand English.' [1]

It was perhaps as well for the Cornishman's reputation that the recipient of this letter was *not* a very good judge of English, or it might perhaps have occurred to him that Mr Antony's own epistolary style was susceptible to some improvement.   Still less, apparently, did it ever occur to Mr Antony that *he* might have found a friend to write his Italian letters !

In time of war, the overseas market for pilchards was, of course, greatly restricted, with the result that prices slumped, and the fishermen became deprived of one of their principal sources of revenue. In 1801, ten thousand hogsheads of pilchards were sold at St Ives for manure, at tenpence per cart load, owing to lack of other sale.[2] 'Last season, before the peace (of Amiens),' states the *Cornwall Gazette*, 31 July 1802, ' the price of pilchards per hogshead was as low as twenty-eight shillings. The glad tidings of peace, however, immediately raised it to forty-seven shillings. The number

[1] Formerly in the possession of Sir Edward Hain, St Ives.
[2] 'Notes on Pilchard Fishery,' Royal Cornwall Polytechnic Society, Report 1878.

of seans afloat this season on the coast of Cornwall exceeds two hundred, and the value of this dead property amounts to £160,000 (at £800 per sean), exclusive of the current expense of wages which, at eighteen men to each sean at seven shillings per week per man, is £1,260 per week more.' Penzance alone had thirty-six seines afloat in the following month, with a complement of sixteen men to each, and nearly a hundred and fifty driving boats which carried three or four men apiece. The seiners here received wages of about ten shillings a week, and the huers a guinea, besides a small percentage of the fish taken.[1]

Whereas the seines were owned in almost every case by parties of ' adventurers ', who were commonly merchants or men possessed of substantial property, the driving boats or drifters were usually the property of the more respectable fishermen themselves. The latter, accordingly, received no wages, their remuneration being entirely dependent on the success or otherwise of the season's fishing. Such profits as were made, were divided into eight shares, of which one was set aside for the upkeep of the boat, three for the nets, the remaining four going to the men. The master of the boat claimed no more than one of his crew, but the boy who usually formed one of the latter, was held to be sufficiently rewarded with the fish that fell into the sea when the nets were drawn. In order to secure this portion, which was sometimes considerable, he was furnished with a bag-net at the end of a rod, known as a ' keep ' net.[2]

In a good year, such as that of 1802, the share-fishermen were said to be gaining as much as eighteen shillings a week. The quantity of fish on the north coast, however, during this summer appears to have been phenomenal. ' The pilchards have brought the other fish in with them,' states the *Cornwall Gazette*, ' and our markets are supplied with the greatest abundance and variety—cod, ling, hake, pollock, whiting, mullet, bass, soles, turbot, etc.—all at very low prices, and pilchards almost for nothing.'[3] Five years later, however, the fishing showed a very different aspect. ' The season is now almost come,' states the *Cornwall Gazette*, 18 July 1807, ' when it was usual to commence our great pilchard fishery ; but for the present season, scarcely a single pilchard has

---

[1] *Cornwall Gazette*, 7 August 1802.
[2] Courtenay, Royal Cornwall Polytechnic Society, Report 1838.
[3] *Cornwall Gazette*, 14 August 1802.

appeared. This, however, is of less consequence as the want of a market for the fish last year, and the still more discouraging prospects of the present, have extinguished all hope and expectation from this once fruitful source of our prosperity. Ten or a dozen seines will, we are informed, be the outside of what will be put to sea this year, and those to provide only for our own markets, and the trivial demands of the West Indies. The mackerel fishery of the present year also, as in the last, has been most unprofitable. In some seasons, these fish have confined their visits almost entirely to the coasts of Cornwall and Devon. But of late, while very few indeed have been caught here, we find they abound in vast shoals on the coast of Norfolk ! '

As thus shown, in addition to the vagaries of the fish themselves, the renewal of war, after the short peace of 1802, had again presented the industry with the problem of finding markets. The demand for pilchards, it is true, remained unabated. In 1811, a cargo which had been sent out from Cornwall under licence was seized by the French, and through them sold to the Italians at the enormous price of £9 per hogshead.[1] Two years later, another cargo which reached Leghorn in safety, brought a like price to the enterprising Cornish merchants.[2] The outlet for pilchards, nevertheless, was very much restricted, and during this time immense quantities were taken for their oil only, the fish, after pressing, being sold for manure. An attempt, indeed, was made to find a new vent for pilchards in the West Indies, for which market they were treated by pickling. Owing, however, to lack of knowledge, or care, in curing them, the fish got into disrepute, and the trade languished.[3] With the return of peace, and the gradual settlement of Europe after the Napoleonic wars, the exports resumed their accustomed channel and the fisheries benefited accordingly. In 1814 and 1815, the quantities taken were small, but the ports being now open, the fish brought high prices, rising in the latter year to one hundred and eight shillings per hogshead.[4] This was,

---

[1] *West Briton*, 23 July 1812.

[2] J. C. Bellamy, *Guide to the Fishmarket* (1843), 80.

[3] J. S. Courtenay, Royal Cornwall Polytechnic Society, Report 1838, 119–20.

[4] This was exclusive of the oil which varied from two to as much as seven gallons per hogshead of fish. In addition, the Government bounty of 8s. 6d. per hogshead continued, until 1829, to be paid on all pilchards exported to foreign markets. See Cornwall Polytechnic Society, Reports 1835, 1838.

of course, a ' peak ' year, and from that time onwards until 1837, prices fluctuated within the more sober limits of thirty shillings to eighty shillings per hogshead.

Nevertheless, a remarkable stimulus had been given to the industry by the return of normal trade. During the year 1827, the total number of seines in Cornwall, ashore and afloat, was three hundred and sixteen. Persons employed about the seines at sea numbered two thousand six hundred ; those directly engaged in the pilchard fishery on shore six thousand three hundred. In addition to the seines, there were more than three hundred and fifty drift boats, employing one thousand six hundred men. Altogether the full complement of persons employed in connection with these two main branches of the Cornish fishing industry numbered ten thousand five hundred ; whilst the capital invested in the boats, nets, cellars, and other establishments on shore was close on £440,000.[1] In the year 1830, the total quantity of pilchards sent to the Mediterranean ports from St Ives alone amounted to some six thousand four hundred hogsheads ; whilst during the years 1829–38 St Ives supplied the Italian markets with an average of nearly nine thousand hogsheads annually.[2] In the season of 1832, a seine owner at Newlyn is said to have cleared £1,300 as the result of the enormous catches being taken at that time in Mounts Bay,[3] whilst on a yet more memorable occasion, in November 1834, no less than ten thousand hogsheads or thirty millions of fish were enclosed by the seines at St Ives within an hour ![4]

IV

Prior to the middle of the eighteenth century, the season for pilchards frequently extended from July till November or

[1] Yarrell, *British Fishes.* Quoted by J. C. Bellamy, *Guide to Fishmarket.* The number of men and boats engaged in the fishery was subject to considerable fluctuation. In 1877, the total number of seines in Cornwall was 390, employing 1,024 men at sea. Drift boats in this year numbered 538, with 2,241 men afloat. Cf. Royal Cornwall Polytechnic Society, Report 1878, 94 and 98.

[2] *Western Morning News,* 21 September 1921.

[3] *Western Antiquary* (1883), III, 77.

[4] J. Couch, Royal Cornwall Polytechnic Society, Report 1835, 83 and 98.

With "Bushes"

With Trumpet

(*See page 99*)   A HUER SIGNALLING

"BULKING" PILCHARDS IN A FISH CELLAR

(*See page 101*)

December, sometimes even into January or February.   During the last century, however, the season generally commenced about the beginning of August, and lasted until the end of October, or, as the old people used to say :

> *When the corn is in the shock*
> *Then the fish are on the rock.*

As the time for their arrival drew near, a close watch was kept for the pilchards from the shore, and any indication of their approach was triumphantly hailed :

> *See where the bird of force*
> *The quick-eyed gannet marks the pilchard's course,*
> *Darts with the lightning's flight amid the shoal*
> *And fills with rapturous hope the fisher's soul.*
> *Auspicious bird!*
> *Welcome, thrice welcome to our southern shore!*
> *At thy approach the seiner plies his oar,*
> *At thy approach the Huer, watchful still,*
> *Ascends with anxious step the prospect hill*
> *And if his eye discern the scaly host*
> *Waves the known signal and informs the coast.*
> *Then what a scene ensues! the teeming bay*
> *In long discoloured columns marks the prey,*
> *Thousands and tens of thousands, millions pour,*
> *And ' Hevva, Hevva ' rings along the shore.*[1]

At St Ives, the launching of the great fleet of seine-boats, which during the off-season were drawn up on the grassy banks adjoining Porthminster beach, was a joyous occasion for all the children of the town.   Crowding into the boats as they were dragged down across the sand into the sea, the children would sing :

> *A laky (leaky) ship with her anchor down!*
> *Her anchor down, her anchor down!*
> *A laky ship with her anchor down,*
> *Hurrah, my boys, hurrah!*
>
> *We 're loaded with sugar and rum, my boys!*
> *And rum, my boys, and rum, my boys!*
> *We 're loaded with sugar and rum, my boys,*
> *Hurrah, my boys, hurrah!*

[1] *Cornwall Gazette*, 24 July 1802.

Rocking the boats from side to side as they sang, the fleet, with its crew of happy youngsters, was launched into the blue waters of St Ives Bay, and was then rowed round to the harbour to be fitted up with the nets, ropes, and other tackle required for the forthcoming season.

The unit known to the fishermen by the comprehensive term, a ' seine ', comprised three boats and two nets. The largest of the boats was a kind of galley, about forty feet long and twelve wide, combining burden with swiftness. It was equipped with a capstan and a space, called the net room, in which the gear was stored. Whilst lying off-shore, awaiting the arrival of the fish, a canopy or ' tilt ' was commonly erected in the bow, under which the crew were able to shelter in bad weather, and where they did their cooking. This boat, known as the *seine-boat*, was manned by six rowers and a steersman with, frequently, an eighth man to lend further assistance when the time came to ' shoot ', or pay out, the great net which it carried. The second boat, somewhat smaller, but manned by a like number of men, was called in St Ives, the *tow-boat*, and in other places, the *follower*, from its always taking up a post in the rear of the *seine-boat*. The *tow-boat* carried a smaller net called the *tuck-seine*. The third boat, which was the smallest of all, was called, in St Ives, the *follower*, and elsewhere, the *lurker* or *cock-boat*. It generally carried the master seiner and one or two lusty men.[1]

From the beginning of the season onwards, the seines were rowed out early in the morning, and remained throughout the day at anchor in their various stations, each one anxiously awaiting the signal from the huers who kept their watch on the cliff-top above. Owing to the seiners' dependence on wind and tide, and the necessity of speedy and well-ordered action, when once the school or schools of pilchards arrived, the coast line within the waters of the sandy bays was mapped out into clearly defined ' stems ' or stations, which were assigned to the various companies of seine owners at the beginning of each season by drawing lots. In St Ives Bay, the fishing stems lying between Hayle Bar and the Island were known respectively as Carrack Gladden, the Leigh, the Pull, Porthminster, Pednolver, and Carrick Leggoe or Carn Crowse. Each of these was defined by means of two poles erected on the shore, one some distance behind the other, and the fishermen

[1] *Cornwall Gazette*, 24 July 1802.

clearly understood that they must not trespass over the imaginary line which lay between these poles and extended indefinitely out to sea. Considering the great sums of money which were at stake, and the speed with which the schools of pilchards were capable of moving along the coast, some such arrangement was clearly needed, in order to prevent the violent conflicts which must undoubtedly have arisen had all the companies been free to make a rush for the most favourable position at the same time.

At length, perhaps, on some hot sleepy August afternoon, the huers would suddenly be startled into activity by the sight of certain reddish-brown patches of colour moving rapidly along beside the shore, close under the surface of the sea. 'At one moment,' writes Mr Harris Stone, 'the mass or school of pilchards—for such it is—may be a quarter of a mile in length, and even as you look it elongates and shoots out into half a mile, only to thicken up a few minutes later into a regular ball, more or less spherical. Immediately the fish are sighted the huer's trumpet blares forth, and the cry of " hevva ! hevva ! " (Cornish *hesva*, a school of fish) goes up, and is quickly spread through the neighbouring town. Out from the streets and houses pours forth the whole population, for the arrival of the pilchards concerns all, the women and children, not less than the men. Meantime the huer, standing silhouetted on top of the hedge before his hut, is signalling frantically, with a " bush " in each hand, to the boats which are awaiting his orders no less eagerly below. First he waves his two clubs to the eastward, and the men strain at the oars in an answer to his commands, then, with his whole body rapidly bending up and down, he directs the boats to take their course straight out to sea. At length, the psychological moment arrives, and the huer, dropping his bushes for a moment, yells through the long speaking trumpet to the men to shoot the seine.' [1]

The seine-net itself was a formidable affair, being more than a quarter of a mile long, and about seventy feet wide or deep. Cork floats were attached to it at regular intervals along one edge and lead sinkers on the other. Altogether, the net with its floats, sinkers, and ropes weighed close on three tons. On the orders coming to shoot the seine, the fishermen would start to pay out the net, whilst the rowers at the same time pulled the boat through a large semicircle. With such

[1] *England's Riviera*, 43 *et seq.*

vigour and alacrity was this work carried out that it was by no means uncommon for the whole of the net, with its rope, corks, and lead, to be thrown into the sea in less than five minutes.[1] Provided the bottom edge of the seine was touching the ground, and the top was floating properly on the surface of the water, the fish had but little chance of escaping, but as it was difficult to bring the two ends of the great seine-net together all the way to the bottom, the smaller ' stop-net ', manipulated by the tow-boat, was paid out across the opening. Meantime the ' follower ' had also arrived at the starting point and set about joining up the seine- and the stop-nets, the crew at the same time beating the water with their oars in order to frighten the fish back. In this way, provided that everything went well, the fish were at length enclosed by a wall of net from which escape was impossible. By means of the many capstans dotted along the shore, the seine was then drawn into shallow water. Great care and judgment had to be exercised in this, for two or three days, or even as much as a week might elapse (if the catch was heavy) before the nets could be emptied of their haul. It was essential, therefore, that the water should be shallow enough to permit of the clearing process, and yet deep enough at all states of the tide to keep the fish alive until they could be landed.[2]

The net, therefore, having been manœuvred into position, and the weather and tides proving suitable, the work of ' tucking ' began. This consisted of lowering into the seine-net a small ' tuck-net ', one side of which was attached to the attendant boats. The tuck-net had long ropes by which it was raised to the surface of the water when full. ' At the moment when the tuck-seine produces its burthen above water,' states an old writer, ' the sight, if the sun shines out, is beautiful beyond all description. Ten thousand lively little creatures, jumping and springing together, reflect from their burnished scales of blue and silver such a blaze of light and beauty as cannot be conceived by those who have never beheld it.'[3] Meantime, the men, working with baskets, locally known as ' whiskets ', scooped up the fish from the tuck-net into their boats, till they were standing waist high in pilchards. As each of these attendant boats or ' dippers ' was filled, it was pulled for the shore, from whence its contents

[1] J. Couch, Royal Cornwall Polytechnic Society, Report 1835, 74.
[2] Mr William Paynter, *Old St Ives*, 39.
[3] *Cornwall Gazette*, 24 July 1802.

were removed by the ' blowsers ' or carriers to the innumerable cellars with which the fishing towns were furnished.

In places where approach to the cellars was impracticable for carts, ' gurries ' or boxes with four pole-handles were used, each gurry containing about a thousand pilchards. Gurry-watchers, armed with sticks, were frequently appointed to accompany these, in order to prevent people from stealing or ' kaybing ' the fish.[1] The story is told how on one occasion, Mr B——, a leading seine owner, arrived on horseback at St Ives in order to superintend the landing of a large school of pilchards which had just been enclosed on the beach. Riding down to the edge of the sea, he beckoned to a boy who was standing by, to come and hold his horse.

' What 'll 'ee give me ? ' inquired the youth, with Cornish shrewdness.

' Give you ? Oh, I 'll give you sixpence.'

' Shaen't do et,' was the blunt reply. ' Why I can get more 'en that kayben old B——'s pilchers.'

Arrived at the cellars, the blowsers would find the women and children already waiting. Each gurry, as it came, was tipped out on to the ground, and the fish were seized upon by the children and handed to the women who laid them in layers along the cellar wall, with their heads pointing outwards. As each row of pilchards was completed, it was covered with a layer of salt, and on to this another layer of pilchards was laid, and so the pile went on increasing, until it was as high as the women could conveniently reach. This process, known as ' bulking ', often went on far into the night, and when the catch was a big one was continued for many nights in succession, the women and children coming from all the surrounding country-side in order to assist in the work which had to be done at high pressure. ' During these strenuous nights,' as Mr W. Paynter has said, ' the cellars presented scenes of extraordinary interest and activity. The dark background with its heavy shadows relieved at intervals by flickering candles, the burly porters dumping the fish on the ground, the women piling them up hour after hour, the attendant children with their " whiskets " of salt and fish, and the " bulks " themselves gleaming pink and pearly-grey, formed a picture likely to remain long in the memory of those privileged to have seen it.' [2]

[1] Mr William Paynter, *Old St Ives*, 39–40.
[2] Mr William Paynter, *Old St Ives*, 40.

After remaining in bulk for some weeks, the fish were removed and placed in barrels in which they were pressed by means of heavy stones, in order to extract the residue of the oil which they contained. In earlier times, this oil was largely used for lighting purposes, a fact which explains the old saying: 'Meat, money, and light, all in one night'. Pilchard oil was also regarded by many Cornish people as a sovereign remedy for festering cuts and wounds. The squeaking noise made by the bursting of the air bladders whilst the fish were being pressed was called 'crying for more', and was regarded as an omen that further catches of pilchards would soon be brought in to keep the others company. It was likewise said that the advent of a good haul of fish was presaged by a commotion among the 'bullies' or pressing-stones, which between seasons were kept in the cellars, above which the fishermen lived.

At length when all the fish had been saved, the town crier in his 'high-pole' (top) hat was sent round the streets and alleys in order to proclaim to all those who had been employed in connection with the various seines [1]—the 'Amity', the 'Success', the 'Unity', the 'Fisherman's Friend', the 'Friend's Endeavour', or whatever the name of the company might be—that they were to assemble at one or other of the inns in the town in order to be paid. In most cases, the seiners received a cheque for their share of the fish, and this they forthwith proceeded to divide amongst themselves. The writer has been told that in the old days at Sennen Cove it was usual for this cheque to be paid to the landlord of the one and only inn. The latter would then take it to Bolitho's bank in Penzance, and there exchange it for its equivalent value in sovereigns, half-sovereigns, and a good assortment of silver. On his return, all hands who were entitled to a share would assemble round a table at the inn. In addition to the active partners in the seine, there were generally five or six sleeping partners, as on the death of a married man, his share was continued to his widow for life or to his children until they were old enough to look after themselves. The pile of gold being placed in the middle of the table, the landlord would look round and say, 'Well, boys, how much do 'ee think it 'll go?' One of the men might perhaps suggest £5 or possibly £8, on which the landlord would place that amount in front of each. If any gold remained over, another guess would be

[1] Mr William Paynter, *Old St Ives*, 41.

made, and another share-out took place. The same process was then applied to the silver. If at the end a little odd money still remained, it was spent on drinks all round, whilst the few odd coppers were set aside for ' niceys ' (sweets) for the children.[1]

The method still employed in Sennen for dividing the catches of mullet which are sometimes taken there in considerable quantities, is no less interesting, and is probably still older in its origin. On being brought ashore, the fish is thrown on to the ground in piles, each pile being as nearly equal as the men can conveniently make it. Generally there are two piles to each man. When all the fish has been divided thus, one of the men goes round with a basket, and into it the others throw some little personal belonging, such as a knife, a tobacco box or the like. These are then thrown out at random on to the piles of fish, by which means each man is able to identify his share and feels, moreover, that he has received it by a fair and impartial allotment.[2]

In the case of the pilchard seines, the owners, after the men had received their shares, would sometimes contribute towards the cost of a supper for the women whom they had employed during the season. These ' cellar-feasts ', as they were called, were usually held in some sail-loft which had been fitted up for the occasion, and to them each woman was generally allowed to invite a friend. ' Some pretty come out they was too ! ' an old St Ives fisherman once remarked to the writer. ' Every woman used to turn up in a clean sogget (apron), and after the supper there would be singing, dancing, and fiddling, going on till eleven o'clock at night sometimes. Plenty of fun all round, but little or no drinking.' [3]

V

The pilchard fishery was followed by that of the herring which were, as indeed they still are, taken with drift nets, along the north coast, up to Christmas. January and February were, generally speaking, poor months for the

[1] Per Mr J. C. Hoare.
[2] Per Mr Manning-Sanders.
[3] Per Mr Edward Basset.

fishermen, but from March to the end of April, or sometimes later, the mackerel fishery was in full swing. With the disappearance of these fish from the home waters, it was customary for the fast-sailing, lugger-rigged fleets of Porthleven, Newlyn, Mousehole, and St Ives to fit out for the North Sea herring fishery which was conducted principally from the ports of Whitby, Sunderland, Hartlepool, and Scarborough. Many of the Cornish boats, however, from as early as the seventeenth century onwards, were wont to show still greater enterprise, following the herring round the north of Scotland to the Isle of Man, and thence to the coast of Ireland.[1] Much of the Cornish fisherman's prosperity formerly depended on the success or otherwise of this fishery, which occupied two or three months of the year, and carried the men such great distances from home. Their enterprise, however, was not always crowned with the success which it deserved. On 2 August 1839 we learn from the columns of the *West Briton* that the greater part of the St Ives and Mounts Bay boats had returned home from the herring fishery in Ireland, where the season had proved a complete failure. Not only was the number of fish taken very small but, owing to a combination among the buyers, the prices were so low as scarcely to recoup the fishermen for their outlay. ' This,' states the writer, ' represents a great loss to Cornwall. as not less than two hundred and fifty boats from St Ives and Mount's Bay were engaged in the Irish fishery this season.'

During the summer of the same year, however, the pilchard fishery proved more successful, the fresh fish selling in the country districts at one shilling and eightpence per hundred and twenty, and those cured for exportation bringing fifty-two shillings per hogshead at the Mediterranean ports.[2] Throughout the ensuing decades of the nineteenth century, seasons of scarcity continued to alternate with others in which the markets were wellnigh glutted with the huge catches of fish. In the year 1847, the exports of pilchards from Cornwall amounted to 40,883 hogsheads or 122,000,000 fish, whilst the greatest recorded number ever taken in one seine was that of 5,600 hogsheads or 16,500,000 fish, at St Ives in 1868.[3] After such catches, thirty or forty vessels might be seen at

[1] Hobson Matthews, *History of St Ives*, 339.
[2] *West Briton*, 4 October 1839.
[3] *Victoria History of Cornwall*, 584.

one time in the harbour at St Ives, waiting to carry the fish away to Italy.[1]

It is sad, indeed, to have to relate that the whole of the inshore seine fishery, and the stirring life which went with it, has now become part and parcel of the bygone days, and the very memory of it is becoming lost with the death of the older generation. For some years before the end came, a great change had taken place in the method of dealing with the fish. Owing to the invention of curing in tanks, the process of laying the pilchards in bulk was entirely dispensed with, and as a result many hundreds of men, women, and children became robbed of their former means of support. The new process is said to have been introduced first at Mevagissey, and it is certainly a curious fact that not only did the pilchards shortly afterwards begin to desert that bay, but since the introduction of tanks has become general in all the fishing ports, the vast shoals of pilchards which formerly darkened the waters of the Cornish coast have no longer been seen. The year 1907 witnessed practically the last of the really big catches to be taken by the seining method, some eight thousand hogsheads or roughly twenty-four millions of fish having been netted that year in St Ives Bay.[2] Since that time, the industry has steadily and persistently declined, and though a few seines are still kept in readiness at Coverack, and at one or two other coves along the south coast, this branch of the fishing industry may be said, for the time being at any rate, to be extinct.

Among the older generation of fishermen, there are still not a few who regard this fact as being a direct judgment of Heaven on the infamous invention of curing in tanks. Others, seeking a more rational explanation, ascribe it to the absence of the red water which formerly flowed into the sea from the surrounding mines, and which, so far from polluting the fishing grounds, is claimed to have served a useful purpose by thickening the waters of the bays in a manner which attracted the shoals of pilchards to lie therein. A more likely explanation, however, seems to lie in the vast increase of deep-sea trawling, in the Channel and elsewhere, which, by breaking up the shoals, and by destroying huge quantities of the immature fish, is everywhere robbing the inshore fisherman of his livelihood by cutting off his supplies

[1] Per Mr Edward Basset.
[2] See *Western Morning News*, 21 September 1921.

at the source. Though this view is still questioned in some
degree by the 'experts', it is held by every practical Cornish
fisherman with whom the writer has spoken, and it is certainly
a striking fact that during the war, when trawling was largely
in abeyance, mackerel, herring, and other fish were more
plentiful in the inshore waters than they had been for many
years previously.

Though the seining is now defunct, pilchards still represent
an important section of the West Country share-fishing
industry, and, as recently as the summer of 1929, phenomenal
catches of these fish were landed at the Cornish ports. They
are now taken, however, only at considerable distances from
land, and are caught, like the mackerel and herring, in drift-
nets. The latter resemble the seine-nets in so far as they
have corks all along one edge, but no leads are attached to
the other, since they are intended only for fishing in deep
water where they do not reach the bottom. One end of the
drift-net is fastened to the boat, and the other is carried out
by the strong-flowing tide. Frequently twenty or more nets
are fastened one on to the other, so that the whole combination
is generally a mile or more in length, and stands in the water
like a wall. As the fish come up with the tide, their heads
become entangled in the meshes of the nets, from which they
are not easily able to withdraw on account of their gills which
open and operate like barbs.

The 'shooting' of a long train of nets, and the thought
of how much depends on the fortune which may attend them
when once they have passed far out into the dark surrounding
waters, is an occasion the significance of which is far from
being lost upon minds so deeply imbued with religious feeling
as those of the Cornish fishermen. To a visitor out with
them in their boats, it is a moving experience to hear the
murmured utterance of the prayer : ' Lord, spare our labour,
and send them in with a blessing. Amen '—with which words
many crews are (or were formerly) in the habit of consigning
the first of their drift-nets to the deep. Those who know
the Cornish fishermen, moreover, will hardly be surprised to
learn that other practices of a yet older origin still survive
among them, and that, in some cases, there lies embedded
in the first of the cork floats, as it goes drifting out upon the
tide, a silver coin,[1] placed there to-day, no doubt, more
in jest than in earnest, and yet unconsciously fulfilling the

[1] Per Mr George Dunn, St Ives.

custom instituted by their far-off ancestors who thus sought to propitiate the Spirit of the sea. Going below afterwards into their tiny, stuffy cabins, reeking with the smell of fish and strong tobacco, it was not unusual to see one of the older men turning to the pages of his Bible, whilst the good old Methodist hymns, which cheered their forefathers under like conditions, are still often raised by the fishermen of to-day, when riding beneath the stars on the dark rolling waters of the Atlantic.

After some hours of waiting thus, the time at length comes for the nets to be drawn in again on board, and this used to be the signal among the mackerel drivers for the calling of their ancient chant :

Bri' el, mâta, treja, peswara, pempes, wethes! ' A mackerel, a fellow, a third, a fourth, a fifth, a sixth ! ' of which each man cried a word in turn as the first netted fish appeared, ' a formula ', as Mr Nance has observed, ' closely matched by fishermen in Scotland, and on the south and east coasts of England ', [1]—but of special interest in this case as being preserved in the ancient Celtic language of the Duchy.

VI

Until recent times, the drifting for mackerel continued to form one of the most important branches of the Cornish fishing industry, although it was principally confined to the boats of Mounts Bay and St Ives. There were formerly two mackerel fisheries in the year, the one commencing in March and closing about the end of May, and the other extending from September to December. The fish taken in the spring were mostly consumed fresh ; those caught in the autumn, being esteemed of better quality, were salted in in great numbers by the inhabitants of the county, for winter use. In the spring of 1838, over one hundred and twenty boats were engaged in this fishery at Newlyn, Mousehole, and Porthleven.[2] At this time, and, indeed, for many years later, the fish was principally marketed by the wives of the fishermen who hawked their husbands' catches through the adjoining towns

---

[1] *Folklore Recorded in the Cornish Language*, 8–9.
[2] Royal Cornwall Polytechnic Society, Report 1838. 130–1.

and villages. One of the most pleasing and familiar sights of Penzance in those days was that of the Newlyn fishwives, who in their scarlet cloaks and large black beaver hats, might be seen daily in the streets. The fish itself was carried in ' cowals ' or specially-shaped baskets, which were supported on the women's backs by a broad band which passed around their hats. With their fine symmetry, healthy complexions, curling ringlets, and blue eyes, they must indeed have presented a striking contrast to their sisters of the trade in London, and more than one traveller seems to have lost his heart to the beautiful fishwives of this town.[1]

With the opening of the Cornwall railway in 1859, changes of a far-reaching character took place. As a result of the direct communication now established with the metropolis, a new and important market was developed for the Cornish spring mackerel. Newlyn became the local depot for this trade, and thither was brought the whole of the catches of the Mounts Bay fleet. The fish train for London left at 2 p.m., and to get the catches home and landed in time for this, was the supreme effort of the day. To meet this necessity a new class of boat was built, designed especially for speed. By 1884, the number of mackerel drivers belonging to the county had increased to nearly four hundred, employing two thousand seven hundred men, the cost of the newer type of boat, with its full complement of nets and tackle, being approximately £600.[2]

Up to the time when Newlyn harbour was built, the Newlyn fleet had permanent moorings off the shore. At these moorings, each vessel kept a four-oared boat at anchor, by means of which the crew, with their catches, were able to land on their return from the fishing grounds. It was a fine sight to see the great fleet of mackerel drivers riding off the shore, or the same number of small boats waiting at the moorings when the large ones were at sea. The Mousehole mackerel drivers differed from those of Newlyn in using a three-oared jollyboat to bring their fish ashore. Each of these was in the charge of a boy, from ten to fourteen years of age, who was engaged by the fishing lugger to whom the boat belonged at a wage of one shilling and sixpence a week. This ' captain ' of the jollyboat was known as a ' yawler ', a term peculiar to Mousehole where alone he was employed.

[1] Cf. G. A. Cooke, *Topographical Description of Cornwall* (1830).
[2] Royal Institution of Cornwall, March 1884, Journal VIII, 12.

The yawler's duties, as described by Mr William Pezzack, to whom the writer is indebted for the following information, were clearly defined. Whilst the season lasted, he was the absolute slave of the lugger by which he was employed. Early in the morning, often at daybreak, he would shoulder the two long oars required by the crew for pulling ashore and his own short ' paddle ' with which he himself sculled the jollyboat. Thus equipped, he would wend his way to the harbour, where he would find some fifty other yawlers, all busily engaged, if the tide were low, in helping each other to get afloat. As soon as the fleet was sighted in the offing, the flock of small craft would scull away to the best position for bearing down before the wind to ' take ' the lugger to which each one belonged. This ' taking ' was the great event of the yawler's day. As each lugger neared the coast her yawler would drop out of the waiting flock, and get right ahead of his boat, as it bore down upon him under full sail. The faster she was going, the greater his joy. With the jollyboat pointing the same way as the big boat, the yawler would wait with the coiled painter in his hand, ready for the critical moment when, with the foam piled up at her bows, the lugger rushed by. As she did so, the painter was nimbly thrown to those on board, and the yawler would crouch low in expectation of the jerk with which, as the rope became taut, his jollyboat sat up almost on end, with the water boiling up behind the stern as if intent on swamping her. ' To be towed to Newlyn market in this style,' writes Mr Pezzack, ' was a supreme joy. To miss this feat, was a disgrace too deep to be contemplated—and in practice it very rarely occurred, owing to the skill and judgment in manœuvring their craft which the boys attained.'

If there was not enough fish to be worth taking to Newlyn, the yawler had only to come alongside when the big boat anchored, in order to take the crew ashore. At other times, when the fleet of luggers was becalmed, the yawlers would often scull out two or three miles to meet them and take off the fish, which would then be rowed in to Newlyn by one or two of the younger members of the lugger's crew.

Very often, the yawler had a strenuous time getting out, against wind and tide, to the proper position where he could be taken up by the incoming fleet. The jollyboats were always equipped with a kedge rope with a stone attached to one end. When so much exhausted that they could scull no more, the boys would drop anchor for a time, and rest. Then, as they felt able to renew the struggle, they would take to their scull once more and so press on until they reached the desired position for being taken up. Often the fleet itself would be expected about breakfast or dinner-time, and the yawler, in consequence, knew the pangs both of hunger and thirst, as he waited long and patiently at his post. Great was his satisfaction, however, if he could manage to get on board his lugger when at length she arrived and regale himself with the warm black tea, bits of fish, and stale bread left over from the crew's own meal.

Whilst the fleet was at sea, the yawler was at liberty to amuse himself as best he liked. There was no prank with wind or waves that he would not try. Knowing, as he did, every trick and temper of his own jollyboat, he would manœuvre and propel her into nooks and crannies, round the rocks, and in and out of the breaking sea, rejoicing in the dangers which he evaded by his skill.

The yawlers were not all boys, however. A few of them were aged fishermen who, no longer having strength for the strenuous life at sea, had returned to their boyhood's job, and did it well. Some of these old men still continued to wear the tall ' stove-pipe ' hats of their earlier days. The sight of these, tilted on the backs of their owners' venerable heads, caused no small amusement to the boys, as they watched them swaying from side to side in their rolling, pitching boats. But although they sometimes laughed at their old-fashioned ways and notions, the boys respected them too, for when they could be got to talk, these weather-beaten old men would tell of the days long past, of their hairbreadth escapes in open boats, of being hunted by the press-gang, of smuggling and wrecking, and other incidents of their exciting and venturous youth.[1]

The employment of the yawler, as Mr Pezzack has said, produced a class of men supremely expert in the management of small craft, and consequently a type of sailor particularly suited for the handling of yachts, a profession in which many of them were subsequently engaged. With the completion of the harbour at Newlyn, however, the day of the yawler came to an end, since the fishing fleet, by being able to enter port and discharge its catches directly on to the quays, no longer required the assistance of the jollyboats. The con-

[1] ' The Yawlers of Mousehole,' *Cornishman*, 31 October and 13 November 1909.

struction of Newlyn harbour, moreover, was contemporaneous with the beginning of a rapid decline in the prosperity of the Mounts Bay mackerel fishery, a decline which has since resulted in the disappearance of the whole of the famous fleet of drifters once owned by these ports.

The story of the collapse of this great branch of the Cornish fishing industry dates back in its origin to the time when the ' up-country ' trawlers first began to frequent the western waters. As long ago as 1843, the menace of this new type of fishing operation had been noticed by at least one keen observer. Writing in that year, Doctor Bellamy stated : ' Fishing, taken generally, interferes in the slightest way with the habits of the creatures in question ; but the employment of a trawl, during a long series of years, must assuredly act with the greatest prejudice towards them. Dragged along with force over considerable areas of marine bottom, it tears away, promiscuously, hosts of the inferior beings there resident, besides bringing destruction on multitudes of smaller fishes, the whole of which, be it observed, are the appointed diet of those edible species sought after as human food. It also disturbs and drags forth the masses of deposited ova of various species. An interference with the economical arrangement of Creation, of such magnitude, and of such long duration, will hereafter bring its fruits in a perceptible diminution of these articles of consumption for which we have so great necessity. The trawl is already fast bringing ruin on numbers of the poorer orders requiring the most considerable attention. The fishermen of Cawsand complain to me that their profits gradually lessen, and point to the reckless destruction of spawn and young fish by trawlers, as the great source of their misfortunes '.[1]

Elsewhere in Cornwall it seems that the disastrous effects of trawl fishing were not fully appreciated until considerably later than this. Prior to the opening of the Cornwall railway, the number of trawlers, who at that date mostly hailed from Plymouth or Brixham, was small, and the time during which they continued their operations was limited by their having to run to Plymouth, sixty miles off, in order to reach the nearest market. They only, therefore, trawled by day, whilst the local mackerel drivers had the grounds to themselves at night, which was all that they desired.[2] Up to this time not

[1] *Guide to the Fishmarket*, 52, 140.
[2] *Cornish Telegraph*, 2 April 1878.

only did mackerel abound in the home waters in such numbers that in some seasons a single boat might bring in more than four thousand of them as the result of one night's draught, but hook-and-line fish were equally plentiful all along the south coast. In March 1802, ling of the best quality were being taken in Mounts Bay at the rate of ten or eleven hundred a day by single boats,[1] whilst a few years later it is recorded that as many as forty thousand hake were landed at Newlyn and Penzance within the space of twelve hours.[2] In addition to these extraordinary catches, the choicer grades of fish were procurable in the local markets throughout the year.

With the coming of the railway, however, the facilities for speedy communication with London which had so much benefited the local mackerel drivers, also resulted in a vast increase in the number of visiting trawlers. When in the year 1878 the Government at length decided to hold an inquiry, the latter were said to number more than a hundred, many of them being east-country boats. These vessels now trawled over the best mackerel driving grounds, day and night, from February to April, frequently fouling and cutting the nets of the local drifters. Feelings between the two opposing interests ran very high, and many of the witnesses who were called stated that the trawlers not infrequently made zigzag tracks across the drift-nets for the express purpose of destroying them, hoping, by such tactics, eventually to oust the local men from the field.[3]

In addition to the economic factor, religious differences added increased rancour to the dispute. True to their own lights in refusing to go to sea on Sunday themselves, the Newlyn men felt it to be more than they could stand that their rivals, scouting such sentiments, should be allowed to land their ill-gotten catches within their own harbour. At length, in May 1896, the storm which had so long been impending, broke. Seeing the east-country men returning one Monday morning from the fishing grounds, the Newlyn men put out to meet them in their boats, with the intention of throwing the fish overboard. Realizing this, the trawlers turned away and put into Penzance. Back went the Newlyn men to their port, and immediately started breaking up everything they could lay hands on with which to make weapons

---

[1] *Cornwall Gazette*, 13 and 27 March 1802.
[2] J. C. Bellamy, *Guide to the Fishmarket*, 54.
[3] *Cornish Telegraph*, 2 April 1878.

(See pages 86 and 100)

A SEINE OF PILCHARDS

(See page 108) AN OLD FISH "JOUSTER"

for the coming affray. Armed in this manner, they set off for Penzance and here, at the eastern end of the promenade, they met their rivals, and a hand-to-hand fight ensued. In the meantime, however, soldiers had been telegraphed for from Plymouth, and on their arrival very soon succeeded in quelling the riot.[1]

Though peace was restored, the causes which had given rise to the disturbance still remained. There is, indeed, something rather pathetic about this last ineffectual outburst on the part of those who were engaged in an old traditional industry. Faced as the hand-loom weavers had once been, with economic changes which were robbing them of their very means of livelihood, and understanding little of the underlying causes which made such changes inevitable, the Mounts Bay fishermen, in resorting to force, were but following out the blind instinct for self-preservation. Circumstances, however, were too powerful for them, and with the coming in later years, not only of increasing numbers of trawlers, but of the large steam drifters, who are able to use three miles of net to the local fisherman's one, besides being far less dependent upon weather, the fate of the Mounts Bay sailing fleet was sealed. For many years they struggled on against the ever-increasing odds ; but now, at length, the time has come when they have been completely driven from their own ground. As a consequence, therefore, the fishermen of Newlyn, Mousehole, and Penzance may be seen to-day in the mackerel season eking out an existence by acting as porters and carriers to their rivals, who now land their catches on the quays from which, but a few years since, their own fleet so proudly sailed.

VII

It must not be assumed, of course, despite the loss of the inshore pilchard seining, and the rapid decline of the local mackerel drifting, that the Cornish fishing industry is a thing of the past. ' There are still,' wrote Mr Howard Dunn in 1927, ' about eleven or twelve hundred local fishermen, whose numbers are augmented, at various times, by approximately two thousand three hundred North Sea fishermen, and some-

[1] See *Western Morning News*, 13 January 1930.

times as many as a thousand Frenchmen or Bretons, the
latter fishing the waters off the Cornish coast and taking their
catches home to France. The fishermen, therefore, and the
packers, curers, coopers, and box-makers, together with the
capital invested in the boats, nets, gear, stores, smoke-houses
(for kippering) and ice-works, still form no mean part of the
county's stock-in-trade, whilst in recent years the annual
value of the catches landed at the Cornish ports has approxi-
mated to £400,000.' [1]

A quite considerable income is still derived, moreover,
from other types of fishing than those already mentioned,
the more important among these being the long-line, and the
crab and lobster fisheries, both of which take place during
the spring and summer. The results of all these classes of
fishing, however, are subject to great fluctuations, dependent,
as they are, not only on the migrations of the fish themselves,
but on the favourable or adverse conditions of the weather.
In some seasons, one class of fish may be present in abundance,
whilst in another it will be conspicuous by its almost complete
absence. The year 1929, for instance, proved on the whole
to be a very successful one for the Cornish fisherman. During
the long-line season, great quantities of dog-fish were taken
on the hook. This fish, which was formerly of no marketable
value, has of late years become much sought after, being sold
in the up-country markets under the name of 'flake'. [2] The
pilchard season of the same year was likewise a success in
the western waters, where some of the boats grossed about
£600 down over a period of fourteen weeks. On the other
hand, in the south-eastern area, embracing Looe, Polperro,
Mevagissey, and Fowey, this particular fishery was practically
a failure. The herring season, which in that year commenced
rather earlier than usual, gave every promise of success, a
promise, however, which was, in a large measure, offset by the
subsequent violence of the weather, which necessitated the
restriction of operations in Port Isaac, Padstow, and Newquay,
in all of which ports the men made very poor returns. Even
in St Ives, where, with few exceptions, the fleet did remarkably
well in the matter of fish, there were more nets lost than
had ever been previously recorded in any season. Some boats
lost anything up to a whole fleet of nets, a mile in length.
As the boats only, and not the tackle, are insured by the

[1] Cornwall ' Education Week ' Handbook (1927), 115.
[2] *West Briton*, 2 January 1930.

society, such losses detracted very considerably from what might otherwise have been a highly successful season.[1] The great increase in the shoals of pilchards and herrings met with during this year, might reasonably have been supposed to augur well for the next, but yet in the summer of 1930 the pilchard season was described as an 'utter failure', and the worst one on record for fifty years past. The long-line fishery was stated at the same time to have been equally unsuccessful, in some cases the men not grossing enough money to cover their out-of-pocket expenses. Yet in this very year, which proved so disastrous for other forms of fishing, the landings of the boats engaged in the crab fishery exceeded those of the corresponding seasons for ten years past.[2]

These facts, culled from the fishery officer's reports, show clearly enough the precarious and uncertain nature of the fisherman's livelihood. The effect of the unrestricted operations of the deep-sea trawlers is constantly being shown by the 'patchy' nature of such shoals of fish as now find their way into the inshore waters. None know this better than the fishermen themselves, who realize that a successful season to-day is far more a question of luck than ever it was in the past. The result is that, owing to the constant discouragements which the industry has received, the number of young men entering its ranks is small indeed, and year by year the number grows less. 'Scarcity of men to fill the available boats is one of the most serious factors of the fisheries in various Cornish ports,' wrote the local correspondent of the *Western Morning News* on 17 October 1928. 'In Mounts Bay, during the recent pilchard season, a few boats would have been unable to proceed to sea, but for the addition of visiting Newlyn and east coast fishermen to assist in working them. From the port of St Ives owners of boats were yesterday visiting the various Mounts Bay ports in search of men to make up their crews, but were, in some cases, unsuccessful.' During the spring and early summer of 1931, the long-line fishery was also severely handicapped by the difficulty of obtaining men. At one port in the south-eastern area, nearly fifty per cent. of the fleet was laid up through failure to obtain crews to work the boats.[3] It is

[1] *West Briton*, 2 January 1930.
[2] *West Briton*, 18 December 1930.
[3] *West Briton*, 18 June 1931.

clear from this, that if the decline in the number of men continues at its present rate, the nation as a whole will shortly be deprived, not only of a source of its food supply, but of a fine race of seafarers which, until recently, has provided it with a valuable recruitment for the navy and the merchant service.

It is obvious, therefore, that the restoration of the declining fortunes of the inshore fisheries of Cornwall, as elsewhere, is a matter of more than local concern. That this is realized to some extent is shown by the fact that the Government itself is now participating in the research which is being carried out with regard to the migrations of fish. Such a policy, it is hoped, may lead ere long to fruitful results, whilst international agreement with regard to trawling should prove of even greater value in restoring prosperity to the industry. It would seem, however, that something more, even than a partial return of fish to the coast, is necessary, if the fisheries of Cornwall are to be re-established upon an entirely satisfactory basis. The present methods of buying and distributing fish are both antiquated and wasteful. Whilst it is generally agreed by all parties that there exists, throughout the country, a large and unsatisfied demand for fish, yet when, as in the summer of 1929, unusually large quantities of pilchards made their appearance in the home waters, the fishermen were informed by the merchants that their requirements were satisfied, and that they could take no more fish from them, even if they were brought to land. That such a situation could ever arise, would seem due, in no small part, to the subsequent methods employed in distributing the fish. As things stand at present, the local buyers sell to commissioned agents at Billingsgate, who sell in turn to distributors, who sell to the retail traders, who sell to the public. Each buyer, of course, takes his profit from the next until, at length, the price which has been paid to the fisherman may have been multiplied ten times over before it is charged up to the consumer. To the unemployed population of our inland towns, there must, indeed, be a tragic irony in the constantly reiterated slogan : ' Eat more Fish ', when it is realized that the ' rings ' which have adopted this expensive method of gaining new customers are chiefly responsible in making the goods they advertise too dear for those same potential customers to buy.

For the fisherman, of course, the position is equally unsatisfactory although it must be admitted that he, to a certain extent, has himself to blame, having never given to the various attempts at co-operative selling the full measure of his support. Time and again co-operative marketing societies have been established at the Cornish ports. In some cases, these bodies have functioned successfully for three or four years, afterwards dwindling to nothing through the disloyalty of their members. Discussing the matter on a recent occasion with a *Western Morning News* reporter, a Porthleven fisherman remarked : ' We had a co-operative marketing society here at one time, but it failed for the same reason as in other places. We were getting good prices for ourselves, but a private salesman came along and offered better. Some of our members took the short-sighted view and went over with him. This led to the break-up of the society. Personally, I think we should be doing better to-day if we had kept the society going. But that is the chief fault of Cornish fishermen, they are so jealous of each other that they will not work together and, unlike the farmers, we have no union to represent us. I am afraid the industry will be no better until the Cornish fishermen can be taught to realize that unity is strength '.[1]

VIII

Whilst a consistent loyalty in supporting the co-operative marketing societies would undoubtedly help the fisherman to obtain better prices even under present conditions, it is clear that the industry itself must be subjected to a complete overhauling and reorganization if it is to survive in the new ' big business ' era of the twentieth century. As Mr W. D. Jamieson recently pointed out in the *Daily Chronicle*, ' there is little doubt that a large section of the Scottish fishery was suffering twenty years ago from conditions very similar to those under which the West Country now labours. First, in the north, the trawlers killed the prosperous line fishing, then the beam trawl scooped in the white fish, and the outlook for the local fishermen appeared black indeed. Then, a day came when the first of the steam drifters arrived. To the sail-boat, of course, this meant strenuous competition,

[1] *Western Morning News*, 13 February 1931.

but the drifter was seen to be obviously the craft of the future and their number quickly multiplied. Every man who could afford it, built his own. In other cases, whole families combined together, sold their old craft, and invested all their savings in the new. In other cases again, the banker showed himself willing to lend his aid, and to-day many of the small ports in the north of Scotland, in which the outlook was once as dark as it still is in Cornwall, are equipped with fleets of thirty or forty drifters which drive a profitable trade. Where the boats are entirely financed by capitalists, as many of them are, the transition from being his own master to the status of a wage-earner must certainly have been a hard one for the share-fisherman, but it is in keeping with the natural trend of the times, and it is surely better than extinction ? The question has often been asked, is there no available capital for such purposes in Cornwall and Devon ? Are there no men of commerce who can see in this matter a sound investment ? Cornwall, of course, is far from the great markets, and also from some of the newer fishing grounds, but mechanical devices in the steam-driven craft have eliminated distance. The Scottish fishermen now follow the herring far afield round the British Isles, while their women-folk come as far west as St Ives in order to do the work of kippering, which, surely, Cornish girls might learn to do as well ? It is hard to see why things should remain as they now are, or why the Cornish fisherman should not follow where his Scottish brethren have so successfully led the way '.

Such remarks, coming as they do from one who has witnessed changes of such a far-reaching importance in another great branch of the fishing industry of this country, would at any time have provided stimulating food for thought, but to-day their purport has taken on a new significance owing to the appearance of the modern Belgian motor trawler in the western waters. This has given an entirely new trend to the whole industry, and is at present causing embarrassment, not only to the Cornish fishermen, but even, in some degree, to their former vanquishers, the east-country men. It is only, indeed, within the last few years that this new phase of foreign competition has begun seriously to be felt. Prior to the war, the Belgians, so far from rivalling British fleets, were content, in many cases, to buy up out-worn Brixham smacks with which to conduct their own fisheries. Since that time, however, their whole outlook has changed. Assisted, *in part*, by governmental subsidies or cheap loans, the Belgian fishermen have condemned their old craft, and entered upon the construction of the finest type of sea-going vessel, equipped with the very latest form of motive power.[1] During the very time, in fact, when English fishermen, and in particular those of the West Country, have been driven by force of circumstances to lay up their craft, their Belgian confrères have been forging ahead, and the sight of their boats is now a familiar one in almost every port along the south coast. Before the war, Brixham possessed about two hundred and fifty sailing craft—to-day the number is less than fifty, and these are rapidly being sold off for yachts and houseboats. As against this, we have the official figures of the Ostend fleet, which in 1920 consisted of ninety-five sailing smacks, thirty-three steam trawlers, and seven motor trawlers. Since that time Ostend has 'scrapped' all its sailing craft, and now owns some thirty-five steam trawlers, and over two hundred and fifty motor trawlers.[2] Referring to a visit paid to this port at the beginning of 1931, an authority on Cornish fishing stated that he found there more than a dozen new motor vessels under course of construction, whilst the further orders, at that time received, were sufficient to keep the yards busy for another two years to come.

Such trawlers are stated to cost £6,000 apiece, and are fitted with Diesel engines and mechanical devices of the latest type. In competing with these vessels, the English steam-driven craft, costing more to build, and using a more expensive type of fuel, to say nothing of the greater number of hands which they require, seem likely to be relegated to an inferior position in the future.[3] There is, indeed, no little irony in the way in which history appears about to repeat itself. When the east-country boats came to Mounts Bay, they revolutionized the older industry which they found there, and the local fishermen, adhering too conservatively to their old ways, have in consequence been nearly wiped out. But, whilst Cornwall lost its mackerel fishery through the advent of the Lowestoft and Yarmouth drifters and trawlers, it now looks as if it may be the turn of the latter to give way to their still more efficient Belgian competitors. It is, of course, too

[1] See *Western Morning News*, 13 January 1931.
[2] Mr W. J. Modley, *Western Morning News*, 10 June 1931.
[3] *Western Morning News*, 17 January 1931.

early to say yet what steps will be taken by the east-country owners to meet this new situation. But whatever the future may have in store for *them*, it clearly holds out little promise for the Cornish fisherman, equipped only with his tiny craft with which to face a competition which can cause something akin to dismay even among his erstwhile vanquishers.

For the local industry, perhaps one of the most disturbing factors in the present situation is the new type of trawl which the Belgian craft are said to be employing. The trawling operations of the east-country fleets have already proved sufficiently disastrous in destroying immature fish, and in breaking up the larger ' schools ' before they reach the inshore waters, but the new Belgian trawl-nets are alleged to be of smaller mesh than any which have previously been used by British craft. As a local fisherman recently declared : ' Nothing can escape from these trawls. They are worse than fly-nets. They simply murder every immature fish that comes into them '.[1] This, again, is clearly a matter which will have to be dealt with by international agreement, seeing that it is of vital concern, not only to British fishermen, but to all those who make use of the fishing grounds of the Channel and the North Sea. Meantime, intensive trawling is also prejudicing the long-line fishery, which was one of the last remaining assets of the local industry, and which hitherto has partly compensated the Cornish fisherman for the loss of the mackerel drifting. To-day, however, owing to the danger of entanglement of his line of hooks wih the trawl, and still more on account of the fact that the latter is sweeping bare the grounds where the boulter boats formerly went, the Cornish fisherman is being driven to seek more and more distant fields, and when at length he returns to port, it is only to find, in many cases, that his competitors with their fast-driven craft have already taken possession of the quays and landing places.[2] In some instances, the greater portion of the Belgian catches have not only been disposed of, but actually put on rail before the local men's fish can be sold, whilst harder still is the case where the Cornishman, on entering his own ports, is told by the buyers that the present demand is satisfied, and he sees the fish which he has toiled all night to get, being carted away into the country-side for manure.

[1] *Western Morning News*, 16 May 1931.
[2] *Western Morning News*, 23 April 1931.

Were the three-mile limit, which under modern conditions is clearly of little value, to be extended to twelve, as has been suggested, it might aid in ridding the present situation of some of its more grievous anomalies, and help to tide the local industry over a period in which the country at large is deciding whether it shall be reorganized or allowed to perish. For, as has already been pointed out, such reorganization necessitates, first and foremost, the capitalizing of the industry. The western fishermen, whilst clearly recognizing the increased catching powers of their foreign competitors, claim that the new type of vessel which the situation demands is beyond their financial resources to supply. This being the case, the fleets must be modernized, either through the assistance of the financier or by co-operative effort, unless, of course, the work can be entirely effected through state subsidies or loans, which at the moment appears unlikely.

The problem, of course, presents other difficulties besides that of finding the necessary money for the building of new boats. Many of the present Cornish ports are clearly unsuited for the introduction of a larger type of craft, requiring sufficient depth of water for exit and ingress at all states of the tide. The changes which have been suggested would, therefore, undoubtedly mean the partial abandonment of such ports, in favour of others which are better endowed in this respect. Fortunately, Cornwall has no lack of deep-water harbours, especially along its southern shore, and the development in these of a new type of fishing should not present great difficulty.

Harder, no doubt, must be the task of convincing men so ' set ' in their ways as the share-fishermen of Cornwall that the time has come when they, like their northern brethren, must face the facts of the changing economic world in which they live, and subject themselves to a transition which cannot prove other than painful to those who have so long prided themselves on their independence and the personal ownership of their craft. Moreover, Cornish fishermen have never taken to deep-sea trawling, and although a few of them have done a little of this class of fishing, inshore : drifting, long-lining, and crabbing have always (with the addition of seining) been their chief vocations. Faced as they now are, however, with the entire loss of seining, together with a large part of their former drift fishing, and seeing, year by year, the better-equipped fleets of their foreign and east-country rivals scouring the seas from the Eddystone to Trevose, the time cannot be far distant when the realization will be borne in upon them that they *must* reorganize or perish.

Once these facts are recognized, the necessary change in attitude on the part of the men themselves may be rapid. For the fisherman comes of the same stock as the miner. Altering conditions in industry have long ago taught the latter how to adapt himself to new methods, and he is no longer suspicious of the changes which have added so largely to his material welfare. Nor need the older fishermen, who still cling to their former ways, despair of a livelihood. The crab and lobster fishery which now constitutes the most important branch of the industry in the smaller coves, does not stand in need of the same drastic reorganization, and may long continue to flourish on its present lines. But the fact remains that for the industry at large, changes of a radical nature will have to be made if it is ever to regain the status and prosperity which it once enjoyed. In fishing, as in all other forms of economic life, the day of the small unit is over and past. Deep-sea trawling has come to stay, and though the latter is likely to be increasingly regulated in the future by international agreement, it is in the development of this particular branch of fishing that the only hope of a returning prosperity for the sober hard-working seafarers of Cornwall appears to lie.

CORNWALL AND THE
CORNISH

THE WESTERN LAND

I

To the Cornishman who knows anything of the light in which his country was formerly regarded by those who dwelt outside its borders, the present-day renown of the ' Delectable Duchy' still provides cause for surprise, and a certain mild amusement, so great has been the change in attitude towards it on the part of his English neighbours. For Cornwall itself, to all intents and purposes, is still the self-same land which was known to the writers of old, its coastline just as stern and rugged, its climate not appreciably changed through now being advertised as Britain's Riviera. To-day, no less than in the past, Atlantic gales still buffet its cold, cruel line of cliffs for weeks on end, whilst hill and moorland lie soaking and hidden beneath the clouds and driving storms of rain. Four centuries ago, as now, Nature had her other and kindlier moods. Smiling days there must have been when the blue waves broke in creamy whiteness upon the dark rocks and jagged reefs, and sandy coves lay basking in the warmth and sparkle of the summer sun. Autumn came with its soft, still, misty days, and the dying bracken turning to gold, whilst springtime witnessed the yearly miracle of wild anemones transforming the bleakest hills and uplands.

And yet the Duchy was far from being ' delectable' in the eyes of most Englishmen who fought their way into it in the past, and to whom its far out-stretching coastline, its ' horrid mountains ', and desolate moors, appeared only as fit surroundings for the rough half-civilized ' Barbarians ' who dwelt therein, and who, in popular imagination, divided their time between wrecking and smuggling and wresting a miserable subsistence from their labours beneath the earth. 'Cornwall,' wrote Andrew Borde in 1542, ' is a pore and very barren countrey of al maner thing, except Tyn and Fysshe,' [1] whilst even a native poet was fain to write :

> *O Cornwall ! wretched spot of barren ground,*
> *Where hardly aught but rocks and furze is found,*
> *Thy produce scarce provides thy sons with bread,*
> *Nor finds them wood for coffins when they 're dead.* [2]

[1] *Introduction to Knowledge.*
[2] Cf. *Cornish Notes and Queries* (1906), 310.

' I make no doubt,' states a writer describing Cornwall in 1776, ' that thousands of readers know no more of the scenes here described than if it were not a part of this country. Cornwall presents a wild and strange appearance. There are few signs of fertility or cultivation ; so that the eye which is accustomed to and fond of beautiful prospects will here meet with no other entertainment than wonderful heaps of stones, refuse of the Tinners, or people who work the mines. In other respects this country in general has nothing to bespeak the good opinion of travellers. The west end of it must undoubtedly be very unhealthy, being but a few miles across from the Northern to the Southern Channel, by which means it is always subject to heavy, cloudy, rainy weather, so that those people whose business or calling oblige them to be much abroad are almost continually wet to the skin and over shoes in dirt.' [1]

Perhaps, however, when one comes to consider the remoteness and isolation in which Cornwall lay enveloped in the past, the contrast between this and the opinion of latter-day writers is not so greatly to be wondered at. The shipwrecked mariner formerly thrown up upon its coast, or the Englishman driven down into the county by the necessities of business, experienced alike the repugnance natural to the exile who finds himself cut off amidst strange surroundings far removed from home.

It is interesting, however, to note that whilst the older writers are in general agreement as to the harshness and desolation of the country, many of them appear to have been favourably impressed by its inhabitants. In his account of that ' most dangerous and memorable adventure' of rowing from London to Bristol in a small wherry boat, during the year 1589, Richard Ferris speaks well on more than one occasion of the treatment which he and his companion received at the hands of the Cornish people. ' At St Ives,' he writes (whither they had won their way after an exciting escape from a pirate off the Land's End), ' we were well entertained. The next day we put to sea again, but, being within five miles of St Ives, we were constrained to seek for a cove which we found near Godrevy. Here, for that we wanted victuals, our Master was constrained to climb the great cliff (at least forty fathoms high) . . . which none of us durst do, but, blessed be God for it, he had no harm at all.

[1] *St James's Chronicle.*

At this place we stayed two days at Master Arundel's house, where we were greatly welcomed.' Farther up the coast, at ' Bottrick's Castle ' (Boscastle) they stayed with a gentleman called Hender—' full seventeen days '.[1]

John Taylor, the ' Water Poet ' and Thames ferryman, who in the year 1649 ' travelled neere six hundred miles, from London to the Mount in Cornwall, and beyond the Mount to the Land's End and home again ', writes in even more glowing terms of the Cornishmen. Cornwall he describes as the ' Cornucopia, the complete and replete horn of abundance for churlish hills and affable courteous people : they are loving to requite a kindness, placable to remit a wrong and tardy to retort injuries. The country hath its share of huge stones, mighty rocks, free gentlemen, bountiful housekeepers, strong and stout men, handsome, beautiful women . . . in brief they are in most plentiful manner happy in the abundance of right and left hand blessings '.[2]

John Taylor possessed in no small degree the qualities requisite for a boon companion, a fact which perhaps accounts for the number of good dinners and the liberal entertainment which he received at the hands of the gentry with whom he stayed. Those who were less happily endowed by Nature, and who were forced to seek their lodging by the wayside, generally fared but ill. ' Strangers,' wrote Carew, ' occasioned to travaile through the shire, were wont no less sharply than truly to inveigh against the bad drinke, coarse lodging, and slacke attendance which they found in those houses that went for Innes : neither did their horses' better entertainment prove them any welcomer ghests than their masters.' As he goes on to explain, however, this was not so much on account of churlishness on the part of the inhabitants, as simply because wayfarers ' in such an outcorner ' being rarely expected, ' to make great provision upon small hope of utterance, were to incurre a skorne-worthy losse '. At the same time he admits that among the poorer inhabitants, especially in the west, there still survived traces of resentment at the expulsion which they had long ago suffered at the hands of their Saxon invaders, and which resulted, even as late as Elizabethan times, in the gruff reply being sometimes made to an English visitor : ' *Meea navidua cowzasawzneck* ', ' I will speak no Saxon '. ' To their gentlemen, however,' writes Carew, ' they carry a

[1] Cf. Arber reprints, English Garner, VI, 153–63.
[2] *Wandering to see the Wonder of the West* (1644).

very dutiful regard, holding them as Roytelets (little kings) because they know no greater.' [1]

The spirit of clanship which has always been an essential characteristic of the working-classes in Cornwall, was equally observable amongst the gentry of olden times, and was fostered by the great amount of social intercourse which obtained within the borders of the Duchy. So closely indeed were all the chief families knit together by the ties of relationship and marriage that it gave rise to the popular saying : ' All Cornish gentlemen are cousins '. Such families, writes Carew, ' converse familiarly together, and often visit one another. A gentleman and his wife will ride to make merry with his next neighbour, and after a day or twayne these two couples go to a third, in which progress they increase like snowballs till through their burdensome weight they break again '.[2] The easy sociability developed amongst Cornish gentlemen in this manner gave rise to the famous compliment once paid them by Queen Elizabeth, who remarked : ' They are all born courtiers with a becoming confidence '.[3] Courtiers and men of affairs as many of them were destined to be, such Cornishmen generally retained their affection for the place of their birth amidst all the distractions of life in the metropolis. Not a few would have echoed the sentiments of Master Attorney Noy, who was wont pleasantly to say that his house had no fault in it, save only that it was too near unto London, ' though indeed ', adds Fuller, ' it was distanced thence full three hundred miles, in the remoter part of this country '.[4]

II

The poor, of course, were lacking in those opportunities for social intercourse which were such a feature of the lives of the gentry, and such scanty leisure as they enjoyed was for the most part devoted to hardy and active ' pastimes of the body ', of which hurling and wrestling were the chief. Although throughout the Middle Ages, and indeed as late as Elizabethan

[1] *Survey of Cornwall.* Carew's knowledge of the Cornish language was very limited. Properly spelt the sentence should read : ' My nyvennaf cows Sawsnek '.

[2] *Survey of Cornwall.*

[3] W. Borlase, *Natural History of Cornwall*, 304.

[4] *Worthies of England* (1662).

times, wrestling was a common sport all through England, the Cornishmen seem always to have been recognized as among its most skilful exponents. In his poem on the battle of Agincourt, Drayton tells how the Cornish contingent marched to that memorable field beneath a banner proudly depicting two wrestlers ' in a hitch '. Rather less than a hundred years later Henry VIII gave orders, through one of the Godolphins, that a number of Cornish wrestlers should be present to compete at the great Sporting Carnival held at Calais in 1521.[1]   Carew himself when writing towards the end of the sixteenth century states : ' You shall hardly find an assembly of boys in Devon or Cornwall where the most untowardley amongst them will not as readily give you a muster of this exercise as you are prone to require it. Their continual exercises in this play, hath bred them so skilful a habit, as they presume that neither the ancient Greek Palestritae, nor their once countrymen and still neighbours, the Bretons, can bereave them of this Laurell '.[2]

Even the poor, however, were not without their share of intellectual enjoyments. Chief amongst these were the performances of the *Gwaries*, or Cornish miracle plays, whose widespread popularity gives convincing proof of the civilized nature of their audiences. Indeed, from early times, the Cornishmen appear to have enjoyed a definite reputation for their dramatic skill, and in the year 1428 we learn that one of their countrymen, ' Jakke Trevaill ', was accorded the honour of presenting various plays and interludes ' before the King, at Christmas '.[3]   Most of the extant Cornish miracle plays emanated from that once famous centre of learning, Glasney College, at Penryn, and date from the period 1350–1500. Of these plays the most considerable is the series known as the *Ordinalia*, of which two fifteenth-century copies are still in existence. The performance of this particular drama occupied three days. The epilogues which conclude the acting of the first and second day tell the audience ' to come again on the morrow ', and then bid the pipers ' play for the dance ', with which the performances ended. As Mr Morton Nance has pointed out, the playing places of those days having no seats, the audience after standing so many hours must have needed

[1] See Harry Pascoe, Cornwall 'Education Week' Handbook (1927), 153.
[2] *Survey of Cornwall*.
[3] W. Bottrell (quoting William Sandys), *Traditions and Hearthside Stories of West Cornwall*, 2nd Series, 271.

something to unstiffen their joints ! The drama of *The Life of Saint Meriasek*, which was written in 1504, concludes on an even more festive note :

> *Drink ye all with the play*
> *We will beseech you*
> > *Before going hence.*
> *Pipers, pipe ye at once !*
> *We will, every son of the breast,*
> > *Go to dance.*
> *Go ye or stay,*
> *Welcome shall ye be*
> *Though ye be a week here.*[1]

The plays themselves were acted in Cornwall in the open-air theatres or Rounds, of which at least two examples still remain. Of these, the better known, perhaps, is the ' Plen-an-Gwary ' (Place-of-the-Play) at St Just-in-Penwith, a circular embankment, one hundred and twenty-six feet in diameter, and capable of accommodating about two thousand people. Perran Round, near Perranporth, is a similar construction, but in a much better state of preservation. In the bottom of it may still be seen a three-foot pit which perhaps served as the infernal region, concerning which, as Mr Thurstan Peter has said, ' people's ideas were as curious then as they are now '. During the performances the position of the actors in the ' plain ' itself was carefully orientated. God and Heaven took the east ; the Devil and Hell the north ; worldly potentates were assigned to the west ; whilst saints and good characters occupied the south. ' Distinguished characters,' writes Mr Nance, ' had their own " tents ", " palaces ", or " towers ", probably consisting at the most, of sentry-boxes made of wood.' In some cases Heaven appears to have been represented by a scaffold erected above the plain. In 1575 an entry in the borough accounts of St Ives records : ' Spent upon the carpenters that made hevin, 4d '. The number of such playing places must at one time have been very considerable, and ' Plen-an-Gwary ' as a place-name or field-name occurs in several districts in West Cornwall. The ' Plain-an-guare ' at Redruth had already fallen into decay when Borlase visited it about the year 1752. He describes the remaining mound as being ' high but ruinous ', and showing no sign of ever

[1] Edited by Whitley Stokes (1872), viii.

having gone more than half round.[1] By 1842 it had almost completely disappeared, and its existence is now remembered only through having given its name to the suburb which has since been built upon its site.

Although by the middle of the sixteenth century, the great days of the Cornish drama were over, a miracle play, entitled *The Creation of the World*, *with Noah's Flood*, was compiled by William Jordan, of Helston, as late as the year 1611. Large passages of this play appear to have been borrowed from some earlier drama ; but it is interesting to note that Jordan, in his amplifications, still follows the tradition of putting foreign words—English, Latin, and French—into the mouths of unbelievers, torturers, or devils, such creatures by an unwritten law being seemingly forbidden to speak good Christian Cornish !

Of the popularity of these plays, as late even as the end of the sixteenth century, Carew provides ample evidence, a fact which ill accords with the description which Raleigh received of the ' rough and mutinous ' character of the Cornish tinners.[2] Indeed, one may well be permitted to wonder if, with all our advance in education, any audience could now be found who would be willing to stand listening to such dramas, in the open air, for three long days on end.

In addition to the miracle plays, the dramatic sense of the Cornish people received satisfaction from the occasional visits of bands of strolling players from ' up the country '. A reference to ' a player of the lord the King' occurs in the Launceston borough accounts as early as 1531, whilst another entry in 1577 records the payment of money ' to my Lord Stafford's men '.[3] Liskeard has two references to players in the early part of the seventeenth century,[4] and the St Ives borough accounts show no less than seventeen entries with regard to play matters between the years 1573–84. One of these makes mention of money paid ' to my Lord Mounte Joye's men '.[5]

A strange incident is related of the performance of a play called *Sampson* by one of these parties of players in the town of Penryn about the year 1600. On the night of the perform-

[1] Borlase MSS., 1751–8, *penes* Royal Institution of Cornwall.
[2] Cal. S.P. Dom. Eliz. 7 July 1586.
[3] J. T. Murray, *English Dramatic Companies*, II, 297.
[4] J. Allen, *History of Liskeard*, 235 and 239.
[5] Hobson Matthews, *History of St Ives*, 151.

ance it so happened that ' certain Spaniards were landed in the town, unsuspected and undiscovered, with the intent to take the town, spoil it, and burn it '. They were just about to carry out this intention when their ears were assailed by the martial notes of trumpet and drum, and the sound of armed men preparing themselves for battle. A moment afterwards a great shout was raised and the Spaniards, supposing that the alarm had been given, fled precipitately to their boats,[1] leaving the townsfolk to the enjoyment of Dagon's downfall, all unconscious of how nearly the tumult of the players had saved them from their own.

Cornwall, indeed, as appears from the borough and parish records was not without its own bands of players at this date, several of whom, including ' the players of Germal ', ' the players of St Burdocks ', and ' the players of Liskeard '[2] appear to have been in the habit of touring the countryside, ' gathering money for their churches '. The stage clothes and ' properties ' used for these performances generally belonged to the parish, and we learn that in 1585 the ' Robin Hood Players ' of St Columb possessed ' v Coates for Dancers, A ffryer's coate, 24 dansinge belles, a streamer of red moccado and locram, together with vi yards of white woolen cloth '.[3] Armed with this magnificent finery, the St Columb Robin Hood Players several times visited St Ives.[4]

Amongst other recreations of the Cornish people of these times, feasting had a very prominent part. This chiefly took the form of Harvest Dinners, Church Ales, and ' the solemnizing of their Parish Church's dedication, which they term Saint's Feast '.[5] As to the Harvest Dinners, though they bore only the name of a dinner, ' yet ', writes Carew, ' the guests take their supper also with them, and consume a great part of the night after in Christmas rule '. On these occasions rich and poor met together, and the wide friendly kitchens of the old manor houses were transformed into scenes of jollity and mirth. To them would come the Guise Dancers, decked out in their fluttering ribbons and antique finery, ready to perform some Christmas play or dance a ' Latterpooch ' or Morris. At other times some Cornish ' Three

[1] T. Heywood, *Apology for Players.*
[2] J. T. Murray, *English Dramatic Companies*, II, *passim.*
[3] *Journal of Royal Institution of Cornwall*, No. 59, 9.
[4] Hobson Matthews, *History of St Ives*, 155 and 157.
[5] Richard Carew, *Survey of Cornwall.*

Men's Song' would be struck up, among them, no doubt, the Fisherman's Catch, beginning :

> *Ha mî ow-môs, ha mî ow-môs,*
> *Ha mî a moaz in gûn laze,*

which now constitutes the only example of its kind which has survived.[1] The Church Ales held a somewhat different place, for their avowed purpose was to make money which was afterwards converted ' partly to good and godly uses, as relieving all sorts of poor people, repairing of churches, building of bridges, amending of highways, etc., and partly for the princes service by defraying such rates and taxes as the magistrate imposeth for the Countries defence '.[2] With this in view, wardens were appointed who made collection from among the parishioners, and afterwards employed the proceeds in brewing and baking. By Whitsuntide, all things being ready, the grand feast took place, and friends and neighbours from all the parishes round ' lovingly visited one another and frankly spent their money together, for the common good '. In this way, too, as Carew remarks, ' quarrels were appeased and men's minds were conformed to a civil conversation'. Puritan writers of the day, however, were already beginning to condemn the saints' feasts as ' superstitious ', and the Church Ales as ' licentious ', Stubbs remarking with characteristic exaggeration that at the latter ' they spend sometimes half a year together, swilling and gulling, night and day, till they be as drunk as Apes '.[3] That the system of Church Ales was in reality open to many abuses can hardly be doubted, and it was probably this fact, rather than the invective of Puritans which caused its ultimate disappearance. The saints' feasts, on the other hand, were destined to survive, and are not even yet an obsolete feature of Cornish life.

III

The vigorous support which was so long accorded to these ancient customs in Cornwall was in no small part a result of the isolation of the various localities, and the fact that they

---

[1] See R. Morton Nance, *Folk-lore Recorded in the Cornish Language*, 7.
[2] *Survey of Cornwall.*
[3] *Anatomy of Abuses* (1583), edited New Shakespeare Society, 150.

were thereby made dependent, in the matter of recreation and amusement, on their own resources. The local government of the time was similarly independent of all outside influence, the mayors and recorders of each town being for the most part Justices of the Peace for their own area—' a garment (in divers men's opinion) over-rich and wide for many of their wearish and ill-disposed bodies ', as Carew humorously remarks. Under the government of a Mayor or Portreeve, assisted by a number of lesser officials—Market House Wardens, Quay Wardens, Way Wardens, Wardens for the Poor, Wardens for the Coffer, Wardens for the Pewes, Kings and Queens of the Summer Games, etc.—each town pursued its own way, assisting its own poor, providing its own amusements, and above all, jealously safeguarding each of its little industries. Though we smile when we read of such enactments to-day, the authorities at St Ives were only carrying Protection to its logical extreme, when they pronounced in 1603 that ' no person shall buy or sell again any barrel of Bristowe beer, or any other beer, on pain of forfeiture, considering that our own Beer and Ale made within our Town is by common experience found as good and healthful to men's bodies '.[1]

Despotic as the measures adopted by such municipal authorities must now appear, the powers and prerogatives claimed by the great manor lords or their deputies were in certain cases even more startling. In the Pleas of the Crown, 12 Edward I, for instance, we find that the lords of Scilly claimed the right to execute judgment upon felons by carrying the culprit to a certain rock in the sea, and there, ' with two barley loaves and a pitcher-full of water, to leave him until he was drowned by the flowing of the sea '. Writing of the Scilly Islands, as late as 1750, Heath, an officer of the garrison on St Mary's, says : ' The spiritual court of the island is the " ducking chair " at the quayhead, into which offenders in language or morality are put by order of the " Court of Twelve ", and receive their purification in salt or holy water. The punishments in Scilly are fines, whipping, or ducking. There is no prison for the confinement of offenders, through the place being perhaps a confinement in itself '.[2] Probably, however, even the rule of the Island Council was more tolerable than the petty tyranny and exactions of the Lord of the Manor

---

[1] Hobson Matthews, *History of St Ives*, 171.
[2] See J. E. Hooper, *Scilly under the Godolphins*, Old Cornwall, XI.

of Connerton who held sway over the westernmost part of the mainland, and who, until the inauguration of the County Court, held a special court of his own once a month for the trial of small cases. He also maintained a private prison in Penzance for the incarceration of those who had offended his majesty.[1]

That there were plenty of cases to keep such courts busy, and the prisons full, there can be no doubt. For despite their clannishness, the Cornish people of old possessed, as they still do, a tendency to litigiousness and a desire to get the better of their neighbours, which led that quaint old writer, Andrew Borde, to remark, ' A Cornishman will try the law, for the wagging of a straw '. Some excuse for this, however, may perhaps be found in the highly intricate subdivision of the rights of ownership in the mining and fishing industries, and the almost incredibly complicated system of land tenure which has obtained in the Duchy, in some instances, to the present day. Seeing that in the Cornwall of the twentieth century it is possible to find small areas which are divided between as many as fifty different owners, some of whom may possess one-fortieth of the mining rights beneath a two-acre field, it is not surprising that lawsuits should still be frequent. More especially must this have been the case in the past when, owing to the rapid increase in the value of Cornish estates, many of the old customary rights and privileges first began to be subjected to serious question, and when, if contemporary writers are to be trusted, the legal fraternity seem to have been more inclined to foment than allay the possessive fever of their clients. Discoursing on this matter in 1758, Dr William Borlase very effectively summed up the case when he wrote : ' The truth is that in mining as well as fishing there are very numerous and minute subdivisions of property, seeing that every working-tinner, though little or nothing worth, shall oftentimes have one thirty-second or one sixty-fourth, and sometimes less share of the adventure ; which persons, if the adventure is a losing one, being the more unwilling the less they are able to pay the costs incurred. Again : those little adventures do oftentimes shift hands, are bought and sold and bought again ; this produces wranglings and frequent application to the law courts. Again : the number of materials necessary to mining and fishing is so great that it entangles the people with a great

[1] J. S. Courtney, *Half a Century of Penzance* (1825–75), 15.

diversity of sellers of ropes, candles, powder, iron, timber, salt, flax, hemp, line—the more bargains the more disputes, some ill-designing persons being always ready to inflame and exaggerate rather than to appease the numerous dissentions to which such an intricate commerce is perpetually liable. A second reason of litigiousness in Cornwall is that we have as many sorts of law-courts here as in any part of England. Besides the Courts of Assize and Ecclesiastical Courts, there is the Lord Warden's Court, from which there is a farther appeal to the Duke of Cornwall in Council ; the Vice-Warden's Court held every month, and the Stannary Courts, held every three weeks for tin causes. Here are also Court Leets of the Duke of Cornwall and other Lords of Manors for debts and disputes relating to property. By means of all these there is too open and easy access to law contentions for the advantage of private families. Litigiousness is, therefore, partly the fault of the inhabitants, and in part the result of their polity and that multifarious trade to which their mining and fishing unavoidably exposes them, whereas in counties where husbandry is the chief or sole employment, business is in fewer hands, bargains plain and easily adjusted, and the gains not so great as to prompt those of a middle rank immediately to go to law '.[1]

IV

As in the case of their litigiousness, so in other respects the characteristics which had distinguished the Cornish people of Andrew Borde's day were destined for long after to show but little change. Nor was this really to be wondered at in a country-side which, owing to lack of proper roads and the consequent difficulties of transport, was largely cut off from the influences which were continually affecting the outside world. It is true that even in the Middle Ages, Cornwall possessed at least two thoroughfares which might have been dignified by the name of roads, and a traveller, if he were sufficiently well equipped and riding for his life in the king's service, was able by dint of supreme effort to reach the west from London in six or seven days. Thus, in 1342, we learn that a messenger who had been sent from Restormel Castle

[1] *Natural History of Cornwall*, 307.

on 2nd April contrived to reach London with letters for the Receiver, and to bring back other letters from the Council in the space of twelve days, at a total cost of 2s. 6d., of which 6d. was his wages.[1] As late as 1605, however, pack-horses carrying bullion into Cornwall for the purchase of tin by the Crown, were allowed ten days for the journey from London to Truro.[2]

In 1663 the post still took eight days to reach Penzance from London, and ordinary travel was, of course, much slower.[3] The route generally travelled appears to have been by the great ridgeway which follows the backbone of the county out of Launceston, and whose course for the most part still remains unchanged from ancient times. This was by far the oldest and most important of the roads through Cornwall, nor was it without good reason that its course was thus chosen by the primitive people whose footsteps first traced it in the bleak and desolate wilderness through which it passed. For here alone, in contrast to the undrained valley swamps, a view could be obtained on either hand, and a greater security must have been felt from the sudden attacks of lurking enemies man or beast. Evidence of the great antiquity of this upland road may still be seen in the burial mounds of long-forgotten chieftains which stand beside its course, and which have caused it to be likened in this respect to the world-famed Appian Way which led from Rome. Indeed, there is little doubt that Roman conquerors must once themselves have trod this route as they pressed ever westward in their search of Cornish tin ; whilst, as a writer has pointed out, the motorist careering along its course to-day, if he had time to think of such matters at all, might plume himself on ' scorching ' where Tristran rode and ' cutting in ' where once King Arthur's steed curvetted. In medieval times the road became the haunt of footsore pilgrims taking their way from London to the Mount—a mount whose summit was not ' guarded ' then, but the dwelling place of pious monks, and the home of saintly relics.

The only other road through Cornwall which could lay claim to any importance prior to the middle of the eighteenth century, was that which followed the line of the south coast, and from Cremyll Passage (opposite Plymouth), went through

[1] Duchy of Cornwall Office Records.
[2] Receiver General's Account.
[3] Millet, *Penzance, Past and Present.*

Millbrook and Crafthole to Looe and Fowey, afterwards crossing by Tywardreath Ferry to St Austell—and thence on to Tregoney. This was at one period used as the post-road, much to the indignation of several of the inland towns, including Launceston, whose inhabitants in 1703 made representation to the Government, pointing out the disadvantages under which they lay in their correspondence by having to pay an additional fee of 2d. on each letter, through being served only by a by-post.[1]

What the road itself was like may be gathered from the account of that intrepid lady traveller, Celia Fiennes, who, in 1698, entered Cornwall by this route on her way to the Land's End.[2] Her vivid descriptions show clearly enough the nature of the primitive watercourses which still served as thoroughfares in Cornwall, and which made travel in the Duchy, not only an exceedingly laborious, but in many cases a hazardous undertaking. Of her crossing over the River Tamar by Cremyll Ferry she writes : ' I was at least an hour in going over, about a mile, and notwithstanding there was five men rowing, and I set my own men to row also, I do believe we made not a step of way for almost a quarter of an hour, but blessed be God, I came safely over at last. But those ferry boats are so wet, and then the sea and wind is always cold to be upon, that I never fail to catch cold in a ferry boat as I did this day '.

Once over, the roads, even in the eastern part of the county, were still as Carew described them, ' uneasy by reason of their mire and stones—beside many uphills and downhills ' —so that Mrs Fiennes was not ill-pleased when she found that her route descended on to the sandy seashore between Plymouth and Looe, her horse's shoes being by this time almost completely worn off. After Looe, further adventures were in store for the traveller, more particularly at the point where the old high road precipitately descended into the town of Fowey. ' A deep clay road it was,' she writes, ' which by the rain the night before had made it very dirty and full of water in many places. In the road there are many holes and sloughs wherever there is clay ground, and when by the rain they are filled with water it is difficult to shun danger. Here my horse was quite down in one of these holes full of water, but by the good hand of God's providence, which has always been with me, ever a present help in time of need, I, giving

[1] Robins, *History of Launceston.*
[2] *Through England on a Side-saddle in the Time of William and Mary.*

him a good strap, he flounced up again, though he had gotten quite down, his head and all, yet did he retrieve his feet, and got clear off the place with me on his back.'

Somewhat incoherent as the danger and toils of this day's journey had made her, the next stage forward in her route evidently afforded her more satisfaction. For that night when she lay at the little market town of ' St Austins ' (St Austell), she tells how her landlady brought her' one of the West Country tarts, the first I had met with. It was the most acceptable entertainment that could be made me. They scald their cream and milk in most parts of these countries, and so it is a sort of clouted cream, as we call it, and so put it on top of the apple pie '. Less to her taste was the well-nigh universal custom of the country, of smoking : ' Men, women, and children ', she notes, ' have all their pipes of tobacco in their mouths, and soe sit around the fire smoking, which was not delightful to me when I went down to talk with my landlady for information of any matter and customs amongst them. I must say ', she adds, however, ' they are as comely sort of women as I have seen anywhere, tho' in ordinary dress—good black eyes and crafty enough, and very neat.

' In the further west,' she continues, ' the miles are very long ones, but you have the pleasure of riding as if in a grove in most places, regular rows of trees standing on each side of the road.' Tonkin, however, writing a little later than this,[1] appears to have been far from satisfied with the prevailing habit of allowing the hedges to grow unpared, complaining that he himself had received an irreparable injury from riding beneath the overhanging branches. As to the roads, he describes them as being ' full of holes and pools ' into which the country people ' throw muck and straw to make dung ', so that, as Fuller noticed many years before, those who went much a-horseback were accustomed to use ' Gambadoes ' (long Spanish riding boots) ' whereby', as he says, ' whilst one rides on horseback, his leggs are as in a coach, cleane and warm, in those dirty countries '.[2]

Tonkin's assertion, that the only occasions on which the roads were mended was ' when some great man's coach passes by that way ', shows that by the beginning of the eighteenth century, at any rate, *some* wheeled traffic had at least begun to make its appearance in the county. Evidently, however,

[1] See Notes printed in 1811 edition of Carew's *Survey of Cornwall*.
[2] *Worthies of England* (1662), 205.

such an event was rare, for it is said that on the appearance of the first coach in Mevagissey about this time, the whole population turned out, exclaiming in astonishment : ' Why, 'tes nothin' short of a house upon wheels ! ' According to Mr Henderson the earliest reference to a coach in Cornwall occurs in August 1644, when Charles I came down in one to fight the Earl of Essex ; ' but I doubt ', he adds, ' if he would ever have ventured to bring such a vehicle into Cornwall if he had not got an army of ten thousand men with him to pull him out of the mud ! ' [1]

Probably the first coach to make its appearance in West Cornwall was that owned by the Hawkins family, at whose country seat at Trewinnard in St Erth, it remained as one of the show sights, until it was removed to the County Museum at Truro, a few years since. In this old-fashioned ' Noah's Ark upon springs ' the Hawkins family were formerly wont to drive forth through the narrow country lanes, in a great state, as Mr Bottrell has put it, if not in a state of comfort. Riding thus, however, ' with their cavalcade of belles and beaux, they doubtless thought themselves as grand and as glorious as Solomon and the Queen of Sheba—till they stuck fast in some hole, and the half-dozen or more men who attended them with poles, ropes, picks, spades, and led horses, were forced to come to their rescue and set them going once more '—at a rate which may have averaged some three miles an hour where the roads were passable. [2]

Despite the example set by the Hawkins family, it is clear that wheeled traffic continued to be regarded as very much of an innovation in West Cornwall throughout the earlier part of the eighteenth century. ' I have heard my mother relate,' wrote Dr Davy, brother of Sir Humphry Davy, about 1760, ' that when she was a girl there was only one cart in the town of Penzance, and that if a carriage appeared in the streets it attracted universal attention.' [3] It is said that a certain Mrs Treweeke was among the earliest of the inhabitants of Penzance to possess one of these new vehicles, and that in it she on one occasion drove as far as St Ives in order to attend a concert. It would appear, however, that the inhabitants of the latter town must have known as much about concerts as they did about carriages, for on the lady's

---

[1] *West Briton*, 18 July 1929.
[2] *Traditions and Hearthside Stories of West Cornwall*, III, 149.
[3] *Life of Sir Humphry Davy*, I, 8.

arrival in the streets she is reported to have been followed by an admiring crowd, who shouted : ' The concert is come, the concert is come ! ' [1]

In the absence of roads suitable for wheeled traffic, practically the whole of the merchandise of the country districts continued to be carried, until almost the end of the eighteenth century, on the backs of mules and ponies, the latter belonging to the hardy little Goonhilly breed who, as Celia Fiennes noted, tripped along lightly on the stoniest roads, and throve on grass or furze, ' loving not oats or hay because they knew not the taste of them '. She further describes how she saw the harvest being brought in in this way, the corn stacked up on the animals' backs, till the latter looked like moving ricks, whilst by their side ran women and children with naked feet, steadying the rocking burdens. For carrying sand, manure, or other dressing on to the fields, ' dung pots ' were employed, these being slung over wooden pack-saddles, placed across the animal's back. By means of a falling door in the bottom of each pot, the contents could be dropped on to the fields at will, thereby avoiding the necessity of lifting the pots from the saddle. For the carriage of corn, hay, faggots, wood, slate, etc. long or short ' crooks ' (as they were termed) were more generally used, these consisting of arched wooden saddles, with pegs protruding on either side. [2]

It was to Richard Carew, first and foremost of Cornish historians, that the county was indebted for the earliest recommendation of the mule for purposes of draught, this animal being, in his own words, ' a beast which will fare hardly, live verie long, drawe indifferently well, and carrie great burdens, and hath also a pace swift and easie enough for mill and market service '. Such attributes might well have been deemed sufficient in themselves to commend these animals to the Cornish people, yet, such is human prejudice against anything new or untried, that the same author tells us that ' when not long sithence someone brought over an he-asse from France, who, following his kind, begat many moyles, for monsters the countrie people admired them, yea, some were so wise as to knock on the head or give away this issue of his race as uncouth mongrels '. [3] The mule, however, or ' moyle ', as he was more commonly known in Cornwall,

---

[1] G. B. Millett, *Penzance, Past and Present*, 45–6.
[2] See *Letters from West Cornwall* (1826).
[3] *Survey of Cornwall*.

was not destined to remain in disrepute for long, and within a hundred years after this was written, the pleasant winding tracks and ' green lanes ' of Old Cornwall witnessed a constant stream of these patient, hardy animals, bearing coal to the mines and copper ore to the ports, the merchantman's traffic from town to town, and the farmer's produce to mill or market. Incredible as it may seem to-day, it is nevertheless a recorded fact that at Hayle in the year 1758 there might ' usually be seen above five hundred, oftentimes a thousand animals at work ', bearing coal from that port to the mines and manufactories of the surrounding country-side.[1]

The mules frequently travelled in large companies, seventy or more at a time, each one laden with two sacks of ore, placed on either side of a strongly made pack-saddle. The arrival of these processions in the narrow streets of the towns was wont to create a considerable stir, the animals themselves frequently taking possession of such pavements as existed, and forcing the inhabitants to seek refuge in friendly door-ways, in order to avoid coming in contact with the slimy dripping sacks. The men in charge generally walked on foot behind their teams, but after the ore had been deposited in the yards near the quays, they commonly performed the homeward journey seated comfortably on the animals' backs. Some of the paths by which they travelled may still be traced across the rough bleak moorlands of West Cornwall, untrodden to-day, however, even by the tourist, who finds the ' beauty spots ' more quickly accessible by the ubiquitous motor transport of our mechanical age. Elsewhere, in the cultivated districts, the mule tracks and ' pannier-lanes ' of a bygone day may alike be discovered lying deep between their Cornish stone-built hedges, but so over-grown with brambles, furze, and other vegetation now that only rabbits or the shy night-moving badger can betake their way through them. Further than this, it is probably true to say that not a few of the picturesque, winding lanes which are still in use, must originally have been laid down on the lines of still more ancient mule tracks, and their many twists and turns are the chance result of some sagacious animal (leader of the team) thus picking his way betwixt bog and furze-brake, in the long-ago days, before ever the country-side was enclosed.

With such primitive means of transport, and such primitive roads upon which to travel, it is small wonder that the Cornish

[1] W. Borlase, *Natural History of Cornwall*, 45.

people of the past made but few journeys, and were in consequence very ill guides. ' They know little from home, only
to some market town which they frequent, but are none the
less very solicitous to know where you go, how far, from
whence you came, and where is your abode,' wrote Mrs
Fiennes with that shrewd faculty for observation which makes
her diary so entertaining to the modern reader. No doubt
for the bulk of the population it would have been as true to
say then as when Fuller had written at an earlier date : ' When
Cornishmen went (or rather were driven by the violence of
their occasions) to go to London, it was usual with them to
make their wills as if they took their voyage into a foreign
country. Besides,' he added, ' the children of the Cornish
gentry counted themselves above, and those of the poorer
sort beneath, a trade in London, as unable to attain it by
reason of the difference in their language, whose feet must
travel so far to come to the city, whilst their tongues must
travail further to be understood when arrived there.' When
circumstances, however, offered no alternative, and the three-
hundred-mile journey to the metropolis had to be made, those
who could afford to do so rode thither on horseback, though,
even so, not without many sad misgivings, for as the old
couplet pointed out :

Ride to Lunnon on a hoss ?   See what money it do cost !
Rubs us raw and rubs us beer (bare), afore we do get haalf way
    theer.

All the existing evidence goes to show that throughout the
earlier decades of the eighteenth century, the roads of Cornwall
remained for the most part in their primitive state, still following the highland ridges as in ancient times, and descending
only to the valleys by breakneck hills where some river or
creek had of necessity to be crossed. In 1732 a writer in the
Gentleman's Magazine claimed that the roads of the Duchy
' were still what they were after the Flood ', whilst twenty-two
years later another contributor to the same paper added :
' Cornwall, I believe, at present has the worst roads in all
England. A great part are intolerable, remaining in the same
condition in which the Deluge left them, whilst most of those
which have been improved are so extremely narrow and uneven
that they are almost inaccessible to all kinds of wheeled vehicles.
This great inconvenience I look upon as the one grand article

that has so much prejudiced travellers against the county in general, who, I know, are too apt to form hasty judgments of the manners of its inhabitants from a prospect of the rough and mountainous country they pass through'.[1] Significant as this may be as a defence of the character of the inhabitants, it nevertheless shows that the actual conditions which obtained still justified to some extent those writers who continued to dub Cornwall as the land of ' West Barbary '.

From the middle of the eighteenth century onwards, however, a considerable improvement began to take place in the main roads of Mid and East Cornwall. Already in 1754 a new turnpike was in course of construction between Truro and Falmouth, and Truro and Grampound, an undertaking which the above-quoted writer describes as ' a very masterly and complete piece of workmanship '.[2] In 1759 an Act of Parliament was passed ' For making a road, or repairing a road, from Launceston to Camelford, Wadebridge, St Columb, and Truro '. The improvement of this road was largely effected through the zeal of the local inhabitants, and it is recorded that, in order to assist the undertaking, the Rev. Wm. Phillips, Rector of Lanteglos, cut with his own hands the figures on the granite milestones which still remain beside its course.[3] In 1763 Edward Leach, reeve and deputy-steward of Stoke Climsland, described the road from Horsebridge to Launceston as being safe for wheeled traffic, a great part of it being turnpike road. ' From Launceston to Linkinghorne Church Town,' he added, ' is a tolerable good road, and from thence on to Liskeard may also be travelled with wheels, safe.' [4] In the year 1770 a new road was begun from Torpoint to Liskeard, a piece of engineering which must have involved a considerable outlay of public money as, owing to the hilly

[1] See ' Lanje ', *Western Morning News*, 7 April 1927.

[2] In a petition to the House of Commons, dated 16 January 1754, it was stated that the roads radiating from the Borough of Truro ' are become very ruinous, and many places thereof are so narrow that carriages cannot pass each other, especially in winter and the rainy seasons, when they are so deep and founderous that wheel carriages, horses laden, and even travellers pass in great danger '. The Government, in consequence, gave permission for widening and repairing the following roads : those leading south-west to Penryn ; north to Shortlane's End ; west to Redruth ; east to Lostwithiel ; north-east to St Columb, and a sixth leading to Tretheage Bridge. See P. Jennings, *Journal of Royal Institution of Cornwall*, XV, 315 (1903).

[3] Rev. John. Wallis, *Cornwall Register* (1847).

[4] Duchy of Cornwall Office Records.

nature of the district, cuttings had in many places to be made through more than twenty feet of solid rock.

According to ' Lanje ', a well-known contributor to West Country newspapers, the first stage coach between Torpoint and Truro was set up in 1796, by a man named Walter Cross. The latter hailed from Mevagissey, and had at one time followed the sea and smuggling, but having gained £100 by raffling for a curious astronomical clock (made by H. Jenkins of St Austell), he embarked that sum, with other additions, in setting up a coach. This spirited adventure was much resented by the innkeepers along the road, who, however, on finding that it was a paying proposition, eventually set up a rival coach of their own. Both these coaches were heavy, clumsy contrivances, drawn by four horses, at the rate of four miles an hour. They worked alternately from Torpoint to Truro, going down one day, and returning the next, each coach carrying six inside passengers.[1]

Some years earlier than this, another and somewhat speedier stage coach had started to run on the Launceston—Bodmin route, by means of which an energetic traveller might perform the journey of one hundred miles from Exeter to Falmouth in a long day of twenty-one hours. Those who could afford to do so, however, covered the distance more comfortably in post-chaises, stopping the night at Bodmin or Launceston *en route*. A vivid description of the tedium which attended even this improved mode of travel is provided by Robert Southey, the Poet Laureate, who thus describes his impressions on journeying up the country from Falmouth in the year 1802 : ' Early in the morning our chaise was at the door, a four-wheeled carriage which conveniently carries three persons. It has glass in front and at the sides, instead of being closed with curtains, so that you at once see the country and are sheltered from the weather. Two horses drew us at the rate of a league and a half ' (four and one-half miles) ' in the hour to Penryn, whose ill-built and narrow streets seem to have been contrived to make as many acute angles in the road, and take the traveller up and down as many steep declivities as possible in a given distance. In two hours we reached Truro, where we breakfasted. J—— showed me where some traveller had left the expression of his impatience written upon the wainscot with a pencil : " Thanks to the Gods another stage is past ". Our second stage was to a single house called the

[1] *Western Morning News*, 7 April 1927.

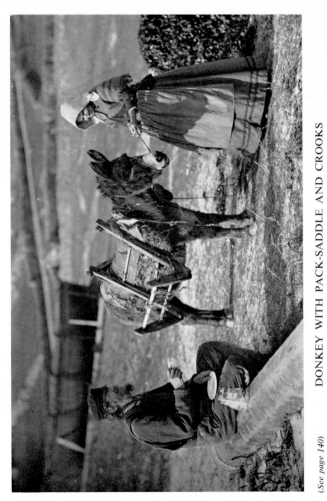

(*See page 140*)

DONKEY WITH PACK-SADDLE AND CROOKS

RUSSELL'S WAGON ON THE WAY TO LONDON

(See page 146)

Indian Queens, which is rather a post-house than an inn. One inconvenience attends this mode of travelling, which is that at every stage the chaise is changed and, of course, there is the trouble of removing all the baggage '.[1]

Moreover, travelling by chaise was anything but cheap. In 1773 the cost of a journey from Cornwall to London, including turnpikes, tips, and the hire of the vehicle, worked out at about tenpence per mile, a sum which would have to be multiplied several times over in order to show its present-day equivalent. Mr Henderson has told how young Mr Christopher Hawkins, returning by post-chaise to Eton after a Christmas holiday in Cornwall in the latter part of the eighteenth century, spent £15 on the journey, which occupied five whole days. To-day, as Mr Henderson has said, we can go to America in as short a time and for about the same expense ! Not being in the position to make such a comparison, however, the traveller of one hundred and fifty years ago, who had accomplished his fourteen leagues in the day, was quite willing, like Southey, when enjoying the comforts of the famous White Hart Inn at Launceston, to exclaim : ' What a country for travelling in is this ! Such rapidity on the roads ! Such accommodation at the resting places ! '[2]

Great as were the changes which were revolutionizing the means of transport, even at this date, it was long before such improvements began to be felt in the more outlying parts of Cornwall. In 1761 the turnpike-road still only reached as far as Marazion,[3] and the St Ives and Land's End districts remained, in consequence, in a splendid isolation which caused no small inconvenience to the growing mercantile interests of those areas. ' You reflect on me for not writing per return of post,' wrote Mr Anthony of St Ives, in 1779, to another fish merchant at Falmouth, ' but you are to understand that at Falmouth they receive their letters in the morning, and do not return before night. On the contrary, our post does not come till two or three o'clock in the afternoon, and never stays more than one hour, sometimes not so long. As St Ives is a cross-penny post, some distance from the established post office, there is no possibility of answering a letter by the same post, and it is so late before it comes here that sometimes

[1] Don Manuel Alvarez Espriella (pseudonym Robert Southey), *Letters from England* (1802), I, 8–11.
[2] C. G. Henderson, *West Briton*, 18 July 1929.
[3] G. B. Millett, *Penzance, Past and Present*.

I fear the man may be too late to meet the back post when he returns to Marazion.' [1]

One very important consequence, however, of the improvement of the *main roads* of the county after 1750, had been the introduction of the stage-wagon—a huge carriage upon four wheels of prodigious breadth, very wide and long, and arched over with canvas like a bower. This monstrous machine was commonly drawn by eight large horses, whose neck bells might be heard from a considerable distance as they approached along the road. The carrier walked or rode beside them, bearing upon his shoulder a whip, as tall again as himself, which he sometimes cracked in the air, rarely having occasion to exercise it in any other manner. ' His dress ,' states a contemporary writer, ' is a sort of tunic or smock of coarse linen, and is peculiar to this class of men. The wagons themselves are day and night upon the road, and are oddly enough called " flying wagons ", though they travel slower than a walking funeral.' [2]

All the same, the stage-wagons served a useful purpose by providing the poor with a less expensive alternative to the coaching or post-chaise system. Through their means it was possible to make the journey to London in the space of about three weeks, the passengers taking their own bedding with them, and sleeping in the vehicle itself at nights. Subject as such journeys were, however, not only to constant tedium and discomfort, but to the very real dangers which were apt to arise from the crossing of rivers and unbridged fords, from highway robberies, sickness, and other adversities, the precaution, common among Cornish people, of making a will before starting was not even then, perhaps, as superfluous as it would now appear.

V

For the majority of the inhabitants of West Cornwall, therefore, even as late as the end of the eighteenth century, to have journeyed as far east as the River Hayle, was to have earned the reputation of being no inconsiderable traveller.

[1] Letters formerly in the possession of Sir Edward Hain, St Ives.
[2] Don Manuel Alvarez Espriella (i.e. R. Southey), *Letters from England*, I, 16–17.

This fact is amusingly illustrated by the story told of an old St Ives woman who, on one occasion, in the early days of Methodism, went to hear Whitefield preach at an open-air meeting on the top of Trencrom Hill, in the neighbouring parish of Lelant. Having never been out of sight of home before in all her fourscore years, the astonishment with which she beheld the distant prospect from this famous hill-top was only equalled by that of 'stout Cortez and his men' when gazing on the Pacific. As she remarked to those about her, 'she never knawed the world was so big before'—and, as to the hills which she beheld in the distance towards Camborne and Redruth, she could only imagine they must be in France or Spain, or possibly in one of those far-off countries she had heard of in the Bible.

This story, whether apocryphal or not, is representative of the intellectual confinement in which the poorer classes of that time lay ; a condition which resulted from the isolation of the county, and the almost complete absence of any means whereby knowledge might reach them concerning the nature of the outside world. One newspaper only, the *Sherborne Mercury*, published by Messrs Goadby of Sherborne, ever found its way into the west. This was carried through the country by a man specially employed in distributing it. Great was the excitement in the small towns and villages on the day on which the 'Sherborne Rider' rode in, dusty or mud-bespattered, as the case might be, and bestriding his bulging saddlebags from which he dispensed to the eager crowd his *Mercury* and *Entertainer*. All too short were the moments in which he remained to take the money, and the orders of the new customers, before departing again 'into the blue'. So closely was the word 'Sherborne' associated in the minds of the older generation with that of 'news' that, as late as the middle of the last century, gossip-mongers were still frequently referred to in Cornish villages as being 'regular Sherborners'.[1]

The majority of the poor, however, who were unable to read, were denied the benefits even of this slight intellectual stimulus. A story told by the Rev. R. Polwhele illustrates the consequent mental darkness which enveloped many of the more isolated villages of Cornwall at this date. 'About the year 1740,' he writes, 'there was no place of worship in a certain large village to the west of Truro, nor was there a Bible to be seen. The only religious book in the place consisted

[1] *Western Antiquary*, III, 50.

of a copy of the New Testament and the Common Prayer Book, bound together in one volume. This valuable rarity was the property of an old woman who kept the village inn, on a shelf in which the volume lay together with a copy of the celebrated history of *Robinson Crusoe* placed alongside it. One summer's day, alarmed by a violent thunderstorm, the villagers sought shelter under the roof which contained this sacred deposit, considering it the only place of safety. To make assurance doubly sure, anxious inquiry was made for Jack, the landlady's apprentice, who had the rare good fortune to have learnt his letters. This lad was considered a prodigy ; and being found, was desired to commence reading prayers to the terrified auditory, who were on their knees in the common drinking room. Jack went to fetch the Prayer Book from the shelf, where it had long rested beside its companion. Unfortunately, as things were, in a state of confusion, he took down the latter, and falling on his knees, began reading from it as fast as he could. From miscalling some words and mispelling others, the boy had continued some time before the error was discovered. At length, having stumbled upon the *Man Friday*, his mistress cried out : " Why, Jack, thee 'st got the wrong book. Why, thee 'st reading prayers out of *Robinson Crusoe !* " The boy, feeling this reproof to be an insult to his superior understanding, pertinaciously continued to read, declaring that " *Robinson Crusoe* would as soon stop the thunder as the Prayer Book ".' [1]

It is scarcely strange perhaps, under such circumstances, that even so patriotic a Cornishman as Dr William Borlase should have occasionally repined at the fates which had destined him to spend the greater part of his long life in so remote a situation as the rectory of Ludgvan must then have been. Writing about the year 1770 to ' a young scion of a Cornish house ' at that time completing his studies in Oxford, he says : ' I should indeed be buried before my time if I was already confined to the narrow limits of this corner of the world, and though I shall always be glad to see you, yet 'tis my earnest intreaty that you stick to a college life, with short excursions to London or Bath, or anywhere with your tutor, for in this country there is nothing to be learned and everything to be forgot. This is my opinion, but to be hinted at, you know, rather than prest '. The tone of this letter, which was written but two years before his death, owes something

[1] *Traditions and Recollections* (1826), 719.

no doubt to the loneliness and disillusionment of an old man, oppressed with growing infirmities and mourning the loss of his associates and companions of other days. The friend of Pope, who once likened him to the Cornish minerals in his own famous grotto at Twickenham—'in the shade but shining'—had forgotten for the moment, perhaps, the happy hours spent with the ' free, frolicking gentry' of the neighbourhood who had been the companions of his youth. ' In the summer time,' he wrote to a friend of those earlier days, ' we meet (some ten or a dozen) at a bowling green. There we have built a little pleasure house, and there we dine ; after dinner play at bowls, and so by frequently meeting together we are, as it were, like so many brothers of one family, so united and so glad to see the one the other.' The original agreement by which this club was formed at Marazion in 1719 is still in existence, as are also the Cornish verses written by William Gwavas, one of its members, in honour of the occasion.[1]

Despite the not unnatural regret with which he sometimes contemplated the loss of intellectual companionship, the learned rector contrived to show better than any other man of his day how many enjoyments of a varied kind could be derived from a well-spent leisure, even in the isolation of a far-off Cornish parish. Not only did he rebuild the rectory, but he transformed the plot of ground before it into a garden which has since, under the hands of his present-day successor, become one of the most famous of its kind in Cornwall. ' It was with the greatest reluctance,' wrote Dr Borlase, when the initial stages of this work were in progress, ' that I could leave the diggers and delvers and withdraw into my study to Horace and Dryden.' [2] Nor were his studies confined to the classics, seeing that almost to the end of his life he retained that passion for literary and scientific investigation which resulted in two large folio works on Cornwall, and the interchange of a voluminous correspondence with a majority of the most eminent characters of the intellectual world of his day.

Nor was Cornwall at that period wholly unprovided with opportunities for enjoying amusements of a more frivolous nature, and at its various assemblies, with their balls, card parties, and routs, the local society contrived to emulate in no mean spirit the doings of the more fashionable world of

---

[1] See *Quarterly Review*, vol. 137 (1875), 374.
[2] See *Quarterly Review*, vol. 137 (1875), 374.

London or Bath.   Such were the prevailing restrictions on travel that even the great families frequently possessed a ' town house ' iń one of the larger Cornish towns, where they were content to take up their abode during the winter months. The ' pride of Truro ' is a phrase which still serves to remind us of the time when the great houses of Princes Street (now converted into offices and shops) were inhabited by a fashionable society which included the Boscawens, the Lemons, and other equally well-known families who resided there during a part of the year in order to enjoy the attractions of the Literary Society, County Library, Theatre, Assembly Rooms and, last but not least, the Cockpit which the town at that time boasted.   The Lemons, who had made money by adventuring in the local mines, had their country seat at Carclew, but a few miles distant from Truro.   This expensively appointed house, replete with all the latest fashions in furnishing, was described by a traveller in 1759 as being surrounded by a garden and walks ' beautiful beyond description, and by far exceeding anything I have seen in Cornwall.   Just as we got to the house ', he continues, ' it began to rain violently, and notwithstanding there was only a maidservant (Mr Lemon being at his house in Truro), we accepted her invitation of a bed, which we thought more agreeable than being exposed to the fury of the weather over the downs, which are all open. We got a very good dish of green tea which served me for my supper, had a good fire, and wanted nothing to make the evening quite agreeable but a pipe and tobacco.   We tried for a pipe, but could not get one, and therefore sat down very contentedly without it.   I went to bed between nine and ten, and lay in a very handsome Chinese bed, and the room hung with very handsome India paper, exactly the same figure with the Chinese.   But, 'tis not magnificence that procures ease and repose, for that night was the most uneasy I had since my being from home '. [1]

Even Penzance in the western extremity of the peninsula, was not without its local society, and boasted an assembly which met at fortnightly intervals throughout the winter at the old Ship and Castle Inn (now the Union Hotel), where the members indulged in music and dancing.   As in Truro, a theatre and a cockpit flourished also in this town. [2]

A pleasant picture of one of the Cornish assemblies of the

[1] See *Penzance Natural History and Antiquarian Society* (1888–92), 281.
[2] G. B. Millett, *Penzance, Past and Present*, 41.

day is to be found in the diary of the Rev. J. Skinner. 'On 7th November 1797,' he writes, ' we proceeded to the assembly at Bodmin. This is a monthly meeting for which the charge is a moderate subscription of 5s. for the season, though the entertainment to be sure does not discredit this vast expense. The room they dance in is perhaps twenty-five feet long, the boards laid the contrary way, and some of them much higher than others, which occasions various trippings as you go down the dance. It is lighted by five or six candles stuck against the wall, and the music usually consists of a blind fiddler and a little scraper, his son. But we were particularly fortunate on the occasion of our visit in having the band of the Somerset Militia, who not only occupied half the room, but stunned us with the noise of their drums, clarionettes, etc. Indeed, I should have been much better pleased if Mr Fiddler had reigned alone. The ladies, however, seemed perfectly charmed and contented, and I was accordingly glad to get away before tea, leaving them to the society of the Red Coats.' [1]

VI

It is clear from these accounts not only that Cornwall during the latter half of the eighteenth century was far from being inhabited by a mere rabble of uncouth ' barbarians ', as so many Englishmen were still inclined to suppose, but that the trade and commerce upon which the existence of a cultivated and leisured class depends, must have been in a flourishing condition. This was particularly true of the mining industry, which, thanks to the discovery of copper about the year 1710, had subsequently developed on an unprecedented scale. Down to the beginning of the eighteenth century, much of the old feudal atmosphere still prevailed, especially in the west where many of the local squires were in the habit of developing the mines on their own estates, ' the frugal fare of the workmen and the consequent low rate of wages, rendering the employment of a considerable number of hands quite within the compass of any man of moderate means '. It is recorded that the father of Dr William Borlase, the antiquary, was himself one of the old squires of this type, and tradition reports that

[1] British Museum, Additional MS. 28793.

every Saturday in the earlier years of the eighteenth century, a troop of miners and ' bal ' maidens, with ' John of Pendeen ' riding at their head, might have been seen wending their way along the rough moorland tracks from St Just to Penzance, in order to receive their wages for the work done at his mines.[1]

The growth of commerce and industry developed in this way had the effect, of course, of greatly increasing the value of Cornish estates, and the rivalry between neighbouring landowners, in consequence, often ran high. Indeed, many of the rough old squires of that day appeared to have regarded it as almost a necessity to be at loggerheads amongst themselves, if it were for no other purpose than to show their mettle and courage. Thus it was said to have been the proud boast of Squire Harris of Kenegie (near Penzance) that there was only one person who would not make way for him on the high road, and that was his old neighbour, Mr Rogers, of ' Trazza ' (Treassowe). Many of the country roads of West Cornwall at this date consisted, as already shown, of little more than grass-grown tracks, divided in some places by rocks or brakes of furze, which offered a choice of ways to the traveller. If, when on his high horse, Mr Rogers could discern from a little distance the track by which his neighbour from Kenegie was approaching, he would be sure to take that one by preference. If the way was deep and miry, so much the better ; the men would then ride up against each other full butt, for all the world like two goats meeting on a plank, and either have a ' scruff ' or a slashing fight with their whips. Yet on the whole, these two old squires, like many others of their kind, were good enough friends, and often hunted together over each other's lands, and visited one another in state upon all ceremonial occasions.[2]

Isolated as they were, however, from the moderating influences of the outside world, and concentrated in their outlook upon their own immediate affairs, it is small wonder that such rivalries should have led upon occasion to more serious displays of the passionate temper which underlies the character of the Celt. Perhaps the most remarkable instance of this kind was seen in the case of Henry Rogers, of Skewes, a farm and tenement situated in the parish of Crowan. This

---

[1] *Quarterly Review* (1875), 373.
[2] Cf. W. Bottrell, *Traditions and Hearthside Stories of West Cornwall*, III, 39.

property had for long been the freehold patrimony of the Rogers family which, about the year 1733, consisted of two brothers. The elder of the two, who was married, but without issue, lived at Skewes, whilst Henry Rogers, who had several children, resided in Helston, where he carried on the trade of a pewterer. According to a belief which generally obtained at this time, freehold lands which had once descended to an heir could not be alienated without the concurrence of the next heir. In the year 1734, however, the elder Rogers died, and by his will gave the whole of the Skewes property to his widow, whose maiden name was Millet. This action aroused all the latent passion of the younger brother, who, believing the will to be spurious, took the law into his own hands, and arriving one day when his sister-in-law was away from home, turned the servants out of doors, and took forcible possession. Up to this point the whole country-side was in favour of ' Pewterer Rogers's ' claim, but the widow appealing to law, the sheriff was at length directed to eject the usurper by force. Meantime, however, Rogers, supported by several of his men, had barricaded himself into the house, and on the arrival of the civil forces commenced to shoot at them from the windows, thereby killing two men and narrowly escaping wounding the sheriff himself. This happened on 8th June 1734. On the following day the under-sheriff arrived with a posse of soldiers, who were similarly fired upon by the inmates of the house, one soldier being killed. After this, strange to say, Rogers was allowed to remain at Skewes undisturbed till the March of the following year, when more soldiers were sent for, and after two of these had been killed, a cannon at length fetched from Pendennis Castle. That night, probably realizing that the game was up, Rogers made his escape. A £350 reward, however, was offered for his capture, as the result of which he was shortly afterwards apprehended whilst asleep at an inn near Salisbury. At his trial Rogers is reported to have appeared ' very penitent ', but to have declared, none the less, that ' had it been in his power he would have killed as many more again, and thought he committed no crime '. The jury, however, were not unnaturally of a different opinion, and on 1st August 1735, Rogers was condemned to death. Although no one attempted to justify the murders which had been committed by him, yet, for long after his death, a strong feeling of compassion was entertained for his case, and it was popularly held in the neighbourhood that none of the subsequent proprietors of old Skewes would ever prosper in its possession.[1]

Whilst it was but rarely, of course, that local rivalries led to such a pass as this, it would be possible to cite other cases wherein the passionate temper of the Cornish Celts has resulted in outbursts of a strangely violent nature. Within the memory of persons still living a certain East Cornwall farmer whose wife had left him, got together a band of companions and besieged the house to which she had retired, threatening to set fire to the building with all its inmates, if she was not instantly surrendered.

Still more often, cunning and sharp practice have been employed in gaining ends which force was unfitted to achieve, and many were the strange artifices resorted to by well-known Cornish landowners of the past, in order to obtain possession of property to which their legal claims were, to say the least of it, ' shady '. Not far from the Land's End there lies a valuable farm, possession of which is said to have been won by an ancestor of its present owner in the following curious way. For some time after the marriage of the individual in question the farm had been held by an illegitimate son of his wife's father. This base son dying intestate, two landowners laid claim to the property, one of whom was the ancestor of the present owner. A lawsuit was accordingly instigated, as the result of which it was decided that the latter gentleman had proved his title to the inheritance, on the strength of his wife's claims. The tenants of the farm in the meantime had been living there for several years scot-free, on the pretext that they did not know to whom the rent was payable, and, finding this arrangement very much to their taste, they now refused to recognize the legally successful claimant as their landlord. In order to obtain an acknowledgment of possession, therefore, it became necessary to devise some other form of payment. On consultation with the lawyers the latter gave it as their opinion that the mere transference of a handful of earth, or even of a stick cut from the hedge, might be said to constitute this. The claimant, accordingly, one day borrowed a lazy horse from a friend, and took a ride past the property. Happening in this way to meet his tenant in the lane, he begged the latter to do him the favour of cutting him a switch, ' as he had left his whip behind '. To this the unsuspecting farmer readily agreed.

[1] See *Parochial History of Cornwall*, I, 269-70.

The stick was cut and handed to the squire, who immediately rode off in triumph ; and it was but a few days later that the farmer received an intimation from the lawyers advising him of the transference of ownership which this simple act of politeness had effected.[1]

Old Mr R——, of Nanpusker, was a similarly notorious land-grabber, whose name was well known in Cornwall during the eighteenth century. The story is told how his ' body-servant ' was always instructed to keep a close watch on forth-coming sales of property, and to give his master due warning of any which were likely to result in good bargains. One day when certain ' quillets ' (small pieces) of land at Gwinear Green were being sold, old R—— was there according to custom, buying up all he could get, and only sorry it wasn't more. ' I tell you what, R——,' at length exclaimed a neigh-bour, who was standing near by, ' you don't know what " enough " do mean. Why, if you was to buy up all Europe, you would still be looking over to Asia for a bit of a furze-croft for your mules ! '

Whilst such was the disposition of a large portion of the squirearchy of those days, glimpses may be got of other men of kindlier character, and more generous feeling, whose presence served to sweeten the whole atmosphere of a con-temporary Cornish life. William Beckford, who visited Trefusis, the ancient home of the family of that name, in the year 1787, has left us a pleasant picture of the old-fashioned Cornish squire at his best. The Trefusis which he describes at that date was ' an antiquated mansion, containing many ruinous halls and never-ending passages. The latter, however could not be said to lead nowhere, for Mrs Trefusis herself terminated the perspective. We should have very much enjoyed her conversation', the writer goes on, ' but the moment tea was over the squire could not resist leading us round his improvements in kennel, stable, and ox-stall, though it was pitch dark, and we were obliged to be escorted by grooms and groomlings with candles and lanthorns. In the course of our peregrinations through halls, pantries, and ante-chambers, we passed a staircase with a heavy walnut railing, lined from top to bottom with effigies of ancestors that looked quite formidable by the horny glow of our lanthorns—which illumination, dull as it was, occasioned much alarm amongst a collection of animals, both furred and feathered, the delight

[1] Per Mr Henry Thomas, St Just.

of Mr Trefusis's existence.   At dinner that night we had on
the table a savoury pig and some of the finest poultry I ever
tasted : and round the table two or three brace of old Cornish
gentlefolks, not deficient in humour or originality.   About
eight in the evening six game-cocks were ushered into the
eating-room by two limber lads in scarlet jackets ; and, after
a flourish of crowing, the noble birds set to with a surprising
keenness.   Tufts of brilliant feathers soon flew about the
apartment, but the carpet was not stained by the blood of
the combatants ; for, to do Trefusis justice, he has a generous
heart, and takes no pleasure in cruelty.   The cocks were
unarmed, had their spurs cut short, and may live to fight fifty
such harmless battles '.[1]

It is probable, however, that comparatively few of Mr
Trefusis's contemporaries shared his humanitarian principles
to this extent, and cock-fighting, in its most brutal form,
continued to be indulged in by many persons almost to within
living memory.   An account of the ' sport ' was given to the
writer not long since by an old Lelant miner whose father
had worked in his younger days with a man named Betty,
who resided at Lelant Downs.   The latter possessed, amongst
other birds, a famous English gamecock which was said not
only to have been capable of beating every rival which was
brought to fight it, but to have possessed such an innate love
of the sport as frequently to visit on its own account another
cock which was kept at Carntisco, a farm about a quarter of
a mile away.   On one of these occasions, Betty's cock broke
its beak in trying to fight its rival through a gate.   Nothing
daunted, Betty soon had the beak ' sharped ' again, ready to
match the bird against the next comer.   Not long after, another
miner in the neighbourhood challenged Betty to bring his
cock to the test in a field behind his house.   The news soon
spread in the neighbourhood, and a large gathering assembled
to see the great fight.   Hardly had the birds settled to their
grim contest, however, before it became apparent that Betty's
cock was still to be the champion.   Time after time the weaker
bird was knocked to the ground, sometimes attempting to
run away, but only to be dragged back to the fight by its brutal
owner.   At length the poor creature was knocked down for
the last time, killed outright by the spurs of Betty's cock which
had pierced it through the head.   It is a strange coincidence
that some little time after this the owner of the defeated bird

[1] *Travels*, II

was himself killed in ' Foxes ' shaft, at Wheal Sisters, by a small stone striking him on the head.[1]

Another cruel old sport, that of bull-baiting, had only ceased in West Cornwall a few years before this. In the year 1813 a famous bull-baiting match was held on Madron ' Feast ' Monday, in a field where the workhouse now stands. The bull was supplied by the squire of Kimyel, an estate in the neighbouring parish of Paul. A ship's anchor was brought up the hill from Penzance, a distance of nearly three miles, and was firmly fixed in the centre of the field. To this the bull was fastened and baited until it died. It is said that the very last bull-baiting match to be held in Cornwall took place but a year later, in a field near Ponsandane Bridge, at Penzance. ' I remember,' wrote an aged witness, a number of years since, ' seeing the black bull being led by four men. The crowd was dispersed early in the evening by a severe thunderstorm, which much alarmed the people, who thought it (I believe) a judgment from Heaven.' [2]

VII

Looking back on these matters in the light in which we have come to regard them now, there seems something oppressive in the deep shadow which ignorance and brutality combined in casting over the day-to-day life of the period. Turning over local records, one may see how petty malefactors were still flogged through the streets of Cornish towns,[3] how public hangings were regarded as a fashionable entertainment for rich and poor, how lunatics were displayed in cages for the amusement of passers-by,[4] whilst honest paupers were sentenced to conditions which now seem scarcely credible in a country paying even lip-service to the principles of Christianity. Whilst the poor were subjected to such treatment as this, it was a time amongst the well-to-do of duelling and hard hitting, of drunkenness and debauchery—an age in which the expression, ' as drunk as a lord ', was still significant of the manner of living in the houses of the great.

[1] Per Mr Nathanial James, Trencrom.
[2] See Miss M. A. Courtney, Cornish Feasts and Folk-lore, 5–6.
[3] G. B. Millett, Penzance, Past and Present (1880), 30.
[4] Mr Silvanus Jenkin, a great-uncle of the writer, remembered seeing a lunatic ' on show ' in a cage, at Redruth, about the year 1835.

Under such circumstances it is not to be wondered at that the poor, uneducated tinner, and the half-starved fishermen of Cornwall, indulged to the full in the common practice of heavy drinking—a practice for which a more than usual facility existed in this county by reason of the inflow of cheap spirit through the smuggling trade. Amongst the working classes, indeed, it had been long observed that the poorer and more uncertain the nature of their livelihood, the more prevalent was the recourse to drink, ' tippling and ale houses ', as Carew remarked, 'ever abounding in all parishes richest in tin '. Commenting on this statement more than a hundred years later, Tonkin was fain to add that, in the mining districts, ' if there were but three houses together, two of them shall be ale-houses '.

' We hear every day of murmurs of the common people of want of employ, of short wages, of dear provisions,' wrote Dr Borlase in 1771. ' There may be some reason for this : our taxes are heavy upon the necessaries of life, but the chief cause is the extravagance of the vulgar in the unnecessaries of life. In one tin-mine near me, where most of the tinners of my parish have been employed for years, there were lately computed to have been at one time three score snuff-boxes ; there may be in any parish about fifty girls above fifteen years old, and I dare say forty-nine of them have scarlet cloaks ; there is scarce a family in the parish, I mean of common labourers, but have tea once if not twice a day, and in the parish almshouses there are several families, but not one without their tea-kettle, and brandy also when they can purchase it . . . in short, all labourers live above their condition.'[1]

Considering that it was estimated that about this time a sum equivalent to £30,000 was annually expended on drink by the working classes of one typical Cornish parish, such as Redruth,[2] there would certainly appear some justification for the writer's criticism. But in point of fact, the latter was directed not so much against intemperance in general, as against the practice of heavy drinking on the part of those who were unable to afford it. For, as the writer goes on, ' If these extravagances were committed only by those who had the wherewithal to pay for them, the vice of excessive drinking would not be altogether shameful ; but the misfortune is that the poorest working tinner shall be credited by the ale-drawer

[1] See *Quarterly Review* (1875), 395.
[2] R. Polwhele, *History of Cornwall*, VII, 108 note.

till his account becomes considerable, and then persecuted by bailiffs till he pays costs as well as scores '.[1] No better exposition of the class-morality of the eighteenth century will be found in all its literature than this naïve statement on the part of one who was alike representative of the landowning community, of the magistracy, and the Church. Dr Borlase's remedy for such working-class excesses was equally characteristic of his position and his age. For they consisted, not in the advocacy of any improvement in the standard of living, nor in the provision of educational facilities which might lead men on to taste those intellectual pleasures in which he himself had found such lasting satisfaction, but merely in the recommendation of stricter laws to prevent public-house keepers from suing any man who had neither freehold nor lease estate. ' This,' he writes, ' would prevent the idle from spending what they have not, for if they had no credit, the ready money they get must go in necessaries and consequently would not be sufficient for purposes of idleness. As it is at present, however, this is certain, that to credit a poor labourer for superfluities, much more for excessive drinking, is to encourage and tempt him to neglect and transgress every serious duty of life.'[2]

In making such a suggestion, however, the writer was clearly reckoning without the ' Trade ', whose influence in political circles was even stronger then than it is to-day. The farmer would certainly have opposed any measures which would have been likely to curtail their profits, no matter how advantageous they might have been for the country at large. Indeed, the attitude of the gentry toward this question was curiously inconsistent. Though they were quick to complain of the debauchery of the labouring classes when it resulted in any interference in the daily routine of their work, they made little attempt either to check the smuggling trade or to regulate the iniquitous ' cider allowance ', which to a certain extent in Cornwall, and to a very large extent in Devonshire, was forced upon the agricultural labourer in part payment of his wages. Furthermore, these same gentry, however much they might censure the intemperance of the poor, were nothing loath at election times to connive at the methods of their chosen candidates for Cornwall's ' rotten boroughs ' who found in the provision of quantities of strong liquor

[1] Borlase, *Natural History of Cornwall*, 308.
[2] Borlase, *Natural History of Cornwall*, 308.

a cheap and effectual means of buying the support of the poorer voters. ' The corruption of our boroughs at the electing members for Parliament,' Dr Borlase himself admitted, ' begins with intemperance and riot ; these dissipate every generous sentiment of freedom, love of country, and inclination to industry. Venality naturally succeeds, and is followed by extravagance and idleness ; these by poverty, and poverty (such is the round !) by abandoning themselves to intemperance again on the first opportunity, and repeating the basest prostitution of the highest privilege. A corruption this both of principle and practice, of patriotism and morality, infesting more counties than one, but so much the more to be lamented in Cornwall as this county has a so much greater number of boroughs than any in Great Britain,' sending (at this date) no less than forty-four members to Parliament, as against forty-five for the whole of Scotland.[1]

THE COMING OF WESLEY

I

INTO this thrusting, striving, hard-hitting world, whose most characteristic feature was its unashamed materialism, there came about the middle of the eighteenth century that little band of Methodist pioneers, preaching the gospel of redemption and warning their hearers to quit the accepted ways, and flee from the wrath to come. The bravery of voicing such ' enthusiasm ' for religious principles anywhere in eighteenth-century England would have been remarkable enough ; but when cultured Oxford men like the Wesley brothers, not content with preaching to the great congregations of London, must needs start pushing their way into the uttermost parts of far Cornwall, and into the very hovels of the poor, the world must have deemed that madness alone could excuse such folly.

Although neither of the Wesleys was actually the pioneer of Methodism in Cornwall, they were early in the field and, in the course of his thirty-nine years of preaching, John Wesley

[1] Borlase, *Natural History of Cornwall*, 308–9.

GWENNAP PIT

(See page 164)

BILLY BRAY, LOCAL PREACHER AND MINER

(*See page 172*)

himself found time to pay the more important centres in the Duchy between thirty and forty visits.[1]

The Reverend Charles Wesley was the first to enter Cornwall in July 1743, and was followed a few weeks later by his brother. The latter was accompanied by the celebrated John Nelson, Mr Shepherd, and Mr Downs. Wesley continued in Cornwall on this occasion for about three weeks. The following extracts from his diary throw light on the indefatigable energy with which he characteristically threw himself into the work. On Friday, 2nd September, he preached at Morvah, a hamlet situated about twelve miles from the Land's End. On Saturday he held a service in the same district at ' Three-Cornered Down ', afterwards riding to Gwennap, some twenty-five miles away, where another service was held. On the Sunday morning, he again preached at Gwennap, and thence proceeded to Treswithian Downs, near Camborne, where he preached in the forenoon and afternoon. At seven in the evening he met the society at St Ives—having delivered six sermons and ridden over fifty miles in three days.

On Tuesday, 6th September, Wesley preached at Morvah ; on Wednesday, at Zennor ; on Thursday, at Kenegie Downs ; on Friday, at St Hilary Downs ; and on Saturday, at St Just in the afternoon and at Sennen in the evening. On Sunday, 11th September, he began by preaching at Sennen between four and five in the morning ; then, between eight and nine, to a very large congregation at St Just ; soon after 1 p.m. to another gathering near Morvah Church ; to yet another at Zennor about five ; ' after which ', he writes, ' I hastened to St Ives, where we concluded the day with joyful lips '. Six sermons and a meeting, and twenty-five miles on horseback in the space of thirty hours !

Notwithstanding this, the next day, 12th September, found the great preacher once more on his way to Camborne, where he addressed a meeting in the morning, returning to St Ives for another the same evening.

On the following day he started for the Scilly Islands, sailing thither from St Ives in a fishing boat, a distance of fifteen leagues. About half-past one the party landed on St Mary's, and immediately waited upon the governor ' with the usual present, viz. a newspaper '. ' The minister,' writes Wesley, ' not being willing I should preach in the church, I preached at six in the street to almost the whole town. It was a blessed

[1] *West Briton*, 18 September 1930, 28 May 1931.

time, so that I scarce knew how to conclude. After sermon I gave them some little books and hymns, which they were so eager to receive that they were ready to tear both them and me to pieces.' After preaching here again on the next day, Wesley and his companions left 'this barren dreary place', and returned to St Ives in the teeth of a strong gale.

On Friday, 16th September, Wesley preached at St Hilary Downs, and again, in the evening, at St Ives. The latter meeting was subjected to disturbances from a violent mob, and Wesley himself received a blow on the head. On the following day, however, he preached at St Just and at the Land's End. Here also he preached again on the Sunday morning ; and at 1 p.m. at Morvah ; in the afternoon at Zennor ; whilst the day concluded, as on the previous Sunday, with a service at St Ives.

It is wellnigh impossible, at this distance of time, to estimate the full extent of the mental and physical toil involved in such a succession of sermons and meetings, interspersed with long rides over a rough country-side. Often the preachers went practically without food during a great part of the day. 'Brother Nelson,' Wesley exclaimed, as they were riding together on one occasion, ' we ought to be thankful there are plenty of blackberries ; for this is the best country I ever saw for getting a stomach, but the worst that ever I saw for getting food. Do the people think we can *live* by preaching ? '

Such was the life of one to whom, as a writer has said, ' high honour, learned ease, and literary fame were all accessible, but who, contemning these, chose to travel in hunger and weariness over the commons of Cornwall, and then, after the day of unparalleled labours, to sleep on a hard floor '.[1]

As it was, the flame of the new teaching touched the old stagnating religious life of Cornwall, causing it to stir uneasily. Men knew not what to think. Such a staggering change of attitude in persons so far their superior, left the poor undecided, for the moment, whether to scoff or to believe. The clergy in many cases found themselves in much the same predicament. Whilst certain of their number—like the Reverend Thomson of St Gennys, and the Reverend Bennet of Laneast —threw open their churches to the new preachers, many more remained apathetic. Others again, foreseeing the ultimate loss of their authority and prestige if such practices were allowed to continue, entered upon a campaign of deliberate persecution ; using as their dupes the unlettered multitude

[1] *The Cornish Banner*, August 1847, 417–20.

who were ready to be swayed by their authority for want of knowing any better. To this end the press-gangs also served a very useful purpose, by supplementing the civil powers which many of the clergy possessed. The Wesley brothers, being themselves clergymen, were freed from this particular danger ; but their assistant ministers, being in the eyes of the law lay-men, could claim no such exemption, and on more than one occasion they suffered intolerable injustice. Maxfield, one of the best of them, was arrested at Wesley's side, at Crowan, and carried off to Marazion. Here he was condemned to a period of service in the Navy by Dr William Borlase, who combined the offices of a clergyman and a magistrate, and was, in consequence, a notorious persecutor.[1]

A short time after this, when Wesley was preaching at St Just, a constable was sent by order of Doctor Borlase to apprehend one of his chief local supporters, Edward ' Greenfield ' (? Grenfell). ' I asked a little gentleman of the place,' wrote Wesley, ' what objection there was to Edward Greenfield. He said : " Why, the man is well enough in other things, but his impudence the gentlemen cannot bear. Why, sir, he says he knows his sins are for-given ! " ' [2] On the occasion of Wesley's second visit to Cornwall, he found the whole country-side greatly excited over the news of Admiral Mathews's victory over the Spanish fleet. ' The crowd at St Ives,' writes Mr Arthur Smith, ' could think of no more congenial way of giving expression to their joy and thanksgiving than by demolishing all the windows and furniture of the Methodist preaching room. Wesley, whose temper and patience were imperturbable, appreciated the humour of the idea, and even found cause for thankfulness, remarking that if Admiral Lestock had fought as well, the mob would probably have killed all the Metho-dists.' [3] In the following year Wesley recorded in his journal : ' I rode with Mr Shepherd to Gwennap. Here also I found the people in great consternation. Word was brought that a great company of tinners, made drunk on purpose, were coming to do terrible things. I laboured much to compose their minds, but Fear had no ears : so that the abundance of people went away '.[4]

[1] H. Arthur Smith, *Cornish Magazine*, I, 247.
[2] *Journal*, I, 501 (edition 1829).
[3] *Cornish Magazine*, I, 246.
[4] *Journal*, I, 506–7.

Still, in spite of every kind of opposition, much of it achieved by underhand and despicable means, Wesley's personality and pertinacity at length succeeded in overcoming the violent prejudices of the Cornish, and long before the end of his life he had filled them with such enthusiasm that his visits came to resemble triumphal progresses.

In these later visitations the usual preaching ' rooms ' belonging to the society proved quite incapable of accommodating the multitudes who gathered to hear the great missioner. It was Wesley's custom, therefore, to take his stand on some elevation out of doors, such as a rock or low wall, where he might the better be seen and heard by the vast congregations. Several of the rocks on which Wesley thus stood to preach are still remembered by his name, and in at least one instance the stone itself has subsequently had a chapel built about it.

It was on the occasion of one of his visits to Gwennap in the year 1762 that the famous ' pit ', which has since become the Mecca of Cornish Methodism, and where a preaching service has been held every Whit-Monday since its founder's death, was first used by Wesley. The day, as it so chanced, was a windy one, and the crowd being greater than ever, it was obviously a question whether the preacher could possibly make himself heard in an unsheltered situation. Near by, however, were some old mine workings, and among them a deep funnel-shaped hollow, formed by the caving in of the more shallow parts of the excavations below. Into this strange amphitheatre the multitude thronged, the preacher taking his stand on a crag-like eminence which formed a natural pulpit. The experiment at once proved a success, Wesley's voice being heard perfectly in all parts of the pit. At a later date, the original crude hollow was improved by cutting circular terraces of seats in the grassy banks and by smoothing and levelling the surfaces. Altogether Wesley himself preached in Gwennap Pit on some fifteen subsequent occasions. In describing one of these services he wrote : ' I think this is the most magnificent spectacle which is to be seen on this side heaven. And no music is to be heard on earth comparable to the sound of many thousand voices, when they are all harmoniously joined together, singing praises to God and the Lamb '.[1]

In 1781, when he was seventy-eight years of age, he once again referred to his preaching in this spot. ' I believe,' he

[1] *Journal*, IV, 54.

writes, ' between two- and three-and-twenty thousand were present, and I believe God enabled me to speak that even those who stood farthest off could hear distinctly. I think this is my *ne plus ultra*. I shall scarce see a larger congregation till we meet in the air.' [1]

Truly astonishing was the change of attitude which Wesley's preaching had brought about amongst those who had once been ready to drive him from their midst. Nor was the seed of that preaching destined to fall upon shallow soil to flourish only for a day. ' You can scarcely enter a farmhouse or labourer's cottage amongst the hills of Zennor, or the moors of Wendron,' wrote a well-known Cornishman thirty years since, ' or an engine-house amongst the mines of Camborne, without finding among the few books displayed a copy of Wesley's hymns. You can scarcely find a village from the Tamar to the Land's End which is not blessed with a little house of prayer and worship, plain and unpretentious indeed, but the cherished centre of a true devotion. These are the real monuments which commemorate the unequalled labours of the great evangelist. The ancient churches perpetuate the names of many saints, the little chapels all preserve the name of one whose heroic life changed the whole of England, but no part of England so thoroughly and so effectually as the land of Tre, Pol, and Pen.' [2]

The fervent spirit of revivalism produced by the new teaching was vividly described in a letter addressed to the founder of the movement by the famous preacher, Adam Clarke, on 31st January 1785. ' At St Austle,' he writes, ' the Lord has bared His arm in a very eminent manner, especially within these eight or ten days. On Sunday 23rd, after I had preached at Mevagissey and Trewarren, I came here (to St Austell) where I found a vast multitude of people gathered together. The house was so crowded that I had great difficulty to get to the pulpit ; they crowding together for some time, we were obliged to make those within to stand on the seats, and notwithstanding this was done, and every interval filled, scores were obliged to return home who could gain no admission, and numbers waited around the house the whole time. Such a death-like solemnity and profound attention I scarcely ever saw before ; every soul seemed to hear for eternity, and departed without noise or confusion.

[1] See *West Briton*, 28 May 1931.
[2] H. Arthur Smith, *Cornish Magazine*, I, 251.

The next morning I preached at six o'clock, and had nearly two hundred people. The same evening I preached again, and the house was so thronged that the people were again obliged to stand on the seats, and the good Lord did not suffer me to speak in vain, and some both of the high and low were much affected. Next morning I preached at six again, and the congregation was computed to be nearly three hundred, so mightily does the word of God run and prevail. Nor is this amazing work manifest among the poorer and more wretched kind of people only, as at Port Isaac, but several of those who are called " the better sort " are induced to cast in their lot among us, inasmuch that curled, tied, and powdered hair, high heads, etc., which were before idolized, are now detested and abandoned, and the lofty looks are brought down. At Mevagissey there is also a revival. Indeed, there is an increase of hearers almost throughout the whole circuit. The houses will not contain them, so that we have been and are yet obliged to preach out of doors in frost, snow, etc. Was I not confident enough that this is the work of God, I believe I could not go through it. From my present disposition I think I can truly say that all the money on earth could not induce me to bear the bodily distressing exercises which I am now enabled by the grace of God to go through—among the rest that of preaching four times on Sundays, three times often on weekdays, and every morning wheresoever it is practicable. Indeed, I think it not a small miracle that my very weak constitution is able to bear these fatigues—but with God there is nothing impossible.'[1]

This stirring up of the people, in a manner so unorthodox, would never have been possible, or indeed desired by the early Methodist leaders, had the Church been alive throughout to its proper responsibilities. The Cornish people themselves, indeed, had ever been by nature of a fervently religious type, sharing with their brother Celts of Brittany the need for a lively expression of their intrinsic yearning for worship and devotion. It was this which at the Reformation, two hundred years before, had inspired the Celts of Cornwall to fight with such desperate energy for the defence of the ' old religion '. ' We will not receive the new service because it is but like a Christmas game, but we will have our old service of Matins, Mass, Evensong, and Procession as it was before. And we, the Cornish, whereof certain of us understand no

[1] See *The Cornish Banner*, June 1847.

English, do utterly refuse the new service'—so ran the prologue of that boldly worded 'petition' sent up from Cornwall in the reign of Edward VI.[1] Nor was this an empty boast, as those in authority very soon found. For, on the petition being rejected, there arose the great 'Cornish Come motion' of 1549, when the Cornish people, under the leadership of not a few of their gentry, marched up through the country in an army ten thousand strong, and laid siege to Exeter. Here they were only repulsed after a display of such 'valour and stoutness' that, as Lord Grey remarked, 'he never, in all the wars he had been in, did know the like'.[2] Their defeat was the death-knell of the old religion, and incidentally of the Cornish language itself, since, owing to the refusal of the authorities to allow the New Prayer Book to be translated into Cornish, the means whereby the old language has been perpetuated to this day in Wales, was lost to the western Celts for ever.

The latent spiritual fervour of the Cornish people, however, though it thus became robbed of its outward form of expression, lay for nearly two centuries, not dead, but sleeping. During this time the Church itself was sinking into a slow spiritual decay, sufficiently alert, it is true, to claim its dues and privileges, but giving little or nothing in return to the 'hungry sheep' who still looked up but were not fed. In the year 1681, John Hingston of Towednack, gentleman, stated that a child of his, and children of other parishioners, had died unbaptized owing to the neglect and absence of the vicar (who also held the parish of Lelant, with St Ives), and that, 'several persons dyeing within the said parish of Towednack, and having noe Priest to bury them according to the Church of England, one of them was left without buryall, which became noysome untill some other minister came to bury him'. The same witness added that 'since the nonresidency of the vicar in the said viccaredge, very often, when he comes to officiate, he comes very unseasonably, viz. sometymes att seaven of the Clocke in the morning, sometymes att Eleven of the Clock, sometymes att one of the Clock, and sometymes towards the Eveninge, about sun sett. And Imediately on his comeing att Church he begins prayer, although very few of his parishioners are present'.[3]

---

[1] Henry Jenner, *Handbook of the Cornish Language*, 13.
[2] W. H. Tregellas, *Cornish Worthies*, I, 60–1.
[3] J. Hobson Matthews, *History of St Ives*, 265.

So things went on from bad to worse till, at the time when the Wesleys arrived in Cornwall, the prestige and authority of the Church had probably reached its lowest ebb. An official return made in the year 1745 by the incumbents of all the parishes of Devon and Cornwall, in response to a printed list of questions circulated by the bishop, provides indisputable proof of the frequency with which plural livings were held by the clergy at this date. Although in many cases the answer to the irritating question : ' Do you reside in your cure ? If not, why not ? ' was left a blank, or with a note to say that the subscriber would send adequate reasons for his absenteeism in a private letter, the number of replies which *were* received are sufficiently illuminating. Thus we learn that Mr John Tregenna was rector of both Mawgan and Roche. Stithians, Perranarworthal, and St Michael Penkivel were likewise in the hands of one man. The vicar of Kenwyn and of Kea lived at Madron, of which he was also the vicar. The parson of Mevagissey lived at board in the parish, ' being unwilling to encumber himself with the cares of a family '. The rector of St Ewe spent most of his time at his other living at St Hilary. Breage, Germoe, Cury, and Gunwalloe were held by a Doctor Collins who, however, resided at St Erth, of which he was also the vicar. Lelant, Towednack, St Ives, and Zennor were similarly in the hands of one incumbent.[1]

Among those clergy, on the other hand, who held but one living, and were content to reside on the spot, not a few belonged to the rollicking, fox-hunting school, who cared more for good liquor and the excitements of the chase than for either the spiritual or material welfare of the parishioners committed to their charge. A story is told by the Rev. Baring Gould of a certain west-country vicar of this date who was fond of having convivial evenings at his parsonage, evenings which only too often ended uproariously.

' Mr Radford,' said the bishop on one occasion. ' I hear, but I can hardly believe it, that men fight in your house.'

' Lor', my dear,' answered Parson Radford in his broad

---

[1] Returns in the Diocesan Registry at Exeter. Cf. C. G. Henderson, *Western Morning News*, 12 July 1921.

Plural livings were not, of course, confined to Cornwall. In 1810 there were six thousand livings in Great Britain in which the incumbent was non-resident. In 1838 there were still over four thousand non-resident clergy in the country. See J. L. and B. Hammond, *Age of the Chartists*, 220.

west-country speech, ' don't 'ee believe it. When they begin
fighting I take and turn 'em out into the churchyard ! '

It is said that the same parson was just about to mount
his horse and gallop off to the meet one day, when word was
brought to him that the bishop was in the village. He had
barely time to send away his hunter, run upstairs and jump,
red-coated and booted as he was, into bed, when the bishop's
carriage drew up at the door.

' Tell his lordship I 'm ill,' was the vicar's injunction to his
housekeeper.

A few minutes afterwards the woman ran upstairs in sore
dismay and entered the parson's room.

' Please your honour, his lordship says he 's fine and sorry,
and can he come up and sit with you a little ? '

' With me ? Good heavens, no ! ' gasped the vicar,
peeping out from beneath the bedclothes. ' Go down and
tell his lordship I 'm took cruel bad with scarlet fever, say it 's
an aggravated case, and very catching ! ' [1]

Whilst many of the clergy were merely slackers at their
posts, there were others whose conduct unfortunately merited
much stronger censure. The Church at this time, it must be
remembered, was still regarded, like the pocket boroughs,
as a great system of patronage and property. In 1810 Lord
Harrowby, criticizing a suggestion which had been made that
the richer benefices should be taxed in order to supplement
the income of the poorer livings, stated : ' The first objection
to a general tax upon the higher clergy, in which the parochial
clergy were included, was this : about three-fifths of the livings
of this country were in lay patronage, and the advowsons
were a part of the estates of the proprietors, bought and sold
like other estates for a valuable consideration, upon the faith
that they were only subject to taxation in common with other
estates '.[2] Whilst the land-owning classes were thus in a
position to exercise such sovereignty within the Church, it
is not surprising that the younger son or the ' fool of the
family ' should have been frequently slipped into some comfortable preferment through the all-powerful influence of
the patron squire. Of such a type was Parson B——, of
whom it is related that he regularly helped himself from the
Sunday offertories, and not infrequently got drunk upon

[1] *The Vicar of Morwenstow* (i.e. Life of Rev. R. S. Hawker).
[2] *Parliamentary Debates*, House of Lords, 18 June 1810. See J. L.
and B. Hammond, *Age of the Chartists*, 220.

the wine which was intended for the sacrament.[1]   Certain people can still remember the ancient, doddering clerk of this parish, who died at the advanced age of nearly one hundred, and who was said to have been an illegitimate son of the parson, from whose hands he had received the appointment as a young man.

Still, despite such scandals, it had clearly never been the original intention of Wesley or of the other Methodist leaders to encourage their followers to break away from the Mother Church.   John Wesley himself had expressly forbidden his preachers to hold services in church hours unless the incumbent happened to be a ' notoriously wicked man ', or one who preached Arian or some ' equally pernicious doctrine '.[2] Neither did the early Wesleyans consider it their business to teach a new theology, their leader justly claiming in matters of religion to be ' for as few innovations as possible.'   The real purpose which had inspired the movement was, as Mr and Mrs Hammond have so well defined it, ' to bring ardour and purpose into a Church whose teaching had become formal and cold, and whose life and conduct reflected and respected too faithfully the spirit and outlook of the world. They were not rebels against the authority of this indolent and comfortable institution ; they were rebels against the easy-going pagan life of the time, with its neglect of the passionate gospel which the Christian Church came to life to preach.   The Methodists desired to supply the fervour which was lacking.   They were not Nonconformists, but revivalists, and they succeeded in reviving both the Established and the Nonconformist Churches '.[3]

Hence it was that, in the early days, the Methodists frequently proved to be among the most devout attendants at their parish churches.   In the churchyard at Altarnun, a tombstone to the memory of Digory Isbell, who ' died ' in 1795, and of Elizabeth his wife, ' who exchanged earth for heaven ' in 1805 (the distinction was perhaps not an unconscious one !), records the fact that ' they were the first who entertained the Methodist preachers in this county, and lived and died in that connection, but strictly adhered to the duties

[1] An entry in a note-book kept by the sexton of Launceston Church records that on one occasion in 1817 ' the clergyman read to the burial what could not be found from the book, from a state of intoxication '. —*Western Antiquary*, IV, 31.
[2] *Works*, VII, 512.
[3] *Age of the Chartists*, 238.

of the Established Church '. A traveller who visited St Just-in-Penwith in 1797 records the fact that he heard there some of the finest singing ' I ever remember to have heard in any country church. After service, I understood there were sometimes one thousand five hundred people present, it being in the midst of the mine country. What is more extraordinary, these people usually attend the (Methodist) meetings before they come there, and afterwards conclude the day by praying and exhorting each other in their own houses '.[1] Truly the profession of Methodism entailed a rigorous mode of life in those early days when the foundations of that great movement were being laid in the spirit of fervour and devotion. ' On 25th December 1781,' we read in the pages of the *Arminian Magazine*, ' many persons met at Gabriel Thomas's house in St Just Church Town at three in the morning, in order to sing and pray. The power of God fell on them, so that six were in an agony, one of whom fainted ; but two others were soon filled with peace. At seven, they removed to the preaching-house, where the same power was present. They continued in prayer till about nine. They met again in the evening, and stayed till one or two in the morning.'[2] Such was Christmas Day for a devout Methodist in the year 1781.

Ready, however, as the early Methodists appear to have been to continue within the body of the Established Church, it became increasingly clear as time went on that the Church itself was becoming less and less inclined to tolerate the Methodists. Already, in 1745, at a time when the Methodist movement was still in its infancy, the temper of many of the clergy towards the new sect can be judged from the tone of the replies sent in to the bishop in response to his inquiry as to the number of dissenters dwelling within their parishes. Under the heading of St Just, Doctor Borlase, its vicar, wrote : ' We have in our Church Town an unlicensed house appropriated to the Methodists, in which several persons do meet at unseasonable hours '. The reply received from the vicar of St Hilary was even more contemptuous : ' We have only one Methodist, who is an infamous woman of Marazion, fit only to associate with so infamous a sect ! ' At St Ives there were stated to be ' many people called Methodists who frequently assemble at the house of Mr John

---

[1] British Museum, Additional MS. 28793, fol. 52.
[2] *Arminian Magazine*, VII, 211.

Nance, at unseasonable hours '. At Gwennap the vicar wrote : ' A sect called Methodists came among us of late, of which there are forty or fifty that follow them. They have an unlicensed meeting-house, and a succession of teachers that run up and down the country '.[1]

II

In proportion as the teaching of Wesley gained strength and support from among the laity, the opposition of the clergy became more and more marked.   As a consequence, therefore, the division between the two bodies showed a tendency to widen and the Wesleyans were driven increasingly into relying upon their own resources.   Probably one of the secrets of the rapidly developed strength of the new movement in those early years lay in the fact that the latter meant more to the Cornish people even than the awakening of their long-dormant religious life.   Whilst it did this, it also brought into their lives new thoughts and responsibilities, and inspired them with a desire for education and an enlargement of their whole intellectual outlook.   The new sect, in fact, possessed both the disadvantages and the compensatory incentives of poverty.   With few of the churches any longer open to them, meeting places had to be provided and a new ministry established and, in the absence of tithes or endowments, the task of shouldering these responsibilities fell upon the people themselves.   So whilst some were gathering the actual sticks and stones out of which to build the little chapels which sprang up like mushrooms through the country-side ; others, labourers by day or night in the mines and fisheries, set themselves to work with single-hearted devotion to equip themselves for the ministry.   All were not alike successful. Crude enough were many of the little chapels raised by the amateur builders, cruder still the efforts of some of the ' local preachers ' who filled the rostrums therein on Sundays, or at the weekday meetings, and attempted to guide the wor-shippers in prayer and praise.   Among such were many working men of the type of Billy Bray, Dick Hampton, Soli Stone, Joe Smitheram, and a hundred others, whose work is

[1] See C. G. Henderson, *Western Morning News*, 12 July 1921.

written large upon the face of the country-side, and in the hearts of the people, though their names have long been forgotten.

' Aw, ais, the loocals do do very well,' remarked an old Cornishwoman in the early part of the last century, ' but they 're worken all the day an' come night they 're ready to drop ; an' es hard for them to maake up a sarmon. And then Sundays, see what miles they do walk to get to all the by-plaaces, an' then lot of them caan't read wan word in a book, but they 're good men f'r all that. I don't knaw what we should do wethout the " loocals ".' [1]

Many persons still living can remember something of these old-style preachers, and the humour and pathos of those services of bygone days. ' I well recollect,' a lady recently told the writer, ' an old man who used to come to preach in our chapel at home, dressed in corduroy trousers and a high silk hat. He always carried with him a large red-spotted handkerchief, which he used to whip out from his pocket with a peculiar " flink ", apply to his brow and then spread carefully on the ground before " pitching " on it to pray.' [2] Very peculiar were the forms which these extempore prayers sometimes took. In the old and now ruined chapel at Tregarthen, near St Ives, a man was said to have prayed one night : ' O Lord, save all the people in the world, me and my wife, our booy Jan and 'es wife, we four and no moore ' (that being the number of his family). Many of the local preachers were most dramatic once they got into the pulpit. Soli Stone always took off his coat when preaching in warm weather, in order to give his arms more freedom. Unlike the other old preacher, Soli knew not the use of a handker-chief, even if he possessed such an article, and accordingly when at the height of his fervour, and the ' sweat going over him like rain ', would make free use of the back of his hand. ' Now, brethren,' he would exclaim, ' I 'm going tell 'ee this evenin' a bit about heaven—'eaven ! why what do a passel of people from up Troon ' (or wherever it might be) ' knaw about 'eaven ? Howsomedever, let 's ask Abr'am 'bout it, 'ee ben up theere a braa while. Hi theer ! Abr'am ! ' (placing his hands to form a trumpet, and straining earnestly towards the ceiling), ' what soort of plaace is 'eaven ? Tell us a bit about it, can 'ee ? ' ' Glory upon glories, my son,' came the solemn reply. ' Oh that so ; es a ? ' said the preacher

---

[1] Mrs Bonham, *A Corner of Old Cornwall*, 68.
[2] Per Mrs J. Davis, Troon.

continuing the dialogue ; ' why I thoft as much, but these 'eer Troon people wouldn't believe it ! Now, my friends, let 's hear what 'Lijah got to tell us.'[1]   Having by such means gained the interest of his listeners, the preacher would suddenly turn upon them and point the earthly application of his parable with a sober power and simplicity which the opening words might scarcely have led an onlooker to expect. ' Come down, thou great Jehovah, and bring thy stone hammer along weth 'ee and scat (break) the hard hearts of this wicked and perverse people,' the preacher would cry on other occasions, when driven to exasperation by his hearers' seeming apathy. Though many doubtless smiled, they did so not in any derisive spirit, for all knew the earnestness which lay behind this humble form of address. ' I know you, you young men,' Billy Bray, the miner preacher, once exclaimed as he gazed down upon his congregation from the pulpit. ' You kneel down and bow your heads, but all you see before your eyes is " Cock, Hatter " ' (that being the maker's name inside their tall hats) ; ' and you young women too, you put up your hands before your eyes, but all the time you 're geeking (peeping) through your fingers and thinking to yourselves : " Is *he* come ? " '

A writer of Cornish dialect has thus described in his own humorous way the excitement which was caused when some well-known character of this sort was planned to preach at the local chapel. ' Never shall I forget the night when Maister Jan Whitnick came to preach up to Hellesveor. He was a proper man, sure enough, and hes faame was so great that the people came to hear 'un like they would flock to a circus ; although other praichers had often to give sarmons to two men and a boy, the deaf chapel-keeper and the band, for their whole congregation. The night Maister Whitnick came, however, they war packed away like matches in a box, or pelchurds in a mawn (basket), an' hundreds were turned away, mad to think they couldn't get in. Scores of people climbed up 'pon the windowsells outside, and geeked in through the glass, where they could see hes arms going up and down like pump-handles, even ef they cudden hear hes sarmint. He took for hes text the words : " Let your light shine ", and, my dear life, 'ee gov 'un fits, I can tell 'ee. He never had nawthen but a blank sheet of paper afore 'un to whet his memory, and the spontaneroushness of hes remarks was

[1] Per Miss E. B. Vivian, Camborne.

amazin'. He deddun stick to his text all the time, and we had
little bits av botony, 'strology, screpture, teetotalism, politics,
an' poetry—an' 'ee jumped from Land's End to the Cape of
Good Hope quicker 'n a man could blink. The more he
talked, the more the steam arose, and the people rejoiced
and shouted " Amen " and " Hallelujahs ! " till the walls
were fit to crack. Aw, soas, it were more excitin' than Daniel
in the lions' den ; and Maister Whitnick's cheeks wor'
glistening with sweat and gladness. Then he winded up his
sarmint with a string of tremenjous words, and cried with a
quiver'n voice : " Brethren and sistern, lev' us sing that grand
old hymn, *Graace is flowin' like a rever !* " Well, the band
strick up the tune, and though we was cliged (stuck fast)
together like bricks, we joined in and made the plaace ring
weth music. The corneter and the fluter and the baass-violer
went at it fer dear life, and the euphonium man nearly blawed
heself to rags. As fer the candles, they was melting away
with the heat and running down in streams 'pon the people.
At last Maister Whitnick's eye happened to light 'pon Sampey
Curnow, what was playen the baass-viol ; an' he saw that
Sampey was right under wan av they candles from which
the grease was flowin' down 'pon hes shoulder, like melted
butter ovver a piece of conger. As Maister Whitnick spied
this, a beautiful smile stole ovver hes features, and as Sampey
digged away at the baass-viol, the gaat man waved hes hands
and cried : " Brethren, lev' us sing that grand verse ovver
again, *Graace es flowin' like a rever !* " Up went the verse
again, and Maister Whitnick's voice sounded like a cheribim's
as he waved hes hymn book with wan hand and kept hes
eye upon Sampey and the drippin' candle with the other.
" My brethren," he hollered forth, before we had sung the
last words, " it es good to be here ! This es a glorious time !
Lev us sing that verse all ovver once again ! " And as we
again sung, " Graace es flowin' like a rever ", the grease from
the candle came down in a graat white splat upon Sampey's
best West of England broadcloth, and then, of a sudden,
the candle spluttered and went out.' [1]

Amongst many of the less educated ' locals ' the readings
from the Scriptures often presented considerable difficulties
and occasions for stumbling. A dear old man of this type
was one day reciting the story of Shadrach, Meshach, and
Abednego, and the burning, fiery furnace. Each time he

[1] Printed in *St Ives Times*, anonymous.

came to the words 'cornet, flute, harp, sackbut, psaltery, dulcimer', etc., he liked the look of them less, and at last as the words swam before his eyes for the fourth time he looked up suddenly from the book and, gazing down upon the congregation, exclaimed : 'You do knaw which I mean, brethren—band as before !' [1] Such naïve simplicity was, of course, by no means confined to the chapels, and was equalled, if not exceeded in many cases, by the clerks of the parish churches a hundred years ago. At Kenwyn, one Sunday, two dogs, one of which was the parson's, were fighting at the west-end of the church. The parson, who was reading the second lesson at the time, being annoyed at the disturbance, rushed out of the pew, and went down to part them. On returning to his place, and being doubtful of where he had left off, he turned to the clerk and asked : 'Where was I, Roger ?' 'Why, down parting the dogs, maister,' was the unlooked-for reply. 'A very short time since,' wrote Polwhele (*Traditions and Recollections*, 1826), ' parish clerks used to read the first lesson. I once heard the St Agnes clerk cry out : " At the mouth of the burning viery vurnis . . . Shadrac, Meshac, and Abednego, come voath and come hether ". A clerk of St Anthony in Meneage used invariably to read " the *ragging* (for the *raging*) of the sea " ; " Thou shalt break their *bones* (for their *bonds*) " ; and for *dragons—dragoons !* The clerk at Lamorran, in giving out the Psalm, " like a timorous bird to distant mountains fly " always said : " Like a temmersum burde ", etc., with a shake of the head and a quavering voice which could not but provoke risibility. At Mevagissey, when non-resident clergymen officiated, it was usual with the squire of the parish to invite them to dinner. Several years ago a clergyman was requested to do duty at Mevagissey on a Sunday when the creed of St Athanasius is directed to be read. Before he began the service the parish clerk asked him whether he intended to read the Athanasian Creed that morning. " Why ? " said the clergyman. " Because if you do, no dinner for you at thesq uire's at Penwarne ! " '

By most, if not by all, of the village congregations of those days—in church and chapel alike—the Scriptures were interpreted in the most literal sense. ' If thy hand offend thee, cut it off and cast it from thee,' was the text of a sermon delivered on one occasion by a Cornish vicar. ' Ais, that 's

[1] Per Mrs Stanley James.

all right, passon, for you rich folk,' commented an old woman afterwards, ' but I got my living to earn.'

' What do the Screpture mean by " gross darkness " ? ' was the rhetorical question asked on another occasion by a local preacher. ' You don't knaw, my friends, but I can tell 'ee. A gross is one hundred and forty-four, so " gross darkness " do mean a hundred and forty-four times darker than pitch dark ! ' [1]

At other times the familiar hymns and scriptural writings were subjected to individual interpretations, which were still more peculiar. Among the sea-going population of St Ives was an old sailor who was a regular attendant at one of the local chapels where, though he had never learnt to read, his voice always rang out loud in the singing of the hymns. One of these was a particular favourite with him on account of the line : ' And view the landscape o'er ', which the old man always sang as : ' And view the land Cape Horn '— magical words which, no doubt, awakened in his own mind memories quite undreamt of by the more sophisticated members of the congregation standing at his side. In the same town another old sailor on one occasion lay dying, and was visited by the parson, who asked him if there was any particular passage from the Scriptures which he would like to have read. ' Why, ais,' was the reply, ' I should dearly love to hear once more where they do tell about the *Lezard Lights*.' Fortunately the vicar was a man ' quick in the uptake ' and, recollecting the description in Genesis of the ' lesser lights ' that ruled the night, was able to gratify his hearer with the story of their creation. Many other stories could be told to illustrate the prevailing simplicity of those days. A Falmouth man had on one occasion to lose two of his toes by amputation. After the operation had been performed he insisted on having these carefully deposited in the churchyard, giving as his reason : ' I couldn't appear before the dear Lord on the Day of Judgment with no toeses, now could I ? ' In another port, not far distant, dwelt a family of fishermen, one of whom lay dying. Just before the end came one of the brothers standing by the bed stepped forward, and bending over the prostrate form, whispered in his ear : ' Good-bye, Jan, and tell Faather when you do see him that the *Meary Jane* ha' ben lengthened ten feet by the starn. He 'll be glad to knaw '.[2]

[1] Per Mr Jim Thomas. [2] Per Mr Morton Nance.

In both the chapels and churches of those days the congregation, when properly moved, were wont to give encouragement to the preacher by such interjections as : ' Praise the Lord, that 's so ' ; ' God grant it ' ; ' Alleluia ' ; ' Blessed be His name ' ; etc. ' I am the King's son,' fervently exclaimed a ' local ' on one of these occasions. ' So am I ! dear brother, so am I ! ' called forth an old woman encouragingly from the back of the chapel. In some instances, however, the comments were apt to be embarrassing. ' It is now nearly thirty years,' cried a preacher, ' since I became a new man, and from that time to this, the Lord knoweth I lie not, in no point have I offended.'

' Oh, the villain,' came a loud ' aside ' from one of the congregation, ' 'twas but laaste Saturday night I seed 'un as drunk as a pig ! '

On another occasion, in a West Cornwall chapel, the preacher announced the opening of his sermon with the solemn words : ' In my Father's house are many mansions '. Immediately a look of incredulity passed over the faces of the congregation, and on his repeating the text for the second time, flesh and blood could stand it no longer. ' 'Tes nothen' more than a great strammin' lie what thee 'rt telling,' cried out an indignant farmer. ' We do all knaw well enough that your father's house haven't got but three rooms in it—and one of them 's no bigger than a pig's crow (sty).'

Similarly plain-spoken comments were sometimes forthcoming even in the churches. One Sunday morning, the vicar of Manaccan had been reading to his congregation the narrative of St Paul's shipwreck. As he finished an old seaman arose to his feet and crushingly remarked : ' Well, all I can say is, passon, St Paul was a damned bad sailor '.

A story, told in Camborne, describes how at one period the thatched roof of the old chapel at Roseworthy had got into a bad state of repair. The trustees, though anxious about its condition, were divided in their opinion as to what ought to be done ; one party being for a new roof, the other for merely patching up the old one. On a certain Sunday evening the leader of the ' patched roof ' party was ' planned ' to preach, and was in the midst of his sermon when a large piece of the ceiling fell away, striking him on the head. The chance of pointing the moral was too good to be missed, and jumping up from his seat at the other end of the chapel, the leader of the opposition called forth in jubilant tones :

' That 's ob 'un, Loord, scat to 'un, scat to 'un. I knawed all along 'twas Thy will we should have a new roof '.[1]

Like certain of the village priests of the Roman Catholic Church on the Continent to-day, the old-style local preachers of Cornwall, being drawn from among the poorest country folk, had had but few chances in their youth of acquiring the accepted habits of polite society. The story is told how Dick Hampton, the famous ' pilgrim preacher ' of the early part of the last century, was on one occasion taking tea in a lady's elegantly furnished drawing-room. A large company was present, and while Mr. Hampton greatly amused the guests by his peculiar sallies, he was the occasion of considerable perturbation to his hostess. Like Dr Johnson, he was a great tea drinker, and could easily dispose of ten or a dozen cups. To the lady's great distress, however, the preacher, previous to the passing of his cup for replenishing, insisted on throwing the ' grooshens ' (tea leaves) over his shoulder on to the carpet. The lady in an endeavour to prevent the recurrence of this peculiar habit, kept a close watch on her guest's cup, and as she noticed it was becoming empty leant forward and remarked : ' Don't trouble, Mr Hampton, pray don't trouble ; pass me the cup, if you please '. ' Oh,' said Dick, ' 'tis no trouble at all,' and over went the grooshens again on to the floor. When tea was finished a gentleman remarked to Mr Hampton that he ought not to have acted so. At this the preacher was much distressed ; but, as he very properly asked : ' Why didn't she tell me not to thraw they grooshens out ? I thought I was saving her trouble. Why can't people be honest and say what they do mean ? '[2]

What the ' locals ' of this type lacked in fashionable manners they frequently made up for in native shrewdness. Billy Bray, on one occasion, chanced to be paying a call at a house where his visit was clearly not unexpected, but proved, for some reason or other, to be untimely. After sounds of considerable scuffling within, the door was opened by a small and rather embarrassed little girl.

' Oh ! good afternoon, Mr Bray,' she exclaimed. ' Mother would so like to have seen you, but she's just had to go out.'

' H'm, that so, is it ? ' said the preacher, glancing towards the bottom of the half-opened door, ' well all I do say is,

[1] Per Mrs Stanley James.
[2] Sir Richard Tangye, *One and All*, 22.

you tell your mawther she 'd better to take her feet with her next time she go ! '

The gifts and qualifications of the local preachers, of course, varied greatly, and in some instances men who were toiling throughout the week as working miners proved in the chapels on Sundays to be speakers of the highest order. Such men would frequently deliver a lengthy sermon, without notes ; entering upon the most subtle metaphysical problems, and quoting poets and prose writers, ancient and modern, with the ease and assurance of scholars.[1] See such a man at his work underground throughout the week, ragged and half-naked, with the perspiration and slime running down over his face and shoulders, and the contrast between him and the well-dressed preacher of the previous Sunday was indeed a striking one.

How such men contrived to gain their education amidst the ceaseless round of toil in which they were engaged, can only be understood by those who have traced their apprenticeship in the biographical sketches which in a few cases record the details of their lives. In a little volume of this sort, entitled *The Miner of Perranzabuloe*, William Murrish, a typical local preacher of his day, has told the story of his life as it was passed in the village of Cocks, near Perranporth, between the years 1818–61. Brought up in a small cottage, on the precarious earnings of a father who worked as a tributer in the adjoining mines, he acquired his alphabet at one of the Church schools, and was already able, through his mother's teaching, to read the Bible by the age of six. Of other books the cottage possessed but few—' an old geography without any covers, two volumes of the *Methodist Magazine* (one for 1804, containing the history of the Irish rebellion), these, with the Bible and a hymn book, constituted our whole library ', he wrote. ' After a while, however, my eldest brother James began to take up the *Youth's Instructor*, and being passionately fond of reading began to get into books in various ways. We took up the *Child's Magazine* and the *Child's Companion*, and at a later date were presented by one of the preachers with Wesley's Hymns

[1] On the occasion of a visit to St Agnes in 1757, Wesley himself listened to a sermon delivered by a working man, who must have been among the earliest of the local preachers of that circuit. ' I could scarce have believed if I had not heard it,' wrote Wesley, ' that few men of learning write so correctly as an uneducated tinner speaks extempore.' See *West Briton*, 6 December 1928.

and the *Life of Mr Silas Todd*. We could all sing, and frequently in the evening struck up a tune. James sang bass, Martin the air, my sisters Nancy and Sally first and second treble, whilst father and mother, who had both been church singers in their day, would also join.' The father, however, being taken with a fatal seizure when on his way homeward one day from Summercourt fair, 'where he had sold a cow and bought a pony', the boy was driven at an early age to work underground. Notwithstanding this, William Murrish continued his studies, in season and out. 'In the summer of 1840,' he writes, 'my cousin, W. Kernick, and myself, for the sake of improvement, agreed to write letters to each other. I wrote first and mentioned music, teetotalism, etc. as subjects which had occupied my thoughts.' In this way ideas were developed, and the habit of expressing them was formed, and soon afterwards the subject of the memoir became 'planned' as a local preacher. The years which followed were strenuous ones, divided between days and nights of labour at the mine and the self-imposed task of preaching and leading prayer meetings in the surrounding village chapels. The end of the story is a sad one. Stricken by the dread 'miner's complaint', brought on by over-exertion and work in close, unventilated places underground, strength and vitality began to fail. Harder to bear than the poverty which ensued from the enforced abandonment of his work, was the realization that his active life at the chapel was over. Cut off from this never-failing source of comfort and refreshment, his last days were spent in cultivating those gifts of patient endurance which showed, perhaps better than anything in the period of his ministry, the stuff of which such men were made.

Outlying places in the early days could only be visited by a 'rounder', or regular minister, perhaps once in three months. On the other Sundays the congregation were entirely dependent on such locals, and when the supply of these failed, they had to have resource to a simple 'prayer meeting'. 'Aw! they rounders do knaw lot 'bout the Bible, 'cause see, they get good schoolen', and can say lots of verses off quite pat, and don't stop for a word,' remarked an old woman on one occasion. 'I wish they cud come to our village oftener than they do, awnly they alles praich too shart to please me.' [1] Such indeed was the attraction of a good preacher to Cornish

[1] Mrs Bonham, *A Corner of Old Cornwall*.

people of the past that fishermen from St Ives would think little of walking to Redruth and back on a Sunday—fifteen miles each way—in order to hear some special sermon, feeling no weariness on the homeward road, so engrossed would they be in discussing the matter which they had heard expounded.

In 1819 Adam Clarke visited Cornwall once again on one of the last of his famous preaching missions. Everywhere he went immense crowds gathered to hear the words of one who had been the friend of Wesley himself, and who was now among the few remaining pioneers of the movement's early days. Amongst other places he visited St Austell where, thirty-five years before, he had done so much towards establishing the cause. Here a memorable adventure befell him which, but for a miracle of Providence, might well have brought his career as a preacher to an untimely end. ' They had just been enlarging the chapel,' he writes, ' building a new end and a gallery to it. When I was about to take my text, the gallery gave way ; the timber fairly came out of the walls, yet it did not fall down, but the confusion was awful. I was close to the gallery, and distinctly saw the peril. Had it come down I knew I must have been the first victim ; but at least two hundred others would also have been killed. I stood in my place ; for had I moved universal terror would have taken place, and many must have fallen victims to an impetuous rush out. The chapel was soon nearly emptied, and no one was hurt. Many came back again, and I preached ; but I knew not till the end of the service all the miracle it required to save us ! Then it was found that owing to the pressure in the gallery, the timbers, being too short, had started out from the walls two feet ; and the gallery actually shook to its centre, having nothing but its pillars to support it. Our son John, being beneath, could see this plainer than I could at the time ; and he saw also that if it fell he must be killed if he kept his place, which was immediately before the pulpit. He knew, however, that his father must be the first victim, and resolutely kept his situation, expecting eternity every moment. But enough of this, it makes one's blood run chill. This is the last crowd I ever wish to see.' [1]

In some of the smaller villages, in the early days, services were frequently held in barns which were lighted only by a few

[1] *The Cornish Banner*, 389–91.

tallow candles placed along the walls, whilst the congregation sat about on heaps of straw or corn sacks, and the preacher stood on the end of a barrel. Not infrequently a few larkish youngsters would suddenly blow out all the lights in the middle of a sermon, and then begin a violent romp amidst the congregation. By the time someone had run out and borrowed a tinderbox and struck a light again, a quarter of an hour or more had often elapsed before the service could proceed. As a consequence of one of these unseemly disturbances which took place in the Methodist chapel at Penryn in 1802, a warrant was issued for the apprehension of the young 'rioters'. One of them, so we read, absconded, another was suffered to compromise for fifteen minutes' exhibition in the stocks.[1]

The music in such chapels often presented considerable difficulties. In many cases the congregation were wont to rely solely on some leader to raise or 'pitch' the tune, which he frequently did with the aid of a penny whistle. As only a sprinkling of those present possessed either hymn books or the ability to read them, two lines of each verse would be given out at a time and were repeated by the singers. If the usual leader, however, chanced to be absent through any cause, great confusion was apt to arise. Some of the congregation would start to sing the hymn in 'common' metre; others in 'long', no one realizing the mistake till they got to the end of the second line, when they had to stop to have the next two read out. ' 'A don't come in 'xactly, do 'a?' one of the congregation would sheepishly remark, 'but theer, never mind, we can all'us double 'un arver a bit when the words wean't hold out.'[2] In many cases, however, even the small villages were able to boast a band, a feeling for music being among the many latent talents which the new communal life of the chapels had evoked. 'My father's first attempt as a musician,' wrote Mr J. C. Hoare in reference to Cornish village life about ninety years ago, 'was made by climbing through the window of the Wesleyan chapel and practising on the bass viol which one of the players sometimes left there from Sunday to Sunday. The result of this was that in a very short time he was able to accompany the service. He was also expert in the fiddle and flute, playing either of these two in church. The psalms in metre were the only songs

[1] *Cornwall Gazette*, 6 February 1802.
[2] Mrs Bonham, *A Corner of Old Cornwall*.

of praise then sung, except for an occasional anthem. About 1862, however, a " seraphine " (harmonium) was installed in place of the instruments.' [1] This was, no doubt, thought a vast improvement at the time ; but, in effect, it might well seem that the changes wrought by its introduction and that of the more recent organ have tended to impoverish the musical life of the average modern chapel.

III

The teaching of John Wesley had gained its hold by supplying opportunities for religious expression which the hearts of the Cornish people had lacked for two hundred years. With the stirring up of the new preaching, all the wild emotional enthusiasm of their forefathers awoke again. This time, it is true, there was no pageantry to catch the eye, no gaily decked images or processions, no interweaving of saintly fairy tales to inspire the daily round and common task. Outwardly these forms were absent, but the old innate desires were still there, and in the barns and bleak little chapels of the new Methodism, the blood of the Lamb, the fires of Hell which go not out, and the wealth and glory of the New Jerusalem still flashed upon the inward eye, causing those wild scenes of fervour which only those who have witnessed ' revivalism ' amidst a passionate Celtic people can well understand. As a writer has said, however, whilst the ' new evangel ' brought hope, peace, and joy to the believer, it cast a dense shadow on the minds of the ' unsaved ' ; for the terrible doctrine of eternal punishment in a material fire was persistently enforced upon the imagination of the people. Even children were once taught to sing :

> There is a dreadful hell
>   And everlasting pains,
> Where sinners must with devils dwell
>   In darkness, fire, and chains.

A catechism ' for the use of children below seven years of age ' taught the doctrine that ' hell is a dark and bottomless pit, full of fire and brimstone, where the bodies of the wicked will

[1] *Reminiscences* (MS).

be tormented with fire for ever, and their souls by the wrath of God '. Nor was such teaching solely confined to the less educated ' local ' preachers. The *Wesleyan Magazine* itself, of eighty years ago, quotes such awful lines as :

Prayers are then idle, death is woo'd in vain—
In midst of death poor wretches long to die ;
Night without day or rest, still doubling pain ;
Woes spending still, yet still their end less nigh ;
The soul there restless, helpless, hopeless lies ;
The body frying roars and roaring fries :
There 's life that never lives, there 's death that never dies.

As may well be imagined, such a doctrine, when expounded by a preacher of active imagination and capable of clothing his ideas in vivid language, created the utmost terror in the minds of the poor, struggling, uneducated people, adding intense mental suffering to their many physical woes. ' Under the influence of such sermons,' wrote an eye-witness, ' people would not infrequently rush to the penitent pew, and in piteous tones plead aloud to be saved from the wrath to come, whilst the elders and members of the church shouted for joy. The din of voices at such times was deafening. Commingled with the cries of the penitents, young and old, for mercy, and the elders' jubilant shouts of " Alleluia ! ", " Praise the Lord ! " and " Glory be to God ! " were the stentorian tones of warning of the preacher and the sobs of many members of the congregation. I have seen women leap off the ground and clap their hands for joy at seeing an " erring " (i.e. unconverted) husband or son approach the penitent pew, and have known strong, middle-aged men swoon in consequence of the high pitch to which their feelings have been wrought.' [1] Such revivals were at one time of frequent occurrence, and on some occasions were prolonged to inordinate lengths. Billy Bray thus describes a great open-air meeting, at which he was called upon to preach to three thousand people : ' After I had announced my text, a mighty power of the spirit of God came upon the people, and many began to cry aloud for mercy. It was soon quite impossible to go on preaching, so I gave out a hymn and went amongst " the slain of the Lord ". The men and women in distress were led into the schoolroom. As one and another found peace we asked them to go out and let others come in. In this way I went on

[1] F. E. A., *Cornish Magazine*, II, 224–5.

until ten o'clock. It will scarcely be credited, but that meeting was prolonged without intermission day or night for eight days after it began '.[1]

Revivals formerly did much to enliven the tedium of everyday life in the remote villages. The sight of the converts jumping over seats and singing and shouting at the tops of their voices in their new-found joy, provided rich food for gossip if it did nothing else. Even the scoffer found pleasure in the spectacle of one of his neighbours crying unto the Lord ' to curtail the works of the devil ', whilst another ' brother ', in his determination to go one better, was beseeching the Almighty ' to cut his tail right off ! ' A story is told how one night in a chapel near Camborne a hulking great miner, who had been roused to the highest pitch of excitement by the power of the preacher, jumped up suddenly, and leaning with all his weight on the pew in front of him, shouted wildly : ' I tell 'ee, friends, I will be saaved to-night—if I do break my bloody neck '. Hardly were the words out of his mouth when the pew on which he was leaning suddenly collapsed under his weight, precipitating the penitent head foremost on to the floor, whence he was carried out unconscious, as one dead. Needless to say, the sensation caused by this incident was immense, everyone taking it as a direct intimation that his prayer had been heard ; though whether in a favourable sense or otherwise it would appear hard to say. Stories, of course, are often told of men of this sort who regularly got converted whenever a revival broke out, and forgot their vows with equal regularity when once the storm of religious fervour had died down again. Clearly, however, the converts made by revivals were not all hypocrites. As an old writer on the subject has well said : ' It is not easy to be a hypocrite in a country place, where every man's actions are open to observation, and the smallest matters of his life are well known. The effects of Methodism in making the drunkard sober, the idle industrious, the profligate moral, in inducing men to provide decently and comfortably for their families, can be attested by thousands of witnesses. Is it not fair to judge of a tree by its fruits ? '[2] For the credit of Methodism no less than of Cornish character, it should never be forgotten that there were many sinners converted in these seasons of revival who became subsequently the very salt of the earth.

[1] Rev. Mark Guy Pearse, *The Ship Where Christ was Captain.*
[2] *Letters from West Cornwall* (1826).

Humble in spirit, as in circumstances, their lives of patient
endurance and self-sacrifice passed unknown and unrecorded ;
but they were the lives none the less of saints—faithful, within
the limits of their understanding, to the example of Wesley
and of that Master to whose service *his* life had been one
long devotion. As another writer has recently stated :
' Volumes might be written about revivals. The real thing
was awesome. I say " real thing " advisedly, because I think
that latterly they have been more or less " worked up ", but
there was no doubt about the spontaneity of those of say even
forty years ago. They got such a hold on the people that
men and women talked of nothing else—in the streets, underground, in the boats at sea—conversation ever returned to the
same subject. We might well ask where all this emotionalism
has gone, and whether perhaps the twentieth century might
not still be the better for a small dose of it ? ' [1]

IV

Whilst the revivals provided one form of outlet for emotions
which in pre-Reformation days had found their expression
in the ritualistic pageantry of the Church, the love of feasting,
and processions became manifested in the all-important
' buryin's ' which still retain such a hold in chapel-going
Cornwall. The extraordinary predilection of the Cornish
people for funerals was admirably expressed by the old lady
who remarked : ' Ais, I do dearly love a good funeral, and I
do go to all that I can. And what I say is this. If you do go
to other folk's funerals, they 'll come to your'n ' (!). Such a
sentiment would have found response in the hearts of many
of the older generation of Cornish people, to whom the
thought of impending death was never far absent. In many
households, indeed, in Cornwall, as in Scotland, it was a
general custom to keep a shroud, a white cap, and a pair of
white stockings always in readiness, in order that the last
journey, when the time for it came, might be made with fitting
decency. There is no doubt that the pomp and ceremony
of the great funerals which were indulged in by the gentry of
former times, set a standard which their poorer neighbours

[1] Per Mrs Stanley James.

have ever since looked up to as the ideal of what a ' burying ' might be. ' Man,' wrote Sir Thomas Browne, ' is a noble animal, splendid in ashes and pompous in the grave,' and whilst fireside stories still recalled those great funerals of t e past, when a Godolphin or a Basset, dying in London, had been brought home in state amidst a splendour as impressive to the eye as it was devastating to the purse, the Cornish people were not lacking in inspiration for their own humbler attempts at honouring their dead. Nor had the magnificence of such funerals declined, amongst those who could afford them, even within the last century, as may be gathered from accounts of the obsequies of Sir John St Aubyn, who died in London in 1839. On 17th August of that year, we learn from the columns of the *West Briton*, the procession attending the corpse left Putney in the following order :

1 Porter	Undertaker on Horseback	1 Porter
1 Porter	Two Mutes on Horseback	1 Porter
1 Porter	Board of Feathers	1 Porter
	Hearse drawn by six Horses dressed with	
6 Porters	Feathers and Velvet	6 Porters
	Seven Mourning Coaches with Four	
Porters	Horses dressed with Feathers and Velvet	Porters
	Sir John's Private Carriage	
C o a c h m e n and Footmen in Black Silk Hat Bands and Gloves	Gentlemen's Carriages 12 in number	All the Porters with Wands and Black Silk Hat Bands and Gloves

On leaving the town the procession was, of course, considerably reduced in order to facilitate a speedier progress, but notwithstanding this it did not reach Devonport until the 23rd. Here the remains were attended by the Mayor and Council, and other dignitaries of the town ; the Board of Commissioners, the Borough Police, the boys of St John's School (of which the baronet had been a patron); the girls of St John's School; the Town Sergeant (with the mace of the Corporation covered with crape) ; four clergymen ; two beadles, and numerous attendants on horseback, not to mention the private carriages of mourners from the locality. All along the route taken by the procession from Stonehouse Bridge to Torpoint Ferry, the shops were closed, and the tolling bells of the neighbouring churches and chapels proclaimed to the 30,000 or more people who had assembled in the streets that a great man was passing to his grave. On Monday the 26th the cavalcade at length arrived at Clowance, the family seat of the St Aubyns, where on Wednesday the 28th the body lay all day in state under a canopy of black cloth, with plumes and feathers. Here it was attended by twelve boys from the Free School, in crape scarfs ; eight poor men in cloaks, standing bareheaded ; eight male servants in crape bands ; twelve girls from the Free School, in crape sashes and bows ; seven female servants in hoods and scarfs ; twelve poor widows in hoods and scarfs ; and two mutes. On the following day the people from the neighbouring towns began to assemble at Clowance at an early hour. The gates of the park were thrown open, and every one who obtained admission to the house was treated with refreshments. Before the hour arrived at which the funeral was timed to start, a double line of spectators, 20,000 or 30,000 in number, had formed up along the road between the house and Crowan Church. Through the midst of this assembled multitude the procession made its solemn way. First came the master of the Free School, followed by a hundred boys, and the mistress of the same with fifty girls, all appropriately dressed for the occasion in the complimentary mourning provided by the family. Following these walked a hundred members of the Order of Freemasons, bearing their banner, Sword of State, a Bible on a black cushion, with the vacant jewel, etc. Then came a hundred tenants wearing silk hat-bands and gloves, an undertaker, two mutes, and thirty poor widows, the latter in black gowns, hoods, and scarfs. Before the body, which rested on a car, ' impelled by tenantry ', walked the officiating clergyman and two leading mourners, whilst behind it in their respective order came thirty relatives, a hundred clergy and gentlemen, twenty-five servants and, finally, a hundred and fifty more tenants in hat-bands and gloves. Throughout the whole of the proceedings, we learn, ' the greatest decorum was preserved, nor was there the slightest movement calcu-lated to disturb the procession on the part of the immense throng '. [1] Only when the ' melancholy ceremony ' was over, and the procession had returned once more to the house and dispersed, might scenes of a more lively, but possibly less decorous nature have been witnessed among those who, not having been worthy to partake of the ' baked meats '

[1] *West Briton*, 6 September 1839.

provided at the family's expense, no doubt celebrated the evening of this great day at their own particular ' port of call '.

Doubtless there were certain aged people, even then, who reflected sadly that such funerals were not what they once had been. Among them were probably some who could recall the death of another great landowner of this district, and tell how the coffin, made from copper obtained in his own mines, had, on the night preceding the funeral, been filled with the strongest rum wherewith his workpeople had ' waked ' the deceased until the dawning of the day, whilst the body lay in state, alongside.[1]

Whilst the poor could never hope to emulate such scenes as these, the two prime essentials of a ' proper ' funeral— the procession and the feasting—continued to characterize the Cornishman's ideal of a burying down to a generation ago. Indeed, the slow walking procession is hardly yet a thing of the past in some country places. Whenever feasible, funerals were arranged to take place on a Sunday afternoon, when the greatest possible number could attend to show their respect and also to assist the principal mourners in th consumption of the food and drink which was regularly provided for these occasions. The thought of how well attended his funeral would be must have brought consolation to many a Cornishman when on his deathbed. Old people in the Camborne mining district were formerly wont to recall with pride how the funeral of a certain ' Cap'n Tom Nicholls ' of their parish had been noted as ' the biggest ever seen in Cornwall '. A certain brother mine captain, who was not by any means a favourite with the men, happened to remark to a friend on this occasion : ' I don't suppose when I die I shall ever have such crowds as this to my funeral '.

' Iss, you would,' exclaimed a miner, who was standing at his side, ' and more besides—ef they thoft they was going to get rid of thee and have Cap'n Tom back again ! '[2]

In the height of the mining prosperity of those days, when vast numbers of men were employed in their dangerous calling underground, funerals of this sort were apt to occur with distressing frequency. A slip on the ladders, a slight movement of the rock, a ' stull ' (timber prop) giving way, or a premature

[1] F. J. Stephens, Trans. *Royal Geological Society of Cornwall*, XV, Pt. IV (1919), 287.
[2] Per Mr Tom Miners, Penponds.

explosion when blasting—any of these disasters might result in some poor woman being suddenly made a widow, and left with the responsibility of bringing up a family of small children.   Little could the poor do at such times, save to show their sympathy by attendance at the funeral.   Preceding the coffin on these occasions went a long double row of singers, usually headed by an elder of the chapel, who read out the hymn, two lines at a time, in loud and solemn tones. Favourite among funeral hymns was the one beginning :

> *Ah, lovely appearance of death !*
> *What sight upon earth is so fair ?*
> *Not all the gay pagans that breathe*
> *Can with a dead body compare !*

' Buryin' ' tunes of this sort were usually sung in a minor key, and in very slow time, the dolorous tones of the singers, mingled with the cries of the mourners, lending a most melancholy air to the whole proceeding.   Behind the coffin came the invited mourners, often fifty or more in number, walking in couples, each man ' leading ' a female at his side. In this matter the strictest etiquette was always observed, and great care had to be taken by the master of the ceremonies to see that no mistake occurred with regard to the placing of the next of kin.   For it was considered an unpardonable slight if any one was assigned a place farther back in the procession than by right of relationship he or she ought to have been, and the most unseemly wrangling sometimes took place on the question as to who was entitled to the honour of walking ' next the corpse '.[1]   After the funeral was over, the whole party proceeded either back to the house or to some neighbouring inn, where the generous nature of the entertainment provided left no doubt as to one of the reasons for the general popularity of funerals in Cornwall.   Cold beer sweetened with sugar, ' poker ' beer slightly mulled, ' shenagrum ', and other drinks were consumed at such times in vast quantities, so much so that, as an old publican once remarked : ' A decent burren' es so good as a feer '.

Whilst the principal mourners were regaling themselves in a room apart, many others contrived to be present in the mixed assembly of lesser mourners outside.   It is to be feared that few of these thought much of the solemnity of the

[1] See Charles Bath, *Uncle Kit's Legacy*, 66–8.

occasion, so long as they got a fair share (and more, if possible) of the victuals and drink which were provided. Zennor people, who, owing to the poverty of their parish, were supposed never to have enough to eat at home, were especially noted for their attendance at funerals. ' Hi, you, do 'ee happen to have a pipeful of the 'bacca you brought away from the last burran' you went to away over to Gulval,' was the kind of banter to which the men of this parish used to be subjected, ' and ded 'ee fill your pockets with biskey to carr' home to the childern ? And how often ded 'ee change your place among the ring of people out in the town-plat (farm-yard), that you might drink twice or three times to every other body's once, when the toddy (grog) was being carried round ? No, you dedn't help the poor people to carry the corpse over the hills to church-town, ded 'ee, after you had busted youself on toddy and cake, and stuffed a few ounces of shag in the palm of your hand instead of the bowl of your pipe, and pocketed pipe and all ! Any one could hear 'ee for miles away, coman' home so jolly, singan', Here's a health to the baarley mow" to the tune of the Old Hundred, more like you had been to a weddin' than a funeral.' [1] If they had been given a chance to excuse themselves, the Zennor folk would have explained that their reputation as singers was sufficient to make them welcome at *any* assemblage where good voices were required, no matter whether it might be at a ' curl ' (carol) singing, a wedding, or a funeral, and that their constant attendance at the latter was in no way connected with the incidental ' baked meats ' ! If this was true, they had their rivals in the inhabitants of another village, east of Hayle, as the still oft-quoted saying : ' Like a High Lanes choir at a funeral ', clearly shows.

Many ludicrous incidents are related of the funerals which were attended by mourners of this sort. Many years ago now, a man who went by the nickname of ' Brother ' died at Rosevin in Sancreed. Amongst those who were present at the funeral was a quaint old tailor, Lewis Grenfell by name, a local 'character', and eccentric. In the absence of any more desirable person, the latter was asked to announce a hymn with which to start the procession. Nothing loath, old Grenfell promptly raised his hand to secure attention and then, whether as a makeshift to cover his woeful ignorance of hymns,

[1] William Bottrell, *Traditions and Hearthside Stories of West Cornwall* 1870), 83–4.

(See page 168) INTERIOR OF ST BREWARD CHURCH
(after Rowlandson)

(See page 178) ROSEWORTHY CHAPEL

WALKING FUNERAL AT MORWENSTOW

(See page 190)

or out of sheer devilry it is not known, gave out in solemn tones :

> *Poor ' Brother ' is dead and gone*
> *And no better is left behind him,*
> *We 'll carry him off and bury him up*
> *Where the Devil shall never find him !* [1]

V

What, in the meantime, has been the attitude of the Church towards Nonconformity since those early years when Methodism first began to exercise a dominating influence over the lives of the Cornish people ? ' On the whole,' wrote the superintendent of the Cornwall Wesleyan Circuit on a recent occasion, ' I think the relationship between the Anglican and Methodist Churches may be said to have been very creditable to both.' Granted the general truth of this statement, it is perhaps only fair to add that the chief credit for this should be assigned to the Dissenters. For despite the importance of the position occupied by Nonconformity, the Church continued throughout to possess all the privileges and prerogatives which it had enjoyed from of old. Many of the clergy, it is true, had been broadminded enough to resign themselves with good grace to the dwindling congregations, and the loss of prestige which the Church was fated to experience, but they still had the satisfaction of knowing that every farmer in their parish was paying tithes for the upkeep of the institution which they represented, irrespective of whether he might ever choose to attend its services or not. There can be no doubt that such a state of affairs must at times have been galling in the extreme to the devout Methodist, who realized that this tax upon his resources was virtually robbing the chapel, in which his whole spiritual life was centred, of the support which he would have wished to give it. The Cornish people, indeed, must have possessed a more than human degree of forbearance if they had never shown their resentment at such a patently anomalous position.

Nor was the Church content in the past always to exact

[1] Per Mr Henry Thomas, St Just.

its legal dues in the most propitious manner. In the 'hungry forties' of the last century it was still a common sight to see notices posted in the mining areas ordering the inhabitants to attend at a specified time and place 'in their best clothes' in order to pay the Church rates. 'Church rates?' wrote an old Camborne resident who well remembered those days of bitter poverty; 'why ninety-nine out of every hundred of those men were Dissenters. Best clothes? Why the poor fellows had only got what they stood up in, apart from their underground rags. When their clothes got wet through, which they did often enough, they had to stay in bed till their wives dried them. They never tasted meat from one week's end to another, and often enough they sat in the dark of an evening because they couldn't afford candles. I've known a tributer[1] work for a whole month for practically nothing at all, in order to do another fellow out of his job, and you couldn't blame him, either, for he was next to starving! Was ever a mockery more bitter than to ask such men for Church rates, and then to tell them to come in their " best clothes " to pay them?'[2]

True, in some parishes the tone of such demands was softened, and a dinner was provided for the tithe payers, which at any rate ensured the pill being administered on a full stomach. Such dinners were generally served in the church school, which meant a holiday for the children who, whatever their parents thought of it, looked forward to the tithe-paying days with genuine pleasure. The fare provided usually consisted of hot roast beef or boiled joints of beef and mutton, plain suet pudding and potatoes, followed by plum pudding. Beer, followed by a glass of gin, was provided to wash down this solid food; whilst a rummer of brandy-grog was served out towards the end, in order to nerve the victims whilst the tithe was actually being paid. 'The tables at Ladock,' writes Mr Hoare, 'used to be laid for about sixty-five people, including four or five women. This system of paying tithes came to an end here in 1890.'[3]

In the days when tithes were still paid in kind considerable ingenuity used to be exercised in giving the parson as poor value as possible, consistent with the letter of the law. Thus out of a litter of pigs, it was always the dwarfed shrivelled

---

[1] Miner working for a percentage of the value of ore he sends to surface.
[2] Per Miss B. E. Paull.
[3] *Reminiscences* (MS.)

little ' veer ' or ' piggy-widden ' which found its way to the clergyman's table for, as an old rebellious couplet boasted :

We 've cheated the Passon—we 'll cheat him again !
For why should we give him the one in ten ?

Tithes in kind formerly included not only the tenth calf, pig, goose, turkey, and other live stock reared on the farm, but also a similar levy on all the ' white sowl ', i.e. butter and milk ; and on the hemp, honey, hay, beans, and other produce of the farmer's labour.[1] In many of the seaports the Church likewise claimed the tithe of fish, and that not only of the catches taken off the Cornish coast, but even of the produce of the Irish herring fishery,[2] to which the hardy Cornishmen formerly sailed in their open boats, a hundred leagues, in order to gain a humble pittance for the support of their families during the slack seasons of the home industry. Payments in kind, however, sometimes led to disputes of a highly unbecoming nature between the clergy and their parishioners. An entry made by a former vicar on the fly-leaf of one of the register-books of Zennor parish, records the fact that ' on Sunday 27th June 1762, a number of parishioners brought Butter and Cheese into the Chancel in the Time of Divine Service, imagining that it would be accepted instead of their Tithes for Cows and Calves ; but not being taken away, either by them or any one else, before it grew offensive, I ordered the Church Wardens, under pain of being cited to the Spiritual Court to remove the same as an Indecency and a Nusance to the congregation. I here insert this, lest my successor should be imposed upon by being told that I accepted of that or any other Butter and Cheese instead of Tithes of Cows and Calves, which I assure him I did not. As Witness my hand this 21st day of July 1762

' Jacob Bullock, Vicar '.[3]

Nor did the clergy of a later date show any tendency to relax the strictness of their demands, as is shown by an interesting story related in the recently published *Memoir* of the Rev. Cornelius Cardew. About the year 1800 this well-known clergyman, who was at one time headmaster of the famous Truro Grammar School, found himself possessed of the two comfortable livings of St Erme and Lelant, the

[1] J. Hobson Matthews, *History of St Ives*, 263.
[2] *Ibid.*, 339.
[3] See *ibid.*, 269.

former worth about £400 a year, the latter £200. Shortly after his appointment, however, the living at Lelant was raised to £350, and then the trouble began. On 30th December 1802, the Lelanters tendered the usual £200, but this was refused, and consequently nothing was paid either in that year or the next. A suit in the Court of Exchequer having failed, after costing the doctor the sum of £314, and the collectors at Lelant still refusing to pay the arrears, 'it had evidently become high time', writes his biographer, 'for the doctor to take some action'. In October 1805, therefore, having settled up his affairs in Truro, he rode off to St Ives, which was at that time a dependant of Lelant,[1] and the chief seat of the trouble. On his arrival he found Mr Halse, who was the ringleader of the opposition, ready to give battle. On the following Sunday, 6th October, the doctor proceeded to address a portion of the parishioners in the church, whilst Mr Halse harangued the remainder in the churchyard. Shortly after this a meeting was held in the Town Hall, at which Halse was appointed sole collector of tithes for St Ives. Disorderly conduct followed. On arriving in church the next Sunday, Doctor Cardew found another clergyman, named Morgan, who lived in the town, already in possession of the desk from which the doctor himself had intended to conduct the service. That night the doctor's windows were broken, and various other attempts were made to intimidate him. Eventually, however, the doctor triumphed in his cause, the arrears were paid, and by the year 1811 he was able to write : ' In asserting what I deemed to be my just rights, I have received many losses, mortifications and indignities from men of selfish and wicked dispositions, and from others who owed me far different conduct. May God forgive them, as I do from my heart '.

Happily, however, as time went on, the relationship between church and chapel grew less strained, and disputes of this kind became of rare occurrence. Until comparatively recent years an amicable compromise may be said to have existed between the Church and the Dissenters in the majority of Cornish towns and villages, and though few church people perhaps ever attended the chapel services, the more broad-minded Nonconformists frequently attended those of the church. The inter-sectarian life of a town like Camborne, for instance, some forty years ago, was typical of this. ' At that date,'

[1] St Ives was constituted a separate benefice in 1826.

writes Mrs James, 'Whitsuntide and the parish feast were the two outstanding festivals of the year; for the latter, although commemorative of the Patron Saint of the Church of England, was kept, and kept well, by both chapel and church alike. All relatives and friends tried to get home for Feast Sunday, and broth, boiled beef and roast suet pudding was the menu of the day. On Feast Monday the church held a great social gathering which started with a tea and ended with an entertainment. This was well patronised by both church- and chapel-goers, hundreds always being turned away, having failed to gain admittance. On Whit-Sunday, the children of the Wesleyan Sunday Schools, numbering nearly two thousand in those days, had their own service in the afternoon and on Whit-Monday *all the schools of every sect* walked in procession through the town headed by bands, each scholar carrying his or her own mug. Arrived at their various fields outside the town, tea and a huge saffron bun was provided for each child, whilst the adults enjoyed a more substantial sit-down meal at tables. This was followed by games such as "Twos and Threes", "Thread the Needle", "Tug of War", "Coils", etc., till about 9 o'clock, when every one went home tired but happy.'

The attitude of chapel people in those days towards the Church was briefly but fairly summed up in the words of an old lady who remarked: 'Ais, we do all have to come it, first and last, though I do say for christenings, marryings and berrins' we must go to church, but for praichin' and anything for the next world give me the chapel'.

Despite the loss of a large part of its spiritual authority, the Church had all along continued to exercise a certain degree of influence over the lives of the poor. In the earlier part of the last century the latter, when attending the church services, were still in the habit of showing the greatest outward deference to the parson. At the conclusion of a service the poorer members of the congregation were accustomed to stand curtsying or touching their forelocks on each side of the aisle, whilst the great man walked down through their midst. The children likewise who attended the Sunday Schools were taught their duty in this respect at an early age. 'Parson Tonkin was Vicar of Lelant when I was a cheeld (child), seventy years or more ago,' an old miner at Carbis Bay once told the writer. 'A great big man he was, tall and upright, and strong as a horse. We used

to have to go to Sunday School at Lelant and then on to
church. After service, we would walk back to Carbis Bay
to dinner, and then be made to go down to Lelant church
again in the afternoon. If, as sometimes happened, we did
not come, parson would examine us next Sunday and then,
perhaps, we would tell him that our parents was too poor
to give us clothes or shoes (I know my toes used often to be
showing through my boots), but he would never take that
as an excuse, but would cane us as hard as he could on the
hands. I tell 'ee we was glad when we was old enough to
start work, so as to stop having to go to school and be able to
miss that seven miles walk every Sunday.'

The parson, however, was not always feared. In many
cases he was looked upon as the friend of the parish, and
retained the good will of its inhabitants without distinction
of sect. By reason of his position as an educated man his
advice was often sought on secular matters. On one occasion
in the middle of the last century, an old road-mender, who was
also a local preacher on the chapel ' plan ', came to the vicar
of his parish to consult him about a census form which he had
received. ' There 's seems a purty lot of questions to answer,
sir,' he remarked. 'And there's one which do ask what my
" occupation " is—do 'ee think I had best put down " Local
preacher and Highwayman " ? '

There were, of course, in every parish those who were willing
to seize the crumbs of patronage which might fall from either
the church or chapel table. Of such a sort was that quaint
old character, Betty R—— of St Just, better known by her
suggestive nickname, ' Betty the Barrel '. Learning on one
occasion of the arrival of a new parson at Sancreed, Betty
made her way thither on the following Sunday ' to hear a bit
of church praichin' '. On his return to the vicarage after
service, the parson was surprised to find the old lady wandering
up and down in his garden. Thinking she must be either
deranged in her mind or there for no good purpose, he went
out and asked her what she wanted. ' Oh, my dear sir,'
was the reply, ' I 've heerd one blessed sarmon this morning
and I 'm going to stay and hear another blessed sarmon
before I go home.' The guileless parson, imagining the old
humbug to be sincere, brought her in and gave her a good
dinner, assuring her that she was welcome to dine there any
Sunday she wished. Some time after this the vicar himself
called one day at Betty's house, where the old woman

happened to be seated over a cup of strong tea and a nice bit
of ' saffern ' cake.   Catching sight of her visitor as he passed
the window Betty had just time to hide the cake and substitute
a dry crust of barley bread, before he entered the room.
At the sight of this poor-looking fare the parson naturally
asked : ' Is that the best you 've got to eat, Betty ? '   ' Oh,
my dear sir,' came her humble reply, ' I 've got Christ with my
crust and a crust with my Christ '—a pious statement, for
which she was promptly rewarded with the gift of a crown ! [1]
Such an incident, it is only fair to say, was by no means typical
of Cornish character ;   for the poor of the Duchy were
generally very independent and resentful of anything which
looked like patronage.

VI

One can hardly conclude a chapter on the story of Methodism in Cornwall without some reference to the position
which the latter occupies in the county to-day, and to its
present relationship to the Church.   On the face of it it must
appear that the spirit of ' sweet reasonableness ' which
characterized, in latter years, the attitude of church and chapel
in their dealings one with another, is less clearly in evidence
to-day.   ' The steady rise of the Anglo-Catholic movement,'
wrote the superintendent of the Cornwall Wesleyan Circuit
in a recent article, ' has inevitably tended to harden denomina-
tional distinctions.'   To such a pitch indeed has this uncom-
promising attitude been carried in at least one parish in
West Cornwall, that not only has the vicar himself consistently
abstained from attending the combined service of prayer on
Armistice Day, but has even forbidden the children of his
Sunday School from joining with those of the chapels.   Even
in many cases where there is personal friendliness between the
representatives of the two bodies, ' the constant insistence
on the Roman views of the Church and ministry make it clear',
states the above writer, ' that easy equal intercourse is
impossible.   When incense is burnt in Truro Cathedral and
confessions are heard there, and in many parish churches ;
when the validity of the sacraments is made to depend on

[1] Per Mr Henry Thomas, St Just.

episcopal ordination and apostolic succession, then, by implication, if not by direct assertion, the Methodists and all Free Churchmen are unchurched. Their only chance of salvation is to return to the orthodox pastures, and to receive the Bread of Life from the duly authorized hands '. The changes in the attitude of the Church towards ritualism, the writer goes on to assert, ' are largely, if not entirely, the work of the clergy. The laity, in an overwhelming number, are happy to acknowledge Methodists as fellow-Christians, and we believe would gladly welcome closer fellowship in worship. The people of the churches are not far from essential union of hearts '.[1]

With this conclusion there should be no need to quarrel, indeed there are the strongest reasons for believing that it is fundamentally true. Meanwhile, however, a large proportion of the older Cornish people continue, perhaps in many cases unreasonably, to object to such outward forms of change as are revealed in the donning of vestments, the lighting of candles, the genuflexions, the crossings with holy water, the burning of incense, and the many other subtler changes which have altered the character of the services in their parish churches of late years. The insistence upon or the resentment against such superficial matters might appear at first sight to be equally lacking in reason, but on closer study the fact emerges that such tendencies are actually representative of a definite change in the doctrine of the Church itself, and one which has unhappily caused a widening of the rift between it and the chapels.

Meantime, in Cornwall as elsewhere, organized religion is engaged in a struggle for which it ought properly to be in possession of a power which can only come from being at peace within itself. Whilst the elders of the churches are beset with the problems of their own differences, the youth of the country is showing by its complete unconcern that it *cares for none of these things*. There can be no doubt that Methodism at the moment is grappling with this essential problem with very little more success than the Church. Almost every year reports come to hand of dwindling congregations, and a lack of interest and support which has already necessitated the closing of a number of the smaller country chapels. The synods and congresses, moreover, too often show a seeming failure to come to grips with the really vital

[1] Rev. J. Herbert Rider, *Western Morning News*, 11 January 1929.

problems of the modern world. The drink trade and prohibition, gambling and Sunday games, though admittedly questions which concern the churches, can hardly compare in their importance with peace, disarmament, and the rectifying of great social injustices. But whilst the former continue to occupy much thought and attention, the latter, until recently, at any rate, have been passed over in comparative silence, and such pronouncements as are made upon them still lack that unanimity which the laity have the right to expect from the leaders of a great Christian fellowship.

Methodism, in fact, seems to stand in need of a new interpretation to-day, if it is to regain the hold which it once had upon the lives of the people. Never was the need for a religious inspiration which might bring peace to a troubled world greater than it is at the present time. Nearly two hundred years ago John Wesley showed by the unparalleled example of his own life the way in which the vital problems of human existence could be brought home to the consciousness of ordinary men. Only the John Wesley of to-day seems lacking who might bring to bear upon the complexities of the present age that vivid interpretation of the Christian message, which alone can relieve the world from all its instability.

CORNWALL THROUGH THE NINETEENTH CENTURY

I

THE coming of Methodism, of course, did not remove all the evils of the old order of society in a day ; and smuggling, wrecking, hard drinking, and other vices against which the great evangelist had inveighed, continued, though in a lessening measure, far into the nineteenth century. In one of his latest books—*The Ship where Christ was Captain*—the Reverend Mark Guy Pearse has recorded the comment made by an old Methodist whose wife had been reading him John Wesley's famous homily, *A Word to a Smuggler*.

' Impidence, downright impidence ! ' grunted the man, when she had finished. ' What do *he* knaw about it ? '

The story, as a reviewer of the book has remarked, illustrates very clearly the spirit of the old isolated Cornwall of the early nineteenth century, ' its insularity, its devoutness, and its rather divine pigheadedness '.

When writing in this period Polwhele was forced to admit that ' the love of malt liquors is peculiarly prevalent in Cornwall, and our aversion to the temperance societies is stronger than in other counties. On our farms the women as well as the men have, at particular seasons, their morning drams before the commencement of work. The brandy-glass circulates briskly among the farmers before any occasional dinner, immediately after the dinner, and a third time before the breaking up of the company '.[1]

True to the principle of *laissez-faire*, the drink trade at this time was allowed wellnigh a free hand, and every enticement was offered for indulging in the ruinous taste for strong liquor. The result of the reduction of the duty on English-made spirits in the year 1825 had tended to make the country more drunken than it had been at any time perhaps since the days of Hogarth. The arguments which had been adduced in favour of this measure must surely have been the most sophistical that have ever led to the passing of any important Act of Parliament. Their substance was, as comprised in the words of Joseph Hume, that ' since it was the disposition of man, when he could only obtain an indulgence occasionally, to get as much of it as he could ; if circumstances enabled him to obtain gratification regularly, the temptation to commit an excess was removed '. How great was the fallacy upon which this argument was based may be gathered from contemporary evidence, which all points to a rapid increase of drunkenness throughout the country after 1825. ' I never saw a female coming out of a gin-shop when I first came to London,' wrote Bishop Bloomfield in 1832 ; ' I have since repeatedly seen females with infants in their arms, to whom they have been giving some part of their liquor. I almost think I have seen more women than men coming out of these shops.'[2]

This increase in spirit drinking, as Mr and Mrs Hammond have recently shown, was one of the chief causes which led to that still more amazing piece of legislation, the famous Beer Act of 1830. Shocked by the gross excesses which had

[1] *History of Cornwall*, VII, 107.
[2] See J. L. and B. Hammond, *Age of the Chartists*, 148.

resulted from the reduction of the spirit duties, social reformers believed that by providing the population with an unrestricted supply of cheap beer, a means would be found of sweeping away gin-drinking with its attendant evils, whilst at the same time assisting agriculture by increasing the demand for barley and hops. Accordingly, in October 1830, this strangely conceived Act became law. After that date any householder, other than a sheriff's officer, could get an excise licence to sell beer, provided he paid two guineas, and produced one surety for £20 or two for £10 each.[1] The only power possessed by the magistrates over these houses was to close them in case of riot. The result was that multitudes of little dram shops, known in Cornwall as ' kiddleywinks ', or simply ' winks ', came into being in every town, village, and hamlet throughout the country. Such beer-houses, of course, had their critics and opponents from the start. The latter claimed that they were the haunts of thieves and profligates, whilst their keepers were accused of acting as receivers of stolen goods. In these houses, it was stated, plots were hatched, and all manner of evil was set on foot against the propertied classes and the State. No doubt many of these charges were gross exaggerations, whilst in not a few cases they were clearly sponsored by the publicans, who were becoming seriously alarmed at the competition created by this new type of drink-shop. At the same time it can scarcely be doubted that within these houses, many of which were situated in lonely places, and all of them exempt from any authoritative supervision, deeds were sometimes perpetrated which lent colour to the worst charges advanced against them by their enemies.

In the Halfway House district, adjoining the main road between Helston and Penryn, there flourished, about a century ago, a number of kiddleywinks, whose customers, by the aid of the smugglers, were often supplied with liquor of a far more potent character than that for which such houses were licensed. One of these kiddleywinks stood in the hamlet of Viscar, another at Carnkie, and a third by the roadside not far from Deadman's Point. Concerning this last an incident is related which is said to have given to the place its sinister name. One Saturday night a group of five or six men visited the shop, where they spent the evening drinking heavily. In the course of conversation it was learnt that one of the party—a gentleman's servant—had a considerable

[1] Hammond, *Age of the Chartists*, 152.

sum of money in his pocket and, accordingly, his companions resolved to murder him on his homeward journey, and divide the spoils. This was done, the man being waylaid on the top of the hill, and stabbed below the ear with a knife. His pockets were then rifled, and his body dragged to the spot now known as Deadman's Point. Later the same night a workman returning from Penryn discovered the corpse of the murdered man. This was buried the next day in a corner of the common near the junction of the roads, it being thought to be a case of *felo de se*, in which burial in consecrated ground was, of course, prohibited. A little child, however, the son of the landlord, subsequently told his parents that he had witnessed the murder, and had seen a man stab the valet ; but scarcely any efforts were made to discover the ruffians, and none of them was ever brought to justice.[1]

In addition to the regular inns and kiddleywinks, there were also a large number of ' bush ' houses, so called from the custom of displaying a bush of furze above their doors, as an indication that liquid refreshment was obtainable within. There are persons still living who remember an alehouse of this description which used regularly to be licensed for the day of the ' October Fair ' at St Lawrence, near Bodmin ; and there were many other houses of a like kind where beer was brewed and sold on such particular occasions.

Queer places some of these old irregular drinking shops must have been. In the midst of the wild fastness of Bostraze Moor, in the parish of St Just, there formerly stood a hovel which went by the name of the ' Bog Inn '. This appears to have been a courtesy title only, since it is doubtful if it had ever received a licence of any sort. Its owner, however, between the years 1850–55 was a man of jovial character, who was in the habit of providing sport for the youths of the neighbourhood on Sundays by offering prizes for any one who could catch a greased pig, which was let loose amidst the banks and pools of the surrounding tin stream works. This merry sport created much enjoyment for every one except the unfortunate animal, which was rarely caught till its legs had been broken. It also had the effect of creating an unwonted thirst among the ' sportsmen ', for whose benefit supplies of porter and smuggled spirit were fetched from the neighbouring town of St Just, and found a ready sale.[2]

[1] *The Eagle*, 1889–90, p. 72.
[2] Per Mr Henry Thomas, St Just.

Despite the undoubted irregularities to which the beershops gave rise, their numbers grew by leaps and bounds. In 1829 there were 50,660 publicans in England licensed to sell beer ; in 1830 the publicans numbered 51,482, but there were 24,342 beerhouses as well. In 1831, whilst the number of publicans remained stationary (51,488), the beerhouses had risen to 30,978, whilst in 1835 the relative numbers were : public-houses, 55,192 ; beerhouses, 44,134.[1] Generally speaking, the better class public-houses in the country districts served as clubs, resembling in this respect the coffee-houses of the previous century. People would meet in them to talk over the events of the day, whilst little groups would often join together to buy a newspaper which was here read aloud and discussed. Inns, too, were distinguished from beershops by making it part of their business to give board and lodging to travellers. With the increasing competition of the kiddley-wink, however, many of the inns were driven to lower their standards, and to rely more and more on the sale of spirits, which the beershops were not officially permitted to sell. The signboards of such inns frequently showed the direction in which their chief prosperity now lay. The old Tinners' Arms, at St Hilary, is still remembered for the following verse which was displayed above its door :

> *Come all good Cornish boys, walk in,*
> *Here 's brandy, rum, and shrub, and gin,*
> *You can't do less than drink success*
> *To Copper, Fish, and Tin.*[2]

In addition to both inns and kiddleywinks, there were also spirit shops. Liquor purchased at these had to be carried away for consumption elsewhere, thereby distinguishing them from the beershops, where it might only be consumed on the premises. The combined effect of all these was to swell the total number of places where drink could be purchased to a prodigious figure. In 1832 Bodmin possessed 29 public-houses and beershops,[3] six years later there were 29 public-houses in the borough of Penzance and 37 beershops in addition,[4]

---

[1] Hammond, *Age of the Chartists*, 152.
[2] This interesting signboard is now preserved at St Michael's Mount.
[3] *Bodmin Register* (1827–38), 57, 238.
[4] R. Edmunds, *Statistical Account of the Borough of Penzance*, 1839.

whilst within the memory of persons still living the small town of St Ives owned no less than twenty public-houses, excluding beer and spirit shops.[1]

Even the Church was not above profiting by the prevailing taste for strong liquor, and from the village inn, which was in many cases situated on glebe property, the ecclesiastical authorities long continued to derive an important revenue. In these comfortable places of resort the congregations were wont to assemble before the service in order to smoke their pipes and sip their ale, till the final strokes of the bell gave warning that the parson was ready to begin. Thither also, a few minutes later, would come the ringers, hot and thirsty from their exercise, and ready to take the places which the congregation had vacated. Weddings and funerals alike made good business for the Church Town Inn, whilst the substantial dinners which followed the vestry meetings were held there as a matter of course, generally with the vicar himself in the chair. From about 1840 onwards, when the friendly societies became a prominent feature of working-class life, these bodies also were in the habit of holding their meetings at the Church Inn, a special flag being hoisted on a pole outside to show when the club was ' in session '.

In justice to its ecclesiastical owners, however, it is only fair to say that drinking was not the only form of amusement which was encouraged at the inn, and almost every respectable house of those days was provided with a ' kayle ' (skittle) alley, for the honest recreation of its customers. Some of these alleys lay out of doors on a piece of flat ground adjoining the inn premises, similar to those which may still be seen in Brittany. More often, however, the alley was housed within a long, low building, with a plank floor and seats on either side of the playing space. The ' men ' or pins were about twelve inches high and three in diameter, and were sometimes furnished with iron collars.[2] The game was usually played for a wager, such as a gallon of beer, and the fact that much drinking went with it at length resulted in its being forbidden on licensed premises. After that, of course, there was nothing left for public-house frequenters to do but to drink the more !

---

[1] William Paynter, *Old St Ives* (1927), 34.
[2] W. J. P. Burton and John Stephens, ' Bodmin Sixty Years Ago ', *Bodmin Guardian*, 5 April 1928.

II

Down to the sixties of the last century it was still the custom for public-houses to remain open all night during the all-important occasion of the local fair. As an old Cornishman once remarked : ' Et belonged for everybody to git drunk on feerday ', and few there were who did not take full advantage of the licence granted them at such times by public opinion and the law. Outstanding amongst the great fairs of the county was Summercourt Fair, an event which is still held annually in the little wayside village of that name adjoining the china-clay district of mid-Cornwall. The business side of this, as of other fairs, has largely declined of late years, and the crowds who still flock to it from all the surrounding country-side are chiefly attracted to-day by the varied round of amusements which it provides. Prior to the establishment of the official cattle markets, however, and the regular opportunities now offered to farmers for the disposal of their stock, Summercourt Fair was one of the chief meeting-places for cattle and horse dealers from all over the county. Here, amidst endless haggling, bickering, hilarity, and stubbornness, thousands of animals of every description annually changed hands, their owners frequently putting up in the village for several days in order to ensure the successful transaction of their business.

Hither also, in the olden days, came the unemployed farm labourers and maidservants, waiting to be hired ; whilst scores of tradesmen and cheapjacks standing behind their stalls displayed wares of every description—boots, clothing, saddlery, cloam-ovens, pitchers, pans, bussas (earthenware pots), broth-basins, knives, forks, plates, ropes, brushes, ornaments, baskets, and other articles too numerous to mention. Quack doctors, then as now, flourished in abundance, their stock-in-trade consisting of sticking-plaster, pills, ' Dutch drops ', and other wonderful nostrums so potent as to be ' positively guaranteed ' to cure every ill from tic-douloureux to corns. Such was the persuasive oratory, indeed, of these salesmen that many who stopped to listen to them out of curiosity, straightway found themselves afflicted with all manner of ailments, of whose very name they had previously been ignorant. Beyond the cheapjacks lay the refreshment booths, at which were obtainable rumps and rounds of beef, hot and cold, bread and potatoes and, last but not least, the ' boiled-roast ' geese for which Summercourt or ' Old Fair ' was erstwhile famous. These geese were killed and boiled a few days before the event, and when fair-day came were roasted over an open fire until they were nicely browned, a way of cooking which earned them the sobriquet by which they were known. Well satisfied with the feasting and drinking, the crowd would then turn their attention to the innumerable sideshows and entertainments, all of which were vociferously eager to win their patronage. These included Sanders's theatre, waxworks, marionettes, penny peeps, giants, dwarfs, and fat women, not to mention the boxing and wrestling booths, which offered substantial prizes to those who were willing to display their athletic prowess.

As the result of these exercises and the continual drinking of beer and spirits which went on from early morning, the majority of those who attended the fair were glad to get home the same night. Some, however, spent one or two days in the vicinity, whilst a few took a whole week, returning home at last looking very crestfallen and dilapidated like an overdue ship, that has long been battling with storms and heavy weather.[1]

For the benefit of the wives of such revellers, a local rhymester, Billy Treglase, used regularly to haunt the fair, singing the following verse of his own composition :

> *All the women of Summercourt Fair,*
> *I'll give 'ee advice, then you can beware.*
> *If your man do drink too much beer or gin*
> *You must scat 'un down with a rolling pin;*
> *So, women, I hope you'll follow this plan*
> *If you should be plagued with a drunken man.*[2]

In the westernmost part of the county the great Corpus Christi Fair, held at Penzance on the Thursday, Friday, and Saturday of the week following Trinity Sunday, still retains much of its former popularity. Although now relegated to a

[1] Per Mr J. C. Hoare.
[2] See *West Briton*, 24 September 1928.

THE OLD MARKET PLACE, ST IVES

(See page 206)

TAMSON BLIGHT, THE HELSTON WITCH

See page 291)

field on the outskirts of the town, Corpus Christi Fair continued within living memory to be held in the main western thoroughfare of Alverton, where for nearly a week it was permitted to hinder the stream of heavy traffic passing in those days to and from St Just. It is recorded that in the year 1842 the shows extended from Buriton House to the front gate of Bellair, and included among their attractions Wombwell's menagerie, and Lawrence's, Morland's, and Hird's theatres ; besides peep-shows, conjurers, roundabouts, boxing booths, and small sideshows of every description. On the ' stannins ' or stalls were sold shellfish, gingerbread ' nuts ' and cakes, the latter flavoured with lemon peel and sometimes cayenne pepper, almonds, comfits, angelica, coloured candies, peppermint, ' clidgey ', ' tomtrot ' (hardbake), and other home-boiled sweets. A large business was always done in these, since every one, besides what he or she might eat at the fair, accounted it a duty to take home a pound or two of such fairings to their households. At the ' stannins ' also were sold great quantities of locally brewed beer. The latter was generally of a very poor quality, but people managed to get drunk on it none the less and, when morning came, several persons might usually be seen lying in the street in a state of helpless intoxication.[1]

Although never equalling Summercourt in the amount of business transacted, St Peter's Fair at Camborne, when in the height of its glory, rivalled both it and Corpus Christi in the extent of its festivities, the spirit of high holiday and carousal being kept up here by the miners for nearly a week on end. During this time drunkenness and disorder reigned supreme, and the constant free fights and public-house disturbances which ensued must have led the single policeman, whom the town at that time boasted, a truly harassing existence. The trouble generally started through a quarrel arising between the Camborne and Redruth men over the perennial question as to which of the two rival towns was the superior. Under the stimulating influence of alcohol, tempers were soon lost, and one or other of the groups would nearly always clinch the argument by knocking down three or four of the opposition.

On one occasion, amusingly described by Mr Charles Bath, the Camborne men had taken the initiative in this respect, and a typical public-house fight had resulted. Whilst the

[1] *Cornishman*, 3 January 1884.

uproar was at its height, ' Stee ', the policeman, arrived and, much to the indignation of the local zealots, insisted on taking into custody a certain Christopher Penpol, who was indicated by the Redruth men as being the originator of the disturbance.

' Christopher Penpol, will you tell us what caused the trouble at the Hoss and Jocks ? ' asked the chairman of the magistrates, when the prisoner appeared in the police court next day.

' Now, I tell 'ee what et were all about,' said Kit, ' yer warship, 'twere Peter's Feer, and everybody got drunk, gentle and simple, 'cause 'twas feer day, yer honour. They that didn't git drunk outdoors, got drunk in. The bettermost sorts were drunk as well as the other sorts, yer warship.'

' Very possibly, very possibly,' remarked the chairman, ' but we must keep to the case before the bench, Christopher, and we want to hear who started this disturbance.'

' Why the Redruth chaps, to be sure,' replied Kit. ' The 'Druth chaps said as how there were bigger shops and more shops in 'Druth than there were out Camburn, an' I sed there warn't and that started the rig, yer warships.'

The case being somewhat difficult to decide, the Bench had a serious conversation lasting for nearly half an hour, at the end of which the chairman announced : ' Christopher Penpol, we are all agreed that you are not guilty of any misconduct on Peter's Fair Day. We find that the Redruth men started the row, by their statement about the number of shops in each town. The one thing that we are all agreed upon is that there are more pawnshops in Redruth than in Camborne. Christopher Penpol, you can go, and you have the good wishes of my fellow magistrates and myself.'

The case was then dismissed, Kit leaving the court amidst loud cheering, in which the Bench heartily joined.[1]

III

Such, if we may rely upon popular tradition, was the attitude of the authorities at fair time. The desire for drink, however, once it had taken hold, was rarely satisfied by such occasional carousals. Every parish in those days had its complement

[1] Charles Bath, *Uncle Kit's Legacy*, 62–3.

of drunkards, many of them, it is true, hard-working men during a great part of their time, but given to regular bouts of drinking as soon as ever they had accumulated sufficient money to indulge their overmastering passion. Sometimes these debauches would last for a week or more, during which time their victims frequently remained away from home, spending the nights in some barn or outhouse, or even in a dry ditch. At length, worn out by their excesses, and sick at heart from the dissipation of all their hard-won savings, such men would return to their homes and daily work, poorer but rarely the wiser for their experience.

A story is told how, at the end of one of these carousals, a certain man was pressed by his companions to have 'just one pint more' before parting. 'No,' was the reply, 'I can't get down a drop moore, but I tell 'ee what you can do. Thraw a pint ovver me if you mind to, so I shall be able to have the smill of un when I do wake up in the morning !'

On another occasion, several Gulval men, returning home from a 'party of pleasure' at the Gurnard's Head, were passing through the village of Newmill. Some of the group suggested going into the Miners' Arms for a last drink all round, whilst others were in favour of going straight home. At length, in order to settle the dispute, one of the men, a well-known farmer of Gulval church-town, exclaimed : ' I tell 'ee what, comraades, I' ll thraw up my hat and if 'ee come down we 'll go in, if not we 'll make for home '. To this proposition all agreed, with what result it is not hard to imagine ! [1]

Although many of the stories of this sort are not without their humour, the heavy drinking of those days resulted as a whole in a vast amount of sordid misery, culminating in some cases in actual tragedy. ' On Saturday last,' states the *West Briton*, 16th August 1839, ' an inquest was held at Carharrack in the parish of Gwennap, on the body of Thomas Michell. It appears that the preceding day, between 6 and 7 o'clock in the evening, a driver of one of Messrs Carne's carts of Falmouth, came to the house of the deceased to borrow a quill, for the purpose as he said, of blowing some salt into one of his horse's eyes, which he had accidentally struck with his whip. The deceased had no quill in the house, but he took some trouble to send for one, and it would appear from this and other circumstances that he knew very well

[1] Per Mr J. C. Hoare.

what the quill was wanted for, and that he had supplied the same person with one before. The quill was eventually procured, and the deceased and the driver proceeded to the cart, which was in the road close by. They then bored a hole in a barrel of spirits, which was in the cart, and begun to suck the contents through the quill. Two or three other carts which happened to be passing at the time, halted at the same spot, their drivers joining the first two. How long they were thus engaged does not appear, but at length a miner, who had been observing them from a distance for about three-quarters of an hour, went towards the group to see what was going on. On his arrival the carts dispersed, and he accompanied the deceased about forty yards towards his home. The deceased did not appear at that time to be the worse for drink, but he told the miner that he had had a " noble drop of brandy " from one of the carts which had just moved off, and that in an hour's time he would be as " drunk as a sack ". He fell asleep shortly after this ; but, on his not waking the next morning, a surgeon was sent for, who found it impossible to rouse him, and he died about five in the afternoon, evidently from the effects of drinking so much raw spirit.'

In the mining districts at this time the Saturday pay-days were still the occasion of much drunkenness, often resulting in some staggering son or husband returning home to wreak his vengeance on the women and children who waited in dread for his arrival. ' We went this morning,' wrote the wife of the vicar of St Hilary, ' in search of a poor woman whose husband had truly beaten her " within an inch of her life ".' A few days before the man in question had announced to his wife, on returning from the alehouse, that he intended to kill her. Sending down his boy for a basin of water and a huge knife, a foot and a half long, which he had had specially made for him at the blacksmith's, he proceeded to double a strong cord in a scourge of nine knots, coiling this round his right hand whilst, with his left, he grasped the woman's mouth. His old mother, over eighty years of age, tottered to the spot in order to shield her daughter-in-law by receiving some of the blows on her own body, whilst his eldest child hung on his collar, entreating mercy for her mother. Such feeble resistance, however, proved of little avail. Having flung his mother out of doors, the man returned once more to his occupation.

'Ever and anon,' writes Mrs Pascoe, 'between the dreadful acts, he took draughts of water to allay the thirst which his victim's blood was insufficient to slake, exclaiming with a fiendish laugh, " Now, this refreshes me ".'

At length deliverance came. A number of people having assembled outside the house, attracted by the shrieks of the women, the wretched wife succeeded in escaping from her husband's grasp whilst his attention was occupied for a moment at the window. Flinging herself downstairs, she drew back the bolts of the door, and made off for her brother's house, where in due course she arrived with her body streaming with blood, half her clothes torn away, and her hair hanging in strings over a death-like face. ' On the day we called to see her,' concludes Mrs Pascoe, ' she had just crawled out to try if she could reach home to see her younger children, but had fainted by the way. The man, in the meantime, had absconded, believing, as he confessed to his brother, that the woman could not have survived his ill-treatment. I can hardly restrain the wish,' she adds, ' that he may long be tortured by this apprehension, so much do our passions need the restraining words : " Vengeance is Mine ".' [1]

Shocked as the reader may well feel at the revelation of such brutal depravity, he has only to turn to the local newspapers of this date to see that the latter was by no means confined to the mining population. Week by week, throughout the year, the earlier files of the *West Briton* and the *Cornwall Gazette* provide a monotonous record of robbery with violence, murder, and drunkenness. ' On Thursday night,' states the *Cornwall Gazette*, 14th November 1801, ' a mob of about 150 persons assembled at Boscarne, in Bodmin parish, some of whom, armed with guns, surrounded the house, whilst others concealed themselves in an outhouse, with the intention, it is supposed, of murdering the miller and his men if they attempted to make an alarm. They then proceeded to destroy the salmon-weir (the property of the Rev. Flamank), that prevented the fish going up the river.'

Owners of land or other property, reading the reports of such incidents, no doubt considered that they were fully justified in regarding the working-classes with hostility and distrust, and were strengthened thereby in their determination to uphold the savage penal code of the time. Certain it is that if both life and property were held in cheap regard, it

[1] *Walks About St Hilary* (1836–8).

was not through any undue leaning towards clemency on the part of the law. At the beginning of the last century there were no less than one hundred and sixty criminal actions which were punishable by hanging, many of which would be regarded to-day as of a trivial character. Thus we read in the report of the Cornwall Summer Assizes held, in August 1808, that Richard Evers, of Lansallos, was sentenced to death for stealing a watch ; that Philip Brenton suffered the same penalty for stealing two oxen ; whilst James Brindell, *alias* ' Jem from Town ', for stealing wearing apparel out of a stage-wagon was committed to seven years' transportation.[1] The latter punishment practically amounted to slavery of the most brutal and disgusting kind, and in many cases was lifelong, since no proper provision was made for the return of the prisoners when the period of their sentence had been completed.

In October 1803 James Nield attended a service in the chapel of the county jail at Bodmin. ' I well remember,' he writes, ' that the psalm read for the day happened, singularly, to be the 79th. Three poor men convicts, then under sentence of death, were present, and appeared very sensibly affected by that pathetic ejaculation in the 12th verse, " Preserve Thou those that are appointed to die ".'

' Pathetic ' though he felt the words to be, it is certain that the writer failed to appreciate the grim humour which they derived from the circumstances, nor realized the irony of their being intoned, in a Christian building, by the encircling warders who, in very truth, were there to ' preserve ' those that were appointed to die !

In 1805 the same writer visited the old Stannary jail at Lostwithiel, where he found a number of miserable wretches confined for debts incurred in connection with the tin-mining industry. The prison he describes as being ' very dirty, not having been washed for near thirty years '. Formerly it had been the practice to allow the Stannary prisoners ' free boundaries ', which extended to the confines of the borough of Lostwithiel. For this indulgence, however, securities had to be given, and seeing that latterly only the poorest, who had nothing to surrender, ever found their way into the prison, such persons were closely confined within its walls. One of the last debtors to be immured here was a certain Salathiel Harris, who was committed on 16th July 1805, and liberated

[1] *Cornwall Gazette*, 20 August 1808.

on 14th November following.   During these four months his wife and children were thrown upon the parish (St Agnes), from which he hailed ; a fact which was no doubt largely instrumental in procuring his release.   No allowance for food was granted to such prisoners whilst they were in jail ; but, in this particular case, in order to prevent the man from actually starving, he ' received the indulgence of being brought down from his room to an iron-grated window next the street, there to solicit the casual charity of passengers by means of a shoe suspended by a cord with which the keeper had humanely provided him '.

Even this description, however, pales before the horrors of Launceston town-jail, which the same writer described in 1812 as being ' in a most filthy and dilapidated state '.   There was no water here, no privy, and no courtyard in which the prisoners might take exercise.   ' Upon asking the keeper when the place had been cleaned and whitewashed,' wrote Nield, ' I well remember his telling me that he had frequently applied to the mayor to have it done, but the answer had always been, " the blacker it is the better ; it has more the appearance of a jail "'.   In some rooms the doors were only four feet high and fifteen inches wide.   In others the only light came from an aperture measuring three feet by nine inches, and that light was almost obscured by an iron bar.   Straw lay scattered about the floor, and there was a fireplace—but no fuel allowed.[1]

Bodmin jail was no doubt better than many of the smaller prisons at this date.   A writer (circa 1799) states that he found the male prisoners here employed on regular tasks, such as gardening and ' polishing moorstone for chimney pieces ' ; and the females in spinning and weaving, and making rugs,[2] in the profits of which they were allowed some small share. Even so, however, he points out that all the women prisoners were herded together ' cheek by jowl ' in one room, and that hardened criminals committed for offences of a brutal character were undergoing the same system of correction as those who had been condemned for the most trifling misdemeanours.[3]

The law itself, as may clearly be seen, recognized no distinction between the thorough-paced criminal, the juvenile offender, and the unfortunate half-wit.   In 1813 a poor, crazy, servant girl was hanged at Bodmin for setting fire to a rick.

[1] James Nield, *State of the Prisons of England and Scotland* (1812).
[2] Rev. J. Skinner, British Museum Additional MSS 28793.
[3] Hamilton Jenkin, *Western Morning News*, 18 February 1928.

In 1827 Mary Ann Benetts, the wife of a respectable farmer, was sentenced to seven years' transportation for shoplifting. The comparative affluence of the latter's circumstances and the trifling value of the articles which she stole show clearly enough that the woman's case was one of kleptomania, a condition which was no doubt aggravated by her having been in an advanced state of pregnancy at the time. Notwithstanding this fact, however, and the prayers of her husband, who was driven by the thought of her fate to a condition 'bordering on distraction', the brutal sentence was carried out.[1]

In 1837 three orphan boys, belonging to the parish of St Hilary, who had long made themselves a nuisance to the neighbourhood by their petty acts of larceny, were found sheltering, together with their booty, in an old deserted ruin among the mines near Redruth. The youngest boy was sentenced to fourteen years' transportation ; but on the special plea of Mr Pascoe, the vicar of St Hilary, this was subsequently reduced to seven years.[2]

IV

Despite the fact, however, that violence and brutality continued in many cases to characterize the action of the law, no less than of the lawbreaker, there is evidence to show that the Cornish people of this date were taming down. The lawlessness, in fact, of which we read, was for the most part confined to certain individuals, and riots and disturbances of a more general order were becoming increasingly rare. ' Till within a very few years,' stated a writer in 1802, ' Cornishmen were famous as wrestlers ; nor is this gymnastic sport entirely discontinued now. But every old inhabitant of this county can tell you how very much it has declined. Formerly we witnessed many matches where parish joined against parish armed with bludgeons and stones : and, in cases of a disputed fall, or some other trifling cause (which seldom failed to arise where men assembled with the weapons and dispositions for riot), the most dreadful battles have

[1] C. G. Henderson, *West Briton*, 16 January 1930.
[2] Mrs Pascoe, *Walks about St Hilary*.

ensued, and death has frequently been the consequence. This savage spirit was, doubtless, the true spirit of war ; and an army of these hardy miners, under proper discipline, would have equalled any soldiers in the world. But these riots are now seldom witnessed. Indeed, the character of the miners has undergone a considerable change, and a stranger who should converse with the tinners of St Austle (*sic*), St Agnes, Gwennap, Redruth, Camborne, or any other mining district in this county, would be surprised at their courtesy and intelligence. From wrestlers and rioters they are become readers ; and, surprising as it may appear, the writings of Milton, Young, Pope, but more particularly of the Wesleys, are as familiar to thousands of them as the favourite pastorals of Alan Ramsey are to the peasantry of Scotland. The Methodists claim to themselves the merit of working this change, and their claim is in part just ; but the magistrates of the country have no less contributed to it by preventing such assemblages of riot and murder.' [1]

Whether the part played by the magistrates in administering the savage criminal laws of the time really contributed to these changes to the degree suggested by the writer, modern sociologists will probably take leave to doubt. That Methodism, on the other hand, did all that its supporters claimed for it, will scarcely be questioned to-day. Indeed, the value of its influence was never seriously questioned by the ruling classes, who, throughout the early years of the nineteenth century, regarded it as a powerful bulwark against the seething forces of Radicalism. In a parliamentary debate on the Preservation of the Public Peace Bill in 1812, Brougham stated that the Methodists had all along proved themselves ' lovers of peace ', and claimed that the absence of any serious disorder in such a time of general impoverishment and distress was owing to ' the happy prevalence of the principles of Methodism '. By inculcating the doctrine that the hardships and brutal inequalities of life were but forms of discipline intended to qualify the poor for a more glorious crown hereafter, the Methodist leaders had ranged themselves on the side of Toryism, however little they may have been conscious as individuals of supporting any one political party. [2] Further than this, Methodism taught the poor the duty of being industrious, whilst at the same time it condemned

[1] *Cornwall Gazette*, 18 September 1802.
[2] See J. L. and B. Hammond, *The Town Labourer*, 278.

almost every form of recreation as a mortal sin.   The results of such a doctrine were not long in showing themselves in all parts of England where Methodism established its hold, and it was no doubt with keen satisfaction that employers of labour and the ruling classes generally learnt of the changes which were characterizing the workpeople of Cornwall at this date.

' Desperate wrestling matches, inhuman cock-fights, pitched battles, and riotous revellings, are now happily of much rarer occurrence than heretofore,' states an historian of the Duchy in 1817.   ' The spirit of sport has evaporated, and that of industry has supplied its place.   The occupations in mining countries fill up the time of those engaged in them too effectually to allow leisure for prolonged revels or frequent festivities ;   and, in other parts of Cornwall, the constant pursuits of steady labour have nearly banished the traditional seasons of vulgar riot and dissipation.' [1]

A very important feature of this period was the growth of the temperance movement which, despite the opposition to which Polwhele has referred, succeeded in gaining a foothold in Cornwall at an early date.   In point of fact, the Society for the Suppression of Drunkenness, established at Redruth in 1805,[2] anticipated by a quarter of a century the Temperance Society of Bradford, which has recently been claimed as the first of its kind in England.[3]

The object of these societies, as the name of their Cornish pioneer suggests, was not so much to forbid the use of alcoholic liquors, as to discourage intemperance.   Though many Methodists at this time were teetotalers, the society as a whole still regarded the question in the light of Wesley's own teaching, which, whilst it was definitely opposed to the use of spirits, had never forbidden ale or light wines.   As an illustration of this, it is recorded that in the year 1827 the children at a Methodist Sunday School treat held at Troon, in the parish of Camborne, were regaled with cakes and beer, a barrel of which had been specially provided for the occasion by a kindly publican.[4]

In 1838 Richard Edmunds, in his *Statistical Account of the Borough of Penzance*, stated that the temperance society

---

[1] C. S. Gilbert, *History of Cornwall*, I, 104.
[2] Rev. R. Polwhele, *History of Cornwall*, VII, 109.
[3] ' The first Teetotal Society was formed in Preston in 1832.'   See Hammond, *Age of the Chartists*, 164.
[4] Rev. Canon S. Carah, *Parish of Camborne*, II, 17.

in the town had in that year grown to the 'extraordinary membership' of 2,100, though he added significantly that a very small proportion of the gentry was among its members.

Twinges of conscience, however, on the score of heavy drinking were clearly making themselves felt among the lower orders at this date, as is shown by the following story told to the writer not long since. One fine summer's day, some ninety or more years ago, two St Ives fishermen, who were out 'driving' for mackerel, chanced to see a keg floating by them in the water. Having with some difficulty got it on board, they discovered to their delight that it was filled with rum. Forgetting all their vows in the temptation of the moment, they started straightway to drink and, sad to relate, in a short time had become so intoxicated that they were unable either to stand or sit. Whilst the elder man had just sufficient sense to climb into his bunk, the other got no farther than the locker below, where he fell on his knees in a stupor. The position in which he found himself evidently suggested a familiar train of thought, and fancying himself at home in chapel, he immediately started praying in a loud voice : ' O Loord, O Loord, have mercy upon me. . . .' The words were hardly out of his mouth before the response came in a sleepy voice from above his head : ' And so the gentleman will, Sam, so the gentleman will ! '

The fervour of Methodist revivalism, however, once it really struck home, left nothing done by halves. From drunkenness and wild living, those who had 'seen salvation' were driven to contrasting lengths of moral earnestness which it is hard to picture to-day. In their perfervid attempts to eradicate all traces of their former sinfulness, the new converts became dead to the world about them, forswearing its harmless pleasures equally with its temptations. Mrs Pascoe, in her inimitable little sketch-book, from which the writer has already quoted, throws a vivid light on the contrasts between the ' sinner ' and the ' saved ', which every village of that day presented. The same pen which depicted the brutal drunkard has left a no less valuable record of the devout and humble-minded poor. Among the many stories which she tells of these, none is more illustrative of character than that of the poor epileptic girl, whose sole pleasure in life consisted in singing the popular hymns and psalm tunes which found favour at that day. Once, and once only, said the governess of the poorhouse where the girl was kept, had she heard from her the scrap of a song, and that was during one of her deranged fits. ' Deep was the concern with which the good woman made this confession,' writes Mrs Pascoe, ' and deeper still the poor wanderer's compunction at hearing from one of the other inmates what she had done. " To see the tears she shed ! " cried the good governess. " She could not put it from her mind, till at length I told her God would not lay to her charge any sins she committed at such times ".'

' Were they bad words she sang ? ' inquired Mrs Pascoe, with not unnatural curiosity.

' Why, no, ma'm,' replied the matron, ' it was not that there was much harm in them either. I believe I can tell them pretty nigh over, for she sang them so pretty and sweet :

> *She trilled like a Linnet,*
> *She mourned like a Dove,*
> *And the words that she sang*
> *Was concerning of Love.*' [1]

Even with her reputation to maintain as wife of the vicar of the parish, Mrs Pascoe must have found it hard not to smile at this mild issue to such a serious avowal. There is no doubt, however, that the pious governess felt very differently, and regarded the incident as an unfortunate scandal which in some measure reflected upon her own authority. So strong, indeed, was the reaction which had set in against all secular musice sinc Wesley's day, that even the most inoffensive popular ditties were viewed with the utmost disfavour by the converted, among whom hardly anything worse could be said of the character of a young man than that ' He edd'n good for nothen' but to go traapsen' round the lanes singing ould songs ! ' Even as late as 1870 such time-honoured favourites as *Sally in our Alley,* or *Come Lasses and Lads* were regarded in Methodist families as ' the Devil's music ',[2] a fact which goes far to explain the paucity of genuine folk songs which have survived in Cornwall.

To the pure indeed, at this time, all things had become impure, insomuch that it would seem difficult to decide whether a converted or an ' erring ' son or husband must have been the harder cross for the womenfolk who had to bear the brunt of these extremes. Meeting ' old George Barnard ' in the

[1] *Walks about St Hilary,* 33.
[2] Dr R. Dunstan, *Cornish Song Book,* 4.

lane one day, Mrs Pascoe had the temerity to offer him a ticket for the local flower show. 'Thank 'ee, ma'm,' was his polite but crushing reply ; 'I would go farther to hear a good sarment than to see the finest flowers the earth doth yield.'

Many of the poorer converts who could not read a letter of the ' Book ' themselves, would entice in one of the village children to read them a chapter now and then, rewarding this service with the ' vall'y of a ha'penny ' set aside from their hard-earned weekly pittance. Throughout their daily lives the minds of such men and women as these never ceased to ponder on the grand question of their ultimate acceptance at the Throne of Mercy. All their visions, sleeping and waking, were tinctured with this spiritual timidity which informed the endless allegories and religious trances which they delighted in relating to the sympathetic listener.

Undoubtedly, in some cases, the new-found piety was not unmixed with the leaven of superstition. One poor child, sadly torn between the temptations of this world and fear of the next, confessed to Mrs Pascoe that after purchasing a pair of ' golden ' earrings for 1s. in Penzance, she had been troubled ever since ' to come athirt the crofts at night for doubting the Old One was behind her ' ; and would not, to gain the world, go to bed without taking the trinkets off and placing them in the farthest corner of her chamber.

Still, the effects of Methodism in supplying the poor with a spiritual fortitude which lifted them above all their material wants and sufferings can never be gainsaid. Entering the home of ' poor William Pearce ' on one occasion, Mrs Pascoe describes how she found the invalid lying on the single bed which served him as a couch by day and the whole family as their resting place by night. For twenty years he had lain thus in one poor tiny room, weak in body, but yet so strong in the power of the Spirit that words scarcely sufficed to express his thankfulness for the mercies which were meted out to him from on high ! Conscious though Mrs Pascoe was of this unseen force from which so many derived their spiritual strength, the conditions she saw about her more than once compelled her to exclaim : ' How *do* the poor get on ? ' In another cottage in the same parish she describes how she found a poor woman with a family consisting of a boy of sixteen, with a cancer in his throat ; three girls, of whom the youngest was a cripple ; and a baby—all dependent on the earnings of a sickly husband, who walked ten miles a day to work for the 25s. a month which was their sole means of support.

Although work itself was plentiful enough, and the mining industry was flourishing, the low standard of wages combined with the high price of all commodities served to make the ' hungry forties ' a byword for the hardships entailed upon the working classes. Owing to the narrow margin of their subsistence, even the more fortunate of the latter lived at all times upon the brink of pauperism, into whose dreaded abyss the loss of the breadwinner was capable of instantly precipitating them. An illustration of this is provided by a brief paragraph in the *West Briton* of 3rd January 1812, reporting the death of George Truran, ' a man of exemplary character ', who had been killed during the preceding week in Wheal Unity mine in the parish of Gwennap. ' He leaves,' states the writer, ' a wife and seven children, the eldest of whom is an idiot. At his death two tenements which he held for his life fell into other hands. A day or two after his death one of the two horses belonging to him which were employed in the mine, was killed, and the other rendered unserviceable. Since that time the widow, who is far advanced in pregnancy, was precipitated from the first floor of her home and now lies seriously injured.'

It has often been said that the shareholder in mines has well deserved the title of ' adventurer ', by which he was formerly known in Cornwall, but with even greater appropriateness could this name have been applied to the workman who staked, not only money, but life itself in this great industrial gamble. ' Poor John King ', of St Hilary, was another of Mrs Pascoe's protégés, whose sufferings had been accentuated by an additional misfortune which was once all too common amongst the mining population. ' Pale and languid ' Mrs Pascoe describes him, as she saw him at work in his little garden, and small wonder, considering that he had survived an accident which must surely have proved a record even in the long list of mining casualties which the parish could number. With graphic force he described to her one day, how when coming up from underground he had missed his footing on the ladder, and fallen away ' two steeples outright ', that is a sheer perpendicular depth of two church spires. When picked up his head was fractured, his collar-bone broken, three ribs were knocked in, his shoulders thrown out of joint, his nose ' laid flat on his face ', and his two ankles ' shot out '. Even more disastrous in some respects was the accident which subsequently befell the club to which the poor man had subscribed for many years. It broke, and with it vanished all his hopes of an independent provision for sickness and old age. Such a fate, as already said, was one which not infrequently befell the more industrious and provident miners of this age, who were thus betrayed into pauperism, and were forced for the remainder of their lives to subsist upon the pittance afforded them by parochial relief.

V

The scale upon which the latter was administered in Cornwall, seems to give little colour to that charge of extravagance which had so much alarmed public opinion as to have led to the appointment of the Poor Law Commissioners in 1834. Pitiful indeed are the stories told of the attempts made at this time to keep body and soul together on the shilling a week allowed by the iron hand of the relieving officer—a sum which little more than sufficed to supply a man and his wife with one meal a day. ' But your clothes ? ' inquired Mrs. Pascoe of one old couple who were dependent on this relief. ' We never look for any, ma'm,' was their meek reply, to which the old man added that he had been forced to wear his one whole shirt for three months without washing.

Adjoining the cottage where these old people lived lay another household with a yet more poignant story. ' Poor Anne Green,' after being newly cured of an abscess on the loin, had gone forth again, all too soon, to work in the fields, in order to supplement her miner-husband's wages. In consequence of this another abscess had developed, as the result of which the woman had become a ' bed-lier '. Meantime the eldest child, a little girl of seven, had taken upon herself the multiplied cares of the family looking after the other children, cleaning the house, ' fitting dinner ' for her father to take to ' bal ' (mine), or to eat on his return. Whilst engaged in these duties one day her flimsy petticoat was caught on fire, and after three weeks of inexpressible agony, she died. Broken down beneath this additional trouble, the father was driven, by sheer necessity, to apply to the Union for help. Three shillings a week was granted to the family, together with the attendance of the Union doctor, ' y-clept in all seriousness Mr. Caudle '. After considerable delay the latter at length arrived, redolent of rum, and by virtue of his professional authority insisted on cutting the woman's tumour, despite the protests of the patient, who was convinced that the proper stage for the lancet had not arrived. Apparently the patient was right, for the subsequent pain became so intolerable that it was obvious that the surgeon had injured a nerve—a fact which perhaps accounted for his straightway resorting to the Falmouth Packet in order to drown the memory of his error. Meantime the husband thought only how he could bestow his leisure hours in walking to Penzance and back (12 miles) in order to lay out the allotted three shillings to the best advantage for the invalid. This matter, however, was soon settled for him, for after walking hither and thither, and being handed from one parish authority to another, with nothing but insults for his pains, the three shillings was cut down to two shillings, to be supplied in kind, viz. 2 lb. of beef and half a pint of wine.

' I drop the pen,' writes Mrs Pascoe, ' in sheer heart-sickness at this more than negro-treatment.'

The story of poor old Susannah Cornish, worn out with labour and short commons, and lying in her tiny one-roomed hovel under the torture of rheumatic fever, provides yet another illustration of pauper treatment. Crippled though she was, she still thought she might be able partially to support herself, if the ' Junion ' would allow her 6d. a week to help out with the house rent. That, thought the kindly Pascoes, should be an easy matter, but they were reckoning without the hard-fisted farmers before whom the poor soul had to appear at the board meeting in Helston. In words which sounded terrible to her ears, they bade her ' go to the place provided for her, and such as her ' ! At length, influence was brought to bear, and she was promised a dole of one shilling for a few weeks. A neighbour going that way promised to call for it, but on making the application was told that an order would be made out to the relieving officer of the division, and that to him the woman must apply. For several weeks she waited on the chance of seeing him, for none knew the time or season when he might choose to visit the parish. When at length he did come, he told Susannah that he had received no such order, and could not pay the money. He need not have troubled, for a few days later the old woman was found dead in her bed. 'After all,' writes Mrs Pascoe with fine sarcasm, ' he did not do it. Cold and hunger killed the woman, the board only withheld the means to live.'

Better off in many respects were the paupers who found asylum in the parish poorhouse, although life even there was certainly hard enough. 'The three old women had gone to bed, tired out with their day's weeding,' wrote Mrs Pascoe on one occasion after visiting this institution. ' Two of them, who will never be eighty again, had spent the day toiling and moiling under a scorching sun " down on their two knees " weeding the onion bed. " Better do that than nothing," observed the governess of the house. " They had been asking leave to go out, and I told them when they had performed their task they should be allowed a half-holiday." '

The supervision of these local poorhouses, prior to the combination of parishes into Unions, lay in the hands of the churchwardens and overseers, who were elected at an annual vestry meeting over which the vicar himself presided. Each of the churchwardens and overseers kept the accounts for one month, in rotation, and the latter provide an interesting record of the treatment of paupers, both within and without the ' house '. The nature of this treatment seems to have varied at different times, and in different parishes, no doubt partly in accordance with the generosity, or otherwise, of the officials who were for the time being empowered to administer the public funds. The account books of the parish of Breage, for example, during the latter part of the eighteenth century, show how relief in money varied from 2d. a week, given in one instance to a widow with two blind children, to as much as 5s. per week in other cases. Extra allowances were made in cases of sickness or accident. Thus we find ' Relief to Stephen Ripper, bad with a flux, 2s.' ; ' Pd. for a quart of brandy for Eliz. Webb attending Mary Robberts when sick, 1s. 6d. ' ; ' Pd. for quicksilver, etc., for curing Thos. Pascoe's family of the itch, 1s. 3d.' ; ' Paid Susanna Williams for curing Rosewarne's children's heads, £1 4s.' ; ' To Jno. Evans for to have a wen cured on his knee, 2s. 6d.' ; ' Relief to Mary Meager when her shoulder bone was struck out and expense putting her to doctor, 2s.' ; ' To Ann Lukey when she fell out of the window, 5s. 6d.' and the like. ' To expense with sundry men drawing Diana Thomas and Richard Dunn out of the plump (well), 3s.' is another interesting item which occurs in the same accounts. Insane persons were commonly chained up, either at the poorhouse or in their own homes, a fact which explains such entries as : ' Wm. Williams for a Bedlam waistcoat in his madness ' ; ' Fetters, chain, and a pair of handcuffs ' ; ' To John Ripper, smith, for chaining Diana Symons ', etc.[1]   In at least one instance, this cruel practice resulted in appalling tragedy. In the year 1817 the poorhouse at Buryan was completely gutted by fire, and two men and four women perished in the flames. One of these unhappy victims was a young woman of nineteen who, being in a state of derangement, had been secured by a chain ' in which ', writes an eye-witness, ' she was seen struggling violently but ineffectually to escape the fury of the merciless element '.[2]

On many occasions the outdoor relief supplied by the overseers was given in kind, showing that the officers both studied economy and also kept in close touch with the poor of their parishes. ' To shifts, caps and whittles for Harvey's child ' ; ' To John Symon's wife to have a jarken (jerkin) and a pair of shoes ' ; ' Ordered Alice Ripper a towser ' (sacking apron for dirty work) ; ' Ordered Thos. Rule's wife to have a cowall ' (fishwife's back-basket or creel) ; ' To 4 yards of blankiting to Mary Tregloan after her clothes was burned ' ; ' To mending the blind man's shoes ' ; ' clothing and bedsheets for the blind man ', are typical entries of this sort. In some cases, the overseers even allowed small luxuries, as the entries for the supply of tobacco to paupers clearly show, but perhaps the most surprising item in the whole of the Breage accounts is that of ' £3 13s. 6d. paid to Wm. Johns for Edward Williams to learn him to play on the violin ', together with ' £1 for a violin and bow for him to learn on '.

Nor was the education of pauper children entirely over-looked. In 1775 the Breage accounts make mention of ' a Bible and spelling book to Richard Thomas, 5s. 6d.' ; ' paper for Lame boy, 4d.' ; ' a quire of paper for Wenches cripple ' ; ' Thos. Rowe for ¼ year's schooling for Wenches cripple, 4s. 3d.' The smallness of the fees perhaps accounts for the fact that the schoolmaster himself was an inmate of the workhouse at this time. To this, however, the vestry appears to have made some objection, and at length orders were

[1] Rev. Canon G. H. Doble, *Breage in the Eighteenth Century*.
[2] *Gentleman's Magazine*, vol. 87, pt. i, 269.

given ' for Thos. Rowe to have no meat, washing, or lodging at the workhouse : unless he will give up the gettings of his school to the parish '. Notwithstanding this, in 1803 we again find the schoolmaster, Richard Thomas, in receipt of relief. By 1808, however, his successor was receiving the princely salary of £1 a month, although as late as 1831 Mary Symons (schoolmistress) was only paid 4s. for four weeks' instruction.[1]

Baptisms, christenings, midwifery, and burial charges occupy another important place in the old parish accounts. ' The latter,' writes Canon H. R. Jennings, in an interesting description of the account books of Madron parish, ' often appear strange to our modern minds, but I think that the quaint entries imply that all efforts were made to do honour to the dead and to ensure that the pauper should be buried as decently as his less unfortunate neighbours.' Certainly many paupers of this date would appear to have enjoyed distinctly better funerals than those which could be afforded by families who were in receipt of no parochial relief. In 1820 the funeral charges for one Madron pauper comprised : ' Coffin, £1 7s. ; stripping, 2s. 6d. ; rum on putting in coffin, 1s. 6d. ; liquor for burial, 5s. 6d. ; four men to carry, 3s. ; beer for the four men, 1s. ; minister, 2s. 6d. ; grave, 3s. 6d.' Weddings also are occasionally mentioned in the parish poor accounts. In 1767 Anne Colenso, pauper of Madron, married John Thomas of Ludgvan. Neither could write their names. The witnesses were the two churchwardens. The expenses paid by the parish on this occasion amounted to £8 19s. 4d., and included : ' Portion for the bride, £5 ; special licence, £2 8s. ; ringers, 4s. ; two days' expenses of the churchwardens and overseers determining about the marriage, £1 6s. 10d.' In some particulars, as Canon Jennings has pointed out, the churchwardens and overseers appear to have been more generous in their treatment of the poor than any Public Assistance Committee would be to-day. Thus we find such extraordinary expenditure as : ' for two bottles of anti-scorbutic pills, £1 11s. 6d.' ; ' for two bottles of Dr Green's drops, 11s.' ; ' Mr Davey for one gallon of wine to mix with the bark for J. E., 12s.' Apparently ' J. E.' did not respond very rapidly to this treatment, and accordingly a more pleasant remedy was prescribed, viz., ' 46 pints of porter on doctor's orders for J. E., 11s. 6d.'

Nor are the old poor accounts always without *conscious*

[1] *Breage in the Eighteenth Century.*

humour, as is shown by the following entry, referring to a certain cripple of Madron parish.

1809, *March 3rd.*

> *Set of casters for Care*
> *To be fixed to his chair*
> *To wheel him about*
> *To enjoy the fresh air.*

Castors, 1s. 4d.   *To fixing Castors,* 8d.[1]

Whilst many subsisted on relief outside ' the house', the inmates of the latter seem for the most part to have consisted of children, the aged, or the infirm. Here again conditions varied greatly in different parishes and at different times. According to a scale of dietary shown in the Breage account book of 1762–1808, breakfast consisted of ' heat broth ' and ' milk porridge ' on alternate days. The same fare was provided for supper, i.e. broth when the breakfast consisted of porridge, and vice versa, except on Saturdays, when porridge was served for both meals. Apparently, on Sunday sufficient broth was made for the week, and no doubt by the time it made its last appearance at breakfast on Friday the inmates felt that they had had quite enough. For dinner there was ' flesh and roots ' on two days of the week, and ' fish and pottateys ' on two others. Wednesday's dinner consisted of ' turnips and pottatey pye ', whilst on Fridays the menu was briefer still—' pottatey pye'. Sunday, however, was a day of almost riotous living, with broth for breakfast and supper, and ' flesh pudding and roots ' at midday.[2]

In some poorhouses, as late as 1829, the inmates appear to have been paid a lump sum weekly, out of which they provided their own food. In such cases, if tradition may be relied upon, the paupers often conducted their affairs with great irregularity, rioting upon beer and pork chops at the beginning of the week, and reduced almost to starvation before their next allowance became due. Even in the more strictly conducted houses, however, the paupers enjoyed an occasional feast, which shows that the administration was not wholly without human understanding and sympathy for their case. In the Breage poorhouse a regular sum was given to the inmates to provide them with beer on Christmas Day. At Madron, in 1832, £1 1s. 2½d. was expended for a dinner at the poorhouse

---

[1] *Journal of the Royal Institution of Cornwall* (1928), 338–49.
[2] See Thomas Pryor, *West Briton,* 3 April 1930.

to commemorate the coronation of King William IV. A tablet in the church of this parish further records the gift of £80 by Captain Thomas Hosking to provide a dinner to the inmates of the poorhouse every year on 10th February, that being the birthday of the said donor.

Of comforts of other sorts there could have been but few. The inventory of the average eighteenth-century poorhouse reveals nothing in the way of furnishing beyond the barest household necessities, and it is to be suspected that the greater part of these were supplied from the belongings of those who became its inmates. The provision of quantities of straw for bedding seems to imply that in many cases the paupers slept on the floor, an arrangement which ensured that room could easily be found when additional persons had to be admitted. The poor, however, at this date were accustomed to live no less hardly in their own homes, and it would at least seem fair to say that, for the majority, conditions of life in the poorhouse can at least have been *no worse* than out of it. Indeed, when due allowance has been made for the general rise in the standard of living, one might reasonably assert that they were as well off as the poor in many workhouses of the country to-day, whilst in comparison with the horrible ' Bastilles ' set up by the Poor Law Commissioners after 1834, the average parish poorhouse seems to have been almost a happy home. It was not without reason, therefore, that Mrs Pascoe wrote so regretfully a few years later : ' I am sorry they talk of breaking up these little district sanctuaries for the old and helpless, to enclose them in one huge mass in some central town where none will have heart or time to enter into their little personal wants and feelings like our good governess, Mrs Treweake. Her very foible is in their favour. Really her administrations to the sick and feeble individuals of her household are exemplary and atone for that little self-importance with which she records the proof of reverential affection shown to her by them '.[1]

VI

Although conditions of life for the poor in the early part of the last century were hard in the extreme, the mercantile and propertied classes appear in comparison to have been but

[1] *Walks about St Hilary.*

little affected by the long continuance of the Napoleonic wars.
Certainly it is true to say that in the period 1800–40 the
fashionable gaiety of such small Cornish towns as Camelford,
Lostwithiel, Grampound, Helston, Penzance, and, in particular,
Truro, reached its zenith. As Mr Henderson has pointed out :
' Prior to 1750 roads were so bad that county families kept
Christmas in their own spacious homes after the old English
fashion. After 1840 railways were so general that London
was already sucking up all the rank and fashion from local
society. The heyday of society in the small country town
was, therefore, the period 1750–1840, and, in especial, that
part of it after 1800 '.[1]

Whatever anxiety the landowning classes may have felt
at the reports which came to them of revolutions and wars
across the Channel, it in no way diminished the number of
balls and the gay assemblies which they continued to patronize
with their presence. On 8th March 1811 we learn from the
columns of the *West Briton* that the Truro assembly ' attracted
almost all the fashionables of the neighbourhood, the dancing
being kept up with great spirit to a late hour '. At the April
assembly it is gallantly reported that ladies ' whose beauty
and fashion render any assembly brilliant were of the airy
party '. The ball on this occasion was opened by Miss Macar-
mick (the Lady Patroness), and Captain Stevenson of the
West Essex. Mr Humphrey Willyams was Master of the
Ceremonies. At the September meeting of the same year
Lord and Lady Falmouth were present, together with Lady
Lemon of Carclew, who brought her four daughters. Mr
Thomas Daniell (of Trelissick) opened the ball with Lady
Falmouth, and they were followed by twenty-five couples.
Among other county families who attended the Truro assem-
blies were the Enyses of Enys, the Willyamses of Carnanton,
the Vivians, and the Trevanions.

Although Truro was always regarded as the chief centre,
the light of fashion shone with a modified brilliance in many
of the lesser towns of Cornwall at this date. In addition to
Helston's Furry-day, the Michaelmas prize-giving at its famous
school—once known as the ' Eton of Cornwall '—provided
occasion for a round of festivities which extended over two
days and concluded with a grand ball at the Angel Hotel.
Even such little places as St Columb shared in the prosperity
engendered by the patronage of the local county families,

[1] *Western Morning News*, 2 April 1930.

and on the occasion of a ball held there on 23rd December 1811, we read that ' the steward led off with the Hon. Louisa Trefusis, and was followed by a dazzling group of beaux and belles. The neighbouring families made a point of attending', adds the writer, ' and it is expected that regular assemblies will shortly be established, a measure likely to meet with the hearty concurrence of that gay town and its vicinity '.[1]

With the cessation of the war with France, a rapid expansion took place in the mining and commerce of the county. This, whilst tending still further to enrich the landowning families, also added very largely to the ranks of the merchant class. Among the latter, a new type of business rivalry begins to be noticeable at this time, a rivalry which, whilst it was imbued with all the untamed passion which had characterized the feuds of the squirearchy, seems to have acquired an added venom by emanating from the ' counting-house ' rather than from the rough-and-tumble of the hunting field.

The story is told how Captain Andrew Vivian, the partner of Richard Trevithick, chanced on one occasion, in London, to meet with a certain Mr James,[2] who was then the leading member of a firm of bankers whose crooked dealings had long rendered their name notorious in Cornwall. The latter told Captain Vivian that, amongst other matters, he had come to London in search of a reliable padlock for his deed boxes, and asked if he would go with him to a locksmith to assist him in making a choice. To this Captain Andrew agreed, and together they inspected many locks, none of which, however, seemed quite satisfactory to the banker. At length the tradesman brought out a padlock which, he assured his customer, was of the latest pattern, and so strong ' that the devil himself couldn't break it '. ' That 's the one for you, James,' exclaimed Captain Vivian, ' and if you take my advice, you 'll buy two or three more whilst you 're about it, to put on your coffin ! '

The words were spoken in jest, but the gibe sank deep, and old James vowed then and there that he would bring ruin on his companion if ever he found the opportunity of doing so. Trivial indeed as the circumstances of their quarrel now appear, it is none the less a fact that to the end of their lives a bitter feud existed between these two men, whose attitude

[1] C. G. Henderson, *Western Morning News,* 2 April 1930.
[2] The names ' James ', ' Richards ', and ' Rowe ' mentioned in this and the following stories are fictitious.

towards one another was characteristic of the jealousy which antagonized many of the local merchant families of this date.

Together with their business of banking, the James family combined an extensive interest in the local mines, for many of which they acted as pursers. It is said that on pay-days old James would always attend in person, and pay the men with cheques drawn on his own bank. Sometimes the miners would raise a mild protest when they were handed a large cheque which might represent the two months' earnings of a ' pair ' of six tributers.[1]

' How are we to get change to divide this ? ' they would ask.

' Why, go down to the Fire Engine Inn,' Mr James would reply, ' you 'll find my son there, and he 'll settle it for you.'

This they had to do, and on arriving would find that the younger James not only charged them a high commission for the favour of granting the change, but also expected them to take drinks all round in the public-house, which formed yet another of the many enterprises in which his family held a controlling interest.

The Jameses were not the only people in Cornwall at this time who were engaged in such multifarious forms of business. Even better known throughout the county at large were the Richardses, whose tentacles spread far and wide over the mining, foundry, banking, shipping, and commercial enterprises of one of the most important industrial areas of West Cornwall. The story is told that on one occasion old Richards, who was renowned for his ability in driving a hard bargain, had successfully negotiated the purchase from a neighbouring landlord of a piece of ground which he suspected of containing mineral deposits. After the business had been completed, the vendor, though not without some misgiving that he had come off second-best in the transaction, invited the other to stay to dinner.

' By the way, Mr Richards,' inquired the host as they sat talking over their wine, ' you 're a churchman, are you not ? '

' Yes,' responded the other, ' I am.'

' And you 've got three sons, I understand. Are they all churchmen, too ? '

' Why, no,' was the reply. ' My eldest son joined the Methodists not long ago, and Nathaniel is a Quaker.'

[1] Tributers were miners who worked on a profit-sharing system in lieu of wages. A ' pair ' was a group of workers consisting of no fixed number.

' Oh, I see, and what place of worship does your third son attend ? '

' Why, to tell you the truth,' answered the other, ' I don't think he goes anywhere in particular.'

' Ah, now that 's a pity,' gravely returned the host, ' but take my advice, Mr Richards,' he continued, tapping him on the shoulder, ' and make a Jew of him as quick as you can. Then you will have the satisfaction of knowing that you can cheat the devil all round ! '

Not far from the residence of the Richards family dwelt another of Cornwall's early captains of industry. The latter was a Mr Rowe, a lawyer by profession but, like the Richardses, a banker also, and a purser or treasurer of several of the local mines. But whilst, it is true, the Richardses were often feared, they were regarded with something akin to respect in comparison with this particular rival, whose business methods had earned him a notoriety which had long been a byword in the county. Among the many stories told of him, it is related that he would often sit up in his brougham drinking throughout the night, being afraid to go to bed lest he should die in his sleep, whilst his sins were so heavy upon him. It so happened that, at a certain stage in his career, Mr Rowe was in a bad way financially. The bank in which he was concerned was about to suspend payment, whilst one of the mines in which he was a leading ' adventurer ' was ' looking very sick ', and its shares had long been a drug on the market. About this time an unofficial agent of the Richardses, who was always on the look-out to do his masters a service, chanced to be seated in a public-house late one evening when a miner, who had just come up from underground, entered the room. From this man the agent learnt that a new lode had been found but a few hours before in the mine in which Mr Rowe was concerned, and that if the prospects turned out as well as they seemed likely to do the future of the ' bal ' (mine) was assured. Without waiting to hear more, the agent hurried off, late as it was, to Mr Richards to inform him of the news. Early the next morning the agent was on his way to Mr Rowe's house. Arrived there, he quickly made his business known.   It appeared, he said, that there were some ' mugs ' up in London who actually wanted to purchase Wheal Fortune shares and so, knowing that Mr Rowe was pretty heavily laden with these, he thought he would do him the service of offering to buy some from him on their behalf. Having spoken thus the agent paused to observe the effect of his oratory. Mr Rowe immediately turned to the most important question —could these ' mugs ', whoever they were, pay, and if so, how many shares would they buy ?

' Why,' replied the agent, ' they will take £1,000 worth if you can spare as many (with a wink), and as to paying, I have actually got the bank-notes for that amount in my pocket.'

Hearing this, the other went to his safe, and passed over the necessary documents, at the same time holding out his hand for the money. His face fell, however, when he saw that the notes being counted out on his table were all of them payable at his own bank and, as he knew well enough, worth little more than the paper on which they were printed. Under the circumstances, however, he could do no other than accept the notes and comfort himself with the thought that at the worst he was only exchanging one valueless possession for another. It was not until some hours later that he learnt of the new lode which had so recently been cut, and understood the extent of his loss on the shares which were now soaring to a value unheard of in all the previous history of the mine.

Notwithstanding the extent of its trade and commerce, it will be seen that Cornwall in the early years of the nineteenth century was still characterized by a certain stubborn individualism which continued to flourish undisturbed by the changes which were taking place in society elsewhere. Original ' characters ', many of them of a whimsical type now rarely to be met with, must have made the Duchy of those days a happy hunting-ground for the traveller who possessed a taste for the curious and the strange. In the year 1803, for instance, we read in the *Gentleman's Magazine* of the death, at the age of eighty, of a Mr J. Rogers, of the parish of Breage, a person truthfully described as being ' of most eccentric manners '. ' He had not been shaved for many months before his death,' states the writer of his obituary notice, ' and his usual practice was at Christmas to go into the sea for the benefit of his health, and when in want of nourishment to lie on his back and suck the goats in the open fields. When he was seen going to market, he always had on his shoulder a sack containing his money, which he carried in this manner to his attorney to lay out at interest.'

Whilst such persons as these were taken more or less for granted in the localities in which they were known, the arrival of a stranger in many of the outlying places was still wont to cause the utmost sensation, calling forth from the womenfolk who flocked to their doors such ejaculations as : ' Who 's that, you ? ' ; ' Where ded '*ee* come from, an ? ' ; ' Drag in the cheeld (child), you ! and don't 'ee lev' un go foorth till 'ee 's gone.' Entering the local chapel on a Sunday, the visitor might experience some embarrassment at hearing himself alluded to by the preacher as ' the outlandish stranger now in their midst ', on whose account the Lord was petitioned that he might not remain ' a foreigner to Him '.

Small wonder, perhaps, if, under these circumstances, the average Londoner still regarded Cornwall as a *terra incognita*, concerning which he entertained many curious notions and prejudices. ' Whenever I arrive in the metropolis safe and sound, without a single broken limb or any other accident in my journey,' wrote a Cornish business man in 1803, ' I observe with a smile the moon-eyed wonder of my London friends, who exhibit me as a kind of outlandish curiosity to all their acquaintance. But I do not judge of the general ignorance with respect to Cornwall from so partial a source ; I form my ideas from the stage itself, where mankind and their opinions are, or should be, faithfully exhibited. Noting that the scene of Mr George Colman's new comedy, *John Bull*, is laid at Penzance, I went to the play when I was lately in town, warm with expectation of being (in imagination) once more at home ; of viewing the beauties of our picturesque bay, and beholding St Michael's Mount rising in awful grandeur, a splendid decoration of the appropriate scene. I expected to see the most charming women of the stage selected to form groups of our Newlyn fish-women, whose delicate complexions and large blue eyes shining under the shade of their wide black hats, arrest the gaze of the admiring traveller. Imagine my surprise at finding the vicinity of Penzance represented as a desert moor, and that too with the uncouth denomination of " Muckslush Heath ".—Horror of horrors !—O abominable trespass upon euphony !—Stable Hobba, Street-on-Nowan, and the Morraps thrown aside for that barbarous phenomenon in acoustics—Muckslush Heath ! An idea, I know, prevails that around Penzance every wind that blows is a storm—that the few houses which are above ground are built of wrecked timber—that the underground inhabitants are the most numerous, and that the above-ground gentlemen are all smugglers—that those who are not stone-eaters are cannibals —and that every horse, at night, is a kind of will o' wisp, and carries a lantern at its tail. Now Mr Colman misnomers our fields and heaths, and so is error propagated. I beg leave, however, to inform Mr Colman that Penzance is a very different place from the commonly received opinion. We have cards for the sedentary, books for the lounger, balls for the light-heeled, clubs for the convivial, picnics for the gay and thoughtless. Turbot and red mullet swim almost at our very doors, our bay is inferior only to the bay of Naples.

' I am Sir, your's,

' A Penzance-Man,

' but no Smuggler, Miner, Wreck-Ravager,

' Cannibal, nor Hottentot.' [1]

VII

Despite the natural indignation felt by a Cornishman at finding his county so grossly maligned, the difficulties of travel in the western part of the Duchy offered sufficient excuse for the ignorance of the average Englishman. Prior to about the year 1820, when the present causeway was constructed, the only direct route between the populous mining districts of Redruth and Illogan and the peninsula of West Penwith, lay across the Hayle river, whose passage at certain states of the tide was not infrequently attended with considerable danger, on account of the quicksands, bars, and deep pools which the estuary contained. The, still extant, Royal Standard Inn, at Hayle, formed the usual starting place for travellers intending to cross to the village of Lelant ' by the mud ', and for their guidance whitewashed posts and balls were erected in order to indicate the most favourable points for making the passage. In broad daylight, and with a trustworthy horse, the crossing presented little difficulty, but at night time, and with a strong flowing or ebbing tide, it was far otherwise, and lives were frequently lost in making the foolhardy attempt. Indeed, those who were most familiar with the estuary would prefer to swim their horses across at high water, rather than risk the passage of the sands when the slime-filled pools and eddies were covered by a half-tide. Those who got over thus, even at the expense of a wet suit of clothes, had always the

[1] *Cornwall Gazette*, 19 November 1803.

consolation of knowing that a comfortable resting-place awaited them at the old Lamb and Flag Inn, where the land-lady provided the best of entertainment for man and beast, including the once famous beefsteaks cooked on hot blocks of tin from the ' Rose-an-grouse ' smelting works next door.[1]

Long, indeed, after the causeway itself had been built, the actual means of travelling between the outlying parts of West Cornwall and places farther east still retained their primitive character. Notwithstanding the fact that the stage coaches could now proceed direct to Penzance, cumbrous ' vans ' still constituted the usual mode of transport for the poorer class of traveller, within the borders of the county. Passengers in the vans were said to be divided into three classes. On any particularly steep hill the first-class retained their seats, the second-class got out and walked, whilst the third got out and pushed ! Since, however, the Cornish people as a whole have never been noted for any undue compassion in their treatment of animals, one may suspect that in reality all the passengers retained their places. A few only may have gone so far as to lift their baskets on to their knees ' to ease the poor horses ', as one old lady used regularly to do when travelling to and from her market town.

In its appearance the van resembled a long, four-wheeled spring cart, covered with canvas stretched over a framework and having curtains both at the front and at the back. The greater portion of the interior was filled with merchandise and parcels, in front of which a few seats were provided for the passengers. The van was a sociable place, where everybody soon learnt about everyone else's business, and where the events of the day were discussed with the utmost animation. The well-known dialect poem describing the company in ' Penna's Van ' provides an excellent illustration of this :

> This notable van, one evening grey,
> Made one of its halts on the road to St Day,
> When a man came up, and he said (it is truth),
> ' I say, es your van, es 'a goin' to Redruth ? '
> ' No, not to Redruth, but unto St Day ;
> I should be glad to take 'ee if you was goin' that way.'
> ' What do 'ee charge, now, for me to ride
> So fur as Comford 'pon the inside ? '

[1] William Bottrell, *Traditions and Hearthside Stories of West Cornwall*, I, 119-21.

' *Sixpence is the price, far as that, my good man ;*
So, if you do please, get at once in the van.'
' *Only sexpence ! iss, sure, then I 'll get in an' ride—*
Mistress, plaise to move on a little furder inside :
Theer now, that 'll do, I 'm in snug enough.
Honly sexpence to ride ! an' the weather so rough.'

The new passenger, having seated himself, begins to take
stock of his companions. It is not long before his interest in
them begins to show itself in the form of questions which,
though possibly a breach of good manners, are wholly without
discourtesy.

' *What be they things, then, mistress, you got 'pon your arms ?* '
' *They are cuffs.*'—' *Be they, sure ? They do look fine and warm.*
And thickey afore 'ee—that edn't no cuff,
Thof it do look just the same ? '—' *Oh ! no, that 's a muff.*'
' *Married are 'ee, 'an, mistress—makin' so bould ?* '
' *Yes* '—' *Up ten year, I spoase ? though you aren't looking old.*
Hav 'ee got any cheldurn ? '   ' *Good man, I have one.*'
' *Well, so have I too—a scape graace of a son.*'
' *What a braave house this es to ride in, then, sure ;*
We 're shut in fine an' loo (sheltered), tho' there esn't no dooar ;
An' we 're a 'spectable company, too, in the van—
No troublesome wumman nor haafe drunken man.' [1]

Notwithstanding these encomiums, the van to persons of
more fastidious taste was apt to prove both cold in winter
and hot in summer ; whilst in wet weather, when all the
curtains had to be closed, its atmosphere was akin to that of
the Black Hole of Calcutta. Closely resembling such vans
were the ' long ' coaches which served a similar purpose in
other parts of England. Robert Southey, the Poet Laureate,
has provided an excellent description of these. ' The long
coach,' he writes, ' is a huge machine, which carries sixteen
inside. It is shaped like a trunk with a rounded lid placed
topsy-turvy. It is not very agreeable to enter one of these
coaches when it is nearly full. The first-comers take possession
of the places nearest the door at one end, or the window at
the other, and the middle seats are left for those who come in
last and who, for that reason, contrary to the parable of the
labourers in the vineyard, may literally be said to bear the

[1] Reprinted in *Old Cornwall*, Second Series, I, 40

heat of the day. There were twelve passengers already seated when we got in, and the atmosphere, indeed, of the apartment, was neither fresher nor more fragrant than that of a prison. To see anything was impossible, the little windows behind us were on a level with our heads, the coachman's seat obstructed the one in front, and that in the doorway was of use only to those who sat by it. Any attempt which we made at conversation was answered with forbidding brevity. The company was too numerous to be communicative, and as half of them went to sleep I endeavoured (though in vain) to follow their example, as the best mode of passing away time so profitless and so uncomfortable.' [1]

No doubt the majority of passengers in the Cornish vans were less sophisticated, and though one occasionally reads of people being made seasick by the vehicle's uneasy motion, the interior of these vans, as already shown, was full of life and animation. In addition to Penna's van, there were many others which did service in various parts of the county. Well known in West Cornwall were those belonging to William Fidock, which plied on the road between Penzance and Truro. These vans left Penzance at 10 a.m., and as there were countless parcels to be delivered, and others to be received, all along the route, stoppages were numerous, and progress was very slow. This, however was taken for granted by passengers and driver alike, since the latter, in order to avoid the ' mileage duty ' which was imposed on all vehicles travelling at more than four miles per hour, had to see that this maximum was not exceeded. Proceeding in this way Copperhouse would at length be reached, and eventually Camborne, where the single horse which drew the van had to be rested and fed. After this, if the roads were not unduly heavy, and nothing untoward occurred, Truro might be reached by five or six in the evening, the journey of twenty-eight miles having occupied over seven hours. Such was the difficulty and expense of getting about that those who had once been so far from home were regarded as no mean travellers, Truro itself being looked upon as the capital of the Far West, and the grandeur of Lemon Street the spectacle of a lifetime. [2]

Penna's and Fidock's vans were but two of a numerous class which flourished, or at any rate existed, in Cornwall,

[1] Don Manuel Alvarez Espriella, i.e. Robert Southey, *Letters from England* (1802), II, 53.
[2] See *Cornishman*, 31 January 1884.

during the last century. Amongst others may be mentioned :
Wall's van from Bodmin to Truro, down one day and up the
next ; Mansell's van, Truro to Wadebridge ; and Sowden's
van, Padstow to Truro. The 'Inkerman' van ran from
Ladock to Truro on market days, taking two hours over the
journey of seven miles. The fare was sixpence each way.
Allen's van ran from Truro to Falmouth daily. Clemo had
three vans on the road, working between Redruth and Truro,
and Falmouth and Penzance. Reynolds's van travelled each
day between Penzance and Helston, connecting there with
vans to Penryn and Falmouth. Other vans plied daily between
Penzance, the Land's End, and St Just. Famous among these
was Coombe's van, which for many years made the latter
journey via Buryan, carrying the mails.[1]

'The majority of these vans,' writes Mr J. C. Hoare, ' were
entered by a step on the shaft, the interior being lighted by a
small window on each side. In course of time a door was placed
at the back, and they then became known as buses, the goods
being carried on the top. It was a great sight on market days
to see the number of vans and buses assembled in each town.
Some of them were known by their owners' names, others
had special names painted in large letters on the sides. In
addition to those which I have already mentioned I can
recollect the Royal Mail, Express, Alma, Fairy, Magnet,
Victoria, Albert, Nevada, New Times, Eagle, North Star, and
Morning Star. The latter left Bodmin for Launceston every
morning at 4 a.m., driven by Hambly. Most of the vans were
one-horse vehicles, but the bus, being of heavier build, was
generally drawn by two horses.'

Meantime, of course, the coaching system had been
developed on a great scale, and provided a far more comfortable and expeditious mode of travel for those who could
afford it. Already, by 1805, according to Polwhele, coaches
had become numerous in Cornwall, and one of them at least
was performing the through journey from London to Falmouth in the space of forty-one hours.[2] This was, in all
probability, the coach which carried the mails to and from
the Falmouth packet boats. 'The perpetual stir and bustle
in this inn ' (at Falmouth), wrote Robert Southey in his Letters
from England, 1802, ' is as surprising as it is wearisome. Doors
opening and shutting, bells ringing, voices calling to the

[1] Per Mr J. C. Hoare of Madron.
[2] History of Cornwall, IV, 139

waiter from every quarter, while he cries " coming " to one room and hurries away to another. Everybody is in a hurry, here ; either they are going off in the packets, and are hastening their preparations to embark ; or they have just arrived and are impatient to be on the road homeward. Every now and then a carriage rattles up to the door with a rapidity which makes the very house shake. The man who cleans the boots is running in one direction, the barber with his powder-bag in another ; here goes the barber's boy with his hot water and razors ; there comes the clean linen from the washerwoman ; and the hall is full of porters and sailors bringing in luggage, or bearing it away—now you hear a horn blow because the post is coming in, and in the middle of the night you are awakened by another because it is going out. Nothing is done without noise, and yet noise is the only thing they forget on the bill ! ' [1]

Within a comparatively few years after this was written the changes foreshadowed in Macadam's famous essay on road-making began to be seen even in this far-off ' angle of Britain '. Not only were many of the old primitive tracks and ' founderous ' by-ways converted into roads with broad well-laid surfaces but, in still more cases, the lines of communication themselves were changed. In order to avoid precipitous gradients, roads began for the first time to be constructed through the valleys, a procedure undreamt of in earlier days. Among such improvements, dating from this period, was the construction of a new road through the valleys of Sheviock, between Antony and Coldrinick. The cost of this undertaking, including that of procuring the necessary Act of Parliament, payment for the land and the execution of the work, amounted to some £15,000,[2] and great was the outcry no doubt among the wiseacres at this unprecedented example of bureaucratic extravagance. The turnpike reformers, however, like the modern Ministry of Transport, cared for none of these protestations, and it is well for the motorist in the county to-day that they did not. As Mr Henderson has truly said : ' Wherever you find a gently-graded hill or a road threading a beautiful valley, you may bless the far-seeing turnpike engineers of a hundred years ago. The vales of Ladock, Glyn, Lanivet, Lamellan, Pentewan, Pencalenick, and Perran Arworthal, to name but a few instances, were innocent of roads before the

[1] *Letters from England*, I, 6–7.
[2] ' Lanje,' *Western Morning News*, 7 April 1927.

turnpike surveyor set to work. The finely-graded hills out of St Austell, Grampound, Ponsanooth, Truro (towards Tresillian), and Helston (towards Penzance), were the creations of their genius, and took the place of precipitous lanes which can still be traced in their neighbourhood' Over these new turnpikes raced the mail-coaches at an average speed of ten miles per hour, their guards wearing bright red coats, high hats with gold bands and huge cockades, and carrying beside them the long brass horns with which they warned the ostlers at the changing houses of their approach.

By the middle of the last century the main roads of Cornwall had attained a high standard of excellence. In 1855 Kellow's ' Fairy ' four-horse omnibus, which left Matthews's Hotel, Camborne, at 6.30 a.m., and called at the Red Lion Inn, Redruth, and the Red Lion, Truro, reached Plymouth at 4.30, in time for the 5 p.m. train to London. On the following day the ' Fairy ' left the New Market Inn, Plymouth, at 7.30, and arrived in Camborne at 6.30 in the evening. Twenty minutes only were allowed the passengers for refreshments at Channon's Hotel, Liskeard, on the way up, and a similar time at Kellow's Hotel, St Austell, on the way down. The single fare was 14s. inside, and 11s. outside. In 1859 the ' Quicksilver ' coach was able to leave Falmouth as late as 11 a.m., and by changing horses at the Norway Inn, Perran Wharf ; Royal Hotel, Truro ; Falmouth Arms, Ladock ; Indian Queens, Goss Moor ; Royal Hotel, Bodmin ; and the Jamaica Inn, Bolventor ; reached Launceston at a comfortable hour the same evening.[1] If, on the other hand, the traveller's business or inclination led him to adopt the southern route, he could proceed from Truro by another coach, which passed through Grampound, St Austell, and Liskeard, and carried him to Plymouth in the space of seven hours.

Owing, however, to the costliness of travelling by coach, it is probably true to say that more people, in the earlier part of the last century, made the journey to and from West Cornwall by sea than by road. From early times the fleet of small vessels engaged in carrying tin from the Cornish ports had provided a recognized means of conveying parcels and goods to London and, in many cases, passengers also took advantage of this cheap mode of transit. It was to the initiative, however, of the enterprising firm of Messrs Harvey and Company, of Hayle, that a regular service was at length

[1] See *West Briton*, 24 March 1927.

established between that port and Bristol. The original boat on this route was the *Herald*, commanded by Captain John Vivian. This was followed by a much larger vessel, called the *Cornwall*. Envious of their success, Messrs Sandys, Carne, and Vivian—the great rivals of the Harveys in local trade—soon afterwards placed a third vessel, known as the *Brilliant*, on the Bristol route.[1] In 1839 the fares to or from Bristol were 21s. ' Cabin ' and 9s. ' Deck ', these including steward's fees. ' A female steward,' states an advertisement in one of the local papers, ' is in attendance on the Ladies' Cabin. Horses, Carriages, Luggage and General Merchandise carefully conveyed. Refreshments of the best description, and at moderate charges, provided on Board.'[2]

The boats generally left Hayle at about 3 o'clock in the afternoon, if the tide served, and arrived in Bristol the next morning. ' The voyage,' states a writer, ' was much too frequently very rough, and passengers were often ill in crossing the bar, before the steamer had even left the headlands.' The boats were generally heavily laden with new potatoes, broccoli, strawberries, or mackerel, according to the season. The very extensive trade in broccoli which Cornwall now enjoys was due in the first place to Mr Sharrock Dupen, the steward of the *Herald*, who, on one occasion when that vegetable was selling at an excessively cheap rate in Cornwall, took a consignment to Bristol, and made a good profit on the transaction.[3] His success encouraged others, and from it has developed one of the most important branches of agriculture obtaining in West Cornwall to-day.

Whenever great catches of fish were taken in Mounts Bay, the night before and early on the day on which the boats sailed, all the carts and horses in Penzance and the neighbourhood were pressed into the service, and the road appeared almost like a race-course, with the number of vehicles on it, each one striving to outstrip the others in the dash to port. ' I have known the *Cornwall*,' says one writer, ' to be delayed two hours after the proper time of starting, taking the baskets of fish on board, whilst, after all, there were always some men too late who, with their steaming horses and carts of fish, were left lamenting upon the quay, to curse their fate and to sell their fish in the neighbourhood for what it would fetch.'

[1] *Cornishman*, 7 February 1884.
[2] *West Briton*, 31 May 1839.
[3] *Cornishman*, 7 February 1884.

At such times, in order to facilitate dispatch, the baskets would be piled up on deck like small mountains, leaving the passengers very little room to walk about. This fact, combined with the warmth of the engine-room, which caused strange odours to emanate from the fish and vegetables, added still further to the troubles of those already inclined to sea-sickness. At times, however, when the sea was really calm, the trip could be very enjoyable—sailing along within sight of the coast, calling at Padstow, then seeing Hartland Point, calling again at Ilfracombe, sighting Lundy Island, then the Flat Holmes and the Steep Holmes, and at length, perhaps, going up the Avon by moonlight, with the nightingales singing in Leigh Woods as the vessel passed through the famous gorge.[1]

VIII

Meantime, the development of commerce and the increasing facilities for travel were effecting changes even in the isolated society of West Cornwall. ' There is a vast number more shops in this place than there was twenty years ago,' stated a resident at Hayle in 1826, ' and in these shops are sold many articles which could not then be obtained. Still, however, the trade here is not properly subdivided. A man who keeps a shop sells almost everything. He is a linen draper, hosier, grocer, tallow chandler, hardwareman, and almost everything else.' [2] In the country districts shops were still sufficiently few in number to provide an excuse for the evil practice of paying part of the farm labourer's wages in kind. Even in the towns master-masons and other employers of labour were in the habit, in many instances, of mulcting their workpeople of a portion of their earnings in return for the bread, groceries, and other commodities which they supplied them at, frequently, well above cost price. Some of the larger mines, too, continued, to within living memory, to keep their own stores or ' tommy shops ', at which the men were virtually compelled to deal.

For the most part, however, the poor were furnished with the common necessaries of life by the weekly markets in the

[1] *Cornishman*, 7 February 1884.
[2] *Letters from West Cornwall* (1826).

towns, to which the country people came from all the surrounding districts in order to lay out their wages. In the earlier part of the last century the old Market House at Penzance, as in other places, had pent-houses along two of its sides, in which a large miscellaneous trade was conducted. On market days these were supplemented by stalls or ' stannins ' erected in all the principal streets, and here food-stuff and merchandise of every kind was displayed for sale. In 1839 the shoemakers of Penzance were so numerous that they had a special benefit society of their own, and on market days between thirty and forty of their stalls—some of them displaying more than two hundred pairs of boots and shoes—occupied a great part of such available space as existed in the narrow streets. Adjoining these stood, or sat, the picturesque Newlyn fish-wives with their ' cowals ' or baskets of fresh and salted fish, and jars of ' train ' (pilchard oil) for supplying the lamps used in the cottages. Beyond them again might be found a dyer, ready to dye the home-made knitted goods which were brought him by the country people. He also did a brisk trade in wools and yarns of all colours for knitting and mending purposes. In addition to these, most of the regular shops were in the habit on market day of placing a large portion of their goods on the pavement outside their premises.[1] The result was that in many cases it was impossible to pass by without stepping off into the muddy street where, at the same moment, the passage of a train of restive mules would sometimes add still further to the liveliness, if not to the enjoyment, of the long-suffering pedestrians.

Among some of the small, but none the less interesting, changes noted by a Cornish writer of the earlier part of the last century was the general introduction of umbrellas. ' Twenty years ago,' he writes, ' there were not above a dozen in this place (Hayle), now they are in universal use. Formerly it was deemed proud for a man to carry an umbrella, just as it was for him to show the collar of his shirt above his cravat. Even the young female Methodists, however,' he adds, ' dress gayer now, though still they have not become so worldly as to wear bows of ribbons on their bonnets.' On the other hand, he noted that the practice of kissing was not so ' prevalent ' as it had been in his earlier days, when, as he says, at all social gatherings, and ' in particular at the Wesleyan prayer meetings, there used to be lots of kissing after service '.

[1] See J. S. Courtney, *Half a Century of Penzance* (1825–75), 12.

At harvest time, too, it had been the custom for the lads to kiss the girls upon the pooks of hay to make it sweet. He also describes the old game of ' Putting round the Pocket-Handkerchief ', which had hitherto been commonly played at midsummer. On this occasion, the young folks would join hands to form a ring around a lighted tar-barrel, which was fixed on top of a pole. One of the lads, taking a handkerchief, would then run round the circle, exclaiming as he did so :

> *' Fire, fire in my glove !*
> *I sent a letter to my love*
> *And by the way I drop't it, I drop't it, I drop't it ! '*

On the latter words he would allow the handkerchief to fall behind some particular girl whom he favoured, and so continue his course around the ring. If he was able to reach the handkerchief again before the girl perceived it, he gave her ' three or four smart kisses '. The girl would then take the handkerchief, and dropping it behind some lad continue in the same way. If she came round again before he discovered it, he received no kiss. But if he noticed that it had been dropped, he could by running after her and catching her before she arrived at his place demand a kiss as his reward.

Perhaps it may have been due to the abatement of these exhilarating pastimes, that whereas, as the writer notes, there had formerly been but one doctor in the whole district, at the time of his writing (1826) there were no less than four in the town of Hayle alone ! [1]

As yet another indication of the way in which the customs of an earlier and less sophisticated age were slowly breaking down, the same writer mentions that the practice of addressing elderly people by the title of ' Uncle ' or ' A'n ' (Aunt) prefixed to their Christian name was yearly growing less common. Whilst this particular usage has since quite disappeared from local speech, the honorary title of ' Cap'en ' (Captain) has continued to within recent years to be the common appellation of all employers of labour. ' Captains ' indeed were formerly as plentiful in Cornwall as Dickens appears to have found ' colonels ' in America. The degree of dignity attaching to the Cornish title was likewise in direct proportion to the local standing of the individual to whom it was applied.

' Who 's that fella you was spakin' to just now ? ' a miner was once overheard inquiring of a friend.

[1] *Letters from West Cornwall.*

' Why, Cap'en Trevanion ! '

' What, the new cap'en from ovver to Wheal Rose ? '

' No, that's another chap.'

' Aw, so he's a say (sea) cap'en, I s'pose ? '

' No, 'e edn' ;   nor yet a Salvation Army cap'en neither. He's a horse-sojer.'

' There, now, I thoft he was only a army cap'en. He didn't look like nothin' more 'n that.'

Despite the outward changes resulting from the commercial development of Cornwall in the earlier decades of the last century, it will be seen that the working classes still retained much of their simplicity of character. Particularly was this the case with the agricultural labourers, whose isolation in the lonely farms and scattered cottages wherein they dwelt was such as to make them regard the inhabitants of a town or village a few miles away as scarcely less ' foreigners ' than those who hailed from across the Tamar or overseas. A good story, and stated by Mr Tom Miners to be a true one, is told of a certain woman at St Keverne, whose daughter had shown her independence of spirit by selecting her future husband from outside the village clan. A visitor calling at the house one day found the mother weeping bitterly. In answer to his inquiry if she was in trouble, she replied : ' Aw, ais, sir ! Why, my daughter is going to get married next week ! '   ' But why are you crying, then,' asked the visitor, ' that should be something to rejoice over, surely ? ' ' Aw dear, no, sir ! ' she replied with a fresh outburst of grief, ' why, she's going to marry a furriner ! '   ' Oh, really, is that so ?   Is he a Frenchman, a Dane, a German, or what ? ' asked her friend. ' My dear life, no ! ' cried the old lady as she flung up her apron to her eyes, ' 'tes worse than that. Why, maister, he's a Cury man ! ' (A parish some six or eight miles distant from St Keverne.) [1]

The young man, indeed, who sought and found his sweetheart outside the village to which he belonged, was not infrequently subjected to a rough handling by the youths who sought to enforce this communal discipline. Sometimes, however, the latter found that they were ' up against ' a tough customer. On one occasion a young man of Illogan Highway, who had recently returned from America, fell in love with a girl who dwelt in a village to the west of Camborne. He had not been coming to see her long ere he was warned that if he

[1] See *Old Cornwall*, III, 36.

persisted in his visits he would be 'put into the wheelbarrow and taken out of the parish'. Naturally he took no notice of this threat, and as a result he was soon afterwards 'arrested' by the young men of his sweetheart's village, placed in a wheelbarrow, and taken a mile or so away to Carnhell Green, where it was proposed to 'dump' him into a pond. On arriving at this spot, however, the occupant of the wheelbarrow suddenly turned upon his persecutors, and pointing a revolver at them coolly remarked : ' Now boys, you 've had your fun, and I 'll have mine—you can take me back again '. Thinking the revolver was loaded, they had no alternative but to agree, and back to the girl's village they went. Arrived there, their faces fell as they received another order. ' You can put me on home, if you mind to, I 'm enjoying this ride first rate ! '—and on to Illogan Highway they had to go, some five miles distant from their own village ! [1]

How astonishingly narrow the limit of such clanships might be was nowhere better illustrated than in St Ives. Fifty years ago the population here was practically separated into two camps—the ' Stennack ' and ' Down-along '. In the Stennack lived the miners who at that time constituted a considerable portion of the inhabitants. Down-along the wharf, and in the narrow streets, courts, and alleyways adjoining the harbour, and extending thence to the foot of the Island and to the Digey, lived the fishermen. Residence within these areas was strictly prescribed. No fisherman would dream of seeking a house in the Stennack, no miner ever lived Down-along. At times feelings ran so high that battles with stones and wooden swords would not infrequently take place between the rival youths of the two camps. Under these conditions it is not surprising that intermarriage was no less discouraged than if the Stennack and the Wharf had been in reality two separate villages.

A story is told that on one occasion a miner chanced to fall in love with a fisherman's daughter who resided in Hicks's Court, off the Digey. He had not been paying his addresses to her for long ere the fisher lads determined to put a stop to the affair. Accordingly, one evening a group of the latter assembled outside Hicks's Court. One of the men was armed with a pistol, another held a ' skeeter ' (syringe), which had been primed with bullock's blood. About 10 o'clock the miner issued from his sweetheart's house. He had hardly

[1] Mr Tom Miners, *Old Cornwall*, III, 36,

stepped into the street before a threatening shout was raised by the waiting mob, and an instant later the pistol was discharged close to the miner's head. Stunned by the report, he fell to the ground and, believing himself to be seriously wounded, placed his hand to his head, only to have his suspicions confirmed by finding that it was streaming with blood. Having done its work, the crowd quickly dispersed, leaving the miner to the gradual discovery of the hoax which had been played upon him, and to reflect on the lesson which it was so plainly intended to teach.

In connection with the marriage rite itself, many curious customs survived in Cornwall till within comparatively recent years. In the Land's End district, it was the practice for the friends and relatives of the bride and bridegroom to visit them after they had retired to their bedroom on the wedding night. If the doors were locked they were burst open, and the bridal pair were then taken out of bed and each was well beaten with a stocking filled with sand. A bush of furze was then thrust into the bed, and the company, having done their duty, departed.[1]

Another infliction frequently suffered by the newly wed was that of the visit of a ' shallal ' or band of infernal music. This was particularly the case with those who were supposed to have been guilty of some moral laxity. In many instances, however, the annoyance of being visited by a shallal was merely the result of the village roughs having conceived a grudge against one or other of the parties concerned. The disturbance produced on these occasions by the beating of kettles, pans, and tea-trays, and the blowing of whistles and horns, was such that in the borough of St Ives shallals had at length to be prohibited by a special by-law.

Closely akin to this was another custom, whereby those who had committed any glaring act of connubial infidelity were held up to public reprobation in what was called a ' Riding '. On such occasions two figures, personating the guilty or suspected pair, were driven through the streets in a cart drawn by donkeys, accompanied by a rabble of men and boys. In the fishing towns these attendants commonly made use of the seiners' speaking trumpets, and signalling horns, wherewith to increase the raucous din and tumult.

[1] Mr Tom Miners, *Old Cornwall*, XII, 23. This custom is said to have been observed in the village of Morvah as recently as the beginning of the present century.

The mummers themselves often recited a ribald dialogue which, whilst just sufficiently disguised to avoid the charge of slander, left no doubt in the minds of the spectators as to whom it was intended to apply to.

About the year 1880 six persons were brought before the magistrates at Stokeclimsland for causing an obstruction when taking part in a ceremony of this sort, locally known as a ' Mock Hunt '. The lawyer, who was responsible for the defence, urged that the parties had merely been upholding a practice which was ' older by far in the counties of Devon and Cornwall than any Divorce Court '. Possibly as the result of this learned pleading the prisoners were let off with a mitigated fine.[1]

Yet another custom, closely resembling these, was the effigy burning which frequently took place on occasions when some local personage had rendered himself obnoxious in the eyes of the populace. ' I remember one night when I was very young,' wrote a Camborne lady not long since, ' my sister and I were taken out of our beds at midnight, and led down to our garden door which opened on to the street. It was a pitch dark night—" black as a shaft ", as Cornish people used to say—without even a glimmer of the stars. Suddenly there was a muffled pad, pad, pad—crowds of people coming up the road, some of them carrying flaming torches whose light threw into weird relief the effigies of a man and a woman mounted on a high pole. The figure of the man, in particular, was so well constructed that, child though I was, I had no difficulty in recognizing the person whom it was intended to represent. The silent procession passed on its way to some adjacent woods, where the effigies were solemnly burnt, the crowd dancing around the fire with malicious joy until the figures had been reduced to ashes. I have often thought of this incident as throwing a curious light on the Celtic strain in Cornish character.' [2]

Other customs of a perhaps more pleasing nature likewise had their place in the simple, unaffected life of the Cornwall of those days. One of the most delightful of these has been described by a writer in the *Western Antiquary* : ' Walking one Sunday near Millbrook we were met in front of some houses by a party issuing from the door, the foremost, an elderly woman, bearing a napkin in which was deposited a

[1] *Western Antiquary*, III, 127.
[2] Mrs Stanley James.

thick round of currant cake, about eight inches in diameter. The woman came to me and presented this cake, saying : " Don't refuse to take it, sir, or it will cause ill-luck to the child ". I then saw that another of the party bore a child in her arms. I took the cake, much to the relief of every one, the giver saying : " Oh, sir, pray that it may have God's grace and grow up a good man " '.[1] This custom of giving a cake to the first person that was met by a christening party on their way to or from the church was once very general.[2] In West Cornwall the cake was known as the ' cheeld's fuggan ' (child's currant cake). In the eastern part of the county it was called a christening ' crib ', or ' kimbly'. The person sent before the party to carry the piece of bread or cake might be of either sex, though a woman was generally preferred. ' I interpret the custom,' writes Mr T. Q. Couch, ' to have some reference to the evil eye and its influence which might fall on the married persons or on the child, but which is sought to be averted by this unexpected gift.' [3]

IX

The country-side in which these ancient practices continued was one which was for the most part innocent of the schoolmaster's attention. A striking commentary on the degree of ignorance which consequently prevailed is provided by the statement of a writer in 1846 who asserted that at a recent trial at which he had been present ' more than one witness did not actually know what a month was, or the name of the present one '. He was further informed, by one of the magistrates, that numbers even of the more respectable miners were alike ignorant, notwithstanding the fact that they were a type of men who were universally allowed to be exceedingly intelligent in relation to all practical matters.[4]

[1] See *Western Antiquary* (1883), II, 165, 182, 190 ; III, 19.
[2] It is still (1932) observed by certain families in St Ives, as I have learnt from a case which has just occurred. In this instance a biscuit was presented to the first person met with on the way to the chapel.
[3] See M. A. Courtney, *Cornish Feasts and Folklore*, 158.
[4] *Cornish Mining Reporter*, 2 October 1846.

The educational opportunities of the poor at this time, however, were of the slightest. In 1840 there were about twenty-seven National and British day-schools in Cornwall, and approximately one hundred and twenty dame-schools, but it was calculated that scarcely more than half the children of the county could have received any instruction in these.[1] The educational standard of the dame-schools was not, in any case, of a high order. An amusing description, given by Mr Charles Bath, of one of these little centres of learning may be taken as fairly representative of them all. ' Peggy Combellack,' he writes, ' who kept the school, was before her time in so far as she " dedn't knaw grammar, but she knawed georgraphe, rithmetic, and the hole of the halfabet ". " Now, cheldren," Peggy would say, " what do ' A ' stand for ? " This was a puzzler to start with, till at last one of the little girls at the bottom of the class held up her hand. " Well, what es 'a, you ? " inquired the mistress. " He do stand for Haape," was the reply. " Right," Peggy would say, " go hup top the class." The next lesson was in geography. This subject was regarded by Peggy as her masterpiece of learning. " Es Coornwall a naation, a hiland, or what es 'a ? " she inquired on one of these occasions. This question completely baffled the whole school, putting the scholars into one continued hubbub. " Ef I ain't got a hanser in five menutes, I'll give 'ee all the custis " (caning on the hands), Peggy exclaimed. " I will have horder, though the owld school do cost more in canes than 'tes worth. Now what es Coornwall, I say. Es 'a a naation, a hiland or a furrin country ? "

' " Boy Kit " was the first to hold up his hand.

' " Please, he hedn't no naation, he hedn't no hiland, nor he hedn't no furrin country, but he's cigged (stuck) on to a furrin country from the top hand," came the bright reply, which was heard with approval by the whole school, Peggy herself included.' [2]

The ' fees ' at such schools varied from a penny to twopence a week, according to the pupil's age and educational requirements. Often such fees were not paid in coin, but in kind. ' Three miners' candles, two " rooty-bakers " (i.e. turnips, a corrupted form of their Swedish name *rutabaga*), or two eggs,' writes Mr Jim Thomas, ' might be tendered for a penny, or a quarter of a pound of cream for twopence. I have

[1] Cornwall 'Education Week' Handbook (1927), 30.
[2] *Uncle Kit's Legacy*, 13–18.

óften seen these used for payment. There were three classes
in the school which I knew—the " A B C " class, the " Go, go "
class, and the " Testament " class. There was only one book,
and this was passed from hand to hand. Bigger children
often taught the smaller ones their letters, the class standing
around in a half circle with their hands behind their backs
until their turn came for the book. The schoolmistress was
also the handy woman of the village, eking out her living by
knitting, or patching and mending clothes for her neighbours,
and so at times would be too busy to teach. The " custis " [1]
I remember well, and how in extreme cases it was laid hard on
both hands. If her "custis" should be mislaid, or purposely
hidden away, our dame had another instrument of torture
ready—the flat wooden " busk " out of an old pair of stays,
or else a switch made out of a bunch of " griglans " (dried
heather).' [2]

Although most dame-schools professed to teach the three
Rs, progress in arithmetic was generally on an even more
limited scale than in the other two sciences. Necessity, however, aided the poor in evolving a system of their own which
served very well for all the common purposes of calculation.
In accordance with this generally-understood method, ' O '
represented a shilling, ') ' sixpence, ' | ' a penny, and ' — ' a
halfpenny. Thus 2s. 7½d. would be written ' OO)|—.'
When the smaller sum became the larger, the penny mark
would be substituted for the two halfpenny marks and, in a
similar way, the sixpenny mark for the equivalent number of
pennies ; so that a comparatively small space would keep an
account up to £1. [3] These signs might commonly be seen
chalked up in public-houses and on the doors of the smithies
at the mines, where the men were charged with the cost of
repairing their tools.

The fact that there were not enough schools in the county
at this date to provide even a percentage of the children with a
grounding of education made less difference than might now
be supposed. For owing to the early age at which they were
put to work, the majority of the children of the poor could
never have availed themselves of the facilities for education,
even if these had existed. In 1867 the commissioners

---

[1] The *custis* was a nearly circular-shaped flat piece of wood, with a
handle about ten inches long.
[2] *Old Cornwall*, IV, 25.
[3] *Western Antiquary*, II, 101–2 (1882).

appointed to inquire into the condition of young persons and women employed in agriculture were told that the hours of work for children were commonly from 6.30 in the morning until 8 or 9 at night. In consequence it is not surprising to learn that very few of them ever received any schooling after they had been taken into farm service, which was usually at the age of ten or eleven.

Despite the fact that the young people themselves would hardly appear to have been responsible for this, one witness solemnly told the commissioners that ' they do not take any *pains* to keep up their education ', whilst a farmer's wife added that although she had often offered the lads pens, ink, and writing materials—' they won't use them '. In certain rare instances the boys did actually receive some instruction in the farmhouses in the evenings, but as another witness had the honesty to admit, ' they are generally too tired after their work to read much '.

For the same reason night schools, where they existed, were for the most part poorly attended. In any case, their distance from the farms, combined with ' the *necessity* of having to have the lads to do up the horses and cattle from 8 to 9 in the evening ' must have made the chances of attending them extremely limited. The farmers themselves, moreover, were in most cases rigidly opposed to any system of compulsory education, fearing both an increase in the rates, and also that the younger generation of labourers would by this means come ' to put themselves above their masters '.[1]

At the time when these words were written the old order of society, as we realize now, was standing upon the threshold of a vast change. In 1870 came the famous Act which made a certain standard of education compulsory for all. The effects of this upon the outlook of the rising generation can hardly be overestimated. Combined with it, a depression in the mining industry began to cause that outward flow of emigration which has since exerted a far-reaching influence upon the character of the Cornish people. As yet, however, these changes were not, and the curtain, therefore, rings down upon the full-blooded life of Cornwall, with its insularity and old traditions, its fervour and devoutness, untouched as yet by even a shadow of the events so near at hand.

[1] Commission on the Employment of Children, Young Persons, and Women in Agriculture, 1867. Appendix Pt. II to Second Report, *passim.*

FOLK-LORE AND SUPERSTITIONS

I

IT is small wonder that a people so isolated from the outside world and engaged, as the majority were before 1870, in the old traditional occupations of mining and fishing, should have retained until recent times a folk-lore inheritance of more than usual richness. One has only to turn to the ever-delightful pages of such a book as William Bottrell's *Tales and Hearthside Traditions of West Cornwall* in order to appreciate this. Related, though his stories are, in the rambling style of the old droll-tellers, they are none the less instinct with many of the qualities of great literature. Humour and romance, lively dialogue, character portrayal and the appreciation of Nature, all find their place in these stories, whilst here and there, in some tale of ' dark imagining ', the narrative rises to heights of dignity and strength which recall the language of the Bible by which its style was unconsciously inspired.

Such was the genuine folk-culture which served to inform the minds of those who once dwelt within the cottage homes of Cornwall, and which must have compensated them in no small degree for their lack of other education. Against this stubborn rock of old belief, the waves of Methodist teaching long broke in vain. As late as the year 1869 the Reverend C. G. Honor was forced to admit that until a recent period ' wonderful stories were still told among the miners and fishermen of the doings of giants, fairies, piskies, mermaids, and demons ', and though he adds that ' under the elevating influence of sobriety and true religion, the Cornish are rapidly rising above their former degrading credulousness ', the tone of his remarks implies that in some respects his wish was still father to the thought.

It is a curious fact, however, that whilst the influence of Methodism never eradicated the ' superstition ' of the Cornish people, yet the latter, by their own act of leaving their native language and taking to English a century before the coming of Wesley, had suffered almost the entire loss of their *older* Celtic folk-lore.

As Mr Morton Nance has written : ' We see this at once when we compare our own traditions that we know to be Celtic, with their parallels that are still related in Wales or in Brittany. To make one example serve for all, it is enough to mention our vague traditions of lost lands and buried cities with the fully-told stories of these which we find in the two Celtic-speaking countries across the Bristol or the British Channel. In Cornwall, the language gone, we have but a faint echo or two of our own Arthur, and something here and there that can only be explained by reference to the folk-lore of Wales and Brittany '.[1]

It is true that considerable space is devoted to Arthurian stories in Robert Hunt's famous collection of *Popular Romances of the West of England*, whilst a great deal more has been written on the subject by professional authors since his day. For the most part, however, this bulky addition to the literature of Cornwall constitutes a mere embroidering of the subject, and has been aptly described as ' visitor lore '. Under this category comes the quite recent association of King Arthur with Dozmare Pool, a summer tale for which there appears to be not a scrap of reliable evidence.[2] Furthermore, as the most recent research seems definitely to prove, Tintagel itself must be regarded as something of a fraud, for, though an interesting old castle, it appears to have no connection with King Arthur or the Knights of his Round Table.[3] Great was the outcry raised, however, by the hotel and lodging-house keepers of Tintagel, when public attention was called to this fact on the occasion of the visit of the International Arthurian Congress to Cornwall in the summer of 1930 ! For some time afterwards the matter continued to be thrashed out in lengthy contributions to the Press.[4] The protagonists consisted on the one hand of a number of scholars and historians anxious only to seek out the truth from the baffling jungle of the romances—and on the other of those residents of Tintagel who regarded the associations of King Arthur with their castle as a valuable commercial asset. It must be

---

[1] *Folklore Recorded in the Cornish Language.*
[2] See Miss B. C. Spooner, *Western Morning News*, 5 November 1928.
[3] See Henry Jenner, ' Tintagel Castle in History and Romance,' *Journal of the Royal Institution of Cornwall*, XXII, Pt. II (1927).
[4] See *Western Morning News*, September 1930.

admitted that the scholars, through having their judgments unhampered by any personal prejudice, and from being in possession of a great deal of evidence of which their opponents were entirely ignorant, fared best in the controversy. Whilst, however, their findings tended to show that Castle-an-Dinas, in the parish of St Columb Major, had a far better claim than Tintagel to having been the birthplace of the king, they established beyond all doubt the association of the Arthurian romance with Cornwall. Indeed, it would have been strange if they had done otherwise, seeing that there is indisputable evidence to prove how deeply the Cornish people were once imbued with reverence for King Arthur, and with the belief in his second coming.

It was in the year 1113 that certain canons of Laon, in France, came to England for the purpose of collecting money for the rebuilding of their cathedral. With them they brought a number of holy relics, by whose aid they effected many marvellous cures. In the course of their tour they arrived at Bodmin, in Cornwall. ' Here,' states an old chronicler, ' a certain man having a withered hand watched before the Feretory (repository of the relics), hoping to receive his health. But as the Britons are wont to strive with the Franks for King Arthur, this man began to argue with one of the servants, saying that Arthur was still alive. Thereupon no small tumult arose, and many rushed into the church with arms, so that if Algar the clerk had not prevented it there would have been bloodshed. This strife in front of the Feretory was, we believe, so displeasing to Our Lady that the man with the withered hand who had made the tumult for Arthur, did not recover his health.' [1]

As Mr Henderson has pointed out, this story is of great interest, for here we have a genuine tradition to the effect that eight hundred years ago Arthur was regarded as belonging to this region, and that it was not even safe for a visitor to scoff at the general belief that he was still alive, and that he would one day return to avenge his people. This idea indeed was even more clearly expressed in the epitaph which was popularly supposed to mark the site of his grave :

Hic jacet Arthurus
Rex quondam—rexque futurus.

[1] See *Western Morning News*, 25 May 1928.

Strong as such beliefs once were, however, the recollection of them has long since faded from the folk-memory of Cornwall. The same may be said of practically the entire body of the older order of folk-lore, which went its way with the disappearance of the Celtic language. The Cornish folk-lore which remains is for the most part of a hybrid type, containing both Celtic and Teutonic elements. Tales in which saints or the Devil play a part, and tales of supernatural beings—some prehistoric, some medieval—have shown the strongest tendency to survive, and these may be found at large in all the popular collections.

As is only natural, a large part of the most characteristic folk-lore of Cornwall is woven around the staple industries of mining and fishing, in which the population have been engaged from time immemorial. Thus, until recent years, Cornish fishermen, who had never so much as heard of the word ' taboo ', still held to the belief that it was unlucky to mention rabbits, hares, or other wild animals, when at sea. So strong was this conviction that, in 1850, it led to a serious case of assault being heard before the Bench at Penzance. It appeared that a Newlyn boat had put out for the fishing grounds and, when nearly at her destination, the crew had discovered the pad of a hare nailed to the mast. In order to obviate the ill-luck, it was deemed necessary to return to anchorage, and then start out afresh. Suspicion, however, rested on the crew of another boat, and so highly were the feelings of the first party outraged by their action that on the following day a fight took place. In consequence, both crews shortly afterwards found themselves before the magistrates for trial.[1]

Clergymen and churches were likewise subjects of taboo, and although the latter, being landmarks, had sometimes to be mentioned when at sea, they were generally referred to by the older generation of fishermen as ' cleeta ', Cornish ' cleghty ' (bellhouse), in order to avoid using the objectionable word ' church '.[2] Such beliefs are, of course, less general now than they once were ; but nevertheless, it is still considered an unfavourable omen if a clergyman is seen standing near the boats when they are about to put to sea. In such cases the men are wont to grumble among themselves : ' No fish for we to-night '. A few months ago a middle-aged and by no

[1] Thomas Cornish, *Cornish Telegraph*, 20 October 1887.
[2] R. Morton Nance, *Folklore Recorded in the Cornish Language*, 14.

means illiterate St Ives fisherman set off one morning with the intention of taking a trip to the Scilly Islands in order to see some friends. Whilst standing beside the steamer on the pier at Penzance, he was greeted by a minister of one of the St Ives chapels who happened to be passing that way. ' I'm very sorry to see you this morning, sir,' remarked the man. ' I'd been thinking of going over to Scilly, but of course I can't go now, since I met you.'

The minister, needless to say, was astonished at these words, but failing to persuade the man to carry out his original intention, the two returned to St Ives by the next train. Whatever embarrassment the minister may have felt, it was certainly not shared by the fisherman, who merely regarded the incident as a warning from on high that he was not to go that day.

At a Methodist Conference held in West Cornwall a short while since, a protest was made at the disrespectful attitude of the children in ' touching cold iron ', in order to avert bad luck, whenever they chanced to meet any of the ministers in the town. It is fairly clear that this practice was not taken so seriously by the children as by those to whom it caused the annoyance ; but it is none the less interesting as proof of the survival of this ancient folk-memory even in the minds of the rising generation of to-day.[1]

Many of the Cornish fishermen's taboos are, or at any rate were, shared by the miner, who is, after all, but a huntsman of metals and imbued with all the huntsman's desire to supplicate or avoid antagonising the spirit of good fortune. Thus, until comparatively recently, ' bulhorns ' (snails) when met with by the miners in their path were commonly propitiated with a bit of tallow taken from their candles. The writer himself recollects being solemnly warned as a child always to speak up clearly when greeted by a miner on his way to work, lest the omission of this slight civility should send the man to his labour with a poor heart and with memories awakened, perhaps, of the once dreaded power of the ' ill-wisher '.

---

[1] Women likewise were commonly regarded as presaging ill-fortune, and formerly no woman was ever invited on board a boat. Canon H. R. Jennings, however, informs me that on one occasion in the year—Peter's Tide—the women at Sennen used to be taken out by the fishermen and rowed around as far as the Land's End. This would appear to be one of those ' exceptions which prove the rule '.

Looking backwards through the ages we find a time when the old alluvial tin 'streamers' of Cornwall preserved the memory of taboos so strongly as to employ a special set of terms to denote the animals and birds which they might meet with at their work. According to an Elizabethan writer, the owl had to be referred to under such circumstances as a 'braced farcer', the fox as a 'long tayle', the hare a 'long ear', the cat a 'rooker', and the rat a 'peep'. Failure to observe the use of these terms was still punished at this time by the serio-comic enforcement of a fine of a gallon or so of ale.[1]

As is well-known, such taboos as these are wont to obtain among hunters in all parts of the world, and far as the cry may seem from Cornwall to India, the connecting link is none the less there for those who have eyes to see it. It is a curious fact, however, that whilst in the East the huntsman still has his code of good omens, in Cornwall only those things which it is unlucky to say or do have been retained in the folk-memory. Thus the hunter of the Orient, whilst dreading the sight or sound of a wild animal, is delighted to meet with a tethered one, and though regarding one woman as unlucky, is much pleased if two women should cross his path. There can be little doubt, however, that Cornwall once possessed a similar belief in fortunate omens and, in common with other Celts, employed a 'triad' form of expressing them. Not long ago a friend of the writer, when conversing with a Cornish labourer, received definite confirmation of this. 'I can mind how the old people would say,' remarked the man, 'there are three things which are the ugliest sights in the world, and three which are the most beautiful. The first is "a fat slatternly woman, a poor lean horse, and an old scat bal" (disused mine). The other is "a woman with child, a ship in full sail, and a field of corn waving in the wind".'[2]

To have discovered, in the third decade of the twentieth century, an unrecorded piece of folk-lore of this nature is in itself something of a triumph, and that it should have been brought to light by a chance conversation with what English visitors are sometimes pleased to call a 'Cornish peasant' adds enormously to its value and interest.

[1] See Hamilton Jenkin, *The Cornish Miner*, 52.
[2] Per Mr W. D. Watson.

II

Stories of the ' knackers ', or underground spirits of the mines, figure so largely in books on Cornish folk-lore that there is little need more than to mention them here. Suffice it to say that belief in the existence of these underground sprites was once very general. The knackers are described as small, wizened, dried-up little creatures, alleged by some to be the spirits of the Jews who had crucified our Lord, and who were placed here to work out their doom. Their presence was not considered altogether unlucky, since they were scarcely ever heard or seen except in the neighbourhood of rich lodes.

' When I was twenty years younger,' an old tinner told Mr Bottrell, ' I worked in Balleswidden Mine, near St Just. One night I was workan' away for dear life, the sweat going over me like rain. I was in good heart, because for every stroke of my tool I heard three or four clicks from the knackers, workan' away ahead of me. By the sound they seemed to be very near. After a few strokes the ground crumbled down loose and easy, and I found that I had broken into a vug (a hollow space in a lode). My eyes were dazzled at first with the glistening of the bunches of crystals of all colours which hung down from the roof and sides of the place, but when I rubbed my eyes and looked sharper into the inner end, there I espied three of the knackers. They were no bigger, either one of them, than a good sixpenny doll ; yet, in their faces, dress, and movements they had the look of hearty old tinners. I took the most notice of the one in the middle. He was settan' down on a stone, his jacket off, and his shirt-sleeves rolled up. Between his knees he held a little anvil, no more than an inch square, yet as complete as ever you saw in a smith's shop. In his left hand he held a boryer (rod for drilling holes), about the size of a darning-needle, which he was sharpening for one of the knackers, whilst the other was waiting his turn to have the pick he held in his hand new cossened, or steeled. When the knacker-smith had finished the boryer to his mind, he rested the end of the hammer-hilt on the anvil, and looked towards me.

' " What cheer, comrade," says he, " I couldn't think where the cold wind was coman' from, and my light es blown out."

' " Aw ! good mornan', es that you ? how are 'ee, an ? " says I ; " and how is all the rest of the family ? I 'm brave and glad to see 'ee, and I 'll fetch my candle in a wink. Your own es too small," says I, " for to stand the draught I 've left into your shop, but I 'll give 'ee a pound of my candles, my dear, weth all my heart I will, ef you 've a mind to have them ! "

' In less than no time I turned round again with my candle in my hand. But what dost think ? When I looked again into the vug there wasn't one of the knackers to be seen nor their tools neither.

' " Arrea, then ! " says I, " where are a' gone to an in such a hurry ? One might think you 'd be glad to shake a paw with an old comrade, who had been workan' on the same lode weth 'ee for months past."

' But all I heard was the sound of them, away some-where in the lode ahead, tee-hee-an' first ; then squeakan' like young rabbits that whitnecks (weasels) had got by the throat.' [1]

The disposition of the knackers, as this story shows, was always capricious, and in many cases proved definitely spiteful. In consequence, it was a common practice among the miners to leave them a ' didjan' (small piece) of their ' croust' (lunch) on resuming work, in the hope, thereby, of purchasing their good will. Failure to observe this ordinance sometimes entailed dire retribution. On one occasion a man named Tom Trevorrow was working in Ballowal Mine, near St Just. ' A queer old " bal " this,' writes Mr Bottrell, ' and one which is said to have been worked " before the flood ". Close by it lies Ballowal " burrow ", one of the most famous prehistoric burial-places in Cornwall. Old " Santusters " (St Just people) used to declare that not only the mine itself, but the barrows, crofts, and " cleves " (cliffs) all around were swarming with knackers and " spriggans " (sprites), so that Tom, if he was wise, would do as the other men did and leave a little of his croust to propitiate these old-time workers whose precincts he was invading. Tom, however, was a scoffer, and cared for none of these things, till one night when he was

[1] William Bottrell, *Traditions and Hearthside Stories of West Cornwall*, I, 74–5.

at work in a place quite by himself he heard ever so many squeaking voices chant :

> " *Tom Trevorrow !   Tom Trevorrow !*
> *Leave some of thy fuggan (heavy cake) for Bucca,*
> *Oh bad luck to thee, to-morrow.*"

' Tom's only reply was to shout in a fury : " Go to blazes, you cussed old Jew's sperrats, or I'll scat (knock) your brains out ". Thereupon the voices suddenly changed to a threatening note, and the miner caught the words :

> " *Tommy Trevorrow !   Tommy Trevorrow !*
> *We'll send thee bad luck to-morrow,*
> *Thou old curmudgeon to eat all thy fuggan*
> *And not leave a didgan for Bucca.*"

' Sure enough on his return to work next day Tom found the truth of their prophecy, for a fall of ground had occurred during the night, burying up all his tools, and the pile of good ore upon which he had been relying for the whole of his two months' pay. It is said that this was only the beginning of the man's bad luck, which so dogged his footsteps that he was eventually compelled to leave the mine.' [1]

In addition to such oft-quoted tales of the knackers, accounts of the haunting of mines by particular spirits were formerly not uncommon. The story of ' Dorcas ', the wraith of a woman who long years ago committed suicide at Polbreen Mine, near St Agnes, is too well known to need retelling here. So likewise are the phenomena of the black dog and white hare at Wheal Vor, whose appearance was always said to presage some fatal disaster at that mine.

It is not generally known, however, that St Ives Consols Mine was also possessed of a familiar spirit. The latter appeared in the shape of a woman, dressed in black, and much muffled up about the face, who used to be seen in the vicinity of the old Wheal Mary shaft. On many occasions the miners had sworn to obtain ' mouth speech ' from this spirit, but always without success. At length, one day, a man shouted at her : ' Thee 'rt a great fool to stand there frightening people like thee dost, and never answerin' nothen

[1] William Bottrell, *Traditions and Hearthside Stories of West Cornwall*, II, 186.

when they do spake to thee '. Hardly were the words out of his mouth when it is said that a gust of wind blew his hat from off his head. On turning to pick it up he was astonished to find that it had utterly disappeared ; and on glancing again towards the figure he observed that it too had done likewise. Next morning his hat was found close to the shaft—torn to shreds and quite useless ! The miner's plain speaking, however, seems to have had its effect, and from that time forth no further appearance of the spirit has been recorded.[1]

A better story than this, because told with far more circumstantial detail, was recently unearthed by the writer in one of the early volumes of the *Arminian Magazine*. The sober manner in which the story is related and the unromantic nature of the source from which it was drawn render it worthy of quotation in full. ' A few days ago,' states the writer, ' I visited John Thomas, of St Just, in Cornwall. He is about sixty-two years of age, and has been a notorious drunkard the greatest part of his life. He told me that on Sunday, 21st December 1783, about 7 o'clock in the evening, he left San Crete (now spelt Sancreed) in order to go to St Just. As it was dark he missed his way, and about midnight fell into a pit about five fathoms deep. On his being missing his friends made diligent search for him, but to no purpose. The next Sabbath day, as one of his neighbours was going to seek his sheep, he saw, at some distance, the appearance of a man sitting on the bank which had been thrown up in digging the pit. On drawing near he saw the apparition go round to the other side of the bank. When he came to the place he could see no one ; but heard a human voice in the bottom of the pit. Thinking that some smugglers had got down to hide their liquors, he went on ; but coming back the same way he again heard the voice. He now listened more attentively, and as he could hear but one voice he concluded it was John Thomas who was missing, and on calling to him he found that he was not mistaken. On this he went and got help, and soon got him out of the pit. But as he had been there near eight days he was very low when he was got out ; but is now in a fair way to do well. In the bottom of the pit he found a small current of water ; which he drank freely of. This, in all likelihood, was the means of keeping him alive. It is said that several other persons saw the apparition, but

[1] Per Mr R. J. Noall.

took no notice of it. As I am not fond of crediting stories of this kind on common report, I resolved to get the account from his own mouth.   'WILLIAM MOORE.

'REDRUTH, 22nd Jan. 1784.'[1]

Stories of this kind, which illustrate the power of clairvoyance, undoubtedly possessed by many Cornish people, are by no means confined to the far-off days of the eighteenth century. Near the village of Wall, in Gwinear, a field path, which formerly led from a mine, emerges through a stile on to the high road. One day, in the earlier part of the last century, a wagoner of notoriously evil habits was found at this point lying dead, having apparently been run over by the wheels of his own wagon. Shortly after the body had been removed a boon companion of the deceased, whose route from the mine followed this pathway, turned up at his home in a very distraught condition. On being questioned by his wife, he stated that the wagoner had joined him at the pathway stile, and had subsequently walked with him for a considerable distance. During that time he had spoken words which the miner could not bring himself to repeat. Their effect upon him, however, was such that from that day he sickened and began to lose all his strength, and not long afterwards died. This incident was well remembered by people living in the district fifty years ago, and was confirmed by the most circumstantial evidence.[2]

A story somewhat similar to this was lately told by a well-known Cornishman—a cousin of Sir Henry Irving—who in his youthful days had worked in a mine near St Ives. One fine summer evening, as he and a comrade were on their way to ' night core ' they were surprised to see a man named Thomas Richards, whom they knew to be working in the preceding shift, already on surface and going off in the direction of his home. They hailed him, but receiving no answer, supposed that, having come up from underground early, he did not wish to be recognized. They, accordingly, passed on without giving the matter another thought. On arriving at the mine, however, they were met by serious faces, and learnt on inquiry that a fatal accident had occurred a few hours before, and that in the engine-house was lying the dead body of Thomas Richards, who had just

[1] *Arminian Magazine*, VIII, 649.
[2] T. Cornish, *Cornish Telegraph*, 20 October 1887.

been brought to surface ! Although, ordinarily, the very reverse of being a superstitious character, Captain John Peters retained to the end of his days an absolute conviction that on this occasion it was none other than the spirit of the dead man which he and his companion had seen.

As might be expected in a county such as Cornwall, where those who were not engaged in mining have so long taken to the sea for a livelihood, kindred stories are related of the appearance of sailors to their friends at the hour of death. Some seventy years ago a seaman, whose home was in the parish of Feock, sailed out of Falmouth in a vessel trading with the Spanish ports. One evening about a week after his departure, his wife began to feel unusually agitated about her husband, and at length, on going upstairs, she heard as it were a sudden gale spring up, and the sound of rushing waters. Looking out of the window into the garden she beheld her husband being carried off the ship by a great wave ; another wave followed and engulfed him, and she saw him no more. In due course she received a letter from the captain of the vessel informing her that her husband had been washed overboard during a gale, and had been drowned. The letter stated not only the day but the hour of the disaster, which exactly corresponded with the time when she had seen the apparition. This story which was told to the writer by Mr Charles Hoare, of Madron, is representative of many others which, as he very properly says, ' are based on facts and related by those who could have had no possible desire of seeing the apparitions which they describe '.

Even to-day, in almost every Cornish seaport town, similarly authenticated stories may be heard by those who have become entitled to the confidence of the inhabitants. On one occasion, but a few years since, a lady living in West Cornwall received a telegram announcing the death by drowning of a young sailor to whom her daughter was engaged. Wishing to break the news as gently as possible, she went upstairs and entered the girl's room, but was greeted on the threshold with the words : ' I know what you 've come to say. My dear has been here already, and told me for himself. He was half-dressed, in his shirt and trousers, with one bracer only over his shoulder. One of his feet was bare, and on the other his boot was unlaced '. Subsequent inquiry revealed the fact that this description exactly tallied with the appearance of the body, when it was recovered from the sea.

There must, one supposes, be many more stories similar to this which, though well known to the families whom they concern, have for obvious reasons never been made public.

III

Considering the lonely nature of their work, ' with darkness and with danger compassed round ', it is small wonder that a sense of the mysterious spirit world was so strongly developed amongst the mixed mining and fishing population of West Cornwall. ' Most everybody was afraid of spirits when they was out by night in those days,' an old man once remarked to the writer, when speaking of Cornwall seventy years ago. It is clear, however, that there were at all times certain people who were ready to play upon their neighbours' superstitious fears to their own advantage. An instance of this was related by a well-known mine manager who died not long since. On one occasion, when a boy, the latter was working with an old man in Providence Mine, at Carbis Bay. It so happened that the day of the local fair at Lelant chanced to fall during one of the weeks in which they were working ' afternoon core '. To the fair the boy was determined to go, however much the chances seemed against it. On the day in question he and his comrade went underground as usual about two o'clock. They had been working for some time in the end of a long level, the old miner beating the ' boryer ' (drill), and the boy turning it, when all of a sudden the latter cried : ' My Loor, whatever 's that, 'en ? ' The words were hardly out of his mouth before the old man, who was known to be highly ' tembersome ', had clapped on his hat and begun making his way out towards the shaft. Arriving on surface, the latter turned to the youngster and said :

' Dedst 'a 'ear anything, booy ? '

' Why no,' replied the other, ' did you ? '

' Well, I aren't sure,' was the old man's guarded reply, ' but no matter for that, I aren't going down to work no more to-day.'

' Well, I 'm some glad for that 'en,' cried the boy, ' 'cause I want to go to Lelant fair '—and without waiting for the other to change his mind off he went.[1]

[1] Per Mr W. P. Veale, St Ives.

In further illustration of the way in which the more reckless and daring were wont to profit by the prevailing superstition, it may be pointed out that the places most celebrated as the haunts of spirits were commonly found to be the favourite haunts of the smugglers too !

On one occasion a woman living in Island Road, St Ives, went out from her house at a late hour of the night in order to draw water for the washing day on the morrow. A few moments later she returned to her husband in great affright. ' What 's all the pore weth 'ee, Jinnifer ? ' he inquired on seeing her terrified countenance. ' Why,' she exclaimed, ' I hadn't gone but a bit of way from the door when I seed a geat wagon coming down the street. I could hear the whip crack, though the hosses' hoofs was muffled. As it passed, I called out " Good night " to the man, but he never answered a word. And then when I looked up against him, I saw all to wance that he 'adn' got no head ! I tell 'ee, Jan, 'twas the devil hisself I seed.'

' Aais, you,' replied her husband, suppressing a smile, ' and what 's more he 'll have 'ee too if you go foorth again. It edn' gone twelve yet, you know ! '

Such devices as these were commonly employed by the smugglers in order to deter gossiping neighbours from prying upon them when they were at their work.

Mr Jim Thomas relates that the hamlet of Crane, near Camborne, was formerly much troubled by spirits, and was in consequence greatly feared by the old people after dark. One moonlight night a certain woman looking out of her bedroom window saw four headless men carrying a coffin through the ' townplace ' (farmyard) below. So much was she affected by the sight that she wisely determined never to risk such an awful vision again. Another haunter of this village, for whose presence it is less easy to account, was the spirit of an old ' bal ' (mine) captain who, during his life, had been a great buyer and seller of mine shares, and who after his death might frequently be seen, on moonlight nights, sitting in the doorway of his office, still doing business with ghostly customers.

On another occasion a well-known mine captain of the Camborne district was passing through Truthall Lane one dark evening when he was met by three female spirits. On his hailing them they replied in sepulchral tones : ' The living have naught to do with the dead '. Upon their repeating this remark for the third time the worthy captain took the hint, and laid heels to the ground with all speed— determined never more to visit Truthall Lane after nightfall.

Like many another piece of Cornish folk-lore this story bears a close resemblance to the Breton tale of the lonely traveller and the three ghostly women whom he discovers at their midnight task of washing clothes in the village pool.

Another story, which, though it is related as having happened in Cornwall, is in reality a widely diffused folk-tale, describes how a certain man took on a wager to enter the parish charnel-house at midnight, in order to bring away one of the skulls which used frequently to be kept in such places. True to his word, on the appointed night the man arrived, and after groping about for some moments in the darkness, laid hold of a skull. He was just making off with it when a sepulchral voice cried out from above his head : ' That 's mine !' Hastily dropping the skull the man waited for some moments and then, spurred on by the thought of the wager, stretched forth his trembling hands and picked up another. He had almost reached the door with this when the voice cried out again in more threatening tones : ' That 's mine !' Once again he made haste to replace the skull on the shelf, then, girding himself for one last effort, grasped hold of a third. Hardly had he done so before the voice snapped out with even greater menace : ' That 's mine ! !'

' What !' exclaimed the man, ' are they all thine ? Thee geat liard, whoever heard of a man living or dead with three skulls ? I tell 'ee I *will* have one !'

Saying which, he grasped the skull under one arm, and dashed from the place with all speed. His action won him the wager, and it was a somewhat crestfallen figure which shortly afterwards dropped down from the rafters, and made its way to the public-house, where the hero of the hour was loudly vaunting of the powers of darkness which he had overcome !

IV

At a time when spirits were believed freely to roam the country-side, the clergy of the Church of England were by no means exempt from personal dealings with their ' ghostly enemy '. Indeed, the fame of many an old Cornish parson was based on his reputed skill as an exorcist, some of them being by no means unwilling to favour the popular superstition in this respect. ' I could mention the names of several persons,' wrote Polwhele in 1826, ' whose influence over their flock was solely attributable to this circumstance.' [1]

Among the most famous ghost-laying parsons of the west was the Reverend Jago, of Wendron, of whose spells it was said that ' no spirit walking the earth could resist them '. By his prayers or powers many a night-wanderer was put back into its grave and so confined that the poor ghost could never get free again. Throughout a long life Parson Jago rode far and wide over the wild moorlands of his parish, never taking a groom with him ; since the moment he alighted from his steed, he had only to strike the earth with his whip and a demon servant was there ready to hold his horse. About a quarter of a mile from Wendron at a certain cross-roads a suicide named Tucker had been buried in accordance with the custom at that time. Passing this dreaded spot one night a drunken farmer, returning from Helston market, cracked his whip and shouted lustily : ' Arise, Tucker ! ' Upon this, it is said, the ghost arose and firmly fixed itself on the saddle behind the farmer. Nothing daunted, the foolhardy drunkard repeated the experiment on several other occasions. At length the spirit became so ' familiar ' that it refused ever to leave the farmer, and eventually the latter was obliged to call in Parson Jago to remove it.

Parson Woods, of Ladock, was another skilled exorcist, who possessed an ebony stick engraved with planetary signs and mystical figures. With this weapon he is said to have belaboured many a ghost and demon.

Famous in East Cornwall was the Reverend Dodge, of Talland, who went to the aid of Parson Mills, of Lanreath, when the latter was pursued by a black coach with headless horses and driver. As Dodge appeared the ghostly coachman shouted : ' Dodge is come ! I must be gone ! ' and the spectral terrors disappeared.[2]

Pre-eminent among the ghost-layers of the more recent past was Parson Richards, of Camborne. On one occasion two miners who had been working ' first core by night ', i.e. 6–10 p.m., were going homeward by a path which lay through the churchyard. In was close on midnight when they reached

[1] *Traditions and Recollections*, 605.
[2] Rev. A. A. Clinnick, *Old Cornwall*, II, No. 2 (1931).

this spot, and accordingly they were much astonished to see the parson himself standing in the porch, a prayer-book in one hand, a candle in the other, and a horsewhip hanging over his shoulder. Their curiosity aroused, they went forward to speak to him, when, to their amazement, he suddenly turned upon them, exclaiming in a fury : ' What ded 'ee want for to go and break the spell like that ? Two minutes more and I should have had 'un fast in hell. Now no one knows when I shall catch 'un again '. With which scarcely Christian sentiments upon his lips he seized his horsewhip and rushed at the men, driving them before him as far as their homes at ' Jethon ' (Treswithian). This story is all the more remarkable from its being handed down in living tradition, Mr Jim Thomas, of Camborne, who related it to the writer, having actually heard in his boyhood the names of the two miners who were concerned.

Another famous exorcist of olden days was Parson Polkinghorne, of St Ives, whose laying of the ghost of ' Wild Harris ', of Kenegie, forms one of the most interesting stories in Mr Bottrell's valuable collection of Cornish folk-tales. The details of how this turbulent spirit, who had long defied the powers of all the other clergy of the district, was at length laid to rest within the ancient ramparts on the adjoining hill of Castle-an-Dinas, form a story too long for retelling here. It is one, however, which should be read by all who wish to know for themselves the ways and means employed by these old-time spirit-quellers, and the extraordinary adventures which not infrequently fell to their lot.[1]

It would seem doubtful, however, if Parson Polkinghorne, for all his skill, was entirely successful in ridding the Harris mansion of the more than one turbulent spirit which formerly haunted it. Although their actual names must be withheld, there are persons still living who can confirm this. About forty years ago the Harris property passed into the hands of another well-known Cornish family, which was represented at that time by two ladies. The elder of these had retired to her bedroom one evening when her sister was much alarmed by suddenly hearing her terrified cries for help. Hastening to her room she anxiously inquired the cause of her distress. It was some time before the other became sufficiently composed to speak, but at length she stated that on being about to get into bed she had suddenly perceived the face of a man outlined

[1] See *Traditions and Hearthside Stories of West Cornwall*, III, 28.

upon her pillow. Of this extraordinary story the younger sister appeared somewhat sceptical, and accordingly the other took up a pencil and proceeded to sketch the face which she had seen. So convincingly was this done that the writer's informant, who had seen the drawing, had no more doubt than had the two ladies that the face was that of ' Wild Harris ', whose portrait remains for comparison with it to this day.

In certain cases the ghostly visitants of such old houses have been known to make themselves so obnoxious as altogether to oust the living from their rights. An instance of this sort was seen in the case of a house which about the beginning of the last century formed part of some old premises near the quay at Penzance. Owing, as it was said, to some nocturnal and ghostly wanderer who, being deprived of rest itself, was resolved that all others should be in a like condition, this particular house had long remained unoccupied. Old people, however, of that date, could recall the time when the place had been a public-house, and stated that a sailor who was known to have possessed money had previously disappeared in its neighbourhood, and had never afterwards been heard of again. At length, in the year 1813, the premises were purchased, and a part of them was taken down ' in order to erect a smelting-house for refining tin for the China market '.

During the work of demolition a human skeleton, greatly decayed, was discovered beneath one of the floors, and this was believed to be none other than that of the unfortunate mariner whose ghost had so long disturbed the precincts wherein the murder had been committed.[1]

In order to prevent the wanderings of such troubled spirits, the latter were frequently imprisoned by the old exorcists in locked rooms. An aged St Ives lady once told the writer that she remembered a room in John Knill's house, in Fore Street, which had long been kept locked on account of the spirit of a lady ' dressed very fine with all her jewellery upon her ', which had been laid to rest therein. She often visited the house in her girlhood, and remembered the fear with which the inhabitants passed the door of this room after dark.

At Clowance there was formerly a room which had remained locked for a hundred years, in consequence of a spirit having been imprisoned within its walls. About a century ago the old house was destroyed by fire, and the haunted room was broken into. It was found to contain a quantity of old-

[1] *West Briton*, 5 November 1813.

fashioned glassware which, apparently not being to the taste
of one of the former owners, had been put aside and locked
up in this room with the spirit.

Lanyon (pronounced ' Lanine ') House, in Gwinear, also had
its sealed chamber. On one occasion two maidservants, out of
curiosity, took up some of the floor boards in the room above
and let down a candle on a string. For some unexplained
reason the haunted room was seen to be half-full of feathers,
which must have at least provided a comfortable resting-place
for the rats, whatever the spirit may have thought about it.

In some cases, however, merely locking the door of a room was
considered an insufficient safeguard, and there are people who
have actually seen a doorway built up with masonry in order to
prevent the escape of some unusually turbulent prisoner.[1]

In large houses it was conceivably not difficult to spare a
room for such purposes, but in smaller establishments the
resultant inconvenience to the living inhabitants must have
been considerable. In consequence, perhaps, of this, spirits
were sometimes ' laid ' under hearthstones, or out of doors in
pigeon-holes, or beneath large rocks. On the tenement of
Treassowe (pronounced ' Trazza '), in the parish of Ludgvan,
near Penzance, there was formerly to be seen a great stone
trough, turned upside down, just in front of a thatched house.
A gentleman inquiring the reason for this was told that there
was a ' spirit ' underneath it which had been ' laid by Passon
Stevens ' many years before. Doubtless there are old people
in the neighbourhood who can still remember this, although
the writer understands that the trough itself has since been
put to a more mundane use.[2]

The study and practice of magic arts was by no means
confined to the clergy in former days. In many instances
the more studious members of the old West Country families
who dwelt in the isolated mansions of West Penwith were
wont to pass much of their time in drawing horoscopes,
concocting drugs, and distilling strange compounds and
cordials, by the aid of which they predicted remarkable
events. Professing such powers, they were naturally held in
awe and respect by their more illiterate neighbours, and were
frequently called upon to raise spirits or to lay them to rest.
Their reputation was still further enhanced by the powers
with which they were accredited of being able to detect

[1] Per Mr Jim Thomas, Camborne.
[2] See Rev. Canon G. H. Doble, *Old Cornwall*, III, 7.

evildoers. As time went on their mantle descended upon the poorer class of conjurer, of whom almost every town and village had its representative. Crude as the methods of the latter often were, they none the less exercised an important influence upon local life.

'About a fortnight since,' states the *Cornwall Gazette*, 20th February 1802, 'there was stolen from the house of John Hockin, a labourer of the parish of Sithney, a small bag, containing cash to the amount of about £10, the property of his son. Suspicion having fallen on two or three of the neighbours, a warrant was procured and their houses searched, but to no effect. The young man, however, being unwilling to give up his money without some further research, resolved last Saturday to go to the *conjurer* and declared his intention to some of the neighbours of going the next morning. Superstition effected what honesty could not ; the terrified thief, in the course of the night, brought back six guineas (perhaps all that was left), and dropped it in at the door of the house whence it had been taken, to the joy of the family, who found it in the morning.'

Polwhele, writing a few years after this of the famous conjurer of Ladock, affirmed that money of great amount had often been recovered through his agency, and added that he himself had witnessed the restoration of twenty guineas to the place whence they had been stolen ' by a wretch who feared the conjurer more than any Justice of the quorum '.[1]

Such beliefs died hard. Not long ago the writer was shown a curiously illustrated treatise on astrology belonging to a certain William Allen, of St Ives (1840–9). At the end of the book the writer had drawn a number of diagrams showing by the position of the stars the most favourable times for going out fishing. Descriptions were also given of the character of various local people, but perhaps the most interesting feature of the book was the attempt which had been made by means of astrology to reveal the perpetrators of petty thefts.

Doctor Jonathan Couch has left an account of a similar character, named John Stevens, who flourished about this time in Polperro. The latter was a shoemaker by trade and, like many of his kind, a man of solitary habits and very studious. If his goodwill was obtained he would employ his art in foretelling the fates of those who came to consult

[1] *Traditions and Recollections*, 605.

him, expecting neither fee nor reward for his labour. In many cases his predictions as to the date of a person's death, or whether or not they would recover from a sickness, were said to have proved very accurate. His library consisted of ephemerides and other books, some in quarto and black letter, on the science of the stars and their government of human actions. He also possessed a round shallow box with three plates of brass, having engraved on them representations of tables and diagrams of planetary motions. One of these plates was a dissected circle with astronomical signs and constellations, and a central hole, in which had been fixed a wire. By moving this over the area the astrologer traced the conjunction of the planets, and so resolved the horoscope of the individual who was consulting him. 'John Stevens,' Doctor Couch concludes, 'was skilful as well as sincere in the exercise of his science, and in intellect was far above the ordinary conjurer and discoverer of witcheries and thefts.'

His local rival, however, a man named Warne, was an astrologer of the latter type. He had not the slightest faith in his craft himself, but since the public at large had a great trust in him he had the skill to use his influence well. His visits to the neighbouring farm-houses were not unwelcome, since, as Dr Couch has written, 'he could turn his hand to anything, and was, moreover, a merry companion'. On one occasion he dropped in on a farmer and engaged to spin some straw for thatching, in return for his dinner. By the meal-time he had spun two bundles of such a size that supernatural aid was suspected. At any rate, he was thought to have well earned his dinner. Soon after this the farmer called in the same conjurer to find out who had stolen his two missing pack-saddles. Harry Warne's oracular reply was: 'They 'll be found after harvest'. This prediction turned out true, for when the time came to use the two prodigious bundles of rope for thatching the ricks, the pack-saddles were disclosed inside them ! [1]

V

'But why seek we in corners for petty commodities?' as Carew would say, seeing that in any account of Cornish folk-lore pride of place must so clearly be given

[1] *History of Polperro*, 125-6.

to the small people or 'piskies' who once haunted the rocks, crofts, fields, cliffs, and cottage homes of old Cornwall.

One of the earliest and most pleasing accounts of these little creatures is to be found in Moses Pitt's letter concerning the once famous Anne Jefferies. The latter was born in the parish of St Teath, in the year 1626, and at one period of her life ' was fed for six months by a small sort of airy people, called fairies '. By their aid she performed many miraculous cures, ' people of all distempers, sicknesses, sores, and agues, coming not only from so far off as the Land's End, but also from London, to be cured by her. She took no money from them, nor any reward. She neither made nor bought any medicines or salves, yet wanted them not as she had occasion. At one time, moreover, she forsook eating victuals, and was fed by these fairies from harvest to the following Christmas Day, upon which, because it was that day, she did eat some roast beef '. In the year 1693 she was visited by a certain Humphry Martyn, from whom the writer of the above letter derived his account. When interviewed she firmly refused to give any details of her intercourse with the fairies, or to describe the cures effected by their aid, saying : ' If I should discover it to you you would make books or ballads of it, and I would not have my name spread about the country in books or ballads if I might have five hundred pounds for doing it '. Anne Jefferies was in all respects a very devout woman, and ' took mighty delight in hearing the word of God read and preached, although she herself could not read '. Here again, however, the small people came to her assistance ; for on one occasion when she was about to be examined before the magistrates and ministers they provided her with the apt quotation : ' Dearly beloved, believe not every spirit, but try the spirits whether they be of God ', turning down the proper page in the Bible in order that she might show it to her judges. In addition to receiving food and counsel from the fairies, Anne Jefferies similarly derived the power of rendering herself invisible, and would often dance with them in her orchard. On one occasion they even went so far at her request as to present a little friend of hers, ' Mary Martyn, aged four ', with a silver cup. At length the time came when the small people warned their friend that ' John Tregeagle, steward to the Earl of Radnor ', had procured a warrant to send her to Bodmin jail, and that she should be kept there for a long time without victuals.[1]

So runs the account given in Pitt's letters. Not long ago, however, the writer when searching through some MSS. in the Bodleian Library came across two papers, dated February and April 1647, which serve to fill in and complete the interesting story of Anne Jefferies. ' I can acquaint you with noe news from these partes,' states the writer, ' save only of a young Girle which foretells things to come and most have fallen out true. Shee eats nothing but sweet-meates, as Alemans (almonds) comfited and the like, which are brought her by small people cladd in greene and some-times by birds. She cures most diseases, the Falling sickness especially and broken bones, only with the touch of her hands. She hath been before the Committee and she bids them do good in their office, for it will not last long. She hath been examined by three able Divines, and gives a good accompt of her religion and hath the Scriptures very perfectly, though quite unlearned. They are fearful to meddle with her, for she tells them to their faces that none of them are able to hurt her. At this present she is at Bodmin, at the Mayor's house, and hath been there ever since the last sessions with a Guard on her. She prays very much, and bids people keep the old form of prayer. She says the King shall enjoy his own, and be revenged of his enemies.' [2]

This frank account of Anne Jefferies' political views put a somewhat different complexion on her long imprisonment which, as the writer of the second article explains, was chiefly ' least her discourses (which are all on behalf of the King, and strangely saucy against the Parliament) should trouble the People's minds, who are apt to revolt from the Parliament's obedience '.[3] These opinions, however, which caused so much concern to the authorities of her own day, seem of small consequence now, and yet we should perhaps be grateful for the fact that by their means she became notorious. For, were it otherwise, we might never have heard of those ' small people cladd in greene ', who fed and comforted her during the lonely days and nights of imprisonment which she suffered through the political fanaticism of her time.

[1] See Rev. S. Baring-Gould, *Cornish Characters and Strange Events*, 531–43.
[2] *Clarendon MS.*, 2443, fol. 102.
[3] *Clarendon MS.*, 2478, fol. 165.

In those days, however, before the vision faded and the eyes of humanity grew dim, the apparition of the fairies was by no means as uncommon as we might now suppose. 'Many strange stories we have,' wrote Thomas Tonkin about the year 1727, 'more especially among the miners, of fairies or, as they call them, piskeys, small people, etc. ; of their discovering mines to them, playing on musick very sweetly in them, etc.—dancing in rings and circles—from whence came the many bare rings and circles which we see in many places, particularly one in a field of my own at Trevaunance, called the Rose Field, where I have been told of above twenty several appearances of them, even in the daytime. I remember that about forty years since, viz. about 1687, one, Agnes Martin, of St Agnes, pretended that she had been carried away by these small people, and gave a long account of her living among them, etc., and that her employment was to look after the children. I have often discoursed with her about it since that time, and by the best conjectures I could make she was carried away by a gang of gipsies (for she was certainly wanting several years, and no one could tell what was become of her, till she was accidentally met with in a fair and brought home), and being very young, not above seven or eight years of age, carried about from place to place generally by night, etc., she verily believed the tale she told, and that she lived with them underground, and was well treated by them, and (no doubt) had this story put into her head by them (i.e. the gipsies). I mention this little story as being within my own knowledge, and not unknown, neither, to many people still living who have had it from her own mouth.' [1]

Tonkin's explanation that Agnes Martin's tale was simply put into her head by gipsies seems, as Mr Morton Nance has pointed out, to be quite unnecessary. For it was a generally accepted belief at that time that young girls were frequently taken away by the small people to look after their children. Any one who is acquainted with Cornish folk-lore will at once recall the similar tales of 'Cherry of Zennor' and 'The Fairy Master', which are recorded by Hunt and Bottrell. No girl would be likely to imagine herself the heroine of a fairy-tale of this sort, unless she had heard it told so often as to make her regard the happening as well within the bounds of possibility. [2]

[1] Thomas Tonkin, *Natural History MS.*, pp. 10–11 (*circa* 1727).
[2] *Old Cornwall*, VI, 40–1.

For a large proportion of the country people of this date, indeed, the presence of the fairies and their participation in human affairs were regarded as matters concerning which there could be no question of doubt. Hence it was that many women would never leave their cottages without first making provision for the small people, or preparations against other less welcome visitants from the spirit world. With this in view the fire hook and prong would be crossed to keep off witches, the brandis (trivet) turned down on the baking-iron to prevent the small people sitting on the former and burning themselves, whilst last, but not least, the hearthstone would be neatly swept, and a basin of spring water left before it, so that the fairies might enter and wash their children under pleasant conditions if they felt inclined to do so.

In a little early eighteenth-century MS. entitled *The Duchess of Cornwall's Progress* the writer states : ' In Madern (Madron) parish a good woman of discretion hath told me of certain, that sitting up late in her father's house she often sawe the fairies (neat little creatures) who familiarly talked with her, and gave her many groats until she bewrayed this converse against their charges and order '.[1]

Throughout the early part of the last century belief in the fairies still remained very general. Late one night about the year 1810 a certain journeyman tailor, named William Dunn, was returning to his home at Sparnick Downs, near Truro. Just as he was passing Kea churchyard he was startled by seeing a troop of small people crossing the path immediately in front of him. They were about eighteen inches high, all dressed alike, with black ' sugar-loaf ' hats, and little red cloaks. They descended the bank from the adjoining common at a run, crossed the road in single file, ascended the hedge and disappeared into the dim churchyard beyond. Dashing his stick after the fairy crew the man climbed the fence and peered over, but the piskies, perhaps offended at his discourteous action, had disappeared, and no further sight of them was vouchsafed him.[2]

It was not always that the small people chose to display themselves to mortal eyes in order to make their presence felt. Though, at times, not unwilling to render useful service to man, they appear more often to have delighted in playing

[1] Bodleian Library, *Lhuyd MS.*, 10,714.
[2] H. Michell Whiteley, *Devon and Cornwall Notes and Queries*, October 1912.

tricks upon him. ' Old Robin Hicks, who formerly lived in a house at Quay Head,' wrote Doctor Couch in his *History of Polperro*, ' was more than once on stormy nights alarmed at his supper by a voice calling sharp and shrill : " Robin ! Robin ! your boat is adrift ". Loud was the laughter and " tacking " of hands when they succeeded in luring Robin as far as the quay, where the boat was lying safely at her moorings.'

Not long since, a middle-aged man, who is well known to the writer, described how his wife had on one occasion been ' pisky-mazed ' whilst going home through a field in the parish of ' Costenton ' (Constantine). Normally, she knew the field perfectly well ; but on this occasion she wandered round and round so long that, at length, she had actually to call for assistance in order to be shown the way out. It was not always, of course, that such help was at hand, and many stories are told of lonely travellers who have been led so far astray as to have at length sunk down exhausted on the bare ground. Others have only released themselves from such situations by following the old people's advice, and turning some garment inside out, in order to break the spell. Again and again the victims of these fairy pranks have described how they have heard the elvish laughter of their invisible tormentors, the expression ' laughing like a piskey ' being still proverbial among the older inhabitants of the Duchy.

Nor did the small people confine these unwelcome attentions to man. About the year 1816 an intelligent farmer, near Lostwithiel, had a pony which he was in the habit of turning out into one of his fields by night. One morning the animal showed signs of being ill. It recovered during the day, but developed the same symptoms during the following night. The farrier was called in, and pronounced that the pony was ' pisky-ridden '. A watch was accordingly set, and that night ' five little men like apes ', the tallest of whom was not more than six inches high, were seen to go into the field and engage in wrestling. The contest was long and, for some time, very equally maintained. At length one of the small men succeeded in throwing each of the others ' a fair back throw '. The victor thereupon jumped on to the pony, and began dancing in the most grotesque manner, and singing very obscene songs, whilst the others, howling with wrath and pain, so terrified the poor animal that, in wild affright, it galloped furiously around the field for upwards of an hour, at length falling breathless and exhausted beside a hedge. In consequence of this the pony was afterwards kept in the stable at night, the door being fastened with a green twig of ' scaw ' (elder), in order to keep out all unnatural intruders. The result was that in a very short time the animal had recovered its normal health.[1]

Down to the end of the last century dealings with the fairies continued to be not uncommon in the more remote country places. A West Cornwall vicar told the writer not long since that an old lady whom he remembered living at Bone, near Penzance, used often to put out money for the small people on a certain rock in a field near her house. It was her proud boast that these gifts were regularly claimed by the fairies, for, as she said, ' by the morning the coins had always gone '.

Though the goodwill of the piskies was sometimes courted in this fashion, their capriciousness made them generally feared. Particularly was this so among the fishermen, many of whom objected to landing from their boats at night on account of their dread of being carried off by these visitants from the spirit world. ' Some little time ago,' wrote Mr H. Michell Whiteley in 1912, ' my brother was staying at a lonely little fishing village on the coast of Cornwall. On one occasion whilst he was there some of the fishing boats came into the harbour in the middle of the night, and he at once went to the pier to see what would happen. He found the fishermen would not come on shore before the morning ; and after much pressing, they told him that the reason why they stopped in their boats until daylight was that they were afraid to land for dread of the " little people ".' [2]

Within the last twenty years a certain man, living at Hayle, was in the habit of regularly putting out a saucer of milk for the small people before going to bed. The latter, he said, only drank the ' astral ' part of the milk, whatever that might be. Apparently the cats drank the rest, and strangely enough one of them which belonged to a friend of the writer became very ill as the result of it.

It would be easy greatly to extend the number of stories relating to the small people by quotation from Mr Bottrell's collections. Among such tales should be mentioned the ' Changeling of Brea Vean ', the ' Piskey Thresher of Boslow ',

[1] *Cornish Mining Reporter*, 6 November 1846.
[2] *Devon and Cornwall Notes and Queries*, October 1912.

or the adventures (recorded by Dr Jonathan Couch) of the Polperro lad who on one occasion was carried away by the fairies on an astonishing visit to the ' King of France's cellar '. The repetition of these stories, however, must be omitted from an account such as this, which aims rather at gathering up the still extant traditionary lore, together with fragments derived from less well-known sources.

The fact that hitherto unrecorded stories are still to be found by those who are willing to make diligent search is illustrated by the following which provides one of the most circumstantial accounts of an appearance of the small people known to the writer. There died at St Ives in the year 1927 an elderly lady, named Mrs Rebecca Noall, who in her youth had been employed as a dressmaker's assistant in a shop in Tregenna Place. In those days it was not uncommon for the girls to be kept at work until eleven, or even twelve o'clock at night, on special occasions when some order had to be executed within a limited time. One evening, when she had been working thus to a late hour, her father went round to the shop to meet her, in order to give her his company home. They started off together, and had reached a spot in Fore Street, known as ' The Cliff ', when an extraordinary sight greeted their eyes. On each side of them appeared a procession of ' little people ' walking in an orderly fashion, arm in arm, with the greatest decorum and dignity. The old lady used to describe them as being the neatest little creatures imaginable, and beautifully dressed in scarlet cloaks and black steeple-crowned hats. Her father had evidently seen them as clearly as herself, for, in a whisper, he bade her keep strict silence and avoid attracting their attention by any exclamation of surprise. Thus they passed by and reached home in safety, none the worse for their strange encounter. To the end of her life, however, the sight which had been vouchsafed them remained deeply impressed upon the lady's memory, and she would often recount the story to her family, who cherish it to this day.[1]

One of the last persons openly to profess a belief in the small people was a certain Sophie Dowrick, an interesting old ' character ', who died in the parish of Philleigh in 1928. Up to within a comparatively few years before her death she still clung to the quaint old crinoline dresses of her girlhood days. Throughout her latter years she boasted much of her

[1] Per Mrs J. H. Hodge, St Ives.

nightly dealings with the small people, who led her, so she affirmed, to the life-giving herbs which she might often be seen gathering on moonlight nights in the fields when the dew was on them.

Many theories have been advanced in attempting to explain the phenomenon of the Small People. The most generally accredited appears to be that they represent a folk-memory of an ancient race of inhabitants, who were conquered by the Celts on their arrival in Cornwall, but who continued for long afterwards to lead a furtive existence in the moorlands and cliffs, till finally they faded away altogether, and were remembered only in old wives' tales and tradition. Such a theory, whilst not in all respects satisfactory, does account for the freakish nature generally attributed to the small people who, in their maliciousness to the inconsiderate, and their kindliness towards those who treated them well, were wont to display the usual characteristics of a conquered race. Further, it explains the tradition (which more especially related to the ' knackers ') of their dwindling size, and the belief that they were destined in time to disappear altogether.

VI

Genuine tales of the fairies are now but rarely to be met with, and any actual belief in their existence may be said to have wellnigh disappeared. The subject of Death, however, is one which still retains many folk-lore associations. Among these may be mentioned the conviction, once commonly held among Cornish people, that the spirit of a person who had been accidentally killed, or who had committed suicide, was bound to ' walk ' in the parish in which death had occurred. On one occasion, some fifty-six years ago, an inhabitant of the parish of Perranuthno fell into a mine shaft which happened to lie so near the boundary that owing to its underlie, the point where the body was found was actually in the adjoining parish of St Hilary. This raised a curious issue, the Perran people maintaining that the man had died where he was found, i.e. in St Hilary, and that he must be buried in that parish, notwithstanding the fact that he was admittedly ' a Perran man '. He was sure to ' walk ', they said, in the parish in which he was killed, and for their part they would rather that he was buried there also. Eventually the curious fact emerged that the unfortunate man, who had certainly fallen down a shaft in Perranuthno parish, and had probably died in St Hilary, had actually to be brought to surface through another shaft in the adjoining parish of Breage. In which parish, therefore, the spirit would eventually decide to walk must have proved a ' puzzler ' even to the most authoritative local wiseacre.

The belief that ' tokens ' or warnings are wont to precede the hour of dissolution is one which still finds very general acceptance. Not long ago a woman living near St Ives told a friend of the writer that when her mother lay dying she was surprised one day to hear a distinct tap at the window of the bedroom. Looking out, she could see nothing to account for the noise, and thought no more of it until some time later, when the tapping commenced again with greater distinctness. She was now convinced that what she had heard was nothing short of a warning of her mother's death, which in point of fact occurred not long after. Her more sceptically minded neighbours, however, explained the phenomenon by the fact that in replacing one of the small window panes which had accidentally been broken a mixture of bread dough had been used instead of putty—a point which the birds had not been slow to observe.

The robin, despite the belief that it was blessed among birds from having plucked a thorn from our Saviour's brow on Calvary, was none the less regarded in Cornwall as foreboding ill if ever it chanced to enter a house. Some three or four years ago a West Cornwall vicar was sitting by the bedside of one of his parishioners who was thought to be dying. The windows were standing wide open in order to give the sick man air, when all of a sudden a robin made its appearance in the room. Roused by the fluttering of its tiny wings, the dying man started up in his bed, and shaking his fist at the bird with surprising vigour, shouted furiously : ' Get out, you——. I aren't going to die yet—with the prettiest field of broccoli that was ever seen on this farm still waiting to be cropped ! ' Either because it realized its mistake, or because it had found the means of escape, it is certain that at these words the robin took its flight from the room, and the farmer, though his life had been despaired of by no less than three doctors, in due course recovered.

On the occasion of a death in the family the old people always made a point of draping the flowers with mourning, and of telling the news to the bees. ' I saw with my own eyes,' wrote Mrs Pascoe of St Hilary, in 1838, ' a little black flag attached to our church-woman's bit of mignonette, which she assured me had begun to quail away since her poor grandson was burnt to death, but had revived after she put on it the piece of mourning. It was not, she added, that she had much faith in it herself, but her daughter in Penzance had twenty-two plants that the ladies used to stop at the windows and admire, which began with one accord to droop from the time the accident happened, and would certainly have died if she had not given them a suit of black apiece. Shall not a poor pew-cleaner,' adds Mrs Pascoe, ' be pardoned for a weakness which moved a President of the Royal Society on the occasion of his mother's death to order, by letter, that his bees in the country should be invested with crape, lest they also should die ? ' [1]

At a meeting of the Penzance Natural History and Anti-quarian Society in 1888, a gentleman mentioned that when a boy he had seen some thirty beehives belonging to Mr Joshua Fox, of Tregedna, tied up in crape because of a death in the family. Another member stated that, ' a few years since ', on the death of the landlady of the First and Last Inn, near the Land's End, not only the flower-pots, but even the bird-cages had been tied up with crape in order to prevent the plants and birds from dying. A year or two later Miss Courtney wrote : ' When inquiring a short time ago what had become of a fine maidenhair fern that we had had for years, I was told that we had neglected, when a near relative of ours had died, to put it into mourning, or to tell it of his death ; and that, therefore, it had gradually pined away '.[2] This curious superstition, it may be added, has not yet died out and, within the last few years, the writer has been told of several cases in which flowers have been draped with black to prevent them ' quailing ' away after the death of their owners.

Perhaps one of the strangest notions of all concerning death was the idea that a soul could not ' pass easily ' if the body lay ' athurt the planshun ' (i.e. across the direction in which the floor boards ran). On one occasion, many years ago now, an old woman had lain for a great while upon the point of

[1] *Walks about St Hilary.*
[2] M. A. Courtney, *Cornish Feasts and Folklore*, 138.

death, but to the surprise of all, the hour of her dissolution was still delayed. At length a consultation took place amongst the relatives and various sympathetic neighbours. ' Well,' said one, ' she edn't gone yet, nor edn't like to, by what I can see.'

' Poor, dear saul,' said another, ' she 's wisht and slow, sure enough.'

' I tell 'ee, soas,' chimed in one of the older women, ' 'tes my belief she wean't never pass as she is, for her body's lying athurt planshun.'

' Why, ais, that 's so,' exclaimed the daughter of the house, ' I never thoft upon it before. Come awver steers and just help me move her round a minute, will 'ee ? '

By dint of much straining and effort the party at length succeeded in shifting the cumbrous old-fashioned bedstead in the tiny room. Some hours later the doctor called to see his patient.

' She 's gone, doctor ! ' cried the daughter as she met him on the threshold, ' we just shifted her bed round, and she went off like a lamb ! ' [1]

Somewhat akin to this was the once common practice of opening doors, windows, and even the drawers of clothes-presses, etc. in order to give the passing spirit free passage. A distressing feature of these deathbed occasions, however, resulted from the custom of inviting in large numbers of persons, who, by their violent exhortations, attempted to procure what was popularly known as a ' beautiful death '. The fact that the writer has himself heard this custom ' preached against ' in a Cornish church proves that it is not yet wholly obsolete, although it is likely before long to have become part and parcel of the bad old days.

VII

If there are two types of ancient superstition which have lasted on more tenaciously than any others in the West Country, they may surely be said to consist of the evil power attributed to the ' ill wisher ' and the magic virtues ascribed to the ' white witch '. Every now and then some case which is

[1] Per Mrs Hodge, St Ives.

illustrative of this still comes up at the local assizes. A man accuses his wife of ill-wishing him by sprinkling salt around his chair ; or a farmer charges some old woman with failing to cure his cattle after receiving money for such a purpose. And startling headlines appear in the papers calling attention to the extraordinary fact that such beliefs can still survive. And yet to those who pass their lives in country districts such news, whilst always interesting, causes less astonishment than might be supposed. For the persistence of these strange practices is indeed a fact which admits of no gainsaying, although it is only on occasion that they chance to gain some notoriety, and the public at large hears anything of them.

It would seem necessary, moreover, to point out that the survival of superstition in this, as in other forms, is by no means confined to Cornwall. As recently as the beginning of the present year (1932) a case appeared before the Wolverhampton Police Court wherein a witness refused to give evidence on the grounds that one of the parties concerned was a witch, and that he feared that a spell would be put upon him. In almost all large towns and cities to-day fortune tellers, astrologers, crystal-gazers, palmists, soothsayers, and others who veil their profession under more abstruse and elaborate names are constantly resorted to, and their number is said to be on the increase. Indeed, as Mr W. H. Paynter, who is an authority on Cornish witchcraft, has recently shown, it is only necessary to acquire a reputation as a student of this subject in order to gain proof of the widespread belief in the efficacy of magic. As may be seen in the portfolio of letters which forms one of the most curious ' exhibits ' in his house— itself a veritable museum of necromancy—requests for his assistance have come to him within the last few years from places as far distant as Manchester. One correspondent writes : ' My husband has been ill-wished with fits. Can you charm him, or send me the name and address of someone who can ? ' Another asks : ' Are you the gentleman that charms diseases ? If so, I should like to see you, as I have been troubled with epilepsy '. Other writers desire to be charmed for warts and rheumatism, whilst one unfortunate woman living at Chesterfield recently implored his aid in winning the affection of a man with whom she was ' madly in love '. ' Will you kindly tell me how I can draw him to me and keep him ? ' she writes. ' It can be done by the power of

" dragon's blood ",[1] but I do not know how to use it.   Please
help me, as I love this man better than anything else in the
world.' [2]   In view of this, it is hardly surprising that, despite
compulsory education and advancing knowledge, belief in
charms and in the power of the evil eye should still survive
in districts which until recently remained so remote as many
parts of Devon and Cornwall.

In former times the advice given by conjurers and witches
not infrequently led to the perpetration of horrible cruelties.
We read in Hone's *Every Day Book* of an ignorant old farmer
who, having met with severe losses in his cattle about the
year 1800, consulted with some equally barbarous neighbours
who, recollecting a tale which tradition had handed down
from remote antiquity, decided to burn alive the finest calf
which he had on his farm, in order to stay the murrain.   This
was actually done, a fire being kindled and the calf pushed
into the flames.   Here it was kept by the group of barbarians
who, being armed with pitchforks or ' pikes ', as they were
called in Cornwall, prevented the victim from escaping the
torture of the flames until the body was finally reduced to
ashes.[3]

A few years later a similar occurrence took place on St
Martin's, one of the Scilly Islands—where a woman, having
lost two or three sheep through sickness, or more probably
starvation, had gained the notion that her animals must have
been bewitched.   On going to Penzance to consult a wizard,
the latter assured her that the malignant spirit which had caused
the mischief resided in the body of an old mare which had
long been kept by the woman in the same field as the sheep.
He further stated that nothing would prosper with her whilst
this mare lived ; but that if the animal was burnt to death
all would subsequently be well with her remaining stock.
Returning home, she assembled her neighbours, who were as
credulous as herself, and the mare was tied to a stake, straws
and faggots were placed about it, and thus, surrounded by the
circle of brutal onlookers, the wretched animal was offered
up as a sacrifice to the genius of superstition.[4]

Though this was probably one of the last occasions when so

[1] *Dragon's blood* is a bright red gum exuding from a kind of palm fruit.
In olden times it had some repute in medicine.   It is now used chiefly for
colouring varnishes.

[2] See Mr W. H. Paynter, *Western Morning News*, 3 March 1932.

[3] Hone, *Every Day Book*, I, 853.

[4] *Cornwall Gazette*, 24 April 1802.

large an animal was made the victim of the sacrifice, similar practices long continued in out-of-the-way places. Some twenty years ago elderly people on the Scilly Islands were still able to recall how a certain farmer who supposed himself to be ill-wished had gone to Penzance to consult a ' doctor '. Arriving there, the latter had informed the man that he had come ' just in time ', and though his horse was dead, his wife who had been ill would recover. Returning to his home, and acting no doubt upon the witch's advice, the farmer proceeded to clear himself and his household of any further evil influences by chaining up a rooster and burning it alive in one of his fields. Whilst he was engaged in this task a woman who happened to be passing by looked over the hedge and, seeing what he was about, started to curse him in no uncertain terms for his cruelty. Though roused to anger by her words, he was yet more afraid of breaking the spell by speaking and had, accordingly, to listen in silence until the woman had finished, which was not before she had exhausted herself in a highly unflattering relation of every detail concerning his life, character, and antecedents ! [1]

Though it is wellnigh impossible that such an occurrence as this could take place to-day, belief in the benefits to be derived from animal sacrifice has survived in various forms to within very recent years. Shortly before the war a doctor, who is still practising in a town in West Cornwall, was attending a patient who had developed a serious illness after childbirth. So critical was her condition that at one point the doctor himself became convinced that there was little hope of her recovery. Arriving one morning, however, during the time when she was lying thus upon the point of death, he was surprised and gratified to note that a distinct improvement had taken place in her condition since he had seen her on the previous evening. On inquiring of the family, he at length elicited the fact that during the night they had cut a live pigeon into half, and had placed the bleeding portions against the feet of the patient, convinced that by so doing her life would be saved. It is certainly a fact that from that time onwards the woman continued to make steady progress, and is alive to-day ; though how far this is attributable to the strange experiment which was conducted upon her, the doctor who gave this account to the writer was unwilling to say.

As further examples of the survival of animal sacrifice,

[1] Per Mr W. D. Watson.

the writer has knowledge of several cases where, in recent years, rats have been buried beneath the walls of houses. Though the act was without conscious purpose beyond that of fulfilling an old custom, there is little doubt that it originated in the once common belief that a new building of any sort requires ' a life '. It is probable that a similar idea of propitiation underlay the practice of placing bottles, containing coins, beneath the ridge tiles of houses, where they are not infrequently found to-day when making structural alterations in old buildings. In some cases the sense of fear which originally inspired such practices is remembered long after the propitiatory act itself has ceased to be observed. On one occasion, some thirty years since, a married couple, who had just moved into a new house, were returning home from Penzance market when the trap in which they were riding overturned, causing severe injury to its occupants. Much sympathy was aroused by this incident, for the young people were very popular in their village, but at the same time, as the vicar of the parish assured the writer, the general comment was : ' Well, there it is, they 'd just gone into a new house, you know '.

Such misfortunes were considered by the old people to be the natural consequence of neglecting to observe the laws of the spirit world. In their opinion, however, the matter did not rest there, for it was generally believed that it was within the power of one human being to bring evil upon another by a definite act of will. One of the most circumstantial stories of ill-wishing known to the writer is related by Mrs J. Bonham in her book entitled *A Corner of Old Cornwall*.

Some ninety years ago a well-known farmer at the Lizard had a trifling quarrel with a neighbour whom he accused of opening one of his gates and causing a valuable mare to stray. In her vexation at being reproved by the farmer, the woman who had been responsible for the act was heard to exclaim : ' I hope old Joslen will never rear a colt from that mare as long as she do live '. Not long afterwards the first colt that was born was killed by falling over a low hedge. The next was drowned in a shallow brook, which had never previously been considered dangerous. To prevent further misfortunes, the mare was shut up with her third colt in the stable. On going out one morning, however, the farmer was amazed to find the little creature dead. It appeared that during the night a puddle of rain water must have leaked in under the stable door, and the colt, having fallen with its mouth in this, and being too weak to rise, had died where it lay. The fourth colt was born with a crooked mouth, and being, in consequence, unable to suck, it, too, pined away and died. No other colt was afterwards borne by this mare, so that the woman's ill-wish was actually fulfilled. The farmer indeed, who was a sober and religious man, believed the series of catastrophes to be nothing more than a remarkable coincidence. Few people at that time, however, would have agreed with him or refrained, under such circumstances, from consulting a ' witch '.

The persons so designated were in some instances wont to ascribe their power to being the seventh son of a seventh son, a contingency which was commonly supposed to entail magical gifts. ' Footlings,' or those who had chanced to be born feet foremost from their mother's womb, were likewise accredited with similar faculties. It was generally thought that the secrets possessed by such individuals could only be handed down from a man to a woman, or vice versa. To attempt to transfer the gift to another person of the same sex was to rob it of all virtue. In not a few instances ' pellar ' families claimed to have inherited their powers from some ancestor who had been fortunate enough to assist a stranded mermaid back into the sea, and who had been granted the faculty of magic in reward for this courteous action.

Famous among the ' pellars ' of West Cornwall was a certain ' Tamson ' or ' Tammy ' Blight of Helston, whose fame is still recounted by old people who can remember her. In the heyday of her powers people regularly resorted to Tamson at certain fixed seasons of the years ' to have their protections renewed ', whilst the ' pellar ' herself frequently made perambulations through the country-side, in order to confer the same benefits upon those who were unable through sickness or other cause ' to call for their protection ' themselves.[1]

A short time ago a portrait of this old lady (possibly by one of the Opie brothers) was discovered by Mr W. H. Paynter in a house at Truro. Mr Paynter, who, as already stated, has made an exhaustive study of Cornish witchcraft, has collected a number of stories concerning the cures effected by Tamson Blight in the course of her professional career. The following may be cited as typical of these. On one

[1] Cf. Bottrell, *Traditions and Hearthside Stories of West Cornwall*, I, 115

occasion a woman living near Helston had a child, which was affected with a mysterious sickness, to cure which medical aid had been sought in vain. As it was generally believed in the neighbourhood that the child was ' ill-wished ', the woman was advised to go to Helston in order to consult Tamson Blight. A visit was accordingly made, and the woman demanded of Tamson the name of her ill-wisher. This she refused to give but, nevertheless, she described the culprit in such detail that the woman ' immediately named the sorcerer ', and returned home resolved ' to bring blood from her '. A few days later the supposedly guilty person passed the woman's door, upon which she rushed out and laid violent hands upon her, scratching her arm, till it bled. From that hour we are told the child began to mend, and was soon able to leave its bed and play with the other children as if nothing had ever been the matter with it.

On another occasion a woman living at Breage was stricken with a severe illness which practically deprived her of all use of her limbs. A neighbour informed her that in all probability she had been ill-wished, and that the best thing she could do would be to go into Helston and see the ' pellar '. Being unable to ' travel ' (i.e. go on foot), it was decided to ask the vicar to take her in his dogcart. The latter at first refused, saying that he did not believe in ' such rubbish ', but at length, in order to humour the poor sufferer's whim, he good-naturedly gave his assent. After certain incantations had been used, Tamson informed the sick woman that, as soon as she arrived home, the one who had ill-wished her would come to the door and say : ' Is my little black cat here ? ' The homeward journey was soon made, and sure enough on reaching the house ' an old woman hobbled in and asked if any one had seen her little black cat '. She had hardly spoken the words before the sick woman arose from her chair and, taking two pitchers, set off to the well to draw water, to the amazement of all the beholders, the vicar himself included.

Such was Tamson's fame that shortly before her death, when she was confined to her bed, people were not infrequently brought to her on stretchers, and laid beside her in her room where, from having been entirely helpless, they were known ' to rise up and go down over stairs perfectly cured '.[1]

Tammy's husband, who was an engine-driver at one of the

[1] *Western Morning News*, 4 June 1928.

mines, laid claim to similar occult powers, and a good deal
of professional jealousy seems to have existed between the
two. On one occasion it is said that the witch, who was in
the habit of picking ' cherks ' (i.e. half-consumed cinders)
from the pile of ashes outside the boiler-house where her
husband worked, was spoken to rather roughly by one of the
captains who suspected her of having stolen some pieces of
timber which were missing from the mine. The old lady said
little at the time, but the next day, when an attempt was made
to start the pumping engine which had been stopped for a
short while for repairs, the machinery would not budge.
The mine itself being very ' quick in water ', matters began to
look serious. At length the captain, suspecting that a spell
had been put upon the engine, decided to send for the witch.
Old Tammy, having enjoyed her triumph, soon arrived on
the scene, and shortly afterwards the pump was doing its
duty once more !

VIII

Although Tamson Blight and her husband were among the
most celebrated ' pellars ' of the county, they had many rivals.
For in their day, almost every town and village boasted one
or more practitioners of the magic art. In the neighbouring
town of Camborne dwelt another ' wise woman ', who had
achieved such renown for effecting cures that people were
often brought to her from places as far distant as the Lizard.
It is said that when Doctor Montgomery, the leading specialist
in Cornwall at that time, had pronounced a case to be hopeless,
the sufferer would commonly be taken to see the white witch
of Camborne, and not a few received their health at her hands.
A few years since, the writer was informed that a woman
who is still living in the district had been cured by this witch
of a hæmorrhage, when lying almost at death's door. It
appears that the only advice given her was to drink warm beer,
but so efficacious did this prove that she rapidly recovered,
and has never known any return of the affliction to this day.
' Uncle Jacky Hooper,' of Blowinghouse, near Redruth,
was another well-known witch-doctor of a somewhat earlier
period. He was frequently resorted to for the cure of sick
cows, which he professed to heal by the simple expedient of

giving the owner a prayer or a chapter from the Book of Proverbs to read over the animal's back. His charge for this was 5s., a very considerable sum of money for poor people in those days. Persons coming to consult him would always be invited into his cottage, where the old man would take tinder and flint, light his lamp, and smoke over a piece of glass. In this he professed to be able to see the business on which his client had called. Sometimes, however, he made a bad 'missment'. One day a man who had a sick cow called to see him.

'Do 'ee knaw what I 've come about, Uncle Jacky?' asked the farmer.

'Why, ais, my dear, of coorse I do,' replied the old man, staring into his bit of glass.

'What es a, then?' inquired the other.

'Why, 'tes in this 'eer glaass so plain as a pike staff. Come ovver here a minute. Now caen't 'ee see 'un for yourself?' asked the conjurer.

'No,' replied the cautious farmer, who was determined not to be drawn out, 'I caen't see nothen theer.'

'Why, how not 'en?' cried Uncle Jacky, driven at length to desperation. ''Tes plain enough to me. Thee 'st ben and lost an underground shart (shirt) up to bal (mine), and you want for me to tell 'ee who 've stolen it!'

On another occasion a lady whose husband was a mining engineer in Spain came to Uncle Jacky, hoping to hear some news about him.

'Come in, my dear, come in,' cried the old man, scenting a good customer. 'Ais, I do know well enough what you 've come for. You do waant for me to tell 'ee somethin' 'bout your husband.'

'Why, how extraordinary that you should be able to tell!' exclaimed the lady; 'but you are perfectly right. Do you know what he is doing and where he is now?'

'Ais,' said Uncle Jacky, 'that I do. He 's a sailor aboard ship, out on the high seas. I can see 'un now in this 'eer bit of glass. He 's just starting to clemb the rigging!' [1]

The smoked glass was not the only piece of paraphernalia employed by the old witch-doctors—wooden hearts, live toads, 'dragon's blood', the hearts of fishes and other curious trifles all going to make up their magical stock-in-trade. What terrifying and yet enthralling places their houses must have

[1] Per Mr Jim Thomas, Camborne.

seemed in consequence to the children, young and old, who came to visit them ! ' " Old Rose " was a character of this sort whom I now dimly recollect,' wrote Mrs Stanley James on a recent occasion. ' Clutching my father's hand we knocked at the door of an old thatch-roofed apology for a house, entered in response to a thin reedy voice piping " Come in ", and stumbled our way across a nearly dark room, lit only by a tiny window, a foot square and mostly stuffed with rags. All sorts of dried herbs and mysterious things were hanging from the rafters overhead, but—most mysterious of all— away by an open fireplace, sitting on a stool, smoking a small pipe, was old Rosie herself, looking in the shadows to be my childish ideal of a witch. What especially appealed to me was her claw-like hands. No one knew her exact age, but she was thought to be over one hundred when she died.'

Witch-doctors, though held in considerable awe and respect, were rarely popular characters, on account of the ill-feeling which their judgments were apt to breed between neighbours. A story recently told by Mr Jim Thomas, of Camborne, is illustrative of this. On one occasion a certain farmer had been having much trouble with his cows, which he believed to be ill-wished. He accordingly sought the advice of a ' doctor ', who instructed him to take a living toad at midnight, and after gathering his family and the servants together, to keep strict silence whilst he roasted it to death on the ' brandis '. As midnight struck the ill-wisher would appear. The farmer followed the advice, and, strange to relate, the clock had barely struck twelve when footsteps were heard outside, and there was a knock at the door. The farmer opened it, and found his brother-in-law with whom he had long been on unfriendly terms, standing on the threshold.

' What do you want at this time of night ? ' asked the owner of the house.

' Why,' came the reply, ' I found your cows straying in the lane, and seeing a light here I thought I would come and tell you that I had driven them into the field.'

It is hardly necessary to add that from that time forth the two men became the bitterest enemies.

As already shown, one of the most effective means of lifting a spell was thought to be that of ' drawing blood ' from the ill-wisher. In the year 1887 an assault of this nature led to the hearing of a case by the magistrates of the Camborne police court. The defendant, a woman whose children were suffering from fever, had been told by one of her neighbours that they were ill-wished. Believing that there was no chance of their recovery until the spell had been removed, she forthwith paid a visit to the reputed sorceress. ' I have not ill-wished your children, I do not go about with fever in my pockets,' replied the latter. To this the mother retorted : ' Then I must see your blood ', which she there and then proceeded to do by attacking the other woman, and scratching her on the face till it bled.[1]

A similar story has recently been told concerning two old women who dwelt in one of the almshouses at Morvah. During one winter the elder of the two occupants had been ill, and at length, all remedies having been tried in vain, she became convinced that a spell had been cast on her by her neighbour, with whom she had long been at enmity. Accordingly, going behind her one day, she suddenly dug a rusty nail deep into the other woman's arm, causing blood to flow. The innocent victim of her aggression not unnaturally raised a protest, and eventually the vicar of the parish had to intervene and threaten the assailant with a summons if she ever repeated her offence.[2]

Another means of lifting a spell was to take the heart of a sheep or bullock, stick it full of pins, and then roast it over an open fire. This was generally done at midnight, sometimes with the following incantation :

> *It is not this heart I wish to burn,*
> *But the person's heart I wish to turn,*
> *Wishing them neither rest nor peace*
> *Till they are dead and gone.*[3]

In some districts an onion stuck full of pins served for a similar purpose. According to a more modern form of the same magic, a photograph of the ill-wisher, with his or her name written across it, is sometimes burnt in the fire.[4]

The extent to which belief in ill-wishing obtained in Cornwall within a comparatively recent period is nowhere better illustrated than in the following story. Between thirty and forty years ago a poor labourer rented a cottage from a farmer living in a parish on the south coast of Cornwall. Prior to his

[1] *Cornish Telegraph*, 20 October 1887.
[2] Miss Gyles, *Old Cornwall*, X, 40.
[3] T. H. Rogers, *Western Morning News*, 5 December 1931.
[4] Miss L. J. Dickinson, *Old Cornwall*, Second Series, II, 21.

removal to the cottage the man had acquired a dog to which he was passionately attached. Unhappily, however, this animal developed an unfortunate propensity for chivying the farmer's sheep. As a not unnatural consequence, the farmer himself became much incensed against the owner of the dog, and at length the cottager realized that he would either have to get rid of the animal or be evicted from his home. One day, therefore, he betook himself to the river, and went on board a barge which lay anchored a short distance from the shore. The men were in the hold, eating their ' croust ' (lunch), and seeing the owner of the dog tying a stone round its neck, preparatory to drowning it, they inquired the reason. The man explained the circumstances, and then coming down into the hold, started to curse the farmer in such terms that even the men, who realized what the loss of the dog meant to him, were astonished at his violence. For this was no ordinary swearing. He cursed the farmer in eating and sleeping, in ploughing and reaping. He cursed his stock, and he cursed his crops, with such awful imprecations and profanity, that at last the men were not sorry to resume work and leave the other to his hell-fire blasphemings. At length he appeared on deck once more, threw the wretched animal overboard, and went home. Strange to relate, from that day onwards misfortunes of every kind pursued the farmer's footsteps. One after another his cattle died. He bought fresh stock, and they had hardly been taken to the farm before they began to sicken. The ' vet.' was there by night and day, sometimes almost living at the farm, but all to no purpose. At last when wellnigh at his wit's end, the farmer met his tenant in the lane, and a bright idea occurred to him. ' John,' he remarked, ' you 're getting up in years, and haven't got too much to live on, I suppose. What if I was to let 'ee have that bit of croft behind your house for to break in and teal (cultivate) some teties (potatoes) ? ' At first the man appeared by no means anxious to accept the offer, but at length his wife persuaded him that, under the circumstances, perhaps the most Christian action would be to let bygones be bygones, and to take the land ! To this he eventually agreed. From that time forth the farmer's luck began to change, and the relationship between the two men became almost amicable. The one creature who does not appear to have profited by the affair was the unfortunate dog, who had served as the unwitting victim of the sacrifice.

Though such incidents are now becoming of rare occurrence, belief in ill-wishing still lingers among old people and in the more remote places. Indeed, a story scarcely less strange than that related above was told to the writer by a West Cornwall doctor only a few months since.

One day, in the year 1929, the latter was called in to see an old woman who was afflicted with a disease which he was forced to pronounce incurable. Shortly after this his patient went to stay with a friend in Penzance. She had not been there long before a violent quarrel broke out, in the course of which the woman cursed her hostess in no uncertain terms, and forthwith departed once more to her own home. A few weeks later the woman at Penzance caught a chill, pneumonia developed, and within three days she was dead. Some months elapsed, and once again the doctor was called in to see the witch, for such she was reputed to be. He found her obviously weaker. ' Can you do anything for me, doctor ? ' she again asked him at the conclusion of his visit.

' No,' he replied, ' I 'm very sorry, but I fear that I cannot.'

' I tell 'ee,' retorted the woman, raising herself in her bed, ' if you don't cure me I shall ill-wish you.'

A few days after this the doctor's wife, who had been driving with him on his rounds, slipped when getting out of the car and broke her leg. She was still in bed as the result of this accident when the story was told the writer. ' But that is not all,' added the doctor, ' for in the same week in which my wife broke her leg I was driving through the town at a very moderate pace when the car (I can only so describe it) literally fell to pieces under me—the back-axle broke, and most of the contents of the gear-box were scattered on to the road. I was naturally much put out by this as, apart from the expense, I was very busy at the time, and was much inconvenienced by having to hire another car whilst my own was being repaired. Then, to add to all these troubles, my dispenser a few days later overset a shelf-full of bottles in the surgery, smashing some expensive glass instruments which were being washed in the sink underneath. About a week after this I received a sudden call from my old patient, who for some time had been in a semi-delirious state. Her mind seemed to clear just as I was leaving her, however, and she suddenly asked after my wife. I told her that she was in bed with a broken leg, at which she seemed half inclined to say something, and then apparently thought better of it, and burst

into tears.   When I left her she was still " crying like rain ".
She died the next week, with a look on her face I shall not
easily forget.   You know what village gossips are, especially
in Cornwall.   They told me that the " devil had been tickling
her "—poor old soul !   You can tell this story if you like,
and add that since the death of this very unusual patient I
have not been troubled with any further disasters ! '

[Whilst correcting these pages for the press I have learnt
that the doctor himself died exactly five months later, aged
only thirty-five years.]

IX

Although this story may well seem to disprove the statement, it is generally speaking a fact that the occult practices
which survive in Cornwall to-day have been purged of their
old-time savagery, and ' charming ', which now constitutes
the commonest form of magic, is entirely beneficent in its
intent.   In times past charms were as numerous and as
varied as the ills to which the flesh itself is heir.   Among
the commonest may be mentioned those for the ' thrush '
(inflammation), deafness, warts, sore eyes, shingles, and
epilepsy.   There are people still living who have seen the
' king's evil ' treated by passing the hand of a dead child over
the affected parts, with the belief that as the body decayed
the scrofula itself would disappear.[1]   Whooping-cough, it is
claimed, can be cured by filling a muslin bag full of spiders,
and tying it round the neck of the patient, who must wear it
day and night.   For asthma, spiders are again made use of.
In this case their webs are collected, rolled up in a little ball
in the palm of the hand, and then swallowed.[2]   Styes on the
eyelid are still commonly treated by touching the inflammation
with a cat's tail ; whilst to cut off a cat's left ear and swallow
three drops of its blood in a wineglass full of spring water
is claimed by one particular ' white witch ' to be an excellent
remedy for measles.
   Many other charms are of a like simple nature.   Some
forty years ago, an acquaintance of the writer, entering a

[1] Per Mr J. C. Hoare.
[2] Miss L. J. Dickinson, *Old Cornwall*, Second Series, II, 20.

cottage at Ludgvan, found an old woman in the act of curing a man of weak eyes by twirling a piece of smouldering bramble stalk in front of his face. He was under the impression that certain words were muttered at the same time. Of this, however, he could not be sure, as he was quickly driven out by the old lady, who had no wish to encourage the curiosity of a prying youngster.

It is evident that the naïve simplicity of some of the village charmers sometimes caused them to be ridiculed by their more sceptical neighbours. Proof of this may be seen in the advice reputed to have been given to a sufferer with toothache, 'to fill his mouth with water, and hold it over the fire till the liquid boiled '—a charm which evidently does not belong to the true canon.

An old folk-tale, recently communicated to the writer, gives further proof that the Cornish, in common with other country people, have always been able to enjoy a good story even when it reflected upon the superstition inherent in their character. Some seventy years ago a certain Cornish parson received an urgent summons from an old lady living on the boundary of his parish. On arriving at her house he learnt that her cow had suddenly been taken ill, and that nothing less was expected of him than to charm away the sickness with which the animal was possessed. Naturally he was somewhat amused at this request, but being inclined to humour the old lady he made a few passes over the animal's back, at the same time muttering with great solemnity : ' If she lives she lives, and if she dies she dies '. In due course he received information that the cow had recovered ! Some years after this the parson himself was taken very ill of a quinsy, so ill indeed that his life was despaired of. News of this soon reached the old lady, who, without waiting for any invitation, hurried off at top speed to the vicarage, forced her way to the parson's bedside, and to the amazement of the nurse, began making certain passes over the sick man, murmuring as she did so the magic words : ' If he lives he lives, and if he dies he dies '. The sound of his own words repeated thus under such very different circumstances so much tickled the clergyman that he burst into a hearty laugh, which had the effect of breaking the quinsy at a critical juncture, and thereby of saving his life. The same story, it is interesting to note, is told in Brittany. It is in fact an ancient folk-tale with many ' localized ' versions of which the Cornish is but one.

Whilst it is easy enough to raise a laugh at the expense of the ' charmers ', the fact remains that in many instances miraculous cures appear to have been achieved through their agency.   It would be outside the scope of this book to attempt any explanation of such phenomena, but the following incidents which relate to persons who are still living, and which have been attested by more than one creditable witness, will show something of the extent to which charming has been successfully practised in recent times.

Some fifty years ago a farmer in West Cornwall was burning rubbish in one of his fields. The stuff was very damp, and in order to make the fire burn more briskly, he had been pouring paraffin on to the pile.   In so doing the can containing the oil slipped from his grasp, and immediately a sheet of flame shot up from the fire, inflicting severe burns on his face and hands.   Being in great pain he returned home with all speed, where his wife applied the usual remedies, but without effect. Night was drawing on, and the man was still in such pain that the family were at their wits' end what to do.   At length one of the farm hands suggested sending for old Betty B——, who had the reputation of being a powerful charmer.   The farmer's son accordingly went off to fetch the old woman, who lived a mile or two away.   On reaching her house he found that the charmer was already in bed.   After hammering for some time on the door, her voice was at length heard inquiring what anyone wanted with a respectable woman at that hour of the night.   The boy explained the circumstances as well as the hurried state of his mind would permit, saying that his father had been badly burnt about the face, was in great pain, and that he hoped the old lady would accompany him home immediately in order to try her powers on the sufferer. ' No need for me to do that, my son,' was the reply, ' go's thy way home, and you'll find all the pain and anger is gone from your father's face by the time you get there.' With this assurance the boy had perforce to be content. True, however, to the old woman's word, he found on his arrival that the pain had completely left his father's face.   The burns on his hands, however, which the boy had forgotten to mention, continued to give him much pain and discomfort all through that night, and showed their effects long after the scars on his face had completely disappeared.

In the same parish there are living at the present time two other persons who are well known as charmers. The one is an old woman, and the other a blacksmith, and both have been instrumental in effecting a number of miraculous cures. Not many years ago a jobbing workman in the district, whilst engaged in repairing the roof of a house, slipped off a ladder and struck his head against a stone. In an instant he was, in the words of the villagers, ' bleeding like a pig '. Realizing the seriousness of the situation, the neighbours tied up his head with towels and rags, and placed him in a trap in order to drive him with all speed to the nearest doctor, who lived some three miles away. The road lay past the blacksmith's shop, where the smith himself chanced to be standing in the doorway. On learning what had happened to the man, he straightway ordered the coverings to be removed from his head, and then began making a series of passes over the wound. Notwithstanding the fact that the latter had been bleeding freely a few minutes before, the beholders were astonished to note that no further blood appeared, whilst the patient himself showed unmistakable signs of recovery. Certain it is that he never visited the doctor, and in a surprisingly short time his wound had completely healed.

In some cases the gift of staunching blood by charming has proved a definite embarrassment to its possessor. Not many years since an intelligent farmer of Cusgarne, in Gwennap, stated that he was a firm believer in blood charms on account of his having been a witness of the following incident. ' When I was a little boy,' he said, ' my father, who was a farmer, slaughtered his own pigs. One day when he was going to kill pigs he said to John, our workman, who could charm blood : " Now, John, mind thee dussn' charm these pigs when I 'm sticking 'em ". John said : " No, maister, I waan't charm 'em ". My father sticked a pig, but he couldn't make 'un bleed. He tried and tried again. At last he said : " John, John, git out of the yard, I shall never kill these pigs whilst thee 'rt here ". So John went out of the yard into the mowhay. Then in a few minutes my father killed they pigs quite easy. When John came back, father said : " I told 'ee not to charm they pigs, and you said you wouldn't. What did 'ee go and do it for afterwards ? "

' " Why, maister," said John, " 'twas like this 'ere. I didn't mean for to charm 'em, but the auld charm keept rising up in my mind, and I couldn't help saying un ! " ' [1]

This, as Mr Thurstan Peter pointed out, is a rather delightful

[1] *Journal of the Royal Institution of Cornwall*, XX, Pt. I (1915), 126–7.

story, since the farmer clearly overlooked the fact that the charm ought to have worked just the same when John was on the other side of the hedge. In all probability it was the farmer's nervousness rather than any supernatural interference which prevented him from slaughtering the animals whilst his labourer was standing by.

It is not always so easy, however, to find a rational explanation for incidents of this sort ; more especially when the individuals concerned belong to the educated classes, as in the following case. On one occasion a lady, who is well known to the writer, was walking with her father through some fields in East Cornwall. The latter in getting over a stile cut his hand very badly on a piece of jagged wire. In an instant the wound had started to bleed profusely. First his handkerchief, and then hers was applied, but as neither sufficed to stop the bleeding, which was becoming serious, they decided to call at a neighbouring cottage for help. The door was opened by a man to whom they explained the situation. ' I wish you would let me charm it for you, sir,' said the cottager.

' What nonsense, indeed ! ' broke out the other, who was somewhat quick tempered. ' I want something to tie this up with. Can you help me or not ? ' He had hardly spoken the words before he realized to his utter astonishment that the bleeding had entirely stopped ! In the face of a complete unbelief—indeed of actual indignation at the suggestion— the unspoken charm had worked its effect, and the wound started to heal from that hour without giving any further cause for trouble or anxiety.

Enough has already been said to show that the age of miracles, for by no other name can these phenomena be termed in our present state of knowledge, is not yet passed. Wrapped in mystery, however, though the subject of charming still is, the results of its practice have frequently been so well attested as to establish the existence of such a faculty beyond all doubt. As recently as the period of the war, a West Cornwall doctor told a friend of the writer that miners not infrequently came to him with wounds which by all appearance should have made them weak from loss of blood. On questioning them, however, they admitted having been in the first place to a charmer, who had staunched the bleeding so effectually that all that they subsequently required was that the wounds should be ' dressed ' to make them heal more quickly.

In recent times charmers are likewise known to have achieved remarkable success in curing such minor ailments as warts. Their usual procedure in such cases is to rub the excrescences with a piece of raw meat, which is subsequently buried. As this decays in the ground so the warts will die away. In order to ensure the secrecy which is essential to the operation, it is sometimes said that the meat should be stolen. A similar cure is claimed to be effected by taking a green pea pod which contains nine peas, ' taking the ninth pea ', and throwing it away with the words : ' Wart, wart, dry away '. As the pea rots the wart itself will disappear. Presumably this method of cure can be practised only in the summer months. For those who prefer a vegetable medium which can be obtained at all seasons of the year, a piece of ordinary turf is said to be equally effective.

Quite recently a lady living at St Ives told the writer that at one period of her life she had been much afflicted with warts on the hand. For months she sought the advice of doctors and chemists, but without avail, none of their remedies doing her the slightest good. At length, though having small faith in such a measure, she agreed to consult a woman who had the reputation of being a good charmer. The latter took her up into a field at Barnoon. Here she explained that she proposed to cut up a piece of turf for each wart, and to replace it on the ground upside down, adding that as the grass withered so the wart itself would die away. ' Do you believe this, my dear ? ' she asked. ' No, Aunt Jinny,' replied her patient, ' I really cannot say that I do, because I don't see how it is possible.'

' Oh, but you must believe it sooner or later,' replied the older woman. It would seem, however, that the charmer's heart must have failed her when she saw the *number* of warts on the lady's hand, for, as she remarked : ' If I was to cut up a separate tobban (bit of turf) for all they, I should have to take up the whole field '.

She accordingly lessened her task by cutting off one piece of turf for every so many warts, at the same time mumbling a few words over the lady's hand. The latter regarded the whole proceeding with a curiosity not unmixed with amusement, nor was it until some weeks later, *when every one of the warts had entirely disappeared*, that her scepticism began to be really shaken.

Nor is this the most recent instance of charming of which

the writer can claim some direct knowledge. In the summer of 1927 some friends who were staying on the Bodmin Moors were definitely assured that a child belonging to the house in which they were staying had been cured of ringworm, only a few months before, by the charms of a local ' white witch '.

It is interesting to note that the people who now possess the gift of charming affect little of the paraphernalia of the witches of olden times. Although they have not yet arrived at the stage of setting up a brass plate on their doors, they would appear generally desirous of being considered within the fringe of professionalism, free lances, as it were, of the great medical fraternity, of whose earliest forerunners they are truly the representatives.

X

Closely allied to the subject of charming is the belief which formerly obtained in the curative properties of certain talismans. Celts and thunderbolts have always been regarded as possessing great efficacy in this respect, and the water in which they had been boiled was commonly administered as a cure for sickness in man and beast. Still more remarkable is the lingering faith in the virtue of ' milpreves '—the name given to a type of prehistoric bead which is found from time to time in the county. These, as their name suggests (Cornish *myl pref*, ' a thousand snakes '), were popularly supposed to have their origin in the gathering together in hot weather of multitudes of adders from whose spittle the bead was produced, sometimes encircled around a hazel wand. This curious belief, as Mr Jenner has recently reminded us, constitutes the last surviving link between the modern inhabitants of Cornwall and the Druids. Pliny in his account of the latter describes how a bead which was worn by them as a badge of office was known as *ovum anguinum*, ' snake's egg ', and states that it was formed from a mass of young snakes enclosed within a shell and blown bubble-like into the air. In his *Survey of Cornwall*, published in 1602, Carew wrote : ' The countrey people retaine a conceite that the Snakes by their breathing about a hazell wand, doe make a stone ring of blew colour in which there appeareth the yellow figure of a snake, and that beasts which are stung, being given to drink of the water wherein this stone hath bene soaked, will there through recover'. He goes on to describe a mil-preve in his own possession which, according to the person who had given it him, had actually been found with a stick in it. A very detailed description of the manner in which these beads were popularly supposed to be formed is given by William Bottrell in his first series of *Traditions and Hearthside Stories*, pp. 148–9. The latest news of them, however, comes from Mr W. A. Pascoe, of St Neot, who writes : 'Some three or four years ago, a gentleman at Cardinham came across nine or ten adders lying on a sunny bank in an orchard, and dispatched the lot with a stick. Thinking it might interest an old country friend, I mentioned the incident to him. To my surprise, he replied solemnly : " Ah, you may depend, they was making an adder-stone ! " Although ', as Mr Pascoe adds, ' the term " milpreve " had become lost from this particular Cornishman's vocabulary, he who had never heard of Pliny or even dipped into Bottrell or Hunt, had received through a long line of Celtic forbears, a belief which extends back into the remote days of pre-Christian Cornwall.[1]

In the judgment of many people the art of ' dowsing ' or divining for water and metals is another subject which properly falls under the heading of ' superstition '. Although the writer does not altogether associate himself with this view, having seen too much of dowsing to regard all its practitioners as humbugs, it is admittedly impossible in our present state of knowledge to treat of the matter as an exact science. Contrary to the usual belief, dowsing is not a practice of very long standing in Cornwall, into which, according to Pryce,[2] it was only introduced in the early part of the eighteenth century. Its practical value, however, had long been an accepted fact in other parts of Europe, particularly in the Hartz mountains of Germany, where, as is shown by the drawings in Agricola's treatise *De Re Metallica* (1556), it was commonly resorted to for the discovery of mineral ores.

Not long ago the writer discovered amongst some papers belonging to Mr Thomas Cornish, formerly a well-known solicitor at Penzance, the following letter, dated 23rd May 1885.

[1] *Old Cornwall*, IX, 45–6.
[2] *Mineralogia Cornubiensis*.

Its contents are of great interest as showing the general attitude towards dowsing at that date. ' Some twenty years ago ' (i.e. about 1865), states the writer, ' a Towednack miner named Henry Berryman emigrated to California. Whilst he was there he dreamt that he was working in a " cross course " to the Baldu lode, in Nancledrea, which was rich in tin. Some years afterwards he came home and went up the adit on the Baldu lode to see if there was any cross course, but found none. He then went to Montana, and whilst there dreamt the dream over again. After some years he came home once more, and on his way dreamt the dream a third time. When he got home he made inquiries about any cross courses known in the district, and ascertained that Samuel Michell had found indications of one whilst " shoding " (digging pits in search of lodes near the surface) in a croft at the back of his house, but that he had gone abroad and nothing had come of it. This pit was about one hundred fathoms north of the Baldu lode. Berryman then came to me and applied for a licence but, with true West Country wariness, said nothing about the dreams. As, however, he did not understand a map, I was obliged to meet him on the ground. Before we met, he had sent for a dowser of great experience, Capt. Matthew Curnow, who dowsed the ground north of the lode from east to west. Just after he had passed, on the surface, the farthest point of the " old men's " underground workings, the dowsing rod began to twitch and presently came to a dead point. The spot was marked, and the dowser blindfolded and taken to a spot west of the " point ", and made to proceed from west to east. As he came across the line of the mark, the rod again became agitated, and again came to a dead point. This dowsing took place within the last ten days, and I picked up the story bit by bit. Several people around the place know it, but they are rather shy of telling it.'

It is certain that those who possess the gift of dowsing to-day are by no means shy of displaying it, and of recent years more serious attention has been given to the subject. Up to the present, however, these tentative inquiries have proved somewhat inconclusive. Accordingly, whilst it is generally felt that the matter is worthy of a fuller investigation, dowsing remains at the moment in that borderland which lies between the realms of science and the supernatural. Meantime, the dowser's aid in finding water continues to be sought, not only by individuals, but by such prosaic bodies as railway companies and local authorities, so that, on the whole, the means must be presumed to be justified by the results. Indeed, those who have frequently seen the dowser at his work, and noted the score-marks left on his hands as the rod turns irresistibly downward when passing over water springs or metals, cannot reasonably doubt that the faculty, mysterious as it is, is a perfectly genuine one in some persons.

No account of the folk-lore of Cornwall would be complete without some mention of the holy wells with which the county is so richly endowed. Owing to the supposed virtue of their waters in curing rheumatism, sore eyes, and various scrofulous complaints, the respect due to these has survived through all the centuries of religious change. The latter, it is true, has resulted in many cases in the desecration of their sites, and in the destruction of the ancient baptisteries with which the Fathers of the Celtic Church had sanctified these natural water springs. But the hearts of the people themselves have been slower to change, and their veneration of the holy wells, allied though it often was to superstition, remained until recently a very real force in their lives. A little more than a century ago Polwhele stated that on the day of the anniversary of the famous well which lends its name to the beach below Cubert, the surrounding villages were ' quite forsaken '. To a stranger coming by chance upon the scene, the great concourse of people gathered together on that wide lonely beach must have provided an impressive sight. It is curious to reflect how closely these assemblies of Methodist Cornishmen must have resembled even at this time the world-famous ' pardons ' which still constitute such an important part of the social and religious life of their Catholic kinsmen in Brittany.

In many cases stories concerning the holy wells which are related to-day as proofs of the Cornishman's superstition, should more truthfully be regarded as survivals of his erstwhile religious veneration. Adjoining the churchyard at Phillack may still be seen the holy well, which is said to have been defiled by a certain Erasmus Pascoe, who used it for washing his sheep. As a consequence of this act all manner of ills are said to have befallen him, culminating in the death of his only son. The truth of this story can hardly be ascertained, although a tombstone in the churchyard bears witness to the fact in 1723 a father and son bearing this name were actually buried here within a couple of months of each other. The really interesting point is that so long after the Reformation the waters of any well should still have been regarded with sufficient veneration to give rise to such a story.

It might perhaps be argued that ' veneration ' is scarcely the word to express the latter-day Cornishman's regard for his holy wells, seeing that it was the curative property of their waters which concerned him rather than their ' saintly ' associations. Until recently almost every well was believed to have its peculiar virtue ; a fact which, as Mr Jenner has said, might have admitted of a rational explanation in the days when personal cleanliness was a very bad second to godliness. Thus Chapel Farm Well at St Breward, Castle Horneck Well in Madron, and ' Joan's Pitcher ' in Lewannick were considered good for sore eyes. St Nun's Well at Altarnon cured insanity. Alsia Well, in Buryan, and St Piran's Well, in Perranzabuloe, were good for rickets, whilst weakly children were bathed in Menacuddle Well at St Austell. Jesus Well in St Minver was reputed to cure whooping-cough. Humours and wounds were said to be cured at Chapel Uny Well in Sancreed. The waters of St Uny's Well at Redruth were said to preserve anyone baptized therein from the danger of being hanged. ' In the neighbouring town of Camborne,' wrote Mr Thurstan Peter, ' they once had a holy well that saved people from becoming foolish. This was destroyed some years ago, and ever since . . .' [1] But we will not conclude this sentence, remembering that Mr Peter himself was a Redruth man ! The Well of St Keyne (properly pronounced ' Kayne ') and St Martin's Well, at Liskeard, are best known for their reputed influence on married life. Constantine's Well in St Merryn, Dupath Well, and the Lady Wells at Mevagissey and at Nance in Colan, were resorted to for sickness of all kinds. Gulval Well, when properly invoked, gave by its bubbling, clearly or turbidly, news, good or bad, of absent friends. [2]

Of all the holy wells of Cornwall none was more richly endowed with folk-lore associations than that of St Madron or ' Madern, ' near Penzance. Here, on the first three Wednesdays in May, children afflicted with shingles, wild-fire, tetters, and other skin complaints were plunged through the waters

---

[1] *Guide to Redruth* (Mate's).
[2] *Cornish Church Guide*, 249–57.

three times ' against the sun ', being afterwards carried nine times around the spring, going from east to west, or ' with the sun '. At the conclusion of the ceremony a piece of cloth torn from the child's clothing was left, either between the stones bordering on the brooklet, or affixed to the thorn tree which grows by the baptistery wall. Such bits of rag have been seen here within living memory. Nor has the repute of Madron Well as a divining fount become quite forgotten. As Mr Bottrell remarked,[1] however, the young people who now visit it and drop in the pebbles, pins, and little crosses which may frequently be seen here, do so more from the pleasure of each other's company than from any real faith in the omens resultant from the sinking of such offerings or from the bubbles which can be made to rise by stamping on the water's edge. The custom of dropping pins into wells in all probability goes back to the time when a metallic offering, however small, was considered to be a necessary tribute to the well spirit.

To a spring, known as ' Figgy Dowdy's ' Well on Carn Marth Hill, near Redruth, it was customary within comparatively recent years for children to take their dolls on Good Friday, in order to have them ' baptized '. An old resident in the neighbourhood used regularly to attend to perform the ceremony. This curious custom was at one time not confined to the Redruth district, as a lady now residing at Hayle informs the writer that when a girl she remembers taking her dolls to a well on Carn Galva, in Morvah, for a similar purpose.

This brief account of the folk-lore of some of the more important wells of Cornwall must by no means be taken as exhausting the subject, which would indeed provide matter for an entire book of greater length than this. Although most of the ancient cults and ceremonies in connection with these wells are no longer regarded, the faith which once inspired them sometimes survives subconsciously. On one occasion a maidservant who was employed at the writer's home at Redruth was seized with a dangerous illness, as a result of which she became delirious. Whilst she was in this condition she constantly called for the waters of different wells, affirming that each in their turn was alone capable of saving her life. For some time every endeavour was made to satisfy her whims, and water was actually fetched from the

[1] *Traditions and Hearthside Stories of West Cornwall*, II, 239–42.

wells she indicated. At length, however, as her demands
gradually extended to wells which lay farther and farther
afield, recourse was had to the town supply which, being
bottled from the tap, and carried thus to her bedroom,
apparently proved equally efficacious, as in due course she
recovered. The remarkable fact is that in her normal state
of mind she would have scorned all such notions, being of the
modern type and inclined to laugh at the ' old people's
superstitions '.

There is little doubt that in former times beliefs and ancient
practices in connection with natural rocks and prehistoric
stone monuments were as widespread as those in connection
with wells. Concerning these, however, there is now little
record, and though one may suspect the existence of fertility
rites, such as are still associated with the dolmens and ' long
stones ' of Brittany, we have practically no knowledge of the
extent to which such customs may have had their parallel
in Cornwall. The delicately poised ' logan ' (pronounced
' loggan ') rocks, however, which are found on many of the
Cornish hills are known to have had their witchcraft associations, whilst some of the fashioned stones of prehistoric
date were certainly regarded as possessing curative properties.
Not far from Madron Well, on the uncultivated moorlands
which lie between it and the north coast, stands the famous
Men-an-Tol, or Holed Stone, sometimes known as the ' Crick
Stone '. Through this, in former days, children were frequently passed ' nine times against the sun ', as a cure for
rickets. Such a practice, though now very rare, is probably
not quite obsolete, since the writer has been informed by
Mr R. J. Noall, of St Ives, that on arriving at the stone one
day not many years since he found a child being hastily
dressed at the conclusion of such a ceremony.

XI

The lingering of these old beliefs was until lately responsible
for preserving many of the barrows, cromlechs, and other
prehistoric remains in which Cornwall was once so rich
but whose numbers in a more ' enlightened ' age have been
sadly reduced. In July 1867 a correspondent wrote to the

Quarterly Review : ' Near Carleen, in Breage, an old cross has been removed from its place, and now does duty as a gate-post. The man occupying the farm where the cross stood set his labourer to sink a pit in the required spot for the gate-post, but when it was intimated that the cross itself was to be erected therein, the man absolutely refused to have any hand in the matter, not on account of any particular love of the beautiful or antique, but for fear of the " old people ". Another farmer related that he had a neighbour who " haeled down a lot of stones called the *Roundags* ", and sold them for building the dock at Penzance. " But," he added, " not a penny of the money he got for them ever prospered, and there wasn't wan of the hosses that haeled 'em that lived out the twelvemonth." '

As recently as the year 1925 the writer learnt that a field called ' Vounder ' (i.e. ' lane '), in the tenement of Pradannack, near Mullion, had never been broken or ploughed on account of the prevailing belief that whoever did so would thereby bring about the death of his eldest son, and other dire misfortune. The reason given for this was that the field had once been a burying ground, a tradition which has lately been confirmed by the discovery of some broken cinerary urns close by.

But whilst such beliefs were formerly the means of preserving many interesting antiquities which would otherwise have found their way into the walls of houses or the metalling of roads, the day when they can be relied upon to afford such protection is over. Unless a determined effort is now made to promote another sort of reverence for these relics of the ancient past, by instruction in the schools, and by educating public opinion, Cornwall's claim to being among the richest antiquarian fields in the country must in time become a matter of history only. Within the last few years a most curious rock, known in the district as the ' Towednack Chair ', has been destroyed for the purpose of building a china clay ' dry ', whilst it would be possible to make a long list of the barrows, earthworks, and other prehistoric remains which have suffered from similar vandalism within the present century. It is true that many of the better-known antiquities are now scheduled under the Ancient Monuments Act, but the eye of the law cannot always be focused even upon these, and unless they are preserved in the hearts of the people their fate must be precarious in the extreme.

It is clear, of course, that such remarks apply no less to the rich inheritance of folk-lore, song, speech, customs, and traditions which once served to endow Cornish life with such infinite charm and variety. Here, again, much has already been lost. Methodism, compulsory education, emigration, and, latterly, the ' discovery ' of Cornwall as a tourist resort have each contributed to the changes which have robbed the Duchy of much of its former individuality. The truth of this is nowhere more apparent than in the case of folk-lore. It is true, of course, as the latter section of this book has shown, that within the hearts of a few old people something of the genuine folk-tradition lingers yet ; whilst here and there, among a smaller proportion of their descendants, fragments of the old-time lore are treasured even now with a secret, half-ashamed, conviction—a conviction which is revealed only in moments of extraordinary crisis, or when in the company of those who have become really at one with the people through long and sympathetic acquaintanceship.

But whilst it is true to say that ' superstition ', as it is loosely termed, is clearly far from having been entirely eradicated, it now no longer manifests itself in the form of ' stories ' for general circulation. In cases where such stories are met with they may generally be assumed to lack genuineness, and one has only to visit the bar-parlour of an average Cornish inn in order to realize that the Cornish people are by no means unwilling to indulge in that kind of ' leg-pulling ' which takes the form of regaling visitors with the type of stories they are all agog to hear. For it is indeed the case that, in coming to Cornwall, most visitors still cling to the impression that they are about to mingle with a highly superstitious and visionary race of people—' mystic ' Celts—whose minds are supposed to be continually preoccupied with tales of the fairies and giants, and romantic daydreams of the past. On the whole the visitors are not to be blamed for this. For the books which they have read, written as so many of them were by former travellers who came into Cornwall at a time when such legendary lore could be picked up ' for the asking ', have all served to encourage the idea. Sooner or later, however, such pleasant fancies are bound to receive a rude shock, and the subsequent disillusionment to which they give place probably accounts for the unflattering descriptions of Cornish character which have appeared in many of the more recent novels about the Duchy.

Be this as it may, the fact remains that the natives of Cornwall to-day no longer conform to the character which was formerly attributed to them. Taken all in all they may be said to consist of a shrewd and calculating set of people, very polite, indeed, to the ' stranger from up the country ', but at the same time fully determined to extract the utmost from the new harvest of wealth which the gods have provided to compensate them for the decay of their former staple industries.

Among the generality of such people it is no exaggeration to say that the folk-lore of the past is wholly forgotten. Of piskies and giants the average Cornishman of to-day knows little and cares less. He has probably never visited the holy wells and prehistoric remains which lie but a few miles from his door, has never seen a Cornish chough, nor heard of its associations with King Arthur. He neither fears to borrow nor lend a bellows because he never uses one. He takes no account of the appearance of magpies, the croaking of ravens, or the howling of dogs. He knows nothing of ' pellars ', of casting spells, or of the charms of ' white witches '. If questioned he would probably be quite unable to rake up a single legend, ghost story, spectre, or romantic belief, unless it might be some tale which a summer visitor had imparted to him from his own study of Hunt's *Popular Romances*, or the railway company's *Guide to Legendland*.

> *The Cornish drolls are dead, each one ;*
> *The fairies from their haunts have gone :*
> *There 's scarce a witch in all the land,*
> *The world has grown so learn'd and grand.*[1]

In many respects, of course, it would be nothing short of sentimentalism to deplore such changes, for the state of being tied and bound by the chains of superstition implies both a servitude of mind and body. And yet there was in the old people's thought much of that beauty which poets seek, many rare flowers of the imagination, which the world of to-day, with all its advance in mechanism and science, can ill afford to lose. Whilst fully admitting the impossibility (even if it were desirable) of engrafting upon such a world the beliefs and outworn notions of a bygone day, there must surely lie between that and the ascendancy of a cheap

[1] ' Henny ' Quick, of Zennor.

materialism some state of compromise ! For now, more than ever, folk-lore is coming to be recognized as an essential part of human knowledge, a magic casement opening on to the past through which the eye of modern man may see, down infinite vistas, the struggles of the awakening mind, and those primitive movements towards the goal of truth which constitute the earliest history of the human race.

CORNISH HOMES AND
CUSTOMS

THE COTTAGE HOME

I

THE old-time cottage homes of Cornwall, like the old-style people who built and dwelt within their walls, are dwindling rapidly in number, and changing standards and conditions of life will soon have swept the majority of such houses from off the face of the country-side. Hundreds, indeed, have disappeared already, leaving, in most cases, ' not a wrack behind '. In other places the fragment of a wall, a few worked stones, an old fuchsia-tree, or some garden herbs still bear witness to the fact that on these spots men and women once lived and loved, worked, played, and slept—and died. With carefulness and anxiety they built those walls, and in the long summer evenings ' teeled ' their little gardens, planning for the day when they would leave them to their children who laughed and played around them at their games. Their life-time of work over, their bones lie resting in the peaceful churchyards. Overhead in the trees, the rooks still build their nests and caw to their mates, but the children of the dead are scattered to the ends of the earth, and their homes stand desolate and forgotten.

Even to-day, however, a sufficient number of these cottages still remain to show us the conditions under which the majority of the Cornish people of the past were born and reared, and the type of dwelling which constituted their homes. Built, as they are, with walls of whitewashed cob (clay) and thatched roofs, or with the local surface stone and slate, such houses make no conscious attempt at the picturesque. Poets indeed may sing of the cottages of rural England, with the honey-suckle twining about their doors, whilst cynics point to the mockery of these vaunted charms when the cold and damp of an English winter descends upon their inhabitants cowering within. The appeal of the Cornish cottage is a less meretri-cious one. Solidity and strength, and the pleasant use of well-tried local materials, harmonizing so well with the surrounding landscape that in time the work of Man seems almost to have become one with that of Nature—these are the qualities which constitute the charm of the cottage homes of Cornwall.

But if the distinctive character of Cornwall is apparent in the types of houses which are met with, still more clearly may it be seen in the plan, or rather absence of plan, upon which the houses are built. No feature is more characteristic of the country-side of England than the little Saxon villages grouped about their ancient greens—the church, with its weathered spire and background of graceful trees, the well-trimmed lawns before the vicarage, the obsequious homes of the poor adjoining the lodge gates and the demesnes of the local squire. But in Cornwall the very absence of these features serves to show the racial differences which existed between its early inhabitants and their neighbours of but even a few miles away across the Tamar. Villages there are, of course, even in Cornwall, but save in the north-eastern corner of the county, where Saxon influence began more early to predominate, such villages bear little or no resemblance to their English counterpart. In most cases the former consist of somewhat forbidding rows of grey-roofed houses, grimly facing the winds and rain which sweep across the treeless uplands in winter. Such villages owe their origin not to any communal spirit, nor to the love of human fellowship and society. Economic necessity, such as the development of mining, clay-working, or quarrying, called them into being, and in the very attitude of the houses one may picture something defiant, as if they shared with their inhabitants a certain resentment at finding themselves in a position so little characteristic of the normal dwelling-place of the Celt. The dwellers in these villages, moreover, owe little or no allegiance to the church of the parish, finding the central focus of their lives in the chapels which their fathers built and which they themselves support. The ' church-town ', indeed, in Cornwall, is something quite apart from the parish at large, a ' town ' which in some instances possesses but one house, and is divorced alike in spirit and situation from the other far more populous groupings which may lie within the parish boundary.

Still more of the inhabitants of Cornwall, in the past, at any rate, lived neither in church-town nor in village, but in lonely farms and scattered cottages, the latter dumped anywhere and anyhow—in odd corners by the roadside, on the rocky ledges above the fishing coves, or amidst the shafts, ' burrows ', and debris of the mines. Hundreds of such cottages were built by the miners themselves in the few short hours of leisure left them between spells of labour underground ; the amateur architects doing everything about the place with their own hands, from the erecting of the walls to the shaping of the timber, and even the setting in of the window-frames and glass—' and never lost an hour's work to bal (mine) when about it either ', as many of them could proudly boast.

Most of these cottage properties were held under the peculiar terms of a lease dependent on ' lives ', a system which, until recent years, obtained very widely in Cornwall. Under such leases a piece of waste ground could be obtained at a nominal rent, and on it the lessee would proceed to erect a house, with the understanding that at the death of the longest-lived of three selected persons, the ground, together with all the buildings and improvements effected thereon, should revert to the original owner. The latter might then retain it for his own use, let or sell it to another, or allow a renewal of the lease to the first tenant on payment of a ' fine '. Heaven alone knows the labour and sacrifice which went into the building of these cottages. The materials were the flesh and bones of the people, and the mortar was mixed with their blood. Small wonder that they should have clung to them through thick and thin, and that they should have proved the magnets which have drawn many a Cornishman back after years in exile, if it were only to view once more the homes their fathers built.

The system of leasing property on ' lives ' formerly proved of immense advantage to Cornish landowners, as by this means thousands of acres of utterly waste land were brought under cultivation which might otherwise have remained unused and unusable to this day.

One of the most extraordinary examples of the industry to which this system lent encouragement was provided by a certain William Pearce, of Landewednack, near the Lizard, who in the year 1804 was awarded a silver medal and a prize of fifteen guineas by the Society for the Encouragement of Arts ' for his unaided enterprise in reclaiming twelve acres of waste ground, the property of Sir Christopher Hawkins, and converting the same into highly-cultivated arable land '. This gigantic and, as it would now appear, almost superhuman task was commenced by the man in question when he had already reached his fiftieth year, and occupied no less than eighteen years of unremitting toil in bringing it to completion. During a considerable part of this time his circumstances were such that, so far from being able to employ labour, he was himself obliged to work for others during five days out of the week, in order to obtain the 1s. a day on which he and his wife and a family of seven children subsisted. ' As to property,' he wrote, ' when I first began this undertaking, I had none, except one mare, and the money which I earned in this way. I worked hard, however, for my employers in order to finish as soon as possible—not to leave off work, but in order to get home to start on again at my own undertaking in improvement.' The land chosen for the purpose was unpromising enough to damp the ardour of any ordinary agriculturist, consisting as it did of a heathy swamp, exposed to all the gales to which the Lizard promontory is subject, its surface soil less than six inches in depth, and beneath this a bed of loose stones, varying in size from half a pound to three hundredweight or more. These circumstances rendering the use of the plough impracticable, the whole of the ground had first to be broken up by hand. This work in itself occupied a number of years, during which time the turf was removed and built up in piles, the latter, when dry, being burnt and the ashes subsequently used for manure. Meantime, a start was made on the removal of the underlying stones which were carried to certain spots, in order to build the fences or Cornish ' hedges '. No less than seventeen of the latter were erected in order to divide the property into the eight different fields or enclosures which were thought necessary for the various kinds of produce it was intended to grow. The ground, as already mentioned, being very swampy, had also to be intersected with various drains, which emptied themselves into deeper ditches, which were dug round the margin of each field. These, indeed, served a double purpose, as thereby a greater height was given to the hedges. At every gateway a bridge capable of supporting a loaded cart was made over these watercourses. Before the land could be cultivated, however, further supplies of manure, consisting for the most part of sea sand, had to be brought from a beach two miles away, the average annual quantity of the material thus used being fifty loads, and the distance travelled in fetching it two hundred miles. In addition to this, at least another two hundred miles a year was traversed during part of the time in delivering coal, a supplementary occupation undertaken by the indefatigable lessee in order to eke out his slender livelihood.

At length the time came when the land on which this incredible amount of labour had been spent actually reached

the producing stage and, in 1803, the proud farmer had the
satisfaction of reaping ten Cornish bushels of barley, nine
trusses of hay, two hogsheads of oats, and ten bushels of
wheat. ' Having dealt with the ground, I began,' he writes,
' to erect a dwelling-house on the spot, the walls of which
were composed of turfs, and the roof rafted and thatched
by myself, although I was bred only to husbandry. To the
house I have added as I was able a barn, stable, cart-shed,
and other convenient outhouses for my cattle, which at present
consist of three horses and one cow, two heifers, two steers,
and one yearling ; to which may be added, as another part
of my small stock, a few bushels of different kinds of grain,
and a small quantity of hay, together with a plough, harrow,
cart, slide, wheelbarrow, and other tools necessary for
husbandry.' [1]

Such perseverance in the face of difficulties would have
been remarkable enough under any circumstances. But in
this case it was rendered all the more astonishing by the fact
that a physical infirmity to which the farmer was subject
necessitated the performance of the whole of the work,
including that of driving the plough, solely with the aid of
one hand.

Judged by every standard of common sense, even a medal
and a prize of fifteen guineas, together with having his achievement recorded in a set of very pedestrian verses, would seem
an inadequate reward for such a vast expenditure of toil, the
fruits of which must in so short a time have redounded to
the benefit of another. Yet such was the temptation of getting
a piece of land on which to erect a home of their own that
the system of leasing on lives continued throughout the whole
of the nineteenth century to prove as attractive to the working
people of Cornwall as it was profitable to their landlords.

Even at this day there are many people still living in houses
which their fathers built, and from which they themselves
are liable to ejection on a mere three months' notice when
the last ' life ' expires. Two old spinsters known to the writer
are living in such a house at the present time. The elder one
is over eighty years of age, and is the last life on the property.
Practically the whole of their joint savings have been sunk in
their little home, which has been their lifelong pride, and
which (very unwisely from a ' business ' point of view) they

[1] *The Turf House, a Poem. With an Appendix of Interesting Facts.*
1807.

have improved out of all recognition. On the death of the elder sister the younger one, who is long past her prime and unfitted for further work, will find herself not only alone in the world but, unless she is able to renew the lease under favourable conditions, faced with the dreaded workhouse in her declining years. Still, on the whole, these tenants have fared better than many of their neighbours, for the entire village in which they dwell lies under the impending shadow of the nearby estate, and many have already seen their properties return to the original owners, as the appointed lives ' fell in '.

In certain instances the hazards of this peculiar form of contract have resulted in extraordinary hardship. In the autobiography of Sir Richard Tangye the story is told of a certain miner who, after a lifetime of toil and economy, had at length contrived to save about £80, a sufficient sum, in those days, to build two cottages. A piece of land was obtained, and the lease was drawn on the usual terms. The man himself had no children, but selected three young and apparently healthy lives, and started to build. Fate, however, was against him, and before the last slate was on the roof all three lives had expired and the poor man was at the mercy of the landowner. So strong was public opinion in this case that the latter was virtually *compelled* to offer the usual composition. By the payment of heavy ' fines ' and other legal charges, the tenant was at length allowed the privilege of placing two new lives on the property. Such, however, was the costliness of the renewal that it swallowed up all the little added comforts and advantages which the rent of the second house would have secured for him in his old age.[1]

It is only fair to say that in many cases Cornish landowners used the power given them under this system in a more generous manner. About the middle of the eighteenth century the tenement of Trevegia-wartha, in the parish of Towednack, was occupied by an old lady who bore the striking name of Zenobia Baragwanath (*bara*, bread ; *gwanath*, wheat). At the age of ninety-nine years her lease, which was on the usual term of lives, had expired, and she was accordingly faced with the prospect of being turned out of house and home. In fear and trepidation, therefore, she made her way to the landlord's agent, in order to state her case and plead for some extension. ' Notwithstanding her age,' wrote an eye-witness,

[1] *One and All*, 33.

'she entered the room, standing upright and robust. She was dressed in what was then called a " Joseph ", which might have been coeval with herself for any remains of colour that it had ; but the quaint riding-dress was perfectly whole and nicely brushed, and so were the silver-buckled shoes that peeped from under it. Her head-dress was " a thing to dream of, not to tell ", so marvellously and inexplicably was it put together. What it was made of none but a milliner of those days could hope to explain. From the waist downwards she wore a " safeguard ", a coarse garment of camlet or serge, which was used to protect her " Joseph ", as well as to cover her feet when she was in the saddle. Her hair was twisted behind into what was then called a " club ", a sort of over-grown pigtail. In her hand she carried a riding-whip with a heavy silver knob.' Thus apparelled she stood before the agent, looking fresh and hearty after her ten-mile ride. Whether the lawyer had previously consulted his client, the Duke of Bolton, is not known, but his response to her appeal was both short and to the point :

' Go 's thy way home, An' Zenoby, my dear, and live so long as thee cust.'

Having thus relieved her mind, and satisfactorily concluded the business, the lawyer invited the old lady to take a glass of wine. This she accepted, but declined the offer of a second, saying that ' she had to ride home in the twilight upon a young colt, and was afraid to make herself giddy-headed '. She lived to enjoy her leasehold another three or four years, dying in 1763, when her body was laid to rest in the old churchyard at Zennor.[1]

Notwithstanding instances of this sort there can be no possible doubt of the hardships caused by the system as a whole ; more especially in the case of elderly women, who were commonly left homeless as well as husbandless by the death of the last life. Much stress was laid on this point by the Radical candidate, Mr Conybeare, during his famous election campaign in the Mining Division in 1885. A con-tributor to *Old Cornwall* has related an amusing incident which occurred at one of his meetings held during that year in the chapel schoolroom at Nancekuke. At the conclusion of a lengthy speech, wherein the candidate had denounced with much eloquence the hardships of the ' three-life ' system, a staunch supporter arose at the back of the hall and, as

[1] Hobson Matthews, *History of St Ives, Towednack, and Zennor*, 464.

though it had been the most apt of illustrations, sprang the following story upon the astonished audience. ' Talking of the troubles of poor old widows, do put me in mind of what poor dear ould Betsy Crowgey said to the Passon when he came to see her once when she were dying. " Well, good-bye, Passon," she said, when he got up to go. " I do wish 'ee well ! Seemin' to me, I shall soon be in Belzybub's buzzum now ! "

' " No ! No ! Betsy," exclaimed the Passon, " I do hope you 're going to a far better place than that ! "

' " Naw, Passon ! Doan't 'ee wesh me no better ; I 'm longen for to go to Belzybub's buzzum ! " says Betsy again.

' " Really now, Betsy," cried the Passon, " I hope you are mistaken, let us pray that it is to Abraham's bosom you are bound ! "

' " Aw, Aber'm, es et ? " returned Betsy. " Well, Passon, you do knaw more than I do 'bout they folks up above, and I caan't tell but what you 're right. But Belzybub or Aber'm, 'tes all wan to me ; for I 've been leven a poor lone widdy-wumman nigh upon fifty year, and so long as 'tes a man's buzzum I 'm bound for, I don't much keer ! " '

For a minute at least the meeting balanced between horror at such a tale in such a place and the mirth that its almost blasphemous telling aroused. Then someone laughed, and the meeting was saved from disaster by everyone following his example.[1]

II

A few cottages, standing to this day in out-of-the-way places, are claimed to have been built under more peculiar conditions even than that of the lease on lives. ' A hundred years ago,' writes Mr J. C. Hoare, ' it was commonly believed that, either by law or prescriptive right, anyone who built a house *in one night* could claim the freehold of it for ever after.'

This concession might appear akin to the offer said to be made to credulous visitors at the Mint when told that they may carry away ' all the bullion they can lift '. Formerly, however, the building of a cottage in one night was apparently not regarded as by any means an impossible feat. Mr Hoare,

[1] *Old Cornwall*, III, 38.

indeed, claims that several buildings which were erected in this manner remained until recent years in his native parish of Ladock.

A young couple of those days, desiring a house and, like many of their descendants in more recent times, seeing small chance of obtaining it by ordinary means, would secretly choose a piece of land, generally some roadside waste, with just enough ground for a one-room cottage, a pig's ' crow ' (sty), and a furze and turf rick. Taking a few friends into their confidence they would then begin to collect the materials, clay for the ' cob ' walls, poles, and thatching ' reed ' (i.e. straw) for the roof, and a ready-made door and a window. ' At length,' writes Mr Hoare, ' the appointed night would arrive. The materials having been secretly gathered near the spot, the conspirators would set to work with a will. Up would go the four walls in almost as few hours, and on them the roof of the new home. A small aperture near the back would be left to act for the moment as a chimney, but later on to develop into a window. Once established in his shanty the owner could make what improvements time and money allowed ; a hearth and chimney would be added in due course, perhaps also an upper room. The hearth was generally made large enough to accommodate a chimney-seat on one side, and sometimes a " cloam " oven on the other ; whilst a " brandis " (trivet) to hold the " kettle " and baking iron, and a turf fork and bellows would also find their place there. Many of these cottages,' he adds, ' have been pulled down and new ones erected on the same spot. In other cases new cottages have been built close by, whilst the old one has served for a linhay, or maybe a stable or a cowhouse. Some are actually owned by descendants of the original one-night builders, others again have been sold to the owner of the adjoining land, perhaps in time of want. Not a few have been retaken, but, as it would seem, unlawfully, for in quite recent years the Duchy of Cornwall claimed one such cottage, but failed entirely in its suit.' [1]

Both in outward appearance and in the scantiness of their furnishings such houses can hardly have differed much from the hovels described by Richard Carew as long ago as the middle of the sixteenth century. At that date, however, ' walls

[1] *Old Cornwall*, VI, 5–7. A similar custom formerly obtained in Devon and in Cheshire. See *Devon and Cornwall Notes and Queries*, XIV, Pt. II, April 1926 ; and Beatrice Tunstall, *The Shiny Night*.

of earth, low-thatched roofs, few partitions, no planchings (wooden floors), or glasse windows, and scarcely any chimnies other than a hole in the wall to let out the smoke : their bed, straw, and a blanket ', and their furniture a ' mazer and a panne or two ', comprised the substance of even the better class of Cornish husbandman. Notwithstanding this, Carew adds that by 1602 these conditions had altogether changed. Indeed, he goes so far as to say that such a fashion of living as described above had since been ' universally banished '. Whilst this may have been true as regards the homes of the wealthier type of farmer in the eastern part of the county, it clearly did not apply to the cottages of the poor.

Of the state of the latter towards the end of the eighteenth century, a good description is found in one of Mr Bottrell's folk-tales. Herein a certain ' Aunt Betty ' describes to a visitor the way in which her family contrived to find sleeping accommodation at night. ' " The babies," she remarks, " I do put in the costan (straw basket), the smaller ones get up on the talfat and stretch themselves in the bed, round the bed, and under the bed, as they like." ' The ' talfat ', to which Aunt Betty referred, consisted of a stage of boards placed immediately under the roof, and extending over one-half of the living room. Sometimes the former was screened off by planks nailed from its flooring to the key beam above ; but more often it simply had a railing, placed so as to prevent any one from falling into the room below. ' " Then look," continued Aunt Betty, " at that little bunk in the top of the wood corner. That was one which Tom (her husband) made out of some wreck timber the other day, so the boys might have a place to themselves. As you see, he put in two strong beams to reach from the wall-plat to the side of the chimney, and then put some planks upon them. To be sure the place isn't so deep as it ought to be for the boys to stretch out full length ; but what matter ? They like it well enough, and their legs hanging down over when they have a mind to stretch will make them grow all the longer ! Half the time they are never in the house at all by night, but sleep down in the boat, where she's moored to the ring-rock, all afloat."

' " Well," says I, " there isn't a healthier nor a handsomer set of boys and maidens in the parish than yours," and, to give the devils their due, no more there isn't.' [1]

Such was the free-and-easy life of a Cornish cottage a

[1] *Traditions and Hearthside Stories of West Cornwall*, I, 216.

hundred and fifty years ago. The sordid side of the picture, however, was not shown by Bottrell. It is rather through the writings of Dr William Pryce, a surgeon of this period, that one learns of the suffering that went with it when some poor miner was carried home ' to his hut full of naked children, but destitute of all conveniences, and almost of all necessaries '. A scene once common enough and yet, as this writer says, ' of such complicated misery and distress as words have no power to describe '.[1]

Elsewhere in the pages of Bottrell may be found a description of another cottage of this period, occupied by an inhabitant of an altogether different class. Poor old An' (aunt) Marget, the witch, belonged to one of the decayed ' poor and proud ' families of the west, but had been disowned in her early youth because of her marriage with a young sailor who had subsequently been killed in an engagement on board the privateer, or pirate ship, which he commanded. At his death she had taken up her habitation in a tiny cottage situated amidst the rocks of Zennor cliff. Here, on two or three particular anniversaries which she kept in each year, she might be seen attired in a blue silk gown, almost thick enough to stand on end, the open front showing a quilted petticoat of white satin, half concealed by an apron of muslin skilfully embroidered with her own needle. On her arms she wore long netted silk gloves reaching to the elbows, and there met by lace ruffles which hung far below her waist. Her silver-grey hair was crowned with a lace cap like a fairy web. Round her neck lay a chain of amber beads, diamond rings bedecked her fingers, whilst a magnificent pair of silver buckles shone on her velvet shoes. The hut in which she lived, with her lambs, kids, cats, tame hares, and poultry (besides the robins, wrens, and sparrows which nested under the thatched roof), was only just large enough to hold her ' turn ' (spinning wheel), table, high-backed carved oak chair, a few stools and, opposite the door, her dresser, which was the pride of the old lady's heart. On the few blue-painted shelves were arranged, with the greatest care and eye to effect, many rare pieces of old china, earthenware of brilliant colours, and of graceful or grotesque forms, besides many singularly-shaped glasses of all hues. Over the fireplace might be seen a large, bright warming-pan, and an hourglass, together with foreign shells, coral, and many other fancy things which had been brought to her from distant lands by

[1] *Mineralogia Cornubiensis* (1778), 177.

the young mariner for whose love she had forsaken her home and proud kinsfolk long ago. An' Marget's bed, her carved oak chest, small treadle-turn for spinning thread, and a few other things, were placed on a talfat which extended over half the length of the hut.[1]

Old Margaret resembled many of her humble neighbours of this period in eking out a slender livelihood by spinning yarn or thread, and weaving. As 'Henny' Quick, the Zennor 'poet' (1792–1857) wrote of his own parents:

> *My father laboured underground,*
> *Mother the spinning wheel put round.*

In the western part of Cornwall Sennen people were especially noted for their skill as weavers. Some of their descendants living at Escols, a little hamlet in this parish, were still known in the latter part of the last century by the nickname of 'Triddles' on account of their forefathers having worked the treadles of the handlooms as their chief employment.

Weavers were much given to singing at their work in order to relieve its tediousness. One of the old weaving farmers of Escols was long remembered by the nickname of 'Uncle Plato' from the fact that, whenever he was overtaken by a fit of weariness in working his treadles, he would begin a solemn tune which ran :

> *Said Plato, Why should man be vain*
> *Since bounteous Heaven has made him great ?*

He seldom finished this ditty, however, since his wife, whenever she was within hearing, would exclaim :

'Peter ! Peter ! may the devil take thee and Plato too. I can hear thee droanan that dreary thing and the treadles gwean (going) lazier and lazier. Come, Peter Vean (*vean*, little, an endearment), strike up :

> *Thinking to lead a sober life,*
> *One Monday morning I took a wife,*

or some other lively catch. I will join in, and thee west make three thraws of the shuttle for one now.' [2]

[1] W. Bottrell, *Tales and Hearthside Traditions of West Cornwall*, I, 78–9.
[2] W. Bottrell, *Traditions and Hearthside Stories of West Cornwall*, II, 196.

The spinning industry, however, was by no means confined to west Cornwall. At a vestry held in the year 1797 in the parish of Stoke Climsland, on the eastern border of the county, it was decided that, owing to the prevailing distress caused by the small quantity of wool being given out by the spinning masters, special assistance should be granted to those parishioners who were dependent upon this form of work for their livelihood. Four years later the matter was again brought to the notice of the parish authorities, who then resolved that ' all persons capable of and accustomed to spinning should continue the practice thereof, notwithstanding the low price of 4d. per lb. given by the yarn jobbers, and that, as an encouragement, an additional 1d. per lb. be given to all spinners belonging to the parish, provided the jobbers do not lower their price any more '.[1]

From the cottage or farm where it was made the homespun cloth was sent to one of the then numerous ' tucking ' or ' fulling ' mills, where it underwent the final process of dipping and stretching. It is interesting to note that in three instances the Cornish word for a tucking mill—' Velyn-druckya ' (*velyn*, mill ; *druckya,* tucking)—still survives as a place-name in West Penwith. Cloth thus made was practically everlasting. It was the proud boast of a certain poor old road-mender, who was a familiar sight to people residing in Gwinear parish seventy years ago, that he had ' twelve suits of clothes home in the " press " ', and only two of them ' biden clath ' (bought cloth).

No doubt many of these suits were family heirlooms, which had been inherited by the old man after they had already proved themselves of more lasting substance than the flesh of their original owners.

Clothing at this period was made up from the homespun material by journeymen tailors who travelled from one house to another, receiving (in the middle of the last century) 1s. per day and their food. Both dressmakers (who got 6d. per day) and tailors took their apprentices with them when they went out to work, the latter receiving their food only. The tailor generally sat crossed-legged on the kitchen table. The

[1] The jobbers, however, failed to maintain their price, so the bounty was not given. At another vestry held on 26 January 1801, it was decided that since the spinners could not work for the yarn-jobbers' price of 3d. per lb., and there was ' a person at Calstock who spins candle-wicks, the Poor Warden should enquire if the poor cannot be employed with better advantage in that profession than in spinning yarn '.

cloth left over from the cutting-out went by the name of
' tailor's cabbage ' and was claimed by the journeyman as his
perquisite ; being afterwards sold by him to poor people for
making or repairing children's clothes. This was the origin
of the old couplet :

> *Little Tommy Tailor, sitting on the board,*
> *Eating more cabbage than I can afford.*[1]

The old tailors were not always completely successful in
their trade. ' Seventy years ago,' writes Mr Jim Thomas,
' we had in Camborne a tailor called Vine, whose chief rival
was a certain Jinny Probis, who lived at " Jethan " (Treswithian). At that time, boys starting to work underground
would generally be provided by their parents with a new white
duck trousers for their first shift or " core ", for it was thought
to be good luck to go down for the first time with a white
garment on. On one occasion a boy at Jethan was about to
start underground, and his mother, according to custom, had
bought him a yard of duck for his trousers. Jinny Probis,
being on the spot, was given the job of making up the clothes
but, alas ! for her reputation, when the trousers were sent
back they were found to be so small that the boy, child as he
was, was unable to get into them. " Jinny must have made
them for a cat," the mother remarked ; so she took them up
to town to Tailor Vine to see if he could put them right. Tailor
Vine looked them over, and said : " Yes, all I got to do is to
leave out the seams a bit and they'll be all right ". So he
" left out " the seams but, in spite of this, when the garments
were returned they were found to be an even worse fit than
before.'

In those days most villages had their local rhymesters,
and this incident was quickly seized upon by one of the
latter, who provided much amusement by the following
doggerel :

My mother bought a yard of duck, a trousers for to make,
And Jinny Probis cut it out and made a grand mistake.
Then Tailor Vine he took a hand, and thought to do it fine,
But when the trousers was tried on—the fore-part was behind ![2]

[1] J. C. Hoare, MS.
[2] *Old Cornwall*, VII, 29–30.

III

It was well indeed that the poor were able to extract amusement from such mishaps as this, for in reality the constant planning and contriving necessitated by the low rate of wages made for conditions which seem the very reverse of humorous. Throughout the ' hungry forties ' of the last century 35s. to 40s. a month was still the standard wage of a surface hand at the mines. The remuneration of farm labourers was even lower, averaging but 1s. a day in most cases, although a skilled man might, with luck, earn 9s. a week, with a cottage ; or 12s. without. On such a meagre income it was scarcely possible to provide even food for a large family and hence, in order to avoid starvation, practically every member of the household was driven into the fields to work. The day began early and finished late. ' My father,' wrote an old woman, not long since, ' was a skilled labourer earning 9s. a week with a good cottage and a garden, when I was a child in about 1850. We were allowed to keep two pigs for our own use, and also to gather as much faggot wood as we wanted from the hedges. Time was obtained to cut this by doing piecework, which began at 4 or 5 a.m. ; the normal hours being from 6 a.m. to 7 p.m.' [1] By 8 o'clock the women and children of the household had likewise found their way to the fields, where they were employed till six in the evening weeding corn, hoeing turnips, picking stones, planting potatoes, rolling barley and oats, hay-making or reaping with the sickle. For such work the children from four or five years of age upwards received 3d. or 4d. a day, according to their size or dexterity ; and the women 6d. or 8d., making, with the husband's wages, some 12s. or 13s. a week.

Meantime the babies of the household had perforce to be left at home to fend for themselves with, at best, an older child to look after them. ' I found little Kitty and her cripple brother (the latter no better than a baby) packed into the window seat brandishing a knife from one hand to the other, and then scuffling for its possession,' wrote Mrs Pascoe after visiting a typical farm labourer's home of this date. ' The young,

[1] J. C. Hoare, MS.

seven-year-old housekeeper, meanwhile, was lighting the fire with a piece of tallow, making repeated excursions to and from the fire-place and the cradle in order to " borrow " a handful of straw from the baby's loose palliasse, and leaving a train of combustibles each time.' [1]

Small wonder under such circumstances that tragedies were frequent. ' On Saturday last,' states the *West Briton*, 25th December 1840, ' the district coroner held no less than three inquests on the bodies of children who had been burnt to death by accidentally setting fire to their clothes whilst left in the house alone during their mother's absence. All of these children were under ten years of age.' In the following week a coroner in East Cornwall stated that he had held eight separate inquests on children who had been burnt to death, within a fortnight, and added : ' Notwithstanding the repeated cautions given to parents (against leaving their children) similar accidents are constantly occurring '.

The doors of the cottages at this date were mostly of the ' hepse ' variety, being divided across the middle into two sections. The upper half was generally kept open so as to admit light and air to the living-room, whilst the lower half was shut in order to keep in the children and to keep out the fowls and pigs. Failure to observe this precaution resulted on occasion in ghastly consequences. ' Last week,' states a newspaper correspondent, ' the mother of an infant child in Gwinear went to fetch water, leaving the baby alone in the cradle. Whilst she was out, a pig entered the house and so dreadfully ate the head and shoulders of the helpless infant that it expired within a few minutes after the mother's return.' [2]

Mrs Pascoe, in her *Walks about St Hilary*, records a similar incident. In this case, however, the pig merely ate the child's hands. Strange to relate, the father, on hearing of the accident, received the news with joy, exclaiming : ' The boy is a gentleman for life, the parish must look after him ! ' ' For the greater part of the year,' adds Mrs Pascoe, ' the child was subsequently exhibited at fairs and markets, and at coach windows, the mother neglecting her other children for this new source of revenue.'

In large families the older boys and girls were almost invariably sent into farm service in order ' to save their meat '. Wages being nominal and luxuries not expected in the way

[1] *Walks about St Hilary* (1836–8), 4.
[2] *Cornwall Gazette*, 30 July 1803.

of food, even the small farmer found it a paying proposition to take a number of such children into his household. The employees of ' Uncle Jan Permewan ', who farmed Penrose, in the parish of Sennen, about the year 1820, have thus been recorded in the rhyme of a local poet :

> *Betsy Pender, Kitty Mann,*
> *Philey Botterell, Gracie Jan,*
> *Boy Sailor, Cousin Kit,*
> *Billy Murley, and Tom Peep.*[1]

The girls would be employed in assisting the farmer's wife in her household chures, and in attending to the pigs, calves, and poultry ; whilst the boys were generally set to driving horses or oxen at the plough. ' In no county does the ox stand in higher estimation for all kinds of work than in Cornwall,' stated a writer in 1826. ' Oxen are everywhere to be met with, drawing the butt (cart), the wain, or the wagon on the road, and the plough and harrow in the fields. They are shod or, as it is locally termed " cued ", and are extremely docile and active, going at a full trot with the empty carriages in the bustling seasons of haytime and harvest, and driven by a little boy who cheers and excites them by the song and the goad.' [2]

In paying turnpikes two oxen were reckoned equal to one horse, and their strength in drawing was calculated to be in the same proportion. In summer they lived on grass, and in winter on wheat straw, rarely receiving any hay. The strength of an ox is said to be in its neck rather than in its shoulder, and the animals were accordingly harnessed to the plough or cart by means of a wooden yoke, without bridle or rein. Their movements were directed solely by word of command, occasionally enforced with a prick from the goad or ' gourd ', which was made from the spindle-wood which grew wild in many of the hedges.[3]

Steers were broken in between the ages of two and three, and were worked for a matter of four or five years, two young ones being added each year to replace the older ones who were put out to fatten for the butcher. In some cases twenty or more oxen were kept on a single farm, and where ' double-furrow ' ploughs were used, eight oxen were harnessed to each

[1] Per Mr Henry Thomas, St Just.
[2] *Letters from West Cornwall.*
[3] J. C. Hoare, MS.

plough, working in four pairs. The same pairs were always yoked together, and bore such attractive names as Diamond and Dainty, Young and Lusty, Young and Beauty, Sport and Pleasure, Star and Stately, Goodluck and Speedwell, Butler and Steward, Neat and Comely, Brisk and Lively, Silk and Golding, Brown and Berry, Spark and Beauty, Forest and Leader, Lad and Virgin.[1] In most cases the oxen required very little ' driving ', and were possessed of a considerable intelligence. During the midday meal, which the men generally ate in the fields, the oxen were released from their yokes, and turned on to the grass. As soon as they were wanted again the ploughboy had only to shout : ' Young, yoke ! ' and the ox referred to would at once look up from his grazing and come of his own accord to the plough, where he would stand patiently waiting for the yoke to be fixed. The remainder of the team were equally familiar with their names, and very rarely did one come to his place out of turn. In order to keep the oxen in good humour it was customary for the boys to keep singing their names in a drawling fashion almost the whole day along. In the busy seasons of the year their voices could be heard thus throughout the whole country-side, as they trudged along behind their teams from dawn to dusk. In some mysterious way the oxen seem to have had an understanding ear for this music, and always worked the better for it.

A strong point in favour of the use of oxen for ploughing in the West Country was that, unlike horses, they took a straight line of their own accord, and however steep the gradient of the field might be, they breasted it direct. Moreover, the working of oxen never seemed to impede their growth. Many of them attained a huge size, and after rendering useful service for four or five years would make 10 cwt. of beef when they were eventually sold to the butcher. ' I inquired,' says one old writer, ' if the flesh of a working ox was as good as that of one which was not worked, and I was told it was better! When they intend to fatten an ox they work him down thin. They then turn him into the pastures till he fattens again. All his flesh is then new flesh, and makes excellent beef.'[2] Possess-

---

[1] An old farmer in the Meneage district more than a hundred years ago is said to have provided his team of eight oxen with the somewhat more original names : ' Rule and Reason, Time and Season, Sweat and Labour, Madcap and Shaver '.

[2] *Letters from West Cornwall.*

ing such advantages, it may seem strange that oxen should ever have ceased to be employed for farm work. The great drawback to their use, however, was their slowness, it being estimated that it required four oxen to do the work of two horses. In addition to this it was considered necessary, latterly at any rate, to employ a man as well as a boy to work one team in a plough, whereas one man with three horses could work the same plough unassisted.[1]

Owing to their poverty, the working-classes of former times could rarely afford the clothing proper to protect them from the cold and wet. In the earlier part of the last century the farm labourer's working dress consisted of a coarse shirt, a pair of ' duck ' trousers not quite reaching to the ankles, a waistcoat, a smock (also made of ' duck '), and low-quartered shoes—without socks or stockings. At a later date, when boots came into general use, their leather was frequently so hard from exposure that it was only with the utmost difficulty they could be drawn on. ' Every worker in those days,' writes Mr Charke, ' had a lace hook, for our boot leather and the laces were too obdurate for fingers alone. If you could only conceive how the men suffered in their feet in summer time from the hot earth which got into their boots, and the perspiration, you would pity them. I dare say they walked from twenty-five to thirty miles a day in the course of their work, with raw and blistered feet, and there were many squeals at night when the stockings came off. The wounds !—wounds with blood ! All to live, and feed others.' [2]

In winter, when the fields were heavy with water, and deep in mud, straw ropes or ' thumb binds ' were wound around the legs from the top of the boots to the knee, like a modern puttee. These thumb binds were made of oaten straw, and received their name from being spun around the thumb, an operation quickly performed by those who had had the necessary practice. The upper part of the body was covered with an apron and a shawl made of old sacks, whilst an ancient ' billycock ' hat served as the usual headgear for all weathers.

Having only one suit of clothes for everyday wear, when the men came home at night soaked to the skin, they were obliged to dry themselves before the fire; whilst the same clothes had to be put on again in the morning, often still wet and icy

---

[1] See *Western Morning News*, 4 May 1925. Oxen were retained for ploughing at Bodrugan farm, in the parish of Goran, as recently as 1895.
[2] ' Remembrances of Life on a Farm,' *Old Cornwall*, II, No. 2.

(See page 318)

A COTTAGE HOME IN THE MINING DISTRICT

OXEN AT WORK NEAR MEVAGISSEY

(See page 334)

cold. Rheumatism in consequence was a wellnigh universal malady amongst the poor. At fifty many a man had become practically an ' ancient ', having to walk on two sticks, and so stiff in his joints that when he sat down he could scarcely ' rise up ' again. The children and women suffered from exposure hardly less than the men. The former were almost invariably underclothed, being frequently without shoes or stockings, or any change of linen. On Saturday nights they had to go to bed early, and naked, in order that their mothers might wash and dry such underclothes as they possessed, to be ready for use again on the Sunday morning.[1] During a frost, or in snowy weather, it was not uncommon to see boys of nine or ten years of age in the fields crying bitterly on account of the cold, and their hands so blue and numbed that they were scarcely able to grasp the frozen turnips which they would be engaged in pulling. After a long day's toil of this sort men, women, and children would return to their homes at night, worn out with fatigue, but still having the household duties—cooking, baking, sewing, or fetching water—to perform before retiring to rest. During the busy seasons of the year, indeed, the men would often contrive to cultivate their gardens by moonlight, whilst within the cottage the womenfolk were ' catching up ' their various chures which had to be done in readiness for the next day's toil, which started with the dawn.

By such means a semblance of comfort and decency was often maintained even in the poorest homes. But where the wife was a slattern or a poor ' contriver ', or the husband preferred to spend his scanty leisure in the public-house or in ' eating sun ' under a warm hedge, dirt and destitution combined in producing a condition of squalor beyond words to describe.

' Never did my eyes behold such a loose, slammerkin, smiling, snuff-taking slattern as Mary Anne Hodge,' wrote Mrs Pascoe on one occasion, ' with her red hair streaming down under her tattered cap, her snuffy nose and chin, her light gown " all in squads ", and her ultra-fashionable sleeves dipping every now and then into the washing-tub over which she was loitering. As I advanced farther into the room I caught sight of a girl blowing the fire. She was a squalid-looking little thing, about eight years old, pale as ashes, and marked with the smallpox—one of those poor creatures that shrink from

[1] Dr R. Dunstan, *Western Morning News*, 2 December 1929.

the light and blink when they get into it. But she had an additional motive now for trying to keep out of sight—her clothing being simply and solely nothing but her shift. " Where are the other children ? " I asked. The woman grinned sheepishly, as she made reply : " I won't tell 'ee no lies, they 're up in bed while I 'm washing their clothes to put on them "."

Adverting to the woman's approaching confinement, and the dilapidated state of the premises, Mrs Pascoe inquired : ' " What will you do with those open beams ? You will catch your death ". " Yes," was the laconic reply, " I suppose I shall, John was saying it oft to be boarded—dangerous too, for any one slipping their foot—I was nearly down through yesterday."

' " Is that your only chamber ? "

' " Oh, yes, fie, and a clever chamber it will be, when we have got a winder to let in some light, and a bit of stairs to get up by." '

On returning home Mrs Pascoe reported what she had seen, with the result that the kind-hearted vicar at once offered to lend the husband a few pounds in order to ' planch ' the upper floor. ' This loan,' wrote Mrs Pascoe, ' the trusty John returned more promptly and thankfully than many of his so-called betters do. The flooring was bought at Marazion, and in order that the mason might not lose his day's wages at the mine, was brought home by the females those two miles on their backs.' [1]

IV

In most of the cottages of those days, the rooms, where there was more than one, were simply divided by wooden partitions. These, as a writer has pointed out, through not being raised as high as the roof, ' allowed a free circulation of air through every room '. Well as this sounds from the point of view of hygiene, in practice ventilation thus secured can hardly have added to the comfort of the family. Whilst, in addition to this, the ill-fitting door and the open chimney provided ' draught enough to feed a pig ', the window alone could be relied upon to exclude both air and sunshine. Such windows were commonly about two feet square. Their glass

[1] *Walks about St Hilary.*

was of the most wretched description, full of ' eyes ' and knots, the better quality costing 1s. 4d. a foot, and being altogether beyond the pockets of the average cottager. In many cases the windows, small as they were, were stuffed with rags or had a slate inserted to take the place of an absent pane. If the window kept out cats and dogs it was about as much as was expected of it ! Wall-paper was, of course, an unheard-of luxury, the inside of the cob being generally—though not always—whitewashed. In the older cottages the ground floor simply consisted of the trodden-down earth, which was levelled once a week with a shovel. Later, floors of lime-ash were introduced. These, at their best, were bare, damp, and cold. It was formerly a common sight to see the inhabitants stepping gingerly from one piece of wood to another when the holes, which were constantly being made in this surface by the hob-nailed boots, had been newly filled. The single downstairs room possessed by most cottages had to serve for all the purposes of kitchen, wash-house, nursery, and sitting-room combined. The furniture in this apartment commonly consisted of a rude table, resembling a carpenter's bench ; and, in some cases, three or four straight-backed chairs. The majority of people, however, had to be content with a long form and a three-legged stool, whilst the children sat on blocks of wood. The grand seat for the head of the household was often formed out of an old tree-trunk. A few earthenware cups, saucers, and basins, some wooden or tin plates, an iron crock for boiling purposes, and a ' kettle ' or ' baker ', practically completed the downstairs equipment.[1]

In the one, or at most two, tiny bedrooms above, the furnishings were equally scanty, consisting only of a couple of bedsteads, with crossed ropes to sustain the mattress. The latter was little better than a straw mat, about half an inch thick, feather ties being at that time a luxury for the rich only. How the family contrived to pack themselves in at night was indeed a marvel. In cases where there was but one bedroom the two youngest children lay with the parents, the infant on the mother's arm, and the next youngest outside the father ; whilst a mattress placed on the floor sometimes accommodated as many as six other children, four lying side by side, and two across their feet. Very frequently both the mattresses and bedding were rotten and filthy. In the cold of winter, coats, dresses, petticoats, and even sacks were utilized for bed

[1] See Dr R. Dunstan, *Western Morning News*, 2 December 1929.

coverings, a fact which tended to increase the normally fetid atmosphere. Where the roofs of the cottages were of thatch winter storms frequently rifled them, and when, as was not infrequent, the thatcher was unable to attend for several days, the rain which trickled through on to the floors of the bedrooms, and on to the beds, added still further to the discomforts of the family.[1]

In such cottages as these sanitary arrangements were, of course, entirely lacking, whilst in many cases ' their dung pits lay immediately before their doors '.[2] Hot-water systems were, naturally, alike unknown, with the result that the inhabitants had little opportunity for washing either their clothes or bodies. In some districts the women were accustomed to take the heaviest part of their laundry to some neighbouring well. Thither also they would carry a ' brandis ' (trivet) and a boiler, the surrounding furze brakes providing the necessary fuel. After being washed the clothes were spread out on the bushes to dry. Water itself was often a scarcity in the mining districts, where in many cases the wells had been drained dry by the pumping engines. In some instances people were obliged to go nearly three miles for their supply.[3]

It speaks well for the character of the Cornish people that they should have retained a reputation for cleanliness and decency even under such conditions. It is true that some of them possessed peculiar ideas on the question of washing. Many of the older generation regarded it as highly dangerous to wash their backs, believing that by so doing they would wash away their strength. Some forty years ago a friend of the writer was riding on top of one of the old-fashioned horse buses which at that time plied between Helston and the Lizard. In the course of the drive a discussion arose among the passengers as to how frequently it was desirable to wash one's hair.

' How often do you do it, John ? ' asked one of the party, turning to the old man who drove the bus.

' Wash me 'ead ? ' exclaimed the latter in tones of righteous horror, ' why, I should as soon think of washing me feet ! '

That the latter prejudice was widespread is illustrated by

---

[1] ' The Good Old Days,' *Cornish Magazine*, II, 114.
[2] R. Polwhele, *History of Cornwall*, VII, 75.
[3] At the present day there are villages in which water is still so scarce as to be retailed to the inhabitants at a penny a bucket.

another conversation overheard quite recently in the streets of St Ives. ' Ais, my dear,' one old woman was explaining to another, ' I was down 'Mester beach the other day, and some passel of people there was too, bathing and widdy-waddying (paddling). I don't knaw what they want with so much of it. I haben' washed me feet for twenty years—and they 're white as lilies now ! ' It would seem probable that this objection to washing the feet arose out of a fear of softening the tough hide which forms their natural protection and had its origin in times past when the majority of the poor were accustomed to go barefooted.

The consequences of overcrowding and of the lack of sanitation and a proper water-supply were bad enough in the scattered homesteads of the country-side, but in the slums and back streets of the towns these evils were greatly intensified. Shut off alike from sun and air, with piles of offal and manure stacked up in their courtlets and backyards, and their only drainage an open ' catchpit ', it is small wonder that in such premises typhus was endemic, and that cholera should have taken further toll of their unfortunate inhabitants. In some instances as many as six out of ten persons residing in one house are said to have been stricken with the latter plague at a time, and having no nurse to attend them, and bereft of even the barest necessities of life, the misery of their condition can be better imagined than described.

During the last outbreak of cholera in the town of Redruth it is said that the old house adjoining the tennis courts (formerly the 'count-house of Wheal Union mine) was set aside as a mortuary for the victims. In the churchyard a short distance away great numbers of the dead lie buried in a common grave.

Some years prior to this an epidemic of cholera had broken out in the district round Penzance. On that occasion it happened that whilst the plague was rife at Newlyn, the neighbouring village of Mousehole remained immune. In order, therefore, to prevent the spread of the disease, barriers were set up between the two villages, the Mousehole people being thereby forced to make a long detour in order to reach their market town of Penzance. This state of affairs continued for some time until at length a Newlyn woman is alleged to have thrown some clothing over the barrier with the avowed intention of introducing the plague amongst her neighbours. Bitter as the rivalry is known to have been between the two places, such an act of savagery would hardly appear credible, were it not supported by what appears to be reliable evidence.

That the Cornish people of this date were of hardy constitution is illustrated by the following incident. During the great cholera outbreak of 1838, a man who was at work in the one hundred and seventy fathom level of the Consolidated Mines at Gwennap was seized with violent vomitings, and the usual symptoms of the disease. With great difficulty he was brought in a ' kibble ' (bucket) to surface, when he was found to be speechless and motionless, and apparently on the point of death. It being then the middle of the night, and no doctor at hand, one of the miners suggested wrapping the head of the unfortunate man in a flannel, and then immersing him up to the neck in the hot-water cistern of ' Bawden's ' engine, the temperature of which was 112°. The experiment was tried and proved successful. After being a quarter of an hour in the water the cramp and pain entirely disappeared, and the patient only complained of great weakness. His abdomen was then bound round with more flannel, after which he set off to *walk* to his home, which was more than two miles away from the mine ! [1]

Cholera and typhus were not the only plagues through which, in popular parlance, the anger of God was made manifest. In many cases these were followed by frightful epidemics of smallpox. In 1870 the latter disease was raging in the district round St Ives. It is recorded that in one or two instances during that year whole families lay awaiting burial at the same time. Some of the cottages in this neighbourhood were never afterwards inhabited for fear of the infection. One of these, the writer has been informed, stood at the entrance to the lane leading off from the main St Ives-Land's End road towards Trevail. Another, situated near Nancledrea, is still roofed and until recently was used as a slaughter-house. A third cottage stood beside the Zennor road, not far from the ' Eagle's Nest '. The people in this house are said to have buried three sons in one week.

That such plagues were a direct consequence of over-

---

[1] ' How d'ee git ? ' ' No bet ' (no better). ' Cusda sweat ? ' (Can you sweat ?) ' Not yet.' This curious greeting, formerly used among the ' bal maidens ' (mine girls) may possibly be reminiscent of the days when cholera was rife and when to ask a person if he could sweat was synonymous to inquiring if he were in good health.

crowding and the low standard of living will scarcely be questioned to-day. How low that standard was the report of the commission appointed to inquire into the condition of persons employed in agriculture in 1867 makes amply clear. In the western part of the county the wages of mal labourers were said to approximate to 11s. or 12s. a week. 'including perquisites'. The nature of the latter can best be understood by a comparison with mid-Cornwall, where the average wage was given as 8s. a week, 'with wheat and barley at a fixed price per bushel'. In St Columb Minor, farm labourers were said to earn 12s. a week, but part of this took the form of grist corn and potato ground in substitution for cash payment. Fewer women on the whole were engaged in agriculture than formerly, but their wages when so employed were still as low as 8d. a day. Children entered the ranks of labour at an early age. Thomas Oliver, of Gulval, aged seven years, told the commissioners : ' I have been out putting down potatoes and got 4d. a day, working from 6 a.m. to 6 p.m., half an hour being allowed for dinner '. Ellen Pierce (eleven years old), described by the schoolmaster of the same village as being very irregular in her attendance, stated in explanation : ' I have been out pulling radishes at 7d. a day, the hours of work being from 8 a.m. to 6 p.m. I go home to dinner from 12 to 1 o'clock. Men, women, boys, and girls all work together when it comes to potatoing. We were seven girls, five boys, and three women, with one man to fill in the drills. The older girls go away early from the morning school to cook or carry dinner for their mothers in the gardens. My aunt works in the gardens and gets 5s. or 6s. a week. In my cottage we have one kitchen, one bedroom, and a dairy. Mother, aunt, grandmother, and myself live there together.'

John Carter, of Ruan Minor (ten years of age), also revealed something of what life had meant for him. ' I was out at work last year and this driving horses for a farmer, and putting in potatoes. I got 1d. a day and three meals ; milk for breakfast, meat and no drink for dinner, bread and milk for supper.'

Although these may have been somewhat exceptional cases, it would appear that the majority of children started work at ten or eleven years of age, receiving at the most but 6d. a day.

The inquiry shows that the cottages of the agricultural

labourer at this date varied considerably in different parts of the county. In almost every instance, however, they are described as being overcrowded. 'I was lately in a labourer's cottage in the parish of St Martin,' stated the Looe relieving officer, ' where the family consisted of nine persons with only one room.' 'The only means of ventilation is by opening the windows,' the commissioners were solemnly informed by the occupant of another cottage in an adjoining parish ! In the Liskeard district the rent of a cottage with a garden was said to vary from 50s. to £5 5s. a year. Near Penzance, however, where the land was particularly fertile, house property was more expensive and rents ranged from £4 to £6 a year. Few even of the better type cottages possessed privies, or had anything in the nature of a water supply. But, as if in compensation for this, it was stated that in some instances the floors of the downstairs rooms were ' as damp as the roads outside ' ! [1]

V

Whilst the cottages of the labourer were often wretched in the extreme, Cornwall at this date possessed many other houses of a small but substantial type which reflected the higher standard of living enjoyed by their inhabitants. The latter, indeed, had in most cases risen from the ranks of the working-class, but in the ' precipice face ' to which society has been likened, their particular niche or ledge lay somewhere above the ranks of the labourer, whilst still being below that of the merchant of the town or the yeoman farmer of the country-side. To this order belonged the mine ' captain ', the skipper of the little coasting vessel, or the foreman of one of the many small works and foundries which at that time flourished in the western part of the county. ' I should think this place is now four times as big as it was twenty years ago,' stated a resident of Hayle in 1826. ' Most of the new houses are covered with helling stones (i.e. slates), which are sold at 12s. to 15s. per thousand. The roofs inside are ceiled, and the floors planched (boarded) or laid with bricks. This was very seldom the case, formerly, and is not universal even now.

[1] *Second Report of the Commission on the Employment of Children, Young Persons, and Women in Agriculture* (1867). Appendix, Part II.

In the lower rooms if you look up, you see the floor of the next story with pieces of wood nailed across from beam to beam. On this the people put their bacon and other things instead of putting them in a cupboard. Before the copper-smelting works had ceased, houses used to be built with slag. These slags were made in moulds, and were hard as adamant, though brittle enough to be broken with a blow. Those persons who built on the company's land had slags for nothing, others were charged 6d. a score. The commoner sort of houses, now that slag can no longer be obtained, are built half-way up of stone and the upper half with a sort of brown mortar called clob. Stones are paid for at 6d. a load to the owner of the quarry, and cost 6d. a load for digging them out. Carting may cost another 1s. The clob only costs the labour of making it.' [1]

In the country districts such houses as these were almost invariably placed somewhere in the ' lewth ' or shelter, in marked contrast to the positions chosen by the average bungalow-builder of to-day. These old dwellings, however, were intended for no mere summer resorts, but were built by a people who had sufficient experience of wind and rain in the course of their working lives to make shelter the prime essential of the sites in which they laid their homes. In such spots, safe from the roaring gales of winter, gardens could be cultivated and flowers grown. For it is a fact, despite much that has been written to the contrary, that the old Cornish people took a pride in the surroundings of their homes, and loved the sweetness of a flower patch wherever Nature permitted them to possess one.

From the garden gate, made of pleasant ironwork beaten at some local foundry, the approach to such houses as these commonly led through borders gay with sweet-williams and other blooms to the substantial porch, built like the rest of the dwelling of moorstone granite. Beside the porch might often be seen an old laburnum-tree or some beautiful lilacs. Four-square these houses stood, their low symmetrically-placed windows commonly gazing down some little valley through which ran the ' river ', red, as often as not, with the water from the adjacent mines. Very frequently the top of the roof was ornamented with a central ridge-tile representing a ' knight ' on horseback. Children were told that whenever this stiff little figure *heard* the chimes of midnight it would

[1] *Letters from West Cornwall.*

start to gallop along the roof ! Another form of decorative ridge-tile was the 'piskey pow' on which, so it was said, the 'small people' footed it gaily during the midnight hours.

The front door was generally so low that it was necessary to stoop on entering, in order to avoid striking one's head against the massive granite lintel. Two steps down and one landed safely into the front passage, which led into the 'hale' or parlour, the kitchen, the back kitchen, and the dairy. The furniture of the 'hale' usually consisted of three chairs, sometimes painted and always carefully polished (though no one ever sat on them) ; an old-fashioned corner cupboard called the 'buffette', and an arm-chair. The centre of the room was occupied by a large 'growder-scrubbed' table. On the mantelpiece might be seen a copper kettle, a pair of 'cloamen' (china) dogs, a couple of tall brass candlesticks, and a 'jinny quick', or Italian irons for frilling the old ladies' caps. In the midst of these, occupying the place of honour, there generally stood or hung a figure or portrait of John Wesley. In the small grate underneath, fire was only lighted on rare occasions, the chief of these being Christmas and the Feast.

The 'buffette' or corner cupboard was always an interesting piece of furniture. 'In height,' writes Canon Carah, 'it was about six feet, with a wooden door (or doors) below, and a glass door above. Almost invariably this door was a thirteen-paned one, like that of a Chippendale cabinet. Inside was displayed the best china and glass. There were fashions in those days and they altered very little. The china must be put below, the glass above. Tumblers must be put upside down ; rummers (grog glasses) right way up. The best tea-spoons must be shared between two rummers, handles down, bowls upward, and spread out like a fan.' It was rarely safe, as the writer points out, to accept the owner's figures with regard to the age of these treasures, the mode of reckoning being : ' " This jug was my grandmother's, she died when she was ninety. She gave it to mother, and mother lived until she was seventy-seven, and I'm seventy "—90+77+70=age 237. Nothing was ever allowed for overlapping ! ' [1] In some cases this mode of reckoning produced astonishing results. Not long ago an aged miner, whose youth had been spent in the days when reading was regarded as an unnecessary accom-

[1] *Old Cornwall*, VII, 7.

plishment for the poor, was showing the writer a ' Cornish penny ', which had chanced to come into his possession. The coin, one of a numerous class of locally-minted 'tokens', bore the clear inscription, ' Dolcoath mine, 1812 '. ' Yes, sir,' remarked the old man, ' that 's a braa ould coin, sure enough. Why, they do say there 's only one mine in Cornwall older than Dolcoath, and that 's Ding Dong, which was worked before the time of Jesus Christ. So I reckon that theer penny 's close upon two thousand years ould.' Then, with the air of conceding a great favour, he added : ' But I 'll sell it to 'ee for £50, if you 've a mind to ' !

In many cases the ' hales ' of the older houses were so packed with delicate trifles that, on the rare occasions on which this room was entered, visitor and host were kept alike in a prickly heat of anxiety, lest by an unwary movement some treasure might be overset. On the mantel-shelves might be seen china cattle, dogs, cats, rearing circus horses, and sheep (the latter attended by the most unconvincing shepherds and shepherdesses) ; whilst this menagerie was scarcely able to ' sit, lie, or stand ' on account of the quartz crystals, Cornish ' diamonds ', tropical shells, ships fixed into bottles, and all manner of other bric-à-brac by which they were surrounded.

Cupboards in other parts of the room contained still further curios ; fine old punch bowls, plates, basins, and small cups without handles, made of rare Indian china, not to mention curious glasses (the latter often coloured) with high twisted stems and patterns cut on their inner surface. Then more shelves and drawers filled with trifles brought home by sailors from foreign parts. Amongst these might often be seen moccasins and pouches of strange design, the work of Indian squaws ; together with strings of rare seeds and shells formed into necklaces. The surrounding walls were commonly decorated with oleographs of the Bay of Naples, showing Vesuvius in the background looking quite obviously red hot. Illuminated texts from the New Testament also decked the walls in great abundance. These were sold for the most part by *Jews*, who drove a profitable trade in hawking them through the country-side.[1]

Altogether it was not without a sense of relief that the company returned to the kitchen which was the everyday

[1] See W. Bottrell, *Tales and Hearthside Traditions of West Cornwall*, III, 52–5.

living-room of the house, and the door closed upon the more sumptuous but far less comfortable parlour, until the next feasten tide came round. The kitchen also had its showpiece of furniture in the form of the dresser, but in this room there was at least space for the inhabitants to move about, and the danger of accidents was less imminent. The old-time dresser, no less than the buffette, was carefully arranged according to fashion. The bowls here and larger basins stood on a side shelf, with a strip of linen under them. Glasses occupied the top row, and beneath them, on the middle shelf, the ' daffer ' (tea-set)—smuggled often as not, like the tea which went in it. At the back of each shelf stood the largest dishes and plates, placed on edge in order to show their patterns. In older times sets of brightly-burnished pewter, locally made from Cornish tin, constituted the chief glory of the dresser. These, however, had practically disappeared from all ordinary houses a hundred years ago, although services of block tin continued to be used for the dinners at some of the mines within living memory.

In most of the farms a long table occupied much of the available space in the kitchen. At meal-times the adults sat down to this on ' firms ' (benches), whilst the children were placed in the low window seat opposite. On the other side of the kitchen, by the foot of the stairs leading to the rooms above, there commonly stood a large settle capable of seating three or four persons. In some settles the high back, which served to keep off the draught, could be lowered at will so as to rest on the arms and form a convenient table. Underneath the seat strips of wood were occasionally nailed between the legs, forming a kind of pen which might accommodate a sitting duck or goose. Not infrequently the latter showed its resentment at this indignity by administering a shrewd nip to the legs of the visitor who unwarily seated himself above. The remaining furniture of the kitchen generally included a grandfather or a ' head and hinge ' (i.e. Dutch) clock, a warming-pan, a hutch to hold half a sack of flour, various pitchers and paddicks for drinking water and, near the fire-place, a ' bellis ' (bellows), salt box, and candle box.

Hanging from the rafters overhead there were usually several bunches of herbs, neatly tied in bags to preserve them from the dust. For the old people were firm believers in the dage that ' there is a doctor in every hedge '. ' There re some plants,' wrote Polwhele in 1826, ' which are disallowed or neglected by botanists, but whose qualities brought into action by some " church-town " crony will sometimes cure a disease which has been given up by her betters as irremediable. For instance, to the wound occasioned by the bite of an adder, a decoction of plantain and sallad-oil has been successfully applied by our cottage doctors. A woman of Edles, a few years ago, bitten in the thigh, was soon cured by this process.' [1] For colds in the head mugwort was regarded as a sovereign remedy, a draught being made by pouring boiling water over a handful of the herb and swallowing the same very hot and sweetened with treacle. Elderflower or ' scaw blowth ', to give it the old people's name (scaw= Cornish ' elder ') was similarly used for fevers, and horehound for coughs. Camomile tea was the usual corrective for a sick stomach, whilst a mixture of elder and camomile was employed as a purgative. For whooping-cough an onion was cut into thin slices and placed, with alternate layers of brown sugar, in a basin. This mixture was allowed to stand overnight, two teaspoonfuls of the resulting syrup being taken three or four times a day, or whenever the cough was raging. An extract of burdock burs was commonly used for scurvy, being carried on board ship by sailors on all long voyages.[2] Mallow prepared in the form of an ointment was applied to inflammations. ' Coltsfoot ' (winter heliotrope) was smoked by the Cornish miners as a precaution against lung diseases. Earache was commonly treated by applying a piece of cooked onion to the affected part, whilst a pounded-up mixture of ' bullorns ' (snails) and groundsel was used as a poultice for gatherings or poisoned wounds.

Poultices, indeed, were formerly regarded as possessing an almost supernatural efficacy. Many years ago an old Cornish doctor recounted to a friend of the writer how on one occasion he had prescribed hot fomentations for a man suffering with pneumonia. On calling at the house next day he found the patient's wife standing at the door.

' Well, how is your husband this morning, Mrs Trevarrack ? ' he inquired before going upstairs.

' Aw, my dear life, doctor,' replied the woman, ' he was some bad laast night—swilled up like a hosgit (hogshead). But with the help of the Loord and the pultice we 've pulled 'un through, I bla.'

---

[1] *Traditions and Recollections*, 607.
[2] J. C. Hoare, MS.

Nor were the old people without their ' patent ' medicines.[1]
Amongst these was a certain mixture known in the Camborne
district as ' Dutch oil ', a few drops of which taken on sugar
was regarded as a panacea for almost every kind of ill.   This
medicine was retailed by an old man who jealously guarded
the secret of its preparation.   At length one of his neighbours,
who was an early riser, chanced to see him one morning in
the garden diligently gathering worms. Seeing that in Cornwall
the earthworm is commonly known as an ' angle-dutch ' the
making of this famous oil ceased from then to be regarded
as a secret process !

Whilst patent medicines of this type have now fallen into
disrepute, great reliance is still placed in herbal remedies.
Almost every Cornish town can boast at least one herbalist's
shop, where juniper berries, cherry bark, and other similarly
attractive nostrums still find a ready sale.   Nor has the
knowledge of remedial herbs by any means died out amongst
the people themselves.   Shortly after the war a friend of the
writer was staying in a very remote village in West Cornwall.
Remarking on the fact that the nearest doctor lived five miles
away, he inquired of a fisherman how they had fared during
the then recent epidemic of influenza. ' Well, sir,' replied the
man, ' we don't hold much with doctors out here.   There 's
an ould woman living next door that do gather all the harbs
we want up 'pon the downses.   One day last winter I had the
'flu, so I took a drop of her mixsher.   I tell 'ee I hadn't sat
by the fire more than half an hour before you could see the
sweat rising through the planshun ovver steers (floor-boards
upstairs).   There edn't no doctor's traade (medicine) would
do that for 'ee ! ' [2]

[1] The following is a list of sundries advertised by M. Allison, Book-
seller on the Market Strand in Falmouth in 1762 :

Bibles, Stationery, Musical Instruments, Glassware, Mathematical
Instruments, and *inter alia* Medicines.

Dr Hills Balsam of Honey	Bateman's Pectoral Drops
Tincture of Valerian	Anderson's Scots Pills
Essence of Water Dock	Bostock and Godfrey's Cordial
Essence of Bardana	Pittans Nervous Drops
Dr Walker's Jesuits Drops	Hungary Water
Greenoughs Tincture for the teeth	Eau de Luce
Turlington's Balsam of Life	Court Plaster
Dr James's Fever Powder	Perfumed Wash-ball
Daffy's and Stoughtons Elixir	Roll & Pot Pomatum

also fine Garden Seeds, Parchments for Lawyers, Printing and Book-
binding.
[2] Per Mr Morton Nance.

VI

Beyond the kitchen, from which we have wandered, lay another room with a lean-to roof which commonly extended across the full length of the dwelling. Here all the sloppy work was done, leaving the kitchen dry and comfortable, and fit at all times for the reception of visitors. At one end of this scullery or back-kitchen a portion was often screened off to form a dairy, whilst at the other end lay the ' spence ', or larder. Between the two an outer door opened on to a court, wherein lay the ' peeth ' (well), fuel ricks, etc.

In the hill country, where stone was cheap and plentiful, the floors of the downstairs rooms were generally laid with great slabs of moorstone (surface granite). Over this the housewife scattered dry sand, which ' took up ' the dirt from the men's boots, and could be easily swept away and renewed. Sanding was often done in patterns, which gave the floor a pleasing appearance. The sand necessary for this purpose was sold in the inland villages by blinded miners or old women who thus contrived to eke out a slender livelihood. Well known amongst these hawkers was a certain Mary Deem, who fifty years ago might often be seen in the Camborne district driving a shaggy white donkey laden with the sacks of fine 'Connor Bar' sand, which she fetched from the towans near Gwithian. Mary Deem was reputed to have come of a good family, but had gone astray in her youth. Her relations, it is said, would have received her back had she been willing to express repentance. This, however, she refused to do, preferring to marry and live in independence as the wife of ' Old Tom ', the bone buyer.

Another character in the same district was Margaret Retallack, who supported life by the sale of ' griglan besoms ', i.e. brooms made from the ' griglan ' or heather which she gathered in the crofts near her home. In addition to selling these to private houses she did a good trade with the mines where such brooms were formerly used in large quantities on the ' floors ' and tin streams. Among her best customers was the famous Dolcoath mine. Here, however, she would sometimes be met by ' Cap'n Josiah ' with the remark :

' Marget, didn't I tell you not to bring any more brooms till after the next count ? '

' Well, perhaps so, Cap'n 'Siah,' would be her ready reply, ' but theer, I had them by me and I said to myself : " What's a bur'n (bundle) of brooms to a great bal (mine) like this ? " '

This piece of persuasion rarely failed in its effect, for ' Marget ' was a widow woman, with a dozen children to support, and the manager well knew her poverty.

Other hawkers of a similar type provided the housewives with ' gaird ' or ' growder '. This substance, formed from the soft, decomposed granite, was largely used for scouring pots and pans, and also for cleaning the floors of the bedrooms. The latter even in the larger and more substantial farms were bare and uncarpeted. The rooms themselves contained little furniture beyond the bedsteads, with a possible addition of an oaken ' press ', in which was stored the household linen, an extra supply of homespun blankets, and the family's ' Sunday best '. Many people at that date had never so much as seen a mirror. Mr Jim Thomas tells the story of a certain old couple living at Breage, who on one occasion had been into Penzance to sell their pig. Owing to the time spent in haggling over the bargain they missed the ' van ' home, and were forced in consequence to stay the night at one of the more up-to-date inns in the town. As they were undressing for bed the old man suddenly called to his wife : ' Stop, Betty, dost'na take off another rag, there's a man looking in upon us through that little window ovver theer '.

' Why, ais, so there is,' cried the old lady, coming to look over his shoulder, ' and what's more, there's an ugly ould witch of a woman 'longside of 'un. They oft to be ashamed of themselves, people of theer age, to come geeking (peeping) in upon decent folk.'

' Now mind,' shouted the old man, working himself into a passion, ' I wean't tell 'ee to go no more ; another minute I 'll give 'ee a scat (blow) upon the 'ead with my stick to larn 'ee proper manners.'

This threat producing no effect, he struck out at the mirror with all his force, splintering the glass to atoms. ' Why, my dear life,' they exclaimed in chorus, ' that wadn't no window after all. It must ha' ben the devil hisself we seed.'

It is said that the price which the poor old couple had to pay

(*See page 353*)   THE OPEN HEARTH OF AN OLD CORNISH KITCHEN

(See page 405)

A HARVEST SCENE
(after Rowlandson)

for their experience was nearly as much as they had received from the sale of their pig.

In the kitchens of all the older houses, great or small, the fire-place invariably consisted of an open hearth, resembling in its appearance a cave let in to one of the walls. The opening was generally five or six feet wide, four or five deep, and somewhat more in height. The foundation of the hearth was raised about a foot higher than the floor of the room, and was constructed, like the side posts and 'cravel' (lintel), of great slabs of stone. The fire burnt in the centre of the hearth, simply on the flat foundation. There were no bars to keep it in like an ordinary grate. Within the hearth stood the three-legged ' chimney stool ', seated on which one could look right up through the open chimney to the sky above. From the lintel hung a white valance known as the ' chimney cloth '. Everything around the fire was kept spotlessly clean, for the old people venerated the hearthstone as if it were an altar.

On the right-hand side of this friendly cavern lay the ' ookener ' (wood corner), in which was kept the day-to-day supply of furze and turf. The furze was cut in the early summer from some selected ' splat ' in the neighbouring crofts, where the growths often attained a height of eight or ten feet. The men engaged in the cutting wore thick leather gloves and on their right leg a long legging which reached nearly to the thigh. A ' tash ' or armful of the furze was seized with one hand, and the stems severed with a hook, just above the ground. Each tash, as it was cut, was laid aside and afterwards made up into faggots, the latter consisting of four tashes bound round with thin green branches. A thousand faggots constituted the usual winter supply for a substantial farm, and of these a skilful labourer would cut and prepare as many as fifty in a day. When thoroughly dried by the sun, the furze was removed to a spot near the house, where it was built into a rick. From this the faggots, seven or eight at a time, would be withdrawn by the aid of a furze-hook, and taken indoors to the ' ookener '. A good deal of skill was needed to fill the latter properly. In a tidy wood-corner the furze was so placed that the sticks were kept out of sight, the blossom ends only facing the room.[1]

In addition to furze, which burnt far too quickly to serve as a fuel by itself, huge quantities of bog turf were annually brought in from the surrounding moors. In the ' high

[1] Miss Carkeek, *Old Cornwall*, IX, 20–3.

country' districts, most of the farms possessed 'turbary' rights which endowed their tenants with the privilege of cutting turf over so many acres of moorland. The average farm required about a thousand 'squares' annually, and a good man would often cut as many as six or seven hundred of these in a day, using for the purpose a heavy iron digger known as a 'piggal'. As soon as they were cut, the turfs were placed in little piles on their sides, thus allowing the wind to blow through them, whilst exposing the widest possible area to the sun. When sufficiently dry the turf also was carried into the 'town-place' (farmyard), and built up into another rick alongside the furze.

In earlier times dried cow-dung or 'glaws' (Cornish *gloas*) was often used by the poor as a fuel. This was collected from the pasture fields during the summer evenings by women and children. The same substance still serves for fuel in many parts of Brittany, where it may often be seen drying on the walls beside the road.

Notwithstanding the fact that from the early part of the eighteenth century onwards coal was being freely imported for the use of the mines, furze and turf long continued to serve the needs of the people for all domestic purposes. In 1799 the overseers of Mylor parish were paying but 9d. a hundred for furze faggots for the use of the poorhouse,[1] a price with which coal, however cheap, must have found it hard to compete. Indeed, until almost the end of the last century many Cornish houses knew no other fuel than that which came to them from within a short distance of their doors. In one or two instances these turf fires are said to have been actually kept alight for a hundred years, faithfully serving the needs of the inhabitants from birth to death. Each night, the embers were banked up before going to bed, and the kettle hooked on to the cross-bar in the chimney. On coming down the next morning the water was always boiling, whilst sufficient fire still remained to fry the bacon and mashed potatoes for breakfast.[2] After the meal the hearth was swept clean, fresh turf was put on, and so the old fire entered on another day of service and companionship to the household.

With the aid of such fires as these the Cornish housewife contrived to do all the cooking for the largest family, asking nothing more than a 'kettle' for baking and a 'crock' for

---

[1] H. P. Olivey, *History of the Parish of Mylor*.
[2] See *The Western Antiquary*, III, 94.

boiling. The kettle, it should be explained, in no way resembled the ordinary utensil of that name (which was distinguished in Cornwall by being termed a ' tay (tea) kettle '), but was simply an iron bowl with three legs capable of being stood on the ground like a small crock. Whenever baking had to be done, the ' brandis ' or heavy iron trivet was first drawn forward into the centre of the hearth and on it was placed a round sheet of iron, known as the ' baking ire '. With the aid of the ' fire-hook ', which took the place on the open hearth of a poker in ordinary grates, the smouldering embers were raked around the brandis and under the baking iron, and were fanned into flame with the ' bellis ' (bellows). As soon as the baking iron had been heated in this way to the proper temperature it was taken off the brandis, carefully wiped and greased, and replaced on the hearth. On to it the bread or other food was then laid and covered by the inverted kettle. Hot embers were raked around, and a fire of furze and ' bruss ' (dried hedge gatherings, etc.) built up over the whole. Beneath this the bread, protected from all dirt and ash, was left to cook for about an hour and a half, at the end of which time the embers were removed, the kettle lifted off, and there was the loaf baked to perfection ! All sorts of dishes —heavy-cakes, pasties, and pies—were prepared in the same way, the only variation being that in some instances a ' baker ' was used instead of a kettle. The former resembled in shape a heavy iron frying-pan without a handle, and differed from a kettle chiefly in having no legs. For boiling and stewing the crock was used, either placed on the brandis or hung from a cross-bar in the chimney. Occasionally, when very large joints of meat had to be roasted, the crock itself would be inverted over the baking iron in place of a kettle.

The methods employed in cooking on the open hearth required both skill and experience ; there was a ' knick ' in them, as the old people used to say. In addition to the art of regulating the fire, there was also the difficulty of ascertaining how the food progressed beneath the pile of embers. To aid them in this some people employed a short tube of iron, one end of which was applied to the baker, and the other to the ear, on the principle of a doctor's stethoscope ! Notwithstanding these drawbacks, all those who have tasted food cooked in this manner agree that no modern oven (which allows the best of the juices to evaporate in the form of steam) can ever compare with ' baking under '.

'Iss, slabs es handy, I deer saay—
There 's piles o' new things maaken—
But give me mother's baaker, soas !
That theer 's the thing for baaken !

Seems now I see her clutten down,
The fire-'ook in her haand
A-foochen 'bout the burnen sticks,
And doin' paasties graand !

And then she'd saay, ' They're ready, 'bleeve ! '
Just as the fit wud taake her,
And slip a knife right in between
The bake-ire and the baaker.

' Aw, they're done beautiful,' she'd saay,
'F'rall wan's burnt a bit—
Well, niver mind—'tes luck I s'pose,
We taake what we can git ! ' [1]

In the central and eastern part of the county the method of cooking somewhat differed, the open hearths of these districts being generally provided with a ' cloam ' or earthenware oven, built into their sides. These ovens are square in shape, with a slightly domed top. They are now made by the Devon potteries and are still supplied in considerable numbers for districts where suitable fuel is obtainable. Before cooking, a fire of furze, chaff, or bruss is kindled within the oven, and allowed to burn until the latter has been heated to the proper temperature. The embers are then swept out with a little broom or rag mop called a ' malkin ', after which the food is placed inside, the earthenware door of the oven ' put home ', and the contents left to cook in the gradually diminishing heat. Until recently the majority of towns in the eastern part of the county had ' common ovens ' of this sort, which were worked for the accommodation of the poorer class of inhabitant. To these the cottagers would take their food to be cooked, the charge for baking a dish of meat and potatoes varying from ½d. to 1d. according to their size. Thousands of faggots of wood were yearly brought into the towns for this purpose, the fuel being built up into ricks adjoining the premises. [2]

[1] Mr Morgan Anthony.
[2] *Cornish Guardian*, 5 April 1928.

The open hearth, however, served many other purposes beyond that of cooking. It was, in fact, the social meeting-place of the household, the very core and centre of the home. In the evenings when the men had come in from their work, the water had been boiled and the tea been made, the house-wife would lay on the red-hot embers two or three 'tashes' of furze, and on to this an apron-full of bruss. Next came several handfuls of 'stubbins' or 'stogs' (tough, slow-burning roots of furze, etc.), and over the whole a complete covering of turfs. A fire thus built would last without further attention for hours, burning with a slow dull heat which kept the family warm and comfortable without being 'scroached'. Seated around such a fire on a winter's night with the chimney-stool in its proper corner, close to the warmth but clear of the smoke, and the high-backed settle brought round in front of the hearth, what snugger or happier place could be found in all Christendom than an old-fashioned Cornish kitchen?

It is true that there was work for all even here, since the old people could rarely afford to be idle. But whilst hands were busy, spinning or carding wool, picking 'smuts' from a pile of grain, stripping goose feathers, making brimstone matches or other similar tasks, tongues kept pace with them, and gossip and songs and fine old folk-tales whiled away the hours till at length nodding heads and sleepy eyes proclaimed that the time had come for 'Men to bed, dogs to door, and maidens to rake out the ashes'.

VII

Where something more was required in the way of illumi-nation than that which came from the glowing embers of the fire, it was supplied in earlier times by the 'stonen chill'. This was a kind of earthenware lamp, shaped like a heavy candlestick, but having at the top, instead of a small socket-hole, a 'well' large enough to contain one or two cupfuls of oil. The edge of the well was provided with a lip in which rested the wick or *purvan*, a Celtic Cornish word signifying 'rush'. At a later date the wick, whilst retaining its ancient name, was generally composed of cotton. When neither this nor the pith of rushes could be obtained, strips of linen were often plaited together, the wick thus formed being known in the Lizard district as a *booba*.[1] ' Do 'ee take the griglan, my dear, and fooch forth the purvan of the chill,' was a remark which might often be heard in the old cottages when the light from one of these lamps was growing low. One wonders how many *Cornish* people, even, would understand to-day the meaning of this request or realize that what was asked was that someone should take the heather-stalk (griglan) and push up (fooch) the wick (purvan) of the lamp (chill) !

Another lamp of a slightly different type was the iron ' chill '. This consisted of a little square metal dish, ' cribbed ' or crinkled up at the corners to hold the wicks which protruded over the edge. Chills of this sort could be either stood on the table or hung from a nail in the wall. Both forms of chill consumed ' train ', the name given to the oil expressed from pilchards. Down to the beginning of the last century train was as commonly sold in Cornish towns as paraffin is to-day. It was brought to market by the fishwives in big jars, and retailed to the country people who included it amongst their regular weekly purchases.

The tiny glimmer of light given by a chill was considered quite sufficient for ordinary occasions. For closer work, where something more than an ' idle light ' was required, the chill was replaced by ' candles ' made from the pith of rushes dipped in tallow. These rushlights were generally held by a clip attached to an upright iron stand. Being pliable they could be bent round and each end lighted. This, however, was considered a somewhat extravagant thing to do, and from it arose the proverbial warning against ' burning the candle at both ends '. Gradually the place of the rush candle and the chill was taken by the ' hempen-wick ' candle, as used by the miners of eighty years ago. This in reality was not much of an improvement, as the ' smeech ' (acrid smell) made by them equalled, if not exceeded, the ' odour ' emitted from the burning of fish oil. Such candles, moreover, required constant snuffing, and though snuffers were beginning to find their way even into the cottages at this date, it was not always that their purpose was clearly understood. Many people, therefore, continued to snuff the wicks with their fingers in the old way, afterwards opening the snuffers and carefully popping the bits inside !

In course of time the hempen candles likewise went their

[1] *Journal of the Royal Institution of Cornwall*, XVII (1875).

way, and were succeeded by ' tallow dips '. These derived their name from the process of manufacture, which consisted of plunging the wicks, when stretched on a frame, into a bath of hot tallow, a certain amount of which adhered. The wicks were then withdrawn and allowed to cool, after which they were again plunged into the fat. This process was repeated until the dip had attained the requisite size. They were usually sold in bunches, tied together by their long protruding wicks, and in this way could be conveniently hung on a button of the miner's coat or from a nail in the cottage.

The tallow candle or ' gressack ', as it is still called in St Just, had other uses, being regarded by the old people as a sovereign remedy for colds when rubbed on to the nose or chest.

These candles, smoky as they were, continued until the coming of the paraffin lamp to provide the only form of light in the cottages, the vastly improved but much more expensive composite candle being reserved for very special occasions, such as Christmas or the Feast.

Prior to the introduction of the modern match the people of Cornwall, as elsewhere, had of course to rely on the tinder and flint. The tinder consisted of a piece of cotton rag which had been soaked in a solution of saltpetre and then dried. Sparks were produced by striking a piece of flint against the steel, from which they fell on the tinder, causing it to ignite. This in itself was a tedious process, and when, either through sickness or for other reasons, a light was required suddenly in the middle of the night, altercations were very apt to arise between husband and wife, each accusing the other of failing to keep the tinder dry. The ' matches ' of those days were likewise home-made. They consisted of thin strips of wood about five inches long, and a quarter of an inch wide. Each end was dipped in a crucible of melted brimstone kept for the purpose. When the tinder had been ignited one end of the match was applied to it and the brimstone burst into flame.

Notwithstanding the laboriousness of this process the modern ' strike-a-light ' matches were at first regarded with considerable distrust. Mr Jim Thomas tells the delightful story of a certain old lady who on one occasion was presented with a sample of these for trial. Being of a cautious turn of mind she thought it would perhaps be as well if she were to test them before going to bed. Accordingly, taking up one in her trembling old hands, she struck it gingerly against the box.

Instantly a little blue flame appeared. ' Ais, that wan's alright,' she muttered to herself, blowing it out and carefully replacing it before picking up another. The remainder proving equally satisfactory she retired to bed with an easy mind. Next morning one of her neighbours inquired how she liked the new strike-a-lights. ' Why, my dear,' was the reply, ' they aren't no good 't oall. Come the middle of the night when I wanted to see for a bit of lozenger for me cough not wan of they blessed matches would strike, for all they was right enough last night. No, my dear, give me the ould tender and flent, that 'll see me to the end of my days, I reckon.'

The ' stream of Time ', which has long since swept away the chill, the rushlight, and the tinder and flint, has wrought many other changes in the character and appearance of the Cornish kitchen. Not the least of these has been the abandonment of the open hearth, and the old methods of cooking which went with it. It is true that here and there in the Land's End district, and still more frequently in the moorlands of central and north Cornwall, the turf rick may still be seen outside the farms, whilst the sweet wholesome smell which is wafted from their chimneys proclaims the surviving use of the older type of fuel. No doubt amongst their inhabitants there are still some who could say with truth :

> Of all the fires that I do knaw,
>   The furze and turf is best ;
> Give me an open chimbley, soas,
>   And you can have the rest.
> Some people like the gas, I s'pose,
>   And some the 'lectric heat:
> But me, I love the sunshine best
>   That's stored in stogs and peat.[1]

For the most part, however, the open hearth has now become a rarity, and with it has gone the turbary rights which formerly pertained to many of the farms. The reason for this, of course, is that during the last fifty years the introduction of the now wellnigh universal ' slab ' or Cornish cooking range has rendered coal the ordinary fuel of Cornwall as elsewhere. To begin with, this coal, like so many other commodities, was hawked through the towns and villages in donkey carts, and retailed to the people at their doors. Most of these

[1] Miss Carkeek, *Old Cornwall*, IX, 23.

old-fashioned coal merchants had their own peculiar cries. Betty R——, a well-known character in the Camborne district, used regularly to proclaim : ' Caul ! caul ! one hundred more and I sell all '—a statement apparently made in the hope of stampeding her customers into an instant purchase ! Much of this coal came from Porthcawl, near Swansea. This, combined with the fact that coal was locally pronounced ' caul ', produced an embarrassing situation for the hawkers. At St Ives, one old man, out of fear of being ridiculed if he shouted ' Porthcawl caul ', regularly adopted as his cry the longer but more euphonious : ' Poortcawl 'ouse caul ! Poortcawl 'ouse caul ! ' [1]

VIII

Towards the end of the last century, and even more throughout the Edwardian period of the present one, it was customary amongst many Cornish people who wished to be thought genteel, to smile somewhat derisively at the mention of the ' old people ' and their simple, homely ways. Through living in an age in which life had been made easy by the inventiveness of others, such persons frequently possessed an unreasoning belief in their own superiority, and were apt to regard with a mixture of amusement and pity that laborious struggle against material circumstances which they had never been called upon to share. Perhaps, on the whole, it was the war, with its lesson that life may still demand of all the labour of hand as well as brain, which caused the change of attitude which is now evident towards the past. Experience gained from life in the trenches, or perhaps of post-war housework, has enabled many to understand for the first time the capacity for labour, and the patient ingenuity which the poor of a hundred years ago possessed. As one thinks of those cramped and tiny cottages, with four or five men and boys, perhaps—some out at work by night and coming in to sleep by day ; with different sets of meals to be prepared at all hours ; with the baking, sewing, and washing to be done ; water to be fetched ; turf to be cut ; potatoes to be ' teeled ' ; fish to be salted ; and the hundred and one other things requiring attention—one

[1] Per Mr R. Morton Nance.

can hardly escape a sense of astonishment at the organizing ability of their inhabitants.

Their life, indeed, was hard and laborious, but it provided that variety of occupation for hand and brain which is so singularly lacking in our own age. Though none would wish to return, perhaps, to those long dark evenings of the past, lit only by the feeble rushlight or the miner's tallow dip, yet more and more is the realization growing that the old people found something therein which gave them both character and a philosophy of life—gifts which, perhaps, were more than compensatory for the absence of the gramophone, the cinema, the cheap newspaper, and even the wireless.

FOOD—ORDINARY AND EXTRAORDINARY

Gurty milk an' bearly-bread no lack,
Pudden-skins an' a good shaip's chack,
A bussa o' salt pelchers, 'nother o' pork,
A good strong stummick and a plenty o' work.

Old Rhyme.

I

THE devil, it used to be said, never came into Cornwall for fear of being made into a pie. Though this statement may seem hard to reconcile with the existence of ' Devil's Quoits ', ' Devil's Cauldrons ', ' Devil's Frying Pans ', and other tokens of his presence which abound in the Duchy, it does at least serve to indicate the strange ingredients which often composed a Cornish pie. It is certainly no exaggeration to say that in times past pies were pre-eminently the medium through which the culinary art of the Cornish housewife was revealed, and though latterly their place has been somewhat usurped by the ' pasty ' for which Cornishmen are now famous, pies still figure largely in the diet of the natives. So highly were these dishes once esteemed that a small cottage, in the parish of St Merryn, is said to have been held for many years by one family in return for the sole quit-rent of a pie composed of limpets, figs, and various sweet herbs.[1]   The flavour of this strange hotchpot is said to have been excellent.

Cornish housewives, as may thus be seen, had original ideas, and everything was grist that came to their mill. Nothing was too big or too small, too tough or too greasy—nothing was considered too ' common or unclean ' to compose a Cornish pie. Proof of this may be seen in the mackerel pies, pilchard pies, conger pies, bream pies, ram pies, muggety pies, taddago pies, nattlin pies, curlew pies, squab pies, lammy pies, giblet pies, leek pies, ' tatty' pies, 'herby' pies, and many more which formerly graced the tables of old Cornwall.

Of all the various fish pies, that made from pilchards was certainly the most odd. This pie formerly went by the nick-name of ' starry-gazy ', from the fact that the fish were cooked therein whole, with their heads projecting through the crust, and their eyes goggling towards the ceiling ! Accidents some-times happened in the small cottages where one room had to serve all the purposes of kitchen, parlour, and children's nursery combined. A stranger on one occasion eating starry-gazy pie is said to have exclaimed with some astonishment at the hardness of the fish's backbone.

' Let me see, my dear ! ' cried the woman, coming forward to the table, ' why, that edn' no fish bone at all. That's our little Johnny's hair comb, what he lost two days ago—careless little emp ! '

Starry-gazy pie is a dish which is now but rarely seen, nor do muggety pies and nattlin enjoy the same degree of popu-larity as formerly. These pies were made respectively from the entrails of sheep (or calves), and of pigs, and were flavoured with parsley, pepper, and salt, and often enriched by the addition of cream.

Somewhat resembling these were taddago pies and lammy pies, the former made from prematurely-born ' veers ' (sucking pigs), and the latter from stillborn or overlaid lambs. Lammy pasties were at one time the favourite ' feasten ' dish of a certain parish in the neighbourhood of Penzance.   In this parish, as elsewhere, it was the custom on the Feast Sunday morning for all those who were not actually engaged in preparing the dinner to resort to church in order to listen to the music and to meet their friends. On one of these occasions a strange clergyman happened to be in the pulpit.

[1] H. P. Olivey, *History of the Parish of Mylor*, 40.

Highly gratified by the presence of such a large congregation and anxious to do the occasion full justice, he entered upon the delivery of one of his lengthiest sermons. Time went on, and still no end to the discourse seemed in sight. At last an old man arose and addressing the preacher, said : ' Sir, 'tes a braa fine sarmon, and I 'm sure we 're much obliged to 'ee for 'un, but the lammy paasties 'es gettin' cold, and we caan't stay no longer ! ' Saying which he picked up his hat and solemnly walked out of the church, being quickly followed by the rest of the congregation.[1]

Another dish much favoured by old-fashioned Cornish people was squab pie. The contents of this are described by Charles Kingsley in *Hereward the Wake* as consisting of layers of apple, bacon, onions, and mutton, and having at the bottom ' a squab or young cormorant which diffused through the pie and through the ambient air a delicate odour of mingled guano and polecat '. In point of fact this description is somewhat libellous, for although on occasions a cormorant may have been used, the word ' squab ' really connotes a young pigeon. Nowadays, the bird which gave the dish its name is generally omitted, but even so the mixture of apple, bacon, onions, and mutton, enriched as it often is by the addition of cream, is sufficiently piquant to excite the most jaded appetite.

No less highly regarded than this was giblet pie, which was composed of the neck, liver, and other entrails of a goose, flavoured with raisins, sugar, and apples. This dish was once commonly served at mine dinners. On one of these occasions two boys entered the kitchen where the goose was being prepared and, whilst the woman's back was turned, contrived to substitute some chopped-up bits of india-rubber for the gizzard. At the dinner which followed two elderly mine captains appeared to find great difficulty in mastication.

' 'Av 'ee lost heart for your meat ? ' at length exclaimed one.

' No, my dear,' was the reply, ' it edn't that at all, but all the same if I hadn't knawed this here were gizzard I should have thought it were a bit of injy.'

' Herby ' pie, as its name suggests, was mainly of a vegetarian character, being composed of nettles, pepper-grass, parsley, mustard, and spinach. Frequently, however, thin slices of pork were added to lend it additional flavour.

[1] *Cornishman*, 15 November 1883.

Leek or, as it is generally called, ' likky ' pie is a dish which still remains a prime favourite in the Duchy. Formerly, in order to give this pie sufficient ' body ' for hungry men, it was the practice to line as well as cover the dish in which it was made with pastry. When nearly cooked a small hole is broken in the top crust, and through this is poured an egg which quickly cooks in the steaming contents. Served thus, ' likky ' pie is food fit for a king and, as some say, is preferred by *Cornish* saints to the ambrosia of heaven !

To strangers, the Cornish custom of enriching savoury dishes by the addition of cream or sugar is apt to appear bizarre, and has been commented upon by many writers.

> *Dear to Cornish palates, ' one and all ',*
> *Appeared in crusted pomp to grace the hall,*
> *The pie, where herbs with veal in union meet,*
> *The tasteful parsley, the nutricious beet,*
> *The bitter mercury wild, nor valued less,*
> *The watery lettuce and the pungent cress ;*
> *When ravishing with odours every nose,*
> *The leek o'er layers of the pilchard rose,*
> *Or, in a gentler harmony, with pork,*
> *Ere yet of mouths it claim'd the playful work,*
> *Attack'd the nostril with a tempting steam,*
> *As opening, it ingulphed the golden cream.*[1]

So wrote of Cornish cookery the author of *The Old English Gentleman*, with mingled admiration and surprise. In point of fact the custom of adding *sugar*, at any rate to savoury dishes, was formerly dear not only to Cornish palates, but to those of English people generally, for, as King has written in the *Art of Cookery :*

> *Our fathers most admired their sauces sweet*
> *And often asked for sugar with their meat,*
> *They buttered currants on fat veal bestow'd.*
> *And rumps of beef with virgin honey strow'd.*
> *Hence mack'rel seem delightful to the eyes,*
> *Tho' dres't with incoherent gooseberries.*[2]

---

[1] Quoted by H. P. Olivey, *History of the Parish of Mylor*, 39.
[2] Quoted by H. P. Olivey, *History of the Parish of Mylor*, 39–40.

II

The food of the Duchy to-day has many claims to popularity, but it is not always that the county has enjoyed such an enviable reputation in this respect. When in 1542 that strange old gossip, Andrew Borde, set himself the ambitious task of writing a universal Baedeker for travellers, he found little good to say of Cornish food. 'Their meat,' he writes, ' and their bread and drink is marred and spoilt for lack of good ordering and dressing,' and he goes on (somewhat unfairly) to make a *native* say :

> *I am a Cornishman, ale I can brew,*
> *It will make one to kake, also to spew,*
> *It is thick and smoky and also it is thin,*
> *It is like wash as pigs had wrestled therein.*[1]

So ill was the reputation of the food of Cornwall, and in particular of its beer, that it seems to have seriously curtailed Borde's own travels beyond the Tamar.

Sir Thomas Elyot, on the other hand, writing about the same date, found cause for congratulation in the ascetic nature of the Cornishman's diet. ' Water,' he writes, ' hath pre-eminence above all other lycoures, and was the very naturall and fyrst drynke to all manner of creatures. Moreover, we have sene men and women of great age and stronge body whyche never, or verye seldome, dranke other drynke than pure water. As by example in Cornwall, although that the countrey be in a very colde quarter—which proveth that if men from their infancye were accustomed to none other drinke, it should be sufficient to kepe naturall moysture and to cause the meat that is eaten to perce and descende unto the places of digestion, which are the purposes that drynke serveth for.'[2] Such an opinion, whilst doubtless based on sound judgment and reason, can have had little appeal for the traveller arriving tired and hungry at a Cornish inn ; and

[1] *Introduction of Knowledge* (spelling modernized).
[2] *Castel of Healthe* (1539).

Borde was no doubt justified in warning his readers of what they must expect in the land beyond the Tamar.

By the time that Richard Carew, the first and foremost of Cornish historians, published his ' Survey ' of the county in 1602, the manner of living of the Cornish people seems to have already shown considerable improvement.   Yet even so, as he admits, ' within the remembrance of some still living, the husbandmen rubbed forth their estates in the poorest plight—their drink, water, or at best but whey : for the richest farmer in a parish brewed not above twice a year, and then God wott what liquor—their meat "whitsul", as they call it, namely milk, sour milk, cheese, curds, and such like as come from the cow and ewe who were tyed by the one legge at pasture: their apparel coarse in matter, ill-shapen in manner : and their legges and feet naked and bare, to which sundrie old folk had so accustomed their youth, that they could hardly abide to wear any shoes, complayning how it kept them over hot '.   Critics of modern fashions and dietetics, who counsel a return to-day to a condition of a life resembling this, should find encouragement in the examples of great physical strength and longevity which it produced.   Carew himself describes how a certain John Bray, a tenant on his estate, had on occasion ' carried upon his back, at one time, by the space of welneere of a butte length, six bushels of wheaten meal, and the miller, a lubber of four-and-twenty years of age, upon the whole ' ; whilst another prodigy, John Romane, ' a short clownish grub ', could carry without difficulty the whole carcass of an ox.   Nor in mere strength alone did such diet prove its worth, seeing that, according to Carew, an age of eighty or ninety years was commonly attained, accompanied in most cases ' with an able use of the body and his senses '.   This testimony is all the more remarkable at a time when men lived hard, worked hard, and, as we are generally led to believe, died younger than to-day.

It is certainly a fact that animal food has always been eaten very sparingly in Cornwall where, until comparatively recent times, fish, rather than butcher's meat, may be said to have formed the staple diet of the poor.   In 1591 Thomas Celey, of St Ives, protesting against the ' pressing ' of fishermen for sailors, wrote :   ' If the men do not continue their fishing the country round will miss their best relief.   The country is poor, and there is little flesh and less butter or cheese '.[1]

[1] *Calendar of State Papers Domestic* (1591–4), 73.

This statement, which throws an interesting light on the prevailing scarcity of food, is confirmed by the account of two travellers who, on reaching Mousehole one night in the year 1590 were unable to purchase meat or drink in the whole village, and were accordingly forced to return to Penzance to satisfy their needs.[1] Such a state of affairs was largely produced by artificial causes. Owing to the multitude of petty regulations enforced by a fatherly government, fish caught in one area might not be exported to another without special licence, or until after so long an interval that it had frequently become bad.[2] Similarly, corn was subject to great scarcity and sudden rises in price owing to bad roads, lack of transport, and the consequent narrowness of the areas from which the supply could be drawn.

To offset the lack of other food, and to create some variety in an age which possessed little in the way of vegetable produce, sea birds of many kinds were formerly consumed. Amongst these were sanderlings, sea-larks, seapies, puffins, shags, and even gulls, ' all of which ', as Carew sagely observed, ' content not the stomacke with a like savourinesse, some being good to be eaten while they are young, but nothing toothsome as they grow elder '.

At this time and, indeed, long afterwards, seals, or ' soyles,' as they are known in the West Country, were frequently included in the dietary of the people. ' In making and growth,' wrote Carew, ' the soyle is not unlike a pigge, being ugly, faced and footed like a moldwarp (mole). He delighteth in musike or any loud noise, and thereby is trained to approach neer the shore, and to show himself almost wholly above water.'

In the year 1825 Robert Stephen Hawker, the famous parson-poet and eccentric, arrived one day with a friend at the old Ship Inn at Boscastle, kept at that time by a certain Joan Treworgy. Having agreed upon the price of their rooms, they proceeded to order dinner.

' What had she got in the house ? ' they asked.

' Meat,' replied the landlady, ' meat and taties.'

The specific difference between beef, mutton, veal, etc., seemed to be utterly or artfully ignored ; and to every frenzied inquiry her calm, inexorable reply was : ' Meat—nice wholesome meat and taties '.

[1] Richard Ferris's *Dangerous and Memorable Adventure*, Arber reprints, English Garner, VI, 153–63.
  Hamilton Jenkin, *Western Morning News*, 24 October 1929.

' In due time,' continues Hawker, ' we sat down to a not unsatisfactory meal, but it is a wretched truth that by no effort could we ascertain what it was that was roasted for us that day by Widow Treworgy, and which we consumed. " Was it a piece of Boscastle baby ? " I suggested to my companion. The question caused him to rush out and inquire again ; but he came back baffled and shouting : " Meat and taties ". There was not a vestige of bone, nor any outline that could identify the joint ; and the not unsavoury taste was something like tender veal. It was not until years afterwards that light was thrown on our mysterious dinner that day by a passage which I accidentally turned up in an ancient history of Cornwall. Therein I read " that the people of Bouscastle and Boussiney do catch in the summer seas divers young soyles (seals) which, doubtful if they be fish or flesh, conynge housewives will nevertheless roast, and do make thereof savoury meat ".' [1]

About the year 1690 there came riding into Cornwall on a side-saddle that intrepid lady traveller, Celia Fiennes. Unlike Andrew Borde, Mrs Fiennes comments more than once on the excellence of Cornish food, in especial the rich ' clouted cream ' which she met with for the first time at St Austell, and the very good bottled beer discovered by her in some of the cottages near the Land's End. [2] Perhaps Mrs Fiennes was lucky—it is certain that she was well-to-do. When not staying with her friends, the Boscawens, or in one or other of the great houses of the county, she probably put up at the best inns, and ordered with an unstinting hand. For the poor, indeed, conditions of life during this period were scarcely less hard than they had been in former centuries. Writing of the tinners in 1697 a Cornish gentleman claimed that the only flesh meat ever tasted by such men was that of sheep or bullocks which had died in the fields through disease or want of pasture. ' Their ordinary food,' he writes, ' is potatoes and barley bread (as coarse as horse bread), with gruel thickened oftener with barley meal than oat meal. By which reason and from having not rags enough to cover them, men are so reduced from well-grown persons as to be now (comparatively) meer pigmies in stature and strength, which is lamentable to behold.' [3]

---

[1] Rev. S. Baring-Gould, *The Vicar of Morwenstow.*
[2] *Through England on a Side-Saddle in the time of William and Mary.*
[3] *Tinners' Grievance.*

III

Notwithstanding the fact that the supply of corn and the means of transporting it were destined to show considerable improvement during the next sixty years, the population also increased so much during the same period that the position described by Borlase in 1758 showed relatively little change. ' Though the low lands,' he writes, ' especially along the Tamar and Alan, may yield more corn than the inhabitants of those parts, and the less fruitful hundreds of Stratton and Lysnewth, can dispense with, yet, the hundreds of Poudre, Kerrier, and Penwith, and the western parts of Pydre (far the most populous tracts of our county) do not yield corn near sufficient to supply the inhabitants. Upon the whole, if those parts entirely addicted to husbandry will yield a sufficiency of grain to make up, in a moderate year, what is wanting in the parts less cultivated, and more addicted to mining, this is full as much as can be asserted in this particular.'[1]

The practice of the merchants, moreover, of exporting corn in order to make higher prices overseas still further imperilled the home supply, and resulted during this century in the outbreak of constant riots among the wellnigh starving population. During some of the worst periods of scarcity the poor in the maritime districts are said to have subsisted almost wholly on limpets and other coarse shell-fish gathered from the rocks, whilst snails even were used to make the ' broth ' which has ever been a stand-by in the Cornishman's diet.[2]

Of all the famine periods which marked the course of the eighteenth century, the year 1794-5 was perhaps the most grievous. ' A very great scarcity of corn prevailed this year over England, and indeed all Europe,' states an entry in the Helston parish register. ' 3,597 Cornish bushels of barley, 172 barrels of flour, and 3,000 pounds of biscuits were imported by subscription into Gweek and sold in this town for the use of the inhabitants and those of the parishes of Wendron, Crowan, Breage, and Germoe.' The scarcity at this time made itself felt even among the well-to-do. ' If

---

[1] *Natural History of Cornwall*, 89–90.
[2] See Hamilton Jenkin, *The Cornish Miner*, 149–56.

you think proper,' wrote the Reverend Charles Penneck. of Tregemba, to a fellow clergyman, ' I will readily join in taking any quantity (of corn) you may approve. The price, I apprehend, will be about 14s. 6d., but Capt. Gundry assures me that the tinners will gladly give 12s. 0d. for this corn rather than 10s. 6d. for our own corn, the quality being so far superior as to produce 40 gallons of meal per bushel more than the corn grown in this country.' [1]

During this same year a dramatic incident was caused by the arrival one day of a band of three or four hundred tinners in the streets of Flushing. ' Dressed,' states an eyewitness, ' in the mud-stained frocks and trousers in which they worked underground, and armed with large clubs and sticks, and speaking an uncouth jargon which none but themselves could understand, they struck terror wherever they went, and seemed like an irruption of barbarians invading some more civilized country than their own. Their numbers were quite equal to that of the whole of the male population of the little village, so that the men stood aghast, the women retired into their houses and closed their doors, and the children seemed struck dumb with affright.' The moment of their visit chanced to be particularly ' inopportune ', since a large amount of grain had arrived in a coasting vessel that day, and was even then being stored in one of the warehouses on the quay. Resistance, if not bloodshed, appeared inevitable when, as the writer, James Silk Buckingham, records, a trifling incident (and one very illustrative, be it said, of the character of the tinners) turned the tide of feeling.

' A few boys about my own age and myself taking courage from our companionship, and strongly stimulated by curiosity, went towards the warehouse where the captains were collected, and where the grain was being stored away, a body of " tinners " being then remonstrating against the act. Captain Kempthorne, an old friend of my father, and with whom I had always been a great favourite, seeing me in the group of boys, came to me, took me up in his arms, and planting me on one of the sacks of corn then leaning against the wall, bade me give out a hymn, which he had often heard me do before—for I had nearly all Dr Watts' collection by heart— and having an excellent voice, with some ear and great fondness for music, I was equally acquainted with the most popular of the hymn tunes. I asked him : " Which hymn ? "

[1] Printed in *The Cornish Telegraph*, 17 November 1869.

He replied : " Any will do, but be quick, and pitch the tune ! " The captain then called out : " Silence for a hymn !" and the tinners, struck with his appeal, hushed their murmurs, and took off their hats as tho' attending worship. The first verse began with : " Salvation, oh, the joyful sound ", and as almost the whole body of miners were at this period followers of Wesley, and many extremely devout, they joined in the simple melody of the hymn verse by verse, as it was given out, and at its close again covered their heads and retired in peace, crossing the ferry to Falmouth in the boats that had brought them over, and relieving all the villagers from any further apprehension.' [1]

Whilst the people of Flushing were concerned only with the immediate problem of saving their skins, it was generally recognized by the more liberal-minded that the real need of the tinners was food rather than ' religious dope '. In many instances genuine efforts were made to alleviate their sufferings by purchasing cargoes of corn through public subscription. ' Getting corn for the poor ' ; ' going to the south in search of corn ' ; ' fetching barley from the Meneage (Lizard district) ', are typical of the entries found in many west Cornwall parish accounts of this date. At Breage, the record books show no less than 1,170 entries of persons receiving corn from the overseers during the year 1800. More than one cargo appears to have been imported here during this period, and the distribution of the corn, which was sold at a reduced rate, kept the parish officials busy for many weeks afterwards. [2]

Despite these measures food riots continued to spread. ' On Monday last,' states the *Cornwall Gazette*, 4th April 1801, ' a great number of women assembled at Plymouth, and obliged the farmers, butchers, and bakers to sell their provisions at reduced prices. On the next day another band of about two hundred women collected at Launceston and plundered a farmer of the parish of Lezant of ten Winchester bushels of wheat. The farmer himself ran off in a fright, and was followed by the women, who pelted him out of the neighbourhood. The corn was afterwards delivered to the poor at 10s. a bushel.'

During the following week disturbances occurred in almost every town and village from the Tamar to the Land's End,

[1] *The Autobiography of J. S. Buckingham.*
[2] See Rev. Canon G. H. Doble, *Breage in the Eighteenth Century*, 21.

'insomuch that we might fill our paper with a detail of their particulars', wrote the editor of the *Cornwall Gazette*. 'Whilst scarcely a town in the county has escaped the contagion, in the markets it has been chiefly confined to the lower order of women only. In the mining districts, however, large bodies of tinners have assembled, particularly in the neighbourhood of St Austell, where they went round to the farmers, carrying a written paper in one hand and a rope in the other. If the farmers hesitated to sign this paper, which pledged them to sell their corn at a reduced price, the rope was fastened about their necks, and they were terrified into compliance.' [1] Similar tactics were adopted in St Ives and elsewhere.

By many people at this time the sole responsibility for the high price of corn and meat was laid at the door of the farmer, on the common principle of attaching blame for any uncomfortable situation to the nearest scapegoat in sight. In point of fact this attitude was not a little unjust. For whilst the farmers themselves were faced with soaring prices in the shops, with an increase in rents and wages, a rising Poor Rate and the inexorable demands of the Church for its tithes, it was clearly impossible that they should have supplied the needs of the community at other than enhanced prices. As regards the price of flour the millers obviously bore a large share of the responsibility, yet they at any rate displayed no intention of sacrificing their profits for the common good. In 1812 best quality wheat was selling in Truro from 38s. to 40s. a bushel. Meantime the millers' price for flour varied from 50s. to 52s. per bushel, the trifling charge of 12s. to 14s. for grinding the corn being accounted for by the scarcity of water. [2]

It is true that the tyranny of the small country miller was beginning to be threatened, even at this date. An announcement which appears in the *West Briton* of 17th September 1812, states that a steam engine, about to be erected at Trengrove in the parish of Illogan, was capable of grinding one hundred and fifty bushels of corn a day at the rate of 6d. a bushel. But although time was destined to show the significance of this announcement, it can have brought little consolation to those who were so nearly bordering on starvation. Nor did

[1] *Cornwall Gazette*, 4 April 1801.
[2] *West Briton*, 17 September 1812. In 1802 when the price of wheat was standing as low as 23s. the Cornish bushel, 'best bag flour', was selling at 60s. in Falmouth.—*Cornwall Gazette*, 6 March 1802.

the events of the day justify optimism. During the same year the policy of the merchants of hoarding grain resulted in the almost complete disappearance of flour from many of the most populous centres of West Cornwall. As a result, fresh riots broke out, striking terror through the country-side. In response to this the justices declared that ' whilst exerting themselves to the utmost, in a time of such scarcity, for the relief of the miner, they were yet determined to punish all rioters and disorderly assemblies according to the laws entrusted to their execution '. The militia was, therefore, called up, and troops summoned from Pendennis Castle. The latter, however, soon learnt by personal experience that there was reason enough to justify the miners' discontent, the officer in charge complaining that he himself had found it impossible to obtain any bread for his men in the whole town of Redruth.[1]

In point of fact, though their sufferings were wellnigh intolerable, the current fears of a general insurrection among the tinners was wholly unwarranted. As Polwhele, who was himself a magistrate, readily admitted, ' though in his conduct rash and daring, the (Cornish) miner is intelligent, and may always be " reasoned with ". With little pretensions to courage, I had no fear in accompanying the sheriff to Liscus, in Kenwyn, where a large body of miners was occupied in seizing upon, threshing out, and carrying away the corn of the farmer. We appealed to their sense of right and wrong ; their leaders were ashamed of themselves ; the flails and the sacks were abandoned, and the crowd dispersed '.[2]

How closely conditions at this time resembled those of the Great War, a century later, may be gathered from the contemporary files of the local newspapers. At a meeting held in Truro on 7th April 1812, we learn that the Associated Attornies of Cornwall resolved that owing to the prevailing scarcity of corn they would not permit pastry or puddings of any kind, in which flour formed an ingredient, to be used by their respective families, whilst at the same time they pledged themselves to contribute in all other ways towards lessening the consumption of flour.[3] No less familiar are the recipes contributed to the papers at this date explaining how the use of flour could be diminished by the addition of rice.

[1] *West Briton*, 10 April 1812.
[2] *Traditions and Recollections*, 582.
[3] *West Briton*, 10 April 1812.

' Bread thus prepared will keep moist for a fortnight,' states one writer with a confidence which the modern reader may find it hard to share, ' and is very pleasant and extremely nutritious.' [1] Nor were queues outside the food shops unknown at this period. In April 1801 the magistrates and constables at Falmouth were forced to attend at the markets daily in order to preserve and to guard the property of the sellers. ' The confusion here,' states an eye-witness, ' is chiefly occasioned by the eagerness of the inhabitants to purchase a small share of the scanty supply which the market affords. Those who do not struggle hard while it is going are compelled to return with empty baskets. A temporary enclosure has now been erected on the Market-Strand to keep off the people from the sellers, who will henceforth hand their goods over the rails to the proper purchasers.' [2]

IV

Nor were these the only ways in which conditions at this time were paralleled by those of little more than a century later. For just as in 1920 when a shortage of food was being experienced in many parts of Europe, and famine was raging in Russia, electrical generating stations in America were burning wheat, and locomotives in the Argentine were running on maize ; so in Cornwall in 1812 pilchards through lack of sale were actually being used by the farmers for manure. It is true that the landings of fish during this year were exceptionally large. ' In addition to pilchards,' states the *West Briton* of 27th August, ' a great quantity of hake, pollock, and conger has been taken on the coast this week. On Tuesday last one boat at Newlyn had six hundred hakes on board which were sold for 2s. 9d. a " burn " of twenty-one fish. One person at East Looe received £400 for fresh fish sold by his people during the last week. In fact the great quantity of pilchards already taken has quite glutted the markets—at Plymouth the former have been sold for 6d. per hundred, and in some cases for 3d.'

Under normal conditions pilchards formed an essential

[1] *West Briton*, 10 April 1812.
[2] *Cornwall Gazette*, 4 April 1801.

part of the diet of the poor. That they should have lacked a sale at a time when all other food was so scarce was solely attributable to the salt tax. 'Each cottager,' wrote Warner in 1809, ' on an average is wont to lay in about a thousand fish for winter use. The quantity of salt necessary is about seven pounds to a hundred fish. Till the late rise in the duty of that article salt might be procured at 1½d. per lb., and the whole stock cured at an expense of 8s. 9d. But *tempora mutantur ;* salt is now increased to 4d. per lb., and a thousand fish cannot be cured under £1 3s. 4d., a sum of unattainable magnitude to a poor man who gets only 6s. or, at most, 7s. per week for his labour.' [1]

The evil consequences of this tax were apparent everywhere, but in the case of the Scilly Islands its incidence amounted to disaster. ' The situation of the poorer inhabitants here during the last winter was truly distressing,' wrote an eye-witness. ' These persons are chiefly dependent for their support in winter upon the fish caught and cured by them during the summer months, but such has been the pressure of the times, even upon these poor islanders, that they have been unable to purchase the salt necessary for curing their summer's catches and, there being no market to which they could have resource, their sufferings have in consequence become very alarming.' So desperate, indeed, was their plight, that the matter at length came to the ears of the Bishop of Exeter, who ' most humanely ' laid their case before the Lords of the Treasury. These, in turn, gave orders for a quantity of salt to be shipped from Penzance, which was eventually sold to the poor of the islands, free of duty, in quantities not exceeding half a bushel to each person. [2] But for this timely intervention it appears certain that many of the inhabitants must have died of actual starvation during the ensuing winter.

The salt duties, as thus appears, were as disastrous to the poor of this country as they had already proved themselves in France, and have since done, in our own time, in India.

As early as the sixteenth century the records of the Cornish ports bear constant witness to the popular resentment which this tax aroused, and the continual efforts to evade it by importing smuggled salt had led to many lively passages-at-arms between the excise officers and the local population.

[1] Rev. R. Warner, *Tour Through Cornwall* (1809).
[2] *West Briton*, 25 June 1812.

In 1597 a certain Captain William Morgan, who was engaged in the profitable business of privateering in the Channel, brought into Mount's Bay ' two barques or pynnaces ' laden with salt and earthen pots.   These, together with another cargo of salt taken near Rochelle, were subsequently shipped to St Ives.   On an attempt being made to land them here trouble arose, and a certain ' Peter Newman did ill intreat and abuse Lawrence Birde, the deputy-customer of the port, calling him Jack and Knave, and vowing to cut off his ears, afterwards giving the said Lawrence a blow, for the reason that the said deputy did stay the landing of the said salt until he might be satisfied that the custom due upon it to the Queen's Majesty was paid '.[1]

A hundred years later a writer on Cornwall describes how he had commonly seen the poor forced to eat the flesh of animals long after it had become unwholesome, simply through their inability to afford the salt necessary for curing the same.   Notwithstanding this, the salt tax was twice renewed during the eighteenth century, and by the time of the Napoleonic wars had reached a figure of approximately £35 a ton.   At this date it was estimated that it took practically the value of one side of the carcass of a pig to procure enough salt to preserve the other.

As a concession to the vested interests of the merchants, salt purchased in *wholesale* quantities for the curing of pilchards was nominally entitled to a rebate of the whole amount of the duty.   This fact not infrequently gave rise to a great deal of ' vexatious interference ' on the part of the excise officers.   Particularly was this the case in the fishing towns where many of the inhabitants dwelt over the cellars where the salt was stored and were wont, by means of a bag let down on a line through a trap-hatch in the floor, to supply their own needs from the duty-free salt below.   This went on all right, as a character in one of Mr Bottrell's stories describes, ' until one day a harum-scarum fool of a woman hurried away from home without taking care to see that the hatch-boards were snug upon the beams.   During her absence the exciseman, going his rounds, entered the cellar, and saw the contrivance.   On putting his head up through the hatch he saw that the sand which covered the floor of the living-room had been swept away, and there, by the trap, still lay a good pile of salt.   On examining other dwellings over fish cellars

[1] Hobson Matthews, *History of St Ives*, 127.

he found trap-hatches in nearly all of them. There 's been a devil of a row amongst them ever since,' added Aunt Jinnifer, ' and all the other women are ready to kill that thoughtless fool—and serve her right. I only pray to goodness they may find some other way to fool the plague of an exciseman, I do '.[1]

Meantime, in order to supplement the supply of food, the cottager who could contrive to rent or own a little ' quillet ' of ground generally cultivated a considerable quantity of pease. This was eaten in the form of porridge, and in some measure compensated for the shortage of flour. Another cereal widely grown in Cornwall at this date was ' pillas ', a small yellow grain, described by an eighteenth-century writer as being the ' oatmeal of the poor '. In form pillas was not unlike rye, but the straw was much finer, and was largely used for plaiting hats, being much softer and tougher than wheat straw. Pillas was seldom ground into flour, but was usually boiled into a sort of porridge, known ' gurts '. The traditional mode of preparing pillas gurts was to take two or three quarts of the grain, damp it, and then put it to stand in a little tray in the warmth of the chimney corner. As soon as the pillas began to ' cheeny ' (i.e. show signs of sprouting), it was placed in a ' baker ' (iron pan), and stirred over a slow fire until it was thoroughly dry and a little ' scroached ' (scorched). Roasting pillas was a fine art, and required great judgment. Nevertheless, it was well worth all the labour, in the opinion of the old people. When roasted, the grain was spread out on a cloth to cool, and afterwards crushed, a handful or two at a time, in a little granite trough. The crusher or pounder employed for this purpose was generally a nicely-rounded ' bowel ' or pebble, picked up on the beach. Pillas gurts in addition to being eaten in the form of porridge, with milk, were often used instead of flour or rice for puddings. Small quantities were also added by the old housewives to the malt, when they wanted their ale extra strong. On this account the gurts came in time to be regarded with suspicion by the excisemen, who at length threatened to fine old women who continued to put their grain to cheeny—calling it malt, forsooth, ' like the cussed ould interfering devils that they were '.[2] This

---

[1] *Tales and Hearthside Traditions of West Cornwall*, III, 67.

[2] See W. Bottrell, *Tales and Hearthside Traditions of West Cornwall*, III, 67–8.

fact, combined with the increase in the cultivation of potatoes, was ultimately the means of driving pillas from the field. ' The last crop I saw harvested,' writes Mr J. H. Thomas of St Just, ' was in 1867 in Sancreed. It was a cereal peculiarly adapted to cold regions and high altitudes, or to rough and exposed ground as in West Penwith.'

At what date the potato first became known in Cornwall it is impossible to say. By the end of the seventeenth century it was already in general use, but its cultivation, until somewhat more than a hundred years ago, was practically confined to two varieties. These were the ' Painted Lord ' and the ' Painted Lady ', both of which were of a red sort, the latter taking precedence at table.[1] During the year preceding that in which it was intended to sow a field with wheat, it was customary to allow the poor to ' teel ' the ground with potatoes, an act of philanthropy which was said to pay the farmers well, since an increase in the wheat crop generally resulted. This, in all probability, was not so much due to any virtue in the potatoes themselves as to the quantities of manure brought on to the land by the people who planted them.

In former times considerable benefit was derived by the Cornish cottager from the keeping of goats. Throughout the eighteenth century these animals were pastured in great numbers on the hill-sides and rough moorlands of the west. Being fattened, they were sold in the markets about Christmas time, and were stated by one writer to be ' not much inferior to venison '. ' Zennor goats,' the nickname by which the inhabitants of that rugged little parish are still known, commemorates their former avocation. The industry itself is now, for no very obvious reason, defunct. It may, however, be doubted whether, even in the past, the inhabitants often tasted the flesh of the animals they reared, since the poverty of this parish was such that the very cows therein are reputed to have kept themselves alive by eating the straw bell ropes in the church !

In addition to goats the moorlands also provided pasture for large numbers of sheep. These were mostly of an inferior type, degenerated from the old Cornish breed. They are described by Worgan as having ' grey faces and legs, short thick necks, narrow backs, flattish sides, and a fleece of coarse wool (" Cornish hair "), weighing about two or three pounds of eighteen ounces '. These mongrel flocks lived upon the

[1] *Letters from West Cornwall* (1826).

downs throughout summer and winter alike, and their mutton was said to be very good. They were certainly a hardy breed, cropping the furze and heath equally with the grass, and were as active as deer. 'If they cannot leap over a fence,' wrote Worgan, ' they will contrive to creep through it, so that they are a great nuisance to any enclosures near the common, particularly when they have got the skab.' [1]

In contrast to these, there was found on the towans or sandy hillocks of the north coast a small compact type of sheep, the mutton of which was of a particularly choice flavour and the fleece approaching that of the South Downs breed. These sheep were said to derive their quality from feeding on the multitudes of little snails which appear on the sandy surface of the towans during the mornings and evenings.

V

On the south coast of Cornwall, where the pastures were more fertile and conditions less exposed, dairy farming of a primitive kind was being widely practised by the middle of the eighteenth century. ' In the parish of Constantine,' wrote a traveller in 1754, ' are one thousand cows kept for milk and their method is this. If any man hath a fancy to keep a dairy of ten or twenty cows, he will agree with a man for that number by the year, giving 48s. a year for the whole increase of each cow, in which the calf is included. The man that lets them finds pasture and keeps them on ground proper for them in summer, and about Michaelmas turns them into their winter's keeping which had remained till then unpastured. But the number of cows so greatly overstocks the place that you would imagine they could not live the winter without hay ; but if they don't they may die, for there is never none given, and unless 'tis a very careless man they are so hardy as to do tolerably well without it.' [2]

The system, herein referred to, of providing separate

---

[1] G. B. Worgan, *General View of the Agriculture of Cornwall* (1811).
[2] *Notes from a Journal made during a Riding Tour of Sixteen Days in Cornwall in 1754*, Penzance Natural History and Antiquarian Society (1888–92), 283.

pastures for summer and winter use was once as general in Cornwall as it still is in the more mountainous countries of the Continent to-day. Confirmation of this is found in the Cornish place-names *gwavas* and *laity*, which mean respectively, winter-house and milk-house (or dairy). The Welsh language also includes the word *hafod* or *haffoty*, meaning summer quarters. Although the Cornish equivalent of this is no longer known, there is little reason to doubt that the western Celts once possessed such a word. From these facts a picture may be formed of the ancient pastoral system of Cornwall wherein, when summer came, the herdsmen would leave the *gwavas* or winter homestead and proceed into the high-country moorlands which, although too exposed for permanent settlement, yielded sufficiently good pasture for the flocks during a few months of the year. In these summer quarters dairy-work would form the chief occupation. Hence the Cornish word *laity* or milk-house may be considered to have had much the same meaning as the Welsh *haffoty* or summer-house. With the fall of the year the herdsmen would leave their summer pastures and return once more to the shelter of the *gwavas* or *hendra* (old homestead).[1] Evidence of the late survival of this system in Cornwall may be found in the files of the local newspapers of little more than a century ago. An advertisement in the *West Briton* of 21st February 1812, announcing the sale of the tenement of Smallcombe in the parish of St Cleer, states: ' Excellent summer pasture for cattle is to be found here, all of which is well supplied with stock from every part of the county during the summer months. If not let by Lady-day, cattle will be taken in as usual from 1st May to Michaelmas, at . . . per head, according to the quality of the pastures, and proper herdsmen will be appointed to take charge of them '. Many other summer pastures are advertised in the same paper, including ' Botreaux Tor, otherwise Butter Tor, in the parish of Symonward ; and Hawke's Tor, Kerkees, Druglets, and Scribble, in the parish of Blisland '. The latter are described as ' containing upwards of eight hundred acres of the best summer pastures for cattle and sheep in Cornwall '. It is stated by Worgan that in 1808 the prices charged by the herdsmen for minding the farmers' flocks at summer pasture varied from 2s. to 21s. per head of neat cattle, and from 1s. to 3s. per score of sheep. These ' farm ' sheep, however, as distinct from the hardier

[1] R. Morton Nance, *Old Cornwall*, IV, 32–4.

native breed, rarely remained healthy for longer than a month or two when pastured on the open downs. After this they became ' moor-sick ', and had to be removed to the lower, cultivated lands to recuperate. It was this fact, in all probability, which accounts for the discontinuance of the practice, and is at least one of the reasons why, although both cattle and sheep may still be seen in the moorland country, their number is small in comparison with the vast herds which formerly roamed those areas in search of summer pasture.

Notwithstanding the extent to which cattle breeding was prosecuted during the eighteenth century, only the comparatively well-to-do could afford the price of butcher's meat. For the ' lowest sort of people ', as a visitor observed in 1776, living was ' so wretched that our poor in the environs of London would soon perish if reduced to their condition. The labourers in general bring up their families with only potatoes or turnips, or leeks or pepper grass, rolled up in black barley crust, and baked under the ashes, with now and then a little milk. Perhaps they do not taste a bit of flesh-meat in three months. Yet their children are healthy and strong, and look quite fresh and jolly '.[1]

Under this somewhat grimly disguised account of potatoes and other vegetables ' rolled up in a black barley crust ', one may perceive what is perhaps the earliest reference to the now far-famed Cornish pasty. The latter, on account of its convenience for carrying to work, has long been a favourite item in the Cornishman's bill of fare, but it is only of recent times that it has become so largely a meat dish. Hardly less favoured by Cornish workmen of the last century was the ' hoggan ', or lump of unleavened dough, in which was sometimes embedded a morsel of green pork. This fare, although heavy enough to kill anyone who had not been inured to it from early youth, long remained general among the miners. For, as Mr Herbert Thomas has expressed it in his well-known song :

Aw, you don't want fancy denners when you're sweaten bare your bones,
An' feel as ef you could digest a barraful of stones,
'Tes for somethin' braave and solid that you knaw your sperit groans
And a hoggan like stull tember you could chow, comraade !

[1] *St James's Chronicle.*

The Cornish miner, as may thus be gathered, liked a diet which would 'stand up' to his surroundings. In further proof of which the story is told of a certain man who married a cook who had formerly been in the service of a wealthy family. On going to the mine one day shortly afterwards he took with him a pasty of his wife's making.

'How did you like your pasty?' was the question asked on his return.

'Aw, 'a wadn' no good at all,' came the disappointing reply, 'time I got down fifty fathoms 'a were scat to lembs (broken to fragments). The wans mawther made wadn' break if they 'd 'a faaled to the bottom of the shaft. They *was* paasties, you!'

Whilst the hoggan or the pasty formed the working-man's 'croust' (lunch) throughout the week, 'broth' made from scraps of pork or beef, and flavoured with 'rooties' (swedes), cabbage, carrots, shallots, or leeks almost invariably constituted the family dinner on Sunday. In some households, where there were many hungry mouths to feed, suet dumplings were added to give the dish more substance. Occasionally there might even be a little morsel of meat to follow. In this case the broth acted as a 'fo'cer', which was designed to take the edge off the appetite. Such economies, though necessary, were not always appreciated. A small boy, called upon to say grace before a meal of this sort, is reported to have cried in desperation: 'O Lord! deliver us from this great ocean of broth, and land us safely upon that little island of mutton over yonder!' [1]   But whilst the meat course was problematical, the broth was invariable, and on a Sunday morning 'Tallywarn' Street, Camborne, the Digey, at St Ives, or indeed any of the more populous centres of an average Cornish town, fairly reeked with its strong and penetrating aroma. Very welcome, none the less, was the old-time invitation: 'Draa foo'th and bread your basins', which was the signal for the family to draw up to the table and prepare for the meal by crumbling into the basin which was set before each a slice from the appetizing 'kettle' loaf. Eager then were the glances turned towards the crock which stood simmering on the hearth, and from which the savoury liquor was generously ladled out.

A 'sweet' in those days was a rare event, but when provided was of a no less substantial nature.

[1] F. W. P. Jago, *Glossary of the Cornish Dialect*, 169.

Rolly polly in the bag, pudden in the basin,
If you'd 'a been where I have been you'd surely look to taste 'n,

ran an old couplet which throws further light on the plain
and solid fare of this period.

A dish of good broth was rightly looked upon as an excellent
dinner, and on that account was commonly reserved for
Sundays. Throughout the remainder of the week the poor
were forced to content themselves with the everlasting round
of fish and potatoes :

> *Scads and 'tates, and scads and 'tates,*
> *Scads and 'tates and conger,*
> *And those who can't eat scads and 'tates*
> *Oh, they must die of hunger,*

was another old rhyme which, although it had its origin in
the Scilly Islands, applied with equal force to the mainland
of the west. ' Rank as the pilchard may be esteemed by those
who are unaccustomed to eat it,' wrote a traveller in 1809,
' yet, throughout Cornwall it is considered the greatest
delicacy. Happy is that taste which goes hand in hand with
necessity, for I know not what would become of the lower
orders of people here if they turned with disgust from an
article which constitutes their chief support. Though the
fastidious epicure might shrink back with some abhorrence
from a Cornish peasant's table, which rarely exhibits more
than a dish of pilchards, chopt up with raw onions and salt—
eaten with the fingers [1] and accompanied with barley or oaten
cakes—yet, I confess, we never contemplated those honest
people round their board without catching the infection of
hunger and being willing to partake of their humble fare.' [2]

The removal of the salt duty in 1825 had tended to increase
the consumption of fish, by allowing greater quantities to be
cured for winter use. Until recently, therefore, every Cornish
cottage included a large ' bussa ' or earthenware pot as part
of its equipment. In this a sufficient number of pilchards
were laid in salt to last the family throughout the months
when fresh fish was scarce. After every big catch ' jousters '
would hawk the pilchards through the inland towns and
villages where they were commonly sold at the rate of eight

[1] ' Fingers for fish, prongs for mait ' was the saying in Newlyn in 1894.
[2] Rev. R. Warner, *Tour Through Cornwall* (1809).

or ten a penny, and in some cases as low as sixpence per hundred and twenty. A substantial farm would lay in six hundred or more of these fish for winter stock, whilst a dozen or two, which might be left over, would be split and hung up outside the door to dry on a stick. These were afterwards peppered and cooked over an open fire, when they were known as ' scroulers '.

It has been said that in many cases the miners actually preferred salt fish to fresh. This may well have been true, since scientists have recently shown that the popularity of kippers and other salt food amongst colliers is a result of the loss of salt which takes place through excessive sweating when the men are at work in hot places underground. It would be interesting to know whether, in the case of Cornwall, the decrease of mining or the rise in the standard of living has been mainly responsible for the fact that pilchards thus treated are no longer as popular as they once were. Certain it is that pilchards are but rarely salted to-day, although among a few of the older generation they are still held in high esteem as a cure for rheumatism.

In addition to pilchards, large quantities of bream, hake, cod, skate, and ray were formerly stocked for winter use, being preserved by drying in the smoke of the open chimney. When thoroughly ' hardened ' in this way the fish were placed in the rack which lay overhead between the beams, slices being cut off and used for boiling as occasion required. Other fish were treated in similar ways. Ling was salted and dried in great abundance, especially in the Scilly Islands, from whence it was exported to many of the towns in the two western counties. Whiting prepared in the same fashion was sold during winter in the local markets under the name of ' buckhorn '. Dog-fish was also preserved, as well as eaten fresh. In the latter case it was often made into a sort of broth known as ' morgay soup ', from the Cornish *môr*, sea ; *ki*, dog.[1] On the south coast of Cornwall immense quantities of lance or sand-eels used to be obtained from the beaches on moonlight nights where, as the tide went down, they were ' twitched ' out of the sand by women and children using small iron crooks. These eels are remarkably agile, and a sharp eye and lively hand are required to seize their wriggling bodies before they bury themselves again in the sand. The larger sort, which sometimes attain a length of nearly a foot, used

[1] See J. C. Bellamy, *Guide to the Fishmarkets* (1843).

to be sold for about twelve a penny, the smaller ones at the rate of a penny a basinful. Crabs, lobsters, and crayfish were also dragged out of the rocks with crooks at the low spring tides. These, however, were generally sold to the gentry, or more recently to the London markets, being considered ' too good ' for poor people. The latter, however, made much use of the smaller shell-fish, especially cockles and mussels, which were often preserved in vinegar.

The conger eel, on account of its size, was highly valued, and was preserved by drying in the sun, as well as salted. Baked in a dish with vinegar it was known as ' soused ' conger. When eaten fresh it was generally served in the form of a pie. The conger is supposed to be a very clean feeder, but this is not always the case. On the occasion of a disastrous wreck at the Lizard, some forty years ago, huge specimens of these eels found their way in on to the beaches where they were picked up without difficulty, being too bloated by their horrible feasting to attempt to escape. The country people, however, had no qualms. Many of them came with their carts from miles around, and for some weeks after conger—salt or fresh—was all the eating, save only among the incurably fastidious.

VI

In earlier times such an incident as this would have provided little cause for wonder, since the poor were in many cases half-starved, and therefore thankful for anything which would sustain life. ' My father had the standard wages for surface hands, which was £2 5s. a month,' wrote an old miner, describing his boyhood in the forties of the last century. ' I was earning 10s. a month, so that £2 15s. a month had to provide for five of us.' [1] Not only were wages low but prices remained astonishingly high. Sugar in 1841 was 8d. per lb., currants 10d., soap 6d., starch 6½d. Tea cost anything from 6s. to 10s. per lb.,[2] and was bought in minute quantities from hawkers, many of whom were blinded miners led about the country by their children. In substitution for tea the dried leaves of mugwort were frequently used by poor families.

[1] Thomas Oliver, *The Autobiography of a Cornish Miner*.
[2] Report of the Royal Cornwall Polytechnic Society (1871), 51.

Jam was, of course, unheard of, the usual form of sweetening being a species of thick black treacle.

Poor as they were, the old people were endowed with a sturdy independence which made them resentful of anything which seemed like charity. The late Dr Dunstan, writing of his boyhood days, recalls an incident which is illustrative of this. Zeke Pearce was an old roadman, supporting a wife and family on the miserable wage of 6s. or 7s. a week. The dinner which he usually took with him when working at a distance from home rarely consisted of anything better than a few slices of barley bread, covered with a thin scraping of treacle. Sometimes, however, he would call at one of the neighbouring houses for a ' dish of tay ' to wash down this humble fare, and on these occasions would not infrequently be asked to stay and partake of the family dinner. Great as the temptation must have been, the old man's reply was invariably the same : ' Why, no thank 'ee, missus, I'd as soon 'av a bit of bread and trickle as anything I know ! ' [1]

In some cases, however, the attraction of a good meat dinner proved irresistible. Living at Copperhouse about this time was an old washerwoman by the name of Prudey, who was employed in the household of a tailor. Knowing the woman's poverty the family made it a practice on washing days to have a round of beef, a liberal portion of which was always set aside for her dinner. To this, however, Prudey sometimes thought it her duty to object. ' Lor, master ! ' she would exclaim. ' What, beef again ! Why don't 'ee have a bit of fish ? ' The tailor at length deputed Prudey to get a ' bur'n ' of hake, one of which was dressed on the following washing day, to the accompaniment also of a round of beef. On being asked which she would have, Prudey gazed a while on both as much as to say : ' How happy could I be with either were t'other dear charmer away ' —then quietly remarked : ' Well, master, I think I'll have a bit of beef ! ' [2]

Down to 1846, when the Corn Importation Bill was passed, the price of wheat was nearly double that of barley. The latter, therefore, formed the staple food of the poor, a wheaten loaf when provided for tea on Sundays or at the feast being regarded as a great luxury. Prior to the coming of the railway, food and merchandise were transported in cumbrous wagons,

[1] *Western Morning News*, 24 January 1930.
[2] *Cornish Mining Reporter*, 6 November 1846.

whose rate of progress rarely averaged more than four miles an hour. It used to be said that when corn dropped in price the merchants sent word by the wagons, but that whenever a rise in price took place special mounted messengers were sent posting through the country-side in order to make the announcement with the least possible delay. Happily for the poor, barley grew freely in most parts of the county, and it is recorded that in congenial lands, with a southern aspect, crops were sometimes sown, matured, and gathered in the short space of six weeks.[1] Very often the corn was bought direct from the farmers, and afterwards sent to one of the many grist mills which flourished on the banks of every stream. The amount of business done by these mills was very considerable. Mr Charles Hoare, whose mother was born at the old mill-house near Caerhayes Castle in 1829, records that she had often seen as many as six two-horse wagons arriving on the premises in one day. The miller's recognized toll was one-twelfth, but this, if tradition lies not, was often exceeded. So suspect were their practices that it was once a common saying that every *honest* miller had hair growing on the palms of his hands. To those, however, who commented on its absence, the millers would retort that it was only honest people who could see it !

In damp weather the home-ground flour sometimes became ' milchy ' (i.e. viscous or sticky), whilst in summer the bread was often affected by ' rope ', which rendered it exceedingly nauseous to taste and smell. On the other hand, if the flour was good the home-baked bread remained much fresher than the shop loaf of to-day, and at the end of the week was as moist and palatable as at the beginning. The leaven used for ' raising ' the bread consisted of a large lump of kneaded dough set aside from the previous batch. It was kept moist during the interval by being placed in a saucer containing a little water. By the time the next baking came round the leaven had often become green with mildew, and both looked and smelt most repulsive.[2] It was, nevertheless, mixed with the new dough, and nobody seemed any the worse. At a later date the leavening was done with barm, a bottle of which was purchased each week by the country people when they came to market. When the leaven had been mixed with dough the latter was put before the fire to

[1] Hitchens and Drew, *History of Cornwall*, I, 557.
[2] *Cornish Magazine*, II, 111.

' plummey' (rise). Old people would often throw a red petticoat over it to keep it ' extra warm '.

Bread baked on the open hearth either took the form of ' kettle ' loaves or of ' manshuns ' (French *manchet*). On one occasion, many years since, Billy Bray, the famous miner evangelist, was preaching at the Wesleyan Chapel at St Ives. The verse chosen for his text was the one beginning : ' In my Father's house are many mansions '.

' Just think of that, my friends,' exclaimed the preacher, beating the pulpit with great earnestness—' no moore bearly breed up theer, no moore sky-blue and sinker, but pure wheaten manshuns for one and all, once we get up Faather's house.' [1]

Novel as was this interpretation of the Scriptures, it was accepted with all seriousness by the greater part of the congregation in whose minds it created a vivid picture of the plenitude of Heaven. Nor was such a material view of the hereafter to be wondered at, considering the contrasting poverty of their earthly state.

' They was poor and hard times sure enough,' an old St Ives fisherman once remarked to the writer. ' Sometimes when I 'm up in the bed at night I do think back 'pon when I was a boy and wonder how we was ever dragged up at all. We had nothen to ate all the week but bearly (barley) bread, black treacle, and salt butter from Ireland. I can mind well two old women who used to sell fermades (cured pilchards) in the streets on Saturday nights. The miners was glad enough when they could get these for a few pence and car' (carry) 'em home for Sunday dennur. We scarcely saw a drop of milk in those days, unless we went out to the farms to get it, and then very often they wouldn't sell it to poor people.' [2]

This scarcity of milk in a county now noted for its dairy-farming may appear strange, but it was, none the less, a fact. Commenting on the condition of the poor in 1827 Dr Clement Carlyon wrote : ' The amount of milk eked out to them after the farmer's family and pigs and calves have been fed, is too sparing to be worth mentioning. By far the greater part of them do not taste milk, because they cannot procure it, from one end of the year to another '. [3]

[1] Per Mr R. Morton Nance.
[2] Per the late Mr Edward Basset.
[3] *Observations on the Endemic Typhus Fever of Cornwall.*

By the fifties of the last century agricultural wages in Cornwall, owing to the demand for labour in the mines, had risen in some cases to 12s. a week, thereby attracting many families from the adjoining counties of Devon and Somerset. 'These higher wages, however,' we are told by a contemporary writer, 'in no way tend to increase wealth unless the recipient has been taught to make good use of his superior advantages. Without such education the increase seems to injure rather than benefit the labourer, since it only affords him a greater opportunity of indulging his sensual appetites.' [1] Perhaps if the writer had had rather more first-hand experience of the average farm labourer's home he might have been led to modify this statement. Breakfast, at this date, almost invariably consisted of 'sky-blue and sinkers', a dish prepared in the following way. A crock-full of water having been put on to boil, a small quantity of barley flour was mixed in a basin with some 'scald' milk (i.e. milk from which the cream had previously been extracted by scalding). This was added to the water in the crock and allowed to simmer for a few minutes, after which it was poured out into basins in which sops of barley bread had been placed. These sops remained at the bottom, nothing being visible but the light-blue liquid which gave the mixture its name. In some of the smaller farms this dish remained in use within living memory, causing much indignation to the labourers who 'lived in'. On one occasion a new arrival, who had previously been accustomed to better fare, was seen to be stripping off his smock.

'Why, what in the world are 'ee doing?' asked one of the maids.

'Doing?' replied the man. 'Why I'm going to deeve (dive) into it. The bread 's down theer somewhere, I s'pose, same as there 's a bottom to the sea if you can get to it !'

Such a breakfast, whilst possessing the advantages of cheapness, was scarcely a sustaining meal for men who on it had to pursue five hours of hard manual labour till noon. 'We lived about half a mile from the mine,' wrote an old Cornishman of life in the forties, 'and I had to go home to dinner. I can assure the reader I was sometimes so feeble I could scarcely crawl along.' [2]

Dinner in the small farms and cottages consisted of fish and

[1] *Journal of the Bath and West of England Society* (1858), VI, 130.
[2] Thomas Oliver, *The Autobiography of a Cornish Miner*.

potatoes, varied occasionally by a barley pasty or potatoes
with a few bits of fat bacon. For supper there would be
barley cakes, or perhaps a pie made of stewed potatoes and
turnips, the latter ' not very fattening but sweet and plenty
tummals ', as the farm boys used to say. In large families
the children often had to go to bed hungry and fasting,
without any supper at all. This necessity was sometimes
softened by the offer of a bribe. Children would be asked :
' Who would like to have a halfpenny for going to bed without
supper to-night ? '

' Why, I will, father—and so will I—and I,' would come
the eager response.

Early the next morning, whilst the family were dressing,
the same voice would inquire from the foot of the stairs :
' Who will give a halfpenny for a pilchard for breakfast',
and the same reply would be given, though more plaintively
this time : ' I will, father, I will ! ' [1]

On Saturday nights in many of the towns soup kitchens
did a brisk trade, men and women, and children, being glad
to fill themselves up with a hot ' basin of broth ', which could
generally be procured for a halfpenny. On one occasion
a boy was regaling himself in this fashion at a stall in the
Camborne market house. He had nearly finished his portion
when he was disgusted to perceive a dead mouse at the bottom
of the basin. ' Hi—missus ! ' he shouted to the old woman
who presided over the stall, ' there 's a mouse in my broth.'

' Well, what can 'ee expect for a 'eapenny, booy, thee
dusn't expect to find a rabbit, I suppose ? ' was the ready
reply. [2]

VII

A great stand-by of the cottager in those days was the pig,
which, in Cornwall no less than Ireland, enjoyed the status
due to the ' gintleman that pays the rent '. Its flesh, moreover,

[1] W. J. P. Burton, *Bodmin Guardian*, 5 April 1928.
Another *true* story of this period is recorded by Mr J. C. Hoare, Three
children arrived at school one morning looking very ' wisht and clemmed '.
Noting this, the schoolmaster asked them if they had had any breakfast.
' Yes, sir,' was the reply. ' What did you have ? ' ' Egg broth, sir.' ' What
ever is that ? ' ' Please, sir, bits of bread soaked in the water that father's
egg was boiled in.'   [2] Per Mr Jim Thómas.

constituted a real luxury amongst those who rarely had the opportunity of tasting other meat. The story is told how a certain hard-fisted old farmer lying somewhat late abed one morning was awakened by the sound of frying proceeding from the kitchen below. Creeping downstairs he peeped into the room where he perceived one of the farm lads seated before a plate of savoury ' fry '. He was just about to enter when the boy, hearing his footsteps, hastily slipped the bacon into his hat and clapped it on his head.

' What 's that you got running down your face ? ' asked the farmer, pointing to the tell-tale streaks.

' Aw, maister,' was the reply, ' I was some laate this mornin' and I be'n sweatin' like mud trying to catch up.'

' That so, es 'a ? ' exclaimed the farmer. ' Well, I tell 'ee booy, I 've seen a man sweatin' often enough, but I never knawed one to sweat bacon grease before ! ' [1]

In the western part of the county the inhabitants of the little parish of Sancreed were formerly known as ' Sancras pigs '. This nickname was by no means as unflattering as it might now appear, since the pigs of this parish were in high demand, and of the twenty or thirty porkers who might be seen in Penzance on a market day, ' tinged ' (tied) fast by their legs to the old cross, every one would be described by its salesman as ' genuine Sancreed ! ' This reputation was due to the fact that Sancreed, alone of all the parishes in West Penwith, had no seaboard. Its pigs in consequence were ' dairy-fed ', and their pork of a much superior quality to those of the surrounding districts where the animals were fattened on fish offal and ' train ' (pilchard oil). In the towns the pigs were generally accommodated with special quarters of their own. On the slope of the hill-side, just behind Portreath, may still be seen one of the rows of little sties in which they were kept. At St Ives there were formerly two ' pig towns ', one near the breakwater, the other adjoining Venton Ia—the parish holy well. The latter has since been more completely desecrated by the local council, who have seen fit to build a public lavatory on top of it.

St Ives also still has its annual ' Fair-Mô ', or pig fair. Although this is now only a pleasure event, it is an interesting reminder of the days when pigs were of sufficient importance to the town to warrant their having a fair of their own.

Elsewhere than in the towns the pigs' ' crows ' (sties) were

[1] Per Mr R. J. Noall.

generally erected in close proximity to the house. Not infrequently it happened that, owing to a miscalculation on the part of the amateur builders, the pig had to be killed when only half fat because it had outgrown its quarters. On these occasions one-half of the carcass was sent to market to fetch a little ready money, whilst the remainder was cured for the use of the family who, by dint of careful management, often contrived to lay in a stock of twenty score of bacon and hams yearly.

Young sucking pigs were known to the Cornish people as ' veers ', but after the age of six or eight weeks were referred to as ' slips '. Sixty or seventy years ago ' a nice little slip which could be put in a bag and carried on the shoulder ' would be worth about 16s.[1] These found a ready sale amongst those who had just killed their porkers, and were on the look out for fresh stock. Such were the temptations of poverty, however, that there were some who were not above *stealing* the carcass of a pig if they saw the opportunity. On one occasion an old couple living near St Ives, who had slaughtered their animal, left it hanging in the cart-house to ' harden up ' overnight. Next morning when they came down the pig was gone ! The police were informed, and their suspicions rested upon a family living a few miles away. A search was accordingly made of their premises, but without result. A short time after the police had departed, the family in question were seen to be hard at work in their garden. In the course of removing some newly-planted bushes and digging a little into the soft earth, the carcass of a newly-slaughtered pig was revealed, neatly wrapped in a bed sheet. Needless to say the police were not informed of this very unusual ' treasure-trove ' !

When a pig was killed the Cornish people had a use for everything ' except the squeal '. The legs of the animal were either salted for boiling or used fresh for ' pig-toe ' or ' knuckle ' pie. Of the latter it was popularly said that they contained enough bones to throw at every man's door in the parish. The pudding skins were often presented by the owners to those who had contributed towards the animal's upkeep by providing it with their household scraps. The ' big pot ' was well cleaned, then filled with pastry and roasted in a dish with meat and potatoes. The ' small pot ', after thorough cleaning by being turned inside out with a special

[1] J. C. Hoare, MS.

stick, was made into 'tresses' and boiled till tender. These tresses when cold were cut into half-inch lengths for 'gurty' meat. This was made by putting the strips into a pie-dish in which rice or 'gurts' had previously been cooked in milk. The mixture was then salted and peppered to taste, and baked until nicely brown.[1]

Hog's pudding was, and still is, another popular dish. In the olden days, however, the blood of the pig was sometimes added to this, in which case the preparation was known as 'bloody pudding'—a description eminently suited to it.

'Scrolls' or 'scollops' proved another favourite dish which was often served for supper. These were sold in the towns at the general provision shops, the owners of which used to melt down bacon fat to make 'mord' (lard). The tiny pieces into which the crinkly rind was chopped formed the scrolls. 'On Saturday evenings,' writes Mr William Paynter, 'the shop was often crowded with children sent by their parents for a "ha'p'orth of scrolls", and they could be seen coming out, carefully carrying little paper cornets filled with the hot, greasy dainty which in those hard times served to make many a simple meal more palatable than it would otherwise have been.'[2]

Finally, it may be mentioned that a use was found even for the gall, which was carefully preserved in a bottle and applied as a remedy for cuts and bruises.[3]

VIII

Whilst the poor of the earlier part of the last century lived hardly enough, amongst the more easily circumstanced farmers diet was on a plain but generous scale. 'Not many years ago,' wrote Polwhele in 1816, 'were seen on the hospitable board (and they are not yet banished from the halls of gentlemen-farmers) the fresh-boiled buttock of cow-beef with sippets and onions, the squab pye, the leek and pork pye —on which clouted cream was profusely poured—the goose and parsnip, and the fish and apple pye. At some houses in

[1] J. C. Hoare, MS.
[2] *Old St Ives*, 24.
[3] Per Mrs Stanley James.

West Cornwall the *dash-an-darras* or stirrup cup is scarcely even now out of fashion.' [1]

On the open hearths of such houses barley loaves to the number of twenty or thirty were often baked at one time. Four gallons of blackberries frequently went into the making of tarts for a single meal, whilst a gallon or two of potatoes, baked beneath the ashes and eaten by the light of a ' screech of furze ', served the household as a mere snack before retiring. In the larder of such establishments stood the ' cool ' or salting trough, hewn in many cases out of a great block of granite, and capable of holding anything up to twelve hundred pounds of home-cured pork. These were the days, it must be remembered, when, in addition to families of a dozen or more children and ' maids ' to help about the house, the unmarried farm hands also lived in and took their meals with the family.

When the time came to prepare for the great day of the year —the parish feast—what a sight there was to greet the lover of good cheer ! Some faint idea of the work which this entailed upon the housewife may be gathered from the fact that the latter had often to provide an average of four slices of bread a day for some forty persons of all ages, for a week on end. The bread on these occasions was made by all households who could afford it with wheaten flour, in contrast to the barley used at other times. In addition to the baking of bread, great batches of saffron cake, ' seedy ' cake, potato cake, pasties, ' fuggans ', and gingerbreads had also to be prepared. In some cases a single buttermilk cake, as large as a coster's cart-wheel, and requiring two women to carry it, would be cooked to itself beneath one huge ' baker '. In the midst of all this activity, might be seen the farmer's wife in her close-fitting muslin cap as, with her arms bare to the elbow, she kneaded the huge batches of dough ; whilst one of the maids ran back and forth to the dairy and ' spence ' (larder), bringing in the ' raw ' (fresh) milk, the butter and cream, the eggs, the currants, the nutmeg, and the ' sponge ' or home-made yeast.

Whilst this work was going forward indoors, the farmer himself would be busy preparing the newly-slaughtered lambs which had been specially fattened for the feast. To provide the quantity of ' lammy ' pie necessary for households such as this, as many as four great dishes were often used, these

[1] *History of Cornwall*, VIII, 137.

being lined with a ' bottom ' of pastry a good inch thick.
On to this was put a layer of lamb, well seasoned with pepper
and salt ; then a layer of shredded parsley ; then more lamb ;
and so on, until the dish was full, when thin cream was poured
over the whole, and the top crust put on. The ' sweet '
course which followed usually consisted of a number of
immense puddings, made from rice boiled in raw milk, with
plenty of cream, eggs, and sugar.[1]

Though the cottagers, of course, were unable to make their
preparations on such a scale as this, every household at that
time kept up the feast to the utmost limit of its means. The
following quotation shows how a prosperous miner and his
friends celebrated this occasion at St Just in the early years
of the last century.

' About two o'clock the feasters (who had been sent off to
church in the morning in order to give the women of the
household room for the cooking) came home and found the
big crock lifted off the brandis (trivet) on to the hearth.
In this large vessel were boiled a rump of beef, a couple of
fowls, and a nice piece of streaky pork to eat with them ;
as well as turnips, carrots, and other vegetables, all in kipps
(net bags) to keep them separate and for convenience in
taking up. When ready the vegetables were put to drain
on bars called " kipp-sticks ", placed across the crock ; the
beef was dished up on a round pewter platter ; whilst the fowls
were provided with a sauce of butter and parsley. On the
chimney stool was a rabbit pie, steaming hot ; whilst a baked
figgy (plum) pudding lay on the dresser, turned out of its
baker on to another pewter platter, and powdered over with
white sugar. On one end of the hearth, over a few embers,
stood a little pot, the very model of the large crock, but not
more than a tenth of its size, containing choice red apply
potatoes, steaming under a cloth. If the feasters didn't make
a good dinner it was from no fault of their hosts, for it was
" cut and come again " till all declared they were " choke full
and ready to burst ". Then they had a nip of brandy all
round to settle their stomachs. Jugs of hot toddy were next
placed on the board, with a little tray of shag tobacco and long
pipes. Crocks and pans being put away the fire was gathered
to one end of the hearth, fresh turfs put on, the chimney-stool
put back to its place in the other end of the roomy hearth
so that those who liked best to smoke in the chimney corner

[1] See Mrs Bonham, *A Corner of Old Cornwall*.

might sit there. The men being made as comfortable as their hearts could desire, the females of the party went upstairs to have a cosy chat to themselves ; and there they had a bottle of old sweet-drink (mead) which had been kept for the feast. " Don't 'ee believe it that they ever went short of plenty of good drink in those roaring times, when there was none of your cussed boatmen sneaking about, trying to hinder one from having good brandy from France." '[1]

The ' Santusters ' (parishioners of St Just-in-Penwith) have always been especially noted for the generous nature of their feasts, and it must not be supposed that the latter were celebrated everywhere with the same munificence. In many parishes the inhabitants obviously found it hard to make show of a feast at all. It was a common gibe in mid-Cornwall that the good folk of St Dennis had on one occasion entertained their guests with ' sloney ' (sloe) pie, a fruit which is generally considered more acceptable to the eye than to the palate. So long was this story remembered against them that until recent times to screw up one's mouth and to mention sloes to a St Dennis man was regarded as offering the deadliest insult. Stithians, likewise, is not a rich parish, and its feast was best remembered from the lampoon of some ungrateful guest :

> St'ans bugs, leathern jugs,
> Sour milk and whey,
> Maggots boilin' in the crock,
> Sti'ans feasten day !

Stithians people, however, have long ago had the good sense to overlook this affront, especially since it was discovered that other parishes would fit equally well into the rhyme :

> St Just bugs, leathern jugs,
> Curdey milk and whey,
> Boil the maggots in the crock
> On Allan'[2] feasten day.

[1] W. Bottrell, *Tales and Hearthside Traditions of West Cornwall*, I, 143.
[2] Often called ' Hallantide ', St Just feast being held on the nearest Sunday to All-Hallows '. It is said that more apples are still sold in this parish on the Saturday of the feast than in almost the whole of the rest of the year ; it being the custom for every child and not a few adults to take an apple to bed with them on the night preceding the feast. The fruit is consumed either before sleeping or immediately on awaking the next morning.

is another variant which, although somewhat inappropriate in this case, probably originated with some Stithians patriot.[1]

In addition to beer and spirits many varieties of home-brewed liquor were formerly consumed in Cornwall. Amongst these were ' metheglin ' or mead, blackberry wine, elder wine, gilliflower wine, cowslip wine, parsnip wine, sloe gin, and ' mahogany '. The latter, sometimes known as ' black-strap ', derived its name from its colour. It was composed of two parts of gin and one of treacle, the mixture being well beaten together. The recipe for making this drink was referred to by Mr Eliot, of Port Eliot, at a dinner party given on one occasion by Sir Joshua Reynolds. Boswell, ever eager for new experiences, expressed a desire to taste it, and a brew was accordingly made under Mr Eliot's supervision. ' I thought it,' wrote Boswell, ' very good liquor ; and said it was a counterpart of what is called *Athol Porridge* in the Highlands of Scotland, which is a mixture of whisky and honey. Johnson said : " That must be a better liquor than the Cornish, for both its component parts are better ". He also observed : " *Mahogany* must be a modern name ; for it is not long since the wood called mahogany was known in this country ".' [2]

Mahogany was highly esteemed by the fishermen, on account of its warming properties. Thomas Bond, in his *History of Looe* (1823), tells how at one of the Cornish Assizes a witness, asked what he had been doing at a certain place, puzzled both judge and learned counsel by stating that he had been ' eating fair-maids (cured pilchards) and drinking mahogany ' !

A favourite drink of the Cornish people at Christmas time was ' shenagrum '. The way in which this was prepared varied slightly in different localities. The most usual method was to bring to the boil half a pint of home-brewed beer, adding to it a half-noggin of pure Jamaica rum, a slice of lemon, and soft brown sugar and grated nutmeg to taste. The mixture was served hot and ' in the good old days ' was sold in the public-houses for 6d. a glass. The word ' shenagrum ' or ' schnagram ', ' schnack ', ' shenackerum ', etc., for it is variously spelt, is explained by Mr Morton Nance

[1] Many parishes had their own special feast-tide dishes which were not commonly found elsewhere. Amongst these are reputed to have been ' ram pie ' at Golant, ' canary duff ' at St Austell, ' white-pot and hollick ' at Lanlivery. See *Western Antiquary*, VI, 299.

[2] *Life of Johnson*, 30 March 1781.

as being a distortion (no doubt under the influence of the drink itself) of the once familiar dog-Latin expression *super naculum*—' on the nail '.   ' In the sixteenth century,' he writes, ' when this phrase first appeared in England, it was used in connection with a custom of reversing the glass and letting its last remaining drop fall on the thumb nail, whence it was licked to show that the liquor was not shirked. A little later we find it used of any drink so excellent and rare that no drop of it should be wasted and, still later, an adjective, " supernacular ", was coined to describe such a drink.' [1]

Although Cornwall is no longer a cider county, its decaying orchards bear witness to the fact that this drink was once as popular in the Duchy as it still is in Devonshire.   A hundred years ago almost every substantial farm possessed its own cider ' press ' and, with a good crop of apples, the household was provided with an abundant supply of this wholesome liquor.   ' Siah Penpol,' wrote Mr Bath in his book entitled *Uncle Kit's Legacy*, ' was one of those old-fashioned people who always put a toad into the cask of cider, and by that means the refreshing drink seemed to be purified by passing again and again through the creature's body.   Indeed, no cider was considered up to the mark unless it had a toad to " work " it.'   That this extraordinary practice was once general appears to be an established fact.   Tradition, indeed, affirms that toads sometimes lived for over twenty years in this fermenting work. When the cask was empty the creature would be tipped out through the bunghole and the people standing by would exclaim : ' Mind the toad, mind the toad, save 'un up for the next brewen' ! '

IX

During the last thirty years or more the food of the Cornish people has undergone a considerable change, and many of the old-time recipes described in this chapter have been discarded or forgotten.   In a great measure this is due to the increase of ' chain ' provision shops, wherein food of a single standardized type is now retailed throughout the country.   Nevertheless it is true to say that a sufficient number of ' local ' items still figure in the Cornishman's diet to cause the stranger to realize that once over the Tamar he is in a land which does not yet

[1] *Western Morning News*, 23 February 1929.

entirely conform to English ways. These differences will not be apparent, of course, to those who pass their time in the hotels or boarding-houses of the summer resorts. Only those who go from village to village on foot and who live as the people live, will discern in food, as in many other matters, those features which still distinguish life in Cornwall from that of other shires. To take the most obvious example, where else but in a Cornish cottage can food of such distinctive character be met with to-day as pilchards, scalded cream, and saffron cake ?

How excellent the pilchard can be when served in Cornwall is no new discovery on the part of strangers. Three centuries ago Fuller commended the ' fumadoe ',[1] eaten with oil and lemon, ' as being meat for the mightiest Don in Spain '. The fumadoe indeed, or ' fair-maid ', is now a wellnigh forgotten delicacy, but the old method of ' marinating ' pilchards by cooking them in a dish with vinegar, spice, and bay leaves is still very common. Strange as this preparation may sound, when eaten in moderate quantities with bread and butter and tea, it forms a pleasant adjunct to a meal —at least to Cornish palates. For the average Cornishman still resembles his forebears in loving ' a bit of savour ' with his tea. ' I was visiting a woman once who did not respond very freely to the religion I put before her,' wrote an old parish worker towards the close of the last century. ' She did not say " Hallelujah ", neither did she " praise the Lord ". She sat uninterested. I read on and at last I came to the words : " Man shall not live by bread alone "—immediately the old woman's face brightened, and she leaned forward. " Ais," she said, " I do belaive that. 'Tes what I always say —give me a savour to my tay, if 'tes only a bit of nifflin (Newfoundland cod)." '[2]

Along with the desire for something savoury goes the constant craving for tea, a pot of which accompanies every meal. In former times, when tea was very dear, and a luxury which had to be partaken of sparingly, the frequent indulgence in a ' leak of tay water ' did little harm. Nowadays, tea in the cottages is a very different matter, harsh and black with strength, and frequently stewed on the ' slab ' until its bitterest essence is extracted.

Another favourite accompaniment to the Cornish ' high

[1] Pilchards (originally) dried in smoke, to preserve them.
[2] *Cornish Magazine*, I, 467.

tea' is heavy cake. This is composed of flour, mixed with butter (or sour cream), currants, and a pinch of salt. The dough is rolled out flat, and its surface generally scored in diamond shapes before being baked in a quick oven. Heavy cake, when 'made up light' by a good cook, is by no means as indigestible as its name would signify.

Tarts made from apple, blackberry, whortleberry, and the like are somewhat differently prepared in Cornwall from other parts of England. The fruit here is generally cooked in a soup plate or round shallow dish. When ready the pastry cover is taken off and laid bottom side up on a plate. The fruit is then mixed with sugar, and spread out over the pastry, cream being usually added. In serving, the tart is cut in wedge-shaped portions like a cake.

Setting aside the pasty, the two articles of diet which probably strike the visitor to-day as being most characteristically Cornish are cream and saffron cake. Concerning the origin of scalded cream, and the reason why its making should be almost confined to the two western counties of Cornwall and Devon, speculation has long been rife. There are some who hold that the practice is derived from the Phœnician merchants who in ancient times are supposed to have traded with the Cornish people for tin. If this be the case it clearly places the men of Devon in the position of borrowers rather than originators of this popular delicacy, since no influence, so far as the writer is aware, has ever been claimed for the Phœnicians in Devon. To a Cornishman, therefore, the statement made by Mr Elihu Burritt in 1865 that he had discovered that 'most delectable of luxuries, Devonshire cream', being made at St Germans, reads a little strangely. Nor can he do other than smile at the many visitors who still persist in asking for 'Devonshire cream' in Cornwall. But when all is said and done, these are academic points, and it is not so much where cream originated as where it may be eaten which concerns most people. Moreover, in these degenerate days, the real credit is due to those who continue to make scalded cream whether they dwell in Cornwall or in Devon. For, surprising as it may appear, the genuine cream is now quite unobtainable on the majority of West Country farms, where of late years the machine separator has ousted the old method of scalding. True, the top of the cream often bears a clotted appearance when served at table, but though the practice of scalding *after* separation may satisfy the visitor, it is far otherwise with the Cornishman who knows what the flavour and consistency of the genuine article should be.

Of course, the old method entailed far more labour. In the first place the new milk, after straining, had to stand for a matter of twelve or even twenty-four hours, whilst the cream was rising to the surface. Then each of the pans had to be slowly heated over the fire until the cream began to show a raised ring around the edge. When sufficiently scalded the pans had again to be taken back to the dairy, where they stood for another twelve hours or more in order to allow the firm, yellow crust to settle. Great care was required in moving the pans to and from the fire, to prevent the 'ream' being broken. By many people a turf fire was preferred, the cream thereby acquiring a subtle peaty flavour. This, whilst it might not be universally regarded as an improvement, was preferable to the slight oiliness often discernible in the separated product.

One would not claim, of course, an equal preference for *all* the older methods of the dairy. There appears little to be said in favour, for instance, of the former practice of taking up the cream with the fingers instead of with the, one trusts, more frequently washed skimmer! The churn, too, for making butter is another very welcome innovation, saving as it does the long mixing by hand in hot weather. In many of the old farms the dairies also served the purpose of a general store-room, and contained the winter stock of apples, potatoes, pilchards, and pork. In consequence of this the butter itself, by the time it came to be eaten, was often tinctured with a variety of flavours.

In the small dairy farms, moreover, the butter had often to be kept for a considerable time, till a sufficient quantity had accumulated to make it worth while taking to market. To maintain its freshness in the interval the old people would 'land it down the plump' (i.e. place it in the well). When at length it was retrieved from this position it had often acquired a distinctly grey appearance. But then, as an old woman once explained to a more than usually fastidious customer: 'Anyone but a fool or bucca (scarecrow) do know you must expect grey butter from a grey cow!'

The Cornish custom of using saffron in cakes has proved, like that of scalding cream, to be a subject for much learned controversy. There is little occasion, however, to attribute the use of saffron in Cornwall to Phœnician influences, seeing that the crocus flower was once commonly employed throughout England as in other parts of Europe for giving colour and flavour to cakes. The calling of ' safforn ' is referred to by Lydgate [1] as a familiar London street-cry in the middle of the fifteenth century, whilst the town of Saffron Walden in Essex derives its name from the culture of the saffron plant which was once its principal industry.

But although in earlier times the use of saffron was certainly not *confined* to Cornwall, it has survived in the Duchy long after its abandonment elsewhere, and during the last half-century has been carried out by Cornish people into almost every corner of the globe. It is said that in the early days of the Cornish emigration to the Rand the curiosity of the postal authorities at Johannesburg was aroused by the number of strange-smelling packets passing through their hands. At length, an order was given that one of these should be opened. On inspection its contents were adjudged to be a rank poison, and the package was accordingly returned to the sender, accompanied by a stern warning pointing out the nature of the offence. The officials, however, were soon destined to learn more of the ways of Cornishmen, and twenty years later, when almost every family in the mining districts of Cornwall owned some member working on the Reef, the amount of saffron which yearly found its way to the goldfields must have been worth a small fortune.

So rapidly, however, are fashions changing that even in Cornwall to-day genuine saffron cake is not always obtainable in the shops. In place of the deliciously scented extract of the crocus, a highly coloured concoction is now being marketed which possesses no taste whatever, and is made from one knows not what. The Cornish people themselves, indeed, no longer appear to hold their saffron cake in the same regard as formerly, and at the chapel gatherings and Sunday school ' treats ' its place is surely, if slowly, being taken by the cheaper varieties of ' fancy ' cakes now sold in the multiple shops.

There are those, of course, who will say that this is as well, for the food of the Duchy has had its critics no less than its admirers. To parody Pope's epigram :

> '*Tis with digestions as our watches, none*
> *Go just alike, yet each believes his own !*

[1] *The London Lyckpenny.*

Strong tea and saffron cake, hoggans and pasties, pilchards and cream 'content not all stomackes' alike; and there are always some who are ready to condemn as poison the meat which has proved unkindly to themselves.

In truth it *would* sometimes appear as if there must be some special providence appointed to keep guard over Cornish digestions. Not long since a working-man described to the writer how he had woken up one morning feeling 'very slight'. As soon as he 'got out the bed', the walls seemed turning round and round before his eyes, and he felt so dizzy that he could hardly stand. After consultation with his wife he decided that he 'wouldn't ate no breakfast', and merely contented himself with a cup of strong tea. All the morning whilst at his work he continued to feel 'slight', and when dinner-time came 'he couldn't ate nothen moore than a bit of cold pasty'. After that, strange to say, he felt much better. On his arrival home in the evening he found that his 'missus' had prepared a nice dish of marinated pilchards for their tea. This, he affirmed, was just what he wanted, so he ate up the whole of his share, and after drinking a few more cups of tea went to bed early and arose next morning feeling as gay as a lark.

Strangers, tempted to adopt such measures, may not always find themselves so fortunate in the result. The latter, therefore, will probably continue to complain that Cornish cream is too rich, pilchards too greasy, and pasties too heavy. No doubt they are right in their own case, but let those who think differently say with Mr Morgan Anthony:

> *Good luck to all the Cornish booys*
> *That niver yet was baiten,*
> *A paasty may they niver want*
> *Nor stummicks for to ait 'n !*

One can hardly do better than leave it at that, adding only this one rejoinder to the critics. If Cornish food is unwholesome, it none the less managed to sustain a singularly hardy race of men in the past—miners, who walked six miles to work, put in eight hours' 'loustering' labour underground, and returned home unspent in the evening; farmers who laboured from dawn to dusk bending double over the sickle, or wheeling three hundred barrow-loads of manure on to the fields in a day; fishermen who toiled throughout winter nights in open boats amidst the freezing spray. Bread and pastry they consumed in vast quantities, but the flour of which it was made was coarse and brown and consequently digestible. Their fish came to them straight from the sea, whilst tinned ' delicacies ' were happily unknown. Chocolates and sweet cakes were alike unheard of, with the result that, although tooth brushes were conspicuous by their absence, and they knew no dentist beyond the local blacksmith, they had serviceable teeth.

Granted all this, it may yet be true that that which was the proper diet for one generation may not necessarily serve the next. Those who have exchanged the pick and hammer for the typewriter and pen, who have gone in from the rain and sunshine to sit at office desks, and whose feet no longer carry them beyond the starting points of omnibus or train, should perhaps be content to taste in imagination only the food which sustained their forefathers under such very different circumstances of life.

THE RURAL CALENDAR

I

OF all the pleasant customs and festivities which served to enliven the workaday life of old Cornwall, those of the harvest-tide probably provided the greatest amount of happiness for the poor. Not but what this season entailed strenuous toil for young and old, since prior to the introduction of the mechanical reaper and the other labour-saving devices possessed by the modern farmer, the harvest often lasted for a period of six weeks. During this time almost every man, woman, and child would come to the farmer's aid, expecting little in return save the abundance of food and drink which the latter invariably provided. Nor did this apply only to the purely agricultural population. At such times even the fishermen would leave their boats, whilst many of the miners on coming up from underground would go straight to the harvest field, labouring there till darkness came, in return only for their food and the gift of a few shillings when the corn was finally gathered in. It is a noteworthy fact that the depression in mining which set in during the seventies of the last century, so far from providing the farmers with a surplus of cheap labour, as they expected, resulted, owing to emigration, in a scarcity of labour, from which they have suffered to a greater or lesser extent ever since.

In earlier times, it is true, the actual reaping was done for the most part by women with the ' hook ' (sickle), an occupation in which many of them were extraordinarily expert. Bending nearly double, the procession of reapers might be seen taking their way down the full length of a field, never stopping for an instant till the end was reached, when they would walk back to the starting side once more. So they would continue, from early morning till ten o'clock ' croust ' time. A brief rest, a mug of cider, and a piece of ' fuggan ' (raisin cake) all round, and the women would be off once more, toiling beneath the sweltering sun till dinner-time. After an hour's interval work would be resumed, and so would proceed with only another brief croust time at four, till the shades of evening fell. Most of the reapers of those days were grand women, splendidly developed, healthy, and active ; but for those to whom Nature had been less kind, the pace was a killing one.

Behind the women came the men, clad in blue or white linen trousers and thin loose shirts. Dexterously twisting the straw binders round the armfuls of corn, they tossed them quickly over, gave a strong pull each way, pitched in the ends, and threw down the sheaves upon the ' arrish ' (stubble). Last in the procession came the children garnering the remains of the corn into ' riskans ' (little bundles).

On some farms, even at this date, the work of reaping was performed entirely by men using specially made hooks of extended length. Skilled labourers of this sort, of whom a dozen or more might sometimes be seen at work in one field, would cut down an acre of corn a day per man, using each hand alternately and urging forward the accumulating burden until they had enough for a sheaf. The latter were bound up by women, one of whom was allotted to every two reapers. As the sheaves were laid aside the boys stood ready to carry them off to the ' setters up '. The latter were generally old men, who exercised their skill in placing the sheaves in the proper position necessary for forming the ' shocks '.[1] Despite the tremendous amount of back-breaking labour necessitated by

[1] Lawrence Maker, *Western Morning News*, 23 September 1929.

such a method of harvesting, the work was sustained with a cheerful good humour which showed that its appeal was not merely confined to the lover of the picturesque, but was shared in some measure by the harvesters themselves. It was indeed considered by many people to be an unseemly innovation when the hook was at length supplanted by the scythe and the work of reaping became henceforth confined to men only.

As time went on labourers who had acquired a special reputation for their skill as scythe-men, would be engaged by the farmers several weeks in advance of the harvest. Remuneration for this seasonal work was at the unusually high rate of about £4 a month; with unlimited beer, cider, and the man's food during the period in which he was employed. A week or two before the harvest began the reapers might be seen in the evenings busily engaged in grinding their scythes and setting them at the right angle to the ' snead ' (handle). The men took great pride in the quality of their blades and would often boast of the distance which they would cut without whetting. The ' sharping ' stones themselves were no less carefully selected and preserved. Some scythes had wooden frames or ' crooks ' fitted on to the blade, for the purpose of casting barley or oats more evenly into the swath. On large farms as many as eighteen reapers might sometimes be seen cutting down a field of wheat, each one bending forward to his stroke in perfect unison, like men rowing a boat. These would be followed by an equal number of women or boys taking out the corn, whilst others in the rear bound it into sheaves.

It was reckoned that a first-rate scythe-man could reap as much as two acres in a day. Tremendous rivalry existed amongst these picked labourers as to who should lead the reaping and set the pace which the others were to follow. At a certain farm in St Keverne a man named Pentecost had long claimed this place of honour. One harvest-tide, however another reaper arrived on the scene who also fancied himself for his strength of wind and muscle, and who insisted that he could set a better pace. With the red flag which denoted the leader fixed to the handle of his scythe, the new reaper started off. Overhead was a broiling sun and a sky like brass, whilst the wheat that year was admitted to be particularly heavy. Half-way down the two-hundred-yard field the leader's strength began to fail.

'Hold on a minute, booys,' he called over his shoulder, 'lev' us stop and draw breath.'

'Stop !' cried Pentecost, who was reaping second ; 'I tell 'ee, booy, if thee 'st stop for a moment I'll cut the scythe through thy ankles !'[1]

The leader knew that this threat was no empty one, and on to the end of the field he had to go, though his back was well-nigh breaking. There were many men of the type of Pentecost in those days, men who prided themselves so much on their strength that they would go to the local 'hammer mills' to have outsize shovels specially made for their use, and who were accustomed, when loading wheat, to carry a 'Cornish bushel' sack of 180 lb. under each arm. In the evenings and on half-holidays these same men would attend the local wrestling matches, where they bore away all the prizes. True, in the end many of them developed ruptures, and compara- tively few attained old age, but they recked little of these consequences whilst they were still in the pride of their youthful strength.

The cutting of the last few handfuls of standing corn in the harvest field was marked by a ceremony known as ' crying the neck.' Gathering towards the centre of the field, the harvesters would divide into three bands, and as the reaper severed the last swath and raised it high above his head, the first group would call forth in stentorian tones : ' We have it ! We have it ! We have it !' to which the second demanded : ' What 'av 'ee ? What 'av 'ee ? What 'av 'ee ?' the third replying : ' A neck ! A neck ! A neck !' Then all, together, joined in shouting : ' Hip ! Hip ! Hip ! Hurrah ! Hurrah for the neck ! Hurrah for Mr ——' (the farmer), and so on ; whilst amidst laughter and tumult the neck-cutting buns were consumed and jars of cider or beer were emptied to the relief of parched throats.

Immediately after this part of the ceremony the neck was plaited and dressed with cornflowers, poppies, betony, etc., and carried off at top speed to the farm-house kitchen. Here it was suspended in a place of honour over the chimney-piece, until it was supplanted by a new neck in the following year. On some farms, however, the neck was kept only until Christ- mas Day, when it was given as a token of esteem to the best milch cow. On one occasion a certain miserly farmer, who had given orders for this to be done, was surprised on going

[1] Per Mr Jewell Hill.

out into the ' town-place ' (farmyard) to find the neck thrust
up the spout of the old-fashioned pump.

' Why, what in the world did 'ee want to put 'un theer
for ? ' inquired the farmer of his man.

' Aw, maister, I allus thoft that was the best milch cow *you*
ever had,' was the ready reply.

On the evening of the day on which the neck was cut, the
harvesters would repair to the farm-house kitchen. Here the
numerous company, often consisting of thirty or more persons,
in addition to the farmer's own family, would sit down to a
substantial meal of broiled pork and potatoes brought in in a
crock capable of holding twelve or fourteen gallons. The
second course generally consisted of apple pie, cream, and
' fuggans ', the whole being washed down with cider and
spirits or (more recently) strong-brewed tea.

The ceremony of crying the neck was one of those happy
survivals from the primitive past which formerly endowed
the harvest with much of its interest and charm. ' On a fine
still autumn evening,' stated a Devonshire writer, in the earlier
part of the last century, ' the crying of the neck has a wonderful
effect. I have once or twice heard upwards of twenty men cry
it, sometimes joined by an equal number of female voices.
About three years back, on some high grounds where our
people were harvesting, I heard six or seven " necks " cried
in one night, although I know that some of them were four
miles off. They are heard through the quiet evening air at
great distances sometimes.' [1] Mrs Bray similarly describes
how on one occasion when travelling in Devonshire she saw
a party of reapers standing in a circle on a rising ground,
holding their sickles aloft. ' One in the middle held up some
ears of corn, tied together with flowers, and the party shouted
three times : " A neck, a neck, a neck ; we have 'n, we have 'n,
we have 'n ". They then went home, accompanied by women
and children carrying flowers and shouting and singing.' The
manservant who attended Mrs Bray said ' it was only the
people making their games, as they always did, " *to the spirit
of harvest* " '.[2]

How widespread was this custom among primitive peoples
is shown by Sir James Frazer in the *Golden Bough*. The number
of instances therein adduced ' leave no room to doubt ', he
writes, ' the meaning of the Devonshire and Cornish expression

[1] Hone, *Every Day Book*, 1826.
[2] *Legends of the Tamar and Tavy*.

" the neck " as applied to the last sheaf. The " corn-spirit " is herein conceived in human or animal form, and the last standing corn is part of its body—its neck, its head, or its tail as it is variously described in different parts of the world. Amongst the many animals whose forms the corn-spirit is supposed to take are the wolf, dog, hare, fox, cock, goose, quail, cat; goat, cow (ox, bull), pig, and horse '.[1]

Whilst Sir James Frazer's theory has not found full acceptance amongst all anthropologists, there is little reason to doubt that some such belief as he has described was originally responsible for the veneration with which the last swath of standing corn was treated. It is curious, therefore, to reflect that the introduction of the mechanical reaper should have alone sufficed within a few years to snap this link which formerly united the harvesters of Cornwall with those of almost every nation of the earth and of all time. For it is only within the last thirty or forty years that the custom of crying the neck has ceased to be observed in the Duchy. For centuries before its abandonment, the origin and meaning of the ceremony was, doubtless, but little understood by the people who took part in it, yet whilst it survived the link with the immemorial past was there. To those who had ears to hear, the voice of the harvesters uplifted in the stillness of a summer's night brought home to the imagination the ' oneness ' of all the peoples of the earth and the nature of Man's first supplication as it must be his last : ' Give us this day our daily bread '.

Thanks in a large measure to the initiative of the St Ives Old Cornwall Society, the crying of the neck was heard once again, at Mr Hugh Dunstan's farm at Towednack, in the summer of 1928. Although only a revival on that occasion, yet among those who were present many must have experienced a sense of the old solemnity which lent to the picturesque little ceremony a dignity not unworthy of its agelong tradition. Whether, as was hoped, the remembrance of it could be perpetuated by an occasional revival [2] such as this time alone

---

[1] In support of this, it is interesting to note that in the parish of Buryan, near the Land's End, the neck was still known but a short time since by the Celtic-Cornish name *pedn-yar* (hen's head).

[2] ' The Crying of the Neck has been carried out twice within this last few years, at Gweek Wartha and Gweek Wollasby, by Mr Thomas Richards and myself. How much our combined ages are over one hundred and forty years, I won't tell 'ee, but we can both jump a five-bar gate— if he was laid flat on the ground.'—T. Boulden, *Western Morning News,* 7 September 1931.

will prove, but in any case it is in the highest degree improbable that the crying of the neck will ever again become a regular feature of the harvest-tide in Cornwall.

II

Soon after the neck had been cut, the corn was made up into 'shocks'. This was done by setting one sheaf in an upright position, placing two others on either side of it, then adding two more 'on the cross'. The gaps or 'opes' were filled in with four more sheaves, whilst an additional one was sometimes put fanwise on the top to 'shed' the rain. If, however, bad weather was anticipated, the corn was placed as quickly as possible into 'arrish' or 'hand' mows. These resembled enlarged shocks continued upwards as high as a man could reach from the ground. 'Knee' mows were still bigger, and consisted of a solid cone of sheaves, rising to a height of about twelve feet, with the 'beards' turned inwards, and the butt-ends only exposed to the weather. The upper portions were laid on by a boy to whom the sheaves were pitched from below, and who went round the top on his knees building them up in a circular form. The cone thus made was finished off by inverting one or two sheaves and tying down their bearded ends to the side of the mow.[1] In this way corn was sometimes left to stand in the fields till Christmas, with little chance of damage save possibly from rats.

The 'arrish' (i.e. stubble-field) mow is said to be confined to Cornwall and Devon, and owed its origin to the damp and uncertain climate of these counties. When the weather permitted, however, the corn was carried soon after the harvest in the usual way. A century ago, when the temperance movement in Cornwall was still in its infancy, the storing of the corn in the rickyard was associated with a considerable amount of drinking. Thus it was customary for the man who pitched the first sheaf on to the rick to receive a wineglass of neat gin, a similar allowance being made to the man who placed it in position. When the rick had attained the required height for the 'head' to be made, a number of voices would be heard singing out : 'The ring ! The ring !' at which signal another

[1] W. J. Charke, *Old Cornwall*, second series, II, 7–8.

wineglass of gin was given to all present. Finally, when the topmost or 'crow' sheaf was about to be laid in position, the builder would call out loudly : ' The crow ! The crow !' on which further drinks were provided all round for the finish.[1]

On some farms in north Cornwall it was customary for the builder of the rick to hold the crow sheaf aloft in one hand and a jug of beer in the other, shouting as he did so : ' Crow ! Crow ! Crow ! Crow sheaf we got here ! Time to drink strong beer !'

The rick itself was built on a rough framework of boards, raised some three or four feet above the ground on ' steads '. These consisted of conical-shaped stones capped by flat circular pieces which gave them the appearance of gigantic toadstools. The purpose of the steads was to prevent the rats and other vermin from gaining access to the ricks. The latter were protected from the weather by a thatching of ' reed ' (corn straw) or rushes, bound down with straw ropes. In exposed places nets of rope were often drawn over the whole and weighted at the sides with stones.

When at length the last sheaf had been carried into the mowhay and the precious corn was saved, all those who had taken part in the harvesting would be invited by the farmer to a grand supper. Special reference is made by Richard Carew to these harvest suppers as long ago as 1602. It seems strange, however, that at that date, when the Cornish language was still widely spoken, Carew should not have referred to them by their Celtic name, *Gôl Deis*, ' feast of ricks ', seeing that this title or its variant forms ' Gooldize ', ' Goolandize ', ' Dicklydize ',[2] etc., obtains in West Cornwall to this day.

No livelier picture can be found of one of these suppers than that given by Mr Charles Bath in his account of a Dicklydize held by a certain Uncle Kit Penpol at Burrow Downs Farm. ' At the head of the table,' he writes, ' sat Kit himself, carving-knife in hand, and before him were laid out boiled beef, boiled mutton, cold ham, and chicken enough to satisfy the wants of three sittings of twenty-five in number.'

The utmost simplicity was wont to rule among the guests

---

[1] Charles Bath, *Uncle Kit's Legacy*, 47.

[2] Latterly, the true meaning of ' Dicklydize ' has in some cases been forgotten and the name has become associated with a kind of frumenty occasionally consumed by the farm hands at the supper. The true meaning of the word, however, is as above.

on these occasions, and the comments were as plain-spoken as they were well-intentioned. At another such harvest supper as this the weather happened to be close and sultry, and the men, as they took up their plates of meat, were seen to sniff and whisper among themselves. Observing this, the farmer decided to appeal to his servant boy, of whose support he felt sure.

' Well, Tom,' he asked, ' what do you say about it ? '

' Why, maister,' was the disconcerting reply, ' I got nothen to say, 'cept that the meat 's stinkin'.'

Happily, nothing so untoward occurred to mar the pleasures of the Dicklydize at Uncle Kit's. After the meat course came plum puddings, rice puddings, baked puddings, and apple puddings, the latter in the Devonshire style, but much larger ; whilst cream in abundance, bread and butter, cheese, cakes, and buns were provided as a last resource for those whose hunger the first courses had failed to satisfy. Nor were the thirsty ones by any means neglected, since for them Kit had provided brandy, gin, rum, and punch, not to mention the less powerful stimulants of cider and beer. By the conclusion of the meal many of the guests must have been in a condition resembling that of the famous ' Tommy Dumplens ', whose naïve request —' Car' me home and don't bend me, for I 'm feelin' a bit possed up '—has so vividly epitomized the feelings which such banquets were apt to promote.

After supper, the entertainment commenced with the singing of ' Harvest Home ', ' Green Brooms ', ' The Flag of England ', ' Here 's a Health to the Barley Mow ', and other time-honoured songs and choruses without which no Gooldize would formerly have been considered worthy of its name.

' By this time,' continues Mr Bath, ' many of the guests were talking rather louder than usual and seemed to be fast losing their self-control, though whether this was due to the singing or the state of the atmosphere, it would be hard to say. " Can 'ee see Sally Penpraze ? " remarked Maria Cooper, " she 's glazen like a fitcher ! " (staring like a polecat). " Now, Ginifer," chimed in a friend, turning to Kit's mother, " mind the wemen, an' doesn't thee leave them git drunk." "Lor', poor souls," replied Ginifer, " 'tes only wance a year, so lev 'em enjoy their kick-up, there edn't much of a shindy yet, my dear." But things soon began to get worse until Burrow Downs Farm seemed like a public-house, every one talking at the same time and each one trying who could shout the loudest. Kit called forth " Arder ! Arder ! " several times, but as his own voice was much thicker than usual, he had little effect on his now unruly guests. Jack Tommy having been called upon for another song, decided to render " Brown Beer ", but broke down badly at the second verse. The singing having failed, another form of amusement was suggested and put into practice. A lighted candle was placed on the floor in the centre of the room, and every one, men, women, and children, had to jump over it, from a given distance, without putting it out. Crinolines were then in the height of fashion and every one strove who could wear the largest. Sally Penpraze being one of those ladies who never like being beaten, had on this occasion taken off the hoop from the water barrel in order to increase the size of her own dress. All went well until Sally's turn to jump the candle arrived. In her then condition it would have suited Sally much better to have remained seated, but feeling that it would never do to back out, she got up and gave a jump. The front portion of the crinoline passed safely over the candle, but Sally did not make sufficient allowance for its size, and before any one realized what had happened a flame of fire shot out from the hindmost part of Sally's garment. Whilst some screamed and others ran to get water, Maria Cooper went to Sally's assistance, but her crinoline getting there first was promptly seized by the spreading flame. Consternation ensued, but after twelve buckets of water had been dashed over the hapless couple and all traces of fire had vanished, the guests began to think that they would do likewise, and thus was brought to an end the Dickley Dize at Burrow Downs Farm.' [1]

It was not every Gooldize, of course, which ended so uproariously as this. ' Never shall I forget,' writes Mr Charles Hoare, ' a harvest supper of my childhood at the farm of one of my relatives—the hot joints, the pies, and the feasting— followed by the lovely walk home afterwards through the quiet lanes with a bright moon and the brilliant stars overhead, and the glow-worms shining in the hedges. The very air seemed to smell of goodness.'

Although the harvest supper is now a very mild affair in comparison with what it used to be, it is not yet wholly obsolete. In West Cornwall it is still customary on some farms to give the men not only their meals and a regular allowance of beer during the harvest, but also, at the conclusion, a

[1] *Uncle Kit's Legacy*, 48–51.

Gooldize (or ' Godize ') supper, consisting of beef, pork, tarts, and pudding. Occasionally this is washed down with a curious drink known as ' lamb's wool ', composed of beer, eggs, sugar, and milk. Portions of the Gooldize pudding, which resembles a Christmas pudding in contents and shape, may sometimes be seen also in the cottages after the harvest, whither they have been sent round by the farmer as a mark of appreciation to those extra hands who were not invited to the feast itself. In place of this it is customary in many districts to present every man, woman, and child who has assisted in the harvest with a saffron bun of about two pounds in weight.

III

The festivities of the harvest-tide had their counterpart in many other convivial occasions which marked the changing seasons of the year. The ' Twelve Days of Christmas ' was a phrase which meant much to the Cornish people of old who, were they to come to life again, would find in our modern Christmas but a faint echo of the mirth and joy with which they celebrated this period of the year. Nowhere in the pages of Dickens himself will a more satisfying picture be found of Christmas cheer than that given by Bottrell of the way in which this day was formerly kept by the Lovell family at their old mansion of Trewoofe (Trove), near Penzance.

Long before daylight on the Christmas morning the women of the household were up and busy with the preparation of the pies, meat, game, and poultry, and all the roasting, boiling, and baking which had to be done in readiness for the feast. Before the break of dawn, too, the men themselves had left the hall, and the valleys and hills resounded to the winding of the bugle horn which roused the neighbouring villages to join in the hunting and hare-tracing over the newly-fallen snow. As soon as the men were gone, the great open fire-place in the hall was filled from end to end with logs of oak, ash, and elm, and sweet-smelling bog-turf laid between. Before this great fire were placed the spits on which were roasted the huge joints of meats, whilst woodcock, snipe, plover, teal and other game were cooked in the dripping-pans beneath. Meantime, the kitchen chimney and oven were taken up with pies of every sort, pigeon, poultry, giblet, rabbit, hare, mullet, bass, veal, besides those of parsley and sweet herbs. In addition to all these were puddings, pasties, cakes, and other knick-knacks designed to tempt the more delicate appetites. About midday the squire, with some of the elderly hunters and the ladies who had been up on the hills to see the chase, would return home ; the table was then laid, and from that time till long after dark company after company kept coming in laden with the game and ' hungry as hounds '.

Splendid indeed the old house must have looked at such times—with its branches of holly, box, and bay ; garlands of ivy on window and wall ; and the great burnished candlesticks standing on the table between steaming bowls and tankards, piles of apples roasted and raw, and the heaps of sweet cakes. Long after the weary attendants had retired to bed and the ladies themselves had tucked up their fine dresses and fallen with right good will to the task of serving, the feasting continued. At length the company, weary of ' eating the good things to save them ', fell to dancing to tunes beaten out on pewter and brass pans, and the strains of the ' crowd ' (tambourine). Daylight had often come before the party at last broke up amidst cheers for the squire, the draining of stirrup cups, and voices bidding a ' Merry Christmas and a Happy New Year to one and all '.[1]

> *Welcome Christmas which brings us all good cheer,*
> *Pies and puddings, roast pork and strong beer.*

Chorus :   *Come let me taste your Christmas beer*
> *That is so very strong,*
> *And I do wish that Christmas time*
> *With all its mirth and song*
> *Was twenty times so long.*

So ran the opening verse of one of those quaint old secular carols for which the county has long been famous, and which so admirably expressed the sentiments of those who formerly sang them.

Long, indeed, before the modern world has even begun to consider the approach of Christmas, the old people would be engaged in deciding upon the all-important question of the ' curl ' (carol) singing which formed such a prominent

[1] *Tales and Hearthside Traditions of West Cornwall*, I, 233 *et seq.*

feature of this festive season. Printed copies of these carols being almost unknown, the singers had either to write out their own parts in MS., or where, as was frequently the case, the choirs consisted entirely of persons who were unable to read musical notation, the parts themselves had to be memorized. All this entailed strenuous work, and as the Christmastide approached, longer and longer became the sessions and more and more arduous the practices ; for the leader, generally some old man chosen by mutual consent, was hard to please, and would have everything done just ' fitty ' or not at all. Eleven o'clock or more had often come before the various bands broke up, and on their way homewards their voices might still be heard raising the fine old melodies with which their forefathers had wakened those selfsame lanes and rugged moorlands for centuries before them.

A week or so before Christmas the arrival of the ' curl ' singers was eagerly awaited in the towns and villages, and the surrounding farms. Then, on some dark night, when the family were seated before the fire blazing cheerfully on the open hearth, shuffling footsteps would be heard in the outer kitchen, accompanied by the scraping of throats and a voice giving directions in a stage whisper. A minute afterwards a question from the leader : ' Are 'ee ready, boys ? ' would be followed by the order : ' Sound for it, then ! ' and the voices would be raised in a long-drawn-out ' do–o–o ', to try the pitch. This preliminary accomplished, the leader would hastily call forth in a sort of chanting tone the first line of the carol :

As I sat on a sunny bank.

At the word ' bank ' the whole choir took up their parts and burst forth in full harmony from the beginning :

> *As I sat on a sunny bank,*
> *A sunny bank, a sunny bank,*
> *As I sat on a sunny bank*
> *On Christmas Day in the morning.*

Other carols followed, among them such time-honoured favourites as ' The First Nowell ', ' The Seven Joys of Mary ', ' The Holy Well ', ' The Holly and the Ivy ', ' The Twelve Days of Christmas ', ' Born is the King of Israel ' (always pronounced ' Isery-hell '), or the old ' Rejoice '. These and many more of a like kind have recently been published in Dr Ralph Dunstan's *Cornish Song Book*, and are now often rendered by the Old Cornwall Societies at their Christmas festivals.

The Cornish people not only rejoiced in their carols when at home, but introduced them wherever they were scattered in the New World or the Old. A few years since, an interesting collection was brought to light at Dalton-in-Furness, in Lancashire, whither they had been brought by the organist of one of the local chapels from his native village in Cornwall. This collection, which was compiled by a certain Francis Woolcock, of Tregoney, rather more than a hundred years ago, is now regularly used each Christmas at the Dalton Methodist Chapel, and no doubt will come in time to be regarded as traditional Lancashire carols.[1] As was the case with other carol collections of this date, much of the music which Francis Woolcock copied in his notebook was evidently written for the curious old wind instruments which were formerly so popular among rustic choirs, and which Hardy describes with such memorable effect in *Under the Greenwood Tree*. In Cornwall, according to Dr Dunstan, the favourite instruments were the flute, clarinet, and an occasional hautboy; and for the bass, bassoons and serpents. 'String instruments,' he adds, 'were sometimes included, but Cornwall was behind Yorkshire and some other counties in this respect. At a later date the serpent was replaced by the ophicleide, sax-horn, or euphonium—but the bassoon long maintained its pre-eminence. On one occasion in Feock Church seven bassoons played the bass; and my informant added, " when they all closed down on the low F it was like heaven ".'[2]

The old carolers always sang in four parts, viz. 'air' (treble), 'seconds' (alto), 'counter' (tenor), and 'bass'. The favourite carols, therefore, were those which gave most opportunity for the 'parts' to exercise their skill, and as many of them contained numerous 'repeats', sometimes of one line, sometimes of the whole verse, the time that a carol would take to sing could rarely be judged by its length on paper.

It is sometimes urged by strangers that the carols most frequently heard in Cornwall to-day lack the tunefulness of

[1] *Old Cornish Carols*, arranged by Ben Barnicoat (1927). See also *Western Morning News*, 17 December 1925.
[2] *Tre, Pol, and Pen* (1928), 89.

English church carols, and appear somewhat melancholy by reason of their ' repeats ', which are often ' drawn out ' in a minor key. How far this criticism is justified it is perhaps difficult for a native to say, but it is quite certain that among the old pre-Reformation carols there are many which give full scope to the ' air ' and possess the liveliest of tunes. Unfortunately these carols are almost entirely neglected by the modern chapel choirs, and were it not for the work of the Old Cornwall Societies their very existence would be in danger of being forgotten.

But although the Cornishman of to-day has lost or neglected much that he should have treasured as his birthright, were his ancestors to return once more to their beloved land they would still find even in the dying embers of a modern Cornish Christmas other features besides the carols to remind them of the past. Amongst these should be mentioned the picturesque custom of hanging up the Christmas ' bush '. The latter, when properly constructed, consists of two little wooden hoops fastened one into the other at right angles, the framework thus formed being decorated with evergreens, furze blossom, apples, oranges, etc. This pleasing form of decoration, which is known in some districts as the ' kissing bush ', is usually suspended in the front window of the house, and when illuminated at night by a lighted candle set inside it, has a peculiarly festive appearance. Considering how easily and cheaply the bush can be made, it is regrettable that this old British form of decoration should have been so widely supplanted by its German counterpart—the Christmas tree.

In the days when open hearths were still universal in the farm-houses, the burning of the Christmas ' stock ' (as the ' Yule-log ' of other parts of Britain was known in Cornwall) was not without its ceremonial. In many cases the stocks had the figure of a man roughly chalked upon them, and were often ignited with a piece of charred wood which had been saved from the last year's fire. A curious story relating to one of these logs is told in an early number of the *West Briton* newspaper. One evening during the Christmas of 1838 a certain Mr Lukey, of Carminow, near Helston, was sitting by the fire when his ears were suddenly assailed by cries resembling those of a child which apparently proceeded from the chimney wherein the stock lay burning—' as it had been for three successive days, according to the universal custom of the country folk at this season'. On examining the log he noticed that it contained a little hole, which being too small to admit his fingers he split open with an axe, only to discover to his great astonishment a large toad entombed in the centre ! [1]

In many cases the fires of Christmas were continued until Twelfth Night or ' Old Christmas Day '. It is recorded that about the year 1830 a number of Sennen farmers assembled on this occasion at a dinner, of which one of the dishes consisted of a ' four-and-twenty blackbird pie '. After the feast, some of the boldest of the young men went out at midnight in order to see the cattle kneel, facing the east.[2] On their return they brought with them rushes which they threw on to the fire, and from the way in which these crackled or the particular form which they assumed in burning they told their fortunes for the ensuing year.[3]

It would certainly appear to be more than a coincidence that these ceremonial fires of midwinter should have so nearly corresponded with the season when the sun reaches its lowest elevation at noon, and, like the bonfires of midsummer, there is reason to suppose that they owed their origin to practices far older than the Christian festival with which they had become associated.

Another ancient custom of this season which, unlike the burning of the Christmas stock, is not yet wholly obsolete was Wassailing.[4] This practice, which was formerly observed throughout England generally, is thus described by Chambers. ' The head of the house,' he writes, ' would assemble his family around a bowl of spiced ale, from which he drank their healths, then passed it to the rest that they might drink too. The word that passed among them was the ancient Saxon phrase, *Wæs hæl*, that is, " to your health ". Hence this came to be the wassail or wassel bowl. The poorer class of people carried round the neighbourhood a bowl adorned with ribbons, begging for something wherewith to obtain the means

---

[1] *West Briton*, 2 February 1838.

[2] An honest countryman, living on the edge of St Stephen's Down, near Launceston, informed me, October 1790, that he once watched several oxen in their stalls at the above time, and that he observed the two oldest oxen only fall upon their knees, making ' a cruel moan like Christian creatures '.—Brand, *Popular Antiquities*, I, 473 (Bohn edn.).

[3] *Cornishman*, 18 October 1883.

[4] Its most notable exponent in Cornwall to-day is Mr Ben Little, of Truro, who, despite his age of eighty-six years, still regularly visits the surrounding districts with his bowl.

of filling it that they, too, might enjoy wassail as well as the rich.' [1]

In Cornwall the bowl, generally made of wood, was decorated and looped around with furze blossom, flowers, ivy, and ribbons. [2] Armed with this magnificent trophy, the wassailers visited the neighbouring farms and houses of the gentry, before whose doors they struck up the following song :

> The mistress and master our warzail begin,
> Pray open your door and let us come in,
>> With our warzail, warzail, warzail, warzail,
>> And joy come to our jolly warzail.

> The mistress and master sitting down by the fire
> While we poor warzailers are travelling the mire,
>> With our warzail, etc.

> The mistress and master sitting down at their ease,
> Put their hands in their pockets and give what they please,
>> For our warzail, etc.

> I hope that your apple trees will prosper and bear
> That we may have cider when we come next year,
>> With our warzail, etc.

> And where you've one hogshead, I hope you'll have ten,
> That we may have cider when we come again,
>> With our warzail, etc.

> I hope that your barley will prosper and grow,
> That you may have some and enough to bestow
>> On our warzail, etc.

> Now we poor warzail boys growing weary and old,
> Drop a small bit of silver into our bowl,
>> For our warzail, etc.

> I wish you a blessing and long time to live,
> Since you've been so free and willing to give
>> To our warzail, etc.

[1] *Book of Days*, I, 27–9, 55–6.
[2] Generally the bowl was empty, but in some cases it was filled with a drink made of boiled ale, roast apples, sugar, and spice.

Additional verses :

> *If the missus is upstairs I hope she 'll come down,*
> *Put her hand in her pocket and give us a crown,*
>   *For our warzail, etc.*

> *Pray, mistress and master, don't take it amiss*
> *But send out your daughter to give us a kiss,*
>   *For our warzail, etc.*[1]

In one or two places in the West Country the wassailers still visit the orchards, sprinkling the trees with cider, to ensure their bearing plentifully in the coming year. Formerly guns were fired off also at such times, in order to scare away malign spirits. At the conclusion of the ceremony, as the song suggests, the wassailers were assured of a warm welcome, which generally took the form of a glass of ' shenagrum ' and a slice of the Christmas cake.

The latter is still a regular feature of the Christmastide in Cornwall, and there will hardly be found a cottage, however poor, which does not attempt to provide something of the sort at this season for the entertainment of chance visitors. In the towns it is customary for old women, commonly known as ' Christmas widows ', to visit their well-to-do neighbours at this time in order to gather money or ingredients for their ' bit of Chrestmas caake '. This is generally known as ' going a-gooding ', and is still observed in Redruth, as doubtless in other places.

IV

The period between Christmas Day and Twelfth Night (the latter still kept by Cornish miners in 1760 as ' Old Christmas Day ') has from time immemorial been devoted to Guise Dancing. During this cold and wintry season of the year the streets of St Ives and the villages about Penzance are still nightly invaded by bands of young people attired in strange and grotesque costume. In almost every case the boys are

[1] This traditional version of the Wassail song was communicated to the author as a child by Miss L. Eddy, of Stithians. According to her statement it was well known in this district at the beginning of the present century.

dressed as girls and the girls as boys, some of them cleverly representing historical or local characters, others merely disguised with blackened faces and Nottingham lace veils —but all enjoying themselves as much as if they were frolicking beneath a midsummer sky. If the night is fine, parties will often group themselves together at the street corners, where an impromptu dance takes place, to the accompaniment of drums, mouth organs, and concertinas. The police, meanwhile, look on benignly, for guise dancing is recognized by law no less than custom, and little rowdyism ever mars the proceedings during the fortnight in which they are now officially permitted.

Writing in 1750 of ' goose dancing ' [1] in the Scilly Islands, Robert Heath tells how the custom had received much encouragement from the military officers formerly stationed there, and who had been wont in this way to distinguish themselves among the ladies. ' They used to go, ' he writes, ' in party-coloured dresses, half of one colour to the right and left, or above and below, exercising drawn swords in their dancing at the houses, where they entered and retired by procession of two and two. At this time, serenades in the night were in practice under the windows of the fair Islanders, which at this day are not quite forgot.'

Indeed, at the time of his writing the custom was still vigorously maintained among the natives, nor was it noticeably lacking in its former spirit of gallantry. The part of the officers, however, was then assumed by the maidens who ' would be dressed up for sea-captains ', and in this manner displayed their graces to the ' ladies ' of the opposite sex. Thus disguised they visited their neighbours in bands and companies, making jokes upon what had happened in the islands, and ' telling every one his own ', without offence being taken. ' After which,' continues Heath, ' the scene shifts to music and dancing, which being over, they are treated with liquor, and then they go to the next house of entertainment. By this sort of sport,' he adds, ' according to yearly custom

[1] This term is still used in the Scilly Islands, but its inhabitants are in error if they suppose that the custom has any connection with geese. The pronunciation of the word ' guise ', both in French and in ancient English (from which it survives in Cornwall), has for many centuries been ' geeze ', and *this should certainly be adhered to*. The meaning of ' to guise ' is ' to go mumming ', and its traditional pronunciation is indicated in the English slang term ' old geezer ', which simply means ' old guise-dancer ', and is used in ridicule of a queerly dressed person who looks like a masquerader. See R. Morton Nance, *St Ives Times*, 30 December 1927.

and toleration, there is a spirit of wit and drollery kept up among the people.' [1]

A writer describing guise dancing at Penzance in 1831 likened it to an Italian carnival, and recalled the days when people of every class, including ' the rich and the great ', came masked and disguised into the streets, or entering the houses which were left open for their reception, carried on ' highly humorous and piquant conversations ', to the delight of all present. He tells further how the young men would assume with the rich old heirloom dresses of their grand-mothers and great-grandmothers the finest of old-ladyfied manners and talk, and how whimsical personages met one on every hand, many of them turning out to be fine ' gentle-men of the fair sex.' During the early part of the last century the costume of the guise dancers often consisted of an antique finery such as would now raise envy in the heart of a collector. Male players were to be seen in long-waisted, gay-coloured coats, resplendent with buttons of brass or tin as large as crown pieces, and having long ruffles at their breasts and wrists. Beneath this were worn breeches of blue, red, or buff ; slashed, puffed, and tricked out with ribbons and tassels. Their hose were generally of a bright blue, whilst their feet were shod with high-heeled shoes, adorned with shining buckles, or bows and ribbons. The chief glory of the men, however, lay in their cocked hats, which were surmounted with plumes and decked with streamers of ribbons. The girls and women were no less magnificently attired : with steeple-crowned hats, stiff-bodied gowns, bag-skirts or trains, and ruffles hanging from their elbows.[2]

Of the origin of guise dancing it is impossible to speak with any degree of certainty. It seems safe to say, however, that it dates back to a period long before the introduction of Christianity to these islands—to those far-off days, in fact, when, like the throwing up of the silver ball in the hurling game, it was probably endowed with a magical significance. In former times its practice was certainly widespread, being common not only to Great Britain but to a large part of Europe. Within the last century the part played by the ' guisards '—that is, masquers—still constituted a prominent feature in the New Year festivities of Scotland. The genuine guisards here, as in Cornwall, did more than merely parade

---

[1] Robert Heath, *Account of the Scilly Islands*, 125.
[2] W. Bottrell, *Traditions and Hearthside Stories of West Cornwall*, II, 2.

the streets in disguise ; they formed themselves into bands or parties, and entering the kitchens of the mansions and farms therein acted some Christmas play, generally that of ' St George and the Dragon '. Sir Walter Scott, who loved the ancient folk-customs of his native country and who was far ahead of his time in recognizing their historical importance, invariably encouraged the guisards to perform their play at his house. In Cornwall, despite the lack of any such educated support, the ' St George ' play continued to be acted by the guise dancers down to a century ago. In the towns and villages, the ' theatre ' was commonly the largest chamber of some inn, or else the ' long room ' over a fish cellar. In the country districts, the farm-house kitchen served the same purpose.

A pleasing account of the rendering of this old drama in a West Cornwall farm, a hundred years ago, is given by ' Uncle Jan Trenoodle ' (i.e. William Sandys) in his *Specimens of Cornish Provincial Dialect*. It was a New Year's Eve, the writer tells us, and a goodly party of friends and neighbours was gathered to spend the day at ' Cousin Nic Carnoweth's '. After a dinner consisting of ' broth, a couple of nice pluffy young mabyers (pullets), a starry-gazy (pilchard) pie, a thumping figgy-pudding, and plenty of strong drink to keep out the cold ', the company seated themselves round the Christmas stock blazing cheerfully on the open hearth. Towards ' teening time ', or the fall of dusk, ' there came a grinning gaukum who told us as how the guise dancers were to the door, with the ancient play of St George. Gladly did we give them leave to enter, so in they came. There was old Feyther Chrestmas with a make-wise face possed (stuck) up on top of his own, and his long white wig, trapesing about and getting in his tantrums ; and there was the Doctor, as they called 'un, with a three-cornered piked hat and his face all rudded and whited, with spurticles (spectacles) on top of his nause. And there was one in a maiden's bed-gownd and coat with ribbons, and a nackan (handkerchief) in his hand and a gook (sun bonnet) on his head. Other youngsters were in white, with ribbons tied all over their shirt sleeves, and with nackans and swords, and such caps as I never see'd before. They was half a fathom high, made of pastyboard (cardboard), weth powers (heaps) of beads and looking-glass, and shreds of old cloth strung upon slivers (strips) of pith—and they strutted about so brave as lubber cocks (turkey cocks) '.

And then they gave the word to begin, and old 'Feyther Chrestmas' stepped out and said :

> ' *Here comes I, ould Feyther Chrestmas,*
> *Welcome or welcome not,*
> *I do hope ould Feyther Chrestmas*
> *Will never be forgot.*'

Father Christmas, having introduced the play, steps back into the half-circle of the performers, leaving the stage open for the Turkish knight. The latter struts forth in an arrogant fashion, proclaiming his superiority to any Christian knight, until, of a sudden, St George himself appears. He also is confident of his prowess, and in consequence a fight takes place in which the Turkish knight is knocked down for dead. Here the play seems like to have ended but for the timely intervention of the Doctor who, after a good deal of humorous ' gag ', cures him of his ' deep and deadly wound '. Once more the Turkish knight arises to do battle, but he is speedily laid low by St George, and this time slain for good. Then in comes the Dragon, a fearsome-looking beast ' with long teeth and scurvy jaw '. His part was not played without danger, since he was required to breathe forth sulphurous flames, an effect which was achieved by putting a lighted squib in his ' snout '. An incautious elevation of the latter by throwing the explosive compound inward might, and not infrequently did, cause severe injury to the player. After a fitting display of his fearsome qualities, the Dragon also is slain by St George who, as a somewhat unexpected reward for his valour, is given the hand of ' Sabra, the King of Egypt's daughter ', in marriage.

Versions of this ancient mummer's play are very numerous, and include such ill-assorted characters as ' Old Beelzebub ', ' Oliver Cromwell ', ' Little Man Jack ', besides other comic ' supers ' who were introduced by the players at will. The chief characters in the play, however, are the same in all versions, whilst the essential action hinges upon the fight between the Turkish knight and St George, the slaying of the former, his resurrection by the (now) ' comic ' Doctor, and the final overthrow of both the Turkish knight and the Dragon, which concludes the play. The real interest of these homely dramas, therefore, lies not so much in their treatment of the subject, which was crude enough, but in the tracing of their long descent. By symbolizing, as in its origin it is thought to have done, the defeat of Winter through the reviving miracle of Spring, the play endowed the custom of guise dancing with a meaning which greatly added to its interest.[1]

Although many years have elapsed since the ' St George' play ceased to be a regular feature of this midwinter carnival, it was not wholly forgotten. In 1866 the Rev. W. S. Lach-Szyrma witnessed its performance by the miners of Pensilva, near Liskeard. In 1890 the villagers of Manaccan and St Martin-in-Meneage toured the play through their neighbourhood with great success. Another excellent rendering of the play was given by the boys of the Roskear School, at Camborne, during the Christmas of 1914. The intention, however, of making it an annual event was frustrated by the staff alterations caused by the war.[2]

Though the war was instrumental in killing the play, the custom of dressing up and parading the streets during the New Year season survived even through that period of change and stress. The time came, however, not long after the war, when guise dancing, in St Ives at any rate, had reached a low ebb and the days of this immemorially ancient custom seemed numbered. At length it was suggested by the local authorities that a ban should be put upon it, on the grounds that it led to a rowdyism which was detrimental to the interests of the town. Happily wiser counsel prevailed. It was pointed out that the character of guise dancing, like that of every other popular recreation, depended largely on those who took part in it, and that the best way of raising its status was to give it that educated support which its agelong antiquity warranted. Accordingly the experiment was tried by the St Ives Old Cornwall Society of holding a Guise Dance Parade on a certain night of the New Year, at which small prizes were offered for the best-designed costume, family heirloom dress, character sketch, Cornish dialogue, and the like. The results exceeded the most sanguine expectations of the promoters. Hundreds of guise dancers flooded the streets, among them,

[1] Such ' battles, ' with the more or less conscious intention of assisting the sun to regain its ascendancy after the turning point of the year, were once staged in many parts of Europe. See Sir J. G. Frazer, *Golden Bough.*

[2] Per Mr Tom Miners. The writer himself when living as a child in Redruth regularly took part in ' private ' performances of the ' St George' play. The version used came from Stithians, and may be found in *Old Cornwall*, I, 29–30. This, I think, must have differed from the ' Jack-o'-the-Green ' play which Mr Miners informs me was acted at Stithians as recently as the early years of the war, and which was only discontinued there by reason of the younger men being called away to active service.

as in days of old, many of the leading inhabitants of the town.
The encouragement given in this way has succeeded in raising
the whole standard of guise dancing, and inspired those who
take part in it with a just pride in their ancient ceremony. All
that is now required is that the ' St George ' play should be
revived in order to re-endow the festival with its true significance.

V

In reviewing the many folk-customs for which Cornwall
has long been famous, it is necessary to distinguish to-day
between those which still survive, even if in an imperfect form,
and those which have but lately become obsolete. Practices
such as guise dancing clearly fall within the first category, and
may be likened to old clocks or watches which only require
the occasional attention of some sympathetic hand to keep
them going for many years to come. Other customs there are,
almost too numerous to mention, which, though they survived
within living memory, no longer have their part in the present-
day life of Cornwall. In some cases the passing of these can
hardly be viewed with much regret. Thus as lately as 1881 it
was customary among the young people at Penzance at
Shrovetide to stand at the street corners with well-greased,
sooty hands, with which they attempted to rub the faces of
the passers-by. At this season, too, people were frequently
deluged with buckets of water, whilst gates were unhung,
gardens robbed of their flowers, and general license given to
the Lord of Misrule. No doubt the student of folk-lore will
recognize in these practices a debased form of the carnival
which formerly preceded the coming of Lent. Such survivals,
however, it will be generally agreed, can sometimes be maintained at too inconvenient a price, and the action of the
authorities in putting a stop to this particular custom will
scarcely be regretted to-day by even the most zealous antiquary. On the other hand, it is but fair to point out how much
that was good as well as bad was often lost by discouraging
the folk-spirit which underlay these ancient practices. Whilst
the carnival had degenerated into a rude horseplay, the contemporary custom among the children of bringing eggs to
school on Shrove Tuesday in order to make their master's

pancakes was one of those gracious survivals whose loss has made country life to-day the poorer, without being in any way the more dignified.

Good Friday in Cornwall has long been observed more in the nature of a holiday than a solemn fast. Memories of the latter, however, are no doubt responsible for the general custom of resorting to the seashore on this day, in order to procure limpets, ' wrinkles ', and other shell-fish. This practice was common to the farm labourers and inhabitants of the inland towns no less than to the dwellers by the coast. On Good Friday morning, crowds of people, carrying knives and sacks, might be seen on almost all the beaches where formerly the shell-fish was gathered in such quantities as often to require the aid of mules or carts to bring it home. In the evening, ' horned cattle for supper ' was the general order in the cottages. ' Chacun à son goût,' wrote Mrs Pascoe, ' but it strikes me as shockingly fee-fa-fumish to see a supper party picking these creatures out with a pin and gobbling them down, " scholar's hats " and all.' [1]

Of late years the changes which have revolutionized modern England have gone much further towards secularizing Good Friday than was ever the case in Cornwall. Indeed, the latter in its observance of this day may now be said to show less of the restless bank holiday spirit than any other part of the country. Among the older generation Good Friday is commonly devoted to the sober recreation of gardening. This fact is no doubt in some measure attributable to the once widely-held belief that seeds planted on this day ' would all grow ', passing like their Creator through seeming death towards a sure and certain resurrection. Amongst the children Good Friday is still known in some parts of Cornwall as ' bat and ball ' day, and marks one of those mysterious turning points of the year on which, with no less certainty than if it were ordained by royal decree, the games of one season give place to those of another.

In the St Ives district on this day the children, often accompanied by their fishermen fathers, are accustomed to sail boats on the old engine ponds of Providence mine at Carbis Bay. If the weather is fine, quite a concourse of people may often be seen assembled on the banks, and great enthusiasm prevails amongst the model yachtsmen. Those who are too poor to afford proper boats cleverly make shift with pieces of

[1] *Walks about St Hilary*, 108.

cork into which are stepped little masts carrying chip sails, a contrivance known to all St Ives children as ' cocken barber ' (i.e. *cok an baban*, ' boat of the child '). Any one of these toys proving particularly successful is referred to as ' cock dayka ' i.e. *cok teca*, ' prettier boat ', or possibly *cok deca*, ' tithe boat ', the latter carrying with it the suggestion of a pro- pitiatory use, as an offering to the sea.[1]

That ' votive ' ships of this sort formerly had their place in Cornwall there can be little doubt. As recently as 1887 a model known as the ' Millbrook ship ' was regularly carried through the streets of Devonport on May Day. The ship itself was adorned with flowers and birds' eggs, and was accompanied by a procession consisting of a drum-and-fife band and children gaily decked with garlands.[2]

The observances of May Day in Old Cornwall ranked second only in importance to those of Christmas and Mid- summer. A contributor to Hone's *Every Day Book*, writing from Penzance a century ago, describes how on the eve of May the young people of the town would assemble at some public-house whence, as midnight struck, they issued forth into the streets to the accompaniment of fiddles, drums, and other instruments. Calling upon others who had previously settled to join them, the parties thus formed would visit the various farms of the neighbourhood, where their arrival was regularly expected. Here ' a beverage called junket, made of raw milk and rennet, *alias* " running " ', was prepared for their entertainment, and eaten with the addition of sugar and cream. ' After this,' continues the writer, ' they take tea and " heavy cake ", composed of flour, cream, and currants.' Being by this time fairly elated, as one may imagine, despite the loss of a night's sleep, dancing followed. If the weather was showery, this often took place in a barn lent by some well-disposed farmer, or if fine in one of his fields or even on the high road. Such dances they were too, as old people recall : ' four-handed, six-handed, and eight-handed reels ; riotous quick-steps, danced with a joy and abandon untiring ; followed by the stately Triumph and Cushion Dances, slow and graceful but equally enjoyable '.[3] The refreshments as supplied within living memory by farmers in the Looe district consisted, in addition to junket, of metheglin (mead), sloe and elderberry wine, milk,

---

[1] R. Morton Nance, *Celtic Words in Cornish Dialect*, 6.
[2] *Western Antiquary*, I, 113, and VII, 40.
[3] Miss E. S. Shapcott, *Old Cornwall*, XI, 24.

and that ' rare but now unknown dainty " Whipped syllabub under the Cow " '.[1]

At length, when satisfied with their dancing and feasting, the parties set about the real business of gathering the ' may ' (sycamore). Whilst some were breaking down the boughs, others would be busy in the preparation of the ' May music '. This consisted of cutting a circle through the bark at a certain distance from the end of the branch, when, by a gentle and regular tapping, the loosened bark slipped off from the wood. A hole was then cut in the hollow pipe, which was thus formed into a species of whistle, capable of emitting a shrill thin sound. Everything being ready, they would then ' bring home the may ' by five or six o'clock in the morning, to the accompaniment of bands playing and whistles blowing, and so continue dancing through the town until the time came for them to separate for their respective employments. ' Although May Day,' states an old writer, ' should fall on a Sunday, they observe the same practice in all respects, with the omission of dancing in the town.'[2]

Formerly, not only May morning, but also the first Sunday of May was kept as a general holiday. On the latter occasion pleasure parties consisting of three or four families would betake themselves to some neighbouring village for a picnic. With them they would carry flour and other materials to make heavy cake, whilst not forgetting tea, rum, and ' other comfortable things ' for their refreshment. The farmers themselves, in return for a trifling sum, would provide delicious junkets and sour milk or ' curd '. With these, the young were satisfied, whilst their elders partook of new-made cake, refreshing tea, and exhilarating punch with which to satisfy the stomach, cheer the spirits, and assist the walk home in the evening.[3]

At this date maypoles were still commonly erected in all the towns and villages of the west. Indeed, they remained customary in some of the more outlying parts of East Cornwall until almost the end of the last century. The practice, however, was endowed with little of that spirit of mirth and good-fellowship which is usually associated with its observance in Merry England. Indeed, the reverse was the case. The poles themselves were tall and straight, bare of all decoration save for a strip of bunting at their tops. ' These poles,' writes Mr W. A. Pascoe, ' embodied a challenge, a challenge to the whole country-side, and many a desperate struggle was waged around

[1] *Ibid.*   [2] Hone, *Every Day Book*, May 1826, 561.   [3] See *ibid.*

them when other communities, accepting the challenge, fought for their possession. One of the last instances of this occurred at a farm near St Neot where there was a large family of seven sons and five daughters. When the month came round they upraised their maypole, having firm faith in their ability to defend it. They did not count, however, upon repelling a mass attack which, amid scenes of great confusion, dire threats, firing of shot-guns (fortunately into the air), and discharges of pepper and hot water by the defenders, eventually succeeded. The captured maypole was borne back in triumph by the attacking party as the gallant defenders retired in disgust to their beds. I must then have been very young indeed, but I shall never forget seeing the party of young men marching through the village street in the night, singing lustily, with the huge maypole on their shoulders.' [1]

In order to defeat the object of their attackers maypoles were protected by all manner of devices. In many cases hoop-iron was banded around them to a considerable height so as to prevent their being sawn off. As long as the poles provided the opportunity for a fight, the participants do not seem to have cared much on which side they were ranged. Mr Pascoe has told how on one occasion the young men of a certain village in the Liskeard district had determined to seize a maypole which had been erected on a site a few miles away. On reaching this spot, however, they found themselves forestalled by another party from the village of St Cleer, who were at that moment striving to attempt its capture. Seeing this, the new arrivals immediately joined forces with the defenders, and by their combined efforts succeeded in dispelling the attack. Having thus displayed their prowess the remainder of the evening was passed in fraternizing with the owners of the maypole at the village inn. ' The custom of the challenge of the maypole,' adds Mr Pascoe, ' declined and finally fell into disuse some forty years since. Undoubtedly it made for a certain amount of riotous behaviour if not actual lawlessness, and the establishment of a regular police force thus brought about its decay. One does, however, feel regret at the loss of a custom which, although misused, was an interesting and picturesque symbol of the advent of spring in the Cornish country-side.'

Although the maypole was abandoned somewhat earlier

[1] ' Old Beliefs around St Neot,' *Old Cornwall*, XII, 2–3. See also Miss B. C. Spooner, ' The Maypole ', *Old Cornwall*, second series, I, 21–3

CRYING THE NECK, TOWEDNACK, 1928

(See page 410)

THE PADSTOW HOBBY-HORSE AND "TEAZER"

(See page 444)

than this in West Cornwall, many of the other ancient observances connected with this season were retained here within
the memory of those who are now but middle-aged. Amongst
these may be mentioned the custom of rising early on the
morning of May Day, in order to bring in flowers and green
branches with which to decorate the houses. If the boys
succeeded in fixing a may bough over a farmer's door before
he was up, the latter was considered bound to give them their
breakfast, which commonly consisted of bread and cream,
with a basin of raw milk. In some districts it was customary
for the farmers to provide the young people with a slice of
bread and cream ' as big as the longest fern ' which they had
been able to gather on their way to the house.[1]

Although, with the exception of Padstow and Helston,
the coming of May is now but little regarded, it cannot even
yet be said that the occasion is wholly forgotten. May Day
in St Ives is still celebrated by the children with the blowing
of home-made whistles known as ' feepers ' or ' pee-weeps ',
whilst ' May-horns ' made of tin are also much in evidence.
In some districts, too, bonfires are still occasionally lighted
on May eve. At Hayle parties of children are accustomed to
perambulate the town singing before the houses :

> Oh, crown the Queen of May,
> Oh, crown the Queen of May,
> Around the ring, we 'll dance and sing
> And crown the Queen of May.

To understand the significance of these last remaining
fragments of an ancient folk-tradition it is necessary to realize
in the first place that the month of May, and, in particular,
May Day, was formerly regarded as a season when witches
had especial power. This being the case, there seems little
doubt that the intention of the ' May music ' was to scare
away these evil spirits from the dwellings of the just. Regarded in this light, the children of St Ives, so far from making
a mere nuisance of themselves by their joyful din, are in
reality conferring an inestimable benefit on the town, ridding
it thus of those baleful influences which are possibly none the
less dangerous from being so generally unsuspected.

The custom of placing green branches before the doors of

[1] In Truro, on May Day, the buses plying to and from the railway
station used often to be decked with flowers, and the harness with ribbons,
whilst in some cases the horses' hoofs were gilded.—T. H. Rogers, *Western
Morning News*, 13 April 1926.

houses can hardly be less ancient, and is thought to be derived from the belief, still widely held among primitive peoples, that the spirit of vegetation is present unseen in these boughs, and that in the spring processions (' bringing in the summer and the may, O ! ') the former is conveyed to each house to bestow his blessing. Furthermore, as Sir James Frazer has shown, it appears that in many cases the spirit of life in the boughs was considered to be transferred to the person who plucked them. Hence comes the Jack-o'-the-Green, still represented in many parts of England and the Continent by a person covered from head to foot in a leafy framework, and hence also the still more familiar Queen of the May.[1] From this it will be seen that the custom of visiting the farms on May morning and of carrying thither green boughs was originally imbued with a serious, not to say sacramental, significance. The demands, therefore, for food and drink, so far from being regarded as an imposition, were in the nature of a tribute willingly rendered in return for the blessings which it was in the power of the bearers of the may boughs to bestow. Happy, indeed, were those days when pleasure and profit were so nearly allied, and when the joys of giving and receiving hospitality were the direct outcome of a practical religion.

VI

From the gratulations with which the Cornish people formerly welcomed the coming of spring one passes by a natural step to the even more spectacular festivities of midsummer, whose eve they celebrated with fires and dancing and midnight revelry along the rugged hill-tops of the west.

The custom of lighting bonfires at this season, and of leaping over them and driving cattle through or around them, is older by far than any written history and is, or was, to be found in almost every country of Europe. Various theories have been offered in explanation of this. According to one school of thought, the fires were originally intended to mimic the sun as the source of all heat and life, and thereby, through a process of homœopathic magic, to have had a supposedly stimulating effect on the growth of crops and the welfare of

[1] *Golden Bough* (short edition), 127 *et seq.*

man and beast. According to another, the virtue of such fires was negative rather than positive, tending merely to avert those dangers which threaten man and beast from blight, sterility, disease and, above all, witchcraft. In accordance with the first view, therefore, the fires might be regarded as a stimulant, in the second as a disinfectant. There seems, however, no reason to consider these two theories as necessarily incompatible. For, as Sir James Frazer has written, ' if we assume that the fires were primarily intended to imitate the sun's heat and light, may we not regard the purificatory and disinfecting qualities, which popular opinion certainly appears to have ascribed to them, as attributes derived directly from the qualities of sunshine ? In this way we might conclude that, while the imitation of sunshine in these ceremonies was primary and original, the purification attributed to them was secondary and derivative '.[1]

Granted that those anthropologists are right who see in the original purpose of the fires an attempt to simulate the sun, it is possible that the custom in Cornwall of carrying flaming torches which were swung with a circular motion round the heads of their bearers may have originated in a conscious imitation of the sun's movement in the heavens. Be this the case or not, it is clearly a significant fact that the two chief fire festivals of Europe coincide more or less exactly with the summer and winter solstices, when the sun reaches respectively its highest and lowest elevation at noon. It seems, therefore, no very far-fetched conjecture to suppose that just as the ceremonial fires of midwinter may have originated with the desire to help the labouring sun to rekindle its seemingly expiring light, so in like manner the bonfires of midsummer may have been intended to circumvent the waning of the sun at the season when its life-giving qualities were being manifested to the full. In both cases the character of these festivals was subsequently transformed by Christianity, the fires of midwinter becoming associated with the feast of Christmas, and those of midsummer with the nativity of St John.

Although, as has already been shown, the bonfires of midsummer were once general throughout Europe, the Civil War appears to have been responsible for their decline in England. As John Aubrey quaintly expressed it in 1686 : ' Warres not only extinguish Religion and Lawes but superstition, and no suffimen is a greater fugator of Phantosmes

[1] *Golden Bough* (short edition), 641–2.

than gunpowder'. The truth of this statement folk-lore students of the twentieth century have even better cause to know than Aubrey. But in Cornwall not even the disruptive influences of internecine strife were sufficient to turn the Celtic inhabitants from their ancient ways, and their romantic mysticism continued to find expression in the fires of midsummer long after these had passed out of memory elsewhere. A century ago, although the 'tooth of Time' had no doubt effaced the original motives of the custom, the practice of lighting bonfires was still regarded in the Duchy with a veneration which leaves little doubt as to the magical significance which had once attached to it. Describing these celebrations in the year 1795, a writer tells how he saw 'the people of all ages dancing around the fires until a late hour of the night, swinging their children through the flames, not in such manner as to hurt them, though sometimes to singe their clothes'.[1]

Even within the last century the act of dancing around the fires was still regarded as a precaution against witchcraft, and in many cases men and women might be seen to detach themselves from the encircling band in order to leap through the flames as the fires burnt low. The ashes of the fires were likewise regarded as a talisman against the evil eye, and were often preserved to this end, though not without the secret belief that if they were to attain their full power it was necessary that some living creature should have been thrown into the flames—rabbits, chickens, rats, and 'such small deer' taking the place therein of the older human sacrifice. Moreover, the ceremony a hundred years ago had not yet completely lost its association with the fruits of the earth, and girls might still be seen bearing floral hoops, made of various herbs and wild flowers, which were subsequently committed as an offering to the flames.

To those who witnessed the impressive scale upon which the celebrations of St John's Eve were conducted in the earlier part of the last century, it must indeed have appeared impossible that so great an anniversary should ever cease to be commemorated. 'Early in the morning of 23rd June,' states a writer at Penzance in 1801, 'the young people are all alert in the preparation of their favourite festival. No sooner does the tardy sun withdraw himself from the horizon than the boys begin to assemble in the several parts of the

[1] *Gentleman's Magazine*, Vol. 65, Pt. II, 739.

town, drawing after them trees, branches of wood and furze—all of which had been accumulating week after week from the beginning of May. Tar barrels are presently erected on tall poles, some on the quay, others near the market, and one even on a rock in the midst of the sea. Meanwhile the female children trip up and down in their best frocks, decorated with garlands and hailing Midsummer Eve as the vigil of St John. At length the joyful moment arrives, and the torches make their appearance ! These are carried by youths, and being made from pieces of inflammable material, blazing in the wind, are swung round their heads with a peculiar circular motion. Some of the torches are of considerable weight and require much exertion and no small skill to keep them from approaching too near the body of the bearer. Thus twisting and wriggling along, with the fitful blaze of the torch reflecting on his or her features (for both sexes mingle in the sport), you have, without much stretch of imagination, a strong resemblance to the Furies. With the increase of darkness there is also an increase in the number of torch bearers, whilst heaped-up tar barrels and bonfires start to blaze in every direction.

' Meantime, the ladies and gentlemen parade the streets or walk in the fields and terraces which command the bay, from whence they behold the fishing towns, farms, and villas vying with each other in the number and splendour of their fires. Meantime, also, rockets, crackers, squibs, etc., resound through every street—and the screams of the ladies on their return from the show and their precipitate flight into the first shop, passage, or house that happens to be open, heightens the colouring and diversion of the night. Then comes the finale ! No sooner are the torches burnt out than the inhabitants of the quay quarters (a great multitude), male and female, young and old, virtuous and vicious, sober and drunk, take hands and, forming a long line, run violently through every street, lane, and alley, crying : " An eye, an eye, an eye ". At last they stop suddenly, and an eye to this enormous needle being opened by the last two in the string (whose clasped hands are elevated and arched), the thread of populace runs under, singing as they go :

> *Open the gates as high as the sky,*
> *And let King George and his men pass by.*

So they go on repeating the same till weariness dissolves

the union and sends them home to bed, which is never till past the hour of midnight.

'Next day (Midsummer) the custom is for the country people to come to Penzance in their best clothes about four or five o'clock in the afternoon, when they repair to the quay and take a short trip on the water (known as a " penn'orth of say "). On this occasion a number of boats are employed, many of which have music on board. After one cargo is dismissed another is taken in, and till nine or ten at night the bay exhibits a pleasant scene of sloops, sailing boats, rowing boats, sea-sickness, laughter, quarrelling, drum-beating, horn-blowing, etc. On the quay there is a kind of wake or fair at which fruit and confectionery is sold, whilst the public-houses are thronged with drinkers and dancers. Such is midsummer in this part of Cornwall, and on the eve and feast of St Peter, which follows so closely upon it, the same scenes are enacted over again.' [1]

In some places, indeed, ' Peter's Tide ' ranked as a festival of almost greater importance than midsummer. This was notably the case at Polperro, which formerly possessed a chapel dedicated to the saint and observed his feast with an annual fair. During the days preceding this, the young fishermen were accustomed to go from house to house begging money to defray the expenses of the bonfire. ' At nightfall on the eve of the feast,' wrote Mr Jonathan Couch, ' a large pile of faggots and tar barrels is built on the beach, and amid the cheers of a congregated crowd of men, women, and children (for it is a favour never denied to children to stay up and see the bonfire), the pile is lighted. The fire blazes, and men and boys dance merrily round it, keeping up the sport till the fire burns low enough, when they ven-turously leap through the flames. It is a most animated scene ; the whole valley lit up by the bright red glow, bringing into strong relief front and gable of picturesque old houses, each window crowded with eager and delighted faces ; and around the fire a crowd of ruddy lookers-on, shutting in a circle of impish figures leaping like salamanders through the flames.' [2]

Although St Peter's Tide was marked by celebrations of a similar kind in many parts of Cornwall, those of midsummer always ranked of chief importance in the west. No bank

---

[1] *Cornwall Gazette*, 4 July 1801.
[2] *History of Polperro*, 157.

holiday, no great feast of the Christian Church was more jealously guarded and upheld than this their own high festival by the Cornish people of old, and nothing in history marks with more positive clearness the breaking down of local custom and tradition than that the commemoration of this red-letter day of days should ever have fallen into abeyance.

On the eve of St John, 1864, the managing committee of the festivities at Penzance showed their appreciation of the fact that ' midsummer comes but once a year ' by letting off two hundred and fifty-eight dozen crackers, in addition to great quantities of Roman candles, Jacks-in-the-box, and sky-rockets. Those who only know the very commonplace streets of Penzance to-day wherein, more perhaps than any other town in Cornwall, the hand of the ' improver ' has eliminated all traces of the past, will find it hard to picture the wild scenes of revelry which the old town must have witnessed. It is probable, however, that the festivities of this year represented what was practically the high-water mark of the Midsummer Eve celebrations. By the eighties and nineties of the last century, owing to the increase of traffic and the stricter precautions against fire demanded by insurance companies, the lighting of tar barrels and the letting off of squibs and crackers in the main streets had been formally abolished by order of the mayor. The consequent discouragement caused by these measures, combined with the growing tendency to abandon all local forms of recreation in favour of stereotyped amusements introduced from farther afield, had already by the years before the war reduced the festivities of midsummer to a very low ebb. It is true that within the present century bonfires were still occasionally lighted on Carn Brea and some of the western hills, but with the outbreak of hostilities an end was quickly put to these.

With the renewed interest in local customs which was seen in the period after the war, and which was stimulated to a very large degree by the work of the Old Cornwall Societies, the revival of the midsummer celebrations became once more a possibility. Accordingly, in the summer of 1929, the eve of the feast of St John saw once again the bonfires blazing merrily on almost every hill-top from the Land's End to the Tamar. As the twilight of a perfect summer's evening began to fall across the stern, bleak moorlands of the west, the first of the waiting beacon fires broke into flame upon the rock-strewn summit of Chapel Carn Brea. The signal, once given, was quickly taken up by other groups of watchers standing beside their fires. From Castle-an-Dinas, the people of Penzance passed on the message to their neighbours of St Ives and Hayle, assembled respectively upon the hill-tops of Rosewall and Trencrom. From here it flashed across the intervening country to Camborne and Redruth. Meanwhile other fires were already blazing in the neighbourhood of Helston, from whence the signal was carried southward into the long outstretching promontory of the Lizard. From the top of Carnmarth, Redruth passed on the word to its neighbours of Truro, many of whom had assembled at St Agnes. From here on the beacon-top the fire was quickly seen at Newquay, and so it went to the great ' china-clay ' district of central Cornwall, where other watchers were waiting in readiness upon the top of Hensbarrow. The people of Bodmin next saw the flames, and after them Liskeard, whose inhabitants were gathered in force upon St Cleer Downs. As their fire leapt upwards into the night, an answering gleam from the heights of Kit Hill showed that the message had reached the Tamar borderland, about twenty minutes having elapsed since the first fire was lighted at the Land's End.

Thanks to the success of this revival, the midsummer bonfires have since been continued each year, and now bid fair to become again a regular institution in the county in which they were so long retained in the course of an unbroken tradition. For although the outlook of man on life and the world about him has greatly changed since first his forebears lit these fires, the love of the spectacular still remains as strong as ever. Children yet of the earth which bred us, what memories of the past are not awakened as amidst the roar and crackle and driving clouds of smoke the flames go shooting upwards on some dark, rock-strewn hill-top ; whilst near and far similar messages of joy and good-fellowship are flashing their way across the country-side. Though the fires may soon die down and the stirring of old memories lasts perhaps but a moment, the life to which we return is none the poorer for this strange experience. Rather it may well be that those moments spent in forgetting the present and looking only on the past and to the future may come in time to hold a deeper significance than many hours which at their passing had seemed more profitably spent.

CUSTOMS AND OBSERVANCES

I

In addition to the many customs and popular festivities described in the preceding chapter, there are others (among them some which were once general to Cornwall) which linger only now in single towns or villages [1] where, like jetsam floating in some still sea creek, they await the outgoing tide. Nowhere can this simile be more justly applied than to the little town of Padstow, itself situated near the mouth of a desert estuary where, twice in the twenty-four hours, the salt tides cover the creeks and sands with their smooth flood which the dreaded ' Doombar ' at once imprisons and becalms.

Padstow was once a busy place, a port of embarkation for Ireland, and occupied in a considerable trade in timber and other merchandise with the Baltic countries. In its small but active shipyards many a fine vessel rose on the stocks, grew to completion, and slipped away to the great sea world outside. The hardy and intrepid fishermen of this town, moreover, were early engaged in that most arduous of all sea enterprises, the great Newfoundland trade. Thither they sailed in specially equipped vessels, Padstow-built, often remaining away from home for nearly two years at a time. Changes, however, came. The days of the wooden sailing ship passed, and with them Padstow's prosperity. Though still to some extent a fishing port, it is now for the most part east-country boats which frequent its quays, and when the winter herring season draws to a close, the fish buyers depart, and the last of the visiting ' drifters ' hoots a sad farewell to the sandy reaches and wind-swept headlands, the little town relapses into unbroken peace and memories of its past.

From this sleepy state of peaceful calm, one day in the year

[1] ' A custom once prevalent throughout a nation or tribal settlement may die out gradually until it is represented only in a few isolated places or, it may be, in a single place. Still this meagre representation is of importance. It is the only clue to the archaic original.'—Sir G. L. Gomme, *The Gentleman's Magazine Library* (1885), x.

stands out in contrast—one day in which the little streets awake again to life and the inhabitants enact those scenes which immemorial custom has prescribed. As midnight approaches on 30th April the sound may be heard of people assembling in the courts and lanes which cluster around the ancient harbour. If one chances to be a Cornishman, but a stranger to Padstow, the first thought that probably springs to the mind is—' A wreck ! ' But no, the inhabitants are stirring at this hour in answer to a happier summons than the cry of drowning men. Agelong memories are awakening and the deeps of a folk-consciousness are opening to reveal the past. All unspoken, the instincts which they have inherited are calling the people of Padstow to celebrate once again that most wonderful of mysteries, the rising sap, the bursting blossom, and the birth of a new summer.

Hardly have the echoing chimes of the church clock resounded twelve, when the hobby-horse ' pairs ' [1] or ' gang ' —dim shapes of men and women—issue forth into the night from the Golden Lion Inn, where they have been partaking of supper. Their leader, an old man whose bent appearance suggests a life which has seen more of labour than revelling, calls out the names of one or two of the leading singers, and is answered from the shadows. All being present to his satisfaction, the party proceeds a little way up the street where a halt is made before some house in which lights in the upper window show that the serenaders are expected. A clearing of throats and a drink all round from the flagon of beer which someone has thoughtfully provided, and the leader calls forth in a sort of chanting tone the opening words of the ' Morning Song ', the rest joining in at the finish of the first line :

> *Unite and unite, and let us all unite,*
> *For summer is a-come unto day ;*
> *And whither we are going we all will unite,*
> *In the merry morning of May.*

> *Rise up, Mr ——, and joy you betide,*
> *For summer is a-come unto day ;*
> *And bright is your bride that lies by your side,*
> *In the merry morning of May.*

[1] ' Pair ' or ' pare '—' company ' or ' fellows '.

Arise up, Mrs ——, and gold be your ring,
  For summer is a-come unto day ;
And give to us a cup of ale, the merrier we shall sing,
  In the merry morning of May.

Arise up, Miss ——, all in your smock of silk,
  For summer is a-come unto day ;
And all your body under as white as any milk,
  In the merry morning of May.

The young men of Padstow might if they would—
  For summer is a-come unto day—
They might have built a ship and gilded her with gold,
  In the merry morning of May.

The maidens of Padstow might if they would—
  For summer is a-come unto day—
They might have made a garland with the white rose and the red,
  In the merry morning of May.

With the merry ring, adieu the merry spring,
  For summer is a-come unto day ;
How happy is the little bird that merrily doth sing,
  In the merry morning of May.

In each verse the refrain ' a-come unto day ' (originally one may presume ' a-cuman to-day ') is ' re-echoed ', as it were, by the leading voices, which lends an added impressiveness to the haunting monotony of the tune. As at least seventeen verses have been recorded, the whole song must formerly have occupied a considerable time. Many of the verses, however, are now forgotten by the singers, and few of the latter are word-perfect even in those which they still render. In each case, therefore, the leader gives out the first line, the party doing as well as they can with the rest, although, with a very little trouble, the whole of the verses could easily be restored to use. Two, however, are rarely, if ever, omitted from the midnight serenade, and these commonly conclude the singing before each house :

Rise up, Mr ——, I know you well afine,
  For summer is a-come unto day ;
You 've a shilling in your purse and I wish it was in mine,
  In the merry morning of May.

> *Now fare you well and we bid you all good cheer,*
> *For summer is a-come unto day ;*
> *We 'll call no more unto your house before another year,*
> *In the merry morning of May.*

This last statement is no longer strictly true, seeing that the leader will assuredly call early the next morning in order to collect the ' shilling' to which the previous verse bears reference. It would, however, be doing an injustice to the people of Padstow to imply that the ceremony is now conducted solely with a view to collecting money. Whilst those who take part in it, being drawn, as they now are, from among the poorer inhabitants of the town, have naturally to seek some compensation for the loss of wages which this annual holiday entails, the real spirit of the old-time revelry is there, and no one grudges the little ' demand' which the honour of being called upon implies. Long after the casual onlooker has retired to bed, the singers continue on their way, their voices sounding, now from near, now from afar, till at length their full round of visits is concluded and they return home for a few short hours of sleep and rest.

Not for long, however, for morning soon comes, and with it Padstow's great day of the year. Soon after eight o'clock the men are once more assembling at the inn, busily preparing the ancient hobby-horse for its annual excursion into the streets.[1] The horse is indeed a formidable-looking creature, solemnly black except for the vari-coloured stripes on its tall cap and ferocious face-mask, with flowing plume and tail and savage-looking oaken ' snappers '. The jaws of the latter are studded with nails to imitate teeth, and are worked with a string held by the man inside. The cap-plume and the horse's tail and mane are formed of tufts of real horse-hair. On the front of the cap are painted the letters ' O B ', one on either side of the vertical stripes. The origin of these mystic symbols is unknown, the explanation given by Padstow people that they stand for ' 'O' B' 'Oss ' (i.e. ' 'Obby 'Oss ', the local variant of hobby-horse) being somewhat too facile to be convincing. Out from the shoulder level of the man who

[1] Photographs together with much valuable information concerning the hobby-horse ceremony will be found in articles written by Mr Thurstan Peter and Mr Edgar Tonkin, published respectively in the *Journal of the Royal Institution of Cornwall*, XIX (1913) ; and in *Devon and Cornwall Notes and Queries*, XII, Pt. IV (October 1922). For the music of the songs the reader is referred to Dr Ralph Dunstan's *Cornish Song Book*.

carries the hobby-horse extends a large hoop, measuring about six feet across. From this falls a ' gown ' of black canvas which hides his body and legs, his feet only appearing from beneath. Owing to the weight of the contraption, its tightness around the head and neck, and the lack of air within, the bearer has no easy task when the capering and careering begins in the streets.

Shortly after 10 a.m. the ' horse ' sallies forth from the Golden Lion, the doorways of which are gaily decked for the occasion with sycamore boughs or ' may '. The accompanying ' gang ', grotesquely apparelled in old-fashioned top-hats (decked with cowslips, tulips, or other flowers), frock-coats, women's jumpers, sailormen's ' cast-offs ', or any fancy costume that comes to hand, attend at its side, each armed with some ' musical ' instrument—drum, accordion, cymbals, tambourine, and (formerly) the fife. Before the hobby-horse darts the ' teazer ' or ' dancer ', a sturdy male whose heavy moustache lends additional extravagance to his feminine attire. In his hands he carries a gaily painted ' club ' (a short stick with a padded head fixed to it by a leather hinge), and as he performs his lively step-dance in the van of the procession, the crowd takes up the words of the ' Morning Song ', and the instruments blare forth the music of the preceding night. Ever and anon, the man with the club turns and faces the horse, and the two keep time together, like partners in some old gavotte, then on again through the streets, the horse making wild sallies wherever the crowd is thickest. From time to time it rushes into the doorway of a house, bumping against the women ' for luck ', the nature of which is clearly understood as meaning childbirth. At frequent intervals, and more especially when the horse pursues some woman, the crowd will shout : ' Oh ! wee 'oss ', a cry long associated with the ceremony but of which the meaning is lost.

As already stated, the song now sung in the hobby-horse procession is the same as that of the night before, viz. the ' Morning Song '. At intervals, however, certain verses and the chorus are interpolated from the ' Day Song ', which should, properly, be alone used at this hour. As the music changes, the gang gathers around the horse, which crouches down upon the road in apparent grief and exhaustion, and all mournfully intone together, like a funeral dirge :

Oh, where is St George?   Oh, where is he, O ?
He 's out in his long boat, all on the salt sea, O.

At the last word the horse suddenly leaps up with mischief in its eye, and the crowd breaks forth into the lively chorus :

> *Oh, the merry ring, adieu the merry spring,*
> *For summer is a-come unto day ;*
> *How happy is the little bird that merrily doth sing*
> *In the merry morning of May.*

So the procession goes on its way once more, the dancer and horse performing their wildest antics.

Formerly, the hobby-horse, after visiting the vicarage, was conducted to the neighbouring hamlet of Treator, there to ' drink ' or rather to be ' ducked ' in the pool. This part of the proceedings has been discontinued for some years. Visits, however, are still paid to Place House, the ancient home of the Prideaux-Brune family, and also, of course, to the other houses that have been serenaded on the preceding night. Here, as in the streets, money is freely collected for the benefit of the horse and its attendants.

Being by this time somewhat exhausted by their strenuous exertions and the loss of the greater part of their night's sleep, the ' pairs ' are wont to retire once more to the Golden Lion, where they generally remain until the bar closes at 2 p.m. ' Not to be daunted,' wrote a visitor on a recent occasion, ' I entered the aforesaid place of refreshment, where I found a room crowded to the door, and so low that I removed my hat. The assembled revellers, men of the fisherman type, were strangely attired, though in the dim light and the fog of tobacco smoke I was unable to note details. The company included one or two elderly women. Everyone appeared to have a large tankard of beer and a musical instrument, to which he applied himself alternately. The din was terrific. It was the atmosphere, however, that decided me. A suffocating smell of beer and perspiration (which, to judge by the closed window, was no inconvenience to those present) convinced me that such delights were not for me. I retired, therefore, to a quiet little restaurant nearby to await the afternoon appearance of the hobby-horse. At length the public-house party sallied forth. Most of them were armed with drums or concertinas, and they one and all atoned by vehemence for their inattention to strict time. They danced, too, not as part of the ritual, I think, but because they felt like that, and, though a trifle unsteady on their feet, as they struck up the hobby-horse tune and passed down the street, I could not help wondering if a more sophisticated rendering might not have lost some of the essential character of this May-day music. " Oh, summer is a-come unto day," went up the shout above the blare of concertina and drum. Refinement would make it a different thing. Having learned that after making another collection the revellers would return to spend the proceeds and the rest of the day in the bar, I got my car and left. I was disappointed. I had come to join in the simple pleasures of a simple people, giving spontaneous expression of their joy at the return of summer, and I had found what seemed at first sight a sordid, beer-swilling affair. How different from the Arcadian revels enjoyed by—by whom? Well, when I came to think of it, I had to admit that what I had wanted to see was something entirely artificial, a well-staged scene from the Golden Age, life as it has never been except in fancy. With something of a shock, I realized that the celebration I had witnessed was the real thing, and probably very like it had been for hundreds of years. That early English poet who so inimitably described the gathering of the Canterbury pilgrims at " The Tabard ", in Southwark, would, I was sure, have felt at home among the company in the Padstow inn. It was a wonderful day—a cloudless sky, a fresh breeze, the air full of larks—and as I revelled in it, I found a strange tune running through my head. It was the song of the Padstow revellers : " Oh, summer is a-cuman to-day ".' [1]

By providing, as it does, a popular outlet for that love of gaiety which is none the less strong through lacking other means of expression, it would seem that this ancient form of merry-making may well survive for many years to come. As a manifesto issued by the townspeople in 1830 still proclaims with truth : ' The bones of every Padstow boy are fired by the hobby-horse. As soon as a child is able to lisp its parent's name it will chant the glorious strains of our ancient festival song, and will usher in May's first merry morn with " The summer and the summer and the may, O ! " ' Long before the real hobby-horse makes its appearance in the streets to-day, parties of children wearing cowslips in their hats may be seen with small improvised hobbies known as ' colts '. With these they imitate the ways of their elders, including that of collecting money ! Whilst this is an innovation which

[1] *West Briton*, 8 May 1930.

is not wholly looked upon with favour, it at least ensures a knowledge of the custom being retained among those whose turn it will soon be to carry the great horse with which their forebears have so long disported themselves.

In former times, when shipbuilding was a thriving industry in the port, it was customary to erect a large maypole ninety feet high at the top of Cross Street. This was decorated with furze and sycamore and had a garland at the head consisting of tulips, wallflowers, and other blooms. This picturesque custom was revived soon after the war, and was witnessed by the writer in 1925. Unfortunately in 1926 it had been allowed to drop once more. In the former year the hobby-horse and its attendants danced merrily round the pole throughout the afternoon, being joined by great numbers of people from the country districts. The evening concluded with a fair on the quay.

The hobby-horse ceremony, which is now said to survive only at Padstow and in the Somerset village of Minehead, appears in former times to have been widely disseminated. Among customs which bear a close resemblance to it in Britain may be mentioned that of the ' Hooden Horse ' of East Kent, and the ' Mari Llwyd ' of Wales ; whilst in King's County, Ireland, a hobby-horse festival was formerly held on St John's Eve. Similar ceremonies in which the hobby-horse has a part are, or were, to be found in Rumania, Switzerland, Poland, the Basque country, etc.[1] Going much farther afield, a mask assumed by native dancers in New Guinea bears such extraordinary likeness to the one used at Padstow that one might almost be tempted to suppose the existence of a kindred ceremony in that country. This, however, is mere conjecture, and may have no foundation whatever.

The nearest approach to the Padstow ceremony is the hobby-horsing of Minehead, which also takes place on 1st May. The custom here, however, survives in a much more broken-down form. This is typified by the horse itself, which is now a sadly degenerate animal, lacking the convenience of a head, and having a tail which consists only of a piece of rope, on to which a cow's tail is sometimes spliced. The Minehead horse has also lost its ' snappers ', though it once had these like that of Padstow. The Minehead folk, indeed, allege that the Padstow beast is really theirs, and that it was stolen from them by the crew of a Padstow vessel. Until recently the horse at

[1] H. W. Killie, *Western Morning News*, 22 May 1933.

THE MID-DAY FURRY-DANCE

(See page 455)

THE HURLING GAME AT ST COLUMB

(See page 461)

Minehead was accompanied by ' gullivers ', or men wearing masks, big hooped skirts, and peaked head-dresses. The office of these attendants corresponded to that of the Padstow ' gangs '. The gullivers, however, have ceased to function, so that the ceremony at Minehead, though interesting as a survival, does not possess the same degree of circumstance which still clings to it at Padstow.

Of the history of this strange custom very little can be said. Tradition in Padstow affirms that some time during a war with France (which the natives ascribe to any date between the fourteenth and nineteenth centuries) the town was threatened by an invasion of the enemy. Most of the men being absent at sea, the women folk arrayed themselves in their red cloaks and carried the hobby-horse to Stepper Point. The effect of this ruse was such that the Frenchmen are said to have turned tail and fled, either supposing that the women were soldiers or that the horse was the arch-fiend himself. That the hobby-horse was an alarming spectacle to foreigners can well be believed. Old people in Padstow recall how a certain Mike Fielding, the horse of bygone days, once chased some Norwegians into the rigging of their ship, and only desisted from the pursuit on being handsomely bought off ! Invading enemies, however, are not so easily checked, and the story of the repulsion of the French is clearly one of those popular myths which, interesting as they may sometimes be, are rarely of much assistance in determining the age or origin of antiquities.[1]

From the close resemblance which it bears to the cognate ' Hal-an-Tow ' song at Helston, however, it may be assumed that part at any rate of the Padstow Day Song dates from the sixteenth century, the reference to the ' Spaniards ' in the Hal-an-Tow being altered to that of ' French Dogs ' at Padstow in order to bring this particular verse up-to-date in wars later than the Elizabethan period. Another point of similarity between the Hal-an-Tow and the Padstow Day Song is the introduction of a female personage who appears at Helston as ' Aunt Mary Moses ', and in Padstow as ' Aunt Ursula Birdwood '. Probably these were once well-known

[1] As an amusing illustration of this, a learned friend of the writer was on one occasion examining some prehistoric remains in a field in West Cornwall. ' Well, what do *you* think of them ? ' he asked the farmer who was standing by. ' Aw, sir,' was the reply, ' I do reckon they was putt there by they ould Romans a hundred—or may be two hundred years ago. You can't tell to a year or two in such things as they.'

'characters' in their respective districts whose names, as Mr Morton Nance conjectures, may have been substituted during the Commonwealth for either 'Elizabeth our Queen' or that of some later sovereign. Other commentators have attempted to relate these females to the 'Mollie' of the Hooden Horse of Kent or the 'Maid Marian' of the morris dance, all of which, as Sir Thomas Browne would say, are 'puzzling questions, not to be resolved by man nor easily, perhaps, by spirits, unless we consult the provincial guardians or tutelary observators'. Short of this, one can only say that the custom of hobby-horsing itself would appear to be older by far than any of England's wars or sovereigns. Indeed, it may well be, as Marcu Bezu, an authority on Rumanian folk-lore, claims that the hobby-horse ceremony 'carries us back to that world-wide god of death and resurrection—Dionysus', and that 'out of the Dionysian worship it is the Satyr element that has prevailed in our own survival and left behind, as it were a symbol, the hobby-horse'.[1]

Like the kindred Furry-dance at Helston, the Padstow ceremony clearly bears the characteristics of a pagan festival of revival and fruitfulness. On to this, as Mr Thurstan Peter has said, there has been grafted both folk-lore and actual history, whilst in later times its true origin has been further obscured by the efforts of persons wishing to remove from it elements now regarded as coarse.

II

There is no doubt that, after Padstow, the May festival of Helston, whose 'Furry-day' takes place a week later on the eighth of the month, must prove somewhat disappointing to those who are interested in these ceremonies as an expression of the folk-spirit. Owing in a large measure to the folk-dancing movement, the fame of the Furry-dance itself has now spread far beyond the limits of the ancient borough in which it has so long been annually performed, and to-day may be said to enjoy a national reputation. All this has made for a certain self-consciousness about the proceedings at Helston, where the townspeople, realizing the importance

[1] Quoted by H. W. Killie, *Western Morning News*, 22 May 1933.

of their festival in attracting visitors, have allowed it to become something in the nature of a ' spectacle '.

True, in many respects, Helston shows commendable pride in the manner in which its ceremonies are conducted, and the leading townspeople here still take their proper part in the dance, and in other ways lend to the proceedings that measure of support which is so sadly lacking at Padstow. Despite this, the crowds who now throng the pleasant old-world streets of Helston on Furry-day are for the most part alien crowds, brought there in motor coaches from neighbouring ' resorts ', and come only to gaze in wonder or amusement at a ' quaint ' old ceremony of whose significance they know little, and probably care less. Whilst, therefore, year by year, the festival attracts onlookers in ever-increasing numbers, its underlying purpose—the bringing in of the ' summer and the may, O ! '—has faded more and more into the background, just as the green boughs which once decked the doorways as a symbol of the approach of summer have given way to the flags and bunting with which the streets are now ' brightened up ' to please the money-spending visitors.

The very name by which the festival is now known shows that this desire to ' improve ' upon the original is no new thing. During the latter part of the eighteenth century, the influence of certain classicalists who were seeking to endow almost every English custom with a Greek or Roman origin was instrumental in bringing about a change in the name ' Furry ' to that of ' Flora ', from the supposed connection of the festival itself with the Roman feast of *Floralia*. By what means the Romans who, so far as is known, were never properly established in Cornwall and, beyond a few milestones and one or two possible camps, have left no trace of their invasion here, should have so successfully imposed this single festival upon the Celtic forefathers of the Cornish race, those who defend the word Flora have never yet explained. All the older historians of Cornwall, indeed, agree in condemning the idea as unworthy of credence. Writing at the beginning of the last century Polwhele, himself a classical scholar, speaks of the corruption of the term Furry into Flora as ' a vulgar error ', whilst another historian—Davies Gilbert—states that the true meaning of the festival had been ' obscured by a fanciful allusion to Greek and Roman mythology '.[1] In his Cornish-English vocabulary printed

[1] *Ancient Christmas Carols* (second edition, 1823).

in 1836 Polwhele again refers to ' the silly fashion of sub-
stituting Flora for Furry, but adds that ' in this capricious
age Truth and Reason bow down to female Fancy '. Since
his time modern philology has succeeded in tracing the
derivation of Furry from the Latin *Feriae*, old French *Férie*,
into the Middle English *Ferier*. This, pronounced locally as
' Furry ', was used in Cornwall as the English equivalent of
gol, the word used in the medieval Cornish dramas for a
' parish feasten holiday '. From the concourse of people
who gathered together on such occasions, and from the
booths which were erected to provide them with food and
other refreshment (such as may still be seen at a Breton
' Pardon '), the word gradually took on some of the meaning
associated with the secular ' fair ', a word which like ' Furry '
itself ultimately derives from Latin *Feriae*.

That this is the true explanation of Helston's Furry there
is no longer any reason to doubt. Moreover, as is now
known, the term was used in other parishes. Edward Lhuyd,
who visited Cornwall in 1700, refers to the parish feast of
Illogan as its ' Furri-day ', and states that it took place ' on
the first Sunday before or after St Luke's ',[3] just as Helston's
Furry coincides with the second of the festivals of St Michael
the Archangel, who is the patron saint of the town and church,
and whose ' image ' appears on the ancient borough seal.
The fashion in error, however, set by the old classicalists,
has resulted in the term ' Flora-day ' becoming so strongly
entrenched in popular sentiment that it is by no means easy
to get the true name reinstated. A beginning, however, has
been made in recent years by the official restoration of the
word Furry as applied to the dance. In consequence of
this it is to be hoped that ere long the festival itself will
become once more known by its proper name of Helston
Furry-day.

Although, as has been shown, the term Furry connects
the event with the feast of the patron saint of the parish,
there is little doubt that the custom is actually far older than

[1] Henry Jenner, *Western Morning News*, 12 May 1928. In point of
fact this derivation was suggested in the *Gentleman's Magazine* (1790),
Pt. II, 875.

[2] Henry Jenner, *Western Morning News*, 12 May 1928 ; and 15 May
1931.

[3] Bodleian Library, Rawlinson MS., D 997. Furry-days were also
celebrated at the Lizard and Penryn on the 1st and 3rd of May respectively. Hitchens and Drew, *History of Cornwall* (1824), I, 721.

the Christian festival by which it has been assimilated. Whilst the word Furry is now practically the sole reminder of its former association with the Church, the pre-Christian part of the ceremony still points to the real origin of the day. Prior to the time when the 'Hal-an-Tow' had degenerated into a mere excuse for collecting money, it was customary for the men and maids to go forth into the country to some neighbouring farm to breakfast. About eight o'clock the party returned once more to town, laden with green boughs, with flowers and oak twigs in their hats and caps, and preceded by an old woman or a man dressed as such, riding on a donkey. This last was clearly the 'Aunt Mary Moses' of the Helston 'Morning Song' who, as already suggested, probably corresponds to the 'Aunt Ursula Birdwood' of Padstow and the 'Mollie' of the Kentish Hooden Horse. Towards the middle of the last century these morning celebrations seem to have become merged with another ancient revel, that of the election of the 'Mock Mayor of St John's'. A description of this appears on an interesting poster dated 1857 : 'A grand procession will parade the town on Friday the 8th day of May, in the following order : Outrider on horseback ; a strong body of police ; Aunt Mary Moses, on a white palfry with her squires and attendants ; band ; constables, with their staffs of office : His Worship the Mayor St John's drawn by six Jerusalem ponies,[1] with coachman and two postilions in gorgeous liveries and the mayor's secretary and groom ; city crier, in a carriage and pair ; the councilmen, two and two. The procession will enter the town at nine o'clock precisely '.[2]

As the Hal-an-Tow procession entered the streets, which were gaily decorated for the occasion with flowers and green boughs, the Morning Song was struck up, to the accompaniment of a drum-and-fife band, and the merry pealing of the church bells :

Robin Hood and Little John, they both are gone to fair, O !
*And we will go to the merry green wood, to see what they do
there, O !*
And for to chase, O ! to chase the buck and doe—

[1] i.e. donkeys.
[2] Per Mr A. S. Oates, Helston.

Chorus :

*With Hal-an-Tow, Rum-ble, O ! for we were up as soon as any
    day, O !*
And for to fetch the summer home, the summer and the may, O !
For summer is a-come, O ! and winter is a-gone, O ! [1]

Shortly after nine o'clock the revellers appeared before
the famous Grammar School in Wendron Street—the school
once known as the ' Eton of Cornwall ', and which numbered
Charles Kingsley amongst its scholars, and Derwent Coleridge
(son of the great Romantic poet) as one of its headmasters.
Here a prescriptive holiday was demanded by the boys.
So strictly indeed was the festival observed in past times that
it is said that anyone found working on this day was liable
to be set astride a pole and carried on men's shoulders to a
point on the Cober river known as Pengellow Water. Here
there formerly lay a wide and muddy pool, which was tradi-
tionally claimed to have no bottom. Over this the victim
was sentenced to leap—a wellnigh impossible feat—or else to
compound for his offence by contributing something towards
the entertainment of his captors. It is said that the provision
of a gallon of ale was readily accepted in lieu of the harsher
sentence ! [2]

The original purpose of the Hal-an-Tow was, as the song
makes clear, the bringing in of the ' summer and the may,
O ! ' ; the Furry-dance which followed expressing the lively
feelings of the inhabitants at the conclusion of this event. [3]
Accordingly the principal dance still takes place, not early
in the morning, as might have been expected, but at noon.
At this hour the leading inhabitants and their guests assemble
in the Corn Market, the gentlemen in top-hats and morning
coats, with flowers in their buttonholes, and the ladies in their
brightest dresses. Preceded by the beadles, carrying their
staves of office, the procession files out of the building.
At their head the band, with its gaily decorated drum, strikes
up the merry tune as off they go along Meneage Street. In
through the front doors of the houses the dancers pass,

[1] The music of this song is recorded by ' Uncle Jan Trenoodle ' (i.e.
William Sandys) in his *Specimens of Cornish Provincial Dialect* (1846).
A restored version appears, with the words, in Dr Ralph Dunstan's
Cornish Song Book.

[2] *Gentleman's Magazine* (1790), 520 ; and *Cornishman*, 18 May 1882.

[3] See *Gentleman's Magazine* (1790), 520.

pealing every bell and rapping every knocker as they go, and so out through the back. Sometimes they dance around a garden or through a room. Shop doors are left open for their progress, and in some places the party files in at one entrance, dances through a department, and out by another ; descending in one place even into a cellar.

The Furry-dance, when properly performed to its lively measure, is equally attractive to join in or to watch. The dancers form a column, gentlemen in the left file, ladies in the right. Before starting the master of the ceremonies numbers off the dancers into groups of two couples. While the first part of the tune is being played the dancers walk forward, each gentleman leading his partner and holding her left hand by his right in a raised position. When the second part is played the two gentlemen change places, passing by the right, and turn (for four bars), the first man the second lady, and the second man the first lady. For the last four bars the gentlemen change places again, and turn their own partners.[1] This movement is repeated, of course, all down the set. Then, as the music changes once more, the whole column advances again. In this way the main streets are traversed, the dance concluding with a circuit of the bowling-green which lies at the lower limit of the town. In the evening a ball takes place. This was formerly held at the Assembly Room of the Angel Hotel where, by established custom, the gentlemen were considered bound (one has no reason to believe unwillingly) to give their partners of the morning their ticket, a pair of gloves, and the first dance.

In former times the midday Furry-dance was strictly confined to the gentry of the town and neighbourhood, the domestic servants and smaller tradespeople holding their own respective dances at different hours. One of the most popular features in the present-day celebrations is the children's dance, which takes place at 10.30 in the morning. Although this is a modern innovation, and had no part in the ancient ritual, it may be defended on the grounds of its keeping a memory of the dance alive among the rising generation. It shows also how easily a new feature, or equally the revival of an ancient one, can be engrafted on to a living custom. Attention was called to this fact some years ago by certain members of the Old Cornwall Societies, who were anxious to see the Hal-an-Tow reinstated in its proper place. The

[1] J. D. Hosken, *Helston Furry-Day.*

latter, it was pointed out, had fallen into abeyance because it had degenerated in the hands of the rowdy public-house element, who alone supported it in its last days. Under new auspices it appeared likely that the Hal-an-Tow might again be made one of the most interesting features of the day. For in addition to the stirring tune of the Day Song the bringing in of the ' summer and the may, O ! ' would call attention to the real significance of the festival which, as shown by the diminishing number of may boughs in the streets, was in danger of being forgotten. These arguments so far bore fruit as to result in a revival of the Hal-an-Tow on the Furry-day of 1930. On that occasion about forty schoolboys, accompanied by members of the Helston Old Cornwall Society, made a circuit of the town where the song was sung at certain stations. Since that date the custom has been repeated each year, and may in time be celebrated with something more nearly approaching its former picturesqueness.

III

Within the memory of the older inhabitants the 2nd of May in Helston was the occasion not only of the renewing of the borough bounds, as is still the case, but also of a grand ' hurling ' match, which took place through the streets. This ancient sport, which has been likened to a kind of ' hand football ', was formerly played in many parts of Britain,[1] but more particularly in the Celtic countries of Cornwall, Wales,[2] and Scotland.[3] It is also found in Brittany, more especially in the Chouan district of the south, where the game known as *la soule* is said to bear the closest resemblance to Cornish hurling. In Cornwall the game is played with a so-called ' silver ball ', a globe made of cork, leather, or wood, and covered with a thick casing of silver. When this required renewing, it was formerly the custom to collect the silver in the form of coins which were taken to a smith who beat them on to the ball. Many of the older hurling balls bore

[1] Cf. the Shrovetide ' football ' matches and similar ball games at Derby, Ashbourne, Alnwick, Dorking, Epsom, etc.
[2] Notably at Llanwenog in Cardiganshire and Pwlldu in Pembrokeshire.
[3] Notably at Scone, Melrose, Jedburgh, and Kirkwall.

appropriate Cornish inscriptions, such as : *Guare wheag yu guare teag*, ' Fair play is good play ', whilst some of the mottoes ran into several lines.

Two kinds of hurling are described by Richard Carew in his *Survey of Cornwall* (1602)—Hurling to Goal and Hurling to Country. The former was the more general in the eastern part of the county where the land was earlier enclosed, whilst the latter predominated in the west. Hurling to Goal is said by Carew to have been ' mostly used at weddings, where commonly the guests undertake to encounter all comers '. For the sake of the ' wedding garments ' it is to be hoped that such matches were of a less strenuous nature than those of the Hurling to Country, wherein the object of the players was to run with the ball into the opposing goal, which might be some gentleman's house, a church tower, or a town or village three or four miles away. ' In these matches,' writes Carew, ' the hurlers take their next way over hilles, dales, hedges, ditches ; yea, and thorow bushes, briers, mires, plashes, and rivers whatsoever ; so you shall sometimes see twenty or thirty lie tugging together in the water, scrambling and scratching for the ball '. Those who got away with it, however, ' may not so steale the palme ; for gallop any one of them never so faste, yet he shall be surely met at some hedge, corner, cross-lane, bridge or deep water which (by casting the countrie) they know he must needs touch at, and if his good fortune gard him not the better, hee is like to pay the price of his theft with his owne and his horse's overthrowe to the ground. The ball in this play may be compared to an infernall spirit ; for whosoever catcheth it fareth straightwayes like a madde man, struggling and fighting with those that goe about to holde him : and no sooner is the ball gone from him, but he resigneth this fury to the next receyver and himself becommeth peaceable as before. This game as on the one side it makes their bodies strong, hard, and nimble, and puts a courage into their heart to meet an enemie in the face : so on the other part it is accompanied with many dangers, some of which doe ever fall to the players share. For proofe whereof, when the hurling is ended, you shall see them retyring home, as from a pitched battaile, with bloody pates, bones broken and out of joynt, and such bruses as serve to shorten their daies ; yet all is good play, and never Attourney nor Crowner troubled for the matter.'

Hurling matches of this sort were commonly played

between neighbouring parishes on the occasion of their feasts. In this way an outlet was provided for the zealous local partisanship which was such a characteristic feature of Cornish society. Indeed, if one may judge by the ' punishing ' type of football which has now replaced hurling between such rival towns as Camborne and Redruth,[1] or St Ives and Newlyn, this disposition has little changed. A visitor inquiring on one of these occasions if the game was likely to be a good one, is said to have received the startling reply : ' We have every reason to believe so, there's a lot of bitter feeling between the two teams '.

In the inter-parish hurling matches of former times the rivalry was intensified by the belief that good fortune went with that parish which won the game, and thereby succeeded in retaining the ball throughout the ensuing year. Great was the glory of those heroes, therefore, who were instrumental in rendering such a service to their parish. It is recorded of one of these, a certain John Hockin of Caleane, that when aged only nineteen ' he carried off the ball from Four Borough Downs in " an Out-Ball ", and brought it himself to Camborne, in opposition to a vast number of horsemen and footmen '.[2]

It is possible that this noted hurler formed one of those ' hundred Cornish gentlemen ' who in 1654 went up to London to give an exhibition of hurling in Hyde Park. The *Moderate Intelligencer* of 4th May of that year provides an account of this famous match, wherein were ' fifty Cornish gentlemen on the one side and fifty on the other. One party played in red caps and the other in white. There was present His Highness the Lord Protector, many of the Privy Council, and divers eminent gentlemen, to whose view was presented great agility of body, and most neat and exquisite wrestling at every meeting of one with the other, which was ordered with much dexterity that it was to show more the strength, vigour, and nimbleness of their bodies than to endanger

[1] The rivalry in this case is certainly of no recent growth as may be judged from the following entry in the Camborne Parish Register : ' William Trevarthen buried in Camborne Church, August 13th, being disstroid to a hurling with Redruth men at the high downes the 10th daye of August, A.D. 1705 '. Per Dr J. Hambley Rowe.

[2] He was buried at Gwithian, 15 October 1706. The Hockins were in many respects a remarkable family. It is reco ded of John Hockin (son of the above) that ' himself fired on the crew of the boat of a French ship-of-war and prevented them landing at Godrevy and plundering the neighbourhood '.—Boase and Courtney, *Collectanea Cornubiensia*, 372.

their persons. The ball they played withal was silver, and designed for that party which did win the goal.'

During the reign of Charles II another great display of Cornish hurling was staged in London, and was witnessed by thousands of spectators. A contemporary ballad-monger, after commenting on the ' foul weather ' which had marred the merrymaking at Islington and elsewhere on the Sunday and Monday of the Whitsun-week, describes how on the bright and sunny Tuesday which followed the hurling took place in Hyde Park.

> *The Cornish hurling of the silver ball,*
> *But Hyde Park a man might truly say*
> *Had in it much the glory of that day.*
> *Stout Cornwall, always loyal to their kings,*
> *A hundred brave resolved persons brings*
> *Of their own country to the park that day,*
> *One of their country's exercise to play ;*
> *Where, being come, themselves they do divide*
> *To east and west, their manhood to decide.*
> *I' th' midst o' th' park 's thrown up a silver ball,*
> *Which being done, stoutly to it they fall.*
> *Heels were tript up and bodies came to ground,*
> *The Cornish hug always good play was found.*
> *Long time it lasted, and now east, then west,*
> *At several times had each of them the best.*
> *Thousand spectators stood with greedy eyes,*
> *To see them at this manly exercise ;*
> *His Highness York's great duke beheld the same,*
> *With other persons of renowned fame.*
> *Brave Cornishmen you are to be commended*
> *And will be so until the world is ended.*[1]

In the hurling game between parishes the ' St Tusters ' (men of St Just-in-Penwith) were formerly regarded as the champions of West Cornwall. A hundred years ago it was customary for the latter on their Feast Tuesday to engage in contest with their neighbours of Buryan or Sancreed, or those of Sennen and St Levan combined. At this time, indeed, whenever parties of young men went from one parish to another to join in the wrestling or other games, they would carry their silver ball with them, and practise their hurling

[1] *Western Morning News*, 21 February 1925.

by the way. Many were the exciting runs which thus took place in the rough hill country of the Land's End district, when some swift runner who had captured the ball would be followed by the rest of the players over rocks and carns, and through bogs and streamworks, till he landed it at last in triumph in the appointed goal. Often, after such matches, the hurlers would assemble in the green-court of one of the old decaying mansion-houses of the west, there to drink health and long life to the family from the barrel of strong beer which the squires were wont to provide.[1]

Similar 'out-hurlings' were formerly played between the parishes of Lelant and St Ives. At length, it is said that the inhabitants of the latter came to outnumber those of Lelant so heavily that the game was abandoned and the ball left with St Ives.[2]

Between fifty and sixty years ago a hurling took place annually on the Feast Tuesday at Tregoney, where the ball was thrown up opposite the town clock, and was played along the road, the toll-gates at Grampound Lane (near Carveth Farm) and at Golden (top of Freewater Hill) forming the goals. Here the married men took on the single,[3] as was the custom also at Truro, where the game continued to be played at a yet more recent date. Forty years ago a somewhat broken-down form of hurling was still practised at Germoe on the Monday after the feast. The ball here was thrown up at one end of the village and hurled—sometimes via the top of the church tower—to the other, where it was thrust in through the windows of the Dolphin Inn. One of the group of men assembled inside would then seize the ball and try to escape with it to a certain well at Ninnis, a farm about half a mile distant. If he succeeded in doing this without being caught the hurler was rewarded with a gallon of beer by the landlord who, it is said, was 'bound to give it to him'. The game was believed locally to have been introduced by a Germoe man, who had captured the ball from another parish, and it was said that if a 'stranger' got possession of it again Germoe would lose the custom.[4] Prior to the war hurling used to be played with considerable spirit on the sands at

[1] W. Bottrell, *Traditions and Hearthside Stories of West Cornwall*, I, 55, 146.

[2] Hobson Matthews, *History of St Ives*, 394.

[3] S. J. Bennet, *Western Morning News*, 9 March 1927.

[4] Rev. S. Rundle, *Penzance Natural History and Antiquarian Society* (1884–8), 155.

Newquay, whilst a few years since an attempt was made, but apparently without success, to revive it at St Merryn. To-day this ancient sport may be said to survive only at St Columb Major and at St Ives. At the latter town the game takes place on the Feast Monday, but is now confined to an in-hurling, played between 'gools' which are erected on 'Mester' (Porthminster) beach. A few years ago the hurlers were presented by the St Ives Old Cornwall Society with a new silver ball bearing an appropriate Cornish inscription in verse.

Despite encouragement, however, the hurling at St Ives is now conducted in a somewhat spiritless fashion, and it is to St Columb rather that the credit is due for showing how this ancient game was and should be played. A stranger entering this quiet little country town on Shrove Tuesday or the Saturday of the following week might well rub his eyes in astonishment at the sight which greets him. Throughout the long narrow street, shuttered and barricaded windows and closed doors are seen on either hand. The place has the appearance of being prepared for a stiff siege. Beneath the sign of the post office, a small slit in the woodwork shows where a letter may still be inserted, but entrance to the building there seems none. Across the way the windows and doors of the two banks are heavily shuttered, their brass plates even protected by coverings of wood. Between erections of timber and wire netting glimpses may be caught of a butcher's shop or drapery store, but again all entrance appears barred. Here and there indeed a half-open door shows that some more intrepid tradesman is carrying on, but inside there is a mysterious gloom, for the windows are covered from top to bottom with sheets of galvanized iron. Anyone possessed of a romantic turn of mind might fancy that the days of Napoleon Bonaparte had come again, and that the forces of the invaders were even now closing about the little town. But in truth these preparations are being made for a contest which is older by far than England's wars, and one which has been continued by countless generations of those who have known this district as their home.

The hurling at St Columb is played between Town and Country, the parishioners residing in the former being matched against those who dwell in the rural parts of the parish. Formerly the Country men wore white 'dickeys' (short jackets), but in the present game there is no distinction in the attire of the contestants. Nor is there any limit to the numbers taking part, so that when both sides are gathered in full strength from eight hundred to a thousand men and youths will sometimes join in the affray. The rules are somewhat indefinite, and no written record of them can be traced. The elements of the game, however, as handed down from generation to generation, have probably varied little for centuries past. From the spot where the ball is thrown up in the centre of the town the goals, consisting of stone troughs[1] standing by the roadside, are each one mile distant in opposite directions. The Town goal is situated at Cross-putty on the Newquay Road, the Country goal at Tregamere Corner on the road to Wadebridge.[2] The object of each party is to take the ball to its particular goal or, failing this, to carry it beyond the parish boundary, which may be a distance of from two to four miles, according to the direction. The side that succeeds in accomplishing either of these feats is regarded as the winner, and the individual who touches the goal with the ball or takes the latter out of the parish is entitled to keep the trophy in his possession until the next hurling day. Should the holder of the ball be touched at any time during the game by a player of the opposing side he is bound to ' deal ' it or take the consequences of a rough tackle. Non-parishioners (who are often called ' foreigners ') are not allowed to take sides, but may throw up the ball straight into the air, if it chances to come into their hands. The hurling mostly takes the form of wild rushes, varied by strenuous tackling, which often lasts for more than an hour before anyone succeeds in carrying the ball to the country. It is a game, therefore, which requires not only a nimble hand and a quick eye, but strength of wind and muscle.

By four o'clock in the afternoon the older and sedater portion of the inhabitants are beginning to take their places in the upper windows, from which they will witness the coming affray. Meantime in the streets below the players are assembling in ever-increasing numbers, china-clay workers with the white dust still clinging to their corduroys, farmers in breeches and gaiters, motor mechanics in greasy overalls, men in white collars and Homburg hats—all classes and types are represented, for none are too proud (although some may be too stiff) to take part in the ancient game. Among the latter are the stalwart hurlers of former days, men once hardy to

---

[1] Probably cross-bases originally.
[2] *Western Morning News*, 24 February 1930.

' wrastle ' and swift of foot as the best of them, but now having to content themselves with judicious comments delivered from the safety of doorways as they see son or grandson going by in the tumble and swift chase which once they loved so well.

As the chimes of the clock in the grey church tower strike 4.15 an agile figure swarms the lamp-post in the centre of the square. Holding one hand aloft he gives ' three cheers for the silver ball '—cheers which are echoed by the lusty voices of the players gathered around. The ball itself, composed of apple wood overlaid with a thick casing of silver, is about the size of a cricket ball, but weighs close on thirteen ounces. On its surface, battered and indented from many a blow, appears the appropriate inscription :

> *Town and country do your best*
> *For in this parish I must rest.*

Whilst the crowd is waiting for the game to begin the ball is passed round from hand to hand in order that those who wish may receive something of the virtue conferred by its touch. Here a mother hands it to her child or some girl, with pretended unwillingness, shyly receives it from her lover. At times even the ball has been carried to the bedside of the dying in order that some sick or aged person may handle it for the last time.

Promptly at 4.30 the ball is ' hove up ', either by the last year's holder or some distinguished visitor, and the game begins in earnest. High in the air the ball rises, and with a shout and halloo the crowd rises on tiptoe in sympathy, striving to catch it ere it falls. Into the thick of the press it descends—surely on top of some head one would say. But no ! by a miracle it reaches the ground with a leaden thud, which is immediately drowned by the rush of hobnailed boots. Now they 're off, a swift runner has got it ; but no, in a trice the crowd are on him. Quick as a thought he passes it to another, who in turn hurls it forward again. A sturdy thick-set player next snatches it. No runner he, but a fighting, striving, bull-necked, iron-muscled ' wrastler ', who will not yield it up in a hurry. On to his heels the main guard throw themselves, one seizes him by the knees, another has him round the waist, a third by the neck. In a moment he is down and lost to view, with the whole pack on top of him—iron-plated boots and all. But never a whit the worse he is fighting still, as clenching the ball he struggles and writhes with volcanic energy beneath the sea of bodies and legs. For some moments there is a deadlock. Then, without need of referee or whistle, the players of their own accord draw off, brushing the dust from their clothes and hands. This is not *the game*, and with all the instincts of fair play and good sportsmanship they know it.

A moment's respite, and someone has thrown up the ball. Once more, helter-skelter, they are off through the winding street. After them follows the crowd of onlookers, old men, women, shopgirls, and children. As the players take their way through in wild career heads crane from the windows and advice, humorous and otherwise, is freely given.

They are far away now, having reached almost to the end of the town, and people begin to hang about in groups, talking, and children play in the street once more. Then suddenly there is again the sound of distant shouting, and down the street come women and children, sightseers and all, like leaves driven before the storm. After them come the players, striving, dragging, tumbling, tossing, now forwards, now back, first up, then down ; their shirts open at the neck, clothes torn to rags, sweat running in their eyes, dusty or mud-spattered—and yet good-tempered and happy—no swearing or foul language.

Even in the heat of the chase the players will stop at the request of some old lady who seated in her window catches and fingers the ball in her withered hands, then drops it back to the crowd below. A moment afterwards, down they go towards the square, heels flying, a swift runner in the van. All of a sudden, he swerves and, like lightning, is off through a side street. With a shout the following crowd try to pull themselves up, but too late—he has gained several seconds by his ruse.

Not so easily, however, will this young Townsman bear away the prize. For all his cunning the Countrymen know a thing or two as well. Ever since the beginning of the game two quiet-looking claymen have been waiting here for their opportunity. Now their time has come, and good use they make of it. Straight into their arms the youngster dashes— one twist, and over he goes like a ninepin, but sustains a light fall, for the once champion wrestler is a sportsman, and the road is hard. Before the boy has risen to his feet the ball has gone ! Running lightly up the street the older man thinks to steal a march on the crowd who have probably gone to the market-place. But once again, the unexpected happens. Three-quarters of the way up he meets the pack and, innocent as he may look, they know him for a cunning ' fox ', and rush forward at his appearance. Calmly enough he meets the situation. A swing of his arm and the ball is sailing high over the heads of the crowd, not to mention the neighbouring chimney pots. Crash ! it lands on a roof, ricochets off, strikes a, fortunately, shuttered window opposite, and drops with a thud three yards away from an aged townsman, who has just looked out, thinking the affray was over.

Fooled in their intent, the crowd turns in time to catch the ball as the old man, quite unmoved by his near escape, puts all his energy into this last chance of showing the youngsters that he once was a hurler too ! Off they go again, but this time the champion runner of the parish has got the ball in real earnest. With a good start and the best pair of heels in Cornwall there is none to touch him. Farther and farther behind lags the crowd for, though he may still have to meet other ' foxes ' on the outskirts of the parish, it is unlikely with his pace and lightning swerve that he will be stopped. One by one, therefore, the players turn in towards home, and a hard-earned tea, in readiness for the ' calling up ' of the ball the same evening.

Promptly at eight o'clock, in the presence of almost the whole town, which is gathered once more in the market-place, the winner climbs the lamp-post, and calls for three cheers for ' town ball ' or ' country ball ' as the case may be. After this, the custom is observed of ' drinking the silver ball '. If the victor of the day is a teetotaller, he is escorted to the institute, where the ball is washed and placed in a large receptacle full of cocoa. This is poured out and handed round for all to drink. Where the winner of the ball is other than a teetotaller, a visit is paid to the Ring of Bells. Here the same ceremony is observed, with the difference only that the ball is immersed in a great can of beer. In this way the evening is passed amidst good fellowship, the players at length returning home, ready to redeem their luck or confirm it on the occasion of the next hurling.[1]

[1] Many attempts have been made to explain the origin of hurling. Amongst these is the suggestion that it represented the battle between winter and summer, and that the throwing up of the silver ball possibly symbolized the ascendancy of the sun in the heavens. For an interesting account of this and other ball games, see R. D. Greenaway, *Journal of the Royal Institution of Cornwall* (1927), Pt. II.

IV

Among interesting customs of mid-Cornwall special mention must be made of the Bodmin ' riding ', since although this has been in abeyance for a number of years, it constitutes the sole example of a festival of its kind in the county. Some years ago the writer discovered what is probably the earliest account of the riding in a notebook compiled by Edward Lhuyd, the Celtic scholar, who visited Bodmin about the year 1700. ' Their feast here,' he writes, ' is on the two Mondays next after St Beccets Day, at which time they have a great concourse of people that come a-riding (as they call it), viz. they deck a piece of timber about a man's height with various sorts of flowers and garlands—and carry it to church (formerly, but not of late). Then to sport on Bodmin Down they go in a body (all of one trade riding by themselves). Some ride for sylver shoes (a piece of silver formed so), others run for sylver rings, etc.' [1]

In these hasty notes, no doubt taken down on the spot, Lhuyd has crystallized a great deal of information on the subject of the riding. Notwithstanding the coincidence of the dates, however, and the existence of a ruined chantry chapel of St Thomas Becket, adjoining the present church, the supposition that the festival was held in honour of this saint now finds little support. Tradition affirms rather, and in this case it would appear to be right, that the riding originally commemorated the return of the body of St Petroc, the patron saint of the parish, whose relics in 1177 had been sacrilegiously stolen by a Breton priest and taken to the abbey of S. Méen. The consequences of this untoward act were not long in making themselves felt. ' For when it became known to Roger, the Prior of Bodmin, and to the canons who served God in the same place, the aforenamed prior went to Henry, King of England ; that by his powerful aid (Henry II was at that time overlord of Brittany) they might again get possession of the body of S. Petroc, of which they had been fraudulently deprived.' At the king's order Rolland of Dinan thereupon took a party of soldiers to S. Méen, and required the monks

[1] Bodleian Library, Rawlinson MS., D 997.

to surrender the relics. The latter, ' being unwilling to incur the wrath of the king, handed over that blessed body to the above-named Roger on the Sunday after Pentecost, 19th June, and that sacred body was returned to him whole and entire, without any part of it being detached, by the abbot and monks of the church of S. Mevennus (Méen or Mewan), who swore upon the relics of the same church that they had not kept back any part of the body. On which the above-named Prior of Bothmenia (Bodmin) returning to England with joy, brought back the body of Blessed Petroc in an ivory shrine '.[1]

Although the date of the commencement of the Bodmin Riding, on the Sunday nearest to 7th July, is later than that of the handing over of the body in Brittany, it may well have coincided with its arrival in Bodmin, seeing that the fact is recorded that it was brought first to Winchester ' for the adoration of the king '.

At the beginning of the last century, the ceremonies of the riding were still conducted on a considerable scale. At this period it was customary for large quantities of beer, which had been brewed and bottled in the previous October, to be carried round the town by two or more young men who had been entrusted with the management of the proceedings. These were attended by a band consisting of drums, fifes, and other instruments, playing the riding-tune. Halting before each house the leader of the party saluted its inmates with the words : ' To the people of this house, a prosperous morning, long life, health, and a merry riding '. The owner was then solicited to taste the riding-ale which was carried round in baskets. A bottle was usually taken in and was acknowledged by an appropriate sum of money which was devoted to the festivities.

On the Sunday, the people of the town flocked to church decked out with ribbons, etc. The next morning a grand procession was formed of all the inhabitants, those who could afford to ride being mounted on horse or ass, and cracking long whips. The trade guilds were also represented, their members carrying the emblems of their various crafts. Headed by the band, the party took their way to the priory, where they received from the owner of the house, as representing

[1] Chronicles of Roger of Hovenden and Benedict of Peterborough. The shrine above mentioned is still in existence. It is kept at a bank in Bodmin, and is among the most valuable relics of its sort in the kingdom. A photograph of it is reproduced in Canon G. H. Doble's *Life of St Petroc*, to which the writer is indebted for the above quotations.

the prior, a garland and a pole decorated with flowers and ribbons. From here the procession passed once more through the main streets to a piece of ground at the western end of the town, where the games were formally opened.[1] An interesting account of the latter appears in the *Royal Cornwall Gazette* of 24th July 1824. ' Anticipations of the amateurs of athletic sports relative to the revival of the ancient festivities of Bodmin Riding,' states the writer, ' have been fully realized. The value of the prizes and the spirit with which those who had direction of the amusements exerted themselves drew together a concourse of people greater than was remembered on any similar occasion. The sports commenced on Monday with wrestling, Henry Maberly, of Cardinham, bearing off the first prize, a gold-laced hat.[2] The sports of the second day commenced with a trial of skill in ringing. The first prize of £6 was won by the ringers of Egloshayle ; the second prize, eight fine hats, by the ringers of St Kew ; the third prize, a silver cup, by the ringers of St Tudy ; and the fourth prize, eight favours, by the ringers of Blisland. The prizes for wrestling this day were valuable—£10 for the first, £5 for the second, and £2 for the third.' The evening of the second day of the sports concluded with a grand ball for the servant girls and their ' followers ', which was kept up until 8 or 9 o'clock the next morning. The ladies on these occasions, we are told, often ran into the ' extreme of fashion ' ; some of the girls having been known to expend a ' guinea in a cap, and to come away without it, and never recover it more '.

It is interesting to note in passing the many kinds of entertainment which were provided at the West Country sports meetings of those days. Wrestling was, of course, the chief attraction, and one which proved hardly less popular in West Devon than in Cornwall. In addition to this, however, the programmes commonly included such representative items as ' A jingling-match by thirteen smart dashing lads for a hat worth a guinea ', or ' Cudgel playing for a silver cup '. Other sports or recreations mentioned at this date are foot races, jumping in sacks, grinning through horse collars, bobbing and diving and such-like ' innocent amusements for producing fun and merriment '.

[1] R. Polwhele, *History of Cornwall* (1816), VII, 138–9. See also T. Quiller-Couch, *Journal of the Royal Institution of Cornwall* (1864).

[2] Other wrestling prizes commonly offered at this date include prime pairs of buff breeches, gold-laced gloves, waistcoats, silver spurs, and goblets.

Notwithstanding the scale on which the Bodmin Riding was celebrated somewhat more than a hundred years ago, by the latter part of the last century it had so much degenerated as to reveal little of its original character and meaning. 'At this time,' writes Mr Burton, ' the Sunday had already ceased to be an occasion, neither was there any proper organization of the Monday's procession and sports. At 4 a.m. a rabble of boys and men assembled at the town clock and led by a scratch band playing, not very musically, the tune of the riding, the crowd marched up the main street, halting at every public-house on the way where they were regaled with free drinks. As there were at least five such halting-places, it is not surprising that the quantity of liquid refreshment consumed gradually produced such an effect on some members of the band that they muddled the music as much as they fuddled their brains.' [1] In consequence, therefore, another agelong custom thus became suppressed; through lack, chiefly, of the support of the educated who should have upheld it in its proper character. The tune of the riding, however, is still preserved in the hearts of the older generation of Bodmin inhabitants, and in these days of revivals there appears no reason why the ceremony itself should not again be made a picturesque and attractive feature in the life of the town.

V

In the *Survey of Cornwall*, published in 1602, an account is given of another, and probably still more ancient, ceremony which formerly obtained in the Bodmin area, but which, unlike the riding, has long since passed out of memory.   ' The youthlyer sort of Bodmin townsmen,' writes Carew, ' use to sport themselves by playing the box with strangers whom they summon to Halgaver. The name signifieth the Goat's Moore, and such a place it is, lying a little without the towne, and very full of quavemires. When these mates meet with any rawe serving-man or other young master who may serve and deserve to make pastime, they cause him to be solemnly arrested for his appearance before the Mayor of Halgaver, where he is charged with wearing one spurre or going untrussed

[1] *Old Cornwall*, VI, 35.

or wanting a girdle or some such felony. After he has been arraygned and tryed, with all requisite circumstances, judgement is given in formal terms, and executed in some one ungracious pranke or other, more to the skorne than hurt of the party condemned. Hence is sprung the proverb when we see one slovenly apparelled to say " he shall be presented at Halgaver Court " (or take him before the Mayor of Halgaver).'

At the time at which Carew was writing it was also the custom among the freeholders at Lostwithiel, ' upon little Easter Sunday ', to elect one of their number who, ' bravely apparelled, with a crown on his head, a sceptre in his hand, and a sword borne before him ', was attended by the rest on horseback to church. Here he was met by the curate in his ' best beseene ' who conducted him to hear divine service, after which he repaired with the same pomp to a feast where he was served with kneeling and all other rites due to the estate of a prince.

The custom of electing a mock mayor, which would appear to have descended from this, was celebrated at Lostwithiel as lately as the year 1884. On that occasion the ceremony was conducted by torchlight in the presence of nearly a thousand people. Writing in 1890 Miss Courtney speaks of similar customs as ' still existing ' at St John's, Helston ; and at Buryan ; and adds that the last ' Mayor of the Quay ' at Penzance had only died about ten years previously, i.e. in 1880.[1] As a matter of fact, the election of such mock mayors was at one time more general than perhaps Miss Courtney herself realized, and a complete list of the towns and villages in which this ceremony was observed in Cornwall alone would prove a long one. Typical of many others was the Mock Mayor of St Germans, who was annually elected on 29th May at some ' bush house ' in that village, after having been well primed with ' fair ale '. On receiving office the ' mayor ' was mounted on a wain or cart, and drawn round the famous walnut-tree (at the foot of Nut Tree Hill), where he proclaimed his jurisdiction over the ancient borough for the ensuing year.[2]

At Launceston on mayor-choosing-day it was customary to elect also a mock ' Mayor of the Pig Market '. Prior to his election, the mayor was made tipsy, his hat was removed and his head well powdered with flour. If his hair was sufficiently

[1] M. A. Courtney, *Cornish Feasts and Folklore*, 27.
[2] R. Hunt, *Romances and Drolls of the West of England*, II, 197.

feast. The preceding days having been given over to revelry, shortage of money commonly provided the necessary inducement to accept the office, to which a fee of about 7s. 6d. was attached. The mayor was adorned with a hat, and having taken his place in a cart was dragged through the village by other revellers who, like himself, had generally been well plied with liquor. Not infrequently the mayor was accompanied in the cart by a deputy mayor, whose duty it was to steady the chief official on his feet. ' The procession,' writes Mr James Roberts, of Bradford, who was a ' Costenton boy ' some *eighty* years ago, ' usually started from the Queen's Arms, and halts were made at various places, where the mayor stood up in the cart and delivered a homily in accordance with the promptings of the leading spirits. If there had been any scandal in the village during the year a halt would be made at the house of the chief actor or actors, and advice given as to their future conduct. After a tour of the village, the cart was sometimes drawn down to the river at Ponjeravah, and the worthy mayor toppled in. As the stream was broad and shallow there was no danger of drowning.' The last Mayor of Costenton was a certain John Roberts, who went by the nickname of ' Jack Darky '. His election, which took place in the feast week of 1857, was witnessed by the Rev. R. F. B. Richards, who had been newly appointed vicar of the parish. The affair proved so distasteful to the latter that he used all his influence to prevent its recurrence. In this he succeeded, and from that time forth the mayoral elections of Constantine have ceased to be.[1]

Finally, mention must be made of the Mayor of Halsetown, near St Ives. The chief interest of the custom here lies in its recent engrafting, the village itself having only been built about 1830 by a former parliamentary candidate, on a plan that secured a vote for each householder. The election took place on the same day as that of the official mayor-choosing in St Ives. At the ' council meeting ' which followed the ensuing points were regularly brought up for discussion :

1. *Halsetown must be lit by gas.*
2. *Halsetown must do away with its rubbish heaps.*
3. *Halsetown must have a water supply.*
4. *Attention must be given to Towednack Quay Head (an imaginary structure).*

[1] *West Briton*, 29 January 1931.

The difficulty of accomplishing any of these tasks, which so far have defied even the more regularly constituted authorities, proved so fatiguing to the councillors that the meeting commonly adjourned in favour of a banquet which was held at the inn where the mayoral chair and hat were kept.

Many other mock mayors are described by Mr W. T. Martin in his valuable paper on this subject, including those of St Neot, Pelynt, Budock, Peace, Illogan, Four Lanes, Stithians, and Crowlas. Nor is there any doubt that this list could be further supplemented by inquiry in other parts of Cornwall. As the writer of the paper has pointed out, however, certain features are more or less common to all ; the elections generally took place in the parish Feast Week, the mayor was made gloriously drunk and, to complete the burlesque, was subjected, after his brief spell of authority, to the ignominy of being tipped into the sea, river, or on to the village rubbish heap. Furthermore, this ceremony, though far from edifying in its latter-day form, was popularly thought to be sanctioned by law no less than custom.

Although changing opinion as to the humour of drunken horse-play has of late years caused the discontinuance of these mock elections, they have, none the less, a well-recognized folk-lore interest. Their existence has been recorded not only in many parts of England but, under the varying forms of licence granted to the Lord of Misrule, throughout Europe generally ; whilst kindred practices are said to obtain as far afield as India. Reduced though they had become in Cornwall to the level of apparently foolish and somewhat disreputable village frolics, their characteristics show that the popular belief that they were an assertion of certain but recently lost municipal rights was insufficient to explain them. For, as Sir G. L. Gomme has written: ' Not only do these (ceremonies) present us with examples of the village moot assembling in the open air under a tree . . . but they parallel those significant ceremonies in India, when on special days the non-Aryan castes of the village meet together, elect their own leader, and take possession in wild and riotous freedom of the entire village. All the vagaries and nonsense practised at these festivals in India are so many symbolical expressions of the power of the non-Aryan tribes during the admitted period of licence. There is no reason why in Britain they should not express, in survival, the same village festival with all its significant ethnic symbolism '.[1] According to this view the mock-mayor ceremonial resolves itself into a folk-memory of the election of tribal chieftains—in Britain possibly Celtic or pre-Celtic—but at all events representative of the older conquered inhabitants who were thus permitted by their overlords, for a brief spell, to reassert their former independence.

Other authorities attribute to these ceremonies a yet more ancient lineage, tracing in them the origin of kingship itself. The latter, it is claimed, was based upon the primitive belief that the god-spirit who controls the fortunes and destinies of Man was wont in certain cases to dwell in human form. Those into whom the spirit thus entered were naturally regarded with all the veneration and honour ascribed to such potentates as are now called kings. At the same time it was observed that even the latter were subject to old age and death. Accordingly, in order to avert the catastrophe of the god-spirit departing with the fleshly tabernacle in which it dwelt, it was thought necessary to kill the king at the first sign of failure in his powers, thereby enabling the spirit to transfer itself to a more vigorous successor. In course of time, however, there developed among kings themselves a not unnatural reluctance to undergo this extreme form of personal sacrifice. Temporary substitutes were, therefore, appointed who, after a brief spell of authority during which the king himself abdicated, were finally slain in his stead. With the growth of less savage ideas the penalty imposed even upon substitutes was mitigated and the latter, upon being deposed, were not killed but thrown out of the palace with every symbol of ignominy and shame.[2] Thus, perhaps, in the election and deposition of some comic mock mayor in a Cornish village there may be traced the last vestiges of a practice coeval with the earliest forms of human society.

Obviously such theories as these cannot be pressed too far, but should be regarded rather as tentative suggestions, which a more intimate knowledge of the ways of primitive peoples may eventually confirm as facts. Meanwhile the study of folk-lore has already served to show how many customs, including those described in this book, which were formerly regarded as purely local, are in reality widely disseminated, and have a definite historical significance.

[1] *The Village Community*, 110–11.
[2] Sir J. G. Frazer, *The Golden Bough* (short edition), 264 *et seq.*

As to the worthiness or unworthiness of such customs to survive, the future may be trusted to decide. On the broad bosom of the stream of Time the little thoughts and conceits of Man froth and bubble and have their day. Some of these bubbles travel farther than others, bearing with them memories of those who sent them forth so bravely floating, long ago. Then they, too, break upon the rock of change, and vanish like the rest into thin air.

INDEX